More Precious Than Gold

Commentary on
The Doctrine and Covenants

Volume 1

by

Monte S. Nyman

Published and Distributed by:

Granite Publishing and Distribution, LLC
868 North 1430 West • Orem, Utah 84057
(801) 229-9023 • Toll Free (800) 574-5779 • Fax (801) 229-1924
www.granitepublishing.biz

Page Layout & Design by Myrna Varga
Cover Design by Steve Gray

ISBN: 978-1-59936-027-0
Library of Congress Control Number: 2008937593

Printed in the United States of America
First Printing, November 2008
1 3 5 7 9 10 8 6 4 2

Contents

Introduction

The Doctrine and Covenants is *our* book. It was written to the members of The Church of Jesus Christ of Latter-day Saints. It was revealed to *us*, not to another dispensation and then passed down as was the Bible, the Book of Mormon, and most of the Pearl of Great Price. Its title, taken from a statement of President Joseph Fielding Smith quoted below, represents the value the book has to each member. The importance of the book to the Church collectively, is shown in the statements of the Presidents of the Church that follow.

—Prophet Joseph Smith:

> . . . in consequence of the book of revelations, now to be printed, being the foundation of the Church in these latter days, and a benefit to the world, showing that the keys of the mysteries of the kingdom of our Savior are again entrusted to man; and the riches of eternity within the compass of those who are willing to live by every word that proceedeth out of the mouth of God—therefore the conference voted that they prize the revelations to be worth to the Church the riches of the whole earth, speaking temporally. [*HC,* 1:235]

—President Brigham Young:

> The book of Doctrine and Covenants is given for the Latter-day Saints expressly for their everyday walk and actions. [*Discourses of Brigham Young,* sel. John A. Widtsoe (1951),128]

—President John Taylor:

> To the revelations [Joseph Smith] made known are we indebted for the glorious principles that God has communicated to the world in these last days. We were as much in the dark as other people were about the principles of salvation, and the relationship we hold to God

and each other, until these things were made known to us by Joseph Smith. [*The Gospel Kingdom, Writings and Discourses of John Taylor*, G. Homer Durham, comp. (1987), 33]

—President Wilford Woodruff:

The Doctrine and Covenants [is] a code of revelations which the Lord gave to Joseph Smith. This book contains some of the most glorious revelation upon doctrine, upon principle, upon government, upon the kingdom of God and the different glories, and upon a great many things which reach into the eternal worlds. [*Teachings of the Presidents of the Church: Wilford Woodruff* (2004), 121]

—President Joseph F. Smith:

I know that this book, the Doctrine and Covenants, . . . is the word of God through Joseph Smith to the world, and especially to the members of the Church of Jesus Christ of Latter-day Saints throughout the world. [*Teachings of the Presidents of the Church:* (1998), 42]

President Heber J. Grant:

I . . . bear my testimony . . . that if we will study the Doctrine and Covenants . . . get the Spirit of the Lord, and teach our children in their youth, that God will bless us. Our children will grow up with a love for the gospel. [Heber J. Grant, *Gospel Standards* (1969),154]

—President Joseph Fielding Smith:

In my judgment, there is no book on earth yet to come to man as important as the book known as the Doctrine and Covenants, . . .

But this Doctrine and Covenants contains the word of God to those who dwell here now. It is our book. It belongs to the Latter-day Saints. More precious than gold, the prophet says we should treasure it more than the riches of the whole earth. I wonder if we do? If we value it more than wealth; it is worth more to us than the riches of the earth. [*Doctrines of Salvation,* comp. Bruce R. McConkie, 3 vols. (1956), 3:198–99]

—President Howard W. Hunter:

Consider [the following] reasons why we should regularly read the Doctrine and Covenants and inspired writings of God's servants.

1. This telestial earth is but a temporary place for us to live—a home away from our real home. Our purpose in life is to find and follow the path that will lead *us back to our heavenly home* in the presence of the Father of us all. The Doctrine and Covenants represents *divine instructions* in our day showing us this fact and how this might be accomplished.

2. The Doctrine and Covenants not only tells us what we need *to know*, but also what *we need to do in order to be saved* in the kingdom of God. It tells us of commandments to be kept, ordinances to be done and preparations to be made before the Second Coming. . . . [*The Teachings of Howard W. Hunter*, ed. Clyde J. Williams (1997), 56]

—President Gordon B. Hinckley:

The Doctrine and Covenants is unique among our books of scripture. It is the constitution of the Church. While the Doctrine and Covenants includes writings and statements of various origins, it is primarily a book of revelation given through the Prophet of this dispensation.

These revelations open with a thundering declaration of the encompassing purposes of God in the restoration of His great latter-day work: (quotes D&C 1:1–2). . . .

From that majestic opening there unfolds a wondrous doctrinal panorama that comes from the fountain of eternal truth. . . . All brought together, they constitute in very substantial measure the doctrine and the practices of The Church of Jesus Christ of Latter-day Saints. . . . The Doctrine and Covenants is a conduit for the expressions of the Lord to his people. [*Teachings of Gordon B. Hinckley* (1997), 163–64]

SECTIONS 66 & 67 • OUTLINE

66:1–2 William E. McLellin is blessed for having received the everlasting covenant.

  a. The gospel is sent forth that the children of men might

             have life and partake of the glories to be revealed in the last days (v. 2).

       b.   These glories were written of by the prophets and apostles of old (v. 2).

➤ 66:3–7   William E. McLellin is clean, but not all, repent of the things that the Lord will show unto him, and what is the Lord's will for him.

       a.   He is to proclaim the gospel in the regions round about (vv. 5–6).

       b.   He is to bear testimony in every place and unto every people (v. 7).

➤ 66:8–13   William is to take Samuel H. Smith with him, and the Lord will be with them.

       a.   Lay hands on the sick and they shall recover (v. 9).

       b.   Return not until the Lord sends you; ask and ye shall receive (v. 9).

       c.   Do not be cumbered, forsake all unrighteousness, commit not adultery (v. 10).

       d.   Magnify your office and you will push many people to Zion (v. 11).

       e.   Continue unto the end and ye will have a crown of eternal life (vv. 12–13).

➤ 67:1–3   The elders gathered together had endeavored to believe they would receive the promised blessing (D&C 66:12), but fear in their hearts kept them from receiving it.

       a.   The Lord had heard their prayers and knew their hearts (v. 1).

       b.   The riches of eternity were His to give (v. 2).

➤ 67:4–9   The Lord gave a testimony of the commandments that were lying before them.

       a.   They knew Joseph's language and imperfections but they desired to express knowledge beyond his language (v. 5).

       b.   The Lord challenged them to take the least of the commandments, and select the wisest among them to [write] one like it (vv. 5–6).

    c.   If they cannot make one like it they are under condemnation if they do not bear record that they are true (v. 8).

    d.   The Lord says they know they are true, and came down from the Father (v. 9).

EXPLANATION OF THE FORMAT

The same format is followed for each chapter of the book. The historical setting of when the revelation was received is given in the beginning paragraphs for each of the sections discussed therein. This brief synopsis is taken primarily from Prophet Joseph Smith's *History of the Church*, abbreviated as *HC*.

The next section, the "Introduction," is designed to be a starting point for the reader as he or she begins to study the chapter. For a teacher, it is an attention getter to focus the students on the subject for that class period.

The third section, an outline of the revelations, is intended to give a framework for a deeper study. Some readers may wish to skip, or skim, this section of the chapter, but it seems helpful for many to get the full content of the revelation. Too often we just pick out a few verses and use as a topical point without seeing the context of those verses, and the overall message of the revelation.

In the "Notes and Commentary" section, segments of the text of the revelation are quoted, and followed by comments, cross references, and explanations for a better understanding of the message of those verses.

The last section is a selection of quotations from various presidents of the Church, Apostles and other General Authorities. These quotations are not all inclusive, but were selected to verify and clarify the concepts and teachings referred to within the chapter. There is some duplication of quotations, other materials, and references in the chapters that follow. This duplication is because the material also applies to other sections of the Doctrine and Covenants, and also so that the reader will not have to turn back to previous pages as while reading.

Chapter One

Prelude to the Doctrine and Covenants

D&C 66; 67:1–9; 69; 70:1–4

H<i>istorical Setting:</i> It is unusual to begin a study of the doctrines and the covenants that are made known in this great volume in what is approximately the middle of the book. However, a brief overview of how and when the book came about will set the stage for our study.

Over a year and a half after the Book of Mormon was published (March 26, 1830) and the Church was organized (April 6, 1830) a special conference of the elders of the Church was held at Hiram, Ohio on November 1, 1831. "Many revelations had been received from the Lord prior to this time, and the compilation of these for publication in book form was one of the principal subjects passed upon at the conference" (heading of section 1). The title selected for this first publication was the "Book of Commandments." The revelations discussed herein, chapter 1 of this work, were given around this time period and show the Lord's support for the project.

Introduction

Elder Neal A. Maxwell made this observation about the Doctrine and Covenants:

> If asked which book of scripture provides the most frequent chance to "listen" to the Lord talking, most individuals would at first think of the New Testament. The New Testament is a marvelous collection of

the deeds and many of the doctrines of the Messiah. But in the Doctrine and Covenants, we receive the voice as well as the word of the Lord. We can almost hear him talking. Words like these sink deep into one's marrow as well as into one's mind, for the majesty and power of the Lord are so evident. [*Ensign*, December 1978, 4]

As we examine these revelations about the coming forth of the Doctrine and Covenants, we will read, and hopefully hear or feel what the Lord is saying about this great book.

The Bible is the basic book of scripture to The Church of Jesus Christ of Latter-day Saints. Brigham Young, the second President and Prophet to the Church in this dispensation, stated: "We take this book, the Bible, . . . for our guide, for our rule of action; we take it as the foundation of our faith" (*Discourses of Brigham Young*, 125). The Apostle Paul wrote that the Saints were of "the household of God; and are built upon the foundation of apostles and prophets, Jesus Christ himself being the chief cornerstone; In whom all the building fitly framed together groweth unto an holy temple in the Lord" (Ephesians 2:19–21).

The Book of Mormon and the Doctrine and Covenants are the scriptures that make the Church unique. The Prophet Joseph Smith declared:

> Take away the Book of Mormon and the revelations [Doctrine and Covenants], and where is our religion? We have none; for without Zion, and a place of deliverance, we must fall; . . . and if we are not sanctified and gathered to the places God has appointed, with all our former professions and our great love of the Bible, we must fall; we cannot stand; we cannot be saved; for God will gather out his Saints from the Gentiles, and then comes desolation and destruction, and none can escape except *Teachings of the Prophet Joseph Smith*, sel. Joseph Fielding Smith (1976), 71]

President Ezra Taft Benson, the thirteenth president of the Church of Jesus Christ of Latter-day Saints stated:

> The Doctrine and Covenants is the binding link between the Book of Mormon and the continuing work of the Restoration through the Prophet Joseph and his successors.
>
> In the Doctrine and Covenants we learn of temple work, eternal families, the degrees of glory, Church organization, and many other great

truths of the Restoration (quotes D&C 1:37–38).

The Book of Mormon brings men to Christ. The Doctrine and Covenants brings men to Christ's kingdom, even The Church of Jesus Christ of Latter-day Saints, 'the only true and living church upon the face of the whole earth' (v. 30). I know that.

The Book of Mormon is the keystone of our religion (see Book of Mormon Introduction). The Doctrine and Covenants is the capstone, with continuing latter-day revelation. The Lord has placed His stamp of approval on both the keystone and the capstone. [Conference Report, April 1987, 105]

With these three building blocks, the Bible, the Book of Mormon, and the Doctrine and Covenants, the Latter-day Saints may become, in the Apostle Paul's words, "builded together for an inhabitation of God through the Spirit" (Ephesians 2:22). Of course, we would include the Pearl of Great Price.

TEXT AND COMMENTARY

D&C 66:1–2 • The Fulness of the Gospel

1 BEHOLD, thus saith the Lord unto my servant William E. McLellin—Blessed are you, inasmuch as you have turned away from your iniquities, and have received my truths, saith the Lord your Redeemer, the Savior of the world, even as many as believe on my name.

2 Verily I say unto you, blessed are you for receiving mine everlasting covenant, even the fullness of my gospel, sent forth unto the children of men, that they might have life and be partakers of the glories which are to be revealed in the last days, as it was written by the prophets and apostles in days of old.

This revelation was given to William McLellin at his request (see section heading). The Lord reminded him of the blessing of receiving His everlasting covenant, which He defined as "the fulness of my gospel," sent unto men, to obtain life and partake of the glories that will "be revealed in the last days, as it is written by the prophets and apostles in days of old" (v. 2). The "fullness of my gospel" has been and will be referred to many times in other revelations in the Doctrine and Covenants, and will be discussed later in this work. The Lord's reference to what was written in days of old, by prophets and apostles, supports Brigham Young's statement above regarding the Bible being the basic book of the Church.

D&C 66:3–7 • Proclaim My Gospel

3 Verily I say unto you, my servant William, that you are clean, but not all; repent, therefore, those things which are not pleasing in my sight, saith the Lord, for the Lord will show them unto you.

4 And now, verily, I the Lord will show unto what I will concerning you, or what is my will concerning you.

5 Behold, verily I say unto you, that it is my will that you should proclaim my gospel from land to land, and from city to city, yea, in those regions round about where it has not been proclaimed.

6 Tarry not many days in this place; go not up unto the land of Zion as yet; but inasmuch as you can send, send; otherwise think not of thy property.

7 Go unto the eastern lands, bear testimony in every place, unto every people and in their synagogues, reasoning with the people.

Brother McLellin was told, as promised, why he was not clean, (v. 3), and was then given assignments and admonitions on how to be successful in those assignments (vv. 4–9). These verses seem self-explanatory, but a few observations are added.

- The Lord expects us to always be a missionary (v. 5).

- It should be remembered that the people were in the process of leaving Kirtland and moving to Missouri, the land which the Lord had designated as Zion (see D&C 57:1–3).

- Any financial help would be deeply appreciated (66:6).

- Reasoning with people "in their synagogues" (v. 7).

- Put the Lord's stamp of approval upon proselytizing the Jewish people at this time.

D&C 66:8–13 • Warning to William McLellin

8 Let my servant Samuel H. Smith go with you, and forsake him not, and give him thine instructions; and he that is faithful shall be made strong in every place; and I the Lord, will go with you.

9 Lay your hands upon the sick, and they shall recover. Return not

till I, the Lord, shall send you. Be patient in affliction. Ask, and ye shall receive; knock, and it shall be opened unto you.

10 Seek not to be cumbered. Forsake all unrighteousness. Commit not adultery—a temptation with which thou hast been troubled.

11 Keep these sayings, for they are true and faithful; and thou shalt magnify thine office, and push many people to Zion with songs of everlasting joy upon their heads.

12 Continue in these things even unto the end, and you shall have a crown of eternal life at the right hand of the Father, who is full of grace and truth.

13 Verily thus saith the Lord your God, your Redeemer, even Jesus Christ. Amen.

The faith and love which the Lord had in and for Samuel Smith is strongly implied here (v. 8). The injunction to lay hands on the sick was not limited to sick members of the Church (v. 9), but was still conditional upon their faith (see James 5:14–15). To "ask and ye shall receive" (v. 9) was one of the things written not only by the "apostles in days of old" (see also Matthew 7:7), but apparently also by the Old Testament prophets. Nephi, who lived in Old Testament times; implies this by warning that those who fail to understand his teachings about the tongue of angels do so "because ye ask not, neither do ye knock" (2 Nephi 32:3–4). He may have been quoting or paraphrasing from the plates of brass.

Brother McLellin was to put his eye single to the glory of God, and not seek after the unrighteous things of the world (v. 10; see also D&C 88:67–68). As an example, the Lord showed him that one of those things that "cumbered," or hindered, his spiritual progress, for which he needed to repent was "adultery—a temptation with which thou hast been troubled" (v. 10). The Lord does know the "thoughts and intents "of our hearts" (D&C 6:16). Through magnifying his office, taking the responsibility of teaching the people "the word of God with all diligence" (Jacob 1:19), Brother McLellin would be able to "push many people to Zion" (v. 11)—another prophecy of an Old Testament prophet (see Isaiah 35:10). Brother McLellin was also promised eternal life if he continued "in these things unto the end," (v. 12), a subject that had been discussed in the conferences that were then being held. The Father and the Son are full of grace and truth (v. 12; compare 2 Nephi 2:6; D&C 93:11), and to be with them in eternal life, these attributes must be attained.

D&C 67:1–3 • A Testimony of These Commandments

1 BEHOLD and hearken, O ye elders of my church, who have assembled yourselves together, whose prayers I have heard, and whose hearts I know, and whose desires have come up before me.

2 Behold and lo, mine eyes are upon you, and the heavens and the earth are in mine hands, and the riches of eternity are mine to give.

3 Ye endeavored to believe that ye should receive the blessing which was offered unto you; but behold, verily I say unto you there were fears in your hearts, and verily this is the reason ye did not receive.

Section 67 was given after Oliver Cowdery and John Whitmer had been chosen to take the Book of Commandments manuscript to W. W. Phelps in Independence, Missouri, for publication. Because "some negative conversation was had concerning the language used in the revelations" (see the section heading), the Lord told the assembled "elders of my church" that He had heard their prayers and knew their hearts and desires (v. 1). These elders had "endeavored to believe" the blessings of "the riches of eternity," which was the promise of eternal life (D&C 66:12), but the fears in their hearts was "the reason that ye did not receive" the blessings (vv. 2–3). For the new and inexperienced elders this is understandable, but also a great lesson to all people that the Lord is willing and capable to fulfill any promise that he makes.

D&C 67:4–9 • A Testimony and a Challenge

4 And now I, the Lord, give unto you a testimony of the truth of these commandments which are lying before you.

5 Your eyes have been upon my servant Joseph Smith, Jun., and his language you have known, and his imperfections you have known; and you have sought in your hearts knowledge that you might express beyond his language; this you also know.

6 Now, seek ye out of the Book of Commandments, even the least that is among them, and appoint him that is most wise among you;

7 Or if there be any among you that shall make one like unto it, then are ye justified in saying that ye do not know that they are true;

8 But if ye cannot make one like unto it, ye are under condemnation if ye do not bear record that they are true.

9 For ye know that there is no unrighteousness in them, and that which is righteous cometh down from above, from the Father of lights.

The language of Joseph Smith (v. 5), and D&C 66:10–14 will be discussed in later chapters.

The words of Joseph Smith, as recorded in the *History of the Church,* describe the effects of this testimony and challenge given by the Lord.

> After the foregoing was received, William E. McLellin, as the wisest man, in his own estimation, having more learning than sense, endeavored to write a commandment like unto one of the least of the Lord's, but failed; it was an awful responsibility to write in the name of the Lord. The elders and all present that witnessed this vain attempt of a man to imitate the language of Jesus Christ, renewed their faith in the fulness of the gospel, and in the truth of the commandments and revelations which the Lord had given to the Church through my instrumentality; and the Elders signified a willingness to bear testimony of their truth to all the world. Accordingly, I received the following:
>
> The testimony of the witnesses to the book of the Lord's command-ments, which He gave to His church through Joseph Smith, Jun., who was appointed by the voice of the Church for this purpose; we therefore feel willing to bear testimony to all the world of mankind, to every creature upon the face of all the earth and upon the islands of the sea, that the Lord has borne record to our souls, through the Holy Ghost, shed forth upon us, that these commandments were given by inspiration of God, and are profitable for all men, and are verily true. We give this testimony unto the world, the Lord being our helper; and it is through the grace of God, the Father, and His Son, Jesus Christ, that we are permitted to have this privilege of bearing testimony unto the world, that the children of men may be profited thereby. [*History of the Church,* 1:226]

SECTIONS 69 & 70 • OUTLINE

➤ 69:1–4   It is not wisdom for Oliver Cowdery to go alone to carry the commandments and money to the land of Zion. John Whit-mer is to go with him.

    a.   John Whitmer is to continue to write and make the history of the church (v. 3).

      b.   He should receive counsel and assistance from Oliver (v. 4).

➤ 69:5–8   Other servants who are abroad in the earth should send the accounts of their stewardships to the land of Zion, which is the seat to do these things.

      a.   John Whitmer is to travel from place to place to obtain knowledge (v. 7).

      b.   He should preach, expound, copy, select, and obtain all things for the good of the church and the rising generations (v. 8).

➤ 70:1–4   The six men named are commanded of the Lord to be stewards over the revelations and commandments that have been and will be given.

      a.   An account of their stewardship will be required on the day of judgment (v. 4).

➤ 70:5–18   (The remainder of this revelation is discussed in chapter 21 of this work).

TEXT AND COMMENTARY

D&C 69:1–8 • Companions for Protection and Counsel

1 HEARKEN unto me, saith the Lord your God, for my servant Oliver Cowdery's sake. It is not wisdom in me that he should be entrusted with the commandments and the moneys which he shall carry unto the land of Zion, except one go with him who will be true and faithful.

2 Wherefore, I, the Lord, will that my servant, John Whitmer, should go with my servant Oliver Cowdery;

3 And also that he shall continue in writing and making a history of all the important things which he shall observe and know concerning my church;

4 And also that he receive counsel and assistance from my servant Oliver Cowdery and others.

5 And also, my servants who are abroad in the earth should send forth the accounts of their stewardships to the land of Zion;

6 For the land of Zion shall be a seat and a place to receive and do all these things.

7 Nevertheless, let my servant John Whitmer travel many times from place to place, and from church to church, that he may the more easily obtain knowledge—

8 Preaching and expounding, writing, copying, selecting, and obtaining all things which shall be for the good of the church, and for the rising generations that shall grow up on the land of Zion, to possess it from generation to generation, forever and ever. Amen.

Doctrine and Covenants section 69 was given through the Prophet Joseph as further instructions to Oliver Cowdery as he took the journey to Independence, Missouri with the manuscript of the Book of Commandments (see section heading). In a footnote in the *History of the Church*, Elder B. H. Roberts cautioned that the wording of verse 1 should not be misunderstood to imply that Oliver Cowdery was untrustworthy, but that the territory through which they were to travel was sparsely settled and dangerous because of the gathering of lawless people and the significant amount of money Oliver and John Whitmer had with them for the building up of the Church in Missouri (*HC*, 1:234). This was alluded to in the section heading.

John Whitmer was appointed to be Oliver's companion on the Missouri journey (v. 2). The revelation is the Lord's justification for having companions in his work; for their protection, and for counsel and assistance to each other. It also gives further instructions to John Whitmer in his current position as Church historian (see D&C 47, and 69:3). He was to seek the help of others, and travel "that he may the more easily obtain knowledge—Preaching, and expounding, writing, copying, selecting, and obtaining all things which shall be for the good of the church, and for the rising generation" (vv. 4–8). Such guidelines are still invaluable to historians today. Again, we are reminded that Missouri, or Zion, was designated as the seat, or the center, of church activities at this time (vv. 5–6).

The Preface to the Book of Commandments, now section 1 of the Doctrine and Covenants, was revealed on November 1, 1831; and the Appendix, now section 133 of the Doctrine and Covenants, was revealed on November 3, 1831. These revelations will be discussed separately as they fit into the sequence of this book.

During the fourth and final conference held at this time, the importance of the Book of Commandments was considered. The Prophet's comments, partially quoted in the section heading of section 70, are given in full here.

> In consequence of the book of revelations, now to be printed, being the foundation of the Church in these last days, and a benefit to the world, showing that the keys of the mysteries of the kingdom of our Savior are again entrusted to man; and the riches of eternity within the compass of those who are willing to live by every word that proceedeth out of the mouth of God—therefore the conference voted that they prize the revelations to be worth to the Church the riches of the whole earth, speaking temporally.
>
> The great benefits to the world which result from the Book of Mormon and the revelations which the Lord has seen fit in His infinite wisdom to grant unto us for our salvation, and for the salvation of all that will believe, were duly appreciated; and in answer to an inquiry, I received the following (D&C 70). [*HC*, 1:235–36]

The above endorsement of the revelations that were about to be printed, was given by the Prophet Joseph himself. He eloquently shows that he was the instrument in the Lord's hands to bring forth this great book of revelations. How could anyone have written this beautiful explanation of what the Restoration included, if he had not experienced what he did in bringing it about? The Doctrine and Covenants is indeed worth "the riches of the whole earth."

D&C 70:1–4 • Stewards of the Revelations

> 1 BEHOLD, and hearken, O ye inhabitants of Zion, and all ye people of my church who are afar off, and hear the word of the Lord which I give unto my servant Joseph Smith Jun., and also unto my servant Martin Harris, and also unto my servant Oliver Cowdery, and also unto my servant John Whitmer, and also unto my servant Sidney Rigdon, and also unto my servant William W. Phelps, by way of commandment unto them.
>
> 2 For I give unto them a commandment; wherefore hearken and hear, for thus saith the Lord unto them—
>
> 3 I the Lord, have appointed them, and ordained them to be stewards

over the revelations and commandments which I have given unto them, and which I shall here after give unto them;

4 And an account of this stewardship will I require of them in the day of judgment.

The six men named in the revelation (v. 1) were all involved in the publication of the Book of Commandments in one way or another. The Lord equated the revelations that were to be printed to the law of consecration and stewardship which He had revealed in February, 1831, nine months previously. The implication is that other revelations would be added to this publication from time to time (v. 3), and they have been. This revelation will be understood better after the law of consecration is studied and understood, as revealed in section 42. The remainder of section 70 will be discussed with that revelation in chapter 21 of this work.

The Prophet then dedicated Oliver and John to the Lord by the prayer of faith as they traveled to Missouri, and several other brethren who had assisted with the work were to "be remembered to the Bishop in Zion as being worthy of inheritances among the people of the Lord according to the laws of said Church" (*HC*, 1:236, note 18).

EDITIONS OF THE DOCTRINE AND COVENANTS

The first collected use of the revelations received by the Prophet Joseph Smith was referred to by the Lord in a revelation in October 1830: "And ye shall remember the church articles and covenants to keep them." (D&C 33:14). The "articles and covenants" consisted of our present day sections 20 and 22 of the Doctrine and Covenants. They were again referred to by the Lord in the revelation "embracing the law of the Church" (D&C 42 section heading). The Lord instructed his priesthood holders to "observe the covenants and church articles to do them, and these shall be their teachings, as they are directed by the Spirit" (D&C 42:13). These two revelations were read in church gatherings and in missionary work as the Lord had directed. They were later published in the first official newspaper of the Church, the *Evening and Morning Star*, in June of 1832.

In July 1833, about nineteen months after the conferences, as the Book of Commandments was being prepared for publication, a mob destroyed the printing press and most of the printed materials. The Saints saved and bound what copies they could, but more were planned to be included than the sixty-five sections they had saved. There was no attempt to republish the Book of Commandments; the next publication of the revelations was entitled "the Doctrine and Covenants." The major editions of the Doctrine and Covenants, to which more revelations were added included the following:

1.   The first edition of the Doctrine and Covenants was published in Kirtland in 1835, and contained 102 revelations. Section 101 was a statement on marriage written by Oliver Cowdery. It was later replaced by the present section 132. Section 102 was another statement written by Oliver Cowdery, "Of Government and Laws in General." This is now section 134 in our Doctrine and Covenants. These two articles were read and unanimously approved at a general assembly of the Church on August 17, 1835, which had met to approve the publication of the first edition (see *HC*, 2:243–47). It also contained what became known as the *Lectures on Faith*. A letter to the members of the Church written by the First Presidency including Oliver Cowdery, the Assistant President, stated: "The first part of the book will be found a series of Lectures as delivered before a Theological class in this place, and in consequence of their embracing the important doctrine of salvation, we have arranged them into the following work" (Preface in the 1835 edition, paragraph 2). The seven lectures that were included were given to the School of the Elders in the winter of 1834–35 in Kirtland, Ohio. They were written by the Prophet Joseph and others, and approved by him.

2.   Another edition was published in Nauvoo, in 1844, shortly after the martyrdom of Joseph and Hyrum Smith. There were 111 sections including John Taylor's description of the martyrdom which is now section 135.

3.   In 1876 another edition was published in Salt Lake City, Utah. This edition included 136 sections. Section 132 of our current Doctrine and Covenants replaced the article on marriage written by Oliver Cowdery. In 1879 Elder Orson Pratt added footnotes to the text of the 1876 Edition.

4.   In 1908 the Manifesto, the Official Declaration by President Wilford Woodruff regarding the discontinuance of the practice of plural

marriage was included. The Manifesto had been approved at the October 1908 General Conference.

5.   Another edition was published in 1921. This edition added some introductory materials and deleted the *Lectures on Faith*. The revelations were printed in two columns instead of the previous one column page, and other editing was done.

6.   Our current edition was published in 1981. Two sections, 137 and 138, were added as well as "Official Declaration—2"; the position of the Church on "every worthy man in the Church may receive the Priesthood." Many other supplemental helps to our understanding the revelations were added, edited, and refined.

The Doctrine and Covenants is a "selection" of revelations given to the members of the Church for clarification of doctrine, and personal guidance. The words of Jarom, in the Book of Mormon, appropriately describe the selections that have been included over the years: "I shall not write the things of my prophesying, nor of my revelations. For what could I write more than what my fathers have written? For have they not revealed the plan of salvation? I say unto you, Yea; and this sufficeth me" (Jarom 1:2). Other revelations may and probably will be added periodically, but what we have is also sufficient for our day, particularly if we will listen to and follow the teachings of our current prophets and apostles.

General Authority Quotes

—Elder Marion G. Romney • Doctrine and Covenants

The scriptures that are binding upon us are the ones the Lord has given us in these latter days. He has never required His people of one dispensation to rely solely upon the teachings He gave to former dispensation. But he has revealed his law, given his commandments anew in every dispensation. And in this dispensation the commandments that we are bound by are those in the Doctrine and Covenants. [CR, April 1969, 108]

—Elder Boyd K. Packer • Doctrine and Covenants

True Doctrine, understood, changes attitudes and behavior. The study of the doctrines of the gospel will improve behavior quicker than a study of behavior will change behavior. Preoccupation with unworthy behavior can lead to unworthy behavior. That is why we stress so forcefully the study of the doctrines of the gospel. [CR, October 1986, 20; see also April 1997, 8; and April 2004, 80]

See also the quotes of Presidents of the Church in the Introduction.

Chapter Two

The Lord's Preface

D&C 1

*H*istorical Setting: As noted in the section heading, this revelation was received at the special conference where the publication of the revelations given to the Prophet Joseph Smith was being discussed. Elder B. H. Roberts made the following editorial comment in the *History of the Church.*

> This special conference at Hiram on November 1, 1831, should receive larger notice. The number of copies in the edition of the Book of Commandments to be printed was considered, and the decision reached that ten thousand should be published. The conference lasted two days. In the afternoon of the first day of the conference, according to the minutes of the conference, the preface to the Book of Commandments was "received by inspiration." The same afternoon the following occurred: "Brother Joseph Smith, Jun., said that inasmuch as the Lord had bestowed a great blessing upon us in giving commandments and revelations, he asked the conference what testimony they were willing to attach to these commandments which would shortly be sent to the world. A number of the brethren arose and said they were willing to testify to the world that they knew they were of the Lord."

> In the second day's proceedings of the conference it is recorded: "The revelation of last evening read by the moderator (this was Oliver Cowdery). The brethren then arose in turn and bore testimony to the truth of the Book of Commandments: after which Brother Joseph Smith Jun., arose and expressed his feelings and gratitude concerning the commandments and preface received yesterday. [*HC,* 1:222]

Introduction

The section heading designates this revelation "the Lord's Preface to the doctrines, covenants, and commandments given in this dispensation." The Lord calls the revelation "my preface unto the book of my commandments" (v. 6).

A preface is a preliminary statement about a book or article which outlines its subject, plan and purpose. The revelation can be divided into these three categories, and will be discussed in that order. Also, the revelations selected for inclusion in the Book of Commandments, or the Doctrine and Covenants, would be an extension of these three categories, and would further explain or amplify them. The revelations that do so will be cited here, but their detailed analysis will be left for a discussion on that revelation.

SECTION 1 • OUTLINE

➤ 1:1–3   The voice of the Lord is to all men and none shall escape.

         a.   No eye shall not see, no ear not hear, nor heart not be penetrated (v. 2).

         b.   The rebellious and unbelieving shall have their secret acts revealed (v. 3).

➤ 1:4–10   The warning shall be by the mouths of my disciples, and none shall stay them.

         a.   They go by the authority of the Lord as His servants (v. 4).

         b.   The Lord's preface to His commandments shall be published to all (v. 6).

         c.   Fear and tremble for they have power to seal on earth and heaven, the unbelieving and the rebellious to the day of the wrath of God (vv. 7–9).

         d.   Every man to be measured by his acts toward his fellow-man (v. 10).

➤ 1:11–16   All that will hear may hear; prepare for the day of the Lord, for it is nigh.

         a.   His sword is bathed in heaven and will fall on the earth's inhabitants (v. 13).

         b.   Whoso will not hear the Lord's voice, His servants, or the

words of His apostles and prophets shall be cut off (v. 14).

   c.   They strayed from his ordinances and broke His everlasting covenant (v. 15).

   d.   They seek not the Lord, but walk in the image of their own god (v. 16).

1:17–20   Knowing what was to come, the Lord called upon Joseph Smith, Jun., and gave him commandments.

   a.   He also gave commandments to others to proclaim unto the world (v. 18).

   b.   All this was to fulfill the prophets (v. 18).

   c.   The weak things of the world shall break down the mighty and strong (v. 19).

   d.   Every man might have opportunity to speak in the name of the Lord (v. 20).

1:24–28   The commandments are of God, and were given to his servants after their language and understanding.

   a.   If they erred it might be made known (v. 25).

   b.   If they sought wisdom they might be instructed (v. 26).

   c.   If they sinned they may be chastened and repent (v. 27).

   d.   If they were humble they might be made strong and receive knowledge (v. 28).

1:29   Joseph Smith Jun. was given power to translate the Book of Mormon.

1:30–33   Those who were given commandments might lay the foundation of the church.

   a.   The only true and living church upon the earth (v. 30).

   b.   The Lord cannot look upon sin with the least degree of allowance (v. 31).

   c.   He that repents shall be forgiven (v. 32).

   d.   If he does not repent the Spirit is taken away (v. 33).

1:34–36   The Lord is willing to make all things known to all flesh.

   a.   The day shall come that peace shall be taken from the earth (v. 35).

   b.   The devil shall have power over his own dominion (v. 35).

    c.   The Lord shall have power over His saints and reign in their midst (v. 36).

    d.   The Lord shall come down in judgment upon the world.

➤ **1:37–39**   Search these, for they are true and faithful and the prophecies and promises shall all be fulfilled.

    a.   They will be fulfilled whether spoken by the Lord or by His servants (v. 38).

    b.   The Spirit beareth record and the record is true, which abideth forever (v. 39).

D&C 1:1–3 • The Subject

1 Hearken, O ye people of my church, saith the voice of him who dwells on high, and whose eyes are upon all men; yea, verily I say: Hearken ye people from afar; and ye that are upon the islands of the sea, listen together.

2 For verily the voice of the Lord is unto all men, and there is none to escape; and there is no eye that shall not see, neither ear that shall not hear, neither heart that shall not be penetrated.

3 And the rebellious shall be pierced with much sorrow; for their iniquities shall be spoken upon the housetops, and their secret acts shall be revealed.

The Lord proclaimed that His message, as given in the revelations of the book that is about to be published, is intended for all the inhabitants of the earth in these latter days. This declaration is consistent with John the Revelator's observation of an angel "having the everlasting gospel to preach unto them that dwell on the earth, and to every nation, and kindred, and tongue, and people" (Revelation 14:6). As confirmed in the Appendix of the revelations, the Lord had "sent forth mine angel [Moroni] flying through the midst of heaven, having the everlasting gospel [the Book of Mormon] to every nation, and kindred, and tongue, and people" (D&C 133:36–37). It was intended for this Book of Commandments (Doctrine and Covenants) to follow the same course (D&C 1:1).

The Lord's admonition that none shall escape (v. 2) was further verified by the Prophet Joseph Smith shortly before his death, on May 2, 1844: "You cannot go anywhere but where God can find you out. All men are born to die, and all men must rise; all men must enter eternity"

(*TPJS*, 367–68). According to President Joseph Fielding Smith, those who are not reached by the Lord's message in this mortal probation will be given that opportunity in the Spirit World.

> I do not understand even from this wording [v. 2] that it is necessary that every heart be penetrated and every ear hear in this life. But if they have not heard, if this opportunity has not come to them through the preaching of the elders and through the things that have been published in the word of the Lord that has gone forth by revelation, the opportunity is going to come to them and they must hear it in the spirit world.
>
> The Lord, in his kindness and mercy, intends to bring the truths of this restored Gospel to every soul, living or dead. In this manner every heart shall be penetrated and every ear shall hear.[1]

Those who rebel against the Lord's message will eventually be extremely sorrowful. The warning secret acts that would be revealed from the housetops (v. 3) was explained in a revelation given December 27, 1832. Angels will blow their trumps as the millennium is ushered in, and reveal these things (see D&C 88:108–110). The revealing of these secret acts of the rebellious was also prophesied by the Old Testament prophet Isaiah: "And the day cometh that the words of the book which were sealed shall be read upon the house tops; and they shall be read by the power of Christ; and all things shall be revealed unto the children of men which ever have been among the children of men, and which ever will be even unto the end of the earth (see 2 Nephi 27:11; JST, Isaiah 29:16).[2]

D&C 1:4–10 • The Plan

> 4 And the voice of warning shall be unto all people, by the mouths of my disciples, whom I have chosen in these last days.
>
> 5 And they shall go forth and none shall stay them, for I the Lord have commanded them.

---

[1] CR, October 1916, as quoted in *The Latter-day Prophets and the Doctrine and Covenants*; Roy W. Doxey, 2 vols. [1963] 1:2.

[2] The verses of Isaiah foretelling the secret acts of men being revealed were among the many plain and precious things lost from our present day Bible (see 1 Nephi 13:24–29), but were preserved in the plates of brass which Nephi obtained from Laban (see 1 Nephi 4:3–25). Nephi is quoting Isaiah from these plates in 2 Nephi 27. The secret acts were known by the Lord beforehand, and were recorded upon the sealed portion of the plates which the Prophet Joseph Smith was commanded not to translate. The words of the sealed part of the plates will be read from the house tops at this time (see 2 Nephi 27:7–10).

6 Behold, this is mine authority, and the authority of my servants, and the preface unto the book of my commandments, which I have given them to publish unto you, O inhabitants of the earth.

7 Wherefore, fear and tremble, O ye people, for what I the Lord have decreed in them shall be fulfilled.

8 And verily I say unto you, that they who go forth, bearing these tidings unto the inhabitants of the earth, to them is given power to seal both on earth and in heaven, the unbelieving and rebellious;

9 Yea, verily, to seal them up unto the day when the wrath of God shall be poured out upon the wicked without measure—

10 Unto the day when the Lord shall come to recompense unto every man according to his work, and measure to every man according to the measure which he has measured to his fellow man.

The first phase of the Lord's plan was to warn the inhabitants of the earth by "the mouths of my disciples" (v. 4). This warning must have seemed an enormous task to the relatively handful of Saints who had gathered at the time. The task is still an enormous one, but is becoming more realistic. In 1965, Elder Spencer W. Kimball made this observation:

In 1965, when the Prophet sends out the Twelve, the seventies, and the numerous elders and sisters to teach the gospel to all the world, there are three and a quarter billion people, or about 13 times as many as when the first commission was given 18 centuries ago. It is estimated that there were only 25 million people on the whole earth when Moses led the children of Israel from Egyptian bondage; and a quarter billion when Christ was born; and half a billion when the crusades were marched and when Columbus crossed the Atlantic and when the pilgrims came, the population remaining almost static for six centuries while war, pestilence, and famine offset the natural growth.

It is estimated that there were one billion people on earth when the Church was organized in 1830, another billion one hundred years later when we celebrated the centennial, and another billion 31 years later; and that there may be another billion after 14 more years have passed. There could be 7 billion on earth while most of you are still living. And then in another century, 42 to 45 billion people may be upon earth. So we should get busy before the population explosion loses us.

We are not discouraged, because our ratio is bettering all the time. On April 6, 1830, there was one Latter-day Saint to 166 million people. In 1840, there was one to 35,000; in 1920, one to 3,400; in 1955, one

to about 1,800; and today, approximately one of every 1,500 souls in the world is a member of The Church of Jesus Christ of Latter-day Saints. We are becoming numerous. [*The Instructor*, May 1966, 200][3]

The task is even more realistic when one considers the Lord's promise that "none shall stay them" (v. 5). As later written by Joseph Smith, "As well might man stretch forth his puny arm to stop the Missouri River in its decreed course, or to turn it up stream, as to hinder the Almighty from pouring down knowledge from heaven upon the heads of the Latter-day Saints (D&C 121:33).

The Lord has given His authority to His servants to teach and publish His words to the inhabitants of the earth (v. 6). This authority is not merely permission to go forth, but also a warning that his published word will be fulfilled (v. 7). His disciples will have power to seal both on earth and in heaven the unbelieving and rebellious up unto the day when the "wrath of God shall be poured out upon the wicked without measure" (vv. 8–9). Each person will be judged according to his works (v. 10). Again the words of John the Revelator concerning the Book of Mormon coming forth are a parallel: "Fear God and give glory to him; for the hour of his judgment is come" (Revelation 14:7). The Doctrine and Covenants is a second witness to the world of the message of the Book of Mormon.

D&C 1:11–16 • The Plan Continued—Unto the Ends of the Earth

11 Wherefore, the voice of the Lord is unto the ends of the earth, that all that will hear may hear:

12 Prepare ye, prepare ye for that which is to come, for the Lord is nigh;

13 And the anger of the Lord is kindled, and his sword is bathed in heaven, and it shall fall upon the inhabitants of the earth.

14 And the arm of the Lord shall be revealed; and the day cometh that they who will not hear the voice of the Lord, neither the voice of his servants, neither give heed to the words of prophets and apostles, shall be cut off from among the people;

---

[3] In 2007, with approximately six and one-half billion inhabitants of the world, and thirteen million members of the Church, the ratio is about one member to five hundred and twenty inhabitants.

15 For they have strayed from mine ordinances, and have broken mine everlasting covenant;

16 They seek not the Lord to establish his righteousness, but every man walketh in his own way, and after the image of his own god, whose image is in the likeness of the world, and whose substance is that of an idol, which waxeth old and shall perish in Babylon, even Babylon the great, which shall fall.

The disciples' warning has two purposes: to prepare a righteous people for the Second Coming of Jesus Christ, and to warn the wicked of the Lord's anger against them and their eventual destruction when he comes (vv. 12–13). The preparation of His people will be to "seek to bring forth and establish the cause of Zion" (D&C 6:6; see also 11:6; 12:6; 14:6). Zion is both a place and a condition of purity (see D&C 57:1–3; 97:18–21). The New Jerusalem is the center of Zion (see D&C 84:2–4). Zion and her stakes will be redeemed before the Second Coming (see D&C 103 and 105). To hear the voice of the Lord is to receive personal revelation. To hear the voice of His servants is to follow the directions of the appointed Church leaders. To give heed to the words of the prophets and apostles is to read and follow the written words of the Bible, the Book of Mormon, the Doctrine and Covenants, and the Pearl of Great Price (v. 14; cf. D&C 52:9, 36). Those who will not hear the word of the Lord's servants, or give heed to the published word, will cut themselves off. This will take place in a natural way, and unnoticed by themselves or the world.

The second phase of the Lord's plan to warn the inhabitants of the world will feature the Lord cutting off from among his people, where they have been gathered, those who will not hearken to his word (v. 14). There may be a tendency to associate righteousness with membership, and wickedness with non-membership. Those who are cut off are those who have strayed from his "ordinances, and broken mine everlasting covenants" (v. 15). To stray from an ordinance, or break a covenant, one must have received the ordinance, or have made a covenant (see D&C 45:1–15; 66:2). Therefore the Lord is speaking of cutting off the members of the Church who have failed to live as they have committed themselves to live. They have not walked after the example of the Lord, but sought their own god (v. 16; cf. D&C 124:84–86). They choose to remain in "the midst of wickedness, which is spiritual wickedness" (D&C 133:14).

D&C 1:17–18 • The First Purpose—Fulfill the Prophets

17 Wherefore, I the Lord, knowing the calamity which should come upon the inhabitants of the earth, called upon my servant Joseph Smith, Jun., and spake unto him from heaven, and gave unto him commandments;

18 And also gave commandments to others, that they should proclaim these things unto the world; and all this that it might be fulfilled, which was written by the prophets—

The gospel was restored for the last days and for the last time. The keys of this dispensation were "in connection with all those who have received a dispensation at any time from the beginning of the creation" (D&C 112:30–31). Therefore all the prophets knew of and looked forward to the Restoration.

D&C 1:19–20 • The Second Purpose—Restore the Priesthood

19 The weak things of the world shall come forth and break down the mighty and strong ones, that man should not counsel his fellow man, neither trust in the arm of flesh—

20 But that every man might speak in the name of God the Lord, even the Savior of the world;

The priesthood was restored to eventually give every man an opportunity to speak in the name of the Lord, rather than trust in the philosophies and strength of men (v. 20). In the Book of Mormon, the Prophet Alma linked the holding of the priesthood in this life with the "first place, or the pre-mortal life:

3 And this is the manner after which they were ordained—being called and prepared from the foundation of the world according to the foreknowledge of God, on account of their exceeding faith and good works; in the first place being left to choose good or evil; therefore they having chosen good, and exercising exceedingly great faith, are called with a holy calling, yea, with that holy calling which was prepared with, and according to, a preparatory redemption for such.

4 And thus they have been called to this holy calling on account of their faith, while others would reject the Spirit of God on account of the hardness of their hearts and blindness of their minds, while, if it had not been for this they might have had as great privilege as their brethren.

5 Or in fine, in the first place they were on the same standing with their brethren; thus this holy calling being prepared from the foundation of the world for such as would not harden their hearts, being in and through the atonement of the Only Begotten Son, who was prepared— [Alma 13:3–5]. (See also Numbers 8:5–26; Hebrews 7:11; Acts 17:26.)

There were undoubtedly other reasons that arose in this life for not giving the priesthood to some, whether from God or man-made. However, regardless of the justification of these reasons, one of the major purposes for the restoration of the gospel has come to pass. In the last days, "all worthy members of the Church may be ordained to the priesthood without regard to race or color" (OFFICIAL DECLARATION—2).

D&C 1:21 • The Third Purpose—Increase Faith

21 That faith also might increase in the earth;

Faith in the Lord Jesus Christ is the first principle of the gospel (A of F 4). "Without faith it is impossible to please [God]" (Hebrews 11:6; see also D&C 8:10). In an apostate world, faith was certainly lagging. The Doctrine and Covenants speaks of faith in the majority of its sections.

D&C 1:22–23 • The Fourth Purpose—Establish the Everlasting Covenant

22 That mine everlasting covenant might be established;

23 That the fullness of my gospel might be proclaimed by the weak and the simple unto the ends of the world, and before kings and rulers.

The blood shed by Jesus Christ in Gethsemane, and on Golgotha, is the everlasting covenant (see Hebrews 13:20). The Prophet Jeremiah foretold of a new covenant being established with the house of Israel and with the house of Judah (see Jeremiah 31:31–34). As the Prophet Joseph Smith declared:

"This covenant has never been established with the house of Israel, nor with the house of Judah, for it requires two to make a covenant, and those two parties must be agreed, or no covenant can be made.

Christ, in the days of His flesh, proposed to make a covenant with them, but they rejected Him and His proposals, and in consequence

thereof, they were broken off, and no covenant was made with them at that time." [*TPJS*, 14–15].

The "everlasting covenant, even the fullness of gospel" was received in these last days by the remnant of scattered Israel that was being gathered (see D&C 66:2; 45:9). The fullness of the gospel was to be taken to the ends of the world, and before kings and rulers (v. 23). As well as the voice of warning by the mouth of Christ's disciples, the weak and the simple, proclamations have been sent to the kings and rulers of the world (see D&C 124; CR, October 1975, 46–49; and CR, April 1980, 75–75). The Lord's purposes are going forth.

D&C 1:24–28 • The Fifth Purpose—Perfecting of the Saints

24 Behold, I am God and have spoken it; these commandments are of me, and were given unto my servants in their weakness, after the manner of their language, that they might come to understanding.

25 And inasmuch as they erred it might be made known;

26 And inasmuch as they sought wisdom they might be instructed;

27 And inasmuch as they sinned they might be chastened, that they might repent;

28 And inasmuch as they were humble they might be made strong, and blessed from on high, and receive knowledge from time to time.

The Restoration was to bring understanding to the leaders of the Church. In turn, these leaders could bring understanding to the members of the Church collectively and individually. As Paul taught the Ephesians, the apostles and prophets and other officers and leaders of the Church were "For the perfecting of the saints" (Ephesians 4:11–12). President Spencer W. Kimball listed this as one of the three missions of the Church that were determined by "the Brethren of the First Presidency and the Twelve" after having "meditated upon and prayed about the great latter-day work the Lord has given us to do. . . . To perfect the Saints by preparing them to receive the ordinances of the gospel and by instruction and discipline to gain exaltation" (CR, April 1981, 3). The commandments of the Lord collected to be printed in what is now the Doctrine and Covenants (v. 24) were for this purpose. The various ways the Lord would bring about the Saints' perfection are specified in the verses that followed (vv. 25–28). All of these ways are through revelation from the

Lord. The people of the world are prone to use reasoning rather than revelation to correct their ways. The Prophet Joseph gave this counsel:

> And we shall at last have to come to this conclusion, whatever we may think of revelation, that without it we can neither know nor understand anything of God, or the devil; and however unwilling the world may be to acknowledge this principle, it is evident from the multifarious creeds and notions concerning this matter that they understand nothing of this principle, and it is equally as plain that without a divine communication they must remain in ignorance. [*TPJS*, 205–06]

Revelation is given in the language of the recipients (v. 24). The prophet Nephi taught this same concept: "For the Lord God giveth light unto the understanding; for he speaketh unto men according to their language, unto their understanding" (2 Nephi 31:3). The Prophet Joseph gave us a third witness of the language of revelation: "If He [Jesus] comes to a little child, He will adapt himself to the language and capacity of a little child" (*TPJS*, 162).

D&C 1:29 • Sixth Purpose—Bring Forth the Book of Mormon

> 29 And after having received the record of the Nephites, yea, even my servant Joseph Smith, Jun., might have power to translate through the mercy of God, by the power of God, the Book of Mormon.

The Lord had preserved the Book of Mormon to come forth in these last days to prove "to the world that the holy scriptures are true" (D&C 20:11; see also 1 Nephi 13:39–41). Since the Book of Mormon was written in a language unknown to the world then and now, it was necessary to have it translated. Joseph repeatedly testified that he "translated [the Book of Mormon] into our own language by the gift and power of God" (*HC*, 1:315); through the medium of the Urim and Thummim (*HC*, 4:537; see also 3:28). The Doctrine and Covenants puts the Lord's approval upon the translation by Joseph (see D&C 6:7; 17:6; 18:2–3; 19:26–27). The ancient prophet Mormon bore witness that the Book of Mormon was "written for the intent that ye may believe the [the Bible]; and if ye believe [the Bible] ye will believe [the Book of Mormon] also" (Mormon 7:9; see also 2 Nephi 33:10). "In the mouth of two or three witnesses every word may be established" (Matthew 18:16; see also

Deuteronomy 19:15). The Doctrine and Covenants is the Lord's third witness of his word (v. 24).

D&C 1:30–33 • The Seventh Purpose—Lay the Foundation of Christ's Church

> 30 And also those to whom these commandments were given, might have power to lay the foundation of this church, and to bring it forth out of obscurity and out of darkness, the only true and living church upon the face of the whole earth, with which I, the Lord, am well pleased, speaking unto the church collectively and not individually—
>
> 31 For I the Lord cannot look upon sin with the least degree of allowance;
>
> 32 Nevertheless, he that repents and does the commandments of the Lord shall be forgiven;
>
> 33 And he that repents not, from him shall be taken even the light which he has received; for my Spirit shall not always strive with man, saith the Lord of Hosts.

The bringing of the Church out of obscurity and out of darkness (v. 30) has reference to the Church being driven into the wilderness, or going into a state of apostasy, as shown John the Revelator on the Isle of Patmos (see Revelation 14:1–6). The Doctrine and Covenants announced that "this is the beginning of the rising up and the coming forth of my church out of the wilderness" (D&C 5:14; see also 33:5; 86:3; 109:73).

The laying of "the foundation of this church" (v. 30) was to ordain men the apostleship once more. This ordination of special witnesses was done before the Church was organized (see D&C 20:2–3; 18:9). The Lord's declaration that the restored Church was "the only true and living church upon the face of the whole earth" is in the context of the proper foundation of apostles and prophets (see Ephesians 2:20–21). While all churches have truth and parts of the gospel, they lack the foundation. The authority upon which they must build to have the everlasting covenant and the fullness of the gospel as defined above. The Church of Jesus Christ of Latter-day Saints is a living church because it has the Spirit within it. The Lord's Spirit is there, and gives it life (v. 33).

The collective Church had been established according to revelation and was acknowledged as acceptable God, but the individual members were mortal and subject to the weaknesses of men (1:30). One of the purposes of the Church, as stated above, was to perfect the saints. The Lord, who is perfect (see 3 Nephi 12:48), could not "look upon sin with the least degree of allowance" (v. 31). Notwithstanding, the members could, and should repent. Their repentance would bring forgiveness and the guidance of the Spirit (vv. 32–33). In the words of the Prophet Joseph, "God does not look upon sin with allowance, but where men have sinned, there must be allowance made for them. . . . There should be no license for sin, but mercy should go hand in hand with reproof." (*TPJS*, 240–241).

D&C 1:34–36 • The Lord's Conclusion

34 And again, verily I say unto you, O inhabitants of the earth: I the Lord am willing to make these things known unto all flesh;

35 For I am no respecter of persons, and will that all men shall know that the day speedily cometh; the hour is not yet, but is nigh at hand, when peace shall be taken from the earth, and the devil shall have power over his own dominion.

36 And also the Lord shall have power over his saints, and shall reign in their midst, and shall come down in judgment upon Idumea, or the world.

The truths contained in the revelations about to be published were intended for all flesh who would receive them (v. 34). Nevertheless, men have their agency (see Moses 4:3); but, at the Second Coming they will know that He is the "Alpha and Omega, the beginning and the ending" (Revelation 1:8; D&C 19:1). Prior to his coming, the Lord warns that peace shall be taken from the earth (v. 35). This time of no peace is undoubtedly the same as described by the Savior in his mortal ministry as "wars and rumors of wars" (1:23). Are we not in this time period now? It certainly seems so, and the devil certainly has power over much of the world. But conditions will get worse as the time of His Coming draws nearer. However, the Lord has power over His Saints, those who follow Him; and He will protect them as they gather to Zion and her stakes (see D&C 84:5–6). His "judgment upon Idumea, or the world" (v. 36), was foretold by the Prophet Isaiah (Isaiah 34:1–10). The Doctrine and Covenants sheds much light upon his Second Coming (see D&C 29; 38;

45; 133). His reign will last for a thousand years (see D&C 29:11).

D&C 1:37–39 • Search These Commandments

> 37 Search these commandments, for they are true and faithful, and the prophecies and promises which are in them shall all be fulfilled.
>
> 38 What I the Lord have spoken, I have spoken, and I excuse not myself; and though the heavens and the earth pass away, my word shall not pass away, but shall all be fulfilled, whether by mine own voice or by the voice of my servants, it is the same.
>
> 39 For behold, and lo, the Lord is God, and the Spirit beareth record, and the record is true, and the truth abideth forever and ever. Amen.

In preparation for the judgment that is to come upon the world, the Lord directs us to do three things. First, search the commandments that are contained in the Doctrine and Covenant, for they shall all be fulfilled (v. 37). The Doctrine and Covenants is the book given for this generation (see the quotes of General Authorities in the Introduction and at the end of chapter 1). This statement should not be interpreted to mean that we do not need to search the other Standard Works. It should be remembered that this revelation was given as a preface to the book of the revelations that were about to be, or would later be, printed. A preface is merely an overview of what is contained in the revelations to follow. The following revelations contain the answers to questions about the world conditions that do and will exist.

The second thing we are commanded to do is to seek and to follow personal revelation as well as the voice of His appointed leaders, for these revelations shall also be fulfilled (v. 38). Revelation is the key to understanding both God's will, and the works of the devil, as noted in the Prophet Joseph's teaching above. The Lord will never permit "the President of this Church to lead you astray" (see statement of Wilford Woodruff Regarding the Manifesto, D&C p. 292; (see also, *Journal of Discourses* [1941], 24:192; and Harold B. Lee, Address to Seminary and Institute Faculty, July 8, 1964; and Marion G. Romney, CR, October 1960, 76). President Joseph Fielding Smith testified: "Neither the President of the church, nor the first Presidency, nor the united voice of the First Presidency and the Twelve will ever lead the Saints astray or send counsel to the world that is contrary to the mind and will of the Lord

(*Ensign*, July 1972, 88). Elder Spencer W. Kimball declared: "the Quorum of the Twelve will never lead you into bypaths; it never has and never will. There could be individuals who would falter; there will never be a majority of Council of the Twelve on the wrong side at any time" (CR, April 1951, 104). We must follow the brethren.

The third thing we are commanded to do is to listen to the confirmation of the Spirit that bears record of the truth (v. 39). "They that are wise and have received the truth, and have taken the Holy Spirit for their guide, and have not been deceived—verily I say shall not be hewn down and cast into the fire, but shall abide the day" (D&C 45:57).

Individually we must decide how we will use the Doctrine and Covenants. President Wilford Woodruff said it "contains enough revelations to lead this church into the celestial kingdom of God" (Claude Richards, *Life of J. Golden Kimball* [1967], 296). Will we search it and let it lead us to the Celestial kingdom, or neglect it and wished that we had used it? The Lord is no respecter of persons (v. 35), it is our choice.

General Authority Quotes

—*The Prophet Joseph Smith* • D&C 1:13–17

I prophesy, in the name of the Lord God of Israel, anguish and wrath and tribulation and the withdrawing of the spirit of God from the earth await this generation, until they are visited with utter desolation. This generation is as corrupt as the generation of the Jews that crucified Christ; and if He were here to-day, and would preach the same doctrine He did then, they would put Him to death. I defy all the world to destroy the work of God; and I prophesy that they never will have power to kill me till my work is accomplished, and I am ready to die. [*TPJS*, 328]

—*President Harold B. Lee* • D&C 1:36

Is there anyone here who doubts as to whether this is the time of which the Lord spoke over a hundred years ago, when peace has been taken from the earth and the devil has power over his own dominion? But listen to the calming voice of the Lord, "And also the Lord shall have power over his saints, and shall reign in their midst, and shall come down in judgment upon Idumea, or the world" (D&C 1:36).

As I have thought of that I have asked, "How will the Lord reign in the midst of His people?" The answer is clear. By and through the priesthood of God, loving those who revile against us, feeling sorry for and praying for those who are sinful that they might repent, being rational and using sound minds rather than to allow our people to be tossed about by rumor and perplexities. [*The Teachings of Harold B. Lee,* ed. Clyde J. Williams (1996), 9–10]

Chapter Three

The Heavens Are Not Sealed

D&C 2; 7

Historical Setting—Section 2: When the Angel Moroni appeared to the young Joseph in 1823, he "commenced quoting the prophecies of the Old Testament. He first quoted part of the third chapter of Malachi; and he quoted also the fourth or last chapter of the same prophecy, though with a little variation from the way it reads in our Bibles," regarding the coming of Elijah before the Second Coming of Christ (JS—History 1:36–39). The latter part of Malachi (4:5–6), as quoted by the Angel Moroni, is now D&C section 2.

INTRODUCTION

The early nineteenth century common philosophy of the ministry of angels was that the heavens were sealed. Therefore, Joseph Smith's telling of his "First Vision" brought the response "that there were no such things as visions or revelations in these days; that all such things had ceased with the apostles, and that there would never be any more of them" (JS—H 1:21). In contrast to this philosophy, the Bible, which those who heard Joseph's story professed to believe, admonished the Hebrews to: "Be not forgetful to entertain strangers: for many have entertained angels unawares" (Hebrews 13:2). If one entertained an angel and was unaware of it, the angel must have looked somewhat like a mortal man. This raises the question: What is an angel? "In the broadest sense, any being who acts as a messenger for our Heavenly Father is an angel." (George Q. Cannon, quoted in Lee A. Palmer, *Aaronic Priesthood Through the Ages*

[1964], 298.) Several years after Moroni's visits, the Prophet Joseph Smith gave the following definition of angels.

> 1 There are two kinds of angels in heaven, namely: Angels who are resurrected personages, having bodies of flesh and bones—
>
> 2 For instance, Jesus said: *Handle me and see, for a spirit hath not flesh and bones, as ye see me have.*
>
> 3 Secondly: the spirits of just men made perfect, they who are not resurrected, but inherit the same glory. [D&C 129:1–30]

On another occasion the Prophet qualified another type of angel who has a body of flesh and bones, a translated or transfigured being. A translated personage is someone who, like Enoch, had lived on earth but "was translated that he should not taste death" (Hebrews 11:5). Concerning these types of angels the Prophet Joseph said:

> Many have supposed that the doctrine of translation was a doctrine whereby men were taken immediately into the presence of God, and into an eternal fullness, but this is a mistaken idea. Their place of habitation is that of the terrestrial order, and a place prepared for such characters He held in reserve to be ministering angels unto many planets and who as yet have not entered in so great a fullness as those who are resurrected from the dead. . . .
>
> . . . This distinction is made between the doctrine of actual resurrection and translation: translation obtains deliverance from the tortures and sufferings of the body, but their existence will prolong as to the labors and toils of the ministry, before they can enter into so great a rest and glory." [*TPJS,* 170–71]

On a later occasion, the Prophet explained:

> . . . the difference between an angel and a ministering spirit; the one a resurrected or translated body, with its spirit ministering to embodied spirits—the other a disembodied spirit, visiting and ministering to disembodied spirits. Jesus Christ became a ministering spirit (while his body was lying in the sepulcher) to the spirits in prison, to fulfill an important part of His mission, without which He could not have perfected His work, or entered into His rest. After His resurrection He appeared as an angel to His disciples.
>
> Translated bodies cannot enter into rest until they have undergone a change equivalent to death. Translated bodies are designed for future missions.

The angel that appeared to John on the Isle of Patmos was a translated or resurrected body [i.e., personage]. Jesus Christ went in body after His resurrection, to minister to resurrected bodies. [*TPJS*, 191]

Section 2 of the Doctrine and Covenants connects us with both a resurrected personage [Moroni] and a translated being [Elijah]. Joseph Smith, in answer to the question of where he obtained the Book of Mormon, said:

Moroni, who deposited the plates in a hill in Manchester, Ontario County, New York, being dead and raised therefrom [resurrected], appeared unto me, and told me where they were, and gave me directions how to obtain them. I obtained them and the Urim and Thummin with them, by the means of which I translated the plates; and thus came the Book of Mormon. [*TPJS*, 119]

Elijah became a translated being at the conclusion of his mortal probation (see 2 Kings 2:11). However, his coming in these last days (D&C 110:13–15), at the time a resurrected personage (see D&C 133:53–55), is connected to a translated being. He appeared as a translated being on what is now designated as the Mount of Transfiguration (see Matthew 17:1–3), and "gave the keys to Peter, James, and John, on the mount, when they were transfigured before him"[4] (*TPJS*, 158). He needed a physical body in order to lay hands on and confer the keys to the apostles. The importance of Elijah's mission is shown by the Savior's commandment to the Nephites to write the words of Malachi in the Book of Mormon "that they should be given unto future generations" (3 Nephi 24–25; 26:2). The text of 3 Nephi is basically the same as the biblical text. The variation in the text of Malachi 4:5–6 (D&C 2); as quoted by Moroni, is shown in the comparison below.

TEXT AND COMMENTARY

D&C 2:1–3 • Elijah the Prophet

1 Behold, I will *reveal unto you the priesthood by the hand of* Elijah the Prophet, before the coming of the great and dreadful day of the Lord.

Malachi 4:5–6

5 Behold, I will send you Elijah the prophet before the coming of the great and dreadful day of the Lord:

---

[4] The New Testament translates Elijah as Elias.

2 And he shall *plant in* the hearts *of the children the promises made to* the fathers, and the hearts of the children *shall turn to* their fathers.

3 *If it were not so, the whole* earth *would be utterly wasted at his coming;* (italics added).

6 And he shall turn the heart of the fathers to the children, and the heart of the children to their Fathers, lest I come and smite the earth with a curse.

The differences in the text, as quoted by Moroni, should not be thought of as the original words of Malachi, but more correctly as a plainer translation to fit our own language and understanding. It is an example of the differences in languages, as spoken of in D&C 1:24, and was discussed in the previous chapter of this work. The Lord reveals things to us according to our language. This explanation is supported by the Third Nephi text's being basically the same as the biblical text. It is further supported by the Prophet Joseph quoting the biblical text of Malachi 4:5–6 in a letter to the members of the Church, and then stating: "I might have rendered a plainer translation to this, but it is sufficiently plain to suit my purpose as it stands" (D&C 128:18).

The Prophet Elijah appeared unto Joseph Smith and Oliver Cowdery in the Kirtland Temple on April 3, 1836, and restored the sealing power to the earth. Why was Elijah selected for this restoration? The Prophet Joseph Smith explained:

> Elijah was the last Prophet that held the keys of the Priesthood, and who will, before the last dispensation, restore the authority and deliver the keys of the Priesthood, in order that all the ordinances may be attended to in righteousness. It is true that the Savior had authority and power to bestow the blessing; but the sons of Levi were too prejudiced. . . . Why send Elijah? Because he holds the keys of the authority to administer in all the ordinances of the Priesthood; and without the authority is given, the ordinances could not be administered in righteousness. [*TPJS,* 172]

Elijah did not appear until the first temple was built in the last dispensation. The Prophet Joseph also explained why the temple was needed first.

> It was the design of the councils of heaven before the world was, that the principles and laws of the priesthood should be predicated upon the

gathering of the people in every age of the world. . . . Ordinances instituted in the heavens before the foundation of the world, in the priesthood, for the salvation of men, are not to be altered or changed. All must be saved on the same principles.

It is for the same purpose that God gathers together His people in the last days, to build unto the Lord a house to prepare them for the ordinances and endowments, washings and anointings, etc. . . .

If a man gets a fullness of the priesthood of God he has to get it in the same way that Jesus Christ obtained it, and that was by keeping all the commandments and obeying all the ordinances of the house of the Lord. [*TPJS*, 308]

In the words of Joseph Fielding Smith, "No man can get the fullness of the priesthood outside of the temple of the Lord" except in days "when there was no house prepared in which to receive these things" then they may be received on the mountain tops (*Doctrines of Salvation*, 3:131–132).

The purpose of Elijah appearing in the Kirtland Temple was to "reveal unto you the priesthood" (D&C 2:1). Since the Aaronic Priesthood and the Melchizedek Priesthood were both restored in May or June 1829, what priesthood was revealed by Elijah? In a sermon given on August 27, 1843, the Prophet Joseph read the seventh chapter of Hebrews and commented on the "three grand orders of priesthood referred to here" (*TPJS*, 322). In a revelation "dated March 28, 1835, we learn that "There are, in the church, two priesthoods, namely, the Melchizedek and Aaronic, including the Levitical Priesthood" (D&C 107:1). The orders of the priesthood referred to by the Prophet Joseph were a part of the two priesthoods named therein. Just as the Levitical Priesthood was included with the Aaronic, the Prophet included the patriarchal authority as the second order along with the Melchizedek. The revelation of 1835 stated that "All other authorities or offices in the church are appendages to this [Melchizedek] priesthood" (D&C 107:5). Therefore, the patriarchal order is an appendage to the Melchizedek Priesthood.

The Prophet Joseph explained the role of the patriarchal priesthood: "The 2nd Priesthood is patriarchal authority. Go to and finish the [Nauvoo] temple, and God will fill it with power, and you will then receive more knowledge concerning this priesthood" (*TPJS*, 323). The power to fill the temple was the power of God, and the keys restored by

Elijah were the priesthood ordinances to seal the children to their fathers as an eternal family with a patriarch at their head. The words of Malachi would then be further fulfilled. The promises made to the fathers (D&C 2:2), who knew there would be apostasies, that the gospel would be restored and all their posterity who lived during the periods of apostasy would have the opportunity to hear the gospel and receive its ordinances through the temple work for the dead. The children thus turn to searching out their genealogical records, and vicariously obtaining the temple ordinances for them. This plan was devised and agreed upon in the premortal life.

> The greatest responsibility in this world that God has laid upon us is to seek after our dead. . . . for it is necessary that the sealing power should be in our hands to seal our children and our dead for the fullness of the dispensation of times—a dispensation to meet the promises made by Jesus Christ before the foundation of the world for the salvation of man. [*TPJS,* 356]

The promises to the fathers were not limited to individual families. There were other people who agreed to come at times when a special need existed and the gospel was not upon the earth. The young man Enos, and his forefathers, in the Book of Mormon, were promised that the Lord would preserve a record of the Nephites to be brought "forth unto the Lamanites in his own due time" (Enos 1:13–18). The fulfillment of this promise was fulfilled and verified through the coming forth of the Book of Mormon (see D&C 10:46–52). While there were undoubtedly many such instances, one relating to the United States of America will suffice for us here. Wilford Woodruff, President of the St. George Temple, bore testimony on September 16, 1877 that:

> The dead will be after you, they will seek after you as they have after us in St. George. They called upon us, knowing that we held the keys and power to redeem them.

> Two weeks before I left St. George, the spirits of the dead gathered around me, wanting to know why we did not redeem them. Said they, "you have had the use of the Endowment House for a number of years now, and yet nothing has been done for us. We laid the foundation of the government you now enjoy, and we never apostized from it, but we remained true to it and were faithful to God." These were the signers of the Declaration of Independence, and they waited on me for two days and two nights. I thought it very singular, that notwithstanding so much

work had been done, and yet nothing had been done for them. The thought never entered my heart, from the fact I suppose, that heretofore our minds were reaching after our more immediate friends and relatives. I straightway went into the baptismal font and called upon Brother McCallister to baptize me for the signers of the Declaration of Independence, and fifty other eminent men, making one hundred in all, including John Wesley, Columbus and others; I then baptized him for every President of the United States, except three; and when their cause is just, somebody will do the work for them. [*Journal of Discourses*, 19:229]

Malachi's words warned that the earth would be smitten with a curse if Elijah did not come. Moroni's words were that the whole earth would be wasted at the coming of the Lord if Elijah did not come. Since the Lord's work includes the destruction of the wicked (see D&C 84:96–98), without the work of the patriarchal authority the plan of salvation would be void, and none of this dispensation would obtain eternal life with God in the celestial kingdom (see Moses 1:39). Another aspect might also be considered. Since God is a God of justice, justice requires that all are to receive the opportunity for the gospel and exercise their agency to choose or reject. The spirit world will give all an opportunity for them to hear the gospel, and vicarious work for the dead will give all an opportunity to receive the ordinances. No man can be saved without the ordinances of the gospel (see D&C 84:19–23; 68:8–9; Mark 16:15–16). To guarantee those in the spirit world an opportunity for these ordinances, the Lord has required a welding link from the days of Adam unto the last dispensation (see D&C 128:18). The spirit of Elijah is prevalent in the world if we will respond to it.

THE MISSION OF JOHN THE BELOVED

*H*istorical Setting—Section 7: Doctrine and Covenants 7 "is a translated version of the record made on parchment by John and hidden up by himself" given by revelation "to Joseph Smith the Prophet and Oliver Cowdery . . . through the Urim and Thummim" (section heading). "A difference of opinion [had arisen] about the account of John the Apostle, mentioned in the New Testament" (*HC*, 1:35). The biblical account is not clear on this doctrine In response to Peter's query, "Jesus saith unto him [Peter], if I will that he [John] tarry till I come, what is that to thee? follow thou me. Then went this saying abroad among the brethren, that

that disciple should not die: yet Jesus said not unto him, He shall not die; but, if I will that he tarry till I come, what is that to thee?" (John 21:22–23).

The revealing of this parchment to Joseph and Oliver is another evidence of records of past dispensations that are still in existence and will yet come forth. These records are mentioned in subsequent revelations.

INTRODUCTION

The Doctrine and Covenants gives us the correct interpretation of what John was promised. Also, this incident introduces us to another type of angelic being, a transfigured personage. These beings are often considered as synonymous with translated beings, but there is a difference. A translated being was taken off the earth without tasting death (Hebrews 11:5), as discussed above. A transfigured being has a change come upon their bodies similar to the translated being, but is allowed to remain on earth without tasting death. Both types of personages must experience a further change to reach the resurrected state (see 3 Nephi 28:36–40). The parchment shown to Joseph and Oliver defines the transfigured John.

SECTION 7 • OUTLINE

➤ 7:1–5   John's request of Jesus was to have power over death and live to bring souls to Christ. Jesus granted that John tarry on earth till Christ comes in glory.

        a.   John will prophesy before nations, kindreds, tongues and people (v. 3).

        b.   John explains why Jesus asked Peter what it was to him (v. 4).

        c.   Peter had been given his desire (v. 4).

        d.   Peter's was a good desire, but John desired a greater work (v. 5).

➤ 7:6–8   Why John's work was a greater one.

        a.   He will be made like a flaming fire and a ministering angel (v. 6).

        b.   He will minister on earth to those who shall be heirs of salvation (v. 6).

    c.   He will minister with Peter and James who hold the keys of their ministry until Christ comes (v. 7).

    d.   Both Peter and John have their desires and shall joy in them (v. 8).

TEXT AND COMMENTARY

D&C 7:1–5 • John the Beloved—Power Over Death

1 And the Lord said unto me: John, my beloved, what desirest thou? For if you ask what you will, it shall be granted unto you.

2 And I said unto him: Lord, give me power over death, that I may live and bring souls unto thee.

3 And the Lord said unto me: Verily, verily, I say unto thee, because thou desirest this thou shalt tarry until I come in my glory, and shalt prophesy before nations, kindreds tongues and people.

4 And for this cause the Lord said unto Peter: If I will that he tarry till I come, what is that to thee? For he desired of me that he might bring souls to me, but thou desirest that thou mightest speedily come unto me in my kingdom.

5 I say unto thee, Peter, this was a good desire; but my beloved has desired that he might do more, or a greater work yet among men than what he has before done.

The promise to John is also verified in the Book of Mormon. After Jesus' three day ministry among the Nephites, he appeared to his Nephite Twelve and individually asked them what they desired of him "after I am gone to the Father" (3 Nephi 28:1). To three of them, who were reluctant to speak: he said "Behold, I know your thoughts, and ye have desired the thing which John my beloved, who was with me in my ministry, before that I was lifted up by the Jews, desired of me" (3 Nephi 28:6).[5] Thus we have another witness to the transfiguration of John, along with the Doctrine and Covenants.

John was promised that he would prophesy before nations, kindreds, tongues and people (D&C 7:3). An angel that appeared to John on the

---

[5] 3 Nephi 28 gives much additional information on the nature of transfigured beings that are not included here. For a more detailed analysis, see Monte S. Nyman, "*Divine Ministry, The First Gospel*, chapter 15, Granite Publishing and Distribution LLC, 2003.

Isle of Patmos said unto him "Thou must prophesy again before many peoples, and nations, and tongues and kings" (Revelation 10:11). His work certainly is not documented, but we do have some evidence of the fulfilling of this prophecy. According to John Whitmer's History, at the June 1831 Conference of the Church:

> The Spirit of the Lord fell upon Joseph in an unusual manner, and he prophesied that John the Revelator was then among the Ten Tribes of Israel who had been led away by Shalmaneser, king of Assyria, to prepare them for their return from their long dispersion, to again possess the land of their fathers [quoted in *HC*, 1:176]. Also, according to Heber C. Kimball, at the dedication of the Kirtland Temple "the beloved disciple John was seen in our midst by the Prophet Joseph, Oliver Cowdery, and others." [Orson F. Whitney, *Life of Heber C. Kimball* (1967), 92]

John had the same desire as the three transfigured Nephite disciples, to bring souls unto Christ (v. 4). This was what he did in his earthly ministry, but what was his greater work (v. 5)? John's parchment helps to further understand his mission.

D&C 7:6–8 • John's Greater Work

> 6 Yea, he has undertaken a greater work; therefore I will make him as flaming fire and a ministering angel; he shall minister for those who shall be heirs of salvation who dwell on earth.
>
> 7 And I will make thee to minister for him and for thy brother James; and unto you three I will give this power and the keys of this ministry until I come.
>
> 8 Verily I say unto you, ye shall both have according to your desires, for ye both joy in that which ye have desired.

Not only was he to minister to embodied spirits on the earth (see *TPJS*, 191), but he was given authority to function as did the ministering angels, or "just men made perfect" who did not have a body (v. 6; see D&C 129:3; quoted above). He would attend to those who are sealed unto eternal life on the earth, or had their calling and election made sure (see D&C 131:5–6; *TPJS* 149–151). The Prophet Joseph explained:

> Spirits can only be revealed in flaming fire and glory. Angels have advanced further, their light and glory being tabernacled; and hence they

appear in bodily shape. The spirits of just men are made ministering
servants to those who are sealed unto eternal life, and it is through them
that the sealing power comes down. [*TPJS,* 325]

Because of the sacred nature of this ministering there is no way of knowing
how many people have been ministered to by John the Beloved.

A second additional greater work given to John was to minister for
Peter and James, or as a minister of the First Presidency to whom Jesus
Christ had given the keys of the New Testament dispensation (see
Matthew 17:1–11; *TPJS,* 158). As promised, John the Beloved has been
on the earth continually since the time of his mortal ministry ended. John
the Baptist acted under the authority of Peter, James, and John when he
restored the Aaronic Priesthood, and the keys of the ministering of angels
to Joseph Smith and Oliver Cowdery on May 15, 1829 (D&C 13, and
section heading). Peter, James, and John committed the keys of Christ's
kingdom to Joseph Smith "and a dispensation of the gospel for the last
times; and for the fullness of times" (D&C 27:12–13).

As taught by President Joseph Fielding Smith,

> ". . . the purpose of granting to prophets this great blessing [of transla-
> tion] (or transfiguration) is that they may minister on the earth.
> Moreover, the Lord, of necessity, has kept authorized servants on the
> earth bearing the priesthood from the days of Adam to the present time;
> in fact, there has never been a moment from the beginning that there
> were not men on the earth holding the Holy Priesthood. Even in the
> days of apostasy, and apostasy has occurred several times, the Lord never
> surrendered this earth and permitted Satan to have complete control.
> [*Answers to Gospel Questions,* comp. Joseph Fielding Smith Jr., 5 vols.
> (1957–66), 2:45]

The heavens are not sealed. The angels of God, of one category or
another, are ministering unto men in this last dispensation, and the work
which they restored is going forth. The blessings are available to those
who will listen to his servants when their opportunity comes.

General Authority Quotes
—*The Prophet Joseph Smith* • D&C 2

Now for Elijah. The spirit, power, and calling of Elijah is, that ye have power to hold the key of the revelations, ordinances, oracles, powers and endowments of the fullness of the Melchizedek Priesthood and of the kingdom of God on the earth; to receive, obtain, and perform all the ordinances belonging to the kingdom of God, even unto the turning of the hearts of the fathers unto the children, and the hearts of the children unto the fathers, even those who are in heaven. . . .

In the days of Noah, God destroyed the world by a flood, and he promised to destroy it by fire in the last days: but before it should take place, Elijah should first come and turn the hearts of the fathers to the children, &c. [*TPJS*, 337]

—*President Joseph Fielding Smith* • D&C 7:5–6

From what we understand why Elijah and Moses were preserved from death: because they had a mission to perform, and it had to be performed before the crucifixion of the Son of God, and it could not be done in the spirit. They had to have tangible bodies. Christ is the first fruits of the resurrection; therefore if any former prophets had a work to perform preparatory to the mission of the Son of God, or to the dispensation of the meridian of times, it was essential that they be preserved to fulfill that mission in the flesh. [*Doctrines of Salvation*, 2:110-111]

Chapter Four

The Book of Lehi

D&C 3; 10

*H*istorical Setting— Section 3: Since sections 3 and 10 deal with the loss of the Book of Mormon subject, we will comment on them together. Due to persecution, Joseph Smith did not do any translating from the actual plates until April 12, 1828 when Martin Harris

> . . . commenced writing for me while I translated from the plates, which we continued until the 14th of June following, by which time he had written one hundred and sixteen pages of manuscript on foolscap paper. Some time after Mr. Harris had begun to write for me he began to importune me to give him liberty to carry the writings home and show them; and desired of me that I would enquire of the Lord, through the Urim and Thummim, if I might not do so. I did enquire and the answer was that he must not. . . . After much solicitation I again enquired of the Lord [for the third time], and permission was granted to have the writings on certain conditions. . . . Notwithstanding, however, the great restrictions which he had been laid under, and the solemnity of the covenant which he had made with me, he did show them to others, and by stratagem they got them away from him, and they never have been recovered unto this day." [*HC*, 1:21]

We will leave the further historical evidence of this incident to a study of church history, and focus on the lessons from the revelation that was given to Joseph.

INTRODUCTION

Jacob, Book of Mormon prophet on brother of Nephi was not talking about the loss of the 116 pages, but his words are applicable to this incident. He admonished his "beloved brethren and our children," future readers of his writings, to "learn with joy and not with sorrow, neither with contempt, concerning their first parents" (Jacob 4:3). The parents to whom he referred were Lehi and Sariah, and Ishmael and his wife. An account of these two sets of parents leaving Jerusalem was written in what was called the book of Lehi (see section heading, D&C 3). Those parents had made some mistakes, but had also done as they were commanded.

We should learn from the mistakes of others, and not have to repeat their mistakes to learn the same valuable lesson. The Prophet Joseph gave a similar admonition: "Why will not man learn wisdom by precept at this late age of the world, when we have such a cloud of witnesses and examples before us, and not be obliged to learn by sad experiences everything we know" (*TPJS*, 155). Had Joseph Smith and Martin Harris followed the commandments of the Angel Moroni, the manuscript would not have been lost. The revelation given to the Prophet Joseph "relating to the loss of 116 pages of manuscript translated from the first part of the Book of Mormon" (D&C 3 section heading) is a choice example of learning with sorrow rather than with joy.

SECTION 3 • OUTLINE

➤ 3:1–4   The works of God cannot be frustrated, but the work of man is frustrated.

      a.   God's paths are straight and his course is one eternal round (v. 2).

      b.   Past revelations and works do not prevent a man's fall (v. 4).

      c.   Boasting and following his own will bring the vengeance of a just God (v. 4).

➤ 3:5–8   Joseph was entrusted with [the manuscript], but was given strict commandments and promises.

      a.   He transgressed often and followed the persuasions of men (v. 6).

b.   He should not have feared man more than God (v. 7).

c.   If faithful, God would have been with him in times of trial (v. 8).

➤ 3:9–11   Joseph was chosen for the work of the Lord, but may fail.

a.   God is merciful, repent and he is still chosen (v. 10).

b.   If no repentance, he will be like other men and have no gift (v. 11).

➤ 3:12–15   Joseph delivered sacred things to a wicked man.

a.   God gave him sight and power to translate (v. 12).

b.   The man broke sacred promises, and boasted in his own wisdom (v. 13).

c.   Joseph lost his privilege for a season (v. 14).

d.   Joseph suffered his director to be trampled (v. 15).

➤ 3:16–20   God's work of sending knowledge of a Savior to a world shall go forth.

a.   The testimony of the Jews has come into the world (v. 16).

b.   The testimony of the fathers of the Nephites, Jacobites, Josephites, Zoramites shall go forth (v. 17).

c.   This testimony shall come to the knowledge of the Lamanites, Lemuelites, and Ishmaelites who dwindled in unbelief (v. 18).

d.   The plates were preserved to fulfill the promises made to his people, and the Lamanites might believe the gospel of Jesus Christ and be saved (vv. 19–20).

TEXT AND COMMENTARY

D&C 3:1–4 • The Work of God Is Not Frustrated

1 The works and the designs, and the purposes of God cannot be frustrated, neither can they come to naught.

2 For God doth not walk in crooked paths, neither doth he turn to the right hand nor to the left, neither doth he vary from that which he hath said, therefore his paths are straight, and his course is one eternal round.

3 Remember, remember that it is not the work of God that is frustrated, but the work of men;

4 For although a man may have many revelations, and have power to do many mighty works, yet if he boasts in his own strength, and sets at naught the counsels of God, and follows after the dictates of his own will and carnal desires, he must fall and incur the vengeance of a just God upon him.

The work of God bringing forth the Book of Mormon was not frustrated by the loss of the manuscript, because the Lord in his foreknowledge "knoweth all things, for all things are present before mine eyes" (D&C 38:2). He knew that the manuscript would be lost, and inspired Mormon to include the smaller set of plates that Nephi had kept. These smaller plates covered the same time period and particularly covered the things of God (see 1 Nephi 6; 9; and 19:1–6). Mormon found the smaller plates while he was abridging, and included them with the abridgment he was making. Neither Nephi nor Mormon knew why they were to make or include two sets of plates, other than it was wisdom in God, who knew all things, to include them (see 1 Nephi 9:5–6; Words of Mormon 1:6–7). Mormon did acknowledge, as he was abridging the larger plates, that "a shorter but true account was given by Nephi" (3 Nephi 5:9). Although God knew they would be lost, he honored the agency of man, and after warning those who were involved, allowed them to proceed in their folly. We will see the frustration of the men (v. 3) who obtained the manuscript as we discuss D&C 10.

"A man" who is spoken of in verse 4 is not named. The Lord probably is making a general categorization rather than specific things which Joseph or Martin Harris had done. There are more specific things mentioned in the following verses and in D&C 10.

D&C 3:5–8 • Fear God Not Man

5 Behold, you have been entrusted with these things, but how strict were your commandments; and remember also the promises which were made to you, if you did not transgress them.

6 And behold, how oft you have transgressed the commandments and the laws of God, and have gone on in the persuasions of men.

7 For, behold, you should not have feared man more than God.

Although men set at naught the counsels of God, and despise his words—

8 Yet you should have been faithful; and he would have extended his arm and supported you against all the fiery darts of the adversary; and he would have been with you in every time of trouble.

These verses speak to Joseph Smith, but again may be somewhat generally applied. The Angel Moroni had warned "that I must have no other object in view in getting the plates but to glorify God, and must not be influenced by any other motive than that of building the kingdom" (JS—H 1:46). When the plates were delivered to Joseph, Moroni gave a charge "that I should be responsible for them; that if I should let them go carelessly, or through any neglect of mine, I should be cut off" (JS—H 1:59). Joseph had not willfully or knowingly sinned, but he had yielded to the persuasions of Martin Harris to show others the manuscript (v. 6). He may have done so because he feared to offend his source of physical support (v. 7). Note that the Lord calls his not keeping the commandments transgressions and not sins. While a "sin is a transgression of a law" (1 John 3:4), a transgression of a law may not be a sin. The Book of Mormon defines a sin as "having transgressed the law of God contrary to his own knowledge" (Mosiah 2:33). A sin of omission is when one "knoweth to do good and doeth it not, to him it is sin" (James 4:17). In his youth, Joseph had not realized that God would provide other support for him if the present one failed (D&C 10:8).

D&C 3:9–11 • Joseph Foreordained

9 Behold, thou art Joseph, and thou wast chosen to do the work of the Lord, but because of transgression, if thou art not aware thou wilt fall.

10 But remember, God is merciful; therefore, repent of that which thou hast done which is contrary to the commandment which I gave you, and thou art still chosen, and art again called to the work;

11 Except thou do this, thou shalt be delivered up and become as other men, and have no more gift.

Jesus Christ knows all things (D&C 38:1–2). "The past, the present, and the future were and are, with Him, one eternal now" (*TPJS*, 220). Christ knew that Joseph wouldn't fall. However, Joseph didn't know, and he was subject to the temptations of the devil, and the persuasions of men. The warning given to Joseph was to honor his agency (D&C 3:9), and to help him to achieve the work to which he had been called. The call to repentance was a learning experience for him, but he had to repent or the gift he had would be lost (D&C 10:11). His experience should be a learning experience for all of us to learn with joy and not with sorrow.

D&C 3:12–15 • The Hands of a Wicked Man

12 And when thou deliverest up that which God had given thee sight and power to translate, thou deliverest up that which was sacred into the hands of a wicked man,

13 Who has set at naught the counsels of God, and has broken the most sacred promises which were made before God, and has depended upon his own judgment and boasted in his own wisdom.

14 And this is the reason thou hast lost thy privileges for a season—

15 For thou hast suffered the counsel of thy director to be trampled upon from the beginning.

The process of translating by sight and power (v. 12) will be treated in a later chapter. Martin Harris is again called a wicked man (v. 12). His not obeying the counsels of God refers to his asking Joseph to inquire three times although he had been told no on the first two times (see *HC*, 1:21). These three inquiries remind us of the Old Testament account of Balaam asking permission of God to go and curse Israel. After the third time, he was given conditional permission, which conditions also were not met (see Numbers 22). The Lord likewise gave conditions to Joseph, after the third request: Martin was to: "show them only to [Martin's] brother, Preserved Harris, his own wife, his father, and his mother, and a Mrs. Cobb, a sister to his wife" (*HC*, 1:21). He had shown the manuscript to others, and had "broken the most sacred promises which were made before God" (D&C 10:13). In depending on his own judgment and his own wisdom (v. 14), Martin was guilty of what Nephi warned against: "the very God of Israel do men trample under their feet; I say, trample under their feet but I would speak in other words—they set him at naught, and hearken not to the voice of his counsels" (1 Nephi 19:7). The Lord accused Joseph of suffering [allowing] this to happen (D&C 10:15), but Joseph also learned from this incident, and repented as he was invited to do (v. 10).

D&C 3:16–20 • The Knowledge of the Savior to the World

16 Nevertheless, my work shall go forth, for inasmuch as the knowledge of a Savior has come unto the world, through the testimony of the Jews, even so shall the knowledge of a Savior come unto my people—

17 And to the Nephites, and the Jacobites, and the Josephites, and the Zoramites, through the testimony of their fathers—

18 And this testimony shall come to the knowledge of the Lamanites, and the Lemuelites, and the Ishmaelites, who dwindled in unbelief because of the iniquity of their fathers, whom the Lord has suffered to destroy their brethren the Nephites, because of their iniquities and their abominations.

19 And for this very purpose are these plates preserved, which contain these records—that promises of the Lord might be fulfilled, which he made to his people;

20 And that the Lamanites might come to the knowledge of their fathers, and that they might know the promises of the Lord, and that they may believe the gospel and rely on the merits of Jesus Christ, and be glorified through faith in his name, and that through their repentance they might be saved. Amen.

There are seven groups named by the Lord to whom a knowledge of the Savior was to come (v. 16–18). Lehi's and Ishmael's families divided into these seven groups after they came to the America's. While there were two major divisions, the Nephites and the Lamanites, these seven family units were still recognized among them (see Jacob 1:13–14). The descendants of Sam were "numbered with Nephi's seed" (2 Nephi 4:11). After the Nephites were destroyed (v. 18), as Mormon prophesied, "whoso remaineth, and is not destroyed in that great and dreadful day shall be numbered among the Lamanites, and shall become like unto them" (Alma 45:14; see Mormon 9:24 for the prophecy's fulfillment). These seven tribes were also mentioned in sixteenth century native documents, called Quiche-Mayan Guatemala writing.

The "Totonicapan" record refers to the division into seven tribes. . . . The "Xahila" family. One of the royal lines of the Quiche of the highlands of the Guatemala, left an account in the Maya tongue entitled "Annals of Xahila." It states therein: We were brought forth, coming we were begotten by our mothers and our fathers, as they say. . . . They say that the seven tribes arrived first at Tullan, and we the warriors followed, having taken up the tribute of all the seven tribes when the gates of Tullan were opened. [Milton R. Hunter and Thomas Stuart Ferguson, *Ancient America and the Book of Mormon* (1950), 87]

The purposes of the Book of Mormon are summarized in the above Doctrine and Covenants verses: To bring the Lamanites to a knowledge of their Savior, and bring them to a knowledge of their fathers and fulfill the promises of the Lord to them (vv. 18–20). The sub title of the Book of Mormon, "Another Testament of Jesus Christ,"[6] fully supports the first purpose named, but the Book of Mormon itself gives almost a verbatim declaration of these purposes (see 1 Nephi 15:14; see also Alma 9:16–17).

*H*istorical Setting—Section 10: Section 3 was given in July of 1828 according to Joseph's *History of the Church* (see section heading). The same history, cited in the section heading of D&C 10, states that section 10 was given a few days later. Lucy Mack Smith, in her history of her prophet son, dates the revelation as September of 1828. The exact date is obviously not known, but the date given by Mother Smith is probably the most accurate. There were no revelations recorded between July 1828 (D&C 3) and February 1829 (D&C 4) other than that revelation. Following D&C 10, the Prophet records only this paragraph: "I did not, however, go immediately to translating, but went to laboring with my hands upon a small farm which I had purchased of my wife's father, in order to provide for my family" (*HC*, 1:28). He was still at the farm in Harmony, Pennsylvania, in February of 1829 when section 4 of the D&C was received. On April 5, 1829, Oliver Cowdery came to Harmony, and the translation commenced two days later with Oliver as his scribe (*HC*, 1:32–33). Although there is evidence that some translating was done with Emma as scribe, the work did not seriously begin again until Oliver arrived on the scene. Therefore, section 10 would more appropriately be placed following section 3, as treated here. Of course the two revelations are on the same subject and should be treated together regardless. We

---

[6] The subtitle was added by the First Presidency and the Quorum of the Twelve in 1982, see Boyd K. Packer, CR, October 1982, 75.

might also consider that it took some time for Joseph to recover from his experience of the loss of the 116 page manuscript.

SECTION 10 • OUTLINE

➤ 10:1–13   The gift to translate is restored, be faithful and continue to translate.

    a. Do not run faster nor labor more than you have strength and means (v. 4).

    b. Pray always to conquer Satan and his servants (v. 5).

    c. They and the man you entrusted has sought to destroy you and your entrusted things, and take away your gift (vv. 6–7).

    d. Wicked men have delivered your sacred writings unto wickedness (vv. 8–9).

    e. Satan put it into their hearts to altar the words you have translated (vv. 10–11).

    f. Satan has sought to destroy this work by lying (vv. 12–13).

➤ 10:14–19   God will not suffer that Satan accomplish his evil designs.

    a. Satan put it into their hearts to get you to translate it again (vv. 15–16).

    b. If you bring forth the same words they have altered them (v. 17).

    c. They will say he has no gift and no power (v. 18).

    d. They will destroy him and his work to get the glory of the world (v. 19).

➤ 10:20–23   Satan has great hold upon their hearts to do iniquity against that which is good.

    a. Their hearts are corrupt, they love darkness rather than light (v. 21).

    b. Satan attempts to lead their souls to destruction (v. 22).

    c. God will turn their efforts to shame and condemnation (v. 23).

➤ 10:24–29   Satan stirs their hearts up against this work.

    a. He says: deceive and lie in wait to catch and destroy (v. 25).

      b.   He flattereth and drags their souls to hell (v. 26).

      c.   He goes up and down the earth seeking to destroy the souls of men (v. 27).

      d.   Those who deceive are not exempt from the justice of God (v. 28).

      e.   They altered the words to get thee to tempt the Lord thy God (v. 29).

➤ **10:30–33**   Joseph shall not translate again the words that have gone forth.

      a.   The wicked will say you have altered your words (v. 31).

      b.   They will publish the altered words and stir the people up to anger, and to not believe in your words (v. 32).

      c.   Satan seeks to overpower your testimony, that this work does not come in this generation (v. 33).

➤ **10:34–37**   In God's wisdom, show not what God is about to reveal to the world until the translation is complete, that you might be preserved.

      a.   God did not say to not show it unto the righteous (v. 36).

      b.   You cannot always tell the wicked from the righteous, so hold off until God sees fit (v. 37).

➤ **10:38–43**   An account of what you have written is on the plates of Nephi.

      a.   This more particular part God will bring to his people (vv. 39–40).

      b.   Translate Nephi's record until you come to the reign of King Benjamin, or to that part of the translation which ye have retained (v. 42).

      c.   God will show that His wisdom is greater than the cunning of the devil (v. 43).

➤ **10:44–52**   The wicked only have a part or an abridgment of the account of Nephi, but the plates of Nephi throw greater views upon Christ's gospel, therefore translate it.

      a.   The remainder of this work contains parts of the gospel which Christ's prophets and disciples desired should come forth (vv. 46–47).

      b.   Their faith was it would come to the Lamanites, and those who became Lamanites (v. 48).

    c.   Their faith was to be made known to other nations who possess this land (v. 49).

    d.   They left a blessing upon the land that those who believe in this gospel shall have eternal life, and it would be a free land (vv. 50–52).

10:53–56   If this generation does not harden their hearts, Christ will establish His church among them.

    a.   The church was not to be destroyed, but built up (v. 54).

    b.   Whoso belongs to His church need not fear, they will inherit the kingdom (v. 55).

    c.   Those who do nor fear Christ nor keep His commandments, and build up the kingdom of the devil will shake to the center (v. 56).

10:57–59   I am Jesus Christ, the Son of God.

    a.   I came unto mine own and they received me not (v. 57).

    b.   I am the light that shineth in darkness and is not comprehended (v. 58).

    c.   I said, Other sheep I have which are not of this fold and many disciples understood me not (v. 59).

10:60–63   I will show the people that the other sheep were a branch of the house of Jacob.

    a.   I will bring to light their marvelous work and my gospel to them (vv. 61–62).

    b.   They shall not deny it but build it up, and bring to light my doctrine (v. 63).

    c.   I will establish my doctrine and overcome contention concerning doctrine (v. 64).

10:64–70   I will unfold this great mystery [of the other sheep].

    a.   I will gather [my sheep] as a hen gather her chicks (v. 65).

    b.   They may partake of the waters of life freely (v. 66).

    c.   My doctrine is: repent and come unto my church (v. 67).

    d.   Whoso declares more or less, is against me and not of my church (v. 68).

    e.   Those who endure to the end in my church I will establish upon my rock, and the gates of hell shall not prevail against them (v. 69).

f.   These are the words of your Redeemer, your Lord and your God (v. 70).

TEXT AND COMMENTARY

D&C 10:1–13 • Do Not Run Faster Than You Have Strength

1 Now, behold, I say unto you, that because you delivered up those writings which you had power given unto you to translate by the means of the Urim and Thummim, into the hands of a wicked man, you have lost them.

2 And you also lost your gift at the same time, and your mind became darkened.

3 Nevertheless, it is now restored unto you again; therefore see that you are faithful and continue on unto the finishing of the remainder of the work of translation as you have begun.

4 Do not run faster or labor more than you have strength and means provided to enable you to translate; but be diligent unto the end.

5 Pray always, that you may come off conqueror; yea, that you may conquer Satan, and that you may escape the hands of the servants of Satan that do uphold his work.

6 Behold, they have sought to destroy you; yea, even the man in whom you have trusted has sought to destroy you.

7 And for this cause I said that he is a wicked man, for he has sought to take away the things wherewith you have been entrusted; and he has also sought to destroy your gift.

8 And because you have delivered the writings into his hands, behold, wicked men have taken them from you.

9 Therefore, you have delivered them up, yea, that which was sacred, unto wickedness.

10 And, behold, Satan hath put it into their hearts to alter the words which you have caused to be written, or which you have translated, which have gone out of your hands.

11 And behold, I say unto you, that because they have altered the words, they read contrary from that which you translated and caused to be written;

12 And, on this wise, the devil has sought to lay a cunning plan, that he may destroy this work;

13 For he hath put into their hearts to do this, that by lying they may say they have caught you in the words which you have pretended to translate.

These verses are mainly self-explanatory. Human tendency would cause Joseph to accelerate his efforts, making up for the time lost due to the loss of the manuscript spoken of above. This tendency would be more likely because of the chastisement Joseph had received from the Lord. However, the admonition to not run faster than one has strength (v. 4) is a general principle applicable to most situations. King Benjamin, the beloved Nephite leader, gave the same principle and admonition to his subjects when instructing them before turning over the reign to his son (see Mosiah 4:27). The Lord was apparently more concerned with accuracy in the Book of Mormon translation than He was with the time element. A warning that Satan was not going to sit idly by, but would continue to influence whomever he could, was a timely reminder (vv. 5–13). The Lord knows the end from the beginning (see D&C 38:2–3).

D&C 10:14–19 • The Designs of Satan

14 Verily, I say unto you, that I will not suffer that Satan shall accomplish his evil design in this thing.

15 For behold, he has put it into their hearts to get thee to tempt the Lord thy God, in asking to translate it over again.

16 And then, behold, they say and think in their hearts—We will see if God has given him power to translate; if so, he will also give him power again;

17 And if God giveth him power again, or if he translates again, or, in other words, if he bringeth forth the same words, behold, we have the same with us, and we have altered them;

18 Therefore they will not agree, and we will say that he has lied in his words, and that he has no gift, and that he has no power;

19 Therefore we will destroy him, and also the work; and we will do this that we may not be ashamed in the end, and that we may get glory of the world.

Although the Lord would not allow Satan to accomplish his evil design (v. 14), Joseph needed to do his part if he were to continue to be the Lord's instrument in the translation (see D&C 3:9, discussed above). The plot to get Joseph to retranslate the part he had already done was inspired by Satan (D&C 10:15–16). This plot reminds us of Jacob's admonition to the Nephites: "O that cunning plan of the evil one! O the vainness, and the frailties, and the foolishness of men!" Nephi's words, many of which had been written in the manuscript, were not intended to be pleasing unto the world (see 1 Nephi 6:5–6). The men, who had altered the words of the translation (D&C 10:17–18), had read those words and obviously were not pleased with them. This attitude identifies their wickedness. Their work to destroy Joseph Smith and his work (vv. 19) is a second witness of their wickedness. They were more concerned with their own reputation and obtaining the glory of the world than they were with the truth revealed through God. Continuing Jacob's warning: "When they are learned they think they are wise, and they hearken not unto the counsel of God, for they set it aside, supposing they know of themselves, wherefore, their wisdom is foolishness and it profiteth them not" (2 Nephi 9:28).

D&C 10:20–23 • The Cunning Plan of Satan

20 Verily, verily, I say unto you, that Satan has great hold upon their hearts; he stirreth them up to iniquity against that which is good;

21 And their hearts are corrupt, and full of wickedness and abominations; and they love darkness rather than light, because their deeds are evil; therefore they will not ask of me.

22 Satan stirreth them up, that he may lead their souls to destruction.

23 And thus he has laid a cunning plan, thinking to destroy the work of God; but I will require this at their hands, and it shall turn to their shame and condemnation in the day of judgment.

As Mormon stated: "Wherefore, all things which are good cometh of God; and that which is evil cometh of the devil; for the devil is an enemy to God, and fighteth against him continually, . . . (Moroni 7:12; see also Alma 5:40; James 1:17; 1 John 3:11). Verse 20 is a third witness with the Book of Mormon and the Bible of the source of evil. The scriptures contain additional witnesses with whom and how Satan operates upon the earth. "Their hearts are corrupt, and full of wickedness and abominations" (D&C 10:21) which tells us that these men were not amateurs in wickedness. As the Proverb states: For as he thinketh in his heart, so is he:" (Proverb 23:7). The great and abominable church took "away from the gospel of the Lamb many parts which are plain and precious; and also many covenants of the Lord . . . that they might pervert the right ways of the Lord, that they might blind the eyes and harden the hearts of the children of men" (1 Nephi 13:26–27). The work of the abominable church was a major reason for the preservation of the records which Joseph Smith was now called upon to translate. Satan was on hand to attempt to prevent the restoration of this lost knowledge. In stirring these wicked men up against this great work, he needed men whose hearts were already turned to iniquity. He was endeavoring to lead them to destruction. As Lehi had learned from the plates of brass, "he sought also the misery of all mankind" (2 Nephi 2:17–18). Misery loves company. Those who become Satan's co-workers will be accountable and con-demned at the day of judgment (v. 23). Satan has many other ways in which he attempts to try to stop this great work.

D&C 10:24–29 • Anger, Flattery, and Destruction

24 Yea, he stirreth up their hearts to anger against this work.

25 Yea, he saith unto them: Deceive and lie in wait to catch, that ye may destroy; behold, this is no harm. And thus he flattereth them, and telleth them that it is no sin to lie that they may catch a man in a lie, that they may destroy him.

26 And thus he flattereth them, and leadeth them along until he draggeth their souls down to hell; and thus he causeth them to catch themselves in their own snare.

27 And thus he goeth up and down, to and fro in the earth, seeking to destroy the souls of men.

28 Verily, verily, I say unto you, wo be unto him that lieth to deceive because he supposeth that another lieth to deceive, for such are not exempt from the justice of God.

29 Now, behold, they have altered these words, because Satan saith unto them: He hath deceived you—and thus he flattereth them away to do iniquity, to get thee to tempt the Lord thy God.

Nephi also warns us that Satan stirs the children of men "up against that which is good" (2 Nephi 28:20). In stirring these wicked men up against the work of translating the records given to Joseph Smith (D&C 10:24), it confirms that the message of the Book of Mormon is good. If it were not good, Satan would not have been against its coming forth. Furthermore, the Lord expands on Nephi's message by telling us how Satan had gone about stirring the wicked men up against the translated manuscript. Through deceit and waiting for the opportunity to destroy what had already been accomplished, Satan had rationalized with them that the ends would justify the means (v. 25). It was okay to be deceitful if it was for their personal betterment. He had apparently convinced them that lying for the right reason was okay. Today we refer to this type of rationale as "little white lies."

Another type of operation is also exposed: flattery. Flattery is an overstatement of a truth, or to praise excessively for self-serving motives. We do not know the specifics of how this happened with those who had altered the translated manuscript, but the Book of Mormon is full of accounts where flattery was used for self-serving motives. For example, Sherem the anti-Christ used "much flattery, and much power of speech, according to the power of the devil" (Jacob 7:4). Before Alma the Younger was converted, he "did speak much flattery to the people" and led many to do iniquities (Mosiah 27:8). Korihor the anti-Christ was accused by Alma of trying to bring "many souls down to destruction, by thy lying and by thy flattering words" (Alma 30:47). In all of the Book of Mormon accounts mentioned above—and there are other accounts—the flatterers were caught "in their own snare" (D&C 19:26). As Satan was doing in the time of the biblical Job (Job 1:6), he continues to go "up and down, to and fro in the earth, seeking to destroy the souls of men" (D&C 10:27). In Job's day, the day of Joseph Smith, or our own day, the flatterer is "not exempt from the justice of God" (v. 28) that will come in the day of judgment (v. 23). Flattery had a major role in the iniquity of the wicked men who endeavored to get Joseph Smith to retranslate that which had been translated and had been lost by Martin Harris.[7]

---

[7] 2 Nephi 28, which is very similar to this section of D&C 10, gives one more way that the devil operates that is not stated in section 10. Satan's followers will say: "All is well in Zion; yea, Zion prospereth, all is well." This exclusion is probably because Zion was not clearly defined or known to the Saints as yet.

D&C 10:30–33 • Do Not Retranslate

30 Behold, I say unto you, that you shall not translate again those words which have gone forth out of your hands;

31 For, behold, they shall not accomplish their evil designs in lying against those words. For, behold, if you should bring forth the same words they will say that you have lied and that you have pretended to translate, but that you have contradicted yourself.

32 And, behold, they will publish this, and Satan will harden the hearts of the people to stir them up to anger against you, that they will not believe my words.

33 Thus Satan thinketh to overpower your testimony in this generation, that the work may not come forth in this generation.

As the Lord told Joseph earlier, the work of God would not be frustrated, but the work of men (D&C 3:3). The foreknowledge of God had once more compensated for the errors of men. God had prevented the devil from destroying the Prophet Joseph and his work of translating the plates that had been delivered into his hands. He now explains the wisdom of his new plan.

D&C 10:34–37 • What You Shall Do

34 But behold, here is wisdom, and because I show unto you wisdom, and give you commandments concerning these things, what you shall do, show it not unto the world until you have accomplished the work of translation.

35 Marvel not that I said unto you: Here is wisdom, show it not unto the world—for I said, show it not unto the world, that you may be preserved.

36 Behold, I do not say that you shall not show it unto the righteous;

37 But as you cannot always judge the righteous, or as you cannot always tell the wicked from the righteous, therefore I say unto you, hold your peace until I shall see fit to make all things known unto the world concerning the matter.

Joseph had probably considered that Martin was righteous and could be trusted since he had financed the project. However, through the efforts of his wife, Martin had allowed the manuscript to be shared with the world. Therefore, the Lord would now make the decision of when and to whom the contents of the plates would be shown to others, and to the world (v. 37). The Lord knows the hearts of all men, and man may be deceived. This course of action was to preserve the life of Joseph Smith. His life had been in danger since he had obtained the plates, and would continue to be until his mission was completed.[8] As will be shown later, the Lord would take other steps to protect Joseph as the work continued. He had also taken steps before to preserve the coming forth of the Nephite record.

D&C 10:38–43 • My Wisdom Is Greater Than the Cunning of the Devil

38 And now, verily I say unto you, that an account of those things that you have written, which have gone out of your hands, is engraven upon the plates of Nephi;

39 Yea, and you remember it was said in those writings that a more particular account was given of these things upon the plates of Nephi.

40 And now, because the account which is engraven upon the plates of Nephi is more particular concerning the things which, in my wisdom, I would bring to the knowledge of the people in this account—

41 Therefore, you shall translate the engravings which are on the plates of Nephi, down even till you come to the reign of king Benjamin, or until you come to that which you have translated, which you have retained;

42 And behold, you shall publish it as the record of Nephi; and thus I will confound those who have altered my words.

43 I will not suffer that they shall destroy my work; yea, I will show unto them that my wisdom is greater than the cunning of the devil.

The second record kept by Nephi were called the "Plates of Nephi" (see 1 Nephi 19:2). It was a shorter but "more particular account" (v. 39) referred to elsewhere as the "small plates" (Jacob 1:1–3). The second

---

[8] We will leave the accounts of his life being sought to a study of church history, but point out here that Joseph knew that the Lord had and would protect him. He said: "The Lord has preserved me until today. He will continue to preserve me by the united faith and prayers of the Saints, until I have fully accomplished my mission in this life, and so firmly established the dispensation of the fullness of the priesthood in the last days, that all the powers of earth and hell can never prevail against it." [*TPJS,* 258]

record was included by Mormon, the abridger of the large plates, for a "wise purpose . . . according to the whisperings of the Spirit of the Lord" (Words of Mormon 1:7). Joseph is thus instructed by the Lord to translate "the plates of Nephi" down "to the reign of King Benjamin, or" to the place where he had "translated, which you have retained" (v. 41). Mormon included these the small plates of Nephi, without any abridging. Thus it was to be published "as the record of Nephi" (v. 42). The 116 pages of manuscript was Mormon's abridgement of the large plates of Nephi and called the book of Lehi, although Nephi had recorded much of his own prophecies on the large plates (see 1 Nephi 19:1). In the preface of the first edition the Book of Mormon, Joseph wrote: "I would inform you that I translated by the gift and power of God, and caused to be written, one hundred and sixteen pages, the which I took from the book of Lehi, which was an account abridged from the book of Lehi, by the hand of Mormon.

"I will show unto them that my wisdom is greater than the cunning of the devil" (v. 43), is a direct quote from the ending of 3 Nephi 21:10 regarding the life of His servant who would bring about "a great and marvelous work" in the latter days (3 Nephi 21:9). The servant [Joseph Smith] "shall be marred because of them [the wicked men who obtained the manuscript]. Yet I will heal him" (3 Nephi 21:10). The marring of that servant would thus be shown to be the loss of the 116 pages, and the healing of that marring would be the translation of the plates of Nephi that Mormon had included.[9]

D&C 10:44–52 • Their Prayers For the Lamanites Are Answered

44 Behold, they have only got a part, or an abridgment of the account of Nephi.

45 Behold, there are many things engraven upon the plates of Nephi

---

[9] The space required to justify this statement is too lengthy for examining here, but is based upon the time of the translation being completed. Joseph had translated 3 Nephi by May 15, 1829 and did not complete the translation of the remaining text (67 pages in our current edition) until at least two or more weeks. At the rate of his translating speed, it is suggested by many that the small plates were translated after the May 15 date. See Oliver Cowdery's account of the appearance of John the Baptist in the Pearl of Great Price, 59 for the conclusion that 3 Nephi had been translated by May 15, 1829. For a more detailed explanation, see Monte S. Nyman, *The Divine Ministry, The First Gospel*, Book of Mormon Commentary 5:329–330.

which do throw greater views upon my gospel; therefore, it is wisdom in me that you should translate this first part of the engravings of Nephi, and send forth in this work.

46 And, behold, all the remainder of this work does contain all those parts of my gospel which my holy prophets, yea, and also my disciples, desired in their prayers should come forth unto this people.

47 And I said unto them, that it should be granted unto them according to their faith in their prayers;

48 Yea, and this was their faith—that my gospel, which I gave unto them that they might preach in their days, might come unto their brethren the Lamanites, and also all that had become Lamanites because of their dissensions.

49 Now, this is not all—their faith in their prayers was that this gospel should be made known also, if it were possible that other nations should possess this land;

50 And thus they did leave a blessing upon this land in their prayers, that whosoever should believe in this gospel in this land might have eternal life;

51 Yea, that it might be free unto all of whatsoever nation, kindred, tongue, or people they may be.

52 And now, behold, according to their faith in their prayers will I bring this part of my gospel to the knowledge of my people. Behold, I do not bring it to destroy that which they have received, but to build it up.

The plates that Joseph was to translate, and would replace what he had already translated, gave "greater views upon [Christ's] gospel" (v. 45). This statement is supported by Nephi's own record. Nephi wrote "the things of God" with the intent "to persuade men to come unto the God of Abraham, and the God of Isaac, and the God of Jacob, and be saved" (1 Nephi 6:3–4). His other plates contained "a full account of the history of my people" (1 Nephi 9:2). "All the remainder of this work" (v. 46) refers to that which Mormon (and Moroni) abridged. Enos and his fathers (Jacob and Lehi) had requested and been promised that these records would be preserved that their posterity, including the Lamanites, would be saved (Enos 1:12–18). Mormon and Moroni's abridgment of the records was with the intent to fulfill these promises (Mormon 7:9; Ether 12:22). The Nephites' faith and prayers were also that other nations who possessed this land, now known as the Americas, would be blessed by believing this gospel, and be a free land to all people (D&C 10:47–51). The Lord confirms that these promises will be fulfilled, and will build upon that part of the gospel that they had already received (v. 52). Nephi had been shown that "the book of the Lamb of God, which had proceeded forth from the mouth of the Jew [the Bible]," would come "from the Gentiles unto the remnant of the seed of my brethren" (1 Nephi 13:38).

D&C 10:53–56 • Christ's Church Among the Gentiles

53 And for this cause have I said: If this generation harden not their hearts, I will establish my church among them.

54 Now I do not say this to destroy my church, but I say this to build up my church;

55 Therefore, whosoever belongeth to my church need not fear, for such shall inherit the kingdom of heaven.

56 But it is they who do not fear me, neither keep my commandments but build up churches unto themselves to get gain, yea, and all those that do wickedly and build up the kingdom of the devil—yea, verily, verily, I say unto you, that it is they that I will disturb, and cause to tremble and shake to the center.

The first step for the Lord, in fulfilling the promise to the Nephite fathers, was to establish His Church among the Gentiles (v. 53). The Savior had told the Nephites, during His divine ministry to them in the meridian of time, that the Father would establish His church among the Gentiles who would repent and come unto His Beloved Son. These church members would then be numbered among the remnant of Jacob to whom the land had been given (see 3 Nephi 21:20–22). He had previously given the land to a remnant of the house of Joseph (see 3 Nephi 15:12–13). The Lord, in a revelation given June 7, 1831, instructed the church to assemble "in Missouri, upon the land which I will consecrate unto my people which are "a remnant of Jacob, and those who are heirs according to the covenant" (D&C 52:2). A remnant of Joseph is also a remnant of Jacob. Through revelation and patriarchal blessings we know that the majority of Church members are of the seed of Ephraim and

Mannasseh, sons of Joseph, son of Jacob.[10] Thus the Church to be established among the Gentiles and the Lamanites, descendants of Nephi and his brethren, is The Church of Jesus Christ of Latter-day Saints. Those who are Gentiles have been and are invited to come unto Christ and be adopted into the Church. Those who harden their hearts against this invitation are rejecting an opportunity to be a part of this great latter day restoration (v. 53). The Church is "built upon the foundation of apostles and prophets, Jesus Christ himself being the chief cornerstone" (Ephesians 2:20). The Bible is the basic book of the Church, and the Book of Mormon was given to build up the Church of Christ (D&C 10:54). Those who belong to that Church, without fear of ridicule or persecution, shall inherit the kingdom of heaven (v. 55). Those who do fear the consequences of membership, and follow other desires, shall tremble as members of the kingdom of the devil (v. 56).

D&C 10:57–59 • Other Sheep of Israel

57 Behold, I am Jesus Christ, the Son of God. I came unto mine own, and mine own received me not.

58 I am the light which shineth in darkness, and the darkness comprehendeth it not.

59 I am he who said—Other sheep have I which are not of this fold—unto my disciples, and many there were that understood me not.

These three verses confirm what the Gospel of John tell us about the Savior. He was born into the Jews' lineage and they rejected Him (see John 1:11). He was born as a light unto an apostate religion, but the religion did not comprehend Him (see John 1:5). He told His Jerusalem followers that there were other groups of the house of Israel unto whom he was sent, but they did not know what he was saying (see John 10:16). He then explains what these verses meant.

D&C 10:60–63 • Other Sheep—a Branch of Israel

---

[10] There are 26 revelations in the Doctrine and Covenants that identify the members of the Church as literal descendants of the house of Israel. (See *Ephraim, Chosen of the Lord*, R. Wayne Shute, Monte S. Nyman, Randy L. Bott; [1999], Appendix 1 "The Second Gathering of the Literal Seed.") This entire book was written to show the blessings promised to Ephraim, who has been gathered in these last days.

60 And I will show unto this people that I had other sheep, and that they were a branch of the house of Jacob;

61 And I will bring to light their marvelous works, which they did in my name;

62 Yea, and I will also bring to light my gospel which was ministered unto them, and, behold, they shall not deny that which you have received, but they shall build it up, and shall bring to light the true points of my doctrine, yea, and the only doctrine which is in me.

63 And this I do that I may establish my gospel, that there may not be so much contention; yea, Satan doth stir up the hearts of the people to contention concerning the points of my doctrine; and in these things they do err, for they do wrest the scriptures and do not understand them.

He explained to the Nephites that they were the other sheep, or branch of Israel, to whom He referred (v. 60), and that those in Jerusalem had supposed He was referring to the Gentiles. He then explained why it could not have been the Gentiles: because they had not heard His voice; nor had He manifest Himself unto them except it were by the Holy Ghost. However, the Nephites had both seen Him and heard His voice (see 3 Nephi 15:21–24). Later in the same day, He told the Nephites of still another branch of Israel, the lost tribes, that He was going to visit (3 Nephi 16:1–3; 17:4). He then explained how He was the light of the miracles the Israelites had performed in His name during the Old Testament time period (D&C 10:61), and that it was his gospel they had had among them previously (v. 62). The Nephites had realized that the law of Moses was intended to bring them unto Christ, that they had come to Christ and thus the law had become dead unto them (see 2 Nephi 25:23–27). The lost tribes would also receive His gospel, and would not deny it as had the Jews. He would also teach them the true points of His doctrine and establish it among them. Such teaching would eliminate contention (D&C 10:63). The work of Satan is to cause contention over points of doctrine, and wrest the scriptures. Jesus had earlier taught the Nephites about Satan being the father of contention, and the true points of His doctrine which had previously caused contention among them (3 Nephi 11:28–32). His mission was to do the same among the lost tribes.

D&C 10:64–70 • This Is My Doctrine

64 Therefore, I will unfold unto them this great mystery;

65 For, behold, I will gather them as a hen gathereth her chickens under her wings, if they will not harden their hearts;

66 Yea, if they will come, they may, and partake of the waters of life freely.

67 Behold, this is my doctrine—whosoever repenteth and cometh unto me, the same is my church.

68 Whosoever declareth more or less than this, the same is not of me, but is against me; therefore he is not of my church.

69 And now, behold, whosoever is of my church, and endureth of my church to the end, him will I establish upon my rock, and the gates of hell shall not prevail against them.

70 And now, remember the words of him who is the life and light of the world, your Redeemer, your Lord and your God. Amen.

The great mystery (v. 64) is the gathering of Israel, who had been "scattered upon all the face of the earth, and also among all nations" (1 Nephi 22:3). The world today does not consider anyone but the Jews to be of the house of Israel. They were only one of the twelve tribes. All of Israel was not only scattered, but also promised that someday it would be gathered (see Amos 9:8–9; Jacob 5). As He taught the Jews and the Nephites, He had often given them the opportunity to be gathered as a hen gathers her chicks (Matthew 23:37; 3 Nephi 10:4–7). But, having their agency, both groups had ultimately rejected him. He affirms in this section, that there will be one last gathering. He will again conditional gather them as a hen gathers her chicks, if they do not harden their hearts (D&C 19:65). If they come to His gathering, they may partake of the spiritual water of Christ and obtain eternal life (v. 66; compare John 4:13–14; Isaiah 12:3). This promise is the doctrine of Christ which comes through His Church and through no other source (D&C 10:67–68). The gates of hell will not prevail against those persons who come into His church and endure to the end (v. 69). Those who are gathered and partake of the spiritual water will have total freedom in the kingdom of God.

The Prophet Joseph Smith taught:

One of the most important points in the faith of the Church of the Latter-day Saints, through the fullness of the everlasting gospel, is the gathering of Israel (of whom the Lamanites constitute a part) that happy time when Jacob shall go up to the house of the Lord, to worship Him in spirit and in truth, to live in holiness; when the Lord will restore his judges as at the first, and His counselors as at the beginning; when every man may sit under his own vine and fig tree, and there will be none to molest or make afraid; when he will turn to them a pure language, and the earth will be filled with sacred knowledge, as the waters cover the great deep; when it shall no longer be said, the Lord lives that brought up the children out of the land of Egypt, but the Lord lives that brought up the children of Israel from the land of the north, and from all of the lands whither He hath driven them. That day is one, all important to all men. [*TPJS,* 92–93]

The words of this promise for eternal life is from none other than the Giver of Life through the resurrection (see John 11:25), and the Light of the World (see John 9:5). He also identified Himself to the Nephites as "the light and life of the world. I am Alpha and Omega, the beginning and the end" (3 Nephi 9:18). He is our Redeemer and our Lord and God. What could be more sure than his promise? How could we learn with more joy?

General Authority Quotes
—*The Prophet Joseph Smith* • D&C 3:10–11; 10:12–15

Every man who has a calling to minister to the inhabitants of the world was ordained to that very purpose in the Grand Council of heaven before the world was. I suppose I was ordained to this very office in that Grand Council. [*TPJS,* 365]

After I had obtained the above revelation [section 3], both the plates and the Urim and Thummim were taken from me again; but in a few days they were returned to me, when I inquired of the Lord, and the Lord said thus unto me: [section 10]. [*HC,* 1:23]

—*Elder Neal A. Maxwell* • D&C 10:4

The scriptural advice, "Do not run faster or labor more than you have strength" (D&C 10:4) suggests paced progress, much as God used seven creative periods in preparing man and the earth. There is a difference, therefore, between being "anxiously engaged" and being over-anxious and thus under-engaged. [*Ensign*, November 1976, 12–13]

—*President Joseph F. Smith* • D&C 10:25

By every possible means [Satan] seeks to darken the minds of men and then offers them falsehood and deception in the guise of truth. Satan is a skillful imitator, and as genuine gospel truth is given the world in ever-increasing abundance, so he spreads the counterfeit coin of false doctrine. Beware of spurious currency, it will purchase for you nothing but disappointment, misery and spiritual death. The father of "lies" he has been called, and such an adept he has become through the ages of practice in his nefarious work, that were it possible he would deceive the very elect. [*Juvenile Instructor,* September 1902, 562]

Chapter Five

A Marvelous Work to Come Forth

D&C 4; 6:1–9; 11; 12; 14; 15; 16

Historical Setting: There are seven revelations considered together in this chapter. The first four revelations were given between February and May, 1829, at Harmony, Pennsylvania where the Prophet was farming to provide for his family. He was also endeavoring to begin again the translation of the Book of Mormon after having lost the 116 page manuscript as was discussed in the previous chapter. Joseph Smith Sr. came to visit and while there, section 4 was received. On April 5, 1829, Joseph met Oliver Cowdery for the first time when he came to Joseph's house. Two days later he began to write for him as he translated. Section 6 was received some time later in the month of April. On a subsequent visit of his brother Hyrum to Harmony, section 11 was given to him through the Prophet. About the same time, Joseph Knight, who had assisted them with material goods so that they might not be interrupted in their translating work, came to visit and asked what the Lord wanted him to do in assisting the work. The Prophet inquired and received section 12.

In June of 1829, due to persecution, the Prophet took up residency in Fayette, New York, at the home of Peter Whitmer Sr. to continue the work of translation. During this time, sections 14 through 16 were given through the Prophet to the three Whitmer sons; David, John, and Peter Jr., who were anxious to assist in the work. All seven of these revelations are connected with the Restoration and the translation of the Book of Mormon. (The above information was taken from *HC*, 1:28–51).

INTRODUCTION

Many of the seven revelations referred to above have parts of them that are identical to each other. The question may be asked: Why are they, or parts of them, identical? In answer, the following observations are shared. The seven recipients were all involved in the same work. Their desires were to find out how the Lord wanted them to be of assistance. The same general descriptions and instructions were applicable to all. The importance of the work and the requirements to participate were the same for all. Furthermore, each of the seven recipients was given specific instructions, as well as the general ones in these revelations or other later revelations. For example, even though the revelation to John Whitmer was identical to the one given to his brother Peter, except for the name, both of them, along with their other brother David, were given another revelation fifteen months later (section 30, September 1830). These later revelations were not identical. All seven men, to whom the revelations being considered were given, were deeply involved and guided by revelation for sometime. Some of these were included in the publications of the revelations and some were not. As one studies these revelations, and the history of the Church, their names will appear often.

Another reason for the similarities in the revelations is that they were intended for all people who embraced this great modern work (see D&C 4:3; 6:4; 11:4, 27; 12:7; 14:4). All of these revelations were given before the Church was organized, and as new converts came into the Church (or come in today) the general instructions were—and continue to be—applicable to them. Also, D&C 15:3 and 16:3 suggest that the Whitmer brothers were told specific things that were not recorded. The Lord runs His Church by revelation (see A of F 5).

SECTIONS 4; 6; 11; 12; 14 & 16 • OUTLINE

➤ 4:1, 4   A marvelous work is about to come among the children of men. (Five of the seven revelations begin with this announcement; see also 6:1; 11:1; 12:1; 14:1).

   a.   Give heed unto the word of God (see 6:2; 11:2; 12:2; 14:2; 15:2–3; 16:2–3.)

> b.   The field is white ready to harvest (4:4; see also 6:3; 11:3; 12:3; 14:3).

➤ 4:2–4   Those who serve God should serve with all their heart, might, mind, and strength.

> a.   Those who desire are called to the work (v. 3; see also 6:4; 11:4; 12:4; 14:4).
>
> b.   The diligent harvester brings salvation to his soul (v. 4; see also 6:7; 11:7; 12:7; 14:7).

➤ 4:5–6   Qualifications for the work: faith, hope charity, and love, with an eye single to the glory of God. [v. 6 lists other attributes, see also 12:8]

➤ 4:7   How to do the work.

> a.   Ask and ye shall receive; knock and it shall be opened (4:7; see also 6:5; 11:5; 12:5; 14:5).
>
> b.   Seek to bring forth and establish the cause of Zion (see 6:6; 11:6; 12:6; 14:6).
>
> c.   Declare nothing but repentance unto this generation (see 6:8–9; 11:8–9; 12:8–9; 14:8–9; 15:4–6; 16:4–6).

➤ 6:10–37   Oliver Cowdery is instructed by the Lord (included with sections 8–9).

➤ 11:10–30   Hyrum Smith is given specific instructions and blessings by the Lord.

> a.   Put your trust in the Spirit which shall enlighten your mind and enable you to know all things (vv. 12–14).
>
> b.   Wait to preach until you have my word, rock, church, and gospel (vv. 15–17).
>
> c.   Keep the commandments, seek first to obtain my word, be patient until the translation is complete (vv. 18–22).
>
> d.   Thou art my son, seek the kingdom of God, and all things shall be added, build upon my rock, deny not the spirit of revelation and prophecy (vv 23–26).
>
> e.   I am the Son of God, as many as receive me, to them will I give power to become the sons of God (vv. 27–30).

➤ 12:7–9   Joseph Knight Sr. and all who seek to establish this work are given instructions.

➤ 14:8–11   David Whitmer is given specific instructions and blessings by the Lord.

     a.   You may stand as a witness of things you shall both see and hear (v. 8).

     b.   I must bring the fullness of my gospel from the Gentiles unto Israel (v. 10).

     c.   You are called to assist in this work, and if you are faithful you will be blessed both spiritually and temporally (v. 11).

➤ 15:1; 16:1   John and David Whitmer are instructed by the Lord.

TEXT AND COMMENTARY

D&C 4:1 • A Great and Marvelous Work

1 NOW behold, a (*"great and"* in D&C 6:1; 11:1; 12:1; 14:1) marvelous work is about to come forth among (*"unto,"* D&C 6:1; 14:1) the children of men.

This great and marvelous work had been foretold much earlier by the Prophet Isaiah, as a work which would be necessary because of the state of the christian world. The christian people would do lip service to the Lord, but were not worshipping him correctly. They were taught by the precepts of men (Isaiah 29:13–14; 2 Nephi 27:25–26). The announcement of the christian world's being in this condition—and thus in need of the fulfillment of this prophecy—was made to the boy Joseph Smith in the spring of 1820. In what is known as "the First Vision," in The Church of Jesus Christ of Latter-day Saints, this young man prayed about which church he should join and experienced the following:

17 . . . I saw two Personages, whose brightness and glory defy all description, standing above me in the air. One of them spake unto me, calling me by name and said, pointing to the other—This is My Beloved Son. Hear Him!

18 My object in going to inquire of the Lord was to know which of all the sects was right, that I might know which to join. No sooner, therefore, did I get possession of myself, so as to be able to speak, than

I asked the Personages who stood above me in the light, which of all the sects was right (for at this time it had never entered into my heart that all were wrong)—and which I should join.

19 I was answered that I must join none of them, for they were all wrong; and the Personage who addressed me said that all their creeds were an abomination in his sight; that those professors were all corrupt; that: "they draw near to me with their lips, but their hearts are far from me, they teach for doctrines the commandments of men, having a form of godliness, but they deny the power thereof. [JS—H 1:17–19]

The marvelous work referred to by Isaiah, and in the revelations spoken of above, was the coming forth of the Book of Mormon. This interpretation is given to us by the Book of Mormon prophet Nephi, quoting the Lord:

1 BUT behold, there shall be many—at that day when I shall proceed to do a marvelous work among them, that I may remember my covenants which I have made unto the children of men, that I may set my hand again the second time to recover my people, which are of the house of Israel;

2 And also, that I may remember the promises which I have made unto thee, Nephi, and also unto thy father, that I would remember your seed; and that the words of your seed should proceed forth out of my mouth unto your seed; and my words shall hiss forth unto the ends of the earth, for a standard unto my people, which are of the house of Israel; [2 Nephi 29:1–2]

The recovering "of the house of Israel" the second time (2 Nephi 29:1) is referring to another of Isaiah's prophecies about the latter day restoration (see Isaiah 11:11). When the Angel Moroni appeared to Joseph Smith later, ". . . he quoted the eleventh chapter of Isaiah, saying it was about to be fulfilled" (JS—H 1:40). The words of Nephi and his seed (2 Nephi 29:2) are the words of the Book of Mormon. Furthermore, when the Savior visited the Nephites following his resurrection in Jerusalem, He referred to the coming forth of the Book of Mormon as a great and marvelous work which was to come among the Gentiles. He said: ". . . when these things which I shall declare unto you, and which I shall declare unto you hereafter of myself, and by the power of the Holy Ghost which shall be given unto you of the Father, shall be made known unto the Gentiles . . ." (3 Nephi 21:2) ". . . For in that day, for my sake shall the Father work a work, which shall be a great and a marvelous work among them [the Gentiles]; and there shall be among them those who will not believe it, although a man shall declare it unto them [the Gentiles]" (3 Nephi 21:9). The last part of this 3 Nephi quote is almost the exact words of Habakkuk, the Old Testament prophet, speaking of a work that would cause the heathens [Gentiles] to "wonder marvelously: for I will work a work in your days, which ye will not believe, though it be told you" (Habakkuk 1:5). The coming forth of the Book of Mormon as a great and marvelous work, was long anticipated by both biblical and Nephite prophets.

The labeling of the coming forth of the Book of Mormon as "a marvelous work" is based upon at least four reasons. First, it was the work of the Father, not of man. Second, the learned Gentiles could not do it on their own, but an unlearned man, through an instrument called the Urim and Thummin—furnished by God, would translate it by the gift and power of God (see 2 Nephi 27:19–20; D&C 3:12).[11] Third, the book was written in a language neither known nor understood in that day (see Mormon 9:32–34). Fourth, the book was translated in a miraculous period of time—not more than ninety days but probably closer to a sixty day period; between April 7, 1839 and sometime in June of 1829.[12] This was a much shorter time period than the seven months it took the printers to set the type and print the book, August 1829 to March 26 1830, the date of the publication of the first edition. In the front of the first edition of the Book of Mormon, the "Memorandum, made by John H. Gilbert" states: "The work commenced in August 1829, and finished in March

---

[11] Through the medium of the Urim and Thummim I translated the record by the gift and power of God (*HC*, 4:537).

[12] See *HC*. 1:32–50. Our intent is not to examine the length of time to translate, but to show that it was a short time. Therefore, we will only show the longest possible time period and the probable shorter period of translating. April 7, 1829 is when Oliver Cowdery began writing as the scribe for Joseph (see *HC*, 1:32). From the handwriting of the original manuscript, it has been determined that almost all of the present day Book of Mormon was translated after Oliver arrived. The Title page, which was the last leaf of the plates, was published in the *Wayne Sentinel* of Palmyra, on June 25, 1829. Therefore, the translation had to have been completed by then. This is the general basis of the ninety day period of translating. The copyright for the publication of the Book of Mormon was dated June 11, 1829, which is a key to the 60 day period. There are many other significant facts that favor the shorter 60 day translation period, but will not be treated here.

1830,—seven months." The coming forth of the Book of Mormon was indeed a marvelous work and a wonder.

D&C 6:2; 15:1–3; 16:1–3 • The Word of God— a Two Edged Sword

> **6:2** Behold, I am God; give heed unto [to 11:2; 12:2; 14:2; the rest of the verse is identical] my word, which is quick and powerful, sharper than a two-edged sword, to the dividing asunder of both joints and marrow; therefore give heed unto my words.
>
> **15:1–3** Hearken, my servant **John**. . . ; [the rest of the verses are identical]
>
> **16:1** . . . Peter, [the rest of the verses are identical] and listen to the words of Jesus Christ, your Lord and your Redeemer.
>
> **16:2** For behold, I speak unto you with sharpness and with power, for mine arm is over all the earth.
>
> **16:3** And I will tell you that which no man knoweth save me and thee alone—

"I am God" (6:2) confirms that the Book of Mormon was to come forth under His supervision and power. "Give heed to my words" also confirms that the Book of Mormon would contain his words as revealed to the Nephite prophets. The defining of His words as "sharper than a two edged-sword" is using a symbolic comparison of truth (His word) and the sword of the warrior of ancient times. The book of Revelation uses the same symbolism (see Revelation 1:16; 2:12). The two-edged sword will cut regardless of which way it may be swung. There is no place the blade may be touched without feeling the effect it does or could do. Likewise, the word of God will have a positive or a negative effect upon whomever it contacts. This is illustrated in a comment made by Nephi to Laman and Lemuel when they complained that he had spoken hard things unto them which seemed to be more than they could bear. Nephi responded: "I said unto them that I knew that I had spoken hard things against the wicked, according to the truth; and the righteous have I justified, and testified that they should be lifted up at the last day; wherefore, the guilty taketh the truth to be hard, for it cutteth them to the very center" (1 Nephi 16:2). God's word is described further as having the power of "the dividing asunder of both joints and marrow" (D&C 6:2). While a sword will cut flesh easily, it takes a forceful blow to sever a joint or cut to the center of a bone. The joint is the point of coordination of the parts of the body. With it being severed, or injured, that part of the body is lost or ceases to function. Likewise, the word of Christ can and does penetrate to the coordination and organization of our lives in the Church, the home, and the community. Resisting the power of the word of God may lead to being isolated from the Church, being severed from the family, or being out of harmony with the community—depending on the severity of the resistance.

The marrow of the bone is the innermost part and an essential factor for health. An injury of this depth requires a great healing process. The word of Christ also has the ability to penetrate to the marrow of our soul and thus affect our spiritual and physical health for good or evil. An example of the negative effect is Zeezrom resisting the word of God that was preached by Alma and Amulek:

> . . . Zeezrom lay sick at Sidom, with a burning fever, which was caused by the great tribulations of his mind on account of his wickedness, for he supposed that Alma and Amulek were no more; and he supposed that they had been slain because of his iniquity. And this great sin, and his many other sins, did harrow up his mind until it did become exceedingly sore, having no deliverance; therefore he began to be scorched with a burning heat. [Alma 15:3]

A further insight into this symbolism is the Lord telling John and Peter Whitmer "that which no man knoweth save me and thee alone" (15:3; 16:3). The health or condition of the marrow in the bone cannot be discerned externally, even if the flesh is torn away and the bone opened up. The innermost thoughts of man are hidden to others, but are known to Christ. Just as medicines or proper diet can influence physical health, the Lord's word can and will penetrate to the very center of one's soul for a healing effect, or leave a person sick and troubled if rejected. In a broader sense, a sick and troubled world could be healed if it would accept the Book of Mormon as the word of God. It will have a positive effect upon those who accept it, but will "cause a great division among the people" as the millennium approaches (see 2 Nephi 30:10).

The briefer account of comparing the word of God with a two-edged

sword, given to John and Peter Whitmer (15:2; 16:3), may have been because they had heard the longer account given to their brother David in section 14. Alma did not repeat to Corianton what he had heard him say to Helaman and Shiblon (see Alma 39:1).

D&C 4:4; 6:3–4 • The Field is White Ready to Harvest

4:4 For behold the field is white already to harvest; and lo, he that thrusteth in his sickle with his might, the same layeth up in store that he perisheth not, but bringeth salvation to his soul;

6:3 Behold, the field is white already to harvest; therefore, whoso desireth to reap, let him thrust in his sickle with his might, and reap while the day lasts, that he may treasure up for his soul everlasting salvation in the kingdom of God.

6:4 Yea, whosoever will thrust in his sickle and reap, the same is called of God. [also D&C 11:3–4; 12:3–4; 14:3–4]

When grain is ripened, especially barley, it turns white and is recognized as being ready to be harvested. The symbolism used is a comparison of the ripened grain to the harvest of souls. Jesus used the same symbolism with the Samaritans, a combination of Gentile colonists brought there by the kings of Assyria and Babylon, who had intermarried with some of the house of Israel (see 2 Kings 17:24). These people were a part of the Gentile graft described by the prophet Zenos, and quoted by Jacob, brother of Nephi, in the Book of Mormon (see Jacob 5:8–9, 18). When Jesus went through Samaria, he stopped at Jacob's well and spoke with a Samaritan women. In response to his disciples question of why he spoke with her, whom the Israelites looked down upon, he said of the Samaritans:

35 Say not ye, There are yet four months, and [then] cometh harvest? behold, I say unto you, Lift up your eyes, and look on the fields; for they are white already to harvest.

36 And he that reapeth receiveth wages, and gathereth fruit unto life eternal: that both he that soweth and he that reapeth may rejoice together.

37 And herein is that saying true, One soweth, and another reapeth.

38 I sent you to reap that whereon ye bestowed no labour: other men laboured, and ye are entered into their labours.

39 And many of the Samaritans of that city believed on him for the saying of the woman, which testified, He told me all that ever I did.

40 So when the Samaritans were come unto him, they besought him that he would tarry with them: and he abode there two days.

41 And many more believed because of his own word. [John 4:35–41][13]

The Samaritans were ready for the light and truth of the gospel He was bringing to them. Both the Doctrine and Covenants and the New Testament account emphasize everlasting salvation in the kingdom of God for both him that reaps and those who are harvested. The shorter analogy given to Joseph Sr., included above (4:4), has the same message.

D&C 4:2–3; 6:4 • Serve With All Your Heart, Might, Mind, and Strength

4:2 Therefore, O ye that embark in the service of God, see that ye serve him with all your heart, might, mind and strength, that ye may stand blameless before God at the last day.

4:3 Therefore, if ye have desires to serve God ye are called to the work; [D&C 4:2–3]

6:4 Yea, whosoever will thrust in his sickle and reap, the same is called of God. [see also 11:4; 12:4; 14:4]

To serve God with all of your heart is to put all of your spiritual effort or power into the work. To serve with all of your might is put all of your physical effort or power into the work. To serve with all of your mind is to put all of your intellectual efforts or power into the work. To serve with all of your strength is to coordinate all the spiritual, the physical, and the intellectual efforts or powers towards each task that you undertake. To slacken one or more of those efforts will result in a lesser accomplishment, and make you accountable for what you did not do that you could have done (4:2). If you have a desire to serve God, he will give you that opportunity (4:3), but you must give more than lip service. You must show evidence of your desire by acting upon your desire. "To thrust in

---

[13] For a more complete treatise of the Samaritans, see the Bible Dictionary 568; and John 4:1–42.

[your] sickle" (4:4; 6:4) implies some form of activity on your part as shown in the following verse.

D&C 6:5 • Ask and Receive, Knock it Shall Be Opened

> 5 Therefore, if you will ask of me you shall receive; if you will knock it shall be opened unto you. [see also 4:7; 11:5; 12:5; 14:5]

To ask of Christ is obviously to pray, but to knock is to make physical or intellectual effort. In the admonition of the New Testament: "But be ye doers of the word, and not hearers only, deceiving your own selves" (James 1:22). The Lord will then open the way for you to continue in His work.

D&C 4:5–6; 12:8–9 • Qualifications For the Work

> 4:5 And faith, hope, charity and love, with an eye single to the glory of God, qualify him for the work.
>
> 4:6 Remember faith, virtue, knowledge, temperance, patience, brotherly kindness, godliness, charity, humility, diligence.
>
> 12:8 And no one can assist in this work except he shall be humble and full of love, having faith, hope, and charity, being temperate in all things, whatsoever shall be entrusted to his care.
>
> 12:9 Behold, I am the light and the life of the world, that speak these words, therefore give heed with your might, and then you are called. Amen.

Faith is a principle of action (see Ether 12:6), hope produces works (see Ether 12:4), and "charity is the pure love of Christ" which is "bestowed upon all who are true followers of his Son, Jesus Christ" (Moroni 7:47–48). To be humble and full of love (12:8) is to have "an eye single to the glory of God" (4:5). The additional attributes given in D&C 4:6 are self-explanatory and will not be discussed further. How to do the work of the Lord is amplified in these revelations.

D&C 6:6–7; 14:6–7 • Seek To Establish Zion

> 6:6 Now, as you have asked, behold, I say unto you, keep my commandments, and seek to bring forth and establish the cause of Zion;

6:7 Seek not for riches but for wisdom, and behold, the mysteries of God shall be unfolded unto you, and then shall you be made rich. Behold, he that hath eternal life is rich. [also D&C 11:6–7; 12:6–7; the words of 14:6 below are rearranged but the same message]

14:6 Seek to bring forth and establish my Zion. Keep my commandments in all things

14:7 And, if you keep my commandments and endure to the end you shall have eternal life, which gift is the greatest of all the gifts of God.

Enoch established a Zion society in the early days of the Old Testament by keeping the commandments of God (6:6). The Lord [or Moses?] described His people as being "of one heart and one mind, and dwelt in righteousness; and there were no poor among them" (Moses 7:18). Being of one heart is to "remember the worth of souls is great in the sight of God" (D&C 18:10). Being of one mind is to become one in doctrine through "the gift and the power of the Holy Ghost" (1 Nephi 13:37). The law of consecration, which will be discussed later, will enable the people to dwell in righteousness and have no poor among them (see D&C 42:33–34, 39).

The Prophet Joseph taught: "We ought to have the building up of Zion as our greatest object. When wars come, we shall have to flee to Zion. . . . The time is soon coming, when no man will have any peace but in Zion and her stakes" (*TPJS*, 160–61). The center place of Zion and her stakes will also be discussed in a later chapter (D&C 57). Those who seek to establish Zion, rather than seeking the riches of the world, will come to understand the mysteries of God that lead to becoming a Zion society, and they will obtain real riches—eternal life, the greatest of all the gifts of God (6:7; 14:7).

D&C 6:8–9; 14:8–11; 15:4–6 • Say Nothing but Repentance to This Generation

6:8 Verily, verily, I say unto you, even as you desire of me so it shall be unto you; and if you desire, you shall be the means of doing much good in this generation.

6:9 Say nothing but repentance unto this generation; keep my commandments, and assist to bring forth my work, according to my commandments, and you shall be blessed. [also D&C 11:8–9]

14:8 And it shall come to pass, that if you shall ask the Father in my name, in faith believing, you shall receive the Holy Ghost, which giveth utterance, that you may stand as a witness of the things of which you shall both hear and see, and also that you may declare repentance unto this generation.

14:9 Behold, I am Jesus Christ, the Son of the living God, who created the heavens and the earth, a light which cannot be hid in darkness;

14:10 Wherefore, I must bring forth the fulness of my gospel from the Gentiles unto the house of Israel.

14:11 And behold, thou art David, and thou art called to assist; which thing if ye do, and are faithful, ye shall be blessed both spiritually and temporally, and great shall be your reward. Amen.

15:4 For many times you have desired of me to know that which would be of the most worth unto you.

15:5 Behold, blessed are you for this thing, and for speaking my words which I have given you according to my commandments.

16:6 And now, behold, I say unto you, that the thing which will be of the most worth unto you will be to declare repentance unto this people, that you may bring souls unto me, that you may rest with them in the kingdom of my Father. Amen. [also D&C 16:4–6]

To do good in this generation one must get others to do good. Doing good is accomplished by declaring nothing but repentance (6:8–9) in order that they may change their lifestyles to conform to the gospel principles that they are taught. This principle is applicable to teaching other church members as well to those who are not members. As John and Peter Whitmer were told, declaring repentance was the thing that would be of most worth to them (15:6; 16:6). The teacher learns more than the student, and teaching repentance should likewise change the teacher's life.

The revelation to David Whitmer shows that through prayer and the utterances of the Holy Ghost, he (and we) would know what principles he was to teach that the hearer may repent (14:8). As a personal commandment, David was to be called to be one of the three witness of the Book of Mormon that had been prophesied there would be (see JST,

Isaiah 29:17; 2 Nephi 27:12; Ether 5:3). Therefore his revelation emphasized that he would testify of things that he would both see and hear (14:8). The testimony of three witnesses, published in the front of the Book of Mormon, states that they had *heard* the voice of God and had *seen* the engravings on the plates by the power of God. As David was told in the revelation above, the fulness of the gospel—which was in the Book of Mormon (see D&C 27:5; 42:12)—would come from the Gentiles unto the house of Israel (14:10). This concept will also be discussed in a later chapter. David was also "called to assist" in the work of the restoration, for which he would be blessed (14:11). He did assist and was blessed, but these things will be left for a church history discussion.

D&C 11:10–14 • The Gift Given Hyrum Smith

10 Behold, thou hast a gift, or thou shalt have a gift if thou wilt desire of me in faith, with an honest heart, believing in the power of Jesus Christ, or in my power which speaketh unto thee;

11 For, behold, it is I that speak; behold, I am the light which shineth in darkness, and by my power I give these words unto thee.

12 And now, verily, verily, I say unto thee, put your trust in that Spirit which leadeth to do good—yea, to do justly, to walk humbly, to judge righteously; and this is my Spirit.

13 Verily, verily, I say unto you, I will impart unto you of my Spirit, which shall enlighten your mind, which shall fill your soul with joy;

14 And then shall ye know, or by this shall you know, all things whatsoever you desire of me, which are pertaining unto things of righteousness, in faith believing in me that you shall receive.

Oliver Cowdery and Hyrum Smith were given much longer revelations than the other revelations that are discussed in this chapter. As stated in the outline above, the remainder of Oliver's revelation will be discussed with other revelations to him, in a later chapter.

The gift which Hyrum had is not specified, but probably refers to the Holy Ghost. It was not conferred as a permanent gift upon him as yet, but was given to him as a temporary guide until the Melchizedek Priesthood was restored, and the power to confer this gift to baptized members of the Church. This is concluded from the admonition to "trust in that Spirit which leadeth to do good" (v. 12), and "my Spirit which shall enlighten your mind" and "fill your soul with joy" (v. 13). These are functions promised through the Holy Ghost (see 2 Nephi 32:5; John 14:26; 16:14). The Holy Ghost is given to all members of the Church, but there are conditions upon which it will come to them. Some of these conditions are given to Hyrum above; for example, he was to desire in faith, do justly, walk humbly, judge righteously, and believe that he would receive.

D&C 11:15–22 • Hyrum is Not to Preach Until Called

15 Behold, I command you that you need not suppose that you are called to preach until you are called.

16 Wait a little longer, until you shall have my word, my rock, my church, and my gospel, that you may know of a surety my doctrine.

17 And then, behold, according to your desires, yea, even according to your faith shall it be done unto you.

18 Keep my commandments; hold your peace; appeal unto my Spirit;

19 Yea, cleave unto me with all your heart, that you may assist in bringing to light those things of which has been spoken—yea, the translation of my work; be patient until you shall accomplish it.

20 Behold, this is your work, to keep my commandments, yea, with all your might, mind and strength.

21 Seek not to declare my word, but first seek to obtain my word, and then shall your tongue be loosed; then, if you desire, you shall have my Spirit and my word, yea, the power of God unto the convincing of men.

22 But now hold your peace; study my word which hath gone forth among the children of men, and also study my word which shall come forth among the children of men, or that which is now translating, yea, until you have obtained all which I shall grant unto the children of men in this generation, and then shall all things be added thereto.

Hyrum's instructions to wait a little while until he began to preach confirms several conditions of the world at the time the marvelous work was about to come forth. First; the full and complete word of God was not available prior to the publication of the Book of Mormon. Second; Christ's rock, revelation upon which his Church was to be built, was not yet given. Third, his Church was not then upon the earth. And fourth, his gospel was not understood, or his doctrine surely known (vv. 15–16).

Hyrum was to prepare himself for the time when he would go out to preach. He was to assist in the translation of the Book of Mormon (vv. 17–20). This was apparently not to assist in the translation itself, but to help in ways that would enable Joseph and Oliver to carry on the work without being hindered through temporal chores. He was to study the Bible, in spite of it not containing the fullness of the gospel at this time, and study the Book of Mormon as it was translated and available to him (v. 21). "All which I shall grant" (v. 22) seems to point to the sealed portion of the plates which were not to be translated at this time, but eventually would be translated (see 2 Nephi 27:8, 22).

D&C 11:23–27 • Build Upon My Rock—My Gospel

23 Behold thou art Hyrum, my son; seek the kingdom of God, and all things shall be added according to that which is just.

24 Build upon my rock, which is my gospel;

25 Deny not the spirit of revelation, nor the spirit of prophecy, for wo unto him that denieth these things;

26 Therefore, treasure up in your heart until the time which is in my wisdom that you shall go forth.

27 Behold, I speak unto all who have good desires, and have thrust in their sickle to reap.

These commandments and promises (vv. 23–26) are a summation of what Hyrum had already been told. The warning to not deny the spirit of revelation or prophecy will be discussed in chapter 7 of this work. Again we note that this revelation was intended for all who had good desires, not just Hyrum (v. 27).

D&C 11:11, 28–30; 14:9 • The Light that Shines in Darkness

11:11 For, behold, it is I that speak; behold, I am the light which shineth in darkness, and by my power I give these words unto thee. . . .

11:28 Behold, I am Jesus Christ, the Son of God. I am the life and the light of the world.

11:29 I am the same who came unto mine own and mine own received me not;

11:30 But verily, verily, I say unto you, that as many as receive me, to them will I give power to become the sons of God, even to them that believe on my name. Amen.

14:9 Behold, I am Jesus Christ, the Son of the living God, who created the heavens and the earth, a light which cannot be hid in darkness;

The light which shines in darkness (11:11) and cannot be hid in darkness (14:9) is the light of truth that is restored after a time of apostasy, and the source of this revelation. Christ has often identified Himself as the Life and the Light of the world (11:28). He also identified Himself in the revelation to Joseph Knight Sr., except that there He reversed it, "the light and life of the world" (D&C 12:9). He likewise identified Himself as the Light and Life of the world in his appearance to the Nephites (3 Nephi 9:18; 11:11). During his mortal ministry, at the celebration of Feast of Tabernacles in Jerusalem, (which is sometimes called the Feast of Lights because of the illumination of the temple courts) He declared that He was the Light of the world (John 8:12). The Gospel of John says: "In him was life; and the life was the light of men" (John 1:4). The statement that He came into His own and they received him not (D&C 11:29) is almost a verbatim statement from the Gospel of John (1:11). There is much to be learned from the various ways that Jesus identifies Himself in the Doctrine and Covenants.

The power to become the sons (or daughters) of God through receiving Him and believing on His name (D&C 11:30) is a part of being born again, or being "spiritually begotten [of Jesus Christ] . . . your hearts are changed through faith on his name" (Mosiah 5:7). As the Prophet Joseph said: "Being born again, comes by the Spirit of God through the ordinances" (*TPJS*, 162). The Spirit of God baptizes or immerses you, and the baptism of water is the ordinance.

There are many similarities in these seven revelations, and they are therefore studied together. But there are also unique contributions in each as well that should be emphasized.

General Authority Quotes

—*The Prophet Joseph Smith* • D&C 6:7

Many men will say, "I will never forsake you, but will stand by you at all times." But the moment you teach them some of the mysteries of the kingdom that are retained in the heavens and are to be revealed to the children of men when they are prepared for them they will be the first to stone you and put you to death. It was this same principle that crucified the Lord Jesus Christ, and will cause the people to kill the prophets in this generation. [*TPJS*, 309]

—*President Joseph Fielding Smith* • D&C 6:9; 11:9

When the Lord calls upon his servants to cry nothing but repentance, he does not mean that they may not cry baptism, and call upon the people to obey the commandments of the Lord, but he wishes that all that they say and do be in the spirit of bringing the people to repentance. [*Church History and Modern Day Revelation* (1946), 1:52]

Chapter Six

The Lord's Trial of the World

D&C 5, 17

*H*istorical Setting—Section 5: All that the Prophet Joseph Smith recorded in his history concerning section 5 was, "The following I applied for and obtained, at the request of the aforementioned Martin Harris." The date of the revelation, March 1829, shows that the revelation was given just shortly after the revelation was given to Joseph Smith Sr. (D&C 4). What reason Martin had for being in Harmony, where Joseph was residing, is not known, but it is assumed, from the revelation given to Martin, that he still was seeking evidence that Joseph had the plates. He was apparently still trying to justify to his wife and friends the reason he had given financial aid for the translation of the plates.

INTRODUCTION

President Ezra Taft Benson stated probably the best position of the Book of Mormon in the world today: "We do not have to prove the Book of Mormon is true. The book is its own proof. All we need to do is read it and declare it. The Book of Mormon is not on trial—the people of the world, including the members of the Church, are on trial as to what they do with this second witness for Christ" (*A Witness and a Warning* [1988], 13). As a testimony for the truth of the Book of Mormon the Lord has given us many and various types of witnesses. The law of witness as given in both the Old and the New Testaments has been met: "At the mouth of two witnesses, or at the mouth of three witnesses, shall the matter be established" (Deuteronomy 19:15; Matthew 18:16). Whether we accept or reject those witnesses is up to us. The Lord has left us without excuse.

SECTION 5 • OUTLINE

➤ 5:1–10   The answer to Martin Harris's request for a witness to see the plates.

     a.   Joseph Smith was commanded to stand as a witness (v. 2).

     b.   Joseph has covenanted to show them only to whom the Lord commands (v. 3).

     c.   He has a gift to translate, and will have no other gift until it is finished (v. 4).

     d.   Woe to the earth's inhabitants if they will not hearken to those words (v. 5).

     e.   Joseph shall be ordained to deliver these words to the children of men (v. 6).

     f.   If they do not believe the words, they would not believe if they were shown all the things given to Joseph (v. 7).

     g.   The Lord is angry with this unbelieving generation and has reserved those things for future generations (vv. 8–9).

     h.   This generation shall have Christ's word through Joseph (vv. 8–10).

➤ 5:11–20   In addition to Joseph's testimony, three witnesses shall be called and ordained.

     a.   They shall know of a surety they are true, and shall view them (vv. 12–13).

     b.   None else shall be granted this power in this generation when the church comes out of the wilderness (v. 14).

     c.   The testimony of the three will be sent forth of his word (v. 15).

     d.   Those who believe will receive a manifestation of the Spirit (v. 16).

     e.   Joseph must wait until he is ordained, and then the testimony of the three shall condemn this generation if they harden their hearts against them (vv. 17–18).

     f.   A desolating scourge shall be poured out from time to time, if they do not repent, until Christ comes again (v. 19).

g.   The Lord's word will be verified as was the destruction of Jerusalem (v. 20).

➤ 5:21–22   Joseph is commanded to yield no more to the persuasions of men, and he shall have eternal life, even if he is slain.

➤ 5:23–29   The Lord speaks concerning the man who wants a witness.

    a.   He must humble himself and he shall view the things he desires (v. 24).

    b.   He shall testify he has seen these things by the power of God (v. 25).

    c.   He is commanded to say no more than what the Lord commands (v. 26).

    d.   If not, he shall break the covenant and is condemned, and shall not view them, and shall trouble me no more (vv. 27–29).

➤ 5:30–35   If Martin does deny this condition, Joseph shall translate a few more pages and then stop for a season, or he shall lose his gift.

    a.   The Lord sees the lying in wait to destroy Joseph, and Martin falling into transgression, if he does not humble himself (v. 32).

    b.   Many lie in wait to destroy Joseph, to prolong his days the Lord has given these commandments (vv. 33–34).

    c.   If Joseph is faithful, he shall be lifted up at the last day (v. 35).

TEXT AND COMMENTARY

D&C 5:1–4 • No Other Gift Until the Translation is Finished

1 Behold, I say unto you, that as my servant Martin Harris has desired a witness at my hand, that you, my servant Joseph Smith, Jun., have got the plates of which you have testified and borne record that you have received of me;

2 And now, behold, this shall you say unto him—he who spake unto you, said unto you: I, the Lord, am God, and have given these things unto you, my servant Joseph Smith, Jun., and have commanded you that you should stand as a witness of these things;

3 And I have caused you that you should enter into a covenant with

me, that you should not show them except to those persons to whom I commanded you; and you have no power over them except I grant it unto you.

4 And you have a gift to translate the plates; and this is the first gift that I bestowed upon you; and I have commanded that you should pretend to no other gift until my purpose is fulfilled in this; for I will grant unto you no other gift until it is finished.

In answer to Martin Harris's request for evidence of Joseph Smith's having the plates, the Lord's first witness, in the trial of the world, was Joseph himself. The Lord had commanded him to be a witness (v. 2). He also had made a covenant with Joseph that he was to show them only to persons whom the Lord commanded (v. 3). Moroni, as he was abridging the Jaredite record, wrote to the translator [Joseph Smith] these same instructions: "And now I, Moroni, have written the words which were commanded me, according to my memory; and I have told you the things which I have sealed up; therefore touch them not in order that ye may translate; for that thing is forbidden you, except by and by it shall be wisdom in God" (Ether 5:1). It was in the wisdom of God that Joseph do nothing else until his gift to translate the records was accomplished (v. 4). President Ezra Taft Benson made this observation: ". . . the importance of the Book of Mormon is to note where the Lord placed its coming forth in the timetable of the unfolding Restoration. The only thing that preceded it was the first vision" (*A Witness and a Warning*, 16).

D&C 5:5–10 • The Word to this Generation

5 Verily, I say unto you, that woe shall come unto the inhabitants of the earth if they will not hearken unto my words;

6 For hereafter you shall be ordained and go forth and deliver my words unto the children of men.

7 Behold, if they will not believe my words, they would not believe you, my servant Joseph, if it were possible that you should show them all these things which I have committed unto you.

8 Oh, this unbelieving and stiffnecked generation—mine anger is kindled against them.

9 Behold, verily I say unto you, I have reserved those things which I have entrusted unto you, my servant Joseph, for a wise purpose in me, and it shall be made known unto future generations;

10 But this generation shall have my word through you;

The Lord's second witness, in the trial of the world, was the Book of Mormon itself. "My words," as used in the verses above, are the words that were translated and published as the Book of Mormon. Joseph was also the Lord's messenger to deliver these words to this generation (v. 6). "This generation," as used here, refers to the generation of the Gentiles, the time when the gospel would be taken to them (see 3 Nephi 16:10–11). The Lord's knowing that this generation of unbelieving Gentiles would not believe, even if they were shown the plates and the Urim and Thummim (D&C 5:7), reminds us of the Savior's parable of Lazarus and the rich man. Both of these men died, but respectively went to Abraham's bosom and hell. The rich man asked that Lazarus be sent to his father's house with the gospel, but was told that they had Moses and the prophets. The rich man implied that they would not believe Moses and the prophets, but that they would believe if one were sent from the dead. The response was: "If they hear not Moses and the prophets, neither will they be persuaded, though one rose from the dead" (Luke 16:31, see vv. 19–30). People who want sensational witnesses are really just making excuses. If such a witness were given, they would find another explanation to explain it away. "Ye receive no witness until after the trial of your faith" (Ether 12:6).

While these things, for which Martin requested evidence, will be shown to future [believing] generations (D&C 5:9), the Lord's wise purpose was to test the Gentiles through sending them the Book of Mormon (v. 10). The Savior told the Nephites: "And I will show unto thee, O house of Israel, that the Gentiles shall not have power over you; but I will remember my covenant unto you, O house of Israel, and ye shall come unto the knowledge of the fulness of my gospel. But if the Gentiles will repent and return unto me, saith the Father, behold they shall be numbered among my people, O house of Israel" (3 Nephi 16:12–13). The Book of Mormon was not intended for the Gentiles only, but was to go "to every nation, and kindred, and tongue, and people" (Revelation 14:6; see also D&C 133:36; 88:103). Satan seeks "to overpower [Joseph's] testimony in this generation" (D&C 10:33), but the Lord's power will prevail as he grants it (D&C 5:3).

D&C 5:11–15 • The Testimony of Three Witnesses

11 And in addition to your testimony, the testimony of three of my servants, whom I shall call and ordain, unto whom I will show these things, and they shall go forth with my words that are given through you.

12 Yea, they shall know of a surety that these things are true, for from heaven will I declare it unto them.

13 I will give them power that they may behold and view these things as they are;

14 And to none else will I grant this power, to receive this same testimony among this generation, in this the beginning of the rising up and the coming forth of my church out of the wilderness—clear as the moon, and fair as the sun, and terrible as an army with banners.

15 And the testimony of three witnesses will I send forth of my word.

The Lord's third witness, in the trial of the world, is the combined testimony of three of his servants (v. 11). Their calling will be discussed in section 17 later in this chapter, and their ordaining will be discussed in section 18 (see v. 17 to follow). the Three Witnesses were unique to other witnesses of the plates, because it came from heaven, and it was by the Lord's power (vv. 12–13). While others also viewed the plates in this generation, none of them did so by the power of God (v. 14). They viewed it in a temporal setting, in a natural way. Their comparison will be made later. The uniqueness was because it was to begin the "coming forth of [Christ's] church out of the wilderness" (v. 14). The book of Revelation tells us that the "woman fled into the wilderness" (Revelation 12:6). The Joseph Smith Translation identifies the woman as "the church of God" (JST, Revelation 12:7).[14] The testimony of the Three Witnesses that the Lord would send forth (D&C 5:15) had been prophesied: Nephi, quoting the Prophet Isaiah, said that "Three Witnesses would behold it, by the

---

[14] The description of the church, "clear as the moon, and fair as the sun . . ." (D&C 5:14) is almost the same as the Song of Solomon 6:10. The quote from this source may raise a question in some minds. A note in what is called the Bernheisel Manuscript, a copy of the Joseph Smith Translation of the Bible, made by John Bernheisel, says that "Song of Solomon not inspired writing" (see Robert J. Matthews *A Plainer Translation: Joseph Smith's Translation of the Bible* [1975], 87, 215). While the entire book may not be inspired writing, there may be parts of it which are inspired, or the book may be quoting from other inspired writings which are now lost (see 1 Nephi 13:26–29). Evidence for this conclusion is the quoting of the passage in other places (D&C 105:31; 109:73).

power of God, *besides him* to whom the book shall be delivered" (2 Nephi 27:12, JST, Isaiah 29:17; underlining added to show that Isaiah also foretold that Joseph would be a witness). Moroni had also told the translator that "unto three shall they be shown by the power of God" (Ether 5:3).

D&C 5:16–20 • A Fourth Witness

16 And behold, whosoever believeth on my words, them will I visit with the manifestation of my Spirit; and they shall be born of me, even of water and of the Spirit—

17 And you must wait yet a little while, for ye are not yet ordained—

18 And their testimony shall also go forth unto the condemnation of this generation if they harden their hearts against them;

19 For a desolating scourge shall go forth among the inhabitants of the earth, and shall continue to be poured out from time to time, if they repent not, until the earth is empty, and the inhabitants thereof are consumed away and utterly destroyed by the brightness of my coming.

20 Behold, I tell you these things, even as I also told the people of the destruction of Jerusalem; and my word shall be verified at this time as it hath hitherto been verified.

The Lord's fourth witness, at the trial of the world, is the manifestation of the Spirit to each individual who will believe on the words of the Book of Mormon (v. 16). This testimony of the Holy Ghost is promised to the reader of the Book of Mormon by Moroni, as he concluded the record (see Moroni 10:4). This testimony will be followed by the born again experience of a water and spirit baptism if they act upon their testimony and come into the Church that has "come out of the wilderness" (D&C 5:14). The personal testimonies of these individuals will condemn whoever hardens their heart against them (v. 18). The desolating scourge, that the Lord will send, was also prophesied of by Isaiah as an "overflowing scourge" (Isaiah 28:15, 18–19). The Prophet Joseph gave his witness of this scourge: "The servants of God will not have gone over the nations of the Gentiles, with a warning voice, until the destroying angel will commence to waste the inhabitants of the earth, and as the prophet [Isaiah] hath said: "It shall be a vexation to hear the report'" (*TPJS*, 87). This scourge will apparently vary in content as well as in times, and will conclude with the Second Coming (D&C 5:19). The people of Lehi were warned of the destruction of Jerusalem after their leaving in 600 B.C., and it happened eleven years later.[15] The date of the Second Coming is not known to man, but will certainly come and verify the Lord's word (v. 20).

D&C 5:21–22 • Warnings and a Promise

21 And now I command you, my servant Joseph, to repent and walk more uprightly before me, and to yield to the persuasions of men no more;

22 And that you be firm in keeping the commandments wherewith I have commanded you; and if you do this, behold I grant unto you eternal life, even if you should be slain.

Joseph's call to repentance for losing the 116 pages of manuscript (v. 21) also included a conditional promise of eternal life. "Even if you should be slain" (v. 22) is an intimation of his eventual martyrdom. At what point Joseph knew he would be slain is not known, but in 1842–43 he stated: "I shall not be sacrificed until my time comes; then I shall be sacrificed freely" (*TPJS*, 274). Like Abinadi, the Nephite Prophet, he knew it would not be before his mission was completed (see Mosiah 13:3–5; *TPJS*, 258; 328). He sealed his testimony with his blood (see D&C 136:38; Hebrews 9:16–17).

D&C 5:23–27 • The Man that Desires the Witness

23 And now, again, I speak unto you, my servant Joseph, concerning the man that desires the witness—

24 Behold, I say unto him, he exalts himself and does not humble himself sufficiently before me; but if he will bow down before me, and humble himself in mighty prayer and faith, in the sincerity of his heart, then will I grant unto him a view of the things which he desires to see.

25 And then he shall say unto the people of this generation: Behold, I have seen the things which the Lord hath shown unto Joseph Smith, Jun., and I know of a surety that they are true, for I have seen them, for

---

[15] Lehi left in the first year of the reign of Zedekiah, and Jerusalem was destroyed in the eleventh year of his reign. While the traditional year of Jerusalem's destruction is 607 B.C., we will not discuss the date variance here.

they have been shown unto me by the power of God and not of man.

26 And I the Lord command him, my servant Martin Harris, that he shall say no more unto them concerning these things, except he shall say: I have seen them, and they have been shown unto me by the power of God; and these are the words which he shall say.

27 But if he deny this he will break the covenant which he has before covenanted with me, and behold, he is condemned.

28 And now, except he humble himself and acknowledge unto me the things that he has done which are wrong, and covenant with me that he will keep my commandments, and exercise faith in me, behold, I say unto him, he shall have no such views, for I will grant unto him no views of the things of which I have spoken.

29 And if this be the case, I command you, my servant Joseph, that you shall say unto him, that he shall do no more, nor trouble me any more concerning this matter.

Martin Harris did not know about the three special witnesses at the time of this revelation. He learned of them about two months later, as will be shown when section 17 is discussed. The above verses seem to be intended to prepare him for this special calling. He would have to humble himself before he could have that opportunity (v. 25). Although verses 25–26 imply he would see them, it does not mention how he would. He is told that he must learn to control his tongue (see James 3:5–8) before he would see them. Apparently, he was prone to embellish. The Lord commanded what he was to say and to say no more. The Lord was giving him a second chance to be involved in the work, but this was to be the last time (D&C 5:27–29).

D&C 5:30–35 • Many Lie in Wait to Destroy Joseph

30 And if this be the case, behold, I say unto thee Joseph, when thou hast translated a few more pages thou shalt stop for a season, even until I command thee again; then thou mayest translate again.

31 And except thou do this, behold, thou shalt have no more gift, and I will take away the things which I have entrusted with thee.

32 And now, because I foresee the lying in wait to destroy thee, yea, I foresee that if my servant Martin Harris humbleth not himself and receive a witness from my hand, that he will fall into transgression;

33 And there are many that lie in wait to destroy thee from off the

face of the earth; and for this cause, that thy days may be prolonged, I have given unto thee these commandments.

34 Yea, for this cause I have said: Stop, and stand still until I command thee, and I will provide means whereby thou mayest accomplish the thing which I have commanded thee.

35 And if thou art faithful in keeping my commandments, thou shalt be lifted up at the last day. Amen.

The Lord gave Joseph another plan to implement if Martin were to fail again (v. 30). Certainly the Lord knew what would happen, but Joseph and Martin did not know. He was granting them their agency, but was giving them a warning (vv. 31–32). Again the Lord warns Joseph of his impending danger, but again promising them an eternal reward (vv. 32–35).

H istorical Setting—Section 17: The sectional heading, and the *History of the Church*, tells us that the three men, Oliver Cowdery, David Whitmer, and Martin Harris, had learned from the translation of the Book of Mormon plates that, "three special witnesses would be designated." Martin had come to Fayette, New York, where the work of translation was now in process. Section 5 was given in Harmony, Pennsylvania, about two months earlier, and thus Martin had not known of the "Three Witnesses" when section 5 was given, as was mentioned above. Note that Ether 5, and 2 Nephi 11; 27 were the sources sighted for learning of the Three Witnesses. Also note the sequence of those cited. Apparently, the book of Ether was translated before 2 Nephi 11, and 2 Nephi 27 were translated. This sequence is evidence that the small plates of Nephi were translated last, or after the abridgment of the large plates was translated. From Oliver Cowdery's account of John the Baptist's appearance to him and Joseph, May 15, 1829, we have another evidence of the small plates being translated last. Oliver states: "After writing the account given of the Savior's ministry to the remnant of the seed of Jacob upon this continent . . ." By this date the translation of 3 Nephi was completed. Thus, less than seventy pages of the current edition of the Book of Mormon were left to translate, unless the small plates were not yet translated. Since the translation was not completed until sometime

in June, it seems that the small plates had not yet been translated.

The three men, Oliver Cowdery, David Whitmer, and Martin Harris, requested of Joseph if they might be those three special witnesses.

SECTION 17 • OUTLINE

➤ D&C 17:1–4   Oliver, David, and Martin are conditionally promised to see the plates, the breastplate, the sword of Laban, the Urim and Thummim, and the miraculous directors.

    a. It shall be by their faith (v. 2).

    b. They will testify by the power of God (v. 3).

    c. Their testimony shall keep Joseph Smith from being destroyed and bring about the righteous purposes of the Lord (v. 4).

➤ D&C 17:5–8   Testify you have seen [these things] even as Joseph has seen them.

    a. Joseph has translated the book as commanded (v. 6).

    b. You have received the same power like unto him (v. 7).

    c. The gates of hell shall not prevail against you (v. 8).

    e. You will be lifted up at the last day (v. 8).

➤ D&C 17:9   Jesus Christ has spoken to bring about his righteous purposes.

TEXT AND COMMENTARY

D&C 17:1–4 • Joseph Smith To Not Be Destroyed

1 Behold, I say unto you, that you must rely upon my word, which if you do with full purpose of heart, you shall have a view of the plates, and also of the breastplate, the sword of Laban, the Urim and Thummim, which were given to the brother of Jared upon the mount, when he talked with the Lord face to face, and the miraculous directors which were given to Lehi while in the wilderness, on the borders of the Red Sea.

2 And it is by your faith that you shall obtain a view of them, even by that faith which was had by the prophets of old.

3 And after that you have obtained faith, and have seen them with

your eyes, you shall testify of them, by the power of God;

4 And this you shall do that my servant Joseph Smith, Jun., may not be destroyed, that I may bring about my righteous purposes unto the children of men in this work.

The five items that the three men were promised they could view are all prominent in the Book of Mormon, and were handed down with the records from generation to generation (see Words of Mormon 1:10–11; Mosiah 28:20; 4 Nephi 1:48). The first item, the set of plates that were made, and the abridgment that was engraven upon them by Mormon, after whom the Book of Mormon was named, had been preserved and hid up unto the Lord for over 1400 years (see Words of Mormon 1:3; Mormon 1:3, 4:23, 6:6; Ether 15:3).

The second item, the breastplate, was used to hold the Urim and Thummim while translating. Joseph Smith was told of it by the Angel Moroni (JS—H 1:35, 42), and saw it and obtained it when he went to the hill Cumorah (JS—H 1:52, 59).

The third item the three men were promised to see was the sword of Laban. Nephi took the sword from Laban, which was made of pure gold and precious steel (1 Nephi 4:9), when he was commanded to kill him (1 Nephi 4:9, 18–21). He later used it as a pattern to make other swords (2 Nephi 5:14). It was also handed down with the other sacred items (see Mosiah 1:16).

The fourth item, mentioned above in connection with the breastplate, was prepared by God "for the purpose of translating the book" (JS—H 1:35). This poses the question of whether there was more than one Urim and Thummim? Abraham had one (Abraham 3:1, 4), and it was had among the Israelites in the day of Moses (see Exodus 28:30). The Urim and Thummim given to Joseph Smith, with the plates, was the one "given to the brother of Jared upon the mount" (D&C 17:1). This statement suggests that there was more than one, but the Lord could have transported it to others when there was a need, as it was brought to Joseph by Moroni. The condition of the three men seeing these things was that their faith be even as "was had by the prophets of old" (v. 2). This suggests that these items were the same ones that were had by others. However, we do not know the answer to the question, nor does it matter.

The last item mentioned, to be shown to the Three Witnesses, was "the miraculous directors which were given to Lehi" (D&C 17:1). The Book of Mormon people gave it a name, the Liahona, but also called it a ball, or director (Alma 37:38; Mosiah 1:16). It was given to Lehi to direct his people in the wilderness (1 Nephi 16:10). It was certainly miraculous. The seeing of these items would surely be evidence of the validity of the Book of Mormon. After they had seen them, they were to testify by the power of God (D&C 17:3). Such power would come by the Holy Ghost and would bring a sure knowledge, not just evidence.

Again, the Lord states his purpose of protecting Joseph Smith from being destroyed (17:4). The Lord knows the thoughts and intents of the heart (see D&C 6:16), and will protect His servants until their mission is fulfilled (see comments on D&C 5:32–33).

D&C 17:5–9 • As Your Lord and Your God Lives the Book of Mormon is True

> 5 And ye shall testify that you have seen them, even as my servant Joseph Smith, Jun., has seen them; for it is by my power that he has seen them, and it is because he had faith.
>
> 6 And he has translated the book, even that part which I have commanded him, and as your Lord and your God liveth it is true.
>
> 7 Wherefore, you have received the same power, and the same faith, and the same gift like unto him;
>
> 8 And if you do these last commandments of mine, which I have given you, the gates of hell shall not prevail against you; for my grace is sufficient for you, and you shall be lifted up at the last day.
>
> 9 And I, Jesus Christ, your Lord and your God, have spoken it unto you, that I might bring about my righteous purposes unto the children of men. Amen.

As stated in chapter 5, concerning David Whitmer (D&C 14:8–11): The Testimony of Three Witnesses, published in the front of the Book of Mormon, states that they had **heard** the voice of God and had **seen** the engravings on the plates by the power of God (emphasis added). Martin Harris had likewise been prepared for his special calling (see D&C 5:23–25 and comments above). As will be discussed in the next chapter, Oliver Cowdery had previously been prepared for this special calling. Now there would be three special witnesses to go with the testimony of Joseph Smith Jr. of his role in the great and marvelous work. The Three Witnesses were to testify of Joseph as well as of what they had seen.

JESUS' PARABLES FULFILLED

Joseph's role was to fulfill the parable, given by Jesus from a ship on the Sea of Galilee, to bring forth "the kingdom of heaven [which] is like to a grain of mustard seed, which a man took and sowed in his field" (Matthew 13:31). The Prophet Joseph, who was commissioned to expound "all scriptures unto the church" as given him by the Comforter (D&C 24:5, 9), gave us this inspired interpretation of that parable: "Let us take the Book of Mormon, which a man took and hid in his field, securing it by his faith, to spring up in the last days, or in due time; let us behold it coming forth out of the ground" (*TPJS*, 98).[16]

The role of the Three Witnesses was to fulfill another parable given by Jesus at the same time: "The kingdom of heaven is like unto leaven, which a woman took, and hid in three measures of meal, till the whole was leavened" (Matthew 13:33). Joseph gave this interpretation: "It may be understood that the Church of the Latter-day Saints has taken its rise from a little leaven that was put into Three Witnesses. Behold how much this is like the parable! It is fast leavening the lump, and will soon leaven the whole" (*TPJS*, 100). As Jesus told His disciples concerning these parables; "blessed are your eyes, for they see: and your ears, for they hear" (Matthew 13:16).

The confirmation by the Lord, that the translation of the Book of Mormon was true, was given in the words of an ancient Hebrew oath: "as your Lord and your God liveth it is true" (D&C 17:6). This was a sacred and binding oath as illustrated by Nephi's using it to assure Zoram, the servant of Laban, that he would be a free man in traveling with them in the wilderness (see 1 Nephi 4:31–33).

The Lord concludes His revelation to the Three Witnesses with

---

[16] Joseph's complete interpretation is not included above, just the first part of it. The entire sermon recorded in Matthew 13 was interpreted by him to show the sequence of events from the time of his ministry to the end of the dispensation of the fullness of times (see *TPJS*, 94–102).

another promise. The promise, on the condition of their keeping these last commandments, was two fold: first, the gates of hell would not prevail against them, and the second was that they would be lifted up at the last day (D&C 17:7–8). Jesus gives the same promise in the New Testament (Matthew 16:18). In both instances, He has reference to following revelation that is available to them and us, and it is sufficient (through His grace) to direct us into returning unto Him when our mortal test is completed. His righteous purposes (D&C 17:10) are "to bring to pass the immortality and eternal life of man" (Moses 1:39).

The young Prophet Joseph records the fulfilling of the three men seeing the aforementioned items. We will give a brief sketch of his account, leaving the details to the study of Church history.

> Not many days after the above commandment was given, we four . . . agreed to retire into the woods . . . having knelt down, we began to pray in much faith to Almighty God. . . .
>
> We beheld a light above us in the air, of exceeding brightness; and behold, an angel stood before us. In his hands he held the plates which we had been praying for us to have a view of. He turned over the leaves one by one, so that we could see them, and discern the engravings thereon distinctly. . . . We heard a voice from out of the bright light above us, saying, "These plates have been revealed by the power of God, and they have been translated by the power of God. The translation of them which you have seen is correct, and I command you to bear record of what you now see and hear." [*HC*, 1:54–55]

To appreciate what pressure Joseph was under prior to this time, and to realize how the Lord kept him from being destroyed, after the three had seen and heard the voice of the Lord, his mother relates this experience:

> On coming in, Joseph threw himself down beside me, and exclaimed; "Father, mother, you do not know how happy I am: the Lord has now caused the plates to be shown to three more besides myself. They have seen an angel, who has testified to them, and they will have to bear witness to the truth of what I have said, for now they know for themselves, that I do not go about to deceive the people, and I feel as if I was relieved of a burden which was almost too heavy for me to bear, and it rejoices my soul, that I am not any longer to be entirely alone in the world. [*History of Joseph Smith by his Mother*, 152]

The Testimony of the Three Witnesses is included in each copy of the Book of Mormon. We encourage you to read it at this time. The Testimony of the Eight Witnesses, also included in the front of the Book of Mormon, was obtained soon after (see *HC*, 1:57). To appreciate the difference and significance between the two, we quote Elder B. H. Roberts, a member of the First Council of Seventy until his death.

> It is to be observed that what may be called two kinds of testimony to the truth of the Book of Mormon is found in the statements of the three and the eight witnesses respectively: vis: what men would call miraculous testimony, and ordinary testimony. Had there been but one kind of testimony the matter would have been much simplified for the objector. Had the testimony of the Three Witnesses been the only kind given; that is, if the plates had been exhibited to the eight witnesses in the same manner as they had been revealed to the three, then, perhaps, mental hallucination might have been urged with more show of reason. Or, if the Three Witnesses had seen the plates in the same manner as the eight did, in a plain, matter-of-fact way, without display of the divine power, then the theory of pure fabrication, with collusion on the part of all those who assisted in bringing forth the work, would have been more standing. But with the two kinds of testimony to deal with it is extremely difficult for objectors to dispose of the matter. [*A Comprehensive History of The Church of Jesus Christ of Latter-day Saints* (1930), 149–150]

Indeed the world is on trial, not the Book of Mormon, and the Lord has left the world without excuse.

General Authority Quotes

—*President Brigham Young* • D&C 5:10

> It was decreed in the counsels of eternity, long before the foundations of the earth were laid, that he, Joseph Smith, should be the man, in the last dispensation of this world, to bring forth the word of God to this people, and receive the fullness of the keys and power of the Priesthood of the Son of God. The Lord had his eyes upon him, and upon his father, and upon His father's father, and upon their progenitors clear back to Abraham, and from Abraham to the flood, and from the flood to Enoch, and from Enoch to Adam. He has watched that family and that blood as it has circulated from its fountain to the birth of that man. He was fore-ordained in eternity

to preside over this last dispensation. [*Discourses of Brigham Young*, 108]

—*Elder Marion G. Romney* • D&C 5:19–29

The Lord always warns the people of a new dispensation through prophets raised up unto them in their own day. This He has done for this generation through the great prophet of the restoration, Joseph Smith Jr. Through him the Lord repeatedly declared that the world was ripening in iniquity and that unless men repented destruction would overtake them. For example, in March, 1829, he said: (quotes D&C 5:19–20). You will note that this prediction, as were like predictions in the past, is conditional. "If they repent not," is the condition. For this generation, as for all others, the Lord has provided the means of escape. This means is now, and has always been, the gospel of Jesus Christ. [CR, April 1958, 128]

Chapter Seven

The Spirit of Revelation

D&C 6:10–37; 8; 9

Historical Setting—Section 6:

> On the 5th of April, 1829, Oliver Cowdery came to my house, until which time I had never seen him. He stated to me that having been teaching school in the neighborhood where my father resided, and my father being one of those who sent to the school, he went to board for a season at his house, and while there the family related to him the circumstances of my having received the plates, and accordingly he had come to make inquiries of me. Two days after the arrival of Mr. Cowdery (being the 7th of April) I commenced to translate the Book of Mormon, and he began to write for me, which having continued for some time, I inquired of the Lord through the Urim and Thummim, and obtained the following: [*HC*, 1:32–33]

INTRODUCTION

Who was Oliver Cowdery? He was a very important man in the founding of the restored Church. As noted above, he began acting as Joseph's scribe for translating the Book of Mormon two days after they met. In addition, he filled the roles of Second Elder of the Church, Joseph's spokesman, church historian, and the first Assistant President. We will enlarge on his other callings in later chapters, and focus on his role as Joseph's scribe in the three revelations discussed here.

SECTION 6 • OUTLINE

➤ 6:1–9   Discussed in chapter five

➤ 6:10–16   Oliver had been given the gift of revelation which was sacred and from above.

      a.   His gift could reveal mysteries and bring others to know their errors (v. 11).

      b.   Make thy gift known to only those of thy faith (v. 12).

      c.   If good and faithful, he can receive salvation, the greatest gift of all (v. 13).

      d.   Thou wast instructed by my Spirit, or you would not have come here (v. 14).

      e.   You now know that I have enlightened you by my Spirit (v. 15).

      f.   None but God knows the thoughts and intents of thy heart (v. 16).

➤ 6:17–21   The words or the work that thou hast been writing are true.

      a.   Stand by Joseph in whatever difficult circumstances there be (v. 18).

      b.   Admonish him in his faults, and receive admonition from him (v. 19).

      c.   Treasure these words, keep the commandments, and I will encircle you in my love (v. 20).

      d.   I am Jesus Christ, I was rejected by mine own, and I am the light in darkness and the darkness comprehendeth it not (v. 21).

➤ 6:22–24   Cast your mind on the night that you cried to know the truth of these things and I spoke peace to your mind.

      a.   What greater witness can you have than from God? (v. 23).

      b.   I have told you things which no man knoweth (v. 24).

➤ 6:25–31   I grant to you a gift, if you desire, to translate even as Joseph.

      a.   I have records that have been kept back because of wickedness (v. 26).

b.   If you have good desires, you can assist to bring these to light (v. 27).

    c.   I give unto you and Joseph, two witnesses, the keys of this gift (v. 28).

    d.   If they reject my words, they can do no more to you than they did to me, but ye shall dwell in glory (v. 29–30).

    e.   If they accept your words, you shall have joy in your labors (v. 31).

➤ 6:32–37   Where two or more are gathered in my name, I will be in thy midst.

    a.   Fear not to do good, what you sow you shall reap (v. 33).

    b.   Let earth and hell combine against you, for if you are built on my rock, they cannot prevail (v. 34).

    c.   I do not condemn you, go and sin no more, perform the work with soberness, look unto me with every thought (v. 35).

    d.   Behold the wounds in my side and in my hands and feet, be faithful (v. 37).

TEXT AND COMMENTARY

D&C 6:10–16 • The Gift of Revelation

10 Behold thou hast a gift, and blessed art thou because of thy gift. Remember it is sacred and cometh from above—

11 And if thou wilt inquire, thou shalt know mysteries which are great and marvelous; therefore thou shalt exercise thy gift, that thou mayest find out mysteries, that thou mayest bring many to the knowledge of the truth, yea, convince them of the error of their ways.

12 Make not thy gift known unto any save it be those who are of thy faith. Trifle not with sacred things.

13 If thou wilt do good, yea, and hold out faithful to the end, thou shalt be saved in the kingdom of God, which is the greatest of all the gifts of God; for there is no gift greater than the gift of salvation.

14 Verily, verily, I say unto thee, blessed art thou for what thou hast done; for thou hast inquired of me, and behold, as often as thou hast inquired thou hast received instruction of my Spirit. If it had not been so, thou wouldst not have come to the place where thou art at this time.

15 Behold, thou knowest that thou hast inquired of me and I did enlighten thy mind; and now I tell thee these things that thou mayest know that thou hast been enlightened by the Spirit of truth;

16 Yea, I tell thee, that thou mayest know that there is none else save God that knowest thy thoughts and the intents of thy heart.

The gift of revelation that Oliver had been given (v. 10) was the Holy Ghost. This conclusion is further substantiated in D&C 8:2–3. Many who have not been given the gift of the Holy Ghost are given its guidance from time to time. Every reader of the Book of Mormon, whether in the Church or not, can know of the truthfulness of the book—indeed, of all things—by the power of the Holy Ghost (see Moroni 10:4–5). The mysteries of God are things which are not known except through revelation from God, and are given to bring truth and salvation to the children of men (D&C 6:11; see also Alma 26:22). It is sacred because it is given only to a few, those who believe in faith (v. 12). As Jesus said: "Give not that which is holy unto the dogs [Gentiles], neither cast ye your pearls before swine" (Matthew 7:6; 3 Nephi 14:6). Those who follow their faith and do good, and hold out faithful to the end shall receive the greatest of all the gifts of God, which is salvation (D&C 6:13).

Oliver had been given this gift of guidance many times, whenever he had asked for it. Apparently he was a praying man and was being guided by the Spirit, including his visit to the Smith home and then to Harmony to see Joseph. The Lord moves His people to be where they are needed, and where he wants them to be (v. 14). Oliver was not cognizant of how much he had been influenced by the Spirit of truth (v. 15). The Lord further explained to Oliver that none but "God knoweth thy thoughts and the intents of thy heart" (v. 16). Since thoughts and feelings are personal, the blessings that come from them are not usually associated with God. The Book of Mormon gives many examples of the Spirit revealing a person's thoughts to one of God's servants (see Jacob 2:5; Alma 10:17; 12:3; 17:16).[17] This is usually done to bring about blessings to someone.

---

[17] Some have used D&C 6:16 as a reference to show that we should not pray vocally, lest Satan thus learn our thoughts and prevent us from accomplishing what we are praying for otherwise unknown. However, the Lord commands us to "pray vocally as well as in thy heart" (D&C 19:28; 23:6). The Lord's power is greater than the devil's, and He will answer our vocal prayers as well as our silent ones.

D&C 6:17–21 • The Book of Mormon Is True

17 I tell thee these things as a witness unto thee—that the words or the work which thou hast been writing are true.

18 Therefore be diligent; stand by my servant Joseph, faithfully, in whatsoever difficult circumstances he may be for the word's sake.

19 Admonish him in his faults, and also receive admonition of him. Be patient; be sober; be temperate; have patience, faith, hope and charity.

20 Behold, thou art Oliver, and I have spoken unto thee because of thy desires; therefore treasure up these words in thy heart. Be faithful and diligent in keeping the commandments of God, and I will encircle thee in the arms of my love.

21 Behold, I am Jesus Christ, the Son of God. I am the same that came unto mine own, and mine own received me not. I am the light which shineth in darkness, and the darkness comprehendeth it not.

Oliver is told that the words of the translation of the Book of Mormon are true (v. 17). This is the first of three times that the Lord verifies the translation in the Doctrine and Covenants. His purpose in doing so is to give further instructions to Oliver. He is to stand by Joseph in defending the translation in all circumstances. There would still be critics of the translation, and there still are critics, but the Lord desired Oliver to help answer those critics—"for the words [Book of Mormon] sake" (v. 18). Nevertheless, Oliver is to point out any faults and take corrections from him as he continues, but the translation so far is acceptable to God (v. 19). Oliver was probably following the Lord's instructions to admonish Joseph in his faults when he differed with Joseph "about the account of John the Apostle, mentioned in the New Testament" (*HC*, 1:35), which led to the receiving of the revelation now published as section 7.

The counsel to Oliver to treasure up the words of the Book of Mormon in his heart (v. 20), would give him a further witness by the Holy Ghost of their truthfulness (see D&C 8:2). This feeling in the heart would help him to be faithful in keeping the commandments, and he would eventually be encircled in the loving arms of the Savior (D&C 6:20). What greater reward could there be for him or for us? Should we not treasure up those same Book of Mormon words, that we not be one of those whom Isaiah foretold, in speaking about the Book of Mormon's coming forth, "that make a man an offender for a word" (Isaiah 29:21; 2 Nephi 27:32) by questioning Joseph's use of the language, or endeavoring to explain the meaning away? Jesus Christ, although rejected by His own people in His mortal ministry (see John 1:11), was the light that shineth in the darkness of an apostate world. That Light, through the Urim and Thummim, came to translate the Book of Mormon and gave us His words [Book of Mormon], even though many in the darkness of the world will not comprehend it (D&C 6:21).

D&C 6:22–24 • Oliver's First Witness

22 Verily, verily, I say unto you, if you desire a further witness, cast your mind upon the night that you cried unto me in your heart, that you might know concerning the truth of these things.

23 Did I not speak peace to your mind concerning the matter? What greater witness can you have than from God?

24 And now, behold, you have received a witness; for if I have told you things which no man knoweth have you not received a witness?

The following was recorded in the Prophet Joseph's history, and is the divine manifestation referred to in the heading of section 6:

After we had received this revelation, Oliver Cowdery stated to me that after he had gone to my father's to board, and after the family had communicated to him concerning my having obtained the plates, that one night after he had retired to bed he called upon the Lord to know if these things were so, and the Lord manifested to him that they were true, but he had kept the circumstance entirely secret, and had mentioned it to no one; so that after this revelation was given, he knew that the work was true, because no being living knew of the thing alluded to in the revelation, but God himself. [*HC*, 1:35]

D&C 6:25–31 • Other Records to Translate

25 And, behold, I grant unto you a gift, if you desire of me, to translate, even as my servant Joseph.

26 Verily, verily, I say unto you, that there are records which contain much of my gospel, which have been kept back because of the wickedness of the people;

27 And now I command you, that if you have good desires—a desire to lay up treasures for yourself in heaven—then shall you assist in

bringing to light, with your gift, those parts of my scriptures which have been hidden because of iniquity.

28 And now, behold, I give unto you, and also unto my servant Joseph, the keys of this gift, which shall bring to light this ministry; and in the mouth of two or Three Witnesses shall every word be established.

29 Verily, verily, I say unto you, if they reject my words, and this part of my gospel and ministry, blessed are ye, for they can do no more unto you than unto me.

30 And even if they do unto you even as they have done unto me, blessed are ye, for you shall dwell with me in glory.

31 But if they reject not my words, which shall be established by the testimony which shall be given, blessed are they, and then shall ye have joy in the fruit of your labors.

The records to which the Lord refers (vv. 26–27), would include but not be limited to: the parchment of John (now section 7), the scrolls of the book of Abraham (Pearl of Great Price), and other records of the Nephites and Jaredites (see Helaman 3:15). More will be said of these records, and Oliver's translating, when we discuss sections 8 and 9. The law of witnesses, two or more (Matthew 18:16), is again followed by Oliver's being given the keys of the gift of translation with Joseph (D&C 6:28). When these records are brought forth, the world will still be on trial. The inhabitants must accept them or reject them, which will bring eternal life or condemnation (see D&C 20:13–15). Those who bring those records forth may also be martyred as were Joseph and Hyrum Smith, but their eternal glory with Jesus is promised. As Jesus told Joseph and Oliver: "they can do no more unto you than unto me" (vv. 29–31).

D&C 6:32–37 • Behold the Wounds Which Pierced My Side

32 Verily, verily, I say unto you, as I said unto my disciples, where two or three are gathered together in my name, as touching one thing, behold, there will I be in the midst of them—even so am I in the midst of you.

33 Fear not to do good, my sons, for whatsoever ye sow, that shall ye also reap; therefore, if ye sow good ye shall also reap good for your reward.

34 Therefore, fear not, little flock; do good; let earth and hell combine against you, for if ye are built upon my rock, they cannot prevail.

35 Behold, I do not condemn you; go your ways and sin no more; perform with soberness the work which I have commanded you.

36 Look unto me in every thought; doubt not, fear not.

37 Behold the wounds which pierced my side, and also the prints of the nails in my hands and feet; be faithful, keep my commandments, and ye shall inherit the kingdom of heaven. Amen.

The Lord quotes several New Testament promises to Joseph and Oliver: His being with his gathered disciples (v. 32; Matthew 18:19); you reap as you sow (v. 33; Galatians 6:7–8); build upon my rock (v. 34; Matthew 16:18); and you are not condemned, sin no more (v. 35; John 8:11). The gospel principles are the same in all generations. The Lord's invitation to "Look unto me in every thought" (v. 36) was probably to always remember Him as we should when we partake of the sacrament. The invitation to "Behold the wounds which pierced my side," (v. 37) may have been an allusion to His future appearance in the Kirtland Temple on April 6, 1836, or to another appearance He would make. It could also be an expression that the veil could have been parted at that time if they had the necessary faith. Again, we have no answer, but we do know who was giving the invitation.

*H*istorical Setting—Sections 8; 9:

> Whilst continuing the work of translation, during the month of April, Oliver became exceedingly anxious to have the power to translate bestowed upon him, and in relation to this desire the following revelations were obtained. [*HC*, 1:36]

Oliver's anxiety was natural since he had been told he held the keys (6:28). However, the Lord had said he had other records which he could assist with their translation (6:26–27). The Lord does grant his desire, and gives him the opportunity to try and translate.

Sections 8 & 9 • Outline

➤ 8:1–5   Oliver is granted the gift to translate old records as the Lord had promised.

    a. The Lord would tell him in his heart and in his mind, by the Holy Ghost (v. 2).

    b. This was the spirit of revelation that was given to Moses at the Red Sea (v. 3).

    c. This gift will deliver you from your enemies who would destroy you (v. 4).

    d. Remember these words and keep my commandments (v. 5).

8:6–12 Oliver has another gift, the gift of Aaron, which has told him many things.

    a. Only the power of God can cause this gift to be with you (v. 7).

    b. Hold it in your hands and it will do marvelous works (v. 8).

    c. It will give you knowledge of whatever you ask (v. 9).

    d. Ask in faith; do not ask for what you ought not (v. 10).

    e. Ask in faith to receive knowledge from the sacred records (v. 11).

    f. I who speak am the same from the beginning (v. 12).

9:1–9 Since Oliver did not translate as desired, he should continue to write for Joseph.

    a. He will be able to assist to translate other records (v. 2).

    b. Be patient and write for Joseph (vv. 3–4).

    c. You did not continue as you commenced, so do not murmur (vv. 5–6).

    d. You did not understand, you took no thought but to ask (v. 7).

    e. You must study it out in your mind, then ask if it is right. If right, your bosom will burn within you, and if wrong, you will have a stupor of thought (vv. 8–9).

9:10–14 If you had known this you could have translated, but it is not expedient now.

    a. I have given Joseph sufficient strength to do it, neither are condemned (v. 12).

    b. Do as I command and you shall prosper, yield to no temptation (v. 13).

c. Stand fast and you shall be lifted up at the last day (v. 14).

TEXT AND COMMENTARY

D&C 8:1–5 • The Book of Abraham

1 Oliver Cowdery, verily, verily, I say unto you, that assuredly as the Lord liveth, who is your God and your Redeemer, even so surely shall you receive a knowledge of whatsoever things you shall ask in faith, with an honest heart, believing that you shall receive a knowledge concerning the engravings of old records, which are ancient, which contain those parts of my scripture of which has been spoken by the manifestation of my Spirit.

2 Yea, behold, I will tell you in your mind and in your heart, by the Holy Ghost, which shall come upon you and which shall dwell in your heart.

3 Now, behold, this is the spirit of revelation; behold, this is the spirit by which Moses brought the children of Israel through the Red Sea on dry ground.

4 Therefore this is thy gift; apply unto it, and blessed art thou, for it shall deliver you out of the hands of your enemies, when, if it were not so, they would slay you and bring your soul to destruction.

5 Oh, remember these words, and keep my commandments. Remember, this is your gift.

The book of Abraham, that is now published by the Church of Jesus Christ of Latter-day Saints, was translated by Joseph Smith from an ancient papyrus that miraculously came into his hands.[18] It was certainly a part of the "old records" to which the Lord referred (v. 1; 6:26). What is not commonly known is that Joseph only translated a small portion of the papyrus. After the translation had begun, Oliver Cowdery wrote: "When the translation of these valuable documents will be completed, I am unable to say, neither can I give you a probable idea how large volumes they will make; but judging from the size and the comprehensiveness of the language, one might reasonably expect to see a sufficient to develop much upon the mighty acts of the ancient men of God" (*Messen-*

---

[18] We will not go into the account of how Joseph obtained this papyrus. For those who desire to understand how he came to obtain this document see H. Donl Peterson, *The Story of The Book of Abraham* [1995].

ger and Advocate, an early Church newspaper), December 1835, 2:236). Something that is even less commonly known is that there were also writings of Joseph, who was sold into Egypt, included in the papyrus. In the *History of the Church* we read: "I commenced the translation of some of the characters or hieroglyphics, and much to our joy found that one of the rolls contained the writings of Abraham, another the writings of Joseph of Egypt" (*Messenger and Advocate,* 2:236). That a record of Joseph of Egypt was kept is verified in the Book of Mormon (see 2 Nephi 3:4–22). Whether the one Lehi quoted from, just referred to, is the same as the one obtained in the Egypt papyrus, we do not know, but someday it will be known. We are also told by the Lord of another ancient record: things were "written in the book of Enoch, and are to be testified of in due time" (D&C 107:57). The Lord does have ancient records yet to come forth. Oliver could have translated some of them had he, and or the Church collectively, exercised their faith.

The spirit of revelation as defined (D&C 8:2–3) has two parts, the mind and the heart. The mind is an intellectual experience. The heart is a spiritual witness. One without the other may be false. If it is only in the mind, it may be the reasoning of man and not agree with the reasoning of God. If it is only an internal feeling, it may be caused by emotion or excitement. The combination of the two; reasoning with God, and edification of the Spirit is verification of it being a revelation from God (see D&C 50:10–12, 22–23). The experience will help us grow in the principle of revelation. Joseph Smith taught:

> . . . A person may profit by noticing the first intimation of the spirit of revelation; for instance, when you feel pure intelligence flowing into you, it may give you sudden strokes of ideas, so that by noticing it, you may find it fulfilled the same day or soon: (i.e.) those things that were presented unto your minds by the Spirit of God, will come to pass, and thus by learning the Spirit of God and understanding it, you may grow into the principle of revelation, until you become perfect in Christ. [*TPJS*, 151]

The example of Moses and the Red Sea (v. 3) was probably not used without purpose. Although the Book of Mormon states five times that Moses parted the Red Sea (1 Nephi 4:2; 17:26; Mosiah 7:19; Alma 36:28; Helaman 8:11), the reasoning of man says that it could not have been the Red Sea, but it was the Reed Sea.[19] The Doctrine and Covenants adds this witness to the correctness of the Red Sea. Furthermore it adds it from an updated source, the last dispensation. Another modern source tells us that Moses was blessed by God to "be stronger than many waters; for they shall obey thy command as if thou wert God" (Moses 1:25). This blessing would supersede the reasoning of man. Through the spirit of revelation, and the power of God, miracles are performed.

The spirit of revelation would deliver Oliver "out of the hands of [his] enemies" (D&C 8:4). Nephi said that "the Holy Ghost . . . will show unto you all things what ye should do" (2 Nephi 32:5). The Prophet Joseph explained: "The first Comforter or Holy Ghost has no other effect than pure intelligence. It is more powerful in expanding the mind, enlightening the understanding, and storing the intellect with present knowledge. . ." (*TPJS*, 149). Therefore, the spirit of revelation would guide Oliver so that he would avoid the enemy's plans to engulf him and take his life both physically and spiritually. To have this blessing, Oliver must remember this promise and keep the commandments (D&C 8:5). The Lord is "bound when ye do what [he says]" (D&C 82:10).

D&C 8:6–12 • The Gift of Aaron

6 Now this is not all thy gift; for you have another gift, which is the gift of Aaron; behold, it has told you many things;

7 Behold, there is no other power, save the power of God, that can cause this gift of Aaron to be with you.

8 Therefore, doubt not, for it is the gift of God; and you shall hold it in your hands, and do marvelous works; and no power shall be able to take it away out of your hands, for it is the work of God.

9 And, therefore, whatsoever you shall ask me to tell you by that

---

[19] See virtually any Bible commentary. Even the conservative New International Version (NIV) Study Bible cites the Hebrew text to claim it was the Reed Sea. The plain and precious parts lost from the Bible (see 1 Nephi 13:26–29) were taken away long before any of the present texts were written, regardless of language. We have no original texts. The Massoretic text (A.D. 900) was the oldest until the Dead Sea texts were discovered. The Dead Sea texts are dated to between 100 B.C. and A.D. 100. The Plates of Brass, from which the Book of Mormon people were basing their teaching, were written at least before 600 B.C., about 500 years before the Dead Sea texts, and will someday be given to us (see 1 Nephi 5:18–19; Alma 37:3–4). The Lord will further verify his records in time. For now we must rely on the witnesses the Lord has given us.

means, that will I grant unto you, and you shall have knowledge concerning it.

10 Remember that without faith you can do nothing; therefore ask in faith. Trifle not with these things; do not ask for that which you ought not.

11 Ask that you may know the mysteries of God, and that you may translate and receive knowledge from all those ancient records which have been hid up, that are sacred; and according to your faith shall it be done unto you.

12 Behold, it is I that have spoken it; and I am the same that spake unto you from the beginning. Amen.

The gift of Aaron, Oliver's other gift, was apparently another instrument for receiving revelation. It had told him many things (v. 6), and he would be able to hold it in his hands (v. 8). In this dispensation, "the dispensation of the fullness of times (see D&C 112:30), Christ would "gather in one all things . . . both which are in heaven, and which are on earth" (Ephesians 1:10). Was this gift the miraculous rod of Aaron (see Numbers 17:6–10; Hebrews 9:4)? There has been some evidence and speculation of Joseph having this instrument,[20] but we will wait for further evidence, or the time when it is publicly made known, to answer the question. For now it falls into the category of: "Trifle not with these things; do not ask for that which ye ought not" (D&C 8:10). We must concentrate on seeking to understand the mysteries of God that will bring us salvation. We must prepare ourselves to receive those ancient records, which Oliver was told he could translate, that are hid up and are sacred (v. 11). When we fully accept that which we have already been given; the Book of Mormon, the Doctrine and Covenants, the Pearl of Great Price, and the Joseph Smith Translation, we will be given more (see 3 Nephi 26:9).

D&C 9:1–4 • Not Expedient to Translate

1 Behold, I say unto you, my son, that because you did not translate according to that which you desired of me, and did commence again to write for my servant, Joseph Smith, Jun., even so I would that ye

---

[20] For evidence, see Hyrum L. Andrus, *Doctrinal Commentary on the Pearl of Great Price* [1967], 5–6.

should continue until you have finished this record, which I have entrusted unto him.

2 And then, behold, other records have I, that I will give unto you power that you may assist to translate.

3 Be patient, my son, for it is wisdom in me, and it is not expedient that you should translate at this present time.

4 Behold, the work which you are called to do is to write for my servant Joseph.

In addition to the comments preceding the verses just quoted, we are reminded of the words of Alma: "I know that which the Lord hath commanded me, and I glory in it. I do not glory of myself, but I glory in that which the Lord hath commanded me; yea, and this is my glory, that perhaps I may be an instrument in the hands of God to bring some soul to repentance; and this is my joy" (Alma 29:9). Oliver was apparently content to do as the Lord now commanded him, to write for Joseph.

D&C 9:5–9 • Study It Out in Your Mind

5 And, behold, it is because that you did not continue as you commenced, when you began to translate, that I have taken away this privilege from you.

6 Do not murmur, my son, for it is wisdom in me that I have dealt with you after this manner.

7 Behold, you have not understood; you have supposed that I would give it unto you, when you took no thought save it was to ask me.

8 But, behold, I say unto you, that you must study it out in your mind; then you must ask me if it be right, and if it is right I will cause that your bosom shall burn within you; therefore, you shall feel that it is right.

9 But if it be not right you shall have no such feelings, but you shall have a stupor of thought that shall cause you to forget the thing which is wrong; therefore, you cannot write that which is sacred save it be given you from me.

Although the Lord's instructions to Oliver were regarding how to translate, part of the wisdom of dealing with him as He did (v. 6), was to teach all of us how to make decisions by revelation. The Lord expects us to use our reasoning power, but to do so as taught to Oliver. We must do more than just ask (v. 7). We must study our situation out in our minds, and then ask if our reasoning is in agreement with him. The burning of the bosom will come if we are right, or the stupor of thought will come if our conclusion was wrong (vv. 8–9). Elder Melvin J. Ballard counseled:

> You do not know what to do today to solve your financial problems, what to plant, whether to buy or sell cattle, sheep or other things. It is your privilege to study it out; counsel together with the best wisdom and judgment the Lord shall give you, reach your conclusions and then go to the Lord with it, tell him what you have planned to do. If the thing you have planned to do is for your good and your blessing, and you are determined to serve the Lord, pay your tithes and your offerings and keep the commandments, I promise that he will fulfill that promise upon your head, and your bosom shall burn within by the whisperings of the Spirit that it is right. But if it is not right, you shall have no such feelings, but you shall have a stupor of thought, and your heart will be turned away from that thing. [CR, April, 1933, 37–38]

All of us can profit by using this decision-making process.

D&C 9:19–14 • Joseph Given Sufficient Strength

> 10 Now, if you had known this you could have translated; neverthe-less, it is not expedient that you should translate now.

> 11 Behold, it was expedient when you commenced; but you feared, and the time is past, and it is not expedient now;

> 12 For, do you not behold that I have given unto my servant Joseph sufficient strength, whereby it is made up? And neither of you have I condemned.

> 13 Do this thing which I have commanded you, and you shall prosper. Be faithful, and yield to no temptation.

> 14 Stand fast in the work wherewith I have called you, and a hair of your head shall not be lost, and you shall be lifted up at the last day. Amen.

Fear is often a detriment to our accomplishments. Oliver feared he would not be able to translate (v. 11). "There is no fear in love" (1 John 4:18). Therefore, if we love God, we will have no need to fear, and he will strengthen us to be able to accomplish what he has commanded. The Lord strengthened Joseph to be able to meet the work of translation (D&C 9:12). Oliver did do as he was commanded and stood fast in the work that he was called to do (vv. 13–14).

Oliver Cowdery describes these events thus:

> These were days never to be forgotten—to sit under the sound of a voice dictated by the inspiration of heaven, awakened the utmost gratitude of this bosom! Day after day I continued, uninterrupted, to write from his mouth, as he translated with the Urim and Thummim, or, as the Nephites would have said, 'Interpreters,' the history or record called 'The Book of Mormon.' [JS—H, footnote, 58]

We also should stand fast in the work wherewith the Lord calls us.

General Authority Quotes

—*President Brigham Young* • D&C 8:1; 9:2

> . . . I tell these things to you, and I have a motive for doing so. I want to carry them to the ears of my brethren and sisters, and to the children also, that they may grow to an understanding of some things that seem to be entirely hidden from the human family. Oliver went with the Prophet Joseph when he deposited these plates. Joseph did not translate all of the plates; there was a portion of them sealed, which you can learn from the book of Doctrine and Covenants. When Joseph got the plates, the angel instructed him to carry them back to the hill Cumorah, which he did. Oliver says that when Joseph and Oliver went there, the hill opened and they walked into a cave, in which there was a large and spacious room. He said he did not think, at the time, whether they had the light of the sun or artificial light; but that it was as light as day. They laid the plates on a table; it was a large table that stood in the room. Under this table was a pile of plates as much as two feet high, and there were altogether in this room more plates than probably many wagon loads. The first time they went there the sword of Laban hung upon the wall; but when they went again it had been taken down and laid upon the table across the gold plates; it was unsheathed, and on it were written these words: "This sword will never be sheathed again until the kingdom of this world become the kingdom of our God and his Christ." I tell you this as coming not only from Oliver Cowdery, but others who were

familiar with it, and who understood it just as well as we understand coming to this meeting. . . . Carlos Smith was a young man of as much veracity as any young man we had, and he was a witness to these things. Samuel Smith saw some things, Hyrum saw a good many things, but Joseph was the leader. [*JD*, 19:38]

—*Elder Richard G. Scott* • D&C 9:8–9

It is so hard when sincere prayer about something you desire very much is not answered the way you want. It is difficult to understand why your exercise of deep and sincere faith from an obedient life does not grant the desired result. The Savior taught, "Whatsoever ye ask the Father in my name it shall be given unto you, that is expedient for you" (D&C 88:64 see also vv. 63, 65). At times it is difficult to recognize what is best or expedient for you over time. Your life will be easier when you accept that what God does in your life is for your eternal good.

You are asked to look for an answer to your prayers (D&C 6:23; 8:2–3, 10; 9:9). Obey the Master's counsel to "study it out in your mind" (D&C 9:8). Often you will think of a solution; as you seek confirmation that your answer is right, help will come. It may be through your prayers; or an impression of the Holy Ghost, and at times by the intervention of others. [*Ensign*, May 2007, 9]

Chapter Eight

The Keys of the Aaronic Priesthood

D&C 13; 20:45–59

*H*istorical Setting:

> We still continued the work of translation, when, in the ensuing
> month (May, 1829), we on a certain day went into the woods to pray
> and inquire of the Lord respecting baptism for the remission of sins, that
> we found mentioned in the translation of the plates. While we were thus
> employed, praying and calling upon the Lord, a messenger from heaven
> descended in a cloud of light, and having laid his hands upon us, he
> ordained us. [JS—H 1:68]

INTRODUCTION

The mission of John the Baptist is one that is greatly misunderstood
in the christian world. It is generally supposed that his mission was
completed with his preparing the way before the Christ in the meridian
of time. However, a careful examination of the scriptures used to support
this theory would show that this is not the case. In Matthew's account,
as John's entry is described, a verse from Isaiah is quoted as having been
fulfilled. "For this is he that was spoken of by the prophet Esaias, saying,
The voice of one crying in the wilderness, Prepare ye the way of the Lord,
make his paths straight" (Matthew 3:3). The verse quoted, with some
variation, is Isaiah 40:3 of our present King James Version text. While
the verse in Isaiah does refer to John the Baptist, the complete mission
of John the Baptist could not have been completed in the meridian of
time because of what Isaiah says in the verses that follow.

> 4 Every valley shall be exalted, and every mountain and hill shall be
> made low: and the crooked shall be made straight, and the rough places
> plain:
>
> 5 And the glory of the LORD shall be revealed, and all flesh shall see
> it together: for the mouth of the LORD hath spoken it. [Isaiah 40:4–5]

Certainly the valleys were not exalted and every mountain and hill made
low at the time of John's earthly ministry and, as verse 5 is apparently
describing the Lord's Second Coming, it is evident that his mission
extended to that time. It seems apparent that John was to prepare the way
before both times. The events spoken of in D&C 13 are the inauguration
of John's preparing the way for the Second Coming.

TEXT AND COMMENTARY

D&C 13 • The Aaronic Priesthood Restored

> Upon you my fellow servants, in the name of Messiah, I confer the
> Priesthood of Aaron, which holds the keys of the ministering of angels,
> and of the gospel of repentance, and of baptism by immersion for the
> remission of sins; and this shall never be taken again from the earth until
> the sons of Levi do offer again an offering unto the Lord in righteousness.

The restoration of the Aaronic Priesthood was the first of two
priesthoods that were restored upon the earth in the Spring of 1829.
"There are, in the church, two priesthoods, namely, the Melchizedek and
Aaronic, including the Levitical Priesthood. . . . The second priesthood
is called the Priesthood of Aaron, because it was conferred upon Aaron
and his seed, throughout all their generations. Why it is called the lesser
priesthood is because it is an appendage to the greater, or the Melchizedek
Priesthood, and has power in administering outward ordinances" (D&C
107:1, 13–14). The priesthood confirmed "upon Aaron and his seed,
through out all their generations, . . . continueth and abideth forever with
the priesthood which is after the holiest order of God" (D&C 84:18).
John the Baptist "acting under the direction of Peter, James, and John,
the ancient apostles" exemplifies the Aaronic Priesthood as being an
appendage to the Melchizedek Priesthood. The outward ordinances, that
are administered by the Aaronic Priesthood, are referred to in the Book
of Mormon as the ordinances of the law of Moses, and are probably the

same as the carnal commandments (see Alma 25:15). In the Doctrine and Covenants, the Aaronic Priesthood "is to administer in outward ordinances, the letter of the gospel, the baptism of repentance for the remission of sins, agreeable to the covenants and commandments" (D&C 107:20). These outward ordinances may also be called "the temporal things" (see D&C 107:68).

The Aaronic Priesthood holds the keys of the "preparatory gospel" (D&C 84:26). It was to prepare one for the Melchizedek Priesthood. It is also called lesser because it has less responsibility and less power (see JS—H 1:70 below). It is referred to as the Levitical Priesthood because under the Mosiac dispensation, only the tribe of Levi was privileged to hold the priesthood, and that priesthood was the Aaronic (see Deuteronomy 10:8).

The keys are the directing power of that priesthood. The idea of the Aaronic Priesthood holding the keys of the ministering of angels may not be fully understood. Do angels minister to all holders of the Aaronic Priesthood? No, but they can if directed to do so. We learn much about the ministering of angels from the Book of Mormon. Asking if miracles have ceased, Mormon states:

> 29 Nay; neither have angels ceased to minister unto the children of men.
>
> 30 For behold, they are subject unto him, to minister according to the word of his command, showing themselves unto them of strong faith and a firm mind in every form of godliness.
>
> 31 And the office of their ministry is to call men unto repentance, and to fulfil and to do the work of the covenants of the Father, which he hath made unto the children of men, to prepare the way among the children of men, by declaring the word of Christ unto the chosen vessels of the Lord, that they may bear testimony of him. [Moroni 7:29–31]

An angel ministered to Laman and Lemuel and called them to repentance, undoubtedly because of the strong faith and firm mind of Nephi (1 Nephi 3:28–30). After the birth of Christ, "to do the work of the covenants of the Father," among the Nephites:

> 15 Nephi —having been visited by angels and also the voice of the Lord, therefore having seen angels, and being eye-witness, and having had power given unto him that he might know concerning the ministry

of Christ, and also being eye-witness to their quick return from righteousness unto their wickedness and abominations;

16 Therefore, being grieved for the hardness of their hearts and the blindness of their minds—went forth among them in that same year, and began to testify, boldly, repentance and remission of sins through faith on the Lord Jesus Christ.

17 And he did minister many things unto them; and all of them cannot be written, and a part of them would not suffice, therefore they are not written in this book. And Nephi did minister with power and with great authority.

18 And it came to pass that they were angry with him, even because he had greater power than they, for it were not possible that they could disbelieve his words, for so great was his faith on the Lord Jesus Christ that angels did minister unto him daily. [3 Nephi 7:15–18]

Although there are no accounts in the Book of Mormon of keys being restored, when Alma the Elder, as he baptized at the waters of Mormon, said: "Helam, I baptize thee having authority from the Almighty God . . ," implies that he has received the keys. Mormon later supports this implication; as Alma ordained others to the priesthood it is recorded that he was "the founder of their church. And it came to pass that none received authority to preach or to teach except it were by him from God" (Mosiah 23:16–17). He was one of the priests of King Noah (Mosiah 18:1), and may have already been ordained to the priesthood, but he would still have to have been given the keys to organize the Church.

Regardless, we do know that "divers angels, from Michael or Adam down to the present time, all declaring their dispensations, their rights, their keys," appeared to Joseph Smith (D&C 128:21). President Wilford Woodruff testified:

"I had the administration of angels while holding the office of a priest. I had visions and revelations. I traveled thousands of miles. I baptized men, though I could not confirm them because I had not the authority to do it.

I speak these things to show that a man should not be ashamed of any portion of the priesthood." [*Discourses of Wilford Woodruff,* G. Homer Durham, comp. (1946), 298]

We must also remember that angels may minister without being seen.

In writing to the Hebrews Paul said: "Be not forgetful to entertain strangers: for thereby some have entertained angels unawares" (Hebrews 13:2). Angels ministering to Aaronic Priesthood holders, and to many others in this manner, is probably much more prevalent than we realize.

The keys of the Aaronic Priesthood are further explained in another revelation: "and the preparatory gospel; . . . is the gospel of repentance and of baptism, and the remission of sins, and the law of carnal commandments, which the Lord in his wrath caused to continue with the house of Aaron . . . until John [the Baptist]" (D&C 84:27). The carnal commandments ". . . consisted only in meats and drinks, and divers washings, and carnal ordinances, imposed on them until the time of reformation" (Hebrews 9:10).

The carnal commandments were also an appendage to the law of Moses. Joseph Smith quoted John the Baptist thus:

> 70 He said this Aaronic Priesthood had not the power of laying on hands for the gift of the Holy Ghost, but that this should be conferred on us hereafter; and he commanded us to go and be baptized, and gave us directions that I should baptize Oliver Cowdery, and that afterwards he should baptize me.

> 71 Accordingly we went and were baptized. I baptized him first, and afterwards he baptized me—after which I laid my hands upon his head and ordained him to the Aaronic Priesthood, and afterwards he laid his hands on me and ordained me to the same Priesthood—for so we were commanded. [JS—H 1:70–71]

That the Aaronic Priesthood "shall never to be taken again from the earth until the sons of Levi do offer again an offering" (D&C 13) suggests that it will be taken later. However, Oliver Cowdery's account of the angels words are slightly different: ". . . I confer this Priesthood and this authority, which shall remain upon the earth, *that* the sons of Levi may *yet* offer an offer unto the Lord in righteousness" (JS—H, footnote, 59; emphasis added). An alternate use of the word "until" is "up to the time that" (Websters Ninth Collegiate Dictionary). This seems to be the intent of Joseph's statement as well as Oliver's. The Prophet Joseph, speaking of the sacrifices of the sons of Levi declared: "These sacrifices, as well as every other ordinance belonging to the Priesthood, will, when the Temple of the Lord shall be built, and the sons of Levi be purified, be fully restored and attended to in all their powers, ramifications, and blessings"

(*TPJS*, 173). The purification of the sons of Levi was given in the context of the restoration of all things in the dispensation of the fullness of times, and refers to literal sons of Levi. This purification will take place in the future.

The following year, April 6, 1830, on the date of the organization of the Church, more was revealed on the offices of the Aaronic Priesthood. We will consider some of what was revealed at that time, since we are talking about the keys of that Priesthood.

D&C 20:46–52 • The Priest's Duties

46 The priest's duty is to preach, teach, expound, exhort, and baptize, and administer the sacrament,

47 And visit the house of each member, and exhort them to pray vocally and in secret and attend to all family duties.

48 And he may also ordain other priests, teachers, and deacons.

49 And he is to take the lead of meetings when there is no elder present;

50 But when there is an elder present, he is only to preach, teach, expound, exhort, and baptize,

51 And visit the house of each member, exhorting them to pray vocally and in secret and attend to all family duties.

52 In all these duties the priest is to assist the elder if occasion requires.

These duties seem self-explanatory. We emphasize only the priest being called to assist the elder, and only to lead when no elder is present. Visiting the house of each member is what we know today as the home teaching program of the Church. The Lord later gave this instruction, which is a part of the preparatory gospel.

107 Therefore, take with you those who are ordained unto the lesser priesthood, and send them before you to make appointments, and to prepare the way, and to fill appointments that you yourselves are not able to fill.

108 Behold, this is the way that mine apostles, in ancient days, built up my church unto me. [D&C 84:107–108]

D&C 20:53–59 • The Duty of the Office of Teacher

> 53 The teacher's duty is to watch over the church always, and be with and strengthen them;
>
> 54 And see that there is no iniquity in the church, neither hardness with each other, neither lying, backbiting, nor evil speaking;
>
> 55 And see that the church meet together often, and also see that all the members do their duty.
>
> 56 And he is to take the lead of meetings in the absence of the elder or priest—
>
> 57 And is to be assisted always, in all his duties in the church, by the deacons, if occasion requires.
>
> 58 But neither teachers nor deacons have authority to baptize, administer the sacrament, or lay on hands;
>
> 59 They are, however, to warn, expound, exhort, and teach, and invite all to come unto Christ.

All that we learn about the deacon's duties, from this revelation, is that he is to assist the teachers. We look to today's instructions to see more of the deacon's duties. As the Church has grown, these duties have been outlined by the Church leaders.

Returning to Joseph and Oliver at the Susquehanna River, we learn:

> The messenger who visited us on this occasion and conferred this Priesthood upon us, said that his name was John, the same that is called John the Baptist in the New Testament, and that he acted under the direction of Peter, James and John, who held the keys of the Priesthood of Melchizedek, which Priesthood, he said, would in due time be conferred on us, and that I should be called the First Elder of the Church, and he (Oliver Cowdery) the second. It was on the fifteenth day of May, 1829, that we were ordained under the hand of this messenger, and baptized. [JS—H 1:72]

THE IMPORTANCE OF JOHN'S MISSION

Joseph Smith taught us about the statement of Jesus Christ regarding the greatness of John the Baptist (Matthew 11:11):

> The question arose from the saying of Jesus—"Among them that are

born of women there hath not risen a greater than John the Baptist: notwithstanding he that is least in the kingdom of heaven is greater than he." How is it that John was considered one of the greatest prophets? His miracles could not have constituted his greatness.

First. He was entrusted with the divine mission of preparing the way before the face of the Lord. Whoever had such a trust committed to him before or since? No man.

Secondly. He was entrusted with the important mission, and it was required at his hands, to baptize the Son of Man. Whoever had the honor of doing that? Whoever had so great a privilege and glory? Whoever led the Son of God into the waters of baptism, and had the privilege of beholding the Holy Ghost descend in the form of a dove, or rather in the sign of the dove, in witness of that administration? The sign of the dove was instituted before the creation of the world, a witness for the Holy Ghost, and the devil cannot come in the sign of the dove. The Holy Ghost is a personage, and is in the form of a personage. It does not confine itself into the form of the dove, but in sign of the dove. The Holy Ghost cannot be transformed into a dove; but the sign of a dove was given to John to signify the truth of the deed, as the dove is an emblem of truth and innocence.

Thirdly. John, at that time, was the only legal administrator in the affairs of the kingdom there was then on the earth, and holding the keys of power. The Jews had to obey his instructions or be damned by their own law; and Christ Himself fulfilled all righteousness in becoming obedient to the law which he had given to Moses on the mount, and thereby magnified it and made it honorable, instead of destroying it. The Son of Zacharias wrested the keys, the kingdom, the power, the glory from the Jews, by the holy anointing and decree of heaven, and these three reasons constitute him the greatest prophet born of a woman. [*TPJS*, 275–76]

The importance of John's appearance, and his mission extending to preparing the way before Christ's Second Coming, cannot be over-emphasized.

We again return to the Susquehanna River.

Immediately on our coming up out of the water after we had been baptized, we experienced great and glorious blessings from our Heavenly Father. No sooner had I baptized Oliver Cowdery, than the Holy Ghost fell upon him, and he stood up and prophesied many things which should shortly come to pass. And again, so soon as I had been baptized by him, I also had the spirit of prophecy, when, standing up, I prophesied concerning the rise of this Church, and many other things connected with the Church, and this generation of the children of men. We were filled with the Holy Ghost, and rejoiced in the God of our salvation. [JS—H 1:73]

The gift of the Holy Ghost had not yet been conferred on Joseph and Oliver, for the Melchizedek Priesthood was not yet restored (but would be in due time, as the heavenly messenger had informed them.) But, as stated before, the Holy Ghost can witness to anyone without it being given as a gift. Joseph and Oliver had that witness at this time, and it continued with them for a while as the following verse tells us.

> Our minds being now enlightened, we began to have the scriptures laid open to our understandings, and the true meaning and intention of their more mysterious passages revealed unto us in a manner which we never could attain to previously, nor ever before had thought of. In the meantime we were forced to keep secret the circumstances of having received the Priesthood and our having been baptized, owing to a spirit of persecution which had already manifested itself in the neighborhood.

> We had been threatened with being mobbed, from time to time, and this, too, by professors of religion. And their intentions of mobbing us were only counteracted by the influence of my wife's father's family (under Divine providence), who had become very friendly to me, and who were opposed to mobs, and were willing that I should be allowed to continue the work of translation without interruption; and therefore offered and promised us protection from all unlawful proceedings, as far as in them lay. [JS—H 1:74–75]

Nephi's warning about how the devil will operate at the last day certainly fits the description given above. "For behold, at that day shall he rage in the hearts of the children of men, and stir them up to anger against that which is good (2 Nephi 28:20). However, the kingdom of God did and will continue to roll forth, and those who trust in the Lord will inherit eternal life as Joseph and Oliver had been promised (see D&C 10:69–70; 6:35–37).

The keys of the Melchizedek Priesthood were conferred, and the Church was restored with Joseph and Oliver as the first and Second Elder respectively, as promised by John the Baptist on the above occasion

(JS—H 1:72, as previously quoted). These events will be discussed in the following chapter.

General Authority Quotes

—*Elder Heber C. Kimball* • D&C 13

Supposing that there was a tub standing here and the people perishing for want of water, could not I, were I beyond the veil, come and pour in water? Yes and you could not see me. Unless your eyes are touched by the power of God, you cannot see an angel [a just man made perfect, or not resurrected]; . . .

Angels are ministering spirits, and do you believe that they will see this people want? . . . [*JD*, 4:7]

—*Elder Parley P. Pratt* • D&C 13

Whenever the keys of the Priesthood, or in other words, the keys of the science of theology, are enjoyed by man on the earth, those thus privileged are entitled to the ministering of angels, whose business with men on the earth is to restore the keys of apostleship when lost; to ordain men to the apostleship when there has been no apostolic succession; to commit the keys of a new dispensation; to reveal the mysteries of history, the facts of present or past times, and to unfold the events of a future time. They can also be present without being visible to mortals. They are sometimes commissioned also to execute judgments upon individuals, cities or nations. They can be present in their glory, or they can come in the form and appearance of other men. They can also be present without being visible to other men.

When they come as other men, they will perhaps eat and drink, and wash their feet; and lodge with their friends. Hence it is written [quotes Hebrews 13:1]. [*Key to the Science of Theology* (1966), 113]

Chapter Nine

The Apostolic Calling

D&C 18; 20:1–4

*H*istorical Setting: Very little is recorded in the *History of the Church* between the last of May, 1829, and the organization of the Church on April 6, 1830 (see *HC*, 1:61–74). Suffice it to say that D&C 18 was given around the first of June 1829. The exact date of the restoration of the Melchizedek Priesthood by Peter, James, and John is not known, but from the content of the revelation, it was most probably restored before this revelation was given. It is quite evident that Joseph is recounting this event when writing to the Church on September 6, 1842. "The voice of Peter, James, and John, in the wilderness between Harmony, Susquehanna County, and Colesville, Broome County, on the Susquehanna River, declaring themselves as possessing the keys of the kingdom, and of the dispensation of the fulness of times!" (D&C 128:20).[21] However, we have no further account to confirm the event.

INTRODUCTION

A foundation is an extremely important part of a building. Without a proper foundation, no structure will be permanent. The Apostle Paul taught the newly founded Church at Ephesus: "Now therefore ye are no

---

[21] The best evidence for dating the appearing of the three ancient apostles to Joseph Smith Jr., and the Three Witnesses of the Book of Mormon is in an article by Larry C. Porter, "Dating the Restoration of the Melchizedek Priesthood," published in the *Ensign*, June 1979, 5–9, 16. Brother Porter gives ample evidence for the dating being between May 15 and about May 29, 1829.

more strangers and foreigners, but fellowcitizens with the saints, and of the household of God; And are built upon the foundation of the apostles and prophets, Jesus Christ himself being the chief cornerstone" (Ephesians 2:19–20). As a church structure is built on the foundation, the foundation must always align with the chief cornerstone, Jesus Christ. He is the Rock, the source of revelation (Matthew 16:16–18) to guide "all the building fitly framed together groweth unto an holy temple in the Lord" (Ephesians 2:21). The "foundation of apostles and prophets," being plural, suggests the Quorum of the Twelve as a unit upon which the Church is built. However, there was no Quorum of the Twelve until February of 1835. A careful analysis of section 18 and 20, verses 1–4, will show that the foundation of the Church is the apostolic calling of men. Joseph Smith and the Three Witnesses were Apostles. The Quorum of the Twelve Apostles became a part of the foundation later.

SECTIONS 18 & 20 • OUTLINE

➤ 8:1–5   Oliver is cautioned to rely on the things he has written, which are true.

       a.   They are concerning the foundation my church, my gospel, my rock (v. 4).

       b.   If you build on this foundation, the gates of hell shall not prevail (v. 5).

➤ 18:6–8   The world is ripening in iniquity, and must be called to repentance, both the Gentiles and the house of Israel.

       a.   Oliver was baptized according to what Joseph was commanded (v. 7).

       b.   Joseph was called for the Lord's purpose, and will be blessed if diligent (v. 8).

➤ 18:9–16   Oliver and Joseph are called with the same calling as Paul.

       a.   The worth of souls is great in the sight of God (v. 10).

       b.   The Redeemer suffered death and the pains of all men that they might repent and come unto Him (v. 11).

       c.   He rose from the dead that all may come on conditions of repentance (v. 12).

       d.   Great joy comes to the soul that repents, you are to cry repentance (vv. 13–14).

       e.   If you bring one soul to Christ how great shall be your joy with him (v. 15).

       f.   How great shall be your joy if you bring many (v. 16).

➤ 18:17–20   You have my gospel before you, my rock, and my salvation.

       a.   Ask the Father in my name and you shall have the Holy Ghost with you (v. 18).

       b.   If you have not faith, hope, and charity, you can do nothing (v. 19).

       c.   Contend against no church, except the church of the devil (v. 20).

➤ 18:21–25   Take upon you the name of Christ and speak the truth in soberness.

       a.   As many as repent, are baptized, and endure to the end shall be saved (v. 22).

       b.   No other name is given whereby man can be saved in the last day (v. 23).

       c.   If they know not the name they cannot be saved (v. 25).

➤ 18:26–30   Twelve disciples will be called to declare my gospel to the Gentile and the Jew.

       a.   If they desire to take my name with full purpose they are called (vv. 27–28).

       b.   They are ordained to baptize according to what is written (v. 29).

       c.   You must perform according to what is written (v. 30).

➤ 18:31–36   Christ speaks to the Twelve—you must walk uprightly before me.

       a.   You are to ordain priests and teachers by the power of the Holy Ghost (v. 32).

       b.   These words are not of men but of Christ, you shall so testify (vv. 33–34).

       c.   You can testify that you have heard my voice (vv. 35–36).

➤ 18:37–42   Oliver and David shall search out the Twelve who have those desires.

  a. You shall know them by their desires and their works (v. 38).

  b. You shall show them these things and fall down and worship (vv. 39–40).

  c. You must preach repentance and baptism to those accountable (vv. 41–42).

➤ 18:43–47 Keep my commandments and you will work a marvelous work to bring men to the kingdom of my Father.

  a. The blessings given are above all things (v. 45).

  b. After this, if you keep not my commandments, you cannot be saved (v. 46).

  c. By the power of my Spirit has Jesus Christ spoken this (v. 47).

➤ 20:1–4 The rise of the Church in last days, one thousand eight hundred and thirty years since the coming of the Lord in the flesh.

  a. Joseph Smith was called and ordained to be an Apostle and the First Elder (v. 2).

  b. Oliver Cowdery was called of God, to be an Apostle and Second Elder (v. 3).

  c. According to the grace of our Savior, to whom be all glory forever (v. 4).

TEXT AND COMMENTARY

D&C 18:1–5 • Rely Upon the Book of Mormon

1 Now, behold, because of the thing which you, my servant Oliver Cowdery, have desired to know of me, I give unto you these words:

2 Behold, I have manifested unto you, by my Spirit in many instances, that the things which you have written are true; wherefore you know that they are true.

3 And if you know that they are true, behold, I give unto you a commandment, that you rely upon the things which are written;

4 For in them are all things written concerning the foundation of my church, my gospel, and my rock.

5 Wherefore, if you shall build up my church, upon the foundation

of my gospel and my rock, the gates of hell shall not prevail against you.

Two of the many instances where the Lord had manifested the truth of the Book of Mormon to Oliver (v. 2), that are recorded, are in section 6 verse 17; when He told Oliver "the words or the work which thou hast been writing are true," and in section 17 verse 6, when He said "as the Lord and your God liveth it is true." There were certainly many others as he was translating, but with this third recorded statement, "the things which you have written are true," the law of witnesses is met: "In the mouth of two or three Witnesses every word may be established" (Matthew 18:16). Actually, the whole section testifies of the truth of the Book of Mormon; it repeatedly refers to it (see section 18 verses 2, 3–4, 17, 30, 34, 39).

Oliver's commandment to rely upon the things that were written (D&C 18:3) refers to the Book of Mormon which he had written as Joseph translated. The foundation of Christ's church is likened, in the Sermon on the Mount and its equivalent in the Book of Mormon, to a wise man that builds his house upon a rock (see 3 Nephi 14:24–27; Matthew 7:24–27). The foundation of Christ's gospel is given in the Book of Mormon (3 Nephi 27:13–21). Christ's rock is the rock of revelation, the source of his doctrine The Prophet Joseph testified: ". . . Jesus in His teaching says, 'upon this rock I will build my Church, and the gates of hell shall not prevail against it.' What rock? Revelation" (*TPJS*, 274). His doctrine is given throughout the Book of Mormon. It is specifically treated in 3 Nephi 11:23–40, when Christ tells them how to build upon His rock so that "the gates of hell shall not prevail against you" (3 Nephi 11:39–40; D&C 18:5; Matthew 16:18).

D&C 18:6–8 • His Name Is Joseph

6 Behold, the world is ripening in iniquity; and it must needs be that the children of men are stirred up unto repentance, both the Gentiles and also the house of Israel.

7 Wherefore, as thou hast been baptized by the hands of my servant Joseph Smith, Jun., according to that which I have commanded him, he hath fulfilled the thing which I commanded him.

8 And now, marvel not that I have called him unto mine own purpose, which purpose is known in me; wherefore, if he shall be diligent

in keeping my commandments he shall be blessed unto eternal life; and his name is Joseph.

It has been nearly 180 years since the Lord said the world was ripening in iniquity (v. 6). When a people or the world is ripe in iniquity, or their iniquity is full, the Lord destroys them (see Genesis 15:16; 1 Nephi 17:35; Ether 2:9, 9:20). The world seems to be close to that ripened stage. The Second Coming is nigh at hand. We should follow the example of Joseph and do the things the Lord commands us, as did he (D&C 11:7–8), that we might escape the coming destruction of the wicked (see D&C 61:31; 101:11).

D&C 18:9 • The Same Calling As Paul

9 And now, Oliver Cowdery, I speak unto you, and also unto David Whitmer, by the way of commandment; for, behold, I command all men everywhere to repent, and I speak unto you, even as unto Paul mine apostle, for you are called even with that same calling with which he was called.

It is not clear whether the Lord is now calling Oliver and David[22] to the Apostleship, or referring back to the time of their having been called. The evidence of the Melchizedek Priesthood being restored between May 15, and about May 29, 1829 (see fn. 40), suggests it was already restored by the time this revelation was received. Furthermore, nothing is said about the keys of the Melchizedek Priesthood being restored, as stated below, or of their ordination, which apparently happened at the same time.

12 And also with Peter, and James, and John, whom I have sent unto you, by whom I have ordained you and confirmed you to be apostles, and especial witnesses of my name, and bear the keys of your ministry and of the same things which I revealed unto them;

13 Unto whom I have committed the keys of my kingdom, and a dispensation of the gospel for the last times; and for the fulness of times, in the which I will gather together in one all things, both which are in heaven, and which are on earth; [D&C 27:12–13; see also D&C 128:20 quoted in the *Historical Setting*]

---

[22] Martin Harris would have probably been included in this revelation but he was not in good standing with the Lord at this time. See section 19 discussed in the next chapter.

With the apostolic calling of men to receive revelation from Christ, the foundation of the Church and the kingdom of God was ready to be established. It will be remembered that the Three Witnesses of the Book of Mormon and Joseph Smith were given a special witness through the power of God which was to be the "beginning of the rising up and the coming forth of my church out of the wilderness" (D&C 5:11–14). Having been ordained (D&C 27:12), and qualifying as special witnesses, the foundation of the church was laid.

D&C 18:10–16 • The Worth of Souls

10 Remember the worth of souls is great in the sight of God;

11 For, behold, the Lord your Redeemer suffered death in the flesh; wherefore he suffered the pain of all men, that all men might repent and come unto him.

12 And he hath risen again from the dead, that he might bring all men unto him, on conditions of repentance.

13 And how great is his joy in the soul that repenteth!

14 Wherefore, you are called to cry repentance unto this people.

15 And if it so be that you should labor all your days in crying repentance unto this people, and bring, save it be one soul unto me, how great shall be your joy with him in the kingdom of my Father!

16 And now, if your joy will be great with one soul that you have brought unto me into the kingdom of my Father, how great will be your joy if you should bring many souls unto me!

The calling of these special witnesses was to cry repentance and save souls (vv. 10, 14). The worth of souls (v. 10) was also emphasized in the Book of Mormon. The sons of Mosiah suffered that they may "be the means of saving some soul" (Alma 26:30). Alma sought to "be an instrument in the hands of God to bring some soul to repentance (Alma 29:9). He recognized that the Zoramite "souls are precious" and sought "power and wisdom" to bring them to the Lord (Alma 31:35). When we realize how much Christ suffered for us (D&C 11:11), we should desire to help Him save souls. When we labor to save souls by crying repentance, we save our own soul, and great is Christ's joy (v. 13). We will have great joy with those to whom we cry repentance and they are saved, and it is multiplied by the number of souls that are saved (vv. 15–16). This is the joy of missionary work, and with our own family unto whom the Lord has entrusted us.

D&C 18:17–20 • Contend Against No Church

17 Behold, you have my gospel before you, and my rock, and my salvation.

18 Ask the Father in my name, in faith believing that you shall receive, and you shall have the Holy Ghost, which manifesteth all things which are expedient unto the children of men.

19 And if you have not faith, hope, and charity, you can do nothing.

20 Contend against no church, save it be the church of the devil.

The gospel, the rock, and the salvation through Christ were before them (v. 17) in the Book of Mormon. Hyrum Smith was told to wait until he had his word before he sought to declare it (D&C 11:16, 21). Joseph, Oliver, and David were now to declare the word. By asking the Father, they would know, through the Holy Ghost, what principles of the gospel they should teach the various individuals to whom they cried repentance (D&C 18:18). They were also to acquire the attributes of faith, hope, and charity (v. 19). Faith would enable them to have the principles of action, power, and salvation in their lives (see 1 Nephi 3:7, 7:17, 2:2). Hope would make them abound in good works (see Ether 12:4). Charity is the pure love of Christ that is poured out on the true followers of Christ, and would purify them (see Moroni 7:48). They were admonished to contend against no church, but to speak the truth in soberness (D&C 18:20 and 21; quoted below). They were to contend against the Church of the devil, or to oppose the doctrines and evil procedures of the devil. Truth must prevail.

D&C 18:21–25 • None Other Name For Man to be Saved

21 Take upon you the name of Christ, and speak the truth in soberness.

22 And as many as repent and are baptized in my name, which is Jesus Christ, and endure to the end, the same shall be saved.

23 Behold, Jesus Christ is the name which is given of the Father, and there is none other name given whereby man can be saved;

24 Wherefore, all men must take upon them the name which is given of the Father, for in that name shall they be called at the last day;

25 Wherefore, if they know not the name by which they are called, they cannot have place in the kingdom of my Father.

To take the name of Christ upon them (v. 21), they must become His children, be born again or be spiritually begotten of Christ (see Mosiah 5:7). Through the covenant of baptism (D&C 18:22), they would come into the fold of God, and be called His people (Mosiah 18:8). They must serve Christ or they cannot know His name, the only name of salvation (vv. 23–25, compare Mosiah 5:12–14).

D&C 18:26–30 • Twelve Disciples Called

26 And now, behold, there are others who are called to declare my gospel, both unto Gentile and unto Jew;

27 Yea, even twelve; and the Twelve shall be my disciples, and they shall take upon them my name; and the Twelve are they who shall desire to take upon them my name with full purpose of heart.

28 And if they desire to take upon them my name with full purpose of heart, they are called to go into all the world to preach my gospel unto every creature.

29 And they are they who are ordained of me to baptize in my name, according to that which is written;

30 And you have that which is written before you; wherefore, you must perform it according to the words which are written.

In preparation for the growth of the Church hereafter, the Lord plans to lay a more permanent foundation for the Church. The Twelve Disciples who are to be called are those who desire to take upon them Christ's name with full purpose of heart. They will declare Christ's gospel to both Jew and Gentile (vv. 26–27). They were given the same mission (v. 28) as the Apostles called by Christ in the meridian of time in the land of Jerusalem. "And he said unto them, Go ye into all the world, and preach the gospel to every creature. He that believeth and is baptized shall be saved; but he that believeth not shall be damned" (Mark 16:15–16). "According to that which is written," or "the words which are written" (vv. 29 and 30), is again the Book of Mormon. That record tells of Jesus calling and instructing twelve Nephite disciples. He taught them the correct manner of baptism, and the baptismal prayer to be used, and many other doctrines (see 3 Nephi 11:18–13:34). He also taught them their relationship to the Jerusalem twelve (see Mormon 3:18–19). The same pattern was to be followed and is followed today.

D&C 18:31–36 • The Lord Speaks to the Twelve

31 And now I speak unto you, the Twelve—Behold, my grace is sufficient for you; you must walk uprightly before me and sin not.

32 And, behold, you are they who are ordained of me to ordain priests and teachers; to declare my gospel, according to the power of the Holy Ghost which is in you, and according to the callings and gifts of God unto men;

33 And I, Jesus Christ, your Lord and your God, have spoken it.

34 These words are not of men nor of man, but of me; wherefore, you shall testify they are of me and not of man;

35 For it is my voice which speaketh them unto you; for they are given by my Spirit unto you, and by my power you can read them one to another; and save it were by my power you could not have them;

36 Wherefore, you can testify that you have heard my voice, and know my words.

The Lord outlines four duties for the Twelve, who were yet to be called. First, they were to walk uprightly before Him, or to be an example to the Church (v. 31). Second, they were to ordain other officers in the Church (v. 32). Third, they were to preach the gospel as directed by the power of the Holy Ghost, within the various assignments and individual gifts of the Spirit given to them individually (v. 32). Fourth, and the most unique calling of all, they were to testify of the words of Christ that He has spoken and will yet speak to them (v. 33–36). When they were called, almost six years later, February 14, 1835, the Lord revealed this description of them: "The twelve traveling councilors are called to be the Twelve Apostles, or special witnesses of the name of Christ in all the world—thus differing from other officers in the Church in the duties of their calling" (D&C 107:23). Other duties of the Twelve are given in later sections of the Doctrine and Covenants.

D&C 18:37–42 • The Witnesses Search Out the Twelve

37 And now, behold, I give unto you, Oliver Cowdery, and also unto David Whitmer, that you shall search out the Twelve, who shall have the desires of which I have spoken;

38 And by their desires and their works you shall know them.

39 And when you have found them you shall show these things unto them.

40 And you shall fall down and worship the Father in my name.

41 And you must preach unto the world, saying: You must repent and be baptized, in the name of Jesus Christ;

42 For all men must repent and be baptized, and not only men, but women, and children who have arrived at the years of accountability.

Oliver and David's call to search out the Twelve (v. 37) was later extended to Martin Harris, when he regained favor with the Lord, and became one of the Three Witnesses of the Book of Mormon as discussed in chapter six. These three men were qualified to search out these men because they were Apostles and special witnesses themselves. They had proven their desire and shown their works by helping in bringing the translation of the Book of Mormon to completion (see *HC*, 1:52–56, including the footnotes). The same requirements of desire and works were to be evident in the Twelve (v. 38). "These things" that the Three Witnesses were to show unto the Twelve after they were found (v. 39) are not clearly specified. Do they refer to the words of this revelation, or do they refer to the five sacred Nephite items that had just been seen by the Three Witnesses (see D&C 17:1)? Since the Three Witnesses saw these items in this time period, the selected twelve being shown them is an interesting possibility. The remainder of the instructions to be given to the Twelve, by the Three Witnesses, are similar to those given previously (vv. 29–39). The exception was the qualification of who were to be baptized; men, "women, and children who have arrived at the age of accountability" (v. 42).

D&C 18:43 • The Witnesses Must Keep Christ's Commandments

43 And now, after that you have received this, you must keep my commandments in all things;

44 And by your hands I will work a marvelous work among the

children of men, unto the convincing of many of their sins, that they may come unto repentance, and that they may come unto the kingdom of my Father.

45 Wherefore, the blessings which I give unto you are above all things.

46 And after that you have received this, if you keep not my commandments you cannot be saved in the kingdom of my Father.

47 Behold, I, Jesus Christ, your Lord and your God, and your Redeemer, by the power of my Spirit have spoken it. Amen.

Oliver and David, because of the special witness they had received, must now "keep my commandments in all things" (v. 43). They were expected to be fully involved in the marvelous work of the Restoration and of spreading the gospel of repentance (v. 44). They had seen the heavens opened and knew of a surety of the truthfulness of the Book of Mormon, and they had heard His voice (vv. 2, 35, and the Testimony of Three Witnesses). These blessings were from above (v. 45). "For of him unto whom much is given much is required; and he who sins against the greater light shall receive the greater condemnation" (D&C 82:3, see Luke 12:48). Salvation in the kingdom of God would come only if they endured to the end (vv. 22, 46). This revelation came from their Redeemer through the power of his Spirit (v. 47), another blessing from above.

*H*istorical Setting—D&C 20:1–4:

> . . . the word of the Lord came unto us in the chamber, commanding us that I should ordain Oliver Cowdery to be an Elder in the Church of Jesus Christ; and that he should also ordain me to the same office; and then to ordain others, as it should be made known unto us from time to time. We were, however, commanded to defer this our ordination until such times as it should be practical to have our brethren, who had been and who should be baptized, assembled together, . . . [*HC*, 1:61]

The date of their ordination is not known, as stated above, but was prior to receiving this revelation (D&C 20). Following section 18 in the *History of the Church*, Joseph recorded: ". . . we obtained the following, . . . but also pointed out to us the precise day upon which, according to His will and commandment, we should proceed to organize His Church once more here upon the earth" (*HC*, 1:64). We include the first four verses here because the subject is the same as section 18; the organization of the Church, and the ordination of Joseph and Oliver to the Melchizedek Priesthood and the Apostleship.

D&C 20:1–4 • The Church is Organized

1 The rise of the Church of Christ in these last days, being one thousand eight hundred and thirty years since the coming of our Lord and Savior Jesus Christ in the flesh, it being regularly organized and established agreeable to the laws of our country, by the will and commandments of God, in the fourth month, and on the sixth day of the month which is called April—

2 Which commandments were given to Joseph Smith, Jun., who was called of God, and ordained an apostle of Jesus Christ, to be the First Elder of this church;

3 And to Oliver Cowdery, who was also called of God, an apostle of Jesus Christ, to be the Second Elder of this church, and ordained under his hand;

4 And this according to the grace of our Lord and Savior Jesus Christ, to whom be all glory, both now and forever. Amen.

The date of the organization of the Church, April 6, 1830 (v. 1), has long been considered in the Church as falling on the mortal birthday of Jesus Christ. Although there has been controversy over this date, particularly over the year, it has been accepted by many of the Church Presidents and Apostles, as shown in the general authorities' quotes at the end of this chapter. The day of the week on which the Church was organized was a Tuesday. This day seems further evidence of the significance of the date.

The laws of the state of New York, in which the Church was officially organized, required that six men sign the Articles of Incorporation. Although there were many more present at the organization meeting, the six men were: Joseph Smith Jr.; Hyrum Smith; Samuel Smith; Oliver Cowdery; David Whitmer; and Peter Whitmer Jr. The laws of the country had been met (v. 1).

When John the Baptist appeared to Joseph and Oliver on May 15,

1829, they were told: "that he acted under the direction of Peter, James and John, who held the keys of the Priesthood of Melchizedek, which Priesthood, he said, would in due time be conferred on us, and that I should be called the First Elder of the Church, and he (Oliver Cowdery) the second" (JS—H 1:72). The directive given by John was thus confirmed in this revelation. Their ordination to the apostleship is not known, but is assumed to have been at the time of the conferral of the Melchizedek Priesthood (see comments under D&C 18:9). As also noted there, their ordination was by Peter, James, and John, and their ordination was verified in section 27 verses 12–13.

General Authority Quotes

—*Oliver Cowdery* • D&C 18:2–3

I wrote with my own pen, the entire Book of Mormon (save a few pages) as it fell from the lips of the Prophet Joseph, as he translated it by the gift and power of God, by the means of the Urim and Thummim, or, as it is called by that book, "holy interpreters." I beheld with my eyes, and handled with my hands, the gold plates from which it was translated. I also saw with my eyes and handled with my hands the "holy interpreters." That book is true. [As quoted in Roy W. Doxey, *The Latter-day Prophets and the Doctrine and Covenants* (1963), 1:239]

—*The Prophet Joseph Smith* • D&C 18:8

Christ was the head of the Church, the chief cornerstone, the spiritual rock upon which the church was built, and the gates of hell shall not prevail against it. He built up the kingdom, chose Apostles, and ordained them to the Melchizedek Priesthood, giving them power to administer in the ordinances of the gospel. John was a priest after the order of Aaron before Christ. [*TPJS*, 318]

—*President Brigham Young* • D&C 18:9

Joseph Smith was a Prophet, Seer, and Revelator before he had power to build up the kingdom of God, or take the first step towards it. When did he obtain the power? Not until the angel had ordained him to be an Apostle. Joseph Smith, Oliver Cowdery, and David Whitmer were the first apostles of this dispensation, though in the

early days of the Church David lost his standing and another took his place. . . . When a man is an Apostle, and stands at the head of the kingdom of God on the earth, and magnifies his calling, he has the keys of all the power that ever was bestowed upon mortal man for the building up of the kingdom of God on the earth. [*JD*, 6:320]

—*The Prophet Joseph Smith* • D&C 18:20–21

. . . the elders would go forth, and each must stand for himself, as it is not necessary for them to be sent out, two by two, as in former times, but to go in all meekness, in sobriety, and preach Jesus Christ and Him crucified; not to contend with others on account of their faith, or systems of evil, but pursue a steady course. This I delivered by way of commandment; and all who observe it not, will pull down persecution upon their heads, while those who do, shall always be filled with the Holy Ghost; this I pronounce as a prophecy. [*TPJS*, 109]

—*President Joseph Fielding Smith* • D&C 18:20–21

When we are commanded to "contend against no church save it be the church of the devil," we must understand that this is instruction to us to contend against all evil, that which is opposed to righteousness and truth. James declares that "every good gift and every perfect gift is from above, and cometh down from the Father of lights, with whom there is no variance, neither shadow of turning," and the scriptures also teach, "for there is nothing which is good save it comes from the Lord; and that which is evil cometh from the devil" (Omni 1:25). All who go forth to teach should do so in wisdom and not contend with the churches or engage in profitless debates, but teach in the spirit of kindness and try to persuade people to receive the truth. [*Church History and Modern Day Revelation* (1946), 1:83]

—*The Prophet Joseph Smith* • D&C 20:1

. . . it [April 6, 1833] being just 1800 years since the Savior laid down His life that men might have everlasting life, and only three years since the Church had come out of the wilderness, preparatory for the last dispensation. [*HC*, 1:337]

—Elder James E. Talmage • D&C 20:1

Without attempting to analyze the mass of calculation data relating to this subject [the time of the Messiah's birth], we accept the Dionysian basis as correct with subject to the year, which is to us B.C. 1, and, as shall be shown, in an early month of that year. In support of this belief we cite the inspired record known as the "Revelation on Church Government, given through Joseph the Prophet, in April, 1830," which opens with these words: [quotes D&C 20:1, and his further comments]. [*Jesus the Christ* (1983), 97]

—President Harold B. Lee • D&C 20:1

April 6, 1973, is a particularly significant date because it commemorates not only the anniversary of the organization of The Church of Jesus Christ of Latter-day Saints in this dispensation, but also the anniversary of the birth of the Savior, our Lord and Master. [CR, April 1973, 4]

—President Spencer W. Kimball • D&C 20:1

The name of Jesus Christ and what it represents has been plowed deep into the history of the world, never to be uprooted. Christ was born on the sixth of April. Being one of the sons of God and His only Begotten, his birth is of supreme importance. [CR, April 1975, 3–4]

Chapter Ten

Endless Is My Name

D&C 19

*H*istorical Setting:

No words of the Prophet introduces this revelation in his History [except the sentence in the section heading], "*A commandment of God and not of man, to Martin Harris, given* (Manchester, New York, March 1830,) *by Him who is Eternal.* Nothing is known of the circumstances which called it forth. And yet there are few revelations that have been given in the present dispensation of the Gospel more important than this one. [*HC*, 1:72]

March 1830 was almost two years after the loss of the first 116 pages of manuscript that was translated and lost (June–July 1828), as discussed in chapter 4 of this work. This event is associated with this revelation (see *HC*, 1:20–22).

INTRODUCTION

The sections in the Doctrine and Covenants give several titles of Jesus Christ as He identifies Himself as the giver of the revelations, or concludes His message with an identification or description. Most of these identifications and descriptions are given in the New Testament, and verify His ministry in the land of Jerusalem. Thus far in the eighteen revelations we have discussed, He has identified Himself by saying; "Behold, I am God" (D&C 6:2); and ". . . the Lord liveth, who is your God and your Redeemer" (D&C 8:1). He has ended the revelations by saying; Behold the Lord is God, and the Spirit beareth record. . . (D&C 1:39). Behold the wounds which pierced my sides, and also the prints of the nails in my hands and feet; . . . (D&C 6:37). "And now, remember the words of him who is the life and light of the world, your Redeemer, your Lord and your God. Amen (D&C 10:70). "I am the same who came unto mine own and mine own received me not; . . ." (D&C 11:29). "Behold, I am Jesus Christ, the Son of the living God, who created the heavens and the earth, a light which cannot be hid in darkness;" (D&C 14:9). Other beginnings or endings were not included because they were duplications of how He had already identified Himself, but we learn a great deal about our Savior just from these descriptions. Probably the single most explanatory revelation declaring His attributes and mission is section 19. Some of His titles are unique to His nature, and are not found in the Bible.

SECTION 19 • OUTLINE

➤ 19:1–5   I am Alpha and Omega, the beginning and the end, the Redeemer of the world.

    a.   I finished the will of the Father and subjected all things unto myself (v. 2).

    b.   I have retained all power even to the destruction of Satan and his works at the end of the world (v. 3).

    c.   I will judge every man according to his works and his deeds (v. 3).

    d.   Every man must repent or suffer, for I am endless (v. 4).

    e.   There will be weeping, wailing, and gnashing of teeth for those found on my left hand (v. 5).

➤ 19:6–12   It is not written no end to punishment, but it is written endless torment and eternal damnation.

    a.   It is more express that it might work upon the hearts of men (v. 7).

    b.   You should understand this mystery even as mine apostles (v. 8).

    c.   I speak to you even as one that you may enter into my rest (v. 9).

    d.   My punishment is endless punishment, for endless is my name (v. 10).

e.   Eternal punishment and endless punishment is God's punishment (vv. 11–12).

➤ 19:13–19   I command you to repent and keep the commandments you received from Joseph Smith in my name.

a.   By my almighty power he received them (v. 14).

b.   Repent lest I smite you by the rod of my mouth, you know not how sore, exquisite, and hard your suffering will be (v. 15).

c.   I, God, suffered for all that they might not suffer if they repent (v. 16).

d.   If they do not repent they must suffer even as I (v. 17).

e.   My suffering caused me to tremble with pain and bleed at every pore (v. 18).

f.   Glory be to the Father, and I finished my preparations unto men (v. 19).

➤ 19:20–23   The Lord commands Martin to repent and confess his sins lest he suffer the punishments of which he had spoken.

a.   He tasted the punishment in the least degree when the Spirit withdrew (v. 20).

b.   Preach only repentance, show not these things to the world until I say (v. 21).

c.   The world cannot bear meat, but must receive milk (v. 22).

d.   Learn of Christ, walk in meekness of spirit, and you shall have peace (v. 23).

➤ 19:24–27   Jesus Christ came by the will of the Father, and He does His will.

a.   Martin is not to covet his neighbor's wife nor seek his life (v. 25).

b.   Do not covet your own property, but impart it to print the Book of Mormon (v. 26).

c.   It is true and my word to the Gentiles, it may soon go to the Jews, of whom the Lamanites are a remnant (v. 27).

d.   The Jews are not to look for a Messiah to come who has already come (v. 27).

➤ 19:28–31   Martin is commanded to pray vocally as well as in his heart, before the world as well as in secret, in public as well as in private.

    a.   Declare glad tidings upon the mountains, and among all people (v. 29).

    b.   Do it with all humility, trusting in Christ, revile not against revilers (v. 30).

    c.   Do not speak of tenets, but declare repentance, faith, and baptisms (v. 31).

➤ 19:32–38   This is the great and last commandment on this matter unto the end of your life.

    a.   Slight these counsels, and destruction of you and your property await (v. 33).

    b.   Impart thy property save for the support of thy family (v. 34).

    c.   Pay your debt to the printer and release yourself from bondage (v. 35).

    d.   Leave your house and home except when ye desire to see your family (v. 36).

    e.   Speak freely to all, preach, exhort, declare truth, with a loud voice (v. 37).

    f.   Pray always and I will pour out my Spirit, and great blessings (v. 38).

➤ 19:39–41   Canst thou read this without rejoicing, and being lifted up with gladness?

    a.   Canst thou run longer as a blind guide? (v. 40).

    b.   Canst thou be humble and meek, and conduct thyself wisely? (v. 41).

    c.   Come unto me thy Savior (v. 41).

TEXT AND COMMENTARY

D&C 19:1–5 • Alpha and Omega

1 I am Alpha and Omega, Christ the Lord; yea, even I am he, the beginning and the end, the Redeemer of the world.

2 I, having accomplished and finished the will of him whose I am,

even the Father, concerning me—having done this that I might subdue all things unto myself—

3 Retaining all power, even to the destroying of Satan and his works at the end of the world, and the last great day of judgment, which I shall pass upon the inhabitants thereof, judging every man according to his works and the deeds which he hath done.

4 And surely every man must repent or suffer, for I, God, am endless.

5 Wherefore, I revoke not the judgments which I shall pass, but woes shall go forth, weeping, wailing and gnashing of teeth, yea, to those who are found on my left hand.

Alpha is the first letter of the Greek alphabet and Omega is the last letter; therefore, Christ is repeating Himself in the second part of the sentence as the word "yea" indicates. He identifies Himself with the same wording in the New Testament (Revelation 1:8). He is the beginning because He was the creator (John 1:10). He is the ending because He has redeemed the world and will bring it into its celestial glory (D&C 88:25–26).

The will of the Father that He fulfilled (D&C 19:2) was the atonement: "I came into the world to do the will of my Father, because my Father sent me. And my Father sent me that I might be lifted up upon the cross; and after that I had been lifted up upon the cross, that I might draw all men unto me, that as I have been lifted up by men even so should men be lifted up by the Father, to stand before me, to be judged of their works, whether they be good or whether they be evil" (3 Nephi 27:13–14). All things are subjected unto Him because "he suffereth the pains of all men, yea, the pains of every living creature, both men, women, and children, who belong to the family of Adam" (2 Nephi 9:21).

Christ's power to destroy Satan and His works at the end of the world (D&C 19:3) is the binding of him at the beginning of the millennium, which is the end of the telestial world. (D&C 45:55). Christ will bind him by destroying the wicked and bringing about the righteousness of the people who will not be destroyed, leaving Satan with no power (see 1 Nephi 22:26). The last great day of judgment will be the final assignment of each person to the kingdom of glory that has been attained through the works and deeds of each individual (19:3). At that great day, all will be resurrected and will have an "immortal body" (Alma 11:45). Those who did not repent will suffer the agony of knowing what they could have attained (D&C 19:4). They will know that "Where God and Christ dwell they cannot come, worlds without end" (D&C 76:112). The Lord will not and cannot revoke His judgment because of the law of justice; mercy cannot rob justice (see Alma 42:22–25). Thus there will be "weeping, wailing, and gnashing of teeth" among those who are found on the left hand of Christ (D&C 19:5).

D&C 19:6–12 • Endless Torment Is God's Torment

6 Nevertheless, it is not written that there shall be no end to this torment, but it is written *endless torment.*

7 Again, it is written *eternal damnation*; wherefore it is more express than other scriptures, that it might work upon the hearts of the children of men, altogether for my name's glory.

8 Wherefore, I will explain unto you this mystery, for it is meet unto you to know even as mine apostles.

9 I speak unto you that are chosen in this thing, even as one, that you may enter into my rest.

10 For, behold, the mystery of godliness, how great is it! For, behold, I am endless, and the punishment which is given from my hand is endless punishment, for Endless is my name. Wherefore—

11 Eternal punishment is God's punishment.

12 Endless punishment is God's punishment.

"Nevertheless," the beginning word of v. 6, identifies an exception to the concept just described. There is a difference between "no end to this torment" and "*endless* torment" (v. 6). The same distinction is given "for *eternal* damnation," with an explanation of why it is used (v. 7). While it does make an impression on the hearts of men, it has also led to the false concept among many religions and people that it is a torment that never ends. Christ labels this concept as a mystery. A mystery of God is a principle that is understood only by those to whom God reveals it (see Alma 26:22). He desired Martin to understand the mystery in order for him to know even as His Apostles knew (D&C 19:8). As one who would be an apostle, or who would "Search out the Twelve" (D&C 18:37) one of the three special witnesses of the Book of Mormon, he needed to understand. The need to know is extended to those who are chosen that they may be one, and that they may enter into his rest (v. 9). The rest of the Lord "is the fullness of his glory" (D&C 84:24). The requirements for entry into His glory are to become, through the priesthood and the Holy Ghost, "sanctified and their garments . . . washed white through the blood of the lamb" (Alma 13:11; see also 13:12).

The principle the Lord revealed was that whatever punishment is meted out (which is a perfect balance of justice and mercy), is not a never ending punishment, but that prescribed by the judgment of an immortal Being who is Endless and Eternal (D&C 19:10–12). He cannot make a mistake, or "God would cease to be God" (Alma 42:25). One of the purposes of the Book of Mormon is "to the convincing of the Jew and Gentile that Jesus is the Christ, the Eternal God" (Title page). Therefore, the punishment by an Eternal God is eternal punishment. An example of someone suffering such punishment that had an unmistakable "end," is Alma the Younger.

> 28 Nevertheless, after wading through much tribulation, repenting nigh unto death, the Lord in mercy hath seen fit to snatch me out of an *everlasting* burning, and I am born of God.
>
> 29 My soul hath been redeemed from the gall of bitterness and bonds of iniquity. I was in the darkest abyss; but now I behold the marvelous light of God. My soul was racked with *eternal* torment; but I am snatched, and my soul is pained no more. [Mosiah 27:28–29; italics added]

Alma is recounted his rebirth experience to his son Corianton many years later, having served the Lord diligently since then (see Alma 36:24).

D&C 19:13–19 • Christ Suffered For All If They Repent

> 13 Wherefore, I command you to repent, and keep the commandments which you have received by the hand of my servant Joseph Smith, Jun., in my name;
>
> 14 And it is by my almighty power that you have received them;
>
> 15 Therefore I command you to repent—repent, lest I smite you by the rod of my mouth, and by my wrath, and by my anger, and your sufferings be sore—how sore you know not, how exquisite you know not, yea, how hard to bear you know not.
>
> 16 For behold, I, God, have suffered these things for all, that they might not suffer if they would repent;

17 But if they would not repent they must suffer even as I;

18 Which suffering caused myself, even God, the greatest of all, to tremble because of pain, and to bleed at every pore, and to suffer both body and spirit—and would that I might not drink the bitter cup, and shrink—

19 Nevertheless, glory be to the Father, and I partook and finished my preparations unto the children of men.

As taught by Jacob, brother of Nephi, salvation comes only "through the grace of God," and consists of two parts. God raises "you from death by the power of the resurrection, and also from everlasting death by the power of the atonement," (2 Nephi 10:24–25). Although the atonement covered the sins of all mankind, it was based on the condition of repentance (v. 17). "For if we sin willfully after that we have received the knowledge of the truth, there remaineth no more sacrifice for sins" (Hebrews 10:26). An unforgivable sin is one which Christ, although he has paid the demands of justice for it, will not apply His suffering towards its payment, because mercy cannot rob justice.

The Atonement was an infinite [all-inclusive] and an eternal sacrifice [of a God] (2 Nephi 9:7; Mosiah 3:7; Alma 34:9–10). The suffering of the atonement took place first, in the Garden of Gethsemane. Later, on the cross, according to this writer's understanding, Christ experienced the most extreme suffering that could come upon man in the flesh. This suffering enabled him to know "how to succor [aid or help] his people" (see Alma 7:12). In Gethsemane, Christ, knowing all things, suffered for the sins of every person in the world (2 Nephi 9:20; Alma 13:13). There, the intensity of his suffering caused him to bleed at every pore (D&C 19:18). Luke is the only gospel writer to include the account of his bleeding at every pore (Luke 22:44), but it is verified in this revelation and in the Book of Mormon: "blood cometh from every pore, so great shall be his anguish for the wickedness and the abominations of his people" (Mosiah 3:7). His bleeding was a suffering of the body, and it was caused by the mental anguish of experiencing every person's sin—thus a suffering of "both body and spirit" (D&C 19:18). The bitter cup, which He "would that I might not drink . . . and shrink," (v. 18) was His experience in Gethsemane "And he went a little further, and fell on his face, and prayed, saying, O my Father, if it be possible, let this cup pass from me: nevertheless not as I will, but as thou wilt" (Matthew 26:39). That He did partake of the cup, to the glory of the Father, and for the benefit of the children of men (D&C 19:20) was confirmed to the Nephites: "I have drunk out of that bitter cup which the Father hath given me, and have glorified the Father in taking upon me the sins of the world, in the which I have suffered the will of the Father in all things from the beginning" (3 Nephi 11:11).

The world's concept of hell is also clarified by the verses here considered. Hell is both a condition and a place. The condition is the suffering of the mind and the body, and the place is where the wicked go when they leave this mortal life. Jacob, brother of Nephi, a Book of Mormon prophet, taught:

> 10 O how great the goodness of our God, who prepareth a way for our escape from the grasp of this awful monster; yea, that monster, death and hell, which I call the death of the body, and also the death of the spirit.
>
> 11 And because of the way of deliverance of our God, the Holy One of Israel, this death, of which I have spoken, which is the temporal, shall deliver up its dead; which death is the grave.
>
> 12 And this death of which I have spoken, which is the spiritual death, shall deliver up its dead; which spiritual death is hell; wherefore, death and hell must deliver up their dead, and hell must deliver up its captive spirits, and the grave must deliver up its captive bodies, and the bodies and the spirits of men will be restored one to the other; and it is by the power of the resurrection of the Holy One of Israel.
>
> 13 O how great the plan of our God! For on the other hand, the paradise of God must deliver up the spirits of the righteous, and the grave deliver up the body of the righteous; and the spirit and the body is restored to itself again, and all men become incorruptible, and immortal, and they are living souls, having a perfect knowledge like unto us in the flesh, save it be that our knowledge shall be perfect. [2 Nephi 9:10–13]

Alma, another Book of Mormon prophet taught his errant son Corianton:

> 11 Now, concerning the state of the soul between death and the resurrection—Behold, it has been made known unto me by an angel, that the spirits of all men, as soon as they are departed from this mortal

body, yea, the spirits of all men, whether they be good or evil, are taken home to that God who gave them life.

12 And then shall it come to pass, that the spirits of those who are righteous are received into a state of happiness, which is called paradise, a state of rest, a state of peace, where they shall rest from all their troubles and from all care, and sorrow.

13 And then shall it come to pass, that the spirits of the wicked, yea, who are evil—for behold, they have no part nor portion of the Spirit of the Lord; for behold, they chose evil works rather than good; therefore the spirit of the devil did enter into them, and take possession of their house—and these shall be cast out into outer darkness; there shall be weeping, and wailing, and gnashing of teeth, and this because of their own iniquity, being led captive by the will of the devil.

14 Now this is the state of the souls of the wicked, yea, in darkness, and a state of awful, fearful looking for the fiery indignation of the wrath of God upon them; thus they remain in this state, as well as the righteous in paradise, until the time of their resurrection. [Alma 40:10–14]

The Prophet Joseph Smith declared:

"There has been much said about the word hell, and the sectarian world have preached much about it, describing it to be a burning lake of fire and brimstone. But what is hell? It is another modern term, and is taken from hades. . . .

Hades the Greek, or Sheol the Hebrew, these two significations mean a world of spirits. Hades, Sheol, paradise, spirits, are all one: it is a world of spirits.

The righteous and the wicked will all go to the same world of spirits until the resurrection. . . .

The great misery of departed spirits in the world of spirits, where they go after death, is to know they come short of the glory that others enjoy and that they might have enjoyed themselves, and they are their own accusers. . . . [*TPJS*, 310–11]

Therefore, a person may experience endless torment and eternal damnation, but that torment does not have to be never-ending. As Jesus taught to both the Jews and the Nephites: "Verily, verily, I say unto thee, thou shalt by no means come out thence until thou hast paid the uttermost senine" (3 Nephi 12:26; Matthew 5:26).

D&C 19:20–23 • Tasted in the Least Degree

20 Wherefore, I command you again to repent, lest I humble you with my almighty power; and that you confess your sins, lest you suffer these punishments of which I have spoken, of which in the smallest, yea, even in the least degree you have tasted at the time I withdrew my Spirit.

21 And I command you that you preach naught but repentance, and show not these things unto the world until it is wisdom in me.

22 For they cannot bear meat now, but milk they must receive; wherefore, they must not know these things, lest they perish.

23 Learn of me, and listen to my words; walk in the meekness of my Spirit, and you shall have peace in me.

Martin was commanded to repent lest he suffer [Eternal] punishment of which the Lord had spoken (v. 20). The experience to which the Lord refers, when Martin had tasted endless punishment in the least degree when the Spirit had withdrawn (v. 20), was probably his visit to see the Prophet Joseph after the 116 pages of manuscript of the translation of the Book of Mormon had been lost. The Prophet's mother describes the event:

> . . . at half past twelve we saw him walking with a slow and measured tread toward the house, his eyes fixed thoughtful upon the ground. On coming to the gate, he stopped, instead of passing through, and got upon the fence, and sat there some time with his hat drawn over his eyes. At length he entered the house. Soon after which we sat down to the table, Mr. Harris with the rest. He took up his knife and fork as if he were going to use them, but immediately dropped them. Hyrum, observing this, said; "Martin, why do you not eat; are you sick? Upon which Mr. Harris pressed his hands upon his temples, and cried out in a tone of deep anguish, O I have lost my soul! I have lost my soul!"
>
> Joseph who had not expressed his fears till now, sprang from the table, exclaiming, "Martin have you lost the manuscript? Have you broken your oath, and brought down condemnation upon my head as well as your own?"
>
> "Yes, it is gone," replied Martin, "and I know not where." [*History of Joseph Smith by his Mother*, 127–129]

One must remember that this was only a taste that Martin had experienced. Later revelations in the Doctrine and Covenants call this type of punishment "the buffetings of Satan" (see D&C 78:12, 82:21; 132:26).

Zeezrom, a lawyer in the land of Ammonihah who had stirred up the people against Alma and Amulek, is another good example of the suffering caused by the withdrawal of Christ's Spirit. After he repented he tried in vain to correct his misrepresentations to the people, who cast him out of the city. The record says:

> . . . also Zeezrom lay sick at Sidom, with a burning fever, which was caused by the great tribulations of his mind on account of his wickedness, for he supposed that Alma and Amulek were no more; and he supposed that they had been slain because of his iniquity. And this great sin, and his many other sins, did harrow up his mind until it did become exceedingly sore, having no deliverance; therefore he began to be scorched with a burning heat. [Alma 15:3]

Zeezrom was paying for those things which he had knowingly done. From the time that he became conscious of his own guilt, he was encircled about by the pains of hell (Alma 14:6). He was healed, baptized, and began to preach unto the people (Alma 15:4–12). To repent and receive the benefits of the Atonement is a much more pleasant experience.

Martin was commanded to confess his sins, and show not the sacred things unto the world until it was wisdom in the Lord (D&C 19:21). He was cautioned to preach the milk of the gospel—repentance—and not the meat (v. 22). This same caution was given by the Apostle Paul: "I have fed you with milk, and not with meat: for hitherto ye were not able [to bear it], neither yet now are ye able (1 Corinthians 3:2; see also Hebrews 5:11–14; 1 Peter 2:2). Milk is the symbolism for the basic principles of the Gospel (see A of F 4). To speak of such things as eternal progression to Godhood is the symbolism for the meat. Just as a child is fed milk, and slowly progresses to eating more and more solid food, the investigators and new members of the Church must be slowly prepared for some of the deeper doctrines of the Gospel. In the positive sense, Martin was promised peace if he would learn of Christ, and walk in the meekness of the Spirit (D&C 19:23). Again we are reminded of the Apostle Paul: "And the peace of God, which passeth all understanding, shall keep your hearts and minds through Christ Jesus" (Philippians 4:7).

D&C 19:24–27 • Christ's Word to the Gentiles— the Book of Mormon

24 I am Jesus Christ; I came by the will of the Father, and I do his will.

25 And again, I command thee that thou shalt not covet thy neighbor's wife; nor seek thy neighbor's life.

26 And again, I command thee that thou shalt not covet thine own property, but impart it freely to the printing of the Book of Mormon, which contains the truth and the word of God—

27 Which is my word to the Gentile, that soon it may go to the Jew, of whom the Lamanites are a remnant, that they may believe the gospel, and look not for a Messiah to come who has already come.

Why Jesus Christ identifies Himself again is probably to remind Martin that he is carrying out His Father's instructions in what He was about to command him (v. 24). We know of no reason why he is warned about his neighbor's wife, nor life (v. 25), but the Lord must have known of some temptation that was going to come to him.

Martin did as the Lord next commanded him concerning his property. He had mortgaged his farm—the "property" mentioned—for three thousand dollars, in order to finance the printing the first five thousand copies of the Book of Mormon (v. 26). This cost was no small amount in that day. This is the fourth Doctrine and Covenants revelation to declare the truthfulness of the Book of Mormon (see D&C 6:17; 17:6; 18:2–3; 19:26). The first two were to Oliver Cowdery, the third to the Three Witnesses, and this one to Martin.

The title page of the Book of Mormon states that it is "Written to the Lamanites, who are a remant of the house of Israel; and also to Jew and Gentile." The Lamanites are remnants of the Jews (D&C 19:27) in two ways. First, the Mulekites were descendants of Zedekiah, king of Judah (see Omni 1:14–16). By direct lineage, or through intermarriage, some of the Lamanites could be descendants of Judah. Secondly, Lehi and Ishmael were cultural Jews because they lived in the divided Southern Kingdom of Judah, although their blood lines, Manasseh and Ephraim, were originally part of northern Israel (see 2 Corinthians 15:8–10). Nephi wrote: "And then shall the remnant of our seed know concerning us, how that we came out from Jerusalem, and that they are descendants of the Jews" (2 Nephi 30:4). He later qualified why they were Jews: "I have charity for the Jew—I say Jew, because I mean them from whence I came" (2 Nephi 33:8).

The time for the Gentiles to receive the gospel is now, and the Book of Mormon is going to them (D&C 19:27). The time for the Jews to receive the gospel is still not here (A.D. 2008), but it will come.

> Wherefore, he shall bring forth his words unto them, which words shall judge them at the last day, for they shall be given them for the purpose of convincing them of the true Messiah, who was rejected by them; and unto the convincing of them that they need not look forward any more for a Messiah to come, for there should not any come, save it should be a false Messiah which should deceive the people; for there is save one Messiah spoken of by the prophets, and that Messiah is he who should be rejected of the Jews. [2 Nephi 25:18]

When that time arrives, the Book of Mormon will be the source of their being taught about their true Messiah (D&C 19:27; see also Mormon 5:12–16).

D&C 19:28 • Of Tenets Thou Shalt Not Speak

> 28 And again, I command thee that thou shalt pray vocally as well as in thy heart; yea, before the world as well as in secret, in public as well as in private.
>
> 29 And thou shalt declare glad tidings, yea, publish it upon the mountains, and upon every high place, and among every people that thou shalt be permitted to see.
>
> 30 And thou shalt do it with all humility, trusting in me, reviling not against revilers.
>
> 31 And of tenets thou shalt not talk, but thou shalt declare repentance and faith on the Savior, and remission of sins by baptism, and by fire, yea, even the Holy Ghost.

Prayer should not only be an everyday event, but an every moment event. Alma tells us to "watch and pray continually" (Alma 13:28). The Savior told the Nephites; "ye must watch and pray always" (3 Nephi 18:15). He commanded the Nephite multitude and His disciples "that they

should not cease to pray in their hearts" (3 Nephi 20:1). These instructions fit those given to Martin (v. 28).

"Glad tidings" (D&C 19:29) is the Hebrew root for our word "gospel" (compare Mosiah 15:14). To publish it upon the mountains (v. 29) may refer to the Americas (see Genesis 49:26). However, it is Isaiah's description of those who publish peace, and the Lord "is the founder of peace" (Mosiah 15:15–18, Isaiah 52:7). The gospel is for all people, but is to follow the Lord's timetable for those "thou shalt be permitted to see" (D&C 19:29). To whomever we are sent, we must exemplify humility and trust in the Lord to prepare the way before us, and not be argumentative (v. 30).

The dictionary defines a tenet as "a principle, belief, or doctrine . . . one held in common by members of an organization, group, movement, or profession, *generally* held to be true" (*Websters Ninth New Collegiate;* italics added). A tenet is somewhat the same as the milk and meat concept discussed above. The Lord did not want Martin teaching the theories and philosophies of men, or morals and ethics without any doctrinal foundation. He wanted the basic principles and doctrines of the gospel taught as He has given them to His servants. The gospel includes the baptism of water, but also the baptism of the Holy Ghost (v. 31). The baptism of fire is the cleansing power (see Moroni 6:4), and the baptism of the Holy Ghost is the personal witness given of the divinity of the Church (see 2 Nephi 31:18).

D&C 19:32–38 • A Commandment Unto the End of Thy Life

32 Behold, this is a great and the last commandment which I shall give unto you concerning this matter; for this shall suffice for thy daily walk, even unto the end of thy life.

33 And misery thou shalt receive if thou wilt slight these counsels, yea, even the destruction of thyself and property.

34 Impart a portion of thy property, yea, even part of thy lands, and all save the support of thy family.

35 Pay the debt thou hast contracted with the printer. Release thyself from bondage.

36 Leave thy house and home, except when thou shalt desire to see thy family;

37 And speak freely to all; yea, preach, exhort, declare the truth, even with a loud voice, with a sound of rejoicing, crying—Hosanna, hosanna, blessed be the name of the Lord God!

38 Pray always, and I will pour out my Spirit upon you, and great shall be your blessing—yea, even more than if you should obtain treasures of earth and corruptibleness to the extent thereof.

Although the law of forgiveness had not been revealed to the Church, this revelation resembles the conditions of the law. According to this law, we are required to forgive someone who trespasses against us three times, even if they are not repentant. On the fourth transgression, we are to take the testimonies of these transgressions before the Lord, and then the Lord will deal with that transgression (see D&C 98:41–43).

Apparently the Lord had previously warned Martin three times, and this was the fourth and his last warning (D&C 19:32). If Martin did not respond, he would bring destruction upon himself and his property (v. 33). How this would happen is not stated, but would probably have been in a natural way because the Lord would have withdrawn His Spirit. If Martin paid the debt, he would be out of bondage (v. 35). He was also required to put full effort into the work of the Restoration (D&C 19:36–37). The Lord would not only forgive him with all of His heart, but would reward him with His Spirit and more than the corruption of the treasures of the earth would bring (v. 38). We never get out of the Lord's debt, because he blesses us for every commandment we keep (see Mosiah 2:24).

D&C 19:39–41 • Can You Read This Without Rejoicing?

39 Behold, canst thou read this without rejoicing and lifting up thy heart for gladness?

40 Or canst thou run about longer as a blind guide?

41 Or canst thou be humble and meek, and conduct thyself wisely before me? Yea, come unto me thy Savior. Amen.

The Lord outlines two courses that Martin can follow. He can rejoice in the gladness of heart (v. 39), or he can continue in the course he has been blindly following (v. 40). He has his agency and the decision is his. As Samuel the Lamanite told the Nephites:

30 And now remember, remember, my brethren, that whosoever perisheth, perisheth unto himself; and whosoever doeth iniquity, doeth it unto himself; for behold, ye are free; ye are permitted to act for yourselves; for behold, God hath given unto you a knowledge and he hath made you free.

31 He hath given unto you that ye might know good from evil, and he hath given unto you that ye might choose life or death; and ye can do good and be restored unto that which is good, or have that which is good restored unto you; or ye can do evil, and have that which is evil restored unto you. [Helaman 14:30–31]

The Lord invites Martin to come unto Him. When one understands the nature of Jesus Christ as an Endless and Eternal God, he will do as Martin did and become humble and meek, and conduct himself wisely before his Savior.

General Authority Quotes

—*Elder James E. Talmage* • D&C 19:11–12, 16–18

During this hundred years many other great truths not known before have been declared to the people, and one of the greatest is that to hell there is an exit as well as an entrance. Hell is no place to which a vindictive Judge sends prisoners to suffer and to be punished principally to his glory; but it is a place prepared for his teaching, the disciplining of those who failed to learn here upon the earth what they should have learned. True, we read of everlasting punishment, unending suffering, eternal damnation. That is a direful expression; but in his mercy the Lord has made plain what those words mean. 'Eternal punishment,' he says, is 'God's punishment,' for he is eternal; and that condition or state or possibility will ever exist for the sinner who deserves and really needs such condemnation; but this does not mean that the individual sufferer or sinner is to be eternally or everlastingly made to endure or suffer. No man will be kept in hell longer than is necessary to bring him to a fitness for something better. When he reaches that stage the prison doors will open and there will be rejoicing among the hosts who welcome him into a better state. The Lord has not abated in the least what he has said in earlier dispensations concerning the operations of his law and his gospel, but he has made clear unto us his goodness and mercy through it all, for it is his glory and his work to bring about the immortality and eternal life of man. [CR, April 1930, 297]

—President Joseph Fielding Smith • D&C 19:16–19

We cannot comprehend the great suffering that the Lord had to take upon himself to bring to pass this redemption from death and from sin. He spent a few years upon the earth, and during that short sojourn he suffered the abuse of men. They stoned him; they spat upon him; they cursed him; they ridiculed him; they accused him of almost every crime they could think of, and finally they took and crucified him upon a cross.

We get into the habit of thinking, I suppose, that his great suffering was when he was nailed to the cross by his hands and his feet and was left there to suffer until he died. As excruciating as this pain was, that was not the greatest suffering that he had to undergo, for in some way which I cannot understand, but which I accept on faith, and which you must accept on faith, he carried on his back the burden of the sins of the whole world. It is hard enough for me to carry my own sins. How is it for you? And yet he had to carry the sins of the whole world, as our Savior and the Redeemer of a fallen world, and so great was his suffering before he went on the cross, we are informed that blood oozed from the pores of his body, and he prayed to his Father that the cup might pass if possible, but not being possible, he was willing to drink.

And here is what he said to the Church [quotes D&C 16–19].

Now, when he said that if we do not repent we will have to suffer even as he did, he had no reference to being nailed to a cross, but it was the torment of mind, of spirit, that he had reference to, before he ever got to the cross, and if men will not repent, they will have to suffer even as he suffered. [CR, October 1947, 147–148]

—The Prophet Joseph Smith • D&C 19:20

There is no pain as awful as that of suspense. This is the punishment of the wicked; their doubt, anxiety, and suspense cause weeping, wailing, and gnashing of teeth. [*TPJS*, 288]

—Elder Orson F. Whitney • D&C 19:27

The name Gentile is not with us a term or reproach. It comes from Gentilis, meaning of a nation, a family or a people not of Israel—that is all. "Mormon" is a nickname for Latter-day Saints, but "Gentile" is not a nickname. It simply means, with us, one who does not belong to the Church. . . . [CR, April 1928, 59–60]

Chapter Eleven

The Keystone of Our Religion

D&C 20:5–36

*H*istorical Setting: The Prophet Joseph records in his history following section 18:

> In this manner did the Lord continue to give us instructions in this manner from time to time, concerning the duties which now devolved upon us; and among many other things, we obtained [section 20], by the spirit of prophecy and revelation. [*HC*, 1:64]

It is agreed by many, including this writer, that section 20 was compiled from these "many other things [revelations] "received between June 1829, and April 6, 1830. The frequent "Amens" at the end of several verses (4, 12, 16, 28, and 36) support this thesis. The first four verses, discussed in chapter 9, would constitute the first revelation of this time period; and verses five through thirty-six the second through fifth revelations, which will be discussed here. The remainder of section 20 (vv. 37–84) will be discussed in the next chapter, except those verses (46–59) that were discussed in chapter 8.

INTRODUCTION

Concerning this record the Prophet Joseph Smith said: "I told the brethren that the Book of Mormon was the most correct of any book on earth, and the keystone of our religion, and a man would get nearer to God by abiding be its precepts, than by any other book" (Book of Mormon, Introduction). The keystone is the final stone placed at the top of a rounding arch, and holds the arch together. The verses of section 20 discussed in this chapter, and given on or around the day the Church was legally organized, show us why the Book of Mormon is the keystone.

SECTION 20 • OUTLINE

➤ 20:5–7   The preparation of the Prophet Joseph Smith to translate the Book of Mormon.

     a. The Father and the Son appeared to this First Elder and manifested to him that he had received a remission of sins (v. 5).

     b. God ministered unto him by an angel, and gave him commandments (vv. 6–7).

➤ 20:8–12   The angel gave Joseph power, by means before prepared, to translate the Book of Mormon.

     a. It contains a record of a fallen people, and the fullness of the gospel, written to the Gentiles and to the Jews (v. 9).

     b. It was given by inspiration, confirmed to others by angels, and declared to the world by them (v. 10).

     c. It proves to the world that the holy scriptures are true, that God does inspire men, and calls them to His holy work in all ages (v. 11).

     d. It shows that God is the same yesterday, today, and forever (v. 12).

➤ 20:13–16 Those who come to the knowledge of this work shall be judged by it.

     a. Those who receive it in faith, and work righteousness shall be crowned with eternal life (v. 14).

     b. Those who reject it shall be turned to their own condemnation (v. 15).

     c. The Lord has spoken; the elders of the church bear witness to its words (v. 16).

➤ 20:17–36 By these things [Book of Mormon] we know: (we will not list the various doctrines enumerated here, but will treat them in sequence below).

Text and Commentary

D&C 20:5–7 • Educated By the Angel Moroni

> 5 After it was truly manifested unto this First Elder that he had received a remission of his sins, he was entangled again in the vanities of the world;
>
> 6 But after repenting, and humbling himself sincerely, through faith, God ministered unto him by an holy angel, whose countenance was as lightning, and whose garments were pure and white above all other whiteness;
>
> 7 And gave unto him commandments which inspired him;

The first event of the latter-day Restoration was Joseph Smith's First Vision, the appearance of the Father and the Son to him in the spring of 1820. In that appearance Joseph was told his sins were forgiven.[23] This revelation is obviously referring to THAT great and marvelous event in his life. His being entangled in the vanities of the world (v. 5) should not be misunderstood. Vanity mean uselessness or valuelessness. He described this time in his life between the First Vision and 1823:

> I was left to all kinds of temptations; and, mingling with all kinds of society, I frequently fell into errors, and displayed the weakness of youth, and the foibles of human nature; which, I am sorry to say, led me into divers temptations, offensive in the sight of God. In making this confession, no one need suppose me guilty of any great or malignant sins. A disposition to commit such was never in my nature. But I was guilt of levity, and sometimes associated with jovial company, etc., not consistent with that character which ought to be maintained by one who was called of God as I had been. But this will not seem very strange to any one who recollects my youth, and is acquainted with my native cheery temperament. [JS—H 1:28]

Although the sixth verse of section 20 is easily interpreted as the visit of the Angel Moroni, it does not tell us that he ministered to and educated

---

[23] On four different occasions Joseph wrote or dictated an account of that vision: 1832, 1835, 1838, and 1841. In two of those accounts he stated that he was told that he was forgiven of his sins. The 1838 account that is in the Pearl of Great Price does not include that statement, but the 1832 account in his own handwriting, and the 1835 account do contain the statement. See Milton V. Backman, *The First Vision* [1980] 155–69.

the young man over a four year period (see JS—H 1:29–54). Joseph Smith's history tells us Moroni visited once a year on the anniversary of the first visit in 1823. However, he must have visited the young man and taught him extensively in preparation for the translation of the record. Mother Smith records that in the winter months of 1823—1824, Joseph taught the family about the Nephites: "He would describe the ancient inhabitants of the continent, their dress, mode of travel, and the animals on which they rode; their cities, their buildings, with every particular; their mode of warfare, and also their religious worship. This he would do with as much ease, seemingly as if he had spent his whole life among them." (*History of Joseph Smith by his Mother*, 82–83). He certainly did not learn all of this about the Nephites from one visit in the previous September (1823).

The commandments that Moroni gave to Joseph included his not showing the plates, or the Urim and Thummim, to anyone except those to whom he was commanded (JS—H 1:42). There were undoubtedly many more commandments given, but they certainly regarded the safekeeping and preparation for translating the plates. Moroni also taught him regarding over a hundred passages of scripture,[24] a few of which are explained in Joseph's history (JS—H 1:36–41).

D&C 20:8–10 • The Contents of the Book of Mormon

8 And gave him power from on high, by the means which were before prepared, to translate the Book of Mormon;

9 Which contains a record of a fallen people, and the fulness of the gospel of Jesus Christ to the Gentiles and to the Jews also;

10 Which was given by inspiration, and is confirmed to others by the ministering of angels, and is declared unto the world by them—

Much has been said about the translation of the Book of Mormon in the previous chapters of this work. Another testimony is added in this revelation that was translated by the power of God (v. 8). The Book of Mormon bears the same testimony.

---

[24] See the Oliver Cowdery, Letter VI, April, 1835 *Messenger and Advocate*, Church Newspaper, published in Francis W. Kirkham, *A New Witness for Christ in America* [1942], 402–406.

"Now Ammon said unto him: I can assuredly tell thee, O king, of a man that can translate the records; for he has wherewith that he can look, and translate all records that are of ancient date; and it is a gift from God. And the things are called interpreters, and no man can look in them except he be commanded, lest he should look for that he ought not and he should perish. And whosoever is commanded to look in them, the same is called seer.

. . . and a gift which is greater can no man have, except he should possess the power of God, which no man can; yet a man may have great power given him from God. [Mosiah 8:13, 16]

"The means which were before prepared" (v. 8) was the Urim and Thummim. It was deposited with the plates that were given to Joseph Smith by the Angel Moroni. Moroni also told Joseph that "God had prepared them for the purpose of translating the book" (JS—H 1:35). The Book of Mormon again verifies that they were prepared previously for this purpose: "Now these things [Urim and Thummim] were prepared from the beginning, and were handed down from generation to generation, for the purpose of interpreting languages" (Mosiah 28:14). Joseph Smith repeatedly gave credit to this means for translating: "the record was translated through the medium of the Urim and Thummim and by the gift and power of God" (*HC*, 1:315, 3:28; 4:537).

The contents of the book were two fold: First, "a record of a fallen people;" and second, "the fullness of the gospel of Jesus Christ to the Gentiles and to the Jews also" (D&C 20:9). The reference to a "fallen people" was not limited to the Nephite nation, but included the Jaredites as well. The Jaredites, which occupied the Americas after their founders were "scattered abroad upon the face of all the earth" at the time of the Tower of Babel (Genesis 11:9), had fallen before the Nephites. The Lord calls the Book of Mormon "a record," not a history, for the history of the Nephites was included on the larger plates of Nephi which were not given to Joseph Smith (1 Nephi 9:2; Jacob 1:2–3).

The Book of Mormon also contained the fullness of the gospel (D&C 20:9). Some people do not understand what is meant by the fullness of the gospel. Because it does not mention some principle that was later revealed through the Doctrine and Covenants, they feel that it does not include the fullness. The fullness of the gospel is defined in the Book of Mormon and in the Doctrine and Covenants as the plan of salvation (see

3 Nephi 27:13–21; D&C 33:11–12; 39:5–6; 76:40–43). A number of other revelations affirm that the Book of Mormon contains the fullness of gospel of Jesus Christ. In a revelation given in August, 1830, the Lord referred to Moroni "whom I have sent unto you to reveal the Book of Mormon, containing the fulness of my gospel" (D&C 27:5). In a December 1830, revelation to Sidney Rigdon, the Lord said: "I have sent forth the fulness of my gospel by the hand of my servant Joseph; and I have blessed him" (D&C 35:17; see also 39:11; 42:12). In total, there are at least five revelations in the Doctrine and Covenants that state that the fulness of the gospel is in the Book of Mormon. Moreover, when Moroni first appeared to Joseph Smith in September of 1823 he told Joseph "that the fulness of the everlasting Gospel was contained in [the plates], as delivered by the Savior to the ancient inhabitants" (JS—H 1:34).

In this revelation, section 20, the Lord tells the Church what the Book of Mormon is and what is to be done with it. It "was given by inspiration" (D&C 20:10), and is therefore scripture. Scripture, in the Apostle Peter's words, is the words of "holy men of God [who] spake as they were moved by the Holy Ghost" (2 Peter 1:21). In a later revelation to the Church, the Lord directed His servants to "speak as they are moved upon by the Holy Ghost. And whatsoever they shall speak when moved upon by the Holy Ghost shall be scripture, shall be the will of the Lord, shall be the mind of the Lord, shall be the word of the Lord, shall be the voice of the Lord, and the power of God unto salvation" (D&C 68:3–4; see chapter 29). Certainly the Book of Mormon qualifies as a book of scripture, and this has been confirmed by the ministering of angels (D&C 20:10)—particularly Moroni and those other angels who appeared to the Three Witnesses and Joseph, which events have been discussed. Their testimony is recorded and printed in the front of every copy of the Book of Mormon. Thus, as the Book of Mormon is taken to the nations, their testimony is also "declared unto the world by them" (v. 10).

When the Angel Moroni appeared to Joseph, he fulfilled the prophecy of John the Revelator: "And I saw another angel fly in the midst of heaven, having the everlasting gospel to preach unto them that dwell on the earth, and to every nation, and kindred, and tongue, and people" (Revelation 14:6). In a revelation given in November, 1831, which the Lord initially identified as the appendix of the Doctrine and Covenants (see section

heading), He showed that the prophecy was underway. "And now, verily saith the Lord, that these things might be known among you, O inhabitants of the earth, I have sent forth mine angel flying through the midst of heaven, having the everlasting gospel, who hath appeared unto some and hath committed it unto man, who shall appear unto many that dwell on the earth" (D&C 133:36). Eventually all people will have an opportunity to receive its inspired message.

D&C 20:11–12 • Three Purposes of the Book of Mormon

11 Proving to the world that the holy scriptures are true, and that God does inspire men and call them to his holy work in this age and generation, as well as in generations of old;

12 Thereby showing that he is the same God yesterday, today, and forever. Amen.

The Lord here outlines three purposes of the Book of Mormon. The first purpose was to prove "to the world that the holy scriptures [i.e., the Bible] are true" (v. 11). Nephi saw, in his vision of the nations of the gentiles, the coming forth of other books [probably including the Doctrine and Covenants, Pearl of Great Price, and JST] that would serve the same purpose for the remnant of his seed.

40 And the angel spake unto me, saying: These last records, which thou hast seen among the Gentiles, shall establish the truth of the first, which are of the twelve apostles of the Lamb, and shall make known the plain and precious things which have been taken away from them; and shall make known to all kindreds, tongues, and people, that the Lamb of God is the Son of the Eternal Father, and the Savior of the world; and that all men must come unto him, or they cannot be saved.

41 And they must come according to the words which shall be established by the mouth of the Lamb; and the words of the Lamb shall be made known in the records of thy seed, as well as in the records of the twelve apostles of the Lamb; wherefore they both shall be established in one; for there is one God and one Shepherd over all the earth. [1 Nephi 13:40–41]

The Book of Mormon confirms a number of aspects of the Bible: authorship (Isaiah 48–49, 1 Nephi 19:23; John the Revelator, 1 Nephi 14:25–27), history (e.g. Melchizedek, as confirmed in Alma 13:14–29;

Abraham, Jacob 4:5), text (e.g. compare Matthew 5–7 with 3 Nephi 12–14). It also provides authoritative interpretation of the Bible (e.g. the "other sheep," John 10:14–16, 3 Nephi 11:13–24, the fate of the Apostle John, John 21:21–23, 3 Nephi 28:1–7. These are just a few of many examples, in each of the four categories, which answer the modern critic's questions about the Bible.

The second purpose of the Book of Mormon is "that God does inspire men and call them to his holy work in this age and generation, as well as in generations of old" (20:11). It teaches us that revelation to man is the same yesterday, today, and forever (see Mormon 9:7–10). It teaches us about men being called to the priesthood according to the foreknowledge of God, and that all might have had this privilege had they accepted the preparation for the priesthood in the pre-mortal life (Alma 13:1–5). In this dispensation, that same privilege of all men holding the priesthood was one of the purposes of the Restoration: "that every man might speak in the name of God the Lord, even the Savior of the world" (D&C 1:20).

The third purpose of the Book of Mormon is to show that Jesus Christ is the same God yesterday, today and forever" (D&C 20:12). The Bible and the Book of Mormon bear witness of Him in three time periods, again proving that the Bible is true. He is the pre-mortal God, or the God of the Old Testament (see John 1:1–5; 1 Nephi 19:10). He is the New Testament God, or the resurrected Christ (see John 20:31; 3 Nephi 11:7–11). He is the glorified Christ, or the millennial God (see Acts 1:11; Revelation 1:5–9; 3 Nephi 26:3–4).

The Book of Mormon is indeed "Another Testament of Jesus Christ."

D&C 20:13–16 • The Book of Mormon: A Crown or Condemnation

13 Therefore, having so great witnesses, by them shall the world be judged, even as many as shall hereafter come to a knowledge of this work.

14 And those who receive it in faith, and work righteousness, shall receive a crown of eternal life;

15 But those who harden their hearts in unbelief, and reject it, it shall turn to their own condemnation—

16 For the Lord God has spoken it; and we, the elders of the church, have heard and bear witness to the words of the glorious Majesty on high,

to whom be glory forever and ever. Amen.

It is important to remember that the Book of Mormon is not on trial; the world is on trial. In fact, every person who comes to "a knowledge of this work" will be judged by it (v. 13). Nephi bore the same testimony: "Wherefore, these things shall go from generation to generation as long as the earth shall stand; and they shall go according to the will and pleasure of God; and the nations who shall possess them shall be judged of them according to the words which are written" (2 Nephi 25:22). However, judgments are not always negative. Those individuals who receive it in faith, work righteousness, and follow its precepts will gain eternal life (D&C 20:14). Only those who will harden their hearts, not believe it, and knowingly reject it will bring about their own condemnation (v. 15). There seems to be a difference between not believing and rejecting it. Those who reject it have a tendency to fight against it. They cannot leave it alone, but look for justification for their rejecting it and spread their unjust reasoning to others. Those who fail to believe, but continue in an honorable way of life, may have another opportunity in the spirit world, or may not receive the crown of eternal life, but will gain a higher glory than those who reject and fight against the Book of Mormon.

The Three Witnesses and Joseph Smith, the elders of the Church, heard the voice of the Lord "from out of the bright light above us, saying, 'These plates have been revealed by the power of God, and they have been translated by the power of God. The translation of them which you have seen is correct, and I command you to bear record of what you now see and hear'" (*HC*, 1:54–55). Their testimony of "the words of the glorious Majesty on high" (*HC*, 1:65) conclude this part of section 20. His glory will "be forever and ever" (D&C 20:16), and ours can be also if we will accept and follow his words.

BY THE BOOK OF MORMON WE KNOW THESE DOCTRINES ARE TRUE

The last part of section 20 outlines the doctrines that we learn from "these things" [the Book of Mormon] (v. 17). This conclusion is based on the fact that the subject of verses five through sixteen is entirely based on the Book of Mormon. As just discussed, the verses tell us how the Book of Mormon came about, its content, its heavenly status, and its effect on our lives. The conclusion is further evidenced by the ending of the Prophet Isaiah's detailed prophecy of the coming forth of the Book of Mormon (see Isaiah 29). "They also that erred in spirit shall come to understanding, and they that murmured shall learn doctrine" (Isaiah 29:24).[25] The Book of Mormon is the source of most of the doctrine of the Church.

To demonstrate we will quote the verses from section 20 and annotate them with a teaching from the Book of Mormon. It is recognized that many other verses, or more references, could be added, but we will just list one supporting scripture unless two doctrines are covered in the same verse.

20:17 By these things we know that there is a God in heaven, who is infinite and eternal, from everlasting to everlasting the same unchangeable God, the framer of heaven and earth, and all things which are in them;

a.   There is a God: But Alma said unto him: Thou hast had signs enough; will ye tempt your God? Will ye say, Show unto me a sign, when ye have the testimony of all these thy brethren, and also all the holy prophets? The scriptures are laid before thee, yea, and all things denote there is a God; yea, even the earth, and all things that are upon the face of it, yea, and its motion, yea, and also all the planets which move in their regular form do witness that there is a Supreme Creator. [Alma 30:44]

b.   God is infinite and eternal: ". . . my joy is carried away, even unto boasting in my God; for he has all power, all wisdom, and all understanding; he comprehendeth all things, and he is a merciful Being, even unto salvation, to those who will repent and believe on his name. [Alma 26:35]

c.   The framer of heaven and earth: Behold, I am Jesus Christ the Son of God. I created the heavens and the earth, and all things that in them are. I was with the Father from the beginning. I am in the Father, and

---

[25] For a more detailed account of Isaiah's prophecy, see 2 Nephi 27, and parts of 2 Nephi 26, Nephi quoting Isaiah from the plates of brass before plain and precious parts were taken away (see 1 Nephi 13:26–29)

the Father in me; and in me hath the Father glorified his name. [3 Nephi 9:15]

> **20:18** And that he created man, male and female, after his own image and in his own likeness, created he them;
>
> And because he said unto them that Christ was the God, the Father of all things, and said that he should take upon him the image of man, and it should be the image after which man was created in the beginning; or in other words, he said that man was created after the image of God, and that God should come down among the children of men, and take upon him flesh and blood, and go forth upon the face of the earth. [Mosiah 7:27]
>
> **20:19** And gave unto them commandments that they should love and serve him, the only living and true God, and that he should be the only being whom they should worship.
>
> And now behold, I say unto you that the right way is to believe in Christ, and deny him not; and Christ is the Holy One of Israel; wherefore ye must bow down before him, and worship him with all your might, mind, and strength, and your whole soul; and if ye do this ye shall in nowise be cast out. [2 Nephi 25:29]
>
> **20:20** But by the transgression of these holy laws man became sensual and devilish, and became fallen man.
>
> Wherefore, all mankind were in a lost and in a fallen state, and ever would be save they should rely on this Redeemer. [1 Nephi 10:6]
>
> **20:21** Wherefore, the Almighty God gave his Only Begotten Son, as it is written in those scriptures which have been given of him.
>
> . . . I know that Jesus Christ shall come, yea, the Son, the Only Begotten of the Father, full of grace, and mercy, and truth. And behold, it is he that cometh to take away the sins of the world, yea, the sins of every man who steadfastly believeth on his name. [Alma 5:48]
>
> **20:22** He suffered temptations but gave no heed unto them.
>
> Now the Spirit knoweth all things; nevertheless the Son of God suffereth according to the flesh that he might take upon him the sins

of his people, that he might blot out their transgressions according to the power of his deliverance; and now behold, this is the testimony which is in me. [Alma 7:13]

20:23 He was crucified, died, and rose again the third day;

. . . yea, the God of Abraham, and of Isaac, and the God of Jacob, yieldeth himself, according to the words of the angel, as a man, into the hands of wicked men, to be lifted up, according to the words of Zenock, and to be crucified, according to the words of Neum, and to be buried in a sepulchre, according to the words of Zenos. [1 Nephi 19:10]

But behold, as I said unto you concerning another sign, a sign of his death, behold, in that day that he shall suffer death the sun shall be darkened and refuse to give his light unto you; and also the moon and the stars; and there shall be no light upon the face of this land, even from the time that he shall suffer death, for the space of three days, to the time that he shall rise again from the dead. [Helaman 14:20]

20:24 And ascended into heaven, to sit down on the right hand of the Father, to reign with almighty power according to the will of the Father;

Wherefore, my beloved brethren, have miracles ceased because Christ hath ascended into heaven, and hath sat down on the right hand of God, to claim of the Father his rights of mercy which he hath upon the children of men? [Moroni 7:27]

20:25 That as many as would believe and be baptized in his holy name, and endure in faith to the end, should be saved.

And if they will not repent and believe in his name, and be baptized in his name, and endure to the end, they must be damned; for the Lord God, the Holy One of Israel, has spoken it. [2 Nephi 9:24]

20:26 Not only those who believed after he came in the meridian of time, in the flesh, but all those from the beginning, even as many as were before he came, who believed in the words of the holy prophets, who spake as they were inspired by the gift of the Holy Ghost, who truly testified of him in all things, should have eternal life,

Behold, I say unto you, is not a soul at this time as precious unto God as a soul will be at the time of his coming? [Alma 39:17]

I, Nephi, having heard all the words of my father, concerning the things which he saw in a vision, and also the things which he spake by the power of the Holy Ghost. . . [1 Nephi 10:17]

For, for this intent have we written these things, that they may know that we knew of Christ, and we had a hope of his glory many hundred years before his coming; and not only we ourselves had a hope of his glory, but also all the holy prophets which were before us. [Jacob 4:4]

20:27 As well as those who should come after, who should believe in the gifts and callings of God by the Holy Ghost, which beareth record of the Father and of the Son;

And after this manner did they ordain priests and teachers, according to the gifts and callings of God unto men; and they ordained them by the power of the Holy Ghost, which was in them. [Moroni 3:4]

And this is my doctrine, and it is the doctrine which the Father hath given unto me; and I bear record of the Father, and the Father beareth record of me, and the Holy Ghost beareth record of the Father and me; and I bear record that the Father commandeth all men, everywhere, to repent and believe in me. [3 Nephi 11:32]

20:28 Which Father, Son, and Holy Ghost are one God, infinite and eternal, without end. Amen.

. . . given unto him to dwell in the presence of God in his kingdom, to sing ceaseless praises with the choirs above, unto the Father, and unto the Son, and unto the Holy Ghost, which are one God, in a state of happiness which hath no end. [Mormon 7:7]

20:29 And we know that all men must repent and believe on the name of Jesus Christ, and worship the Father in his name, and endure in faith on his name to the end, or they cannot be saved in the kingdom of God.

. . . according to the commandments which the Lord God gave unto the children of men. For he gave commandment that all men must repent; for he showed unto all men that they were lost, because of the transgression of their parents. [2 Nephi 2:21]

. . . and when that day shall come that they shall believe in Christ, and worship the Father in his name, with pure hearts and clean hands. [2 Nephi 25:16]

. . . I know by this that unless a man shall endure to the end, in following the example of the Son of the living God, he cannot be saved. [2 Nephi 31:16]

20:30 And we know that justification through the grace of our Lord and Savior Jesus Christ is just and true;

. . . whoso repenteth and is baptized in my name shall be filled; and if he endureth to the end, behold, him will I hold guiltless before my Father at that day when I shall stand to judge the world. [3 Nephi 27:16]

20:31 And we know also, that sanctification through the grace of our Lord and Savior Jesus Christ is just and true, to all those who love and serve God with all their mights, minds, and strength.

Nevertheless they did fast and pray oft, and did wax stronger and stronger in their humility, and firmer and firmer in the faith of Christ, unto the filling their souls with joy and consolation, yea, even to the purifying and the sanctification of their hearts, which sanctification cometh because of their yielding their hearts unto God. [Helaman 3:35]

20:32 But there is a possibility that man may fall from grace and depart from the living God;

I saw that the day of grace was passed with them, both temporally and spiritually; for I saw thousands of them hewn down in open rebellion against their God. [Mormon 2:15]

20:33 Therefore let the church take heed and pray always, lest they fall into temptation;

. . . there was peace also, save it were the pride which began to enter into the church—not into the church of God, but into the hearts of the people who professed to belong to the church of God—

And they were lifted up in pride, even to the persecution of many of their brethren. Now this was a great evil, which did cause the more humble part of the people to suffer great persecutions, and to wade through much affliction. [Helaman 3:33–34]

20:34 Yea, and even let those who are sanctified take heed also.

And now, I say unto you, my brethren, that after ye have known and have been taught all these things, if ye should transgress and go contrary to that which has been spoken, that ye do withdraw yourselves from the Spirit of the Lord, that it may have no place in you to guide you in wisdom's paths that ye may be blessed, prospered, and preserved—

I say unto you, that the man that doeth this, the same cometh out in open rebellion against God; therefore he listeth to obey the evil spirit, and becometh an enemy to all righteousness; therefore, the Lord has no place in him, for he dwelleth not in unholy temples. [Mosiah 2:36–37]

20:35 And we know that these things are true and according to the revelations of John, neither adding to, nor diminishing from the prophecy of his book, the holy scriptures, or the revelations of God which shall come hereafter by the gift and power of the Holy Ghost, the voice of God, or the ministering of angels.

And then shall my revelations which I have caused to be written by my servant John be unfolded in the eyes of all the people. Remember, when ye see these things, ye shall know that the time is at hand that they shall be made manifest in very deed. [Ether 4:16]

20:36 And the Lord God has spoken it; and honor, power and glory be rendered to his holy name, both now and ever. Amen.

Wherefore, the things of all nations shall be made known; yea, all things shall be made known unto the children of men.

There is nothing which is secret save it shall be revealed; there is no work of darkness save it shall be made manifest in the light; and there is nothing which is sealed upon the earth save it shall be loosed.

Wherefore, all things which have been revealed unto the children of men shall at that day be revealed; and Satan shall have power over the hearts of the children of men no more, for a long time. And now, my beloved brethren, I make an end of my sayings. [2 Nephi 30:16–18]

The Prophet Joseph Smith made this timely observation:

Take away the Book of Mormon and the revelations [Doctrine and Covenants], and where is our religion? We have none; for without Zion, and a place of deliverance, we must fall; because the time is near when the sun will be darkened, and the moon turned to blood, and the stars fall from heaven, and the earth roll to and fro. Then, if this is the case, and if we are not sanctified and gathered to the places God has appointed, with all our former professions and our great love for the Bible, we must fall; we cannot stand; we cannot be saved; for God will gather out his Saints from the Gentiles, and then comes desolation and destruction, and none can escape except the pure in heart who are gathered. [*TPJS*, 71]

The Lord has given us the Book of Mormon and the Doctrine and Covenants to teach us the true doctrine of his gospel. The doctrines within these books are what we learn and know to be true (D&C 20:17), and will inspire us to "work righteousness." They will lead us to that "crown of eternal life" (D&C 20:14). They will also prepare us for the Second Coming when we will honor him, recognize more fully his power, and give glory to his name now, then, and forever (D&C 20:36). May we show our appreciation to the Lord for these great books by using them to improve our lives, and sharing them with many of his children as we have opportunity to do so.

General Authority Quotes

—*President Ezra Taft Benson* • D&C 20:9–10

The Book of Mormon was written for us today. God is the author of the book. It is a record of a fallen people, compiled by inspired men for our blessing today. Those people never had the book—it was meant for us. Mormon, the ancient prophet after whom the book is named, abridged centuries of records. God, who knows the end from the beginning, told him what to include in his abridgment that we would need for our day. [*A Witness and a Warning*, 2]

—*President Harold B. Lee* • D&C 20:11

There is nothing better that we can do to prepare ourselves spiritually than to read the Book of Mormon. Many doctrines of the Bible that are only partially covered there are beautifully explained in the Book of Mormon, the Doctrine and Covenants, and the Pearl of Great Price. [*THBL*, 155]

If you want to fortify your students against the so–called teachings in "higher education," the apostate teachings, the so called higher critics that are going to challenge their faith in the Bible, give them a fundamental understanding of the teachings of the Book of Mormon. Review it again and again. [*THBL*, 157]

With respect to doctrines and meanings of scriptures, let me give you safe counsel. It is usually not well to use a single passage of scripture unless it is confirmed by modern revelation or by the Book of Mormon. [*THBL*, 157]

—*Elder Bruce R. McConkie* • D&C 20:17–36

The greatest truth known to man is that there is a God in heaven who is infinite and eternal, that he is the creator, upholder, and preserver of all things, that he created us and the sidereal heavens and ordained and established a plan of salvation whereby we might advance and progress and become like him. . . .

The second greatest truth in all eternity pertains to the divine Sonship of the Lord Jesus Christ. It includes the eternal verity that he was foreordained in the councils of eternity to come to earth and be the Redeemer of men, to come and ransom men from the temporal and spiritual death brought upon them by the fall of Adam. . . .

The third greatest truth known to mankind is that the Holy Ghost of God is a revelator and a sanctifier, that he is a personage of spirit, that his assigned ministry and work in the eternal Godhead is to bear record of the Father and the son, to reveal them and their truths to men. . . . [*BYU Speeches of the Year* (1980), 79]

Chapter Twelve

The Constitution of the Church

D&C 20:37–46, 60–84; 22; 26

*H*istorical Setting: See the "historical setting" of chapter 11 for section 20. The *History of the Church* explains only that section 22 was given "in consequence of some who had previously been baptized desiring to unite with the Church without rebaptism." There is nothing said in the *History of the Church* about section 26 except it was one of three revelations received.

INTRODUCTION

What is the meaning of the new and everlasting covenant mentioned in section 22? The book of Hebrews refers to the "blood of the everlasting covenant" (Hebrews 13:20). Thus, the everlasting covenant is the agreement that Jesus Christ made with His Father that He would come to the earth and make the Atonement (see 3 Nephi 27:14). The new and everlasting covenant is the restoration of this covenant in the latter days, after the Great Apostasy, to prepare for the Second Coming. It is so defined later in the Doctrine and Covenants: "And even so I have sent mine everlasting covenant into the world, to be a light to the world, and to be a standard for my people, and for the Gentiles to seek to it, and to be a messenger before my face to prepare the way before me" (D&C 45:9).

SECTION 20 • OUTLINE

➢ 20:37   A commandment to the church concerning baptism.

a. Come forth with a broken heart and a contrite spirit.

b. Be willing to take upon you the name of Christ and have a determination to serve him unto the end.

c. Manifest by their works that they have received the Spirit of Christ unto a remission of their sins.

➤ 20:38–45   The duty of elders, priests, teachers, deacons, and members of Christ's church.

a. An apostle is an elder and is called to baptize, ordain, and administer the emblems of Christ's flesh and blood (vv. 38–40).

b. Confirm those baptized by the laying on of hands for the baptism of fire and the Holy Ghost (v. 41).

c. To teach, expound, exhort, and watch over the church (v. 42).

d. Confirm the church by laying on of hands, and giving of the Holy Ghost (v. 43).

e. Take lead and conduct all meetings as led by the Holy Ghost (vv. 44–45).

[The duties of priests, teachers, and deacons, vv. 46–59, was covered in chapter 8]

➤ 20:60   Every priesthood office is to be ordained according to the gifts and callings of God, and by the power of the Holy Ghost.

➤ 20:61–67   The elders are to meet in conference every three months or as directed.

a. The conferences are to do the business of the church (v. 62).

b. Elders receive licenses from other elders, and the vote of the church (v. 63).

c. Those ordained by a priest are to take a certificate to an elder and receive a license to perform his duties or receive it from a conference (v. 64).

d. No person in an organized branch is to be ordained to an office without the vote of that church (v. 65).

e. Presiding elders, traveling bishops, high councilors, high priests and elders may ordain where there is no branch of the church to have a vote (v. 66).

    f.   All presidents and presiding officers are to be ordained by the direction of a high council or general conference (v. 67).

➤ 20:68–71   The duty of the members of the church after baptism.

    a.   Elders and priest are to expound all things of the church before the members partake of the sacrament or are confirmed (v. 68).

    b.   They are to manifest their worthiness by godly walk and conversation (v. 69).

    c.   Children are to be blessed by the elders before the church (v. 70).

    d.   No one can be received into the church before the age of accountability (v. 71).

➤ 20:72–74   Baptism is to be administered to those who repent.

    a.   The words of the prayer are given (v. 73).

    b.   He or she shall be immersed in the water and come out of the water (v. 74).

➤ 20:75–79   The church shall meet together often to partake of the sacrament.

    a.   The elder or priest should kneel with the church and pray (v. 76).

    b.   The blessing on the bread is given (v. 77).

    c.   The blessing on the wine is given (vv. 78–79).

➤ 20:80   Members who have transgressed or been overtaken by faults should be dealt with as the scriptures direct.

➤ 20:81–84   Churches are to send one or more teachers to the conferences of the church.

    a.   They are to take the names of those who have united with the church since the last conference so the names of the church may be kept in order (v. 82).

    b.   They are to take the names of those who have been expelled from the church so they can be blotted out (v. 83).

    c.   Members who move from their residence shall take a letter certifying they are in good standing (v. 84).

Text and Commentary

D&C 20:37 • The Manner of Baptism

37 And again, by way of commandment to the church concerning the manner of baptism—All those who humble themselves before God, and desire to be baptized, and come forth with broken hearts and contrite spirits, and witness before the church that they have truly repented of all their sins, and are willing to take upon them the name of Jesus Christ, having a determination to serve him to the end, and truly manifest by their works that they have received of the Spirit of Christ unto the remission of their sins, shall be received by baptism into his church.

Those who were to be baptized were received on the same conditions as the Nephites when the law of Moses was fulfilled and a higher law was given, a broken heart and a contrite spirit (see 3 Nephi 9:20). One's heart is "broken" when one realizes that he or she contributed to the suffering of the Savior in Gethsemane. One's spirit is contrite when one becomes willing to surrender his or her will to the Savior. The remission of sins comes from the cleansing power of the Holy Ghost (see 2 Nephi 31:17). The determination to serve the Savior to the end can only be shown by one's works.

D&C 20:38–45 • The Duty of the Priesthood and Members

38 The duty of the elders, priests, teachers, deacons, and members of the church of Christ—An apostle is an elder, and it is his calling to baptize;

39 And to ordain other elders, priests, teachers, and deacons;

40 And to administer bread and wine—the emblems of the flesh and blood of Christ—

41 And to confirm those who are baptized into the church, by the laying on of hands for the baptism of fire and the Holy Ghost, according to the scriptures;

42 And to teach, expound, exhort, baptize, and watch over the church;

43 And to confirm the church by the laying on of the hands, and the giving of the Holy Ghost;

44 And to take the lead of all meetings;

45 The elders are to conduct the meetings as they are led by the Holy
Ghost, according to the commandments and revelations of God.

The calling of the Apostles, who are elders, is to baptize (v. 38).[26] The
members of the First Presidency and the Quorum of the Twelve Apostles,
are responsible for the missionary work and the baptism of new converts
(D&C 18:41). They are also to watch over the Church and see that
children are baptized when they "have arrived at the years of accountability" (D&C 18:42).

The other duties listed in the above verses (D&C 20:39–44) give the
general or basic duties of all priesthood holders. These seem self-explanatory, but a question may arise over the difference between verses 41 and
43. The first verse (41) refers to the individuals who are new converts
found in doing missionary work, and the second verse (43) is the baptism
of those who are born in the Church and reach the age of accountability.
It also shows the dual purpose of the laying on of hands after being
baptized; to give them the gift of the Holy Ghost, and to confirm them
members of the Church. Today these ordinances are given in the same
blessing.

Meetings conducted as led by the Holy Ghost are sometimes
interpreted, in parts of the Christian world, as spontaneous and disorga-
nized. When they feel an urge to pray, speak, or read they arise and do
so. There is no previous order or plan to follow. Such an interpretation
may be based on Paul's letter to the Corinthians: "How is it then,
brethren? when ye come together, every one of you hath a psalm, hath
a doctrine, hath a tongue, hath a revelation, hath an interpretation. Let
all things be done unto edifying" (1 Corinthians 14:26). The context of
Paul's instructions are advising against spontaneity, and concludes his
thoughts with: "Let all things be done decently and in order"
(1 Corinthians 14:40, see the whole chapter). Moroni gives a similar
instruction to the Nephites:

And their meetings were conducted by the church after the manner

---

[26] Some reject Peter as the author of his first New Testament epistle because he states:
". . . I exhort you, who am also an elder" (1 Peter 5:1). They rationalize that Peter was an
Apostle, not an elder, and thus the author was some one using Peter's name in writing the
epistle. The declaration of an Apostle being an elder answers the critics on this point.
Today, we address the members of the Twelve who are Apostles as "Elder."

of the workings of the Spirit, and by the power of the Holy Ghost; for as the power of the Holy Ghost led them whether to preach, or to exhort, or to pray, or to supplicate, or to sing, even so it was done. [Moroni 6:9]

The Holy Ghost was certainly an external force in directing the organization of the meetings beforehand, as well as guiding the happenings after the meeting began. The current operation of all the meetings in the Church today has come about exclusively through the power of the Holy Ghost.

Note: D&C 20:46–59 were discussed in chapter eight.

D&C 20:60 • Ordained According to the Gifts and Callings of God

60 Every elder, priest, teacher, or deacon is to be ordained according to the gifts and callings of God unto him; and he is to be ordained by the power of the Holy Ghost, which is in the one who ordains him.

Ordinations to the priesthood, whether Aaronic or Melchizedek, are to be done by the gifts and calling of God. Again the Book of Mormon people used the same pattern. "And after this manner did they ordain priests and teachers, according to the gifts and callings of God unto men; and they ordained them by the power of the Holy Ghost, which was in them" (Moroni 3:4). Since there are many gifts and different callings, each ordination will vary according to the dictates of the Spirit.

D&C 20:60–67 • Conferences and Church Business

60 The several elders composing this church of Christ are to meet in conference once in three months, or from time to time as said conferences shall direct or appoint;

62 And said conferences are to do whatever church business is necessary to be done at the time.

63 The elders are to receive their licenses from other elders, by vote of the church to which they belong, or from the conferences.

64 Each priest, teacher, or deacon, who is ordained by a priest, may take a certificate from him at the time, which certificate, when presented to an elder, shall entitle him to a license, which shall authorize him to perform the duties of his calling, or he may receive it from a conference.

65 No person is to be ordained to any office in this church, where there is a regularly organized branch of the same, without the vote of that church;

66 But the presiding elders, traveling bishops, high councilors, high priests, and elders, may have the privilege of ordaining, where there is no branch of the church that a vote may be called.

67 Every president of the high priesthood (or presiding elder), bishop, high councilor, and high priest, is to be ordained by the direction of a high council or general conference.

Conferences were to be held every three months, but if there was a need for a variance, it was subject to change (v. 61). The business of the Church (v. 62) includes such things as personnel changes in organizations, reorganization of boundaries, and financial matters. Today these periodic meetings are called stake or district conferences for the larger organization, and ward or branch conferences for the local organizations. With the growth of the Church has come the need for area or regional conferences from time to time. A general conference for all the members of the Church is still held semi-annually. Licenses were certificates or letters recognizing authority to perform certain duties (vv. 63–64). All of these appointments were to be approved by the vote of people of the unit involved (v. 65). Today this is called the sustaining of officers. Where there was no branch or unit organized, higher or traveling officers could perform these duties (v. 66). All of the above items were under the direction of the presiding or highest officer of that unit (v. 67). The above explanation simplified and general. But when the situation of the early Church is realized, and how the conference concept still fits the large organization of today, the above guidelines must be recognized as coming from above. The uneducated Joseph Smith did not figure out those conferences.

D&C 20:68–71 • Duties of the Members After Baptism

68 The duty of the members after they are received by baptism.—The elders or priests are to have a sufficient time to expound all things concerning the church of Christ to their understanding, previous to their partaking of the sacrament and being confirmed by the laying on of the hands of the elders, so that all things may be done in order.

69 And the members shall manifest before the church, and also before the elders, by a godly walk and conversation, that they are worthy of it,

that there may be works and faith agreeable to the holy scriptures—walking in holiness before the Lord.

70 Every member of the church of Christ having children is to bring them unto the elders before the church, who are to lay their hands upon them in the name of Jesus Christ, and bless them in his name.

71 No one can be received into the church of Christ unless he has arrived unto the years of accountability before God, and is capable of repentance.

The Lord does not want His people to be ignorant. He expects us to know and understand what the Church standards and teachings are. The partaking of the sacrament unworthily is serious in His eyes (see 3 Nephi 18:28, Mormon 9:29; 1 Corinthians 11:27). In partaking of the sacrament, we rededicate ourselves to live according to His gospel principles. He gives us the Holy Ghost to guide us, and He expects us to know why we are prompted to walk in the order that is given (D&C 20:68). Our example of "a godly walk and conversation" should illustrate what the scriptures teach (v. 69). Again, we may not walk according to the scriptures if we do not know what they teach.

The blessing of little children (v. 70) is not new to this dispensation. Jesus blessed the little children in Jerusalem (see Mark 10:13–16) and among the Nephites (see 3 Nephi 17:21–24). The age of accountability (v. 71) was later revealed to Joseph Smith to be eight years of age (see D&C 68:25), but it was also given to Abraham when the law of circumcision was established (see JST, Genesis 17:11). It has undoubtedly been that same age in all dispensations (see D&C 20:25–27). The Prophet Joseph made this declaration:

> "Do you believe in the baptism of infants?" asks the Presbyterian. No. "Why?" Because it is nowhere written in the Bible. Circumcision is not baptism, neither was baptism instituted in the place of circumcision. Baptism is for the remission of sins. Children have no sins. Jesus blessed them and said, 'Do what ye have seen me do.' Children are made alive in Christ, and those of riper years through faith and repentance. [*TPJS*, 314]

D&C 20:72–74 • Baptism by Immersion

72 Baptism is to be administered in the following manner unto all those who repent—

73 The person who is called of God and has authority from Jesus Christ to baptize, shall go down into the water with the person who has presented himself or herself for baptism, and shall say, calling him or her by name: Having been commissioned of Jesus Christ, I baptize you in the name of the Father, and of the Son, and of the Holy Ghost. Amen.

74 Then shall he immerse him or her in the water, and come forth again out of the water.

The gospel is eternal. Baptism is also an eternal law. Baptism by immersion was practiced in every dispensation (see Moses 6:64–65; Matthew 3:13–16; 3 Nephi 11:24–26). The baptismal prayer is the same as the one given to the Nephites with one slight difference. The prayer given by Alma when he baptized in the waters of Mormon (Mosiah 18:12–17) is different than the one given in this dispensation or by the Savior to the Nephites discussed here. However, the essential parts of the prayer; the authority from God, and the method of immersion, were included. Mormon, the abridger, may have paraphrased the prayer, or Alma was given a different prayer for that time period. (For further discussion see Monte S. Nyman, *These Records are True; Book of Mormon Commentary,* 2:409; Granite Publishing and Distribution, LLC Orem, Utah). The Nephite prayer says: "Having authority given me of" (3 Nephi 11:25), and the prayer given above says, "having been commissioned of;" (v. 73), an insignificant difference. We use the words of the prayer given to this dispensation because it was given to us.

D&C 20:75–79 • The Sacrament Prayers

75 It is expedient that the church meet together often to partake of bread and wine in the remembrance of the Lord Jesus;

76 And the elder or priest shall administer it; and after this manner shall he administer it—he shall kneel with the church and call upon the Father in solemn prayer, saying:

77 O God, the Eternal Father, we ask thee in the name of thy Son, Jesus Christ, to bless and sanctify this bread to the souls of all those who

partake of it, that they may eat in remembrance of the body of thy Son, and witness unto thee, O God, the Eternal Father, that they are willing to take upon them the name of thy Son, and always remember him and keep his commandments which he has given them; that they may always have his Spirit to be with them. Amen.

78 The manner of administering the wine—he shall take the cup also, and say:

79 O God, the Eternal Father, we ask thee in the name of thy Son, Jesus Christ, to bless and sanctify this wine to the souls of all those who drink of it, that they may do it in remembrance of the blood of thy Son, which was shed for them; that they may witness unto thee, O God, the Eternal Father, that they do always remember him, that they may have his Spirit to be with them. Amen.

The sacrament prayers are one of the few set prayers in the Church. The Nephites were told by the Savior what to include in the blessings, but the exact prayers were not recorded until later (see 3 Nephi 18:5–11; Moroni 4 and 5). They were the same. The content of the Nephite instructions are the same as the ones revealed today.

D&C 20:80–84 • Verifying Church Membership

80 Any member of the church of Christ transgressing, or being overtaken in a fault, shall be dealt with as the scriptures direct.

81 It shall be the duty of the several churches, composing the church of Christ, to send one or more of their teachers to attend the several conferences held by the elders of the church,

82 With a list of the names of the several members uniting themselves with the church since the last conference; or send by the hand of some priest; so that a regular list of all the names of the whole church may be kept in a book by one of the elders, whomsoever the other elders shall appoint from time to time;

83 And also, if any have been expelled from the church, so that their names may be blotted out of the general church record of names.

84 All members removing from the church where they reside, if going to a church where they are not known, may take a letter certifying that they are regular members and in good standing, which certificate may be signed by any elder or priest if the member receiving the letter is personally acquainted with the elder or priest, or it may be signed by the teachers or deacons of the church.

We are a record keeping church. With the growth of the Church and the invention of electronic mail, the membership of the Church is now processed in a different manner than attendance at conference, which was followed by regular mail (v. 81). However, the names of those added and blotted out are recorded. The same was done among the Nephites. "And they were strict to observe that there should be no iniquity among them; and whoso was found to commit iniquity, and Three Witnesses of the Church did condemn them before the elders, and if they repented not, and confessed not, their names were blotted out, and they were not numbered among the people of Christ" (Moroni 6:7). The book of Acts implies the Saints in Jerusalem had a similar process (see Acts 2:47, 5:14).

SECTIONS 22 & 26 • OUTLINE

➤ 22:1–4   Old covenants have passed away, this is a new and everlasting covenant which was from the beginning.

    a. A hundred baptisms availeth nothing, you cannot enter the strait gate by the law of Moses, neither by dead works (v. 2).

    b. Because of your dead works, this covenant and church is built up to me (v. 3).

    c. Enter into the strait gate as I commanded (v. 4).

➤ 26:1–2   Study the scriptures, preach, confirm the church in Colesville, labor on the land as required until the next conference.

    a. It shall be made known then what you shall do (v. 1).

    b. All things are done in the church by common consent, prayer and faith (v. 2).

TEXT AND COMMENTARY

D&C 22:1–4 • A New Covenant—A New Baptism

1 Behold, I say unto you that all old covenants have I caused to be done away in this thing; and this is a new and an everlasting covenant, even that which was from the beginning.

2 Wherefore, although a man should be baptized an hundred times it availeth him nothing, for you cannot enter in at the strait gate by the law of Moses, neither by your dead works.

3 For it is because of your dead works that I have caused this last covenant and this church to be built up unto me, even as in days of old.

4 Wherefore, enter ye in at the gate, as I have commanded, and seek not to counsel your God. Amen.

When an apostasy from the gospel of Jesus Christ takes place upon the earth, the Lord in due time will restore it again. Thus a new dispensation is ushered in.

> A dispensation of the gospel is a period of time in which the Lord has at least one authorized servant on the earth who bears the holy priesthood and the keys, and who has a divine commission to dispense the gospel to the inhabitants of the earth. When this occurs, the gospel is revealed anew, so that people of that dispensation do not have to depend basically on past dispensations for knowledge of the plan of salvation. [Bible Dictionary, 657]

This was the case concerning the above revelation (section 22). Therefore all old covenants were no longer in force. A good example of a new dispensation occurring without a prior general apostasy is when Christ came among the Nephites and fulfilled the law of Moses. He had initiated His higher law among them under the Melchizedek Priesthood, but still kept the law of Moses (see 2 Nephi 9:24–27). Nephi, son of Nephi, and others who had been given power to administer among the people before the law of Moses was fulfilled, were baptizing them unto repentance (see 3 Nephi 7:15–26). When Jesus appeared to them, Nephi and others were again given power and authority to baptize (3 Nephi 11:18–22). They were told: "ye shall baptize this people when I am again ascended into heaven" (3 Nephi 11:21). After he had ascended, on the second day, he returned and Nephi was the first one who "went down into the water and was baptized" (3 Nephi 19:11). As stated above, they could not enter in at the strait gate by the law of Moses (D&C 22:2). They were now acting under a new dispensation. To put trust into dead works (v. 3) is to rely on past traditions or authority which has been taken away. When a new authority has been restored, it must be followed (v. 4). The Lord gave the same advice (v. 4) as Jacob, brother of Nephi, told his brethren: "seek not to counsel the Lord, but to take counsel from his hand. For behold, ye yourselves know that he counseleth in wisdom, and in justice, and in great mercy, over all his works" (Jacob 4:10).

D&C 26:1–2 • The Law of Common Consent

1 Behold, I say unto you that you shall let your time be devoted to the studying of the scriptures, and to preaching, and to confirming the church at Colesville, and to performing your labors on the land, such as is required, until after you shall go to the west to hold the next conference; and then it shall be made known what you shall do.

2 And all things shall be done by common consent in the church, by much prayer and faith, for all things you shall receive by faith. Amen.

The admonition given to study, preach, and confirm the Colesville church was another way of saying, you have enough to do without worrying about additional things. They had recently been told the purposes of conferences, and also of the principle of the church members voting to approve things done in the Church (20:62–65). This reminder has brought about terminology often used in the Church, "the law of common consent," for approval of new officers or other transactions.

The everlasting covenant of the blood of Jesus Christ is re-established on the earth, and is preparing the way for His Second Coming.

General Authority Quotes

—President Joseph F. Smith • D&C 20:63, 65; 26:2

President Smith . . . presented the authorities of the Church, first remarking that "we desire that the brethren and sisters will all feel the responsibility of expressing their feelings in relation to the propositions that may be put before you. We do not want any man or woman who is a member of the Church to violate their conscience. Of course we are not asking apostates or non-members of the Church to vote on the authorities of the Church. We are only asking for members of the Church in good standing to vote on the propositions that shall be put before you, and we would like all to vote as they feel, whether for or against. [CR, October 1902, 83]

—President David O. McKay • D&C 20:68

There are three things fundamentally important associated with the administration of the sacrament. The first is self-discernment. It is introspection. . . . We should partake *worthily*, each one examining himself with respect to his worthiness.

Secondly, there is a covenant made. A *covenant* even more than a promise. . . . There is nothing more important than that. . . . A covenant, a promise, should be as sacred as life itself.

Thirdly, there is another blessing, and that is a sense of close relationship with the Lord. There is an opportunity to commune with oneself and to commune with the Lord. . . . [CR, April 1946, 112]

—*The Prophet Joseph Smith* • D&C 20:72–74

Baptism is a sign to God, to angels, and to heaven that we do the will of God, and there is no other way beneath the heavens whereby God hath ordained for man to come to Him and be saved, and enter into the kingdom of God, except faith in Jesus Christ, repentance, and baptism for the remission of sins, and any other course is in vain, then you have the promise of the Holy Ghost. [*HC*, 4:555]

—*The Prophet Joseph Smith* • D&C 20:84

. . . It is a fact, if I now had in my possession, every decision which had been made upon important items of doctrine and duties since the commencement of this work, I would not part with them for any sum of money; but we have neglected to take minutes of such things, thinking, perhaps, that they would never benefit us afterwards; which, if we had them now, would decide almost every point of doctrine which might be agitated. But this has been neglected, and now we cannot bear record to the Church and to the world, of the great and glorious manifestations which have been made to us with that degree of power and authority we otherwise could, if we now had these things to publish abroad. [*HC*, 2:198–199]

Chapter Thirteen

Magnify Thy Office

D&C 21; 23; 24

H *istorical Setting:* . . . We had received a commandment to organize the Church; and accordingly we met together for that purpose, at the house of Peter Whitmer, Sr., (being six in number) on Tuesday, the sixth of April, A.D., one thousand eight hundred and thirty. Having opened the meeting by solemn prayer to our Heavenly Father, we proceeded, according to previous commandment, to call on our brethren to know whether they accepted us as their teachers in the things of the kingdom of God, and whether they were satisfied that we should proceed and be organized as a church according to said commandment which we had received. To these several propositions they consented by a unanimous vote. I then laid my hands upon Oliver Cowdery, and ordained him an elder of the "Church of Jesus Christ of Latter-day Saints," after which he also ordained me also to the office of an elder of said Church. We then took bread, blessed it, and brake it with them; also wine, blessed it, and drank it with them. We then laid our hands on each individual member of the Church present, that they might receive the gift of the Holy Ghost, and be confirmed members of the Church of Christ. The Holy Ghost was poured out upon us to a very great degree—some prophesied, whilst we all praised the Lord, and rejoiced exceedingly. Whilst yet together, I received the following commandment: (section 21). [*HC*, 1:75–78]

There were other members present besides the "six in number." Following the recording of section 21, the *History of the Church* states: "Several persons who had attended the above meeting, being convinced of the truth and came forward shortly after, and were received into the Church; among the rest, my own father and mother were baptized, to my great joy and consolation" (*HC*, 1:79). The "six" indicates the legal number required to meet the New York State law, and "was according to previous commandment." It also suggests that the six men had already been selected. The vote to organize the Church further shows their following the "law of common consent" given in section 20 verses 63 and 65 before it was revealed in section 26 verse 2. The mention of laying on of hands for the receiving the gift of the Holy Ghost, and for confirmation as members of the Church, is also in accordance with previous revelation (D&C 20:41, 43).

The section heading of section 23, referring to "the earnest desires on the part of the five persons named to know of their respective duties," is all that is known of the historical setting of that revelation. Section 24 was the first of the three revelations given with no historical setting explained, as mentioned above (*HC*, 1:101); sections 25 and 26 were the other two.

Introduction

In section 24, Joseph Smith is told twice to "magnify thine office" (vv. 3, 9). What does it mean to "magnify" an office? While the generic meaning is to enlarge or make it look bigger, the scriptural meaning is given to us by Jacob, brother of Nephi:

> And we did magnify our office unto the Lord, taking upon us the responsibility, answering the sins of the people upon our own heads if we did not teach them the word of God with all diligence; wherefore, by laboring with our might their blood might not come upon our garments; otherwise their blood would come upon our garments, and we would not be found spotless at the last day. [Jacob 1:19]

A priesthood holder is accountable for the sins of all the people over whom he has a stewardship. If he does not warn them and teach them he must also answer for their sins (see Ezekiel 33:7–9). The things for which the Lord makes Joseph accountable, and the blessings that are promised if he magnifies his calling, are enumerated in the revelations now being considered.

SECTION 21 • OUTLINE

➤ 21:1–6   A record shall be kept among you and Joseph shall be called a seer, a translator, a prophet, an apostle, an elder of the church.

a.   He was inspired to lay the foundation of the church (v. 2).

b.   The church was organized and established on April 6, 1830 (v. 3).

c.   The church shall give heed unto his words as he receives them (v. 4).

d.   His words are as if they were from the Lord's mouth (v. 5).

e.   By giving heed, the gates of hell shall not prevail against them, darkness shall be dispersed, and the heavens shall shake for their good (v. 6).

➤ 21:7–9   The Lord has inspired Joseph to move the cause of Zion in mighty power.

a.   He has seen his weeping for Zion, and he shall mourn no more; his sins are remitted, the Lord's blessings will be on his head (v. 8).

b.   All those who labor in the Lord's vineyard will be blessed, and will believe on Joseph's words given to him by the Comforter (v. 9).

➤ 21:10–12   Joseph shall be ordained by Oliver Cowdery, mine apostle.

a.   Oliver is to be ordained an elder under the hand of Joseph, the First Elder (v. 11).

b.   Oliver is the first preacher of the church, before the world and Gentiles (v. 12).

TEXT AND COMMENTARY

D&C 21:1–5 • A Seer, a Translator, a Prophet, an Apostle, an Elder

1 Behold, there shall be a record kept among you; and in it thou shalt be called a seer, a translator, a prophet, an apostle of Jesus Christ, an elder of the church through the will of God the Father, and the grace of your Lord Jesus Christ,

2 Being inspired of the Holy Ghost to lay the foundation thereof, and to build it up unto the most holy faith.

3 Which church was organized and established in the year of your Lord eighteen hundred and thirty, in the fourth month, and on the sixth day of the month which is called April.

4 Wherefore, meaning the church, thou shalt give heed unto all his words and commandments which he shall give unto you as he receiveth them, walking in all holiness before me;

5 For his word ye shall receive, as if from mine own mouth, in all patience and faith.

Joseph's five titles (v. 1) are very significant. The first title, a seer, is less understood than the other four. A seer is defined in the Book of Mormon:

16 And Ammon said that a seer is a revelator and a prophet also; and a gift which is greater can no man have, except he should possess the power of God, which no man can; yet a man may have great power given him from God.

17 But a seer can know of things which are past, and also of things which are to come, and by them shall all things be revealed, or, rather, shall secret things be made manifest, and hidden things shall come to light, and things which are not known shall be made known by them, and also things shall be made known by them which otherwise could not be known.

18 Thus God has provided a means that man, through faith, might work mighty miracles; therefore he becometh a great benefit to his fellow beings. [Mosiah 8:16–18]

A seer is also defined in the Book of Mormon as one who has two stones fastened to two rims of a bow, or the Urim and Thummim. King Mosiah used these two stones to translate the Jaredite records (Mosiah 28:11).

13 And now he translated them by the means of those two stones which were fastened into the two rims of a bow.

14 Now these things were prepared from the beginning, and were handed down from generation to generation, for the purpose of interpreting languages;

15 And they have been kept and preserved by the hand of the Lord, that he should discover to every creature who should possess the land

the iniquities and abominations of his people;

16 And whosoever has these things is *called seer*, after the manner of old times. [Mosiah 28:13–16; italics added]

The Lord apparently called Joseph a translator, the second title in this revelation (D&C 21:1), in addition to his being a seer, as another testimony from the Lord that Joseph had indeed been the translator of the Book of Mormon.

The third title, a prophet, has several definitions. As used here, it designates Joseph as the head of the Church.

And again, the duty of the President of the office of the High Priesthood is to preside over the whole church, and to be like unto Moses—Behold, here is wisdom; yea, to be a seer, a revelator, a translator, and a prophet, having all the gifts of God which he bestows upon the head of the church. [D&C 107:91–92]

The fourth title, an Apostle, is a special witness "of the *name* of Christ—thus differing from all other officers in the church in duty of their calling" (D&C 107:23; italics added). He is also "an elder" (D&C 20:38), the fifth title in this revelation, "of the church through the will of God the Father." In other words Joseph was selected by the Father to lead the Church. "The grace of your Lord Jesus Christ" is recognizing "his strength and assistance to do good works that [Joseph] otherwise would not be able to maintain if left to [his] own means" (see LDS Bible Dictionary 697). The revelation then gives the example of Joseph laying the foundation of the Church, and building it up, and the date which was set by divine decree (vv. 2–3). All of this Joseph accomplished through the grace of Jesus Christ.

In recognizing what the Lord has done through Joseph, the Lord expects the Church collectively to follow Joseph's words and commandments as if from the Lord's own mouth (vv. 4–5). This is the same blessing as given in the preface, that "my word . . . shall be fulfilled, whether by my own voice or by the voice of my servants, it is the same" (D&C 1:38). Further verification of the Lord's word coming through the President of the Church was given by President Wilford Woodruff in a sermon regarding the Manifesto: (Doctrine and Covenants, p. 292)

The Lord will never permit me or any other man who stands as

President of this Church to lead you astray. It is not in the programme. It is not in the mind of God. If I were to attempt that, the Lord would remove me out of my place, and so He will any other man who attempts to lead the children of men astray from the oracles of God and from their duty. [Text accompanying Official Declaration 1, Doctrine and Covenants, p. 292. See also Joseph F. Smith *JD*, 24:192, and Marion G. Romney, CR, October 1960, 78]

D&C 21:6 • Three Promises to the Church

6 For by doing these things the gates of hell shall not prevail against you; yea, and the Lord God will disperse the powers of darkness from before you, and cause the heavens to shake for your good, and his name's glory.

There are three conditional blessings promised to the Church collectively if they will receive the words of the President of the Church (v. 6). The first blessing, that "the gates of hell shall not prevail against you," had been mentioned in the previous three revelations: to all members of the Church (10:69); to the Three Witnesses (17:8); and to Oliver Cowdery (18:5). In the context of this revelation, it may refer to a doctrine revealed much later, applicable to the third purpose of the Church given by President Spencer W. Kimball: "to redeem the dead by performing vicarious ordinances of the gospel for those who have lived on the earth" (CR, April 1981, 3). The gates of hell will be opened, by the vicarious ordinance of baptism, for the spirits who died and went there without receiving the restored gospel.

The second promised blessing, "the Lord God will disperse the powers of darkness from before you," has also been mentioned before, but in different terminology. Here it refers to the darkness of the apostasy that is overcome by the first mission of the Church given by President Spencer W. Kimball: "to proclaim the gospel of the Lord Jesus Christ to every nation, kindred, tongue, and people" (CR, April, 1981, 3). Thus the Church would "come out of darkness" as well as obscurity (D&C 1:30).

The third promised blessing, to "cause the heavens to shake for your good, and his names glory," is applicable to the second mission of the Church as given by President Spencer W. Kimball: "to perfect the Saints by preparing them to receive the ordinances of the gospel and by instruction and discipline to gain exaltation" (CR, April 1981, 3).

"Discipline" is an extension of being a disciple; one who follows instructions and is willing to be corrected, to be molded, and to be perfected. He is adherent to the teachings of his master, the Lord Jesus Christ. The shaking of the heavens, in this context, would be to send the angels from their spiritual abode to the earth to restore those ordinances and blessing that had been taken away (see D&C 128:20–21). As summarized by President Kimball, "All three are part of one work—to assist our Father in Heaven and His Son, Jesus Christ, in their grand and glorious mission 'to bring to pass the immortality and eternal life of man' (CR, April, 1981, 3).

The Apostle Paul admonished the Ephesians Saints in what could be interpreted to be the same three purposes: "And he gave some, apostles; and some, prophets; and some, evangelists; and some, pastors and teachers; For the perfecting of the saints, for the work of the ministry [proclaim the gospel], for the edifying of the body of Christ [redeem the dead]" (Ephraim 4:11–12). Therefore, the Church in Paul's day was basically the same as our day.

D&C 21:7–9 • The Cause of Zion

7 For thus saith the Lord God: Him have I inspired to move the cause of Zion in mighty power for good, and his diligence I know, and his prayers I have heard.

8 Yea, his weeping for Zion I have seen, and I will cause that he shall mourn for her no longer; for his days of rejoicing are come unto the remission of his sins, and the manifestations of my blessings upon his works.

9 For, behold, I will bless all those who labor in my vineyard with a mighty blessing, and they shall believe on his words, which are given him through me by the Comforter, which manifesteth that Jesus was crucified by sinful men for the sins of the world, yea, for the remission of sins unto the contrite heart.

The Lord's compliments to Joseph for his diligence, prayers, and weeping (v. 7–8) were surely deserved, and probably known to very few. He had endured persecution, ridicule, and threatenings, but through the Lord's blessings he had accomplished much (v. 8). The Lord took the opportunity to promise all who labor in His vineyard His same blessings. Even as Joseph believed in the words of Christ, those who labored in that time were blessed to believe in Joseph's words and the mission of Jesus Christ (v. 9). The same is true today. Jesus said: "If any man will do [the Father's] will, he shall know of the doctrine" (John 7:17). Those who will follow Joseph's teachings now, will believe in his words, and those who follow the living prophet of their day will know that what he speaks is true.

D&C 21:10–12 • Oliver—Apostle, Elder, First Preacher

10 Wherefore it behooveth me that he should be ordained by you, Oliver Cowdery mine apostle;

11 This being an ordinance unto you, that you are an elder under his hand, he being the first unto you, that you might be an elder unto this church of Christ, bearing my name—

12 And the first preacher of this church unto the church, and before the world, yea, before the Gentiles; yea, and thus saith the Lord God, lo, lo! to the Jews also. Amen.

Oliver was not to ordain Joseph an elder in the Melchizedek Priesthood, he had already done that (*HC*, 1:78). Therefore, he was to ordain him to be the leader of the Church. As an Apostle (D&C 18:9; 21:10), and the Second Elder of the Church, Oliver had that authority. He was "under [Joseph's] hand," but he was also "an elder unto this church of Christ" (v. 11). The same procedure is followed today when a new President of the Church is chosen. The President of the Quorum of the Twelve Apostles, the second in seniority, ordains him to that office.

"On Sunday, April 11th, 1830, Oliver Cowdery preached the first public discourse that was delivered by any of our number. Our meeting was held by previous appointment, at the house of Peter Whitmer, Sen., Fayette. Large numbers of people attended. . . ." (*HC*, 1:81). Seemingly, this was an honor bestowed upon Oliver for his faithfulness, since there is no longer a designation of this calling in the Church. However, his calling to preach before the world and the Gentiles was an ongoing call. The Lord's "lo, lo! to the Jews also" is probably indicating an eventual preaching to the Jews (v. 12). The word "lo" is an oft used biblical word, which means sudden, surprise, or calling attention to. The time for the Jews will come about in that manner.

SECTION 23 • OUTLINE

➤ 23:1–2   Oliver is blessed and under no condemnation.

    a. Beware of pride lest ye enter into temptation (v. 1).

    b. Make known thy calling unto the church and the world, and thy heart shall be opened to preach the truth (v. 2).

➤ 23:3   Hyrum is under no condemnation; his heart is opened, and his tongue loosed.

    a. His calling is to exhort and strengthen the church continually.

    b. His duty is to the church forever because of his family.

➤ 23:4   Samuel is under no condemnation; his calling is to exhort and strengthen the church. He is not yet called to preach.

➤ 23:5   Joseph Smith Sen. is under no condemnation, and is to exhort and strengthen the church forever.

➤ 23:5–6   Joseph Knight is to take up his cross, pray vocally before the world, in secret, in his family, among his friends, and in all places.

    a. It is your duty to unite with the true church (v. 7).

    b. Give your language to exhortation that your voice may receive the reward of the laborer (v. 7).

TEXT AND COMMENTARY

D&C 23:1–2 • Make Known Thy Calling Unto the Church

1 Behold, I speak unto you, Oliver, a few words. Behold, thou art blessed, and art under no condemnation. But beware of pride, lest thou shouldst enter into temptation.

2 Make known thy calling unto the church, and also before the world, and thy heart shall be opened to preach the truth from henceforth and forever. Amen.

Although Oliver had been given many revelations in his past year of association with the Prophet Joseph, either to him or in association with others (sections 6; 7; 8; 9; 13; 17; 18), he was still desirous to know more about his duties in the Church. This revelation is more about his personal standing and feelings than about his duties or callings in the Church. His warning against pride (v. 1) is a good example of the Lord trying to help with the problem that later took him out of the Church. His making his calling known to the Church and to the world (v. 2) may have somehow also helped him avoid his pride issue.

D&C 23:3 • Hyrum Smith's Family

> 3 Behold, I speak unto you, Hyrum, a few words; for thou also art under no condemnation, and thy heart is opened, and thy tongue loosed; and thy calling is to exhortation, and to strengthen the church continually. Wherefore thy duty is unto the church forever, and this because of thy family. Amen.

Hyrum Smith had been told in May, 1829 to "first seek to obtain my word, and then shall your tongue be loosed" (D&C 11:21). Now that the Book of Mormon had been published, and the Church was organized, Hyrum is told that "thy tongue is loosed; and thy calling is to exhortation."

Hyrum strengthening the Church *through* his family has been fulfilled to some extent, and will undoubtedly continue. Hyrum later succeeded his father as the Patriarch to the Church (D&C 124:124). "An evangelist is a Patriarch, even the oldest man of the blood of Joseph or of the seed of Abraham. Wherever the Church of Christ is established in the earth, there should be a Patriarch for the benefit of the posterity of the Saints, as it was with Jacob in giving his patriarchal blessing unto his sons, etc." (*TPJS*, 151). The Prophet Joseph's inspired statement is another evidence that his family were *literal* descendants of Joseph, who was sold into Egypt, and the patriarch Abraham (see D&C 113:1–6; Abraham 2:11). The office of the Church Patriarch remained in Hyrum's family until the need of the office was determined by the brethren to have passed. In the October 1979, General Conference it was announced: "Because of the large increase in the number of stake patriarchs and the availability of patriarchal service throughout the world, we now designate Elder Eldred G. Smith as a Patriarch Emeritus, which means that he is honorably relieved of all duties and responsibilities pertaining to the office of Patriarch to the Church." Stake Patriarchs are under the direction of the

Quorum of the Twelve. "It is the duty of the Twelve, in all large branches of the Church, to ordain evangelical ministers, as they shall be designated unto them by revelation—The order of this priesthood was confirmed to be handed down from father to son, and rightly belongs to the literal descendants of the chosen seed, to whom the promises were made" (D&C 107:39–40). Among the stake patriarchs, there are, and have been, many of the descendants of the Smith family serving as patriarchs.

In addition, two of Hyrum's descendants, Joseph F. Smith and Joseph Fielding Smith, became the sixth and the tenth Presidents of the Church after serving for many years as Apostles in the Quorum of the Twelve or as counselors in the First Presidency. Two other descendants of Hyrum Smith; Hyrum Mack Smith, and M. Russell Ballard, served or now serve as members of the Quorum of the Twelve. Hyrum's duty has truly been "unto the Church forever, and this because of thy family."

D&C 23:4 • Samuel Smith Thy Calling is Unto Exhortation

4 Behold, I speak a few words unto you, Samuel; for thou also art under no condemnation, and thy calling is to exhortation, and to strengthen the church; and thou art not as yet called to preach before the world. Amen.

Samuel, the younger brother of Joseph the Prophet, had just turned twenty-two years of age at the time this revelation was given. Why he was not yet called to preach before the world was probably because he was needed to help Joseph to exhort and strengthen the Church, or to assist his family in their temporal needs. He did serve a mission in the local area. On June 30, 1830, he was set apart by Joseph and later left a Book of Mormon with John P. Greene, a Methodist minister. This led to the conversion of Brigham Young and Heber C. Kimball and their families (*History of Joseph Smith by his Mother*, 169–170). His life came to an end due to over-exertion at the time of the martyrdom of his two brothers, Joseph and Hyrum. Many rightfully consider him a third martyr to the Restoration.

D&C 23:5 • Joseph Smith Sen.—The First Patriarch

5 Behold, I speak a few words unto you, Joseph; for thou also art under no condemnation, and thy calling also is to exhortation, and to

strengthen the church; and this is thy duty from henceforth and forever. Amen.

Joseph Smith Sr. was the first Patriarch to the Church, and upon his death the office was given to his son Hyrum (D&C 124:124). See the comments on Hyrum above.

D&C 23:6–7 • Joseph Knight—Unite With the Church

6 Behold, I manifest unto you, Joseph Knight, by these words, that you must take up your cross, in the which you must pray vocally before the world as well as in secret, and in your family, and among your friends, and in all places.

7 And, behold, it is your duty to unite with the true church, and give your language to exhortation continually, that you may receive the reward of the laborer. Amen.

Joseph Knight had "been so kind and thoughtful towards us while translating the Book of Mormon" (*HC*, 1:81), but had not as yet joined the Church. To take up your cross (v. 6) "is to deny himself of all ungodliness, and every worldly lust, and keep my commandments" (JST, Matthew 16:26). Joseph Knight was baptized by Oliver Cowdery later in the month of June, 1830 (see *HC*, 1:88). That he lived up to the other admonitions given him of the Lord is shown by the Prophet Joseph's statement about him in August of 1842: "for fifteen years he has been faithful and true, and even-handed and exemplary, and virtuous and kind, never deviating to the right hand or to the left. Behold he is a righteous man, may God Almighty lengthen out the old man's days. . . " (*HC*, 5:124).

SECTION 24 • OUTLINE

➤ 4:1–4   Joseph Jr. was called to write the Book of Mormon, and to the Lord's ministry.

     a.   The Lord has lifted him out of afflictions, counseled him, and delivered him from enemies, and from the power of Satan and darkness (v. 1).

     b.   Joseph is not excused from transgressions, go thy way and sin no more (v. 2).

    c.   Magnify thine office, sow thy fields and go to the Coles-ville church, and they shall support thee; I will bless them spiritually and temporally (v. 3).

    d.   If they do not receive thee, they will be cursed instead of blessed (v. 4).

➤ 24:5–9   Joseph should continue to call upon God, writing the things given by the Comforter, and expounding all scriptures unto the church.

    a.   It shall be given in the very moment what to speak and write, and they shall hear it, or they shall be cursed instead of blessed (v. 6).

    b.   He shall devote all his service to Zion and have strength (v. 7).

    c.   If he endure his many afflictions, the Lord will be with him unto the end of his days (v. 8).

    d.   In temporal labors he shall not have strength, attend to his church callings (v. 9).

➤ 24:10–14   Oliver shall bear Christ's name before the world and the church.

    a.   Do not suppose you can say enough, and I am with you to the end (v. 10).

    b.   In Christ he shall have glory, and not himself (v. 11).

    c.   Open thy mouth and declare my gospel, both day and night (v. 12).

    d.   Require not miracles except I command you (v. 13).

    e.   Do no miracles except it be required, that the scriptures be fulfilled (v. 14).

➤ 24:15–19   Wherever you enter and are not received, leave a cursing instead of a blessing, dust your feet as a testimony against them.

    a.   Whoso lays hands of violence on you, command them smitten in my name, and I will smite them according to your words and in my own due time (v. 16).

    b.   Those who go to the law with you shall be cursed by the law (v. 17).

  c. Take no purse, script, nor two coats, the church will give your needs (v. 18).

  d. You are called to prune my vineyard for the last time (v. 19).

TEXT AND COMMENTARY

D&C 24:1–3 • Joseph the Prophet Called and Chosen to Write

1 Behold, thou wast called and chosen to write the Book of Mormon, and to my ministry; and I have lifted thee up out of thine afflictions, and have counseled thee, that thou hast been delivered from all thine enemies, and thou hast been delivered from the powers of Satan and from darkness!

2 Nevertheless, thou art not excusable in thy transgressions; nevertheless, go thy way and sin no more.

3 Magnify thine office; and after thou hast sowed thy fields and secured them, go speedily unto the church which is in Colesville, Fayette, and Manchester, and they shall support thee; and I will bless them both spiritually and temporally;

4 But if they receive thee not, I will send upon them a cursing instead of a blessing.

The Prophet's translation of the Book of Mormon was repeatedly verified by the Lord. The things that the Lord had done for him (v. 1) are also verified, but we will leave that verification to the study of his history. Joseph was human, and had transgressions (v. 2), but they were not errors of translation or doctrine: "When did I ever teach anything wrong from this stand? When was I ever confounded? I want to triumph in Israel before I depart hence and am no more seen. I never told you I was perfect; but there is no error in the revelations which I have taught" (*TPJS,* 368). The Lord's admonition to "go thy way and sin no more" is a recognition that he is still the Lord's servant. It is the same admonition given to a woman in the New Testament (John 8:32), but is not comparable in any other way except in both situations they are invited to repent and change their ways.

The Lord had many important things for Joseph to do. Like the Twelve in Jerusalem, Joseph was not to "serve tables" (Acts 6:2). The Saints in the area would take care of his temporal needs for which they

would be blessed both temporally and spiritually (v. 3). This assistance was based on the same principle as tithing; we need the blessings, the Lord could get the financial needs of the Church elsewhere if he needed to do so. Those who would not give assistance would be cursed instead of blessed (v. 4). They needed those blessings whether they knew it or not.

D&C 24:5–9 • Expound All Scriptures Unto the Church

> 5 And thou shalt continue in calling upon God in my name, and writing the things which shall be given thee by the Comforter, and expounding all scriptures unto the church.
>
> 6 And it shall be given thee in the very moment what thou shalt speak and write, and they shall hear it, or I will send unto them a cursing instead of a blessing.
>
> 7 For thou shalt devote all thy service in Zion; and in this thou shalt have strength.
>
> 8 Be patient in afflictions, for thou shalt have many; but endure them, for, lo, I am with thee, even unto the end of thy days.
>
> 9 And in temporal labors thou shalt not have strength, for this is not thy calling. Attend to thy calling and thou shalt have wherewith to magnify thine office, and to expound all scriptures, and continue in laying on of the hands and confirming the churches.

As mentioned in the introduction above, Joseph was admonished twice to "magnify thine office" (vv. 3, 9). The things he was now instructed to do, he certainly magnified. With the Book of Mormon now published in (June of 1830) just before section 24 was received, he began working on translating or restoring the correct meaning to the Bible. This work is now referred to as the Joseph Smith Translation (see *HC,* 1:98–101). Thus the wording of verse 5, "continue in calling upon God, in my name, and writing the things which shall be given thee by the Comforter." The Joseph Smith Translation, hereafter referred to as the JST, continued as time permitted for many years. His expounding all scripture unto the Church (v. 5) extended to what he spoke as well. The Church was once more given a conditional blessing or cursing dependent on its receiving what he spoke (v. 6).

That Joseph magnified his calling in "expounding all scriptures unto the church" is evident from a study of his own *History of the Church.* In sermons, letters, editorials, and other communications either written by him, a scribe, or taken down in longhand by several men and then written and submitted to Joseph for approval, a vast knowledge of the scriptures and the gospel was given to the Church. According to this writer's count, there are only seven Old Testament Books (Ruth, Ezra, Esther, Lamentations, Micah, Habakkuk, and Haggai) and two New Testament Books (2 John, and 3 John) upon whose text Joseph does not specifically comment in his communications or in the JST. Most of these nine books are small compared to the other fifty-seven of the Bible.

Joseph's service and strength in Zion (v. 7) are illustrated in this statement: "We ought to have the building up of Zion as our greatest object" (*TPJS,* 160). Another statement shows his patience in afflictions (v. 8):

> My feelings at the present time are that, inasmuch as the Lord Almighty has preserved me until today, He will continue to preserve me, by the united faith and prayers of the Saints, until I have fully accomplished my mission in this life, and so firmly established the dispensation of the fullness of the priesthood in these last days, that all the powers of the earth and hell can never prevail against it. [*TPJS,* 258]

That Joseph continued in his spiritual calling at the expense of his temporal labors (v. 9) is also exemplified in the above statement made on August 31, 1842, over twelve years after the revelation being considered was given. As stated about him and Hyrum after their martyrdom, "They lived for glory; they died for glory; and glory is their eternal reward" (D&C 135:6).

D&C 24:10–14 • More Instructions to Oliver

> 10 And thy brother Oliver shall continue in bearing my name before the world, and also to the church. And he shall not suppose that he can say enough in my cause; and lo, I am with him to the end.

> 11 In me he shall have glory, and not of himself, whether in weakness or in strength, whether in bonds or free;

> 12 And at all times, and in all places, he shall open his mouth and declare my gospel as with the voice of a trump, both day and night. And I will give unto him strength such as is not known among men.

> 13 Require not miracles, except I shall command you, except casting

out devils, healing the sick, and against poisonous serpents, and against deadly poisons;

14 And these things ye shall not do, except it be required of you by them who desire it, that the scriptures might be fulfilled; for ye shall do according to that which is written.

Oliver was a "special witness of the *name* of Christ in all the world," and, as specified here, "to the Church" (v. 11; italics added). His calling differed "from other offices in the church" (D&C 107:23). He could not over-proclaim his calling, and the Lord promised to be with him to the end (v. 10). The glory of his calling was not his, but in whom he represented, no matter what the circumstances may bring (vv. 11–12). This admonition to Oliver reminds us of Alma's words in the baptismal covenant given to his people at the waters of Mormon:

> . . . now, as ye are desirous to come into the fold of God, and to be called his people, and are willing to bear one another's burdens, that they may be light; Yea, and are willing to mourn with those that mourn; yea, and comfort those that stand in need of comfort, and to stand as witnesses of God at all times and in all things, and in all places that ye may be in, even until death, that ye may be redeemed of God, and be numbered with those of the first resurrection, that ye may have eternal life— [Mosiah 18:8–9]

To Oliver, as an apostle of Jesus Christ, it was even more poignant.

Christ's Apostles are granted power to perform miracles, (v. 13, compare Mark 16:17–18; Mormon 9:22–24). However, Oliver is cautioned to use them sparingly, or as required to fulfill the scriptures (vv. 13–14). The Apostles must pray unto the Father in the name of Christ and the power to perform miracles will be granted (Mormon 9:21). Nevertheless, the Apostle must learn to "not ask that which is contrary to [his] will" (Helaman 10:5). This seems consistent with what Oliver was told.

D&C 24:15–19 • The Dusting of Feet

15 And in whatsoever place ye shall enter, and they receive you not in my name, ye shall leave a cursing instead of a blessing, by casting off the dust of your feet against them as a testimony, and cleansing your feet by the wayside.

16 And it shall come to pass that whosoever shall lay their hands upon you by violence, ye shall command to be smitten in my name; and, behold, I will smite them according to your words, in mine own due time.

17 And whosoever shall go to law with thee shall be cursed by the law.

18 And thou shalt take no purse nor scrip, neither staves, neither two coats, for the church shall give unto thee in the very hour what thou needest for food and for raiment, and for shoes and for money, and for scrip.

19 For thou art called to prune my vineyard with a mighty pruning, yea, even for the last time; yea, and also all those whom thou hast ordained, and they shall do even according to this pattern. Amen.

The cursing by dusting of feet, as a testimony of the Lord's name (vv. 15–16), was also to be used sparingly by the Apostles, following the same guidelines as given them for the use of miracles. The addition of "in mine own due time" leaves it in the Lord's hands, not the Apostles. Again the Lord knows what and when a dusting is appropriate. The Lord warns those who turn to the law [of the land] against His Apostles. The law will curse them. The Lord controls "the destinies of all the armies of the nations of the earth" (D&C 117:6). He also holds the destinies of the laws of the country, and will justify their actions "in his own due time" (see Matthew 10:18–20).

The things for Oliver to take with him (v. 18) are the same as told to the Jerusalem twelve (see Matthew 10:9–10). As the circumstances and cultures change or vary, the instructions may change, but the Church will provide for her Apostles (v. 18).

The pruning of the vineyard for the last time (v. 19) identifies the time period of the allegory of Zenos given to the house of Israel (Jacob 5:62–75). It is the latter days and the allegory is being fulfilled. Those whom the Lord ordained to restore His gospel in the last days did magnify their offices unto the Lord, especially the Prophet Joseph Smith, and those who have succeeded him are carrying on the marvelous work.

General Authority Quotes

—*President Harold B. Lee* • D&C 21:4–6

We have some tight places to go before the Lord is through with this church and the world in this dispensation, which is the last dispensation, which shall usher in the coming of the Lord. The gospel was restored to prepare a people ready to receive him. The power of Satan will increase. . . . We will see those who profess membership but secretly are plotting and trying to lead the people not to follow the leadership that the Lord has set up to preside in this church.

Now the only safety we have as members of this church is to do exactly what the Lord said to the Church in that day when the Church was organized [quotes 21:4–5]. There will be some things that take patience and faith. You may not like what comes from the authority of the Church. It may contradict your political views. It may contradict your social views. It may interfere with some of your social life. But if you listen to these things, as if from the mouth of the Lord himself, with patience and faith, the promise is that [quotes D&C 21:6]. [CR, October 1970, 152]

—President Harold B. Lee • D&C 23:1

. . . If you want to have an exercise in something that will startle you, read some of the warnings that were given through the Prophet Joseph Smith . . . warnings which had they heeded, some would not have fallen by the wayside. But because they did not heed, and they didn't clear up their lives, they fell by the wayside, and some had to be dropped from membership in the church. [CR, October 1972, 130]

—President Joseph Fielding Smith • D&C 24:3, 9

Sometimes we speak loosely of magnifying our priesthood, but what the revelations speak of is magnifying our callings in the priesthood, as elders, seventies, high priests, patriarchs, and apostles.

The priesthood held by man is the power and authority of God delegated to man on earth to act in all things for the salvation of mankind. Priesthood offices or callings are ministerial assignments to perform specially assigned service in the priesthood. And the way to magnify these callings is to do the work designed to be performed by those who hold the particular office involved. [CR, October 1970, 91]

—*The Prophet Joseph Smith* • D&C 24:9

The Prophet gave a very interesting discourse, which occupied more than two hours in delivery, and was listened to with marked attention, by the vast assembly present. [*TPJS*, 189]

Chapter Fourteen

Emma—the Elect Lady

D&C 25

*H*istorical Setting: Emma Hale was born 10 July 1804 at Harmony Pennsylvania. She met Joseph Smith in October of 1825, and they were married 18 January 1927. She was with Joseph at the Hill Cumorah, and waited in the wagon while he obtained the plates from which he translated the Book of Mormon. Her first child, Alvin, named after the Prophet's brother, was born and died on June 15, 1828. She was baptized into the Church June 28, 1830. [Information taken from Gracia N. Jones, *Emma and Lucy* (2005), 214.] They had been married 3½ years at the time this revelation was received. Those years were filled with persecution and trials, but she stood by her husband.

INTRODUCTION

What was the role of women in the newly restored Church of Christ? What place did music take? These two questions were not only answered, but went hand in hand as revealed in this revelation to Emma.

SECTION 25 • OUTLINE

➤ 25:1–4   Emma, my daughter, all who receive my gospel are sons and daughters.

        a.   If thou art faithful and walk in paths of virtue, I will preserve your life and give you an inheritance in Zion (v. 2).

> b. Thy sins are forgiven thee, thou art an elect lady whom I have called (v. 3).

> c. Murmur not because of what you have not seen, it is wisdom that they are withheld (v. 4).

➤ 25:5–10   The office of thy calling is to be a comfort to thy husband in his afflictions.

> a. Be a scribe while Oliver is sent where the Lord wills (v. 6).

> b. Thou shalt be ordained to expand scriptures, exhort the church according to my Spirit (v. 7).

> c. Joseph shall lay on hands for the Holy Ghost, and thy time shall be in writing and in learning (v. 8).

> d. Do not fear, Joseph shall support thee in the church, as revealed to him (v. 9).

> e. Lay aside the things of this world, and seek for things of a better (v. 10).

➤ 25:11–13   Make a selection of sacred hymns, as given thee, for the church.

> a. The Lord's soul delights in the song of the heart (v. 12).

> b. The song of the righteous is a prayer unto God, and answered with a blessing on their heads (v. 12).

> c. Lift up your heart and rejoice, and cleave unto your covenants (v. 13).

➤ 25:14–16   Continue in meekness and beware of pride. Let thy soul delight in thy husband, and the glory which shall come upon him (v. 14).

> a. Keep my commandments and you shall receive a crown of righteousness. If you do not, you cannot come where I am (v. 15).

> b. This is my voice unto all [women] (v. 16).

TEXT AND COMMENTARY

D&C 25:1–4 • Emma—an Elect Lady

1 Hearken unto the voice of the Lord your God, while I speak unto you, Emma Smith, my daughter; for verily I say unto you, all those who receive my gospel are sons and daughters in my kingdom.

2 A revelation I give unto you concerning my will; and if thou art faithful and walk in the paths of virtue before me, I will preserve thy life, and thou shalt receive an inheritance in Zion.

3 Behold, thy sins are forgiven thee, and thou art an elect lady, whom I have called.

4 Murmur not because of the things which thou hast not seen, for they are withheld from thee and from the world, which is wisdom in me in a time to come.

To receive the gospel is more than being baptized with water. It is also the baptism of fire and the Holy Ghost. The Prophet Joseph said: "You might as well baptize a bag of sand as a man [or woman] if not done in view of the remission of sins and getting the Holy Ghost. Baptism by water is but half a baptism, and is good for nothing without the other half—that is, the baptism of the Holy Ghost" (*TPJS,* 314). The baptism of the Holy Ghost brings a mighty change of heart, and by a righteous covenant with Christ to keep His commandments, you are born again and become His spiritual adopted son or daughter. The Prophet Joseph said "Being born again, comes by the Spirit of God through ordinances" (*TPJS,* 162). King Benjamin explained:

7 And now, because of the covenant which ye have made ye shall be called the children of Christ, his sons, and his daughters; for behold, this day he hath spiritually begotten you; for ye say that your hearts are changed through faith on his name; therefore, ye are born of him and have become his sons and his daughters.

8 And under this head ye are made free, and there is no other head whereby ye can be made free. There is no other name given whereby salvation cometh; therefore, I would that ye should take upon you the name of Christ, all you that have entered into the covenant with God that ye should be obedient unto the end of your lives. [Mosiah 5:7–8; see also vv. 1–6]

Emma had apparently had this born again experience, even though she had not been given the Holy Ghost as a gift. Cornelius was given an experience through the Holy Ghost before he was baptized (see Acts 10, especially v. 34, and v. 47). However, her salvation was not assured. Being born again does not guarantee salvation; it only puts one on the path to eternal life (see 2 Nephi 31:17–20). Emma was told she must "walk in the paths of virtue before [Christ]" in order to have her life preserved, or to receive [eternal] life (v. 2). King Benjamin explained: "Therefore, I would that ye should be steadfast and immovable, always abounding in good works, that Christ, the Lord God Omnipotent, may seal you his, that you may be brought to heaven, that ye may have everlasting salvation and eternal life, through the wisdom, and power, and justice, and mercy of him who created all things, in heaven and in earth, who is God above all. Amen" (Mosiah 5:15). Emma's sins were forgiven (v. 3), another evidence of her having had a spiritual experience.

Emma "as an elect lady" is unique. The only other such designation in the scriptures is the second Epistle of John which begins with "The elder unto the elect lady" (v. 1). The Prophet gave this explanation nearly twelve years later, on March 17, 1842, when he organized the Relief Society and Emma was called as the president of the organization. "I gave much instruction, read in the New Testament, and book of Doctrine and Covenants, concerning the Elect Lady, and showed that the elect meant to be elected to a certain work, and that the revelation [D&C 25] was then fulfilled by Sister Emma's election to the Presidency of the Society, she having been previously ordained to expound the Scriptures" (*HC*, 4:552–53). We assume his reading was from 2 John and the revelation that is now section 25. It would be profitable to have a more complete record of what he said. We also assume that an "elect lady" is not limited to the Relief Society President, but to other positions of leadership.

The reason for Emma's murmuring (v. 4) is not stated, but was probably because she had not seen the plates and the Urim and Thummim. We must admire her for her obedience, both before and after this revelation was given. The Lord's wisdom in not showing her these things was not explained, and we must not speculate or question His reasons.

D&C 25:5–10 • Emma's Callings

5 And the office of thy calling shall be for a comfort unto my servant, Joseph Smith, Jun., thy husband, in his afflictions, with consoling words, in the spirit of meekness.

6 And thou shalt go with him at the time of his going, and be unto him for a scribe, while there is no one to be a scribe for him, that I may send my servant, Oliver Cowdery, whithersoever I will.

7 And thou shalt be ordained under his hand to expound scriptures, and to exhort the church, according as it shall be given thee by my Spirit.

8 For he shall lay his hands upon thee, and thou shalt receive the Holy Ghost, and thy time shall be given to writing, and to learning much.

9 And thou needest not fear, for thy husband shall support thee in the church; for unto them is his calling, that all things might be revealed unto them, whatsoever I will, according to their faith.

10 And verily I say unto thee that thou shalt lay aside the things of this world, and seek for the things of a better.

The first calling or responsibility of Emma's was to be a comfort to her husband (v. 5). This is consistent with the Lord's injunction to Adam: "And I, the Lord God, said unto mine Only Begotten, that it was not good that the man should be alone; wherefore, I will make an help meet for him" (Moses 3:18; Genesis 2:18). It is also applicable to Paul's words to the Corinthians. "Nevertheless neither is the man without the woman, neither the woman without the man, in the Lord" (1 Corinthians 11:11). The Lord's partnership is good and works well when followed.

Emma's calling to be a scribe, while Oliver was sent elsewhere, was for the Joseph Smith Translation. The Book of Mormon was published, and Joseph's work on the Bible had commenced with the revelation on the words of Moses, received the month before (see *HC*, 1:98–101).

Emma's ordination to expound the scriptures and exhort the church, as given by the Spirit (v. 7), was what would be called in the Church today a setting apart. In the true sense of the word, it was the correct meaning, to appoint. Again, as the head of the Relief Society, she would fulfill this role. In the Church today, we ordain to the offices of Priesthood, and we set people apart to callings in the auxiliaries. "As it shall be given thee by my Spirit" (v. 7), indicates her role as a teacher and speaker to her sisters.

Some, not of our faith, may ask how the calling of Emma, to expound scripture and exhort the church can be correlated with Paul's directions to the Corinthians?

34 Let your women keep silence in the churches: for it is not permitted unto them to speak; but [they are commanded] to be under obedience, as also saith the law.

35 And if they will learn any thing, let them ask their husbands at home: for it is a shame for women to speak in the church. [1 Corinthians 14:34–35]

The answer is given in the Joseph Smith Translation of that passage:

34 Let your women keep silence in the churches; for it is not permitted unto them to *rule*; but to be under obedience, as also saith the law.

35 And if they will learn any thing, let them ask their husbands at home; for it is a shame for women to *rule* in the church. [JST, 1 Corinthians 14:35; italics shows changes]

The Priesthood offices are callings to rule, or, better understood, to preside or direct the meetings and activities of the Church. The role of women is outlined in the revelation being considered. Note that they do teach and direct as they expound the scriptures, exhort, write, and learn. Again it is a partnership that recognizes and appreciates the differences and similarities of both roles.

The promise of Joseph is laying his hands on her, to receive the Holy Ghost (v. 8), was fulfilled in early August, 1830 when she was confirmed a member of the Church and given the gift of the Holy Ghost. Although she had been baptized on June 28, 1830, the confirmation meeting was broken up by Joseph's arrest (see *HC*, 1:88–89), and due to continued persecution, she was not confirmed until August. Her being supported by her husband is the other side of the marriage partnership, although even in his calling to the Church, he also had a responsibility to support her (v. 9). Emma was also cautioned to "lay aside the things of the world, and seek for the things of a better" [world] (v. 10). In light of the terrible trials and tribulations she was encountering, the Lord was probably telling her it was worth it, and there were better days ahead.

D&C 25:11–13 • Music—the Song of the Heart

11 And it shall be given thee, also, to make a selection of sacred hymns, as it shall be given thee, which is pleasing unto me, to be had in my church.

12 For my soul delighteth in the song of the heart; yea, the song of the righteous is a prayer unto me, and it shall be answered with a blessing upon their heads.

13 Wherefore, lift up thy heart and rejoice, and cleave unto the covenants which thou hast made.

Another specific role for Emma was to select sacred hymns for the Church. The word "sacred" is a good beginning. The hymns should invite the Spirit of the Lord and not the darkness and spirit of Satan. Emma's selection was made into a small booklet that included the words of ninety hymns. It did not include the musical score for any of the hymns; The words were sung to popular or secular tunes of the day. Thirty four of those songs were written by members of the Church, and the others were collected from other denominations of that day. From that humble beginning, music has been emphasized in the Mormon culture as well as the Church culminating in the world famous "Mormon Tabernacle Choir."

The Lord wants our music to come from the heart, not the emotions or carnal, sensual, and devilish lyrics so common in the world. If our hymns come from a righteous spirit, they are a prayer unto Him which will be answered with a blessing upon our heads collectively and individually. Thus, the words of the hymn should be carefully listened to and internalized. They often carry great doctrinal messages, admonitions, or requests. The same pattern was apparently followed in Old Testament times. The book of Psalms is considered by many to be the Lord's Hymn Book for ancient Israel. The importance of music was also evident in the New Testament. A hymn was sung at the last supper (see Matthew 26:30). The Apostle Paul admonished the saints: "Speaking to yourselves in psalms and hymns and spiritual songs, singing and making melody in your heart to the Lord" (Ephesians 5:19; see also Colossians 3:16). We should follow the admonition given to Emma to rejoice and remember the covenants we have made (v. 14), especially as we sing and partake of the sacrament.

D&C 25:14–16 • Delight In Thy Husband

14 Continue in the spirit of meekness, and beware of pride. Let thy soul delight in thy husband, and the glory which shall come upon him.

15 Keep my commandments continually, and a crown of righteousness thou shalt receive. And except thou do this, where I am you cannot come.

16 And verily, verily, I say unto you, that this is my voice unto all. Amen.

These closing verses to Emma are an encouragement to continue in meekness; a warning against pride; a reminder to delight in her husband and the glory that he shall obtain (v. 14), something the Lord apparently knew he would do. They also admonish her to keep the commandments continually, with a conditional promise of a crown of righteousness. They warn her of not being able to come where Christ is if she does not keep the commandments (v. 15). However, the most important message to all of us is that the entire revelation given to Emma is applicable to all of us (v. 16). Do we honor our husbands and wives, and live up to our partnerships? Do we know and appreciate the role of music in the Church and in our own lives? Are we keeping the commandments continually? Will we be able to go where Christ is?

General Authority Quotes

—The First Presidency and Council of the Twelve Apostles • D&C 25:1

All Human Beings—male and female—are created in the image of God. Each one is a beloved spirit son or daughter of heavenly parents, and, as such, each has a divine nature and destiny. Gender is an essential characteristic of individual premortal, mortal, and eternal identity and purpose. [*The Family: A Proclamation to the World*]

—President Harold B Lee • D&C 25:11–13

My experience of a lifetime, and particularly the last thirty-two years as a General Authority, convinces me that the most effective preaching of the gospel is when it is accompanied by beautiful, appropriate music. [CR, April, 1973, 181]

—Elder Boyd K, Packer • D&C 25:11–13

. . . So often our leaders in music feel the necessity, feel responsible, to "up-grade" and introduce "culture" into our worship services by performing music that is either secular or sectarian, chosen solely because it demonstrates their ability, but not in keeping with the

Spirit of the Gospel. Such music has an important place—but not in our worship services.

Someone will now say that I don't know much about music, to this I quickly confess. I do know, however, when the Spirit of the Lord is present; and it does not often yield itself to music that is merely well-performed or dignified any more than it is called forth by the *speech of the world,* however articulate it might be.

What do you do at a time like this, when the stage of your mind is commandeered by these imps of unclean thinking? Whether they be the gray ones that look almost white; or the dustier ones, more questionable yet; or the filthier ones, which leave no room for doubt, what do you do?

This, then is what I would teach you: Let me suggest that you choose from among the sacred music of the Church one favorite hymn. I have reason for suggesting that it be a Latter-day Saint Hymn; one with lyrics that are uplifting and the music reverent. Select one that, when it is properly rendered, makes you feel something akin to inspiration.

Now go over it in your mind very thoughtfully a few times. Memorize the words and the music. Even though you have had no musical training, even though you do not play an instrument, and even though your voice may leave something to be desired, you can think through a hymn. I suspect you already have a favorite. I have stressed how important it is to know that you can only think of *one* thing at a time. Use this hymn as your emergency channel. Use this as the place for your thoughts to go. Anytime you find that these shady actors have slipped in from the sideline of your thinking onto the stage of your mind, think through this hymn. "Put the record on," as it were, and then you will begin to know something about controlling your thoughts. "Music is one of the most forceful instruments for governing the mind and spirit of man" (William F. Gladstone). It will change the whole mood on the stage of your mind. Because it is clean and uplifting and reverent, the baser thoughts will leave. . . .
[*That All May Be Edified* (1982), 38–39]

—*Elder Jay E. Jensen* • D&C 25:11–13

. . . My testimony and conversion to the restored gospel were strongly influenced by the singing of the hymns of Zion as a young boy. . . . Hymns are an essential part of our church meetings. [They] invite the Spirit of the Lord. They often do this quicker than anything else we can do. President J. Reuben Clark Jr. said, "We get nearer to the Lord through music than perhaps through any other thing except prayer."

Music in church meetings and classes should facilitate a spirit of worship, revelation and testimony. For sacrament meetings, the bishopric or branch presidency is responsible to select or approve music. They ensure that the music, the words, and the musical instruments are sacred, dignified, and will promote worship and revelation. Music becomes a performance when it draws attention to itself. . .

The First Presidency has reminded us:

"Latter-day Saints should fill their homes with the sound of worthy music. . . . We hope the hymnbook will take a prominent place among the scriptures and other religious books in our homes. The hymns can bring families a spirit of beauty and peace and can inspire love and unity among family members.

"Teach children to love the hymns. Sing them on the Sabbath, in [family] home evening, during scripture study, at prayer time. Sing as you work, as you play, and as you travel together. Sing hymns as lullabies to build faith and testimony in your young ones."

Important lessons I have learned and seek to apply about hymns are:

1. Strive to be more punctual to meetings, sit quietly and listen to the prelude music, and experience reverence and revelation.

2. Exit meetings more reverently, allowing the postlude music to extend the spirit of the meeting.

3. Sing the hymns. I see some who have access to hymnals but do not sing.

4. Choose hymns appropriate to the meetings and messages.

5. Use hymns to introduce or to emphasize scriptures and gospel truths in lessons and classes.

6.   Listen to the hymns more frequently in our homes, inviting the Spirit to prevail.

I pray that we may eliminate any inappropriate music from our lives and follow the counsel of the First Presidency: "Brothers and sisters, let us use the hymns to invite the Spirit of the Lord into our congregations, our homes, and our personal lives. Let us memorize and ponder them, recite and sing them, and partake of their spiritual nourishment. Know that the song of the righteous is a prayer unto our Heavenly Father, and it shall be answered with a blessing upon [your] heads. . . . [*Ensign*, May 2007, 11–13].

NOTE: The First Presidency quote to which Elder Jensen refers is from the First Presidency Preface in the front of the *Hymns of the Church of Jesus Christ of Latter-day Saints* [1985]. It is recommended that the entire Preface be read.

Chapter Fifteen

The Whole Armor of God

D&C 27

*H*istorical Setting: Early in the month of August, Newel Knight and his wife paid us a visit at my place in Harmony, Pennsylvania; and as neither his wife nor mine had been as yet confirmed, it was proposed that we should confirm them, and partake together of the Sacrament, before he and his wife should leave us. In order to prepare for this I set out to procure some wine for the occasion, but had gone only a short distance when I was met by a heavenly messenger, and received the following revelation [section 27], the first four paragraphs of which were written at this time, and the remainder the September following. [*HC*, 1:106]

INTRODUCTION

We are commanded to attend sacrament meetings (D&C 59:12). However, there is one sacrament meeting that may only be attended by invitation. That sacrament meeting will be presided over by the Lord Jesus Christ. This revelation tells us who will be in attendance, and how those invited to attend will have to prepare for the meeting.

SECTION 27 • OUTLINE

➤ 27:1–4   It matters not what you eat or drink when ye partake of the sacrament, if done with an eye single to Christ's glory.

    a.   Remember Christ's body which was laid down for you (v. 2).

    b.   Remember Christ's blood which was shed for the remission of your sins (v. 2).

    c.   Do not purchase wine or strong drink from your enemies (v. 3).

    d.   Partake of none except it is made new among you (v. 4).

➤ 27:5–14   The hour cometh when Christ will drink of the fruit of the vine with those of his Father's kingdom.

    a.   Moroni, to whom he committed the keys of the stick of Ephraim (v. 5).

    b.   Elias, to whom he committed the keys of the restoration of all things (v. 6).

    c.   John, son of Zacharias, who ordained Joseph and Oliver to the first priesthood, even as Aaron (vv. 7–8).

    d.   Elijah, to whom he committed the keys of turning the hearts of the fathers to the children, and the hearts of the children to the fathers (v. 9).

    e.   Joseph, Jacob, Isaac, Abraham, your fathers and their promises remain (v. 10).

    f.   Michael, or Adam, father of all, prince of all, the ancient of days (v. 11).

    g.   Peter, James, and John, to whom he committed the keys of the dispensation of the fulness of times (vv. 12–13).

    h.   All whom the Father hath given Christ out of the world (v. 14).

➤ 27:15–18   Gird up your loins and take upon you the whole armor of God.

    a.   Your loins girt about with truth (v. 16).

    b.   A breastplate of righteousness (v. 16).

    c.   Your feet shod with the preparation of the gospel (v. 16).

    d.   Take the shield of faith to quench the fiery darts of the wicked (v. 17).

    e.   Take the helmet of salvation, and the sword of my Spirit (v. 18).

➤ 27:18   Be faithful until I come and ye shall be caught up to be with me.

TEXT AND COMMENTARY

D&C 27:1–4 • Remember My Body and My Blood

1 listen to the voice of Jesus Christ, your Lord, your God, and your Redeemer, whose word is quick and powerful.

2 For, behold, I say unto you, that it mattereth not what ye shall eat or what ye shall drink when ye partake of the sacrament, if it so be that ye do it with an eye single to my glory—remembering unto the Father my body which was laid down for you, and my blood which was shed for the remission of your sins.

3 Wherefore, a commandment I give unto you, that you shall not purchase wine neither strong drink of your enemies;

4 Wherefore, you shall partake of none except it is made new among you; yea, in this my Father's kingdom which shall be built up on the earth.

The ingredients used for the sacrament were and are symbolic. The bread represented the body of Christ which He gave up on the cross (see Luke 23:46, or "laid down for you" (v. 2). He had the power to do this because He was born of a mortal woman, and He had power to take it up again because of His immortal Father (see John 10:17–18). The wine, or now water, represented the blood that was shed from every pore in Gethsemane when He paid the eternal demands of Justice with His merciful suffering "for the remission of your sins" (v. 2), and for all the sins of the world. These things we are to remember as we partake of the sacrament. While we use the traditional elements of bread and water, if circumstances required it, we could substitute either of them.

"An eye single to my glory" (v. 2) is used repeatedly throughout the Doctrine and Covenants. It means to recognize that the death and suffering of Christ was done to bring Him and us glory through "the immortality [resurrection] and eternal life [perfection] of man" (Moses 1:39; see also D&C 132:31). In the words of Joseph Smith: "we came to this earth that we might have a body and present it pure before God in the celestial kingdom" (*TPJS*, 181). Through the literal resurrection and infinite and eternal atonement of Jesus Christ this was made possible. The sacrament is to remind us of this sacrifice.

The age old argument of whether wine was drunk by the Saints in New Testament times is seemingly put to rest with this revelation. If we are not to drink "wine neither strong drink" (D&C 27:3), or "none except it is made new among you" (v. 4), was it not the same in that or any other time period? The fulness of the gospel is the same in all dispensations (see D&C 20:26; Moses 6:59–61).

D&C 27:5 • Moroni, the Americas' Angel

> 5 Behold, this is wisdom in me; wherefore, marvel not, for the hour cometh that I will drink of the fruit of the vine with you on the earth, and with Moroni, whom I have sent unto you to reveal the Book of Mormon, containing the fulness of my everlasting gospel, to whom I have committed the keys of the record of the stick of Ephraim;

At the "last supper" with His beloved apostles in Jerusalem, prior to His crucifixion, Jesus partook of the sacrament with them:

> 26 And as they were eating, Jesus took bread, and blessed it, and brake it, and gave it to the disciples, and said, Take, eat; this is my body.
>
> 27 And he took the cup, and gave thanks, and gave it to them, saying, Drink ye all of it;
>
> 28 For this is my blood of the new testament, which is shed for many for the remission of sins.
>
> 29 But I say unto you, I will not drink henceforth of this fruit of the vine, until that day when I drink it new with you in my Father's kingdom. [Matthew 26:26–29]

The Savior refers to this promised event in this revelation. More detail is revealed about this glorious event in a later revelation (D&C 116), but we might observe now that He again refers to drinking "the fruit of the vine" in both references; implying not a fermented wine, but one of their own make.

Perhaps Moroni was mentioned first among the invited guests to the Savior's great sacrament meeting because of his closeness in time and personal visits to the Prophet Joseph. There are, however, some other considerations. According to Elder Orson Hyde in a speech given on July 4, 1854:

> . . . This same angel [Moroni] presides over the destinies of America, and feels a lively interest in all our doings. He was in the camp of Washington; and by an invisible hand, led on our fathers to conquest and victory, and all this to open and prepare the way for the Church and kingdom of God to be established on the western hemisphere, for the redemption of Israel and the salvation of the world.
>
> This same angel was with Columbus, and gave him impressions, by dreams and by visions, respecting the new world. Trammeled by poverty and by an unpopular cause, yet his persevering and unyielding heart would not allow an obstacle in his way too great for him to overcome; and the angel of God helped him—was with him on the stormy deep, calmed the troubled elements, and guided his frail vessel to the desired haven. Under the guardianship of this same angel, or Prince of America, have the United States grown, increased, and flourished, like the sturdy oak by the rivers of water. [Donl H. Peterson, *Moroni, Ancient Prophet Modern Messenger* (1983), 80]

Support for the truthfulness of Elder Hyde's remarks is given in the "Appendix" to the Doctrine and Covenants section 133: "And now, verily saith the Lord, that these things might be known among you, O inhabitants of the earth, I have sent forth mine angel flying through the midst of heaven, having the everlasting gospel, who hath appeared unto some and hath committed it unto man, who shall appear unto many that dwell on the earth" (v. 36).

The reference to Moroni also substantiates that Moroni's coming was the fulfillment of the prophecy of John the Revelator, "another angel fly in the midst of heaven, having the everlasting gospel to preach unto them that dwell on the earth" (Revelation 14:6–7). It is also one of many verifications of Moroni's declaration to Joseph Smith that "the fulness of the everlasting Gospel was contained in" the plates deposited in the Hill Cumorah (JS—H 1:34). Moroni's having "the keys of the record of the stick of Ephraim" committed to him, also justifies the interpretation of Ezekiel 37:15–20 being a prophecy of the coming forth of the Book of Mormon. Therefore, much of importance to the theology of the Church is contained in just this one verse.

D&C 27:6–8 • Elias—Noah—Gabriel

6 And also with Elias, to whom I have committed the keys of bringing to pass the restoration of all things spoken by the mouth of all the holy prophets since the world began, concerning the last days;

7 And also John the son of Zacharias, which Zacharias he (Elias) visited and gave promise that he should have a son, and his name should be John, and he should be filled with the spirit of Elias;

8 Which John I have sent unto you, my servants, Joseph Smith, Jun., and Oliver Cowdery, to ordain you unto the first priesthood which you have received, that you might be called and ordained even as Aaron;

The Elias spoken of in these two verses is Noah. The Prophet Joseph declared that the keys of the Priesthood were first given to Adam: "Then to Noah, who is Gabriel: he stands next in authority to Adam in the priesthood; he was called of God to this office, and was the father of all living in this day, and to him was given the dominion. These men held keys first on earth and then in heaven" (*TPJS,* 157). The angel who appeared unto Zacharias and told him he would have a son, identified himself as Gabriel (see Luke 1:11–19). Gabriel was acting in the spirit of Elias. "The spirit of Elias is to prepare the way for a greater revelation of God, which is the priesthood of Elias, or the Priesthood that Aaron was ordained unto. And when God sends a man into the world to prepare for a greater work, holding the keys of the power of Elias, it was called the doctrine of Elias, even from the early ages of the world" (*TPJS,* 337).

John the Baptist came to prepare the way before Jesus, and acted in the spirit of Elias, having been given those keys by Gabriel or Noah. Jesus taught Peter, James, and John about two Eliases:

9 And his disciples asked him, saying, Why then say the Scribes that Elias must first come?

10 And Jesus answered and said unto them, Elias truly shall first come, and restore all things, *as the prophets have written.*

11 And *again* I say unto you that Elias has come already, *concerning whom it is written, Behold, I will send my messenger, and he shall prepare the way before me*; and they knew him not, and have done unto him, whatsoever they listed.

12 Likewise shall also the Son of man suffer of them.

13 *But I say unto you, Who is Elias? Behold, this is Elias, whom I send to prepare the way before me.*

14 Then the disciples understood that he spake unto them of John the Baptist, *and also of another who should come and restore all things, as it is written by the prophets.* [JST, Matthew 17:10–14; italics show the additions made by Joseph Smith]

The "another who should come and restore all things" (v. 14) was Gabriel, or Noah. Since Noah restored all things after the flood, he was apparently given the keys to restore all things in the dispensation of the fullness of times. John the Baptist, who restored "the first priesthood, or the priesthood of Aaron," was discussed in chapter 8 of this work. He and Gabriel, or Noah, will attend the great sacrament meeting as part of their work under the "spirit of Elias," or as an Elias.

D&C 27:9 • Elijah—Turning the Hearts of the Children

9 And also Elijah, unto whom I have committed the keys of the power of turning the hearts of the fathers to the children, and the hearts of the children to the fathers, that the whole earth may not be smitten with a curse;

The keys that were committed to Elijah were prophesied by Malachi, the last Old Testament Prophet. This prophecy was quoted by Moroni, when he appeared to Joseph Smith, with a different wording, particularly the first part that is not quoted here (JS—H 1:38–39). This prophecy and the different wording were discussed in chapter 3 of this work. It will be discussed further in section 110 verses 13–15, his appearance in the Kirtland Temple.

D&C 27:10 • Your Fathers—the Literal Seed

10 And also with Joseph and Jacob, and Isaac, and Abraham, your fathers, by whom the promises remain;

The covenant made with Abraham (Genesis 12:2–3; Abraham 2:9–12) was passed on to his birthright successors Isaac, Jacob [Israel], and Joseph. "Your fathers" tells us that Joseph Smith and early Church members are the literal seed of these covenant people. As prophesied by the Old Testament prophet Amos, they were sifted, or scattered, "among all nations" (Amos 8:9). Therefore, these early Saints are some of those who were scattered, but were now gathered back. We will see many other references that show the literal seed was among those who are being gathered. "The promises remain," is telling us that the covenant made to these ancient men is still in force. Furthermore, the Prophet Joseph was told that the covenant made to Abraham would be fulfilled through him (see D&C 124:58). The Book of Mormon tells us that the covenant "should be fulfilled in the latter days" (1 Nephi 15:18). It also tells us that it will be fulfilled after the remnants of the Nephites and Lamanites, who were not destroyed, "have been driven and scattered by the Gentiles" (Mormon 5:20). Those times were after the Americas were rediscovered.

D&C 27:11 • Michael—Adam—the Prince—the Ancient of Days

11 And also with Michael, or Adam, the father of all, the prince of all, the ancient of days;

Michael, or Adam, and his role in the great sacrament meeting will be discussed in section 116. The Book of Mormon verifies that all men belong to Adam (see 2 Nephi 9:21). The Pearl of Great Price and later Doctrine and Covenants revelations verify that Adam was "the first of all men" (Moses 1:34; D&C 84:16). The ancient of days is part of a prophecy of the Old Testament Prophet Daniel that will also be discussed later (D&C 116).

D&C 27:12–14 • Peter, James, and John—the Dispensation Link

12 And also with Peter, and James, and John, whom I have sent unto you, by whom I have ordained you and confirmed you to be apostles, and especial witnesses of my name, and bear the keys of your ministry and of the same things which I revealed unto them;

13 Unto whom I have committed the keys of my kingdom, and a dispensation of the gospel for the last times; and for the fulness of times, in the which I will gather together in one all things, both which are in heaven, and which are on earth;

14 And also with all those whom my Father hath given me out of the world.

The keys committed by Peter, James, and John, link their dispensation with the dispensation of the fulness of times (vv. 12–13), the last dispensation of this earth (see Ephesians 1:10, D&C 112:30). The restoration of the Melchizedek Priesthood was discussed in chapter 9 of this work. Those "out of the world," who are given to Christ by the Father (D&C 27:14), are those who have been assured of eternal life, or had their calling and election made sure (see D&C 131:5 and discussion in the next volume of this work). The original Twelve in Jerusalem, except one, were given to Christ by the Father (John 17:6, 12). Those who attain this status are not made known to the world, or other Church members.

D&C 27:15–16 • The Whole Armor of God

> 15 Wherefore, lift up your hearts and rejoice, and gird up your loins, and take upon you my whole armor, that ye may be able to withstand the evil day, having done all, that ye may be able to stand.
>
> 16 Stand, therefore, having your loins girt about with truth, having on the breastplate of righteousness, and your feet shod with the preparation of the gospel of peace, which I have sent mine angels to commit unto you;

Paul taught the same symbolism in Ephesians 6:11–18. There are a few differences in the wording of the two texts, but none of significance.

There are four vulnerable areas of one's body that need to be protected when a warrior goes into battle; the loins, the heart, the feet, and the head. An injury to the loin area will incapacitate, preventing offensive and defensive ability, but will not usually cause death. One bullet, spear, or other object that penetrates the heart can cause death. An injury to the feet will hamper one's mobility and leave him open to further attack. An injury to the head will leave him less capable to understand and reason as the battle continues. The symbolism used by the Lord in this revelation and by Paul, undoubtedly from the same source, is how to protect these four vulnerable areas from the attacks of Satan and his evil co-workers.

The spiritual armor to protect the loins is a girdle of truth (v. 16). Unchastity is the third most serious sin, and will injure the spirit and the body. The Spirit withdraws from those who are unchaste in mind, or engage in immoral acts of adultery, fornication, homosexuality, pornography, or "do anything like unto it" (D&C 59:6). He who lusts after a woman "shall not have the Spirit" (D&C 42:23; 3 Nephi 12:28–29). "No unclean thing can dwell with God" (1 Nephi 19:21). "I, the Lord God, delight in the chastity of women. And whoredoms are an abomination before me" (Jacob 2:28). Chastity and virtue are the "most dear and precious above all things" (Mormon 9:9).

The spiritual armor to protect the heart is a breastplate of righteousness "to be able to withstand the evil day" (D&C 27:16). "The righteous need not fear, for they are those who shall not be confounded" (1 Nephi 22:22). "The devil has no power over us only as we permit him, the moment we revolt at anything which comes from God, the devil takes power" (*TPJS*, 181). The priesthood has more power than Satan, but "the rights of the priesthood are inseparably connected with the powers of heaven, and . . . cannot be controlled nor handled only upon the principles of righteousness" (D&C 121:36).

The spiritual armor to protect our feet is the preparation of the gospel of peace (D&C 27:16). We, and especially our youth, must set goals to live the word of wisdom, avoid the usage of drugs, prepare to receive the priesthood, serve missions, marry in the temple, and by faith "lay hold on every good thing" (Moroni 7:21). Living the gospel will bring "peace in this world, and eternal life in the world to come" (D&C 59:23).

The three pieces of armor discussed above, and the helmet of salvation spoken of below, are defensive measures to protect ourselves. We must also take the offense to win the battle against Satan. Satan's best tool is for good men to do nothing.

D&C 27:17–18 • The Shield, the Helmet, and the Sword

17 Taking the shield of faith wherewith ye shall be able to quench all the fiery darts of the wicked;

18 And take the helmet of salvation, and the sword of my Spirit, which I will pour out upon you, and my word which I reveal unto you, and be agreed as touching all things whatsoever ye ask of me, and be faithful until I come, and ye shall be caught up, that where I am ye shall be also. Amen.

The shield of faith (v. 17) is primarily defensive, but it can also be used as we take the offense. We must ward off the philosophies of men as well as the doctrines of the devil (see D&C 46:7; 2 Nephi 28:18–32). Moroni warned us against such teachings:

7 And again I speak unto you who deny the revelations of God, and

say that they are done away, that there are no revelations, nor prophecies, nor gifts, nor healing, nor speaking with tongues, and the interpretation of tongues;

8 Behold I say unto you, he that denieth these things knoweth not the gospel of Christ; yea, he has not read the scriptures; if so, he does not understand them. [Mormon 9:7–8]

As we study the scriptures our faith will increase and the power of the priesthood will be more accessible. Jacob bore testimony of this: "Wherefore, we search the prophets, and we have many revelations and the spirit of prophecy; and having all these witnesses we obtain a hope, and our faith becometh unshaken, insomuch that we truly can command in the name of Jesus and the very trees obey us, or the mountains, or the waves of the sea" (Jacob 4:6). When we share the gospel with others we are on the offensive, but we are also protecting ourselves. We are combating the forces of evil, and offensively driving Satan away. When we hold up the light of Christ and His gospel to the world, or people not members of the Church, we are defensively warding off temptations from our lives (see 3 Nephi 18:24–25). When others know we have certain standards of living they often go out of their way to protect us from temptation, or provide other alternatives. For example, they serve us milk, fruit juices, or soft drinks, instead of coffee or alcoholic beverages.

The spiritual preparation to protect our head is the helmet of salvation (D&C 27:18). We will be judged by our thoughts, and the words that we speak, as well as our works. King Benjamin warned: "But this much I can tell you, that if ye do not watch yourselves, and your thoughts, and your words, and your deeds, and observe the commandments of God, and continue in the faith of what ye have heard concerning the coming of our Lord, even unto the end of your lives, ye must perish. And now, O man, remember, and perish not" (Mosiah 4:30). Jesus gave a similar warning: "But I say unto you, That every idle word that men shall speak, they shall give account thereof in the day of judgment. For by thy words thou shalt be justified, and by thy words thou shalt be condemned. (Matthew 12:36–37). The Psalmist put it in the positive: "He that hath clean hands, and a pure heart; who hath not lifted up his soul unto vanity, nor sworn deceitfully. He shall receive the blessing from the LORD, and righteousness from the God of his salvation" (Psalm 24:4–5).

The Spirit is the sword, or the offensive weapon. It will reveal the word [of God] that we should speak, and what we request of Christ in righteousness (D&C 27:18). As used earlier, it is two-edged and cuts to the center (D&C 6:2; 1 Nephi 16:2). We must fight the battle to the end, and then we will be caught up to dwell with Christ who is with our Father.

General Authority Quotes

—*Elder Marion G. Romney* • D&C 27:5

One of the most remarkable things concerning the Book of Mormon is the frequency and the finality with which the Lord himself testified to its truth and divinity [quotes D&C 27:5; 1:17, 29; 17:6]. [CR, October 1970, 27]

—*President Joseph Fielding Smith* • D&C 27:6–7

It was Gabriel who appeared to Zacharias and promised him a son, and who appeared to Mary and announced the coming of the son of God as recorded in Luke. It was also Gabriel as an Elias who is mentioned in the Doctrine and Covenants, section 27, verse 7, and was Gabriel, or Noah, who stands next to Michael or Adam in the Priesthood. [CR, April 1960, 72]

—*Elder Harold B. Lee* • D&C 27:15–18

(Quotes Ephesians 6:11, almost the same as part of D&C 27:15)

But he taught a remarkable lesson. He pictured each of us as a man of armor, clothed on various strategic points of his body with an armor that would protect him against the onslaughts of evil. . . .

We are counseled to put on the breastplate of righteousness over our hearts, suggesting that our conduct in life should always be right and proper. Have our feet shod with the preparation of the gospel of peace, or in other words, our objectives, the goal we set out to achieve in life be in harmony with the gospel of peace; and have on the helmet of salvation and take the shield of faith and the sword of the spirit, which is the word of God. Thus armored, we are now prepared with the weapons common to the warfare of Paul's day, comparable to those things which we have in [a] similar way upon us today, to attack and to fight successfully and to win the battle in

which the forces of evil and the forces of righteousness are contending today. [CR, October 1949, 58]

—Elder Marion G. Romney • D&C 27:15–18

. . . every priesthood member will have to be a man of courage. Someone has said that the courageous man finds a way, and that the ordinary man finds an excuse. No man that holds the priesthood wants to be an ordinary man [quotes D&C 107:99–100; 27:15–18]. [CR, October 1962, 79]

Chapter Sixteen

As If From Mine Own Mouth

D&C 28; 30; 32; 43:1–16

Historical Setting—September, 1830:

> To our great grief, however, we soon found that Satan had been lying in wait to deceive, and seeking whom he might devour. Brother Hiram Page had in his possession a certain stone, by which he had obtained certain "revelations" concerning the upbuilding of Zion, the order of the Church, etc., all of which were entirely at variance with the order of God's house, as laid down in the New Testament, as well as in our late revelations. As a conference meeting had been appointed for the 26th day of September, I thought it wisdom not to do much more than to converse with the brethren on the subject, until the conference should meet. Finding, however, that many, especially the Whitmer family and Oliver Cowdery were believing much in the things set forth by this stone, we thought best to inquire of the Lord concerning the matter; and before conference convened, we received [section 28, September 1830]. [*HC*, 1:109–110]

Section 30: This revelation was given before the people separated from the three day conference, which began September 26, 1830. [*HC*, 1:115]

Section 32 (October 1830):

> At this time (end of the conference) a great desire was manifested by several of the Elders respecting the remnants of the house of Joseph, the Lamanites, residing in the west—knowing that the purposes of God were great respecting that people, and hoping that the time had come when the promises of the Almighty in regard to them were about to be accomplished, and that they would receive the Gospel and enjoy its

blessings. The desire was so great, it was agreed that we should inquire of the Lord respecting the propriety of sending some of the Elders among them, which we accordingly did, and received [section 30]. [*HC*, 1:118]

INTRODUCTION

Both section 28 and 43 were given because someone was receiving false revelations. The Prophet Joseph Smith was reported by David Whitmer to have said: "Some revelations are of God: some revelations are of men: and some revelations are of the devil" (*CHC*, 1:163). His statement is given scriptural support by section 46 verse 7, and 3 Nephi 27:11–12. That Satan has given revelation to man throughout the time periods of the earth is verified in Helaman 6:26–30. The philosophies of men may not be considered by some as being revelation, but the Book of Mormon certainly warns against their ideas whatever the source (see 2 Nephi 9:28; 15:21; 28:15). Our emphasis here will be on how to recognize the revelations that are from God, and not of man or the devil.

SECTIONS 28; 30 & 32 • OUTLINE

NOTE: The outline is out of order to follow a topical sequence. The Text and Commentary follows the same order.

> 28:1–7   Oliver shall be heard by the church when he teaches by the Comforter about the past revelations.
>
> a.   No one shall receive revelations and commandments in the church except Joseph Smith Jun., for he receiveth them even as Moses (v. 2).
>
> b.   Oliver shall declare the things given to him even as Aaron declared the revelations of Moses with power and authority (v. 3).
>
> c.   When led by the Comforter, Oliver may speak or teach by commandment (v. 4).
>
> d.   Oliver shall not write by way of commandment but by wisdom (v. 5).
>
> e.   Oliver shall not command him who is at the head of the church (v. 6).
>
> f.   Joseph has the keys of the mysteries and the revelations until another is appointed in his stead (v. 7).

➤ 28:8–10   Oliver shall go and preach the gospel to the Lamanites, if they receive it, he shall establish Christ's church among them.

  a. He shall have revelations, but shall not write them by commandment (v. 8).

  b. It is not yet revealed where the city of Zion shall be built up, but will be (v. 9).

  c. It shall be on the borders of the Lamanites (v. 9).

  d. Do not leave this place until after conference (v. 10).

  e. Joseph shall preside over the conference by the voice of it (v. 10).

  f. What Joseph says, Oliver shall tell (v. 10).

➤ 30:5–8   Peter Whitmer Jun. shall journey with Oliver to declare the gospel.

  a. Fear not, but give heed unto his words and advice, be afflicted in his afflictions, and lift up your heart in prayer and faith (vv. 5–6).

  b. The Lord has given him power to build the church among the Lamanites (v. 6).

  c. None are appointed over him in church matters except Joseph (v. 7).

  d. Be diligent and you shall be blessed with eternal life (v. 8).

➤ 32:1–5   Parley P. Pratt shall go with Oliver and Peter to declare the gospel to the Lamanites. Ziba Peterson shall also go with them.

  a. Christ also will go with them in their midst, and nothing shall prevail (v. 3).

  b. They shall heed that which is written, and pretend to no other revelation (v. 4).

  c. Give heed to these words, and Christ will bless them (v. 5).

➤ 28:11–16 Oliver is to take Hiram Page between him and thee alone, and tell him that what he has written from the stone is not of Christ, but Satan deceives him.

  a. These writings have not been appointed him, nor to any of the church contrary to the covenants (v. 12).

  b. All things in the church must be done in order, by common consent, and by the prayer of faith (v. 13).

    c.   Oliver is to assist in settling things, according to the covenants of the church, before going among the Lamanites (v. 14).

    d.   Oliver will receive revelations during his journey to the Lamanites (v. 15).

    e.   Oliver must open his mouth and declare the gospel (v. 16).

➤ 30:1–4   David Whitmer has feared man and not relied on Christ.

    a.   Your mind has been on the things of the earth instead of your Maker and the ministry to which you were called (v. 2).

    b.   You have not given heed to my Spirit, and those set over you, and been persuaded by others (v. 2).

    c.   You are to inquire at my hand, and ponder on what you have received (v. 3).

    d.   Your home shall be with your father until further commanded (v. 4).

    e.   You shall attend to the ministry in the church and before the world (v. 4).

➤ 30:9–11   John Whitmer shall commence to proclaim the gospel as with a trumpet.

    a.   Your labor is at Philip Burroughs and the regions round about (v. 10).

    b.   Your whole labor shall be in Zion with all your soul, not fearing man (v. 11).

TEXT AND COMMENTARY

D&C 28:1–7 • Revelations For the Church Only To Joseph

1 Behold, I say unto thee, Oliver, that it shall be given unto thee that thou shalt be heard by the church in all things whatsoever thou shalt teach them by the Comforter, concerning the revelations and commandments which I have given.

2 But, behold, verily, verily, I say unto thee, no one shall be appointed to receive commandments and revelations in this church excepting my servant Joseph Smith, Jun., for he receiveth them even as Moses.

3 And thou shalt be obedient unto the things which I shall give unto him, even as Aaron, to declare faithfully the commandments and the revelations, with power and authority unto the church.

4 And if thou art led at any time by the Comforter to speak or teach, or at all times by the way of commandment unto the church, thou mayest do it.

5 But thou shalt not write by way of commandment, but by wisdom;

6 And thou shalt not command him who is at thy head, and at the head of the church;

7 For I have given him the keys of the mysteries, and the revelations which are sealed, until I shall appoint unto them another in his stead.

It had been only about five and a half months since the Lord had said that Joseph's word was "as if from mine own mouth" (D&C 21:5).[27] How quickly man forgets. As one who had apparently forgotten, Oliver was given a positive reinforcement of his position in the Church. He could command the Church, as directed by the Comforter, to live by the revelations that had previously been given by Joseph the Prophet, and head of the Church (D&C 28:1). However, Oliver is reminded that Joseph is the only one to receive new revelation for the Church (v. 2). Moses was the one who received new revelation for the church in the wilderness (see Acts 7:37–38). Oliver's role was to be the same as Aaron's, who was the spokesman for Moses (see Exodus 4:16; 2 Nephi 3:17). He was to be the spokesman for Joseph (D&C 28:3). He may speak with power and authority, but it had to have been given to Joseph first.

There was an exception to the instructions given above. Oliver may give commandments to the church while speaking, if led by the Comforter, but not in writing. As a hypothetical situation, when Oliver was speaking to an assembled congregation of church members, he may command that assembled body to do or not do certain things that Joseph had not given direction concerning, if directed by the Comforter. This commandment was not for the whole church, but for that particular assembly. If it later was to go to the whole church, that would come from

---

[27] Section 21 was given on April 6, 1830. Section 43 was given sometime in September 1830. Section 28 was also given in September, 1830, some days prior to the conference of September 26, 1839. Thus, the estimated date between the two revelations is five and a half months.

Joseph, and would eventually, if not at that moment, be written. The same is followed today. A member of the First Presidency, an Apostle, or a General Authority Seventy, may make changes in or give a commandment to a stake, a region, an area, or a mission applicable to that assembly, but not the whole church. Any law or commandment to the whole Church would come in writing from the President, or the First Presidency, or the First Presidency and the Council of the Twelve Apostles, but would always include the signature of the President of the Church. This is the order of the Church (see D&C 28:13). Also today, as then, Apostles or other General Authorities may write letters of instructions to Church units, or publish books, but their writing is by wisdom, not to give commandments to the whole Church.

Oliver had previously written to Joseph and commanded him to remove a verse out of section 20. After writing to him and visiting with him, Joseph convinced him that the "sentence was reasonable and according to scripture" (*HC*, 1:105). Oliver was in error because Joseph was his head and the head of the Church (D&C 28:6). Although he was the Second Elder of the Church, and ordained as the Assistant President of the Church (*HC*, 2:176; D&C 124:95), his role was to counsel or advise the Prophet, not command him. Joseph held the keys, and they were sealed upon him until another was appointed in his place (D&C 28:7). Again, this was the order of the Church.

D&C 28:8–10 • Revelations, But Write Them Not

8 And now, behold, I say unto you that you shall go unto the Lamanites and preach my gospel unto them; and inasmuch as they receive thy teachings thou shalt cause my church to be established among them; and thou shalt have revelations, but write them not by way of commandment.

9 And now, behold, I say unto you that it is not revealed, and no man knoweth where the city Zion shall be built, but it shall be given hereafter. Behold, I say unto you that it shall be on the borders by the Lamanites.

10 Thou shalt not leave this place until after the conference; and my servant Joseph shall be appointed to preside over the conference by the voice of it, and what he saith to thee thou shalt tell.

The promise that Oliver would receive revelation for himself, but that it was not to be written (D&C 28:4), would happen when he went to preach the gospel to the Lamanites, to which he was now called (v. 8). This promise was to be in all of his assignments; not just there, but it is an example of how and when revelation will be given. This preaching mission was to begin after the three-day conference, which was held beginning on September 26, 1830. Peter Whitmer was called to go with Oliver before they separated from the conference.

D&C 30:5–8 • Oliver—the Second Elder of the Church

5 Behold, I say unto you, Peter, that you shall take your journey with your brother Oliver; for the time has come that it is expedient in me that you shall open your mouth to declare my gospel; therefore, fear not, but give heed unto the words and advice of your brother, which he shall give you.

6 And be you afflicted in all his afflictions, ever lifting up your heart unto me in prayer and faith, for his and your deliverance; for I have given unto him power to build up my church among the Lamanites;

7 And none have I appointed to be his counselor over him in the church, concerning church matters, except it is his brother, Joseph Smith, Jun.

8 Wherefore, give heed unto these things and be diligent in keeping my commandments, and you shall be blessed unto eternal life. Amen.

The instruction given to Peter Whitmer, in this revelation, gives more guidance in what is expected from a counselor or an assistant (vv. 5–7). It also affirms Oliver's position as the Second Elder (v. 8). Furthermore, those sent out by the Prophet is his representative, and the presiding officer wherever he is sent.

D&C 32:1–5 • Two Other Men Called to Accompany Oliver in October 1830

1 And now concerning my servant Parley P. Pratt, behold, I say unto him that as I live I will that he shall declare my gospel and learn of me, and be meek and lowly of heart.

2 And that which I have appointed unto him is that he shall go with my servants, Oliver Cowdery and Peter Whitmer, Jun., into the wilderness among the Lamanites.

3 And Ziba Peterson also shall go with them; and I myself will go with them and be in their midst; and I am their advocate with the Father,

and nothing shall prevail against them.

4 And they shall give heed to that which is written, and pretend to no other revelation; and they shall pray always that I may unfold the same to their understanding.

5 And they shall give heed unto these words and trifle not, and I will bless them. Amen.

Besides Parley and Ziba, there would be a fifth member of the missionary group: the Savior (v. 3). His going confirms the promise given to His disciples in Jerusalem, that "where two or three are gathered together in my name, there am I in the midst of them" (Matthew 18:29; see also D&C 6:32). Once more the procedure for following and receiving revelation is given. The companions were to follow the written revelations, the scriptures (D&C 32:4–5). However, as Oliver was promised to receive revelation for the group (D&C 28:8), their pretending "to no other revelation" (D&C 32:4) had reference to spurious revelations such as those given to Hiram Page.

The Lamanite mission was short lived. Although they were well received by several Indian chiefs, the excitement of their visit "stirred up the jealousy and the envy of the Indian agents and sectarian missionaries to that degree that we were soon ordered out of the Indian country as disturbers of the peace; and even threatened with the military in case of non-compliance" (*Autobiography of Parley P. Pratt* [1970], 57). Thus ended the Lamanite mission, but there were other by-products of the mission that will be discussed later.

The place of the city of Zion was revealed as promised (see D&C 28:9 above). The center place was Independence, Missouri, and it will be discussed later (see D&C 57:1–3). This was, as the Lord said, on the borders of the Lamanites, just beyond the western frontier of the United States, and known as Indian country.

D&C 28:11–16 • Satan Had Deceived Hiram Page

11 And again, thou shalt take thy brother, Hiram Page, between him and thee alone, and tell him that those things which he hath written from that stone are not of me and that Satan deceiveth him;

12 For, behold, these things have not been appointed unto him,

neither shall anything be appointed unto any of this church contrary to the church covenants.

13 For all things must be done in order, and by common consent in the church, by the prayer of faith.

14 And thou shalt assist to settle all these things, according to the covenants of the church, before thou shalt take thy journey among the Lamanites.

15 And it shall be given thee from the time thou shalt go, until the time thou shalt return, what thou shalt do.

16 And thou must open thy mouth at all times, declaring my gospel with the sound of rejoicing. Amen.

The Lord's way of correction is taught to us in the Hiram Page experience. Apparently Hiram was not deliberately trying to usurp the leadership from Joseph, but in the excitement of the new religion, was the victim of the cunning tactics of Satan. Through his miraculous power unknown to man, the devil had somehow communicated to Hiram until he was grasped "with his awful chains" (2 Nephi 28:22). Rather than embarrass Hiram publicly, Oliver was to take him aside and quietly and kindly explain that his revelations were not of God, but from Satan (D&C 28:11). At the same time he was to give him constructive criticism, showing him the correct order of the church and the law of common consent (vv. 12–13). Oliver was also to help settle the situation with the Whitmer family, of whom Hiram was a son-in-law. Certainly Hiram needed some support in explaining that he had been duped by the devil (v. 14). The Lord then gave similar support to Oliver. He would be given revelation on his mission to the Lamanites (v. 15). Oliver held the highest position in the Church among them, thus revelation was to come to him. The Lord had previously corrected and explained this to Oliver.

The revelations to David and John Whitmer are general, and not pertaining to the main concepts of this chapter. However, they contain good advice for all of us.

D&C 30:1–4 • David Feared Man and did not Follow the Spirit

1 Behold, I say unto you, David, that you have feared man and have not relied on me for strength as you ought.

2 But your mind has been on the things of the earth more than on

the things of me, your Maker, and the ministry whereunto you have been called; and you have not given heed unto my Spirit, and to those who were set over you, but have been persuaded by those whom I have not commanded.

3 Wherefore, you are left to inquire for yourself at my hand, and ponder upon the things which you have received.

4 And your home shall be at your father's house, until I give unto you further commandments. And you shall attend to the ministry in the church, and before the world, and in the regions round about. Amen.

As we will learn in a later revelation (D&C 58:26–28), the Lord expects to use our own reasoning power, and make our own decisions. As we do so, we should check it out with him, as we learned in section 9 verses 8–9. This is part of the principle of agency. Considering what David had experienced in the previous few months, it seems he would have involved the Lord more. The Lord seems to be telling David to: "think it over and pray about it."

D&C 30:9–11 • John to Proclaim the Gospel At Home

9 Behold, I say unto you, my servant John, that thou shalt commence from this time forth to proclaim my gospel, as with the voice of a trump.

10 And your labor shall be at your brother Philip Burroughs', and in that region round about, yea, wherever you can be heard, until I command you to go from hence.

11 And your whole labor shall be in Zion, with all your soul, from henceforth; yea, you shall ever open your mouth in my cause, not fearing what man can do, for I am with you. Amen.

While others were being called to go elsewhere and preach the gospel, John was to remain at home, but do the same thing. As we will learn later, the Lord expects us to share the gospel with all those with whom we associate, and not let them "perish in unbelief" (D&C 61:3), as we hurry away to give others an opportunity for salvation.

We will now skip ahead about five months. The Lord had explained on April 6, 1830 that He would speak to the church through the Prophet Joseph (D&C 21:5). Five and a half months later, around mid-September, He had to explain the order of the Church again (D&C 28:1–7). After about another five months, sometime after September 9, 1831 when section 42 was given, the problem of who was to receive revelation for the Church arose again. The following revelation was thus given.

*H*istorical Setting—D&C 43:

Soon after the foregoing revelation was received [section 42], a woman came making great pretensions of revealing commandments, laws, and other curious matters; and as almost every person has advocates for both theory and practice, in the various notions and projects of the age, it became necessary to enquire of the Lord, when I received [section 43]. [*HC*, 1:154]

This woman's name, according to the history of the church kept by John Whitmer, was Hubble. She professed to be a prophetess of the Lord, and professed to have many revelations, and knew the Book of Mormon was true, and that she should become a teacher in the church of Christ. She appeared to be very sanctimonious and deceived some who were not able to detect her in her hypocrisy; others, however, had the spirit of discernment and her follies and her abominations were manifest. [*HC*, 1:154]

SECTION 43 • OUTLINE

➢ 43:1–7   The elders of the church have received the law of the church from him whom I appointed to receive commandments and revelations.

     a.   None other will be appointed until he be taken, if he abide in Christ (v. 3).

     b.   This gift given to another will come through Joseph, if taken from him, he shall have power to appoint another (v. 4).

     c.   Receive not the teachings of another as revelations and commandments (v. 5).

     d.   I give this revelation that ye may not be deceived (v. 6).

     e.   He that is ordained of Christ shall come in at the gate to teach the revelations you have received (v. 7).

➢ 43:8–16   When the church is assembled together, instruct and edify each other that they may know how to act and direct the church according to the law and commandments.

a. Instructions in church law are to sanctify those who receive them (v. 9).

b. They shall bind themselves to act in holiness before Christ (v. 9).

c. By doing this, glory shall be added to the kingdom, and if not, what you have received shall be taken away (v. 10).

d. Purge out your iniquity and sanctify yourselves (v. 11).

e. If you desire the kingdom's glories, uphold Joseph by the prayer of faith (v. 12).

f. If you desire the mysteries of the kingdom, provide for his needs (v. 13).

g. If you do not provide, he shall remain with the people who receive him (v. 14).

h. You are not sent forth to be taught, but to teach things given by my Spirit (v. 15).

I. Ye are to be taught from on high. Sanctify yourselves and ye shall be endowed with power (v. 16).

TEXT AND COMMENTARY

D&C 43:1–7 • None to Receive Revelation Until Joseph is Taken

1 O hearken, ye elders of my church, and give ear to the words which I shall speak unto you.

2 For behold, verily, verily, I say unto you, that ye have received a commandment for a law unto my church, through him whom I have appointed unto you to receive commandments and revelations from my hand.

3 And this ye shall know assuredly—that there is none other appointed unto you to receive commandments and revelations until he be taken, if he abide in me.

4 But verily, verily, I say unto you, that none else shall be appointed unto this gift except it be through him; for if it be taken from him he shall not have power except to appoint another in his stead.

5 And this shall be a law unto you, that ye receive not the teachings of any that shall come before you as revelations or commandments;

6 And this I give unto you that you may not be deceived, that you may know they are not of me.

7 For verily I say unto you, that he that is ordained of me shall come

in at the gate and be ordained as I have told you before, to teach those revelations which you have received and shall receive through him whom I have appointed.

The Lord repeated to the elders of His church (v. 1) what He had said before; that the law of the church was already received through His appointed servant Joseph, (v. 2). He added a condition in the present revelation, "if he abide in me" (v. 3), which gave a loophole. However, He quickly closed the loophole. Even if Joseph did not abide in the Lord, he would retain the power to appoint another in his stead (v. 4). There-fore, the elders were not to receive the commandments and revelations of this woman, or anyone else (v. 5). Joseph was still abiding in Christ, who did not want His people to be deceived (v. 6). This incident reminds us of a certain damsel in the New Testament:

16 And it came to pass, as we went to prayer, a certain damsel possessed with a spirit of divination met us, which brought her masters much gain by soothsaying:

17 The same followed Paul and us, and cried, saying, These men are the servants of the most high God, which shew unto us the way of salvation.

18 And this did she many days. But Paul, being grieved, turned and said to the spirit, I command thee in the name of Jesus Christ to come out of her. And he came out the same hour. [Acts 16:16–18]

One more condition was added in this revelation. Whoever was ordained to succeed the present Prophet, would "come in at the gate and be ordained as I have told you before" (D&C 43:7). The Lord was most probably referring to a revelation given a few days before, September 9, 1831. "Again I say unto you, that it shall not be given to any one to go forth to preach my gospel, or to build up my church, except he be ordained by some one who has authority, and it is known to the church that he has authority and has been regularly ordained by the heads of the church" (D&C 42:11). Mrs. Hubble did not qualify to receive command-ments and revelations for the church under any of the conditions given by the Lord before, or at this time. Nor did anyone else qualify. Joseph was still the Lord's anointed. Before Joseph was martyred, he anointed the Quorum of the Twelve collectively with all of the keys of this dispensation.[28] When he was taken, the keys were still on the earth. The Twelve had the power and the authority to select and ordain a new President of the Church. The same pattern has been followed in each succeeding President.

D&C 43:8–16 • Church Meetings are to Instruct and Edify

8 And now, behold, I give unto you a commandment, that when ye are assembled together ye shall instruct and edify each other, that ye may know how to act and direct my church, how to act upon the points of my law and commandments, which I have given.

9 And thus ye shall become instructed in the law of my church, and be sanctified by that which ye have received, and ye shall bind yourselves to act in all holiness before me—

10 That inasmuch as ye do this, glory shall be added to the kingdom which ye have received. Inasmuch as ye do it not, it shall be taken, even that which ye have received.

11 Purge ye out the iniquity which is among you; sanctify yourselves before me;

12 And if ye desire the glories of the kingdom, appoint ye my servant Joseph Smith, Jun., and uphold him before me by the prayer of faith.

13 And again, I say unto you, that if ye desire the mysteries of the kingdom, provide for him food and raiment, and whatsoever thing he needeth to accomplish the work wherewith I have commanded him;

14 And if ye do it not he shall remain unto them that have received him, that I may reserve unto myself a pure people before me.

15 Again I say, hearken ye elders of my church, whom I have appointed: Ye are not sent forth to be taught, but to teach the children of men the things which I have put into your hands by the power of my Spirit;

16 And ye are to be taught from on high. Sanctify yourselves and ye shall be endowed with power, that ye may give even as I have spoken.

Having firmly established the doctrine of succession of the President, the Lord took advantage of this background to teach the purpose of their church meetings. The meetings in the church are to instruct and to edify.

---

[28] See *HC*, 7: 230–342. Several testimonies of the Twelve Apostles in Joseph's day are recorded in this volume of church history entitled "*Apostolic Interregnum.*"

The instructions are to give knowledge of the way a church member is to act as an individual, and how the Church is to be directed collectively (v. 8). Proper conduct is expected for the whole Church. The Savior taught: "Ye shall know them by their fruits. Do men gather grapes of thorns, or figs of thistles? Even so every good tree bringeth forth good fruit; but a corrupt tree bringeth forth evil fruit. A good tree cannot bring forth evil fruit, neither a corrupt tree bring forth good fruit. Every tree that bringeth not forth good fruit is hewn down, and cast into the fire. Wherefore, by their fruits ye shall know them" (3 Nephi 14:16–20; Matthew 7:16–20). Jesus set the example for us to follow: "Therefore, what manner of men ought ye to be? Verily I say unto you, even as I am" (3 Nephi 27:27). By following His standards, we can have an effect on others. The Lord told the sons of Mosiah as they embarked on their mission to the Lamanites: "Go forth among the Lamanites, thy brethren, and establish my word; yet ye shall be patient in long-suffering and afflictions, that ye may show forth good examples unto them in me, and I will make an instrument of thee in my hands unto the salvation of many souls" (Alma 17:11). The same effect will be had upon our family, our friends, our co-workers, and our community.

The tragedy of improper conduct is shown by Alma's explanation to his son, Corianton:

> 11 Suffer not yourself to be led away by any vain or foolish thing; suffer not the devil to lead away your heart again after those wicked harlots. Behold, O my son, how great iniquity ye brought upon the Zoramites; for when they saw your conduct they would not believe in my words.
>
> 12 And now the Spirit of the Lord doth say unto me: Command thy children to do good, lest they lead away the hearts of many people to destruction; therefore I command you, my son, in the fear of God, that ye refrain from your iniquities; [Alma 39:11–12]

"How to act and direct my church" (D&C 43:8) is most applicable to priesthood meetings, the business of the ward or stake, but it would also be proper for many other meetings. Also, conferences are "to do whatever church business is necessary to be done at the time" (D&C 20:62). To know "how to act upon the points of my law and commandments" (D&C 43:8) requires the knowledge of those laws and commandments. The doctrine of the Church should be taught in our sacrament meetings. President Boyd K. Packer has emphasized: "True doctrine, understood, changes attitudes and behavior. The study of the doctrines of the gospel will improve behavior quicker than a study of behavior will improve behavior. Preoccupation with unworthy behavior can lead to unworthy behavior. That is why we stress so forcefully the study of the doctrines of the gospel" (CR, October 1986, 20; see also CR, April 1997, 8; and CR, April 2004, 80). To edify (D&C 43:8) is to strengthen spiritually, or to have the Spirit accompany our instruction. "That which doth not edify is not of God, and is darkness" (D&C 50:23). When Jesus spoke to the Nephites, it "did cause their hearts to burn" (3 Nephi 11:3). When we teach the truths of the laws and commandments of the gospel, the spirit is present and all are edified together.

We bind ourselves "to act in all holiness" (D&C 43:9) when we partake of the sacrament. We renew the covenants that we made at the waters of baptism, to take upon us the "the name of Christ" and "serve him to the end" (D&C 20:37). By following the law, which we should have been instructed in at our meetings, we become sanctified (D&C 43:9). Sanctification is a process of becoming "pure and spotless before God" in order to "enter into the rest of the Lord [our God]" (Alma 13:12). The rest of the Lord "is the fullness of his glory" (D&C 84:24).

The Lord promises that "glory shall be added to the kingdom which you have received" (D&C 43:10). This has reference to the kingdom of God on earth. The church will grow and prosper and eventually become the kingdom in heaven (see D&C 65:6). Failure to follow the law and the commandment will result in losing the blessings that have already been given. The Lord warned the Nephites of this same loss (see 2 Nephi 28:30). Purging out "the iniquity which is among you" (D&C 43:11) could also come by properly partaking of the sacrament. As we review the past weeks activities during the sacrament service, we recognize the things for which we must repent, and covenant to change our lives in the coming week. Line upon line we purge out our iniquities individually, and it will have an effect upon the whole church collectively.

The Lord gives us another way in which the church and kingdom may grow and prosper. We must pray for our Prophet in faith (D&C 43:12). He has been appointed by the Lord, and will direct him, but what the Lord tells the Prophet is often dependent upon us. As we indicate our willingness to receive guidance, the Lord will inspire him to give us the direction we need. He will not inspire him beyond our willingness to follow. That is why the law of Moses was given to Israel in the wilderness. We should pray for the Prophet's health in mind as well as in body. The Lord will bless us through him.

The Lord also asks the Church to support the Prophet in all of his temporal needs if they desired to know the mysteries of the kingdom (D&C 43:13). At this time, Joseph was translating the Bible, which came to him by revelation. As he translated, he was given additional revelation on the subjects that were in the Bible text. The book of Moses added extensive knowledge on the early chapters of Genesis. Section 29, which we will study next, was given at that same time, and was associated with some of the things he was translating. Today, we support our Prophet temporally as needed. His whole time is dedicated to building up the kingdom in preparation for the Second Coming of Jesus Christ. The Lord is still working on preparing a pure people to whom he will come (D&C 43:14).

We are the Restored Church of Jesus Christ, therefore, we are to teach the principles of the Restoration, not the learning of the world (v. 15). The Lord will teach us as we teach those to whom we are assigned, or sent. The degree to which we are taught is dependent upon our own spiritual preparation. If we make ourselves worthy, or sanctify ourselves, we will learn to recognize the Spirit and follow it. Wherefore, we can give what the Lord speaks to us (v. 16).

General Authority Quotes

—The Prophet Joseph Smith • D&C 28:2

> I will inform you that it is contrary to the economy of God for any member of the Church, or any one, to receive instructions for those in authority, higher than themselves; therefore you will see the impropriety of giving heed to them; but if any person have a vision or a visitation from a heavenly messenger, it must be for his own benefit and instruction; for the fundamental principles, government, and doctrine of the Church are vested in the keys of the kingdom. [*HC*, 1:338]

—*Elder Marion G. Romney* • D&C 28:11–12

This revelation straightened Hiram Page out, but it did not end Satan's efforts to deceive the brethren. You will remember how they (including some of the leaders of the church) fought the Prophet in the days of Kirtland. At the time of one attack on the Prophet when Brigham Young was present, he arose and said that Joseph was a Prophet and he knew it, "and that they who rail and slander him . . . could but destroy their own authority and cut the thread that bound them to the Prophet of God and sink themselves to hell."

—*The First Presidency* • D&C 28

From the days of Hiram Page (D&C 28), at different periods there have been manifestations from delusive spirits to members of the Church. Sometimes these have come to men and women who because of transgression become easy prey to the Arch-Deceiver. At other times people who pride themselves on their strict observance of the rules and ordinances and ceremonies of the Church are led away by false spirits, who exercise an influence so imitative of that which proceeds from a Divine source that even these persons, who think they are "the very elect," find it difficult to discern the essential difference. Satan himself has transformed himself to be apparently "an angel of light."

When visions, dreams, tongues, prophecy, impressions or any extraordinary gift or inspiration conveys something out of harmony with the accepted revelations of the Church or contrary to the decisions of its constituted authorities, Latter-day Saints may know that it is not of God, no matter how plausible it may appear. Also they should understand that directions for the guidance of the Church will come, by revelation, through the head. All faithful members are entitled to the inspiration of the Holy Spirit for themselves, their families, and for those over whom they preside. But anything at discord with that which comes from God through the head of the Church is not to be received as authoritative or reliable. . . . [in James R. Clark, comp., *Messages of the First Presidency of The Church of Jesus Christ of Latter-day Saints*, 6 vols. (1979), 4:285]

Chapter Seventeen

All Things Are Spiritual Unto Me

D&C 29

*H*istorical Setting: Section 29 was given at the same time as section 28 (see the "*Historical Setting*" of the last chapter). As mentioned at the end of the last chapter, Joseph Smith was translating the Bible when he received these revelations. The original manuscripts of his work were not available to a member of the Church to examine for over a hundred years until 1967, when Robert J. Matthews was permitted by the RLDS Church to make a study of them. He found "that the manuscripts contained dates of their composition, showed frequent changes in handwriting denoting changes of scribes, and yielded other revealing bits of information in addition to the text itself."[29] Oliver Cowdery was Joseph's first scribe; and the handwriting of the original biblical manuscript corrections and additions are in Oliver's handwriting, and he left in October of 1830 for the Lamanite mission. Thus, this section was given as a result of his work on the Joseph Smith Translation. According to the Far West Record, an early church minute book of the general Church meetings, the six elders to whom the revelation was given were Oliver Cowdery; David, John, and Peter Whitmer; Samuel H. Smith; and Thomas B. Marsh.

INTRODUCTION

The 8th Article of Faith states that "We believe the Bible to be the

---

[29] *Selected Writings of Robert J. Matthews,* Contributions of the Joseph Smith Translation in Restoring Doctrine, 1999. The summary of his work that follows is from the same source.

word of God as far as it is translated correctly." We have no original manuscripts of the Old or the New Testaments.

> It is now evident that a space of nearly three hundred years elapsed between the originals and the earliest New Testament manuscripts available today, except for some small fragments in which the gap is "only" one hundred fifty or two hundred years. . . . Some textual scholars realize that the second century A.D. presents an impenetrable barrier to tracing the history and source of New Testament documents. [*Selected Writings of Robert J. Matthews*, quoting Sir Fredrich Kenyon and Dr. Fredrich C. Grant, 318]

The earliest Old Testament manuscripts are even farther removed from the time they were written. The Prophet Jeremiah acknowledged that the Bible had been tampered with. He said: "How do ye say, We are wise, and the law of the LORD is with us? Lo, certainly in vain made he it; the pen of the scribes is in vain" (Jeremiah 8:8) Other translations make it even more evident: "How can ye say, We are wise, and the law of the LORD is with us? But, behold, the false pen of the scribes has made it into a lie" (Revised Standard Version). The New Catholic Edition renders it: "How do you say: we are wise, and the Law of the LORD is with us? Indeed the lying pen of the scribes hath wrought falsehood." Jesus acknowledged in the New Testament that the Old Testament had been altered. "Woe unto you, lawyers! For ye have taken away the key of knowledge, *the fullness of the scriptures;* ye enter not in yourselves into the kingdom; and those who were entering in, ye hindered" (JST, Luke 11:53; italics showing addition). The Book of Mormon (1 Nephi 13:26–29) and the Pearl of Great Price (Moses 1:40–41) confirm that much has been lost from the Bible. The Joseph Smith Translation has played a significant role in restoring the plain and precious parts that were lost. Section 29 is the first revelation in the Doctrine and Covenants that was explicitly given as a restoration and explanation of the lost truths from the Bible.

SECTION 29 • OUTLINE

> 29:1–6   I Am will gather his people as a hen gathers her chicks, even as many as hearken, humble themselves, and call on him in mighty prayer.

                a.   The six elders' sins are forgiven, but they are to sin no more (v. 3).

    b.   They are chosen out of the world to declare my gospel (v. 4).

    c.   Christ is in their midst, their advocate with the Father, whose will it is to give them the kingdom (v. 5).

    d.   As written, what you ask in faith, according to Christ's command, they will receive (v. 6).

29:7–11   The six elders are called to gather the Lord's elect who hear and do not harden their hearts.

    a.   The elect shall be gathered to one place to be prepared against tribulations and desolation against the wicked (v. 8).

    b.   The day soon comes that the earth is ripe, and the proud and wicked will burn as stubble (v. 9).

    c.   What the apostles spoke must be fulfilled (v. 10).

    d.   Christ will reveal Himself with power and glory, and dwell in righteousness with men on earth for a thousand years (v. 11).

29:12–13   The Father wills that the Twelve in Jerusalem come with Him in robes of righteousness and crowns upon their heads.

    a.   The Twelve will judge the whole house of Israel that loved Christ and kept His commandment, and none else (v. 12).

    b.   A trump shall sound as on Mount Sinai, and the dead in Christ will be crowned and be with Him (v. 13).

29:14–21   Before that great day, the sun shall be darkened, the moon turned to blood, and the stars fall from heaven.

    a.   There shall be weeping and wailing among men (v. 15).

    b.   Great hailstorms shall destroy the crops of the earth (v. 16).

    c.   The Lord will take vengeance upon the wicked who do not repent (v. 17).

    d.   Flies shall eat the inhabitants' flesh, and maggots come upon them (v. 18).

    e.   Tongues shall be stayed, flesh fall from bones, and eyes from sockets (v. 19).

    f.   Beasts of the forests and fouls of the air shall devour the inhabitants (v. 20).

         g.   The great and abominable church shall be devoured by fire as spoken by Ezekiel the Prophet (v. 21).

➤ 29:22–25   After a thousand years, men will again deny their God, and the earth will be spared but for a season.

         a.   Heaven and earth shall pass away, there will be a new heaven and earth (v. 23).

         b.   Old things pass away, all things become new; men, beasts, fowls, fishes (v. 24).

         c.   Not one hair nor mote shall be lost (v. 25).

➤ 29:26–29   Michael shall sound his trump, the dead awake, graves opened, all come forth.

         a.   The righteous shall be gathered on Christ's right hand unto eternal life (v. 27).

         b.   The wicked on Christ's left hand, and He will not own them (v. 27).

         c.   Christ will say to the wicked: Depart ye cursed into everlasting fire (v. 28).

         d.   Christ has never declared that the wicked shall return, they cannot come where Christ is, they have no power (v. 29),

➤ 29:30–35   All of Christ's judgments are not given to man, but the first shall be last and the last shall be first.

         a.   By His Spirit's power, Christ created all things spiritual and temporal (v. 31).

         b.   He created the first spiritual, the second temporal in the beginning of His work (v. 32).

         c.   The first temporal, and then spiritual in the last of His work (v. 32).

         d.   Unto Christ, His works have no beginning, neither end (v. 33).

         e.   All things unto Christ are spiritual, He has never given a temporal law to man, or their children, nor Adam whom He created (v. 34).

         f.   Adam was an agent unto himself, I gave him spiritual laws not natural, temporal, nor carnal nor sensual (v. 35).

➤ 29:36–41   Adam was tempted by the devil who was before Adam.

a. The devil rebelled and a third part of the hosts of heaven were turned away because of their agency (v. 36).

    b. The third part was thrust down and became the devil and His angels (v. 37).

    c. A place for them was prepared from the beginning, called hell (v. 38).

    d. The devil was allowed to tempt men so they could have agency, to know bitter from sweet (v. 39).

    e. Adam partook of the forbidden fruit, transgressed the commandment, and became subject to the will of the devil (v. 40).

    f. Adam was cast out of the Garden of Eden, and became spiritually dead; the first death (v. 41).

➤ 29:42–45 Adam and his seed were not to die the temporal death until angels declared repentance, and redemption through faith in the Only Begotten Son.

    a. Man was appointed probationary days to have a natural death, and be raised in immortality and have eternal life if they would believe (v. 43).

    b. Those that believe not are raised to eternal damnation and cannot be redeemed from their spiritual fall (v. 44).

    c. They loved darkness rather than light and do evil deeds (v. 45).

➤ 29:46–50 Little children are redeemed from the foundation of the world through the Only Begotton.

    a. Little children cannot sin. Satan has no power to tempt them until they begin to become accountable (v. 47).

    b. It is given them so that great things can be required of their fathers (v. 48).

    c. Those who have knowledge are commanded to repent (v. 49).

    d. He that has no understanding will be done to as it is written (v. 50).

Text and Commentary

D&C 29:1–6 • The Great I Am Gathers His Chicks

1 Listen to the voice of Jesus Christ, your Redeemer, the Great I AM, whose arm of mercy hath atoned for your sins;

2 Who will gather his people even as a hen gathereth her chickens under her wings, even as many as will hearken to my voice and humble themselves before me, and call upon me in mighty prayer.

3 Behold, verily, verily, I say unto you, that at this time your sins are forgiven you, therefore ye receive these things; but remember to sin no more, lest perils shall come upon you.

4 Verily, I say unto you that ye are chosen out of the world to declare my gospel with the sound of rejoicing, as with the voice of a trump.

5 Lift up your hearts and be glad, for I am in your midst, and am your advocate with the Father; and it is his good will to give you the kingdom.

6 And, as it is written—Whatsoever ye shall ask in faith, being united in prayer according to my command, ye shall receive.

Jesus' introduction of Himself as "the Great I AM" (v. 1) is telling His people that He was the God of the Old Testament (Exodus 3:14), the God who scattered all of the house of Israel (see Amos 9:8–9; 2 Kings 17:23). All of the ten northern tribes were captured and scattered among all nations by Assyria in about 721 B.C. The southern tribes of Israel, Judah and Benjamin, were taken captive by Babylon in 589 B.C. (Book of Mormon dating) and remained there for seventy years (see 2 Kings 25:21, Jeremiah 25:12–13). After the crucifixion of Christ, they were scattered again (see 2 Nephi 10:5–6). "I AM" is another name for Jehovah (see JST, Exodus 6:3, John 8:58). With that background, He announces that the gathering of Israel in the latter days (see Jeremiah 16:14–160) is about to take place. He uses the symbolism that He used in Jerusalem just before He atoned for their sins, and to the Nephites: a hen gathering "her chickens under her wings" (D&C 29:2; Matthew 23:37; 3 Nephi 10:4–6). The verses that follow tell the six elders to whom He addresses this revelation the qualifications for those who will do the gathering. Their sins are forgiven, but they must be careful to sin no more (D&C 29:3). He uses the same admonition He gave in the New Testament to the woman taken in adultery (see John 8:11). Once we are forgiven, whatever the sin may be, if we sin again "the former sins return" (D&C 82:7). We must also suffer the consequences of the present sins that are committed.

The system of gathering is the same as always, to declare the gospel to the world (D&C 29:4). He reminds them, as He does later (discussed in the previous chapter D&C 32:3), that He will be in their midst, and that He is their "advocate with the Father." The Father had shared the kingdom with the Son and was anxious to share it with His present day Saints (D&C 29:5). How to attain a share in that kingdom was written (v. 6) in the New Testament. "And whatsoever ye shall ask in my name, that will I do, that the Father may be glorified in the Son. If ye shall ask any thing in my name, I will do [it]" (John 14:13–14; see also Matthew 21:22).[30]

D&C 29:7–11 • My Elect Hear My Voice

7 And ye are called to bring to pass the gathering of mine elect; for mine elect hear my voice and harden not their hearts;

8 Wherefore the decree hath gone forth from the Father that they shall be gathered in unto one place upon the face of this land, to prepare their hearts and be prepared in all things against the day when tribulation and desolation are sent forth upon the wicked.

9 For the hour is nigh and the day soon at hand when the earth is ripe; and all the proud and they that do wickedly shall be as stubble; and I will burn them up, saith the Lord of Hosts, that wickedness shall not be upon the earth;

10 For the hour is nigh, and that which was spoken by mine apostles must be fulfilled; for as they spoke so shall it come to pass;

11 For I will reveal myself from heaven with power and great glory, with all the hosts thereof, and dwell in righteousness with men on earth a thousand years, and the wicked shall not stand.

The definition of the elect as those who "hear my voice and harden not their hearts" (v. 7) should be taken in the context of those who accept the gospel that the six elders are sent to declare (see also D&C 33:6; Moses 7:62; JS—Matthew 1:27, 37, 39). The elect are also defined in other contexts. Emma Smith was an "elect lady because of her calling" (D&C 25:3). "The salvation of mine elect" (D&C 33:6) seem to be those who

---

[30] The slight difference in the wording between the above quote (v. 6), and the Gospel of John or Matthew quote, may be because of the individual Apostle's wording of what Jesus said, or the translation of His words through the ages.

are of the literal house of Israel. Those who obtain [both] the Aaronic and the Melchizedek Priesthood, and magnify their calling become the elect of God (D&C 84:34–40). "The elect according to the covenant," who should not be deceived in the last days (JS—Matthew 1:22) are probably the combination of all of those listed above.

The gathering "unto one place upon the face of this land" (v. 8), has been interpreted to mean that all members of the Church will have to be gathered to Jackson County, Missouri; the center place of Zion. The Prophet Joseph taught that "When wars come, we shall have to flee to Zion," and has been a part of the above interpretation. However, in the same speech, he said: "The time is soon coming, when no man will have any peace but in Zion and her stakes" (*TPJS*, 160–161). In the general conference of April, 1973, President Harold B. Lee, President of the Church at that time, quoted Elder Bruce R. McConkie of the Council of the Twelve":

> . . . another Nephite prophet said: "The Lord . . . has covenanted with all the house of Israel,' that 'the time comes that they shall be restored to the true church and fold of God'; and that "they shall be gathered home to the lands of their inheritance, and shall be established in all their lands of promise." [2 Nephi 9:1–2]

> Now I call your attention to the facts, set forth in these scriptures, that the gathering of Israel consists of joining the true church; of coming to a knowledge of the true God and of his saving truths; and of worshipping him in the congregations of all the Saints in all nations and among all peoples. Please note that these revealed words speak of the *folds* of the Lord; of Israel being gathered to the lands of their inheritance; of Israel being *established in all their lands of promise*; and of there being congregations of the covenant people of the Lord in *every nation, speaking every tongue, and among every people* when the Lord comes again. [CR, April 1973, 6–7; italics in the original]

The Prophet Joseph also taught: "*The whole of America is Zion itself from north to south, and is described by the Prophets, who declare that it is the Zion where the mountain of the Lord should be, and that it should be in the center of the land.* When elders shall take up and examine the old prophecies of the Bible, they will see it" (*TPJS*, 362; italics in the original; see also Alma 46:17). Therefore, the "one place" (v. 8) of gathering is to one of the stakes as well as to the center place of Zion in Missouri, on the face of all this land. The people are to gather to their "one place" in preparation for tribulation and desolation that will come upon the wicked (D&C 29:8). As Nephi said: "For the time speedily cometh that the Lord God shall cause a great division among the people, and the wicked will he destroy; and he will spare his people, yea, even if it so be that he must destroy the wicked by fire" (2 Nephi 30:10). The Lord confirms Nephi's prophetic words; "when the earth is ripe [in iniquity]; all the proud and they that do wickedly shall be as stubble; and *I will burn* them up" (D&C 29:9; italics added). The Lord is quoting the Old Testament Prophet Malachi with a slight variation. The Angel Moroni also quoted it with some slight variation. Malachi said: "the day that cometh shall burn them up" (Malachi 4:1). The Angel Moroni said: "for they that come shall burn them" (JS—H 1:37). The Lord will send His destroying angels, the angels will destroy, and the glory of the Lord that accompanies Him will burn them. Thus all three wordings may be correct.

The time is nigh means it is near (D&C 29:10). The Lord is speaking of his time, not the time of earth. It has been nearly one hundred and eighty years since this revelation was given. One day with the Lord is a thousand years with man (see 2 Peter 3:2; Psalm 90:4; Abraham 3:4). Therefore, it has been between four and five hours since the Lord said it was nigh. Nevertheless, the seventh seal has been opened and we are in the period of silence before the Second Coming (see D&C 77:7, 13). The time is also now near according to the earth's time. The Apostles in the New Testament, of whom the Lord is obviously speaking, said many things about His Second Coming, and they mainly told of what would happen before He came. They did say He would "come in the glory of his Father with his angels" (Matthew 16:27). We will leave the details of His coming to a discussion of later sections of the Doctrine and Covenants which discuss the topic. The Lord's dwelling on earth in righteousness for a thousand years after the wicked have been destroyed (D&C 29:11) will also be left to a future treatise.

D&C 29:12–13 • The Twelve Apostles Judge the House of Israel

12 And again, verily, verily, I say unto you, and it hath gone forth in a firm decree, by the will of the Father, that mine apostles, the Twelve which were with me in my ministry at Jerusalem, shall stand at my right hand at the day of my coming in a pillar of fire, being clothed with robes

of righteousness, with crowns upon their heads, in glory even as I am, to judge the whole house of Israel, even as many as have loved me and kept my commandments, and none else.

13 For a trump shall sound both long and loud, even as upon Mount Sinai, and all the earth shall quake, and they shall come forth—yea, even the dead which died in me, to receive a crown of righteousness, and to be clothed upon, even as I am, to be with me, that we may be one.

The Apostle Paul said: "For we must all appear before the judgment-seat of Christ; that every one may receive *a reward* of the *deeds* done in *the* body, according to *what* he hath done, whether good or bad" (JST, 2 Corinthians 5:10; *italics* indicates changes). The Doctrine and Covenants revelation states they will be at His right hand to judge the house of Israel (D&C 29:12). A seeming contradiction is given by Jacob, brother of Nephi, who said: . . . and the keeper of the gate [to heaven] is the Holy One of Israel; and he employeth no servant there; and there is none other way save it be by the gate; for he cannot be deceived, for the Lord God is his name" (2 Nephi 9:41). Mormon, one of the Apostles among the Nephites (see 3 Nephi 5:13; Moroni 2:1[31]; *HC*, 4:538), sheds further light on the judgment.

18 Yea, behold, I write unto all the ends of the earth; yea, unto you, twelve tribes of Israel, who shall be judged according to your works by the twelve whom Jesus chose to be his disciples in the land of Jerusalem.

19 And I write also unto the remnant of this people, who shall also be judged by the twelve whom Jesus chose in this land; and they shall be judged by the other twelve whom Jesus chose in the land of Jerusalem.

20 And these things doth the Spirit manifest unto me; therefore I write unto you all. And for this cause I write unto you, that ye may know that ye must all stand before the judgment-seat of Christ, yea, every soul who belongs to the whole human family of Adam; and ye must stand to be judged of your works, whether they be good or evil; [Mormon 3:18–20]

---

[31] "This [Book of Mormon] also tells us that our Savior made His appearance upon this continent after His resurrection; that He planted the Gospel here in all its fulness, and richness, and power, and blessings; that they had the Apostles, Prophets, Pastors, Teachers, and Evangelists; the same order, the same priesthood, the same ordinances, gifts, powers and blessings, as were enjoyed on the eastern continent." The Wentworth Letter (*HC*, 4:538).

The apostles, of both Jerusalem and the Americas, will be with Christ at the judgment bar, but in their role as "special witnesses of the name of Christ" (D&C 107:23). The prophets will also be there. The wording, "even as many as have loved me and kept my commandments, and none else" (v. 12), suggests the apostles will judge only the righteous; but it seems to have reference to those who were living on the earth at the time of His coming and were preserved because of their righteousness. This will include terrestrial type people as well as celestial (see 3 Nephi 10:12). In the judgment, the apostles and prophets will testify of what they taught to the nations of the earth, and their words will either condemn us or exonerate us. We will know or remember what they did and said, and know that the judgment of Christ that is given is justified. Nephi will be there (see 2 Nephi 33:14–15); Jacob will be there (see Jacob 6:13); and Moroni will be there (see Moroni 10:34).

The resurrection of the celestial dead will then take place (see D&C 88:97–98). At the sound of a trump "even the dead which died in me" shall come and receive their crowns, and robes of righteousness "be clothed upon them" (v. 13). The resurrection will take some time; not all who have died will come at the same time. Thus those who died in righteousness, who qualified for the celestial kingdom while living on the earth, will come forth first. These will be followed by those who accepted the gospel and had their ordinances done vicariously. These are also celestial saints, but are not mentioned here because the Lord is only describing the beginning of the millennium. Again, more of these details and order will be given to us as we study the remaining sections of the Doctrine and Covenants.

D&C 29:14–21 • Signs to Precede His Coming

14 But, behold, I say unto you that before this great day shall come the sun shall be darkened, and the moon shall be turned into blood, and the stars shall fall from heaven, and there shall be greater signs in heaven above and in the earth beneath;

15 And there shall be weeping and wailing among the hosts of men;

16 And there shall be a great hailstorm sent forth to destroy the crops of the earth.

17 And it shall come to pass, because of the wickedness of the world,

that I will take vengeance upon the wicked, for they will not repent; for the cup of mine indignation is full; for behold, my blood shall not cleanse them if they hear me not.

18 Wherefore, I the Lord God will send forth flies upon the face of the earth, which shall take hold of the inhabitants thereof, and shall eat their flesh, and shall cause maggots to come in upon them;

19 And their tongues shall be stayed that they shall not utter against me; and their flesh shall fall from off their bones, and their eyes from their sockets;

20 And it shall come to pass that the beasts of the forest and the fowls of the air shall devour them up.

21 And the great and abominable church, which is the whore of all the earth, shall be cast down by devouring fire, according as it is spoken by the mouth of Ezekiel the prophet, who spoke of these things, which have not come to pass but surely must, as I live, for abominations shall not reign.

The first sign to come before the Lord's Second Coming spoken of here; the sun darkened, the moon turned to blood, and the stars falling from heaven (v. 14), is in the category of some of Isaiah's prophecies as were explained by Nephi. "In the days that the prophecies of Isaiah [heavenly signs] shall be fulfilled men shall know of a surety, at the times when they shall come to pass" (2 Nephi 25:7). When they happen we will know that they are fulfilled, but probably not until after. The greater signs both in heaven and in earth (D&C 29:14) must be very catastrophic. They will cause weeping and wailing among the hosts [large populations] of men (v. 15). Perhaps these tragedies have already commenced, with tidal waves, earthquakes, tornados and other acts of nature happening each year. The great hailstorms destroying the crops of the earth are still in the future (v. 16), but certainly other causes of crop failure—drought, frost, or insects—seem to be on the increase. The wickedness of the world, the cause of these destructions (v. 17), is also certainly increasing. We must be careful not to judge particular areas or peoples, but the overall wickedness of the world is evident.

The flies eating the flesh of people, the maggots, their flesh falling from the bones, the eyes falling from the sockets, and the beasts and fowls devouring the inhabitants of the earth (vv. 18–20) seem to be all related. Are they a part of the "desolating scourge" or sickness that was to be poured out from time to time until the earth is utterly destroyed (D&C 5:19; 45:31)? They are definitely a voice of warning from the Lord (see D&C 43:25).

The fall of the great and abominable church is often interpreted to be all evil. That seems to be the context here. The Prophet Ezekiel, in prophesying of the battle of Gog and Magog, included many of the above catastrophes that would come upon the land of Israel: "And I will plead against him with pestilence and with blood; and I will rain upon him, and upon his bands, and upon the many people that are with him, an overflowing rain, and great hailstones, fire, and brimstone" (Ezekiel 38:22). There were other devastations (see Ezekiel 38:20–21). They will apparently be worldwide when fulfilled as prophesied here. The devouring fire that destroys the abominable church, will be the glory of the Lord that will cleanse the earth as the Prophet Malachi foretold, as mentioned above.

D&C 29:22–25 • A New Heaven and a New Earth

22 And again, verily, verily, I say unto you that when the thousand years are ended, and men again begin to deny their God, then will I spare the earth but for a little season;

23 And the end shall come, and the heaven and the earth shall be consumed and pass away, and there shall be a new heaven and a new earth.

24 For all old things shall pass away, and all things shall become new, even the heaven and the earth, and all the fulness thereof, both men and beasts, the fowls of the air, and the fishes of the sea;

25 And not one hair, neither mote, shall be lost, for it is the workmanship of mine hand.

The Lord gives a brief view of what will happen after the thousand year Millennium. The little season when men begin to deny their God (v. 22), shows that agency is still a basic law even during this time period. During the Millennium, "because of the righteousness of the people, Satan has no power" (1 Nephi 22:26). Therefore, he will be loosed because the people again choose to be wicked. The pattern is given us in the Book of Mormon after the time of Christ's visit and all are converted unto the Lord (see 4 Nephi 1:2). A small part of the people revolt and then it gets progressively worse (see 4 Nephi 1:20 to the end). The earth's temporal existence is only seven thousand years (D&C 77:7); Therefore, the little season must be a very short period even by earth time.

The new heaven and the new earth (D&C 29:23–24) were foretold by Isaiah in the Old Testament. All that Isaiah adds is that "the former [earth] shall not be remembered" (Isaiah 65:17). Jesus says in the New Testament "that heaven and earth shall pass away," but does not mention the new heaven and earth. In this revelation, the Lord includes men, the beasts, fowls, and fishes becoming new (D&C 29:24). It is another way of saying they will be resurrected. They will have a literal resurrection; nothing shall be lost, not even a hair, or a mote (a small speck) of the actual body (v. 25). The earth will also be resurrected as a celestial kingdom, for those of this earth who attain a celestial resurrection to abide upon (see D&C 88:25–26).

D&C 29:26–29 • The Graves Opened—the Resurrection

26 But, behold, verily I say unto you, before the earth shall pass away, Michael, mine archangel, shall sound his trump, and then shall all the dead awake, for their graves shall be opened, and they shall come forth—yea, even all.

27 And the righteous shall be gathered on my right hand unto eternal life; and the wicked on my left hand will I be ashamed to own before the Father;

28 Wherefore I will say unto them—Depart from me, ye cursed, into everlasting fire, prepared for the devil and his angels.

29 And now, behold, I say unto you, never at any time have I declared from mine own mouth that they should return, for where I am they cannot come, for they have no power.

The Lord comes back to the resurrection that will take place before the heaven and the earth pass away (v. 26). It will be under the direction of Michael, or Adam, because he is the father of "every living creature, both men, women, and children" and they belong to his family (2 Nephi 9:21). There will be an order in the resurrection. Those who lived before the time of Christ will be resurrected before those who lived after His time (see Alma 40:18–19), although many of the time period before Christ have already been resurrected (see Matthew 27:52–53; 3 Nephi 23:9–13).

Although all men will be resurrected, there will be four different kinds of resurrection: a celestial, a terrestrial, a telestial, and even the sons of perdition, (though they will not receive a glory) (see D&C 88:28–32; 1 Corinthians 15:40–42). The righteous, the celestial and the terrestrial beings, will be resurrected at the beginning or during the millennium (D&C 88:97–99), and the telestial beings and the sons of perdition will be resurrected at the end of the millennium (D&C 88:100–101). The sons of perdition are those who will be cursed and go to the place prepared for the devil and his angels (D&C 29:28). The everlasting fire is their mental torment in knowing what they could have enjoyed (see 2 Nephi 9:12–16). Their end, place and torment are known only to those who go there and are partakers of it (see D&C 76:45–46). They will have no opportunity to come to Christ—another evidence of there being no progression from one glory to another. Nor will there be any way of getting out of the devil's place after the resurrection. The resurrected state is permanent.

D&C 29:30–35 • All Things Are Spiritual Unto Christ

30 But remember that all my judgments are not given unto men; and as the words have gone forth out of my mouth even so shall they be fulfilled, that the first shall be last, and that the last shall be first in all things whatsoever I have created by the word of my power, which is the power of my Spirit.

31 For by the power of my Spirit created I them; yea, all things both spiritual and temporal—

32 First spiritual, secondly temporal, which is the beginning of my work; and again, first temporal, and secondly spiritual, which is the last of my work—

33 Speaking unto you that you may naturally understand; but unto myself my works have no end, neither beginning; but it is given unto you that ye may understand, because ye have asked it of me and are agreed.

34 Wherefore, verily I say unto you that all things unto me are spiritual, and not at any time have I given unto you a law which was temporal; neither any man, nor the children of men; neither Adam, your father, whom I created.

35 Behold, I gave unto him that he should be an agent unto himself; and I gave unto him commandment, but no temporal commandment

gave I unto him, for my commandments are spiritual; they are not natural nor temporal, neither carnal nor sensual.

The first being last and the last being first is usually associated with the preaching of the Gospel to the house of Israel first and then the Gentiles, but reversed in the last days (see Matthew 19:30; 20:16; D&C 90:9). However, Christ applies it to all things that He created (D&C 29:30). It was by the power of His Spirit, not His body, that He created or organized the earth to be inhabited by His Father's spirit offspring (v. 31). The earth was thus a spiritual sphere, and when Adam fell and became a temporal being the earth also fell and became a temporal earth. The Prophet Joseph taught: "This earth will be rolled back into the presence of God, and crowned with celestial glory" (*TPJS,* 181). Isaiah also said: "the earth shall remove out of her place . . . in the day of his fierce anger [the Second Coming]" (Isaiah 13:13). It cannot come back to a place it has not been. The earth, which is now temporal, "abideth the law of a celestial kingdom, for it filleth the measure of its creation, and transgresseth not the law—Wherefore, it shall be sanctified; yea, notwithstanding it shall die, it shall be quickened again, and shall abide the power by which it is quickened, and the righteous shall inherit it" (D&C 88:25–26). This will be the last of His work by our present understanding (D&C 29:32), but His work of creating other worlds will continue, for His work has no end (v. 33; see also Moses 1:37–38). Although there was a temporal earth with mortal or temporal inhabitants, His work was to make them all spiritual. "For behold, this is my work and my glory—to bring to pass the immortality and eternal life of man" (Moses 1:39). Therefore, "all things unto [Christ] are spiritual," and all His laws are spiritual even if given in and for a temporal condition (D&C 29:35). The Word of Wisdom was "for the temporal salvation of all saints in the last days," (D&C 89:2), but was to enable them to take hold of the principles of the gospel that would sanctify them and prepare them for the celestial kingdom (see D&C 89:18–21). The Prophet Joseph taught:

> All things whatsoever God in his infinite wisdom has seen fit and proper to reveal to us while we are dwelling in mortality, in regard to our mortal bodies, are revealed to us in the abstract, and independent of affinity of this mortal tabernacle, but are revealed to our spirits precisely as though we had no bodies at all; and those revelations which

will save our spirits will save our bodies. God reveals them to us in view
of no dissolution of the body, or tabernacle. [*TPJS*, 355]

God speaks to our spirits, and we must direct our bodies to comply to
his instructions.

Christ's creation of Adam needs some explanation. He did not create
Adam's spirit; Adam was the spirit offspring of the Father. However,
Christ created the earth under the delegation of the Father, in which task
was assisted by others (see Abraham 3:24; 4:1). He supervised the placing
of His spirit brothers and sisters on the earth so that they might obtain
bodies. Therefore, He created them in the same sense that a contractor
may construct a building, but may not actually do any of the building
himself. He arranged for and supervised its construction, specified and
approved of the materials and organization. Moroni used the same
symbolism in the Book of Mormon:

> 11 But behold, I will show unto you a God of miracles, even the God
> of Abraham, and the God of Isaac, and the God of Jacob; and it is that
> same God who created the heavens and the earth, and all things that in
> them are.
>
> 12 Behold, he created Adam, and by Adam came the fall of man. And
> because of the fall of man came Jesus Christ, even the Father and the
> Son; and because of Jesus Christ came the redemption of man. [Mormon
> 9:11:12]

The creation was the work of Christ. He was carrying out the plan of
Adam's being placed in the Garden of Eden. He allowed the conditions
of the fall and redeemed man from it. The Lord now explains further:

D&C 29:36–45 • A Third Part of the Hosts of Heaven.

> 36 And it came to pass that Adam, being tempted of the devil—for,
> behold, the devil was before Adam, for he rebelled against me, saying,
> Give me thine honor, which is my power; and also a third part of the
> hosts of heaven turned he away from me because of their agency;
>
> 37 And they were thrust down, and thus came the devil and his
> angels;
>
> 38 And, behold, there is a place prepared for them from the begin-
> ning, which place is hell.

39 And it must needs be that the devil should tempt the children of men, or they could not be agents unto themselves; for if they never should have bitter they could not know the sweet—

40 Wherefore, it came to pass that the devil tempted Adam, and he partook of the forbidden fruit and transgressed the commandment, wherein he became subject to the will of the devil, because he yielded unto temptation.

41 Wherefore, I, the Lord God, caused that he should be cast out from the Garden of Eden, from my presence, because of his transgression, wherein he became spiritually dead, which is the first death, even that same death which is the last death, which is spiritual, which shall be pronounced upon the wicked when I shall say: Depart, ye cursed.

42 But, behold, I say unto you that I, the Lord God, gave unto Adam and unto his seed, that they should not die as to the temporal death, until I, the Lord God, should send forth angels to declare unto them repentance and redemption, through faith on the name of mine Only Begotten Son.

43 And thus did I, the Lord God, appoint unto man the days of his probation—that by his natural death he might be raised in immortality unto eternal life, even as many as would believe;

44 And they that believe not unto eternal damnation; for they cannot be redeemed from their spiritual fall, because they repent not;

45 For they love darkness rather than light, and their deeds are evil, and they receive their wages of whom they list to obey.

The book of Moses, or the Joseph Smith Translation of the book of Genesis, was received a short time before (June—October 1830) and revealed part of the information that is now enlarged upon (Moses 4:1–4). Satan had sought to destroy the agency of man (Moses 4:3), which was a spiritual law to provide an opportunity for men to gain happiness through progression (D&C 29:35 above). Satan had enticed a third part of the spirit children of our Father to rebel with him, and they had been cast out (D&C 29:36). This rebellion had also been shown to John the Revelator (see Revelation 12:1–7). Note that both accounts say a "third part," not one-third, as often heard in the Church. A third part means there were two other parts. How were these divided? Apparently, one was the valiant supporters of the plan of the Father that was presented in that grand council. The other part had not exercised as much faith and works in their pre-mortal life as had the first group, and were not as ready or eager to prove themselves (see Alma 13:1–5). They did not follow Satan, but chose to follow the plan; they were not fence-sitters as some have suggested. There is no indication of the number or the percentage among each group, but they do not have to be equal in number. If the numbers were equal, the number of mortals on earth, no matter what time period is being considered, would be severely outnumbered by the devils and his angels (D&C 29:37). For God to lose that many of his spirit children seems unlikely to this writer. The third part, which are many (Abraham 3:28) (but not necessarily one-third,) that followed Satan is destined to be in hell, the place prepared for them from the beginning (D&C 29:38). They are miserable, and are seeking "the misery of all mankind" (2 Nephi 2:18). Nevertheless, the Lord has used their foolishness to provide the earth's inhabitants to be tested through their agency. They must have the bitter to know and appreciate the sweet (v. 39; see also see 2 Nephi 2:11–25).

Adam broke a physical commandment by eating the forbidden fruit. As taught by President Joseph Fielding Smith; "the forbidden fruit had the power to create blood and change his nature and mortality took the place of immortality" (D.S. 1:77). Adam did not sin; he transgressed the commandment (D&C 29:40). Sin is a willful disobedience, or transgressing "contrary to his own knowledge" (Mosiah 2:33). The veil over his mind left him without knowledge of his life before Eden. His transgression did subject him to the devil; the Prophet Joseph taught: "The devil has no power over us only as we permit him. The moment we revolt at anything that comes from God, the devil takes power" (TPJS, 181). The Lord does not mention Eve's role in this revelation, so we will not comment either. Adam's spiritual death, or severance from the Lord's presence, is the first death and the last death. According to the law, Adam died spiritually first, but it is the last death for the wicked that do not meet the requirements for the celestial kingdom, and do not dwell eternally in the presence of God.

In His mercy, the Lord God preserved Adam from temporal death until after angels had declared "repentance and redemption through faith on the name of his Only Begotten Son (D&C 29:42). This doctrine was taught in the Joseph Smith Translation (see Moses 5:6–11). The Lord seemingly repeated it here to prepare Joseph and the Church for a related doctrine, or to make it more available until the JST was published.

That earth life is our "days of probation" to determine our eternal life or eternal damnation (D&C 29:43–44) had been beautifully expressed by Alma:

24 And we see that death comes upon mankind, yea, the death which has been spoken of by Amulek, which is the temporal death; nevertheless there was a space granted unto man in which he might repent; therefore this life became a probationary state; a time to prepare to meet God; a time to prepare for that endless state which has been spoken of by us, which is after the resurrection of the dead.

25 Now, if it had not been for the plan of redemption, which was laid from the foundation of the world, there could have been no resurrection of the dead; but there was a plan of redemption laid, which shall bring to pass the resurrection of the dead, of which has been spoken. [Alma 12:24–25]

Those who follow Satan love darkness rather than light which is typical of everything that we do or love (D&C 29:45). Alma said:

19 Now I would that ye should see that they brought upon themselves the curse; and even so doth every man that is cursed bring upon himself his own condemnation. . . .

26 And in one year were thousands and tens of thousands of souls sent to the eternal world, that they might reap their rewards according to their works, whether they were good or whether they were bad, to reap eternal happiness or eternal misery, according to the spirit which they listed to obey, whether it be a good spirit or a bad one. [Alma 3:19, 26]

As Jesus said: "No man can serve two masters: for either he will hate the one, and love the other; or else he will hold to the one, and despise the other. Ye cannot serve God and mammon" (Matthew 6:24; 3 Nephi 13:24). And Joshua said, probably quoting Enoch: "And if it seem evil unto you to serve the LORD, choose you this day whom ye will serve; whether the gods which your fathers served that [were] on the other side of the flood, or the gods of the Amorites, in whose land ye dwell: but as for me and my house, we will serve the LORD" (Joshua 24:15; see Moses 6:33, Alma 30:8).

D&C 29:46–50 • Little Children Cannot be Tempted

46 But behold, I say unto you, that little children are redeemed from the foundation of the world through mine Only Begotten;

47 Wherefore, they cannot sin, for power is not given unto Satan to tempt little children, until they begin to become accountable before me;

48 For it is given unto them even as I will, according to mine own pleasure, that great things may be required at the hand of their fathers.

49 And, again, I say unto you, that whoso having knowledge, have I not commanded to repent?

50 And he that hath no understanding, it remaineth in me to do according as it is written. And now I declare no more unto you at this time. Amen.

Joseph Smith had probably learned, while translating the Bible, that children were to be circumcised at eight days of age: "And I will establish a covenant of circumcision with [Abraham], and it shall be my covenant between me and thee, and thy seed after thee, in their generations; that thou mayest know for ever that children are not accountable before me until they are eight years old" (JST, Genesis 17:11). The Prophet Joseph declared, "Circumcision is not baptism, neither was baptism instituted in the place of circumcision. Baptism is for remission of sins. Children have no sins" (*TPJS,* 314). In the Old Testament it was practiced as a form of cleanliness and used as a symbol of accountability. The Lord has not given this dispensation any instructions on its practice.

This revelation (D&C 29) enlarges upon the doctrine of accountability. Little children are redeemed by Jesus Christ from the foundation of the world (v. 46). This doctrine is taught in the Bible: "I write unto you, little children, because your sins are forgiven you for his name's sake" (1 John 2:12). However those religions that baptize little children erroneously interpret this passage as referring to being little children in the gospel, or new members in the church. In truth, Satan cannot tempt actual little children because they are not accountable. They are not capable of understanding the significance of baptism until they are that age (D&C 29:47). The Lord places great responsibility on the children's fathers to teach them the purpose of baptism by the time they are accountable (v. 48). All who are accountable are commanded to repent (v. 49). The Lord gave us the background of the accountability of little children so we would be able to understand the final doctrine of this revelation. There are people who, for one reason or another, are handicapped mentally and cannot intellectually understand the purpose of baptism. These people come under the same doctrine as is written about the little children (v. 50). The Book of Mormon gives us a sermon on the subject that fully explains the doctrine (see Moroni 8), but we will not quote it here. There will be other opportunities to explain further.

The Lord's plan covers everyone, and we must see where we fit into that plan, and know that all things are spiritual unto the Lord. All things should be spiritual to us as well.

General Authority Quotes

—*The Prophet Joseph Smith* • D&C 29 and the JST

The Lord would cut short his work in righteousness and except the Church receive the fulness of the Scriptures that they would yet fail. [*TPJS,* 9]

I resumed the translation of the Scriptures. From sundry revelations which had been received, it was apparent that many important points touching the salvation of men, had been taken from the Bible, or lost before it was compiled. [*TPJS,* 9–11]

I believe the Bible as it read when it came from the pen of the original writers. Ignorant translators, careless transcribers, or designing and corrupt priests have committed many errors. [*TPJS,* 327]

—*Elder James E. Talmage* • D&C 29:1

Jesus of Nazareth, who in solemn testimony to the Jews declared himself the *I Am* or *Jehovah,* who was God before Abraham lived on earth, was the same Being who is repeatedly proclaimed as the God who made covenant with Abraham, Isaac, and Jacob; the God who led Israel from the bondage of Egypt to the freedom of the promised land, the one and only God known by direct and personal revelation to the Hebrew prophets in general. [*Jesus the Christ,* 35]

—*Elder Charles A. Callis* • D&C 29:11

Now the great day of the Lord is coming. It is going to be a terrible day. The wicked are going to be destroyed and when I say the wicked I do not mean everybody outside the Mormon Church. There will

be countless millions of people not of this Church spared because they are not ripe in iniquity and to them we will preach the everlasting Gospel and bring them to Christ. [CR, April 1935, 18]

—President George Albert Smith • D&C 29:16–19

It will not be long until calamities will overtake the human family unless there is speedy repentance. It will not be long before those who are scattered over the face of the earth by millions will die like flies because of what will come.

Our Heavenly Father has told us how it can be avoided, and that is our mission, in part, to go into the world and explain to people how it may be avoided, and that people need not be unhappy as they are everywhere but that happiness may be in their lives—because when the Spirit of God burns in your soul, you cannot be otherwise than happy. [CR, April 1950, 169]

—The Prophet Joseph Smith • D&C 29:29

. . . the Lord never authorized them to say that the devil, his angels, or the sons of perdition, should ever be restored; for their state of destiny was not revealed to man, is not revealed, nor ever shall be revealed, save to those who are made partakers thereof: consequently those who teach this doctrine have not received it of the Spirit of the Lord. Truly brother Oliver declared it to be the doctrine of devils. We, therefore, command that this doctrine be taught no more in Zion. [*TPJS,* 24]

—Elder Wilford Woodruff • D&C 29:46–48

Children are taken away in their infancy, and they go to the spirit world. They come here and fulfill the object of their coming, that is, they tabernacle in the flesh. . . . Our children will be restored to us as they are laid down if we, their parents, keep the faith and prove ourselves worthy to obtain eternal life; and if we do not prove ourselves our children will still be preserved, and will inherit eternal glory. This is my view in regard to all infants who die, whether they be born to Jew or Gentile, righteous or wicked. They come from their eternal father and their eternal Mother unto whom they were born in the eternal world, and they will be restored to their eternal parentage; and all parents who have received children here according to the order of God and the holy priesthood, no matter in what age they may have lived will claim those children in the morning of the resurrection, and they will be given unto them and they will grace their family organizations in the celestial world. . . . [*JD*, June 24, 1835, 18:32]

—President Joseph Fielding Smith • D&C 29:50

We have good reason to believe that all spirits while in the pre-existence were perfect in form, having all their faculties and mental powers unimpaired. It is difficult to believe that in that existence spirits were deficient, for that was a perfect world notwithstanding each spirit had his or her free agency. The reasons for these deformities in body and mind are therefore physical. In other words they are confined to the mortal existence, and they are due to physical injury or impairment which comes because of accident or sickness before birth. We have a case in point in the healing of the man who was born blind. The disciples came to the Savior and asked the question whether this man was suffering this blindness as a punishment because of some personal sin before he was born or was it due to the sins of the parents? The Savior's answer was that neither the parents nor this man had sinned to bring upon him the pre-natal blindness. It like all other cases of deficient powers, was due to a physical condition over which child or parents had no control.

The Lord has made it known by revelation that children born with retarded minds shall receive blessings just like little children who die in infancy. They are free from sin, because their minds are not capable of a correct understanding of right and wrong (refers to and quotes Moroni 8; and D&C 29).

Therefore the Church of Jesus Christ of Latter-day Saints considers all deficient children with retarded capacity to understand, just the same as little children under the age of accountability. They are redeemed without baptism and will go to the celestial kingdom of God, there, we believe, to have their faculties or other deficiencies restored according to the Father's mercy and justice. [*Answers to Gospel Questions*, 3:19–21]

Chapter Eighteen

The Lord Provides Leadership

D&C 31; 33; 34; 35; 36

*H*istorical Setting—Section 31: The five sections included in this chapter were given between the end of September, 1830 and sometime in December 1830. A three day conference had been held beginning on September 26th, and section 31 was the last of four revelations received before the elders had separated to go to their various places. The Lamanite mission, discussed in chapter 16, commenced on this occasion. Thomas B. Marsh, to whom this revelation was given:

> ... [had] joined the Methodist church (in New York), but in comparing its principles with the Scripture, and failing to make them correspond, he withdrew from all sects, but expected and indeed predicted the rise of a new church which should have the truth in its purity. He was moved by the Spirit to make a journey west, during which he heard of the Book of Mormon. He met Martin Harris at the office where it was being printed, and secured proof sheets of the first sixteen pages. He later met Oliver Cowdery, and remained with him two days, receiving from him full information as to the coming forth of the Book of Mormon. Returning to his home near Boston, he kept up a correspondence with the Prophet and Oliver for about a year; and upon hearing of the organization of the Church, he moved to Palmyra in September, 1830, and was baptized by David Whitmer, and a few days later was ordained an elder by Oliver Cowdery. [*HC*, 1:117]

INTRODUCTION

Paul taught the people on Mars Hill at Athens that God "hath made of one blood all nations of men for to dwell on all the face of the earth, and hath determined the times before appointed, and the bounds of their habitation" (Acts 17:26). The men to whom the revelations being considered here were given were part of this pre-mortal determination. Thomas B. Marsh became the President of the Quorum of the Twelve Apostles. Ezra Thayre and Northrop Sweet became missionaries for the Lord Jesus Christ. Orson Pratt became a member of the first Quorum of the Twelve Apostles. Sidney Rigdon became the First Counselor in the First Presidency of the Church, and Edward Partridge became the first bishop in Zion. The Lord had raised them up at this period of time to fulfill these positions. Although many of them left the Church at one time or another, they had their agency and no doubt their actions in these callings will be taken into consideration at the time of their final accounting to the Lord.

SECTION 31 • OUTLINE

➤ 31:1–2   Thomas is blessed because of his faith in the Lord's work.

                a.   He has had many afflictions because of his family (v. 1).

                b.   He and his family will be blessed, the day will come that they will believe, know the truth, and be one with him in the church (v. 2).

➤ 31:3–6   The hour of Thomas's mission is come, his tongue shall be loosed, and shall declare glad tidings of joy to this generation.

                a.   Declare the things revealed to Joseph Smith Jr. (v. 3).

                b.   Preach from this time forth, reap the field which is white ready to harvest (v. 4).

                c.   Thrust in your sickle with all your soul, your sins shall be forgiven you (v. 4).

                d.   You shall be laden with sheaves upon your back, the laborer is worthy of his hire, your family shall live (v. 6).

➤ 31:7–9   The hearts of the people shall receive you, and I will establish a church by you.

                a.   You shall strengthen and prepare them for when they shall be gathered (v. 8).

                  b.   Be patient in affliction, revile not against those that revile (v. 9).

   c.   Govern your own house in meekness, and be steadfast
        (v. 9).

➤ 31:10–13   You shall be a physician to the church but not unto the world,
             for they will not receive you.

   a.   The Comforter will give you what you shall do and where
        to go (v. 11).

   b.   Pray always lest you enter into temptation and lose your
        reward (v. 12).

   c.   Be faithful unto the end and I am with you (v. 13).

   d.   These words are not of men but of Jesus Christ (v. 13).

TEXT AND COMMENTARY

D&C 31:1–6 • I Will Bless You and Your Family

1 Thomas, my son, blessed are you because of your faith in my work.

2 Behold, you have had many afflictions because of your family;
nevertheless, I will bless you and your family, yea, your little ones; and
the day cometh that they will believe and know the truth and be one with
you in my church.

3 Lift up your heart and rejoice, for the hour of your mission is come;
and your tongue shall be loosed, and you shall declare glad tidings of
great joy unto this generation.

4 You shall declare the things which have been revealed to my servant,
Joseph Smith, Jun. You shall begin to preach from this time forth, yea,
to reap in the field which is white already to be burned.

5 Therefore, thrust in your sickle with all your soul, and your sins
are forgiven you, and you shall be laden with sheaves upon your back,
for the laborer is worthy of his hire. Wherefore, your family shall live.

6 Behold, verily I say unto you, go from them only for a little time,
and declare my word, and I will prepare a place for them.

   The first six verses, plus verse 9, a total of seven of the thirteen verses
of this revelation, are centered around the family of Brother Marsh. The
many afflictions he had suffered because of his family (v. 2) are not
enumerated. Apparently his children and perhaps others of his extended
family did not believe in the gospel which he had recently embraced, and
they had not been baptized. The conditional promise for their believing

and knowing the truth, and coming into the Church was his being a faithful missionary (vv. 3–6). The Lord blesses his servants in their absence from their families' while they are doing his work. These blessings are also conditional, because of the families agency. The Lord will manifest the truth to them, but He honors their right to choose to accept it.

The metaphor of reaping the field that was white ready to be burned (v. 4) is an extension of the field being white, ready to be harvested (see sections 4; 6; 11–12; 14–16). Grain, especially barley, is white when it is ready to harvest; and following the harvest it was burned in preparation for the next season of planting. In the gospel analogy, the truth is proclaimed and those who accept it are gathered out while those who reject it will be burned at the Second Coming. "Your family shall live" (D&C 31:5), and "I will prepare a place for them" (v. 6), suggests eternal life in the post mortal life. These blessings will be fulfilled after the Second Coming.

D&C 31:7–13 • Thomas B. Marsh—a Physician to the Church

7 Yea, I will open the hearts of the people, and they will receive you. And I will establish a church by your hand;

8 And you shall strengthen them and prepare them against the time when they shall be gathered.

9 Be patient in afflictions, revile not against those that revile. Govern your house in meekness, and be steadfast.

10 Behold, I say unto you that you shall be a physician unto the church, but not unto the world, for they will not receive you.

11 Go your way whithersoever I will, and it shall be given you by the Comforter what you shall do and whither you shall go.

12 Pray always, lest you enter into temptation and lose your reward.

13 Be faithful unto the end, and lo, I am with you. These words are not of man nor of men, but of me, even Jesus Christ, your Redeemer, by the will of the Father. Amen.

These verses define Thomas' role in the newly established Church. His establishing a church (v. 7) refers to a branch of the church being organized where he is sent to preach, and those who accept are gathered together as a unit of the church. "The time when they shall be gathered"

(v. 8) refers to a spiritual "gathering" accomplished by their accepting the gospel; this gathering is in preparation for the Second Coming when the wicked will be burned.

The admonition to be patient in his afflictions and revile not (v. 9) may have reference to his family again, but also includes those to whom he will preach the gospel. "Revile" means to verbally abuse. However, to be meek and steadfast in governing his family (v. 9) is definitely a current situation. His failure to do so was the cause of his later apostasy (see quote by George A. Smith, at end of chapter).

The Lord's call to Thomas, to be a physician to the church, is significant (v. 10). It probably has reference to his future position as President of the Quorum of the Twelve Apostles, since it is "unto the Church." A physician diagnoses the cause of an illness or the extent of an injury, and then prescribes the necessary medicines or procedures for healing. Brother Marsh's diagnoses (what he shall do) and his prescriptions (where he shall go) would be given him by the Comforter (v. 11). That he not make the wrong diagnosis, or make the wrong prescription, would be dependent on his praying always lest he enter into temptation and lose his reward (v. 12), and his faithfulness to the end (v. 13). The reward of his prayers would be the direction of the Comforter, and his faithfulness to the end would be his following the words of Jesus Christ that had just come to him by the will of the Father (v. 13). Again, the failure to do these things was the cause of his fall.

H istorical Setting—Section 33: Section 33 was given to Ezra Thayre and Northrop Sweet in October, 1830. Both of these men "came in the Church at the time of the preaching of the Lamanite missionaries. It was not long after this that Northrop Sweet left the Church and, with some others, formed what they called 'The Pure Church of Christ,' an organization that soon came to its end." (*Church History and Modern Day Revelation*, 1:152)

SECTION 33 • OUTLINE

➤ 33:1–4   Ezra and Northrop are to open their ears and hearken to the voice of the Lord, whose voice is as a two-edged sword to divide joints and marrow, a diviner of thoughts and intents of the heart.

    a.   Lift up your voices as a trump and declare my gospel unto a crooked and preserve generation (v. 2).

    b.   The field is white ready to harvest and it is the eleventh hour, the last time to call laborers into Christ's vineyard (v. 3).

    c.   Christ's vineyard is corrupt, none doeth good but a few, and they err in many instances because of priestcrafts (v. 4).

➤ 33:5–9   This church is established and called out of the wilderness.

    a.   Christ's elect will be gathered from the four quarters of the earth, as many as labor and hearken to his voice (v. 6).

    b.   Thrust in your sickle and reap with all your might, mind, and strength (v. 7).

    c.   Open your mouths and they shall be filled and become as Nephi of old (v. 8).

    d.   Open your mouths and you shall be laden with sheaves upon your backs (v. 9).

➤ 33:10–14   Open your mouths and say repent, prepare ye the way of the Lord, be baptized, and then cometh the baptism of fire and the Holy Ghost.

    a.   This is my gospel, have faith or you cannot be saved (v. 12).

    b.   Upon this rock I will build my church and the gates of hell shall not prevail against it (v. 13).

    c.   Remember the church articles and covenants to keep them (v. 14).

    d.   Those having faith you shall confirm in my church and bestow the gift of the Holy Ghost (v. 15).

➤ 33:16–18   The Book of Mormon and the holy scriptures are given for your instruction, and the power of my Spirit quickeneth all things.

    a.   Be faithful, prayful, and have your lamps trimmed and burning with oil (v. 17).

b.   I come quickly (v. 1).

TEXT AND COMMENTARY

D&C 33:1–4 • The Eleventh Hour to Prune the Vineyard

1 Behold, I say unto you, my servants Ezra and Northrop, open ye your ears and hearken to the voice of the Lord your God, whose word is quick and powerful, sharper than a two-edged sword, to the dividing asunder of the joints and marrow, soul and spirit; and is a discerner of the thoughts and intents of the heart.

2 For verily, verily, I say unto you that ye are called to lift up your voices as with the sound of a trump, to declare my gospel unto a crooked and perverse generation.

3 For behold, the field is white already to harvest; and it is the eleventh hour, and the last time that I shall call laborers into my vineyard.

4 And my vineyard has become corrupted every whit; and there is none which doeth good save it be a few; and they err in many instances because of priestcrafts, all having corrupt minds.

The comparison of the word of God to a two-edged sword (v. 1) was also used in the early revelations (see sections 4; 6; 11–12; 14–16), and will not be repeated here. The crooked and perverse generation (v. 2) is the generation of the Gentiles who were to receive the gospel first in the last days, and then it would be taken to the house of Israel (see D&C 90:8–10; Matthew 19:30).

The eleventh hour (D&C 33:3) was used in the parable of the labourers in the vineyard (Matthew 20:1–16), and in the parable of the ten virgins (Matthew 15:1–13), both referring to the time of the Second Coming drawing near. "The last time I will call laborers into my vineyard" was used in the allegory of the house of Israel given by the Old Testament prophet Zenos, but lost from the Bible (see 1 Nephi 13:26–29). It was copied from the plates of brass by Jacob, brother of Nephi, and included in the Book of Mormon. The allegory refers to "the end draweth nigh," and "the end is nigh at hand" (Jacob 5:62, 71), or the approaching of the Second Coming.

That none doeth good save it be a few (D&C 33:4) was also a warning given by Nephi in the Book of Mormon (2 Nephi 28:14, see the entire chapter). Priestcraft was also cited as being the cause of the corrupted vineyard and was defined by Nephi: "[the Lord] commandeth that there shall be no priestcrafts; for, behold, priestcrafts are that men preach and set themselves up for a light unto the world, that they may get gain and praise of the world; but they seek not the welfare of Zion" (2 Nephi 26:29). The term is not used in the Bible, probable because of the loss of plain and precious parts (1 Nephi 13:26–29).

D&C 33:5–9 • The Church Called Out of the Wilderness

> 5 And verily, verily, I say unto you, that this church have I established and called forth out of the wilderness.
>
> 6 And even so will I gather mine elect from the four quarters of the earth, even as many as will believe in me, and hearken unto my voice.
>
> 7 Yea, verily, verily, I say unto you, that the field is white already to harvest; wherefore, thrust in your sickles, and reap with all your might, mind, and strength.
>
> 8 Open your mouths and they shall be filled, and you shall become even as Nephi of old, who journeyed from Jerusalem in the wilderness.
>
> 9 Yea, open your mouths and spare not, and you shall be laden with sheaves upon your backs, for lo, I am with you.

The church established and called forth out of the wilderness (v. 5) was foreseen by John the Revelator (see Revelation 12:6; JST, Revelation 12:5–7). The organization of the Church on April 6, 1830 fulfilled that prophecy. With the Church established, the gathering of the Lord's elect—the house of Israel, the sheep who will hear His voice (see John 10:26)—commenced. The house of Israel was scattered among the Gentiles as prophesied by the prophet Amos (see Amos 9:8–9; see also D&C 29:7; 86:8–10; JS—M 1:22; Abraham 2:9–11).

The Gentiles who hearken will also be gathered and adopted into Israel (see 1 Nephi 22:8–9, Abraham 2:10; D&C 84:33–34). The four quarters

of the earth from whence the people are gathered are formed by dissecting the center place of Zion into four equal parts that extend outward.

The harvest of the white field (D&C 33:7), is the gathering of the wheat from the tares (D&C 86:7). To reap with all your might, mind, and strength is to open your mouth and proclaim the gospel with all your physical, intellectual, and social power. The Lord will then fill our mouths, by the direction of the Spirit, with the truths of the gospel as was experienced by Nephi as he journeyed in the wilderness and taught his rebellious brothers (D&C 33:8; see 1 Nephi 15–18). The sheaves with which those proclaiming the gospel will be laden (v. 9) are those who accept the gospel, or the converts that are gathered out of the nations of the Gentiles under the direction of the Lord who will be with them.

D&C 33:10–15 • This Is My Gospel

10 Yea, open your mouths and they shall be filled, saying: Repent, repent, and prepare ye the way of the Lord, and make his paths straight; for the kingdom of heaven is at hand;

11 Yea, repent and be baptized, every one of you, for a remission of your sins; yea, be baptized even by water, and then cometh the baptism of fire and of the Holy Ghost.

12 Behold, verily, verily, I say unto you, this is my gospel; and remember that they shall have faith in me or they can in nowise be saved;

13 And upon this rock I will build my church; yea, upon this rock ye are built, and if ye continue, the gates of hell shall not prevail against you.

14 And ye shall remember the church articles and covenants to keep them.

15 And whoso having faith you shall confirm in my church, by the laying on of the hands, and I will bestow the gift of the Holy Ghost upon them.

The message to come out of the mouth of the missionaries was the same as John the Baptist's in the meridian of time; repent and prepare the way of the Lord (v. 10, see Matthew 3:1–3). The summation of the message in both time periods is that the gospel has been restored. The gospel was then defined (D&C 33:11–12). Although the gospel definition was enlarged upon in other places (see 3 Nephi 27:13–20; D&C

76:40–42), the general one given here is consistent with other definitions in the Doctrine and Covenants (see 39:5–6; 68:8–9; 84:27; 112:28–29).

The gospel is the rock upon which the Church was to be built (D&C 33:13). The Prophet Joseph Smith's definition of the rock as "revelation" (*TPJS*, 274), and as "Christ" (*TPJS*, 318), is not contradictory of the rock being the gospel. The source of the gospel is by revelation given through Christ. In a revelation to Hyrum Smith, the Lord said: "Wait a little longer, until you shall have my word [the Book of Mormon], my rock, my church, and my gospel, that you may know of a surety my doctrine. . . . Build upon my rock, which is my gospel" (D&C 11:16; 24). The gates of hell not prevailing against the Church was often used in connection with the Church (see Matthew 16:18; 3 Nephi 11:39; D&C 10:69; 18:5).

The Church articles and covenants that the missionaries were to keep (D&C 33:14) were the twentieth and twenty-second sections of the present Doctrine and Covenants. These revelations were carried by the missionaries and read to prospective new members of the Church (see *The Evening And The Morning Star*, No. 1, Independence, Missouri, June 1832). The baptism of fire and the Holy Ghost promised above (D&C 33:11) was to come after the baptism of water. It was to follow their being confirmed members of the Church and given the Holy Ghost as a gift by the laying on of hands (v. 15). However, it was not automatic. Alma asks: "And now behold, I ask of you, my brethren of the church, have ye spiritually been born of God? Have ye received his image in your countenances? Have ye experienced this mighty change in your hearts?" (Alma 5:14). The Prophet Joseph said that "Being born again, comes by the Spirit of God through ordinances" (*TPJS*, 162). He later said "You might as well baptize a bag of sand as a man, if not done in view of the remission of sins and getting of the Holy Ghost. Baptism by water is but half a baptism, and is good for nothing without the other half—that is, the baptism of the Holy Ghost" (*TPJS*, 314).

D&C 33:16–18 • The Book of Mormon and the Scriptures

16 And the Book of Mormon and the holy scriptures are given of me for your instruction; and the power of my Spirit quickeneth all things.

17 Wherefore, be faithful, praying always, having your lamps trimmed

and burning, and oil with you, that you may be ready at the coming of the Bridegroom—

18 For behold, verily, verily, I say unto you, that I come quickly. Even so. Amen.

Another purpose of the Book of Mormon is added by the Lord; to instruct His Saints. As the book is studied with the holy scriptures, the power of the Spirit will verify and testify of their truths (v. 16). The Holy Spirit is also the oil that is in the lamps that will light the path to the Bridegroom when He comes (v. 17; see Matthew 25:1–13; D&C 45:57). To have our lamps trimmed and burning, we must have already had the experience of recognizing and following the Holy Spirit before He comes. When He comes He will come quickly (D&C 33:18).

*H*istorical Setting—Section 34: Section 34 was given to Orson Pratt (see section heading):

> In October, 1830, I traveled westward over two hundred miles to see Joseph Smith the Prophet. I found him in Fayette, Seneca County, New York, residing at the home of Mr. Whitmer. I soon became intimately acquainted with this good man, and also with the witnesses of the Book of Mormon. By my request, on the fourth of November, the Prophet Joseph inquired of the Lord for me and received the revelation published in the Doctrine and Covenants . . . [*The Orson Pratt Journals*, ed. Elden J. Watson (1975), 12]

SECTION 34 • OUTLINE

➤ 34:1–3   Orson, hearken to what Jesus Christ says unto you.

    a. He is the light and life of the world, which shines in darkness and the darkness comprehends it not (v. 2).

    b. He so loved the world that he gave his own life that as many as believe might become the sons of God. You are my son (v. 3).

➤ 34:4–8   Orson is blessed because he believed, and more blessed because you are called to believe my gospel.

    a. Cry repentance unto a crooked and perverse generation to prepare for my second coming.

b. The time is soon at hand when I shall come in power and great glory (v. 7).

c. It shall be a great day for all nations to tremble (v. 8).

➤ 34:9–12   Before that great day the sun shall be darkened, the moon turned into blood, the stars refuse to shine, and great destruction.

a. Prophesy and it shall be given you by the Holy Ghost (v. 10).

b. Be faithful until I come, I come quickly (vv. 11–12).

TEXT AND COMMENTARY

D&C 34:1–3 • Christ Gave His Own Life For the World

1 My son Orson, hearken and hear and behold what I, the Lord God, shall say unto you, even Jesus Christ your Redeemer;

2 The light and the life of the world, a light which shineth in darkness and the darkness comprehendeth it not;

3 Who so loved the world that he gave his own life, that as many as would believe might become the sons of God. Wherefore you are my son;

Jesus identifies himself to Orson with almost the same terminology as is used in the introduction of the Gospel of John: the Light and Light of men, or the world, that is not comprehended by the darkness of the world (v. 2; compare John 1:4–5). He adds an extension to one of the most well known passages of the Christian world: "For God so loved the world, that he gave his Only Begotten Son, that whosoever believeth in him should not perish, but have everlasting life" (John 3:16). Jesus also so loved the world that He willingly gave His own life that men might become the spiritual sons and daughters of God (D&C 34:3). Since all men and woman are the offspring of God (Acts 17:28–29), they are His spirit sons and daughters. Through being born again, men and women become the spiritually adopted sons and daughters of Jesus Christ (see Mosiah 5:7). He is their father of eternal life. The above interpretation is verified by His statement to Orson that he is His son (D&C 34:3). Orson had apparently been baptized with fire and the Holy Ghost, or born again.

D&C 34:4–8 • Lift Up Your Voice Both Loud and Long

4 And blessed are you because you have believed;

5 And more blessed are you because you are called of me to preach my gospel—

6 To lift up your voice as with the sound of a trump, both long and loud, and cry repentance unto a crooked and perverse generation, preparing the way of the Lord for his second coming.

7 For behold, verily, verily, I say unto you, the time is soon at hand that I shall come in a cloud with power and great glory.

8 And it shall be a great day at the time of my coming, for all nations shall tremble.

The blessing given to Brother Pratt was taken seriously by him. He literally lifted up his voice both long and loud (vv. 5–6). In the foreword to a biography of Orson, Leonard J. Arrington stated:

> Orson Pratt was one of the great missionaries in Mormon history, crossing the ocean sixteen times to preach and write in Great Britain.... Some Latter-day Saints were inclined to discipline Pratt for public statements that had not been previously cleared by 'headquarters.' Brigham [Young], who fully understood Pratt's value to the community, replied, 'If you were to chop up Elder Pratt into inch-square pieces, each piece would cry out, 'Mormonism is true.' 'Brother Orson,' Brigham declared, 'I want you to do just as you have done in your apostleship.' [Breck England, *The Life and Thought of Orson Pratt*, Daniel H. Ludlow, ed. (1985), x–xi]

Orson Pratt did a lot to prepare people for their own time to meet the Savior, as well as the Church collectively for the day when "all nations shall tremble" (D&C 34:7–8; see Isaiah 64:2).

D&C 34:10–12 • The Sun Darkened, the Moon Turned to Blood

9 But before that great day shall come, the sun shall be darkened, and the moon be turned into blood; and the stars shall refuse their shining, and some shall fall, and great destructions await the wicked.

10 Wherefore, lift up your voice and spare not, for the Lord God hath spoken; therefore prophesy, and it shall be given by the power of the Holy Ghost.

11 And if you are faithful, behold, I am with you until I come—

12 And verily, verily, I say unto you, I come quickly. I am your Lord and your Redeemer. Even so. Amen.

The signs to precede the Second Coming regarding the sun, the moon and the stars (v. 9) were foretold by Isaiah (10:23), Ezekiel (32:7–8), John the Revelator (Revelation 6:12–13), and by Jesus during his earthly ministry (JS—M 1:33). They were also given several times in the Doctrine and Covenants (see D&C 29:14; 45:42; 88:87; 133:49). A similar sign was given at the death of the Lord Jesus Christ (see Helaman 14:20; 3 Nephi 8:21–22), and help us to understand what will happen. These signs will be recognized fully after they happen, as was said by Nephi concerning other prophecies of Isaiah (see 2 Nephi 25:8). They were apparently mentioned to Orson as a catalyst for his calling to prophesy by the power of the Holy Ghost (v. 10). He also took this calling seriously, but with great humility:

> This was a particular point in the revelation that seemed to me too great for me ever to attain to, and yet there was a positive command that I should do it. I have often reflected upon this revelation and have oftentimes inquired in my heart—'have I fulfilled that commandment as I ought to have done? . . . I certainly have had no inclination to prophesy to the people unless it should be given to me by the power of the Holy Ghost;
>
> . . . But still, notwithstanding all this, there is one thing that I have endeavored to do, and that is, to inform my mind by reading what God has revealed to both ancient and modern Prophets, in relation to the future, and if I have not had many important prophecies and revelations given directly to myself, I certainly have derived great advantage and great edification from reading and studying that which God has revealed to others; and hence most of my prophesying throughout my life, so far, has been founded upon the revelations given to others. [*JD*, 17:290–9][32]

In this writer's opinion, the Lord was with Orson Pratt during much of his ministry on earth, as He promised He would be (D&C 34:11). The revelation is ended basically the same way as the previous section, "I come quickly" (v. 12; cf. 33:18).

---

[32] This writer has certainly benefitted and gained great understanding from Elder Pratt's explanations of the Old Testament prophets, especially Isaiah.

*H*istorical Setting—Sections 35 and 36: Sections 35 and 36 were given to Sidney Rigdon and Edward Partridge respectively (See section headings). Both men had learned of the Church when the Lamanite missionaries had come to Kirtland, Ohio:

> . . . where they tarried some time, there being quite a number in that place and vicinity who believed their testimony, and came forward and obeyed the Gospel. Among that number was Mr. Sidney Rigdon, and a large portion of the church over which he presided.
>
> Previous to this, Elder Parley P. Pratt (one of the Lamanite missionaries) had been a preacher in the same church with Mr. Rigdon, and resided in the town of Amherst, Loraine County, in Ohio, and had been sent on a mission, where he became acquainted with the circumstances of the coming forth of the Book of Mormon, and was introduced to Joseph Smith Jun., and other members of the Church. The belief that there were many in the church with which he had formerly been united, who were honest seekers after truth, induced Elder Pratt, while on his journey to the west, to call upon his friends, and make known the great things which the Lord had brought to pass.
>
> The first house at which they called in the vicinity of Kirtland, was Mr. Rigdon's, and after the usual salutations, they presented him with the Book of Mormon, stating that it was a revelation from God. This being the first time he had ever heard, or seen, the Book of Mormon, he felt very much surprised at the assertion, and replied that he had which he believed was a revelation from God, and with which he pretended to have some acquaintance; but with respect of the book they had presented him, he had considerable doubt. Upon this, they expressed a desire to investigate the subject, and argue the matter. But he replied, 'No, young gentleman, you must not argue with me on the subject; but I will read your book, and see what claims it has upon my faith, and will endeavor to ascertain whether it be a revelation from God or not.'
>
> . . . after a fortnight from the time the book was put into his hands, he was fully convinced of the truth of the work, by a revelation from Jesus Christ, which was made known to him in a remarkable manner, so that he could exclaim, 'Flesh and blood hath not revealed it unto me, but my Father which is in heaven,' Accordingly he and his wife were both baptized into the Church of Jesus Christ; and, together with those who had previously admitted to baptism, made a little branch of the Church, in this section of Ohio, of about twenty members. [*HC*, 1:120–125]

Edward Partridge had not been baptized when he came to see Joseph, but requested that Joseph baptize him.

'You are now,' replied Joseph, 'much fatigued, Brother Partridge, and you had better rest to-day, and be baptized tomorrow.'

'Just as Brother Joseph thinks best,' replied Mr. Partridge, 'I am ready at any time.'

He was accordingly baptized the next day. [Lucy Mack Smith, *History of Joseph Smith,* 191–92).

SECTION 35 • OUTLINE

➤ 35:1–2   Listen to the voice of the Lord, Alpha and Omega, the beginning and the end, whose course is one eternal round.

    a.   I was crucified for the sins of the world, that those that believe will become the sons of God (v. 2).

    b.   I am one in the Father as the Father is one in me (v. 2).

➤ 35:3–6   Christ has heard Sidney's prayers and prepared him for a greater work.

    a.   He shall do great things even as John to prepare the way for Elijah (v. 4).

    b.   Sidney baptized by water unto repentance but they received not the Holy Ghost (v. 5).

    c.   He shall now baptize by water and they shall receive the Holy Ghost by the laying on of hands (v. 6).

➤ 35:7–9   There shall be a great work among the Gentiles manifest to all people.

    a.   Christ shall show miracles, signs, and wonders unto all who believe (v. 5).

    b.   Whoso asks in my name in faith shall cast out devils, heal the sick, cause the blind to see, the deaf to hear, the dumb to speak, the lame to walk (v. 9).

➤ 35:10–16 The time speedily cometh that great things will be shown to children of men.

    a.   Without faith nothing will be shown except the desolation of Babylon (v. 11).

  b. None doeth good except those ready to receive the fullness of my gospel (v. 12).

  c. I call upon the weak, the unlearned, and despised to thrash the nations by the power of my Spirit (v. 13).

  d. Their arm shall be my arm, they shall fight for me, I will preserve them (v. 14).

  e. The poor and the meek shall have the gospel preached unto them and be looking for my coming (v. 15).

  f. They shall learn the parable of the fig tree, for the summer is nigh (v. 16).

➤ 35:17–19 I have sent forth the fullness of my gospel by the hand of Joseph Smith, and in weakness have I blessed him.

  a. He is given the keys of the mysteries of things sealed from the foundations of the world, which shall come from time to time if he abide in me (v. 18).

  b. Watch over him that he faint not, and he shall be given the Comforter (v. 19).

➤ 35:20–27 Sidney shall write for Joseph that the scriptures shall be given for the salvation of mine elect.

  a. They shall hear my voice, see me and abide the day of my coming, and be purified as I am pure (v. 21).

  b. Tarry with him and he shall journey with you, forsake him not and these things shall be fulfilled (v. 22).

  c. Joseph shall prophesy, thou shalt prove his words by the holy prophets (v. 23).

  d. Keep my commandments and the heavens shall shake for thy good, Satan shall tremble, and Zion shall flourish (v. 24).

  e. Israel shall be saved in due time, and no more be confounded (v. 25).

  f. Be glad, redemption draws nigh, the kingdom is yours until I come (vv. 26–27).

TEXT AND COMMENTARY

D&C 35:1–2 • The Course of the Lord is One Eternal Round

1 listen to the voice of the Lord your God, even Alpha and Omega, the beginning and the end, whose course is one eternal round, the same today as yesterday, and forever.

2 I am Jesus Christ, the Son of God, who was crucified for the sins of the world, even as many as will believe on my name, that they may become the sons of God, even one in me as I am one in the Father, as the Father is one in me, that we may be one.

That the course of the Lord is "one eternal round" (v. 1) was also stated by Nephi (1 Nephi 10:19). "He is unchangeable from all eternity to all eternity" (Moroni 8:18). His oneness with the Father was also explained beautifully to the Nephites (see 3 Nephi 11:32, 35–36).

D&C 35:3–6 • Sidney Rigdon a Forerunner

3 Behold, verily, verily, I say unto my servant Sidney, I have looked upon thee and thy works. I have heard thy prayers, and prepared thee for a greater work.

4 Thou art blessed, for thou shalt do great things. Behold thou wast sent forth, even as John, to prepare the way before me, and before Elijah which should come, and thou knewest it not.

5 Thou didst baptize by water unto repentance, but they received not the Holy Ghost;

6 But now I give unto thee a commandment, that thou shalt baptize by water, and they shall receive the Holy Ghost by the laying on of the hands, even as the apostles of old.

The greater work for which Sidney had been prepared (v. 3) was extensive. Although he did not know it, he had already been a forerunner, even as John the Baptist had been before Christ's earthly ministry, to bring many of the Campbellites into the Church by teaching them some of the first principles of the gospel, repentance and baptism (vv. 4–5). Now, having proper authority, he would be able to give them not only repentance and baptism, but teach them about and give them the Holy Ghost by the laying on of hands (v. 6). Eventually about 1,000 of the Campbel-

lites, among whom he had been a minister, would be brought into the Church.[33]

The Prophet Malachi taught that Elijah would come "before the coming of the great and dreadful day of the Lord" (Malachi 4:5). Part of Sidney's great work was to prepare a people for that great event, and warn the people what would happen to them if they were not prepared (D&C 35:4). Sidney would be given many other great things to do in the coming years of the newly restored Church.

D&C 35:7–9 • Miracles Are Promised

7 And it shall come to pass that there shall be a great work in the land, even among the Gentiles, for their folly and their abominations shall be made manifest in the eyes of all people.

8 For I am God, and mine arm is not shortened; and I will show miracles, signs, and wonders, unto all those who believe on my name.

9 And whoso shall ask it in my name in faith, they shall cast out devils; they shall heal the sick; they shall cause the blind to receive their sight, and the deaf to hear, and the dumb to speak, and the lame to walk.

The gospel was taken to all nations, or the Gentiles, after the Jews had rejected it in the meridian of time (see Matthew 28:19). The gospel was to go to the Gentiles first in the latter days (see Matthew 19:30; D&C 90:8–10). Therefore, the great work in the land even among the Gentiles (D&C 35:7) was termed the dispensation of, or the times of, the Gentiles (see JST, Luke 21:24–25; 3 Nephi 16:7–9; D&C 45:28–29). The miracles, signs, and wonders designated to Sidney (D&C 35:8–9) are the same as promised to the New Testament Apostles as they were sent to all nations (see Mark 16:17–18). The last had now become first.

D&C 35:10–16 • The Weak Things to Thrash the Nations

10 And the time speedily cometh that great things are to be shown forth unto the children of men;

11 But without faith shall not anything be shown forth except desolations upon Babylon, the same which has made all nations drink

---

[33] "In about three weeks from the time brother Pratt and co-laborers entered Kirtland, 127 persons were baptized. Subsequently the numbers were augmented to about 1000 souls." Matthias Corley, as quoted in *LDPDC*, 1:418.

of the wine of the wrath of her fornication.

12 And there are none that doeth good except those who are ready to receive the fulness of my gospel, which I have sent forth unto this generation.

13 Wherefore, I call upon the weak things of the world, those who are unlearned and despised, to thrash the nations by the power of my Spirit;

14 And their arm shall be my arm, and I will be their shield and their buckler; and I will gird up their loins, and they shall fight manfully for me; and their enemies shall be under their feet; and I will let fall the sword in their behalf, and by the fire of mine indignation will I preserve them.

15 And the poor and the meek shall have the gospel preached unto them, and they shall be looking forth for the time of my coming, for it is nigh at hand—

16 And they shall learn the parable of the fig-tree, for even now already summer is nigh.

Great miracles are promised to be shown unto the children of men (v. 10), but miracles cease when there is no faith and they dwindle in unbelief. If there is no faith, men are not fit to be members of Christ's church (see Mormon 9:20; Moroni 7:37–39). When the righteous are gathered out and there is no faith, the desolations upon Babylon will follow (D&C 35:11). Babylon represents the wickedness of the nations of the world, or spiritual fornication (see D&C 133:14). The "wine of the wrath of her [Babylon's] fornication" (D&C 35:11) denotes a situation where the Saints have been gathered out (see Revelation 18:4; D&C 133:5), the nations have become inhabited by devils and foul spirits, and they embrace the immoral practices of Babylon of old, or commit fornication with her (see Revelation 18:2–3). Therefore, only those who are ready to receive the fullness of the gospel will do good (D&C 35:12). Those who accept the gospel are the weak in the eyes of the world, the unlearned in the ways of the world, and are despised because of their goodly ways (v. 13).

Those who accept the gospel are the gathered of Israel who will thrash the nations of the world by the power of Christ's Spirit, as prophesied by the Prophet Isaiah (see Isaiah 41:14–15). The Lord will fight their battles (D&C 33:14), who will be the poor and the meek who are looking

for the time of Christ's coming, and have recognized the sign of His coming as taught in the parable of the fig tree (vv. 14–15; Matthew 24:32–33; JS—M 1:38–39).

D&C 35:17–19 • Joseph Blessed In Weakness

17 And I have sent forth the fulness of my gospel by the hand of my servant Joseph; and in weakness have I blessed him;

18 And I have given unto him the keys of the mystery of those things which have been sealed, even things which were from the foundation of the world, and the things which shall come from this time until the time of my coming, if he abide in me, and if not, another will I plant in his stead.

19 Wherefore, watch over him that his faith fail not, and it shall be given by the Comforter, the Holy Ghost, that knoweth all things.

All of the latter-day work was administered by the Prophet Joseph Smith. He held the keys of the mystery of those things revealed in the portion of the plates that were not translated, as well as other records yet to come forth, that reveals the end from the beginning (vv. 17–18, see 2 Nephi 27:6–8). The Lord again acknowledges Joseph's agency, although He knew Joseph would not fail (D&C 35:19; see D&C 28:7; 43:3–4). The Saints then and now were and are to sustain him and his successors that they may continue to receive revelation given through the Comforter (D&C 35:19).

D&C 35:20–27 • Sidney to Prove Joseph's Words

20 And a commandment I give unto thee—that thou shalt write for him; and the scriptures shall be given, even as they are in mine own bosom, to the salvation of mine own elect;

21 For they will hear my voice, and shall see me, and shall not be asleep, and shall abide the day of my coming; for they shall be purified, even as I am pure.

22 And now I say unto you, tarry with him, and he shall journey with you; forsake him not, and surely these things shall be fulfilled.

23 And inasmuch as ye do not write, behold, it shall be given unto him to prophesy; and thou shalt preach my gospel and call on the holy prophets to prove his words, as they shall be given him.

24 Keep all the commandments and covenants by which ye are bound; and I will cause the heavens to shake for your good, and Satan shall tremble and Zion shall rejoice upon the hills and flourish;

25 And Israel shall be saved in mine own due time; and by the keys which I have given shall they be led, and no more be confounded at all.

26 Lift up your hearts and be glad, your redemption draweth nigh.

27 Fear not, little flock, the kingdom is yours until I come. Behold, I come quickly. Even so. Amen.

As stated by Robert J. Matthews, the best authority on Joseph Smith's Translation of the Bible, concerning section 35 verse 20:

> The implication is that the current Bibles were not in a condition like "the Lord's own bosom." Such a promise sounds like a statement of restoration. It is either declaring a restoration, or it is saying that the ancient Bible never had the truth in the first place; but this would be contrary to the statement of the angel to Nephi that in the beginning the Bible was plain and precious, easy to be understood, and contained the fulness of the Gospel of Jesus Christ. [*Selected Writings of Robert J. Matthews* (1999), 331]

Sidney's call to write for Joseph (v. 20) was similar to Oliver's call as scribe for the translation of the Book of Mormon. Both records had the same purpose: the salvation of Israel, the Lord's elect (v. 20). Verse 21 is an extension of John 10:27, "My sheep hear my voice." In the context, it implies that His voice will be in Joseph's translation. The Lord certainly spoke though Joseph in this most important work. It also promises those sheep who hear His voice that they will see Him and be purified (D&C 35:21), a condition required to live with Him (see also Moroni 7:48). Sidney is again admonished to support and sustain Joseph, and the work of translation shall be fulfilled (D&C 35:22). Sidney, a learned man of the Bible, is called upon to prove that the translation made by Joseph is correct by calling on the words of the [biblical] prophets to show that they taught the same things that Joseph was inspired to write (v. 23). The heavens shaking for Sidney's own good, and the flourishing of Zion (vv. 24–25) were also promised the entire Church if they would receive the words of Joseph as if from the Lord's own mouth (see D&C 21:5–7). As these promises are fulfilled, Satan will certainly tremble (D&C 35:24). Isaiah prophesied that "Israel shall be saved with an everlasting

salvation" (Isaiah 45:17). The Lord confirms Isaiah's word will be fulfilled in the Lord's own due time (D&C 35:25). The Lord again concludes the revelation with the promise that He will come quickly (D&C 35:27).

SECTION 36 • OUTLINE

➤ 36:1–3   Edward is blessed, his sins are forgiven, and he is called to preach Christ's gospel with the voice of a trump.

    a.   The Lord will lay his hand on him by Sidney Rigdon, and he shall receive the Holy Ghost which shall teach him the peaceable things of the kingdom (v. 2).

    b.   Declare the gospel with a loud voice, saying, Hosanna, blessed be the name of the most high God (v. 3).

➤ 36:4–8   Edward is given a commandment concerning all men.

    a.   As many as come before Joseph and Sidney, embrace this calling and commandment, shall be ordained to preach the everlasting gospel to all nations (v. 5).

    b.   They shall cry repentance, save yourselves from this untoward generation, come forth out of the fire, hating even the garments spotted with the flesh (v. 6).

    c.   Every man who will embrace the gospel with singleness of heart may be ordained and sent forth (v. 7).

    d.   I am Jesus Christ, gird up your loins, I will come suddenly to my temple (v. 8).

TEXT AND COMMENTARY

D&C 36:1–3 • Edward Partridge's Conditional Promises

1 Thus saith the Lord God, the Mighty One of Israel: Behold, I say unto you, my servant Edward, that you are blessed, and your sins are forgiven you, and you are called to preach my gospel as with the voice of a trump;

2 And I will lay my hand upon you by the hand of my servant Sidney Rigdon, and you shall receive my Spirit, the Holy Ghost, even the Comforter, which shall teach you the peaceable things of the kingdom;

3 And you shall declare it with a loud voice, saying: Hosanna, blessed be the name of the most high God.

Edward Partridge had not been baptized when he came with Sidney to see the Prophet Joseph. Therefore, he was promised these blessings on condition of his baptism. Perhaps Sidney was called to confirm him as a fulfillment of the promise that he would lay on hands and give the gift of the Holy Ghost (see D&C 35:6). The commandments were kept and the promises were fulfilled.

D&C 36:4–8 • All Men Ordained and Sent Forth

4 And now this calling and commandment give I unto you concerning all men—

5 That as many as shall come before my servants Sidney Rigdon and Joseph Smith, Jun., embracing this calling and commandment, shall be ordained and sent forth to preach the everlasting gospel among the nations—

6 Crying repentance, saying: Save yourselves from this untoward generation, and come forth out of the fire, hating even the garments spotted with the flesh.

7 And this commandment shall be given unto the elders of my church, that every man which will embrace it with singleness of heart may be ordained and sent forth, even as I have spoken.

8 I am Jesus Christ, the Son of God; wherefore, gird up your loins and I will suddenly come to my temple. Even so. Amen.

The promise concerning all men who would come to Joseph and Sidney [to be baptized and receive the Holy Ghost] would be ordained and sent forth (vv. 5, 7) is in keeping with one of the purposes of the restoration; "that every man might speak in the name of God the Lord, even the Savior of the world;" (D&C 1:20). It is also the theme given by President Spencer W. Kimball: "Every worthy young man should serve a mission."

Hating even the garments that are spotted with the flesh (D&C 36:6) is similar to Paul's admonition to "Abstain from all appearance of evil" (1 Thessalonians 5:22). The Lord's promise to suddenly come to His temple (D&C 36:8) is the first mention of the temple in the Doctrine and Covenants. The promise is in fulfillment of Malachi's prophecy: "Behold, I will send my messenger, and he shall prepare the way before me: and the Lord, whom ye seek, shall suddenly come to his temple, even the messenger of the covenant, whom ye delight in: behold, he shall come,

saith the LORD of hosts" (Malachi 3:1). It was fulfilled with the Lord's appearance in the Kirtland Temple (see D&C 110:1), but should not be limited to that appearance. A temple had to be built before the Lord could appear in it. Many temples have now been built, and there have undoubtedly been other appearances.

CONCLUSION

The calling of these brethren, to whom the revelations in this chapter were given, to important positions in the Church both then and in the future, support the doctrine taught by the Prophet Joseph: "Every man who has a calling to minister to the inhabitants of the world was ordained that very purpose in the Grand Council of heaven before this world was. I suppose I was ordained to this very office in that Grand Council." (*TPJS*, 365)

General Authority Quotes
—Elder George A. Smith • D&C 31:9

The wife of Thomas B. Marsh, who was then President of the Twelve Apostles, and Sister Harris concluded they would exchange milk, in order to make a little larger cheese than they otherwise could. To be sure to have justice done, it was agreed that they should not save the strippings, but the milk and the strippings should all go together. . . .

Mrs. Harris, it appeared, was faithful to the agreement, and carried to Mrs. Marsh the milk and the strippings, but Mrs. Marsh, wishing to make some extra good cheese, saved a pint of strippings from each cow and sent Mrs. Harris the milk without the strippings.

Finally it leaked out that Mrs. Marsh had saved strippings, and it became a matter to be settled by the Teachers. They began to examine the matter, and it was proved that Mrs. Marsh had saved the strippings, and consequently had wronged Mrs. Harris out of that amount.

An appeal was taken from the Teacher to the Bishop, and a regular Church trial was had. President Marsh did not consider that the Bishop had done him and his lady justice, for they decided that the strippings were wrongfully saved, and that the woman had violated her covenant.

Marsh immediately took an appeal to the High Council who investigated the question with much patience . . . Marsh, being extremely anxious to maintain the character of his wife, as he was the President of the Twelve Apostles, and a great man in Israel, made a desperate defense, but the High Council finally confirmed the Bishop's decision.

Marsh, not being satisfied, took an appeal to the First Presidency of the Church, and Joseph and his two counselors had to sit upon the case, and they approved the decision of the High Council.

. . . Thomas B. Marsh then declared that he would sustain the character of his wife, even if he had to go to hell for it.

The then President of the Twelve Apostles, the man who should have been the first to do justice and cause reparation to be made for wrong, committed by any member of his family, took that position, and what next? He went before a magistrate and swore that the "Mormons were hostile to the State of Missouri.

That affidavit brought from the government of Missouri an exterminating order, which drove some 15,000 Saints from their homes and habitations, and some thousands perished through suffering the exposure consequent on this state of affairs. [_JD_, 3:282–84]

—_President Heber C. Kimball_ • D&C 31:12

About the time [Thomas B. Marsh] was preparing to leave this Church, he received a revelation in the Printing Office. He retired to himself, and prayed, and was humble, and God gave him a revelation, and he wrote it. There were from three to five pages of it; and when he came out he read it to Brother Brigham and me. In it, God told him what to do, and that was to sustain Brother Joseph and to believe that what Brother Joseph had said was true. But no; he took a course to sustain his wife and oppose the Prophet of God, and she led him away, . . .

Thomas B. Marsh was once the President over the Quorum of the Twelve—over Brother Brigham and me, and others; and God saw fit to give him a revelation to fore-warn of the course he would take; and still he took that course. We told him that if he would listen to that revelation he had received, he would be saved; but he listened to his wife, and away he went. His wife is now dead and damned. She led him some eighteen years; and as soon as she died, he came to winter quarters—now Florence—and has written to us, pleading for mercy. We have extended it to him, and he will probably be here this season or the next. [*JD*, 5:28–29, July 12, 1857]

Chapter Nineteen

Assemble at the Ohio—
A Commandment

D&C 37; 38; 39; 40

Historical Setting: In December of 1830, as Joseph was working on the translation of the Bible, he was given a revelation he labeled as "Extracts from the Prophecy of Enoch" (*HC*, 1:133). This revelation is now published in the Pearl of Great Price as Moses, chapter 7. "Soon after the words of Enoch were given, the Lord gave the following commandment: [D&C 37]" (*HC*, 1:139; see also the section heading).

> The year 1831 opened with a prospect great and glorious for the welfare of the kingdom; for on the 2nd of January, 1831, a conference was held in the town of Fayette, New York, at which the ordinary business of the Church was transacted; and in addition, the following revelation was received (D&C 38). [*HC*, 1:140]

INTRODUCTION

Why were the saints commanded to go to the Ohio? The simple answer: "Behold, I say unto you that it is not expedient in me that ye should translate any more until ye shall go to the Ohio, and this because of the enemy and for your sakes" (D&C 37:1).

The next revelation gave two reasons: "there I will give unto you my law, and there you shall be endowed with power from on high" (D&C 38:32). All of the above reasons will be discussed in their context. For a more complete answer, as explained by the Prophet Joseph: "The great

Jehovah contemplated the whole of the events connected with the earth, pertaining to the plan of salvation, before it rolled into existence, or ever 'the morning stars sang together' for joy (Job 38:7); the past, the present, and the future were and are, with Him, one eternal 'now'" (*TPJS,* 220). The foreknowledge of God will be more fully discussed in connection with section 38.

Sections 37 & 38 • Outline

➤ 37:1–4   It is not expedient to translate any more until ye go to the Ohio, because of your enemies and for your sakes.

    a. Do not go until you have preached my gospel in those parts, and strengthened the church wherever it is found, especially in Colesville (v. 2).

    b. Assemble to the Ohio when Oliver Cowdery shall return unto them (v. 3).

    c. Every man shall choose for himself until Christ comes (v. 4).

➤ 38:1–6   Thus saith Jesus Christ, the Great I Am, Alpha and Omega, the beginning and end.

    a. He looked upon the wide expanse of heaven and all the seraphic hosts of heaven before the earth was made (v. 1).

    b. He knows all things and all things are present before His eyes (v. 2).

    c. He spake and all things were made (v. 3).

    d. He took Enoch's Zion into His bosom, and pleads before the Father for all who believe on His name, by virtue of the blood he has spilt (v. 4).

    e. He has kept the wicked in chains of darkness until the judgment day, and will keep the future wicked there also (vv. 5–6).

➤ 38:7–12   Christ's eyes are upon you, he is in your midst, but ye cannot see him.

    a. The day will come that you will see him and know that he is, but he that is not purified will not abide the day (v. 8).

b.   Gird up your loins and be prepared, the kingdom is yours and the enemy shall be overcome (v. 9).

    c.   Ye are clean but not all, and He is pleased with none else (v. 10).

    d.   All flesh is corrupted before Him, and darkness prevails (v. 11).

    e.   Eternity is pained, angels await to gather the tares and burn them (v. 12).

➤ 38:13–15   Christ reveals a mystery of men in secret chambers seeking your destruction in process of time, and ye know it not.

    a.   You are blessed, and some are guilty, but He will be merciful (v. 14).

    b.   Be strong and fear not, the kingdom is yours (v. 15).

➤ 38:16–22   A commandment is given for your salvation; the poor have complained, I have made the rich, all flesh is mine and I am no respecter of persons.

    a.   I made the earth rich, it is my footstool, and I will stand on it again (v. 17).

    b.   I design to give you greater riches, a land of promise, flowing with milk and honey, if you seek it with all your hearts (vv. 18–19).

    c.   Christ covenanted the land for you and your children while the earth stands, and you will possess it in eternity (v. 20).

    d.   You shall have no king, but Christ will be your king and watch over you (v. 21).

    e.   [The commandment, v. 16] Hear my voice and follow me, and you shall be a free people, and have no law but my law (v. 22).

➤ 38:23–27   [the Law of the Commandment]

    a.   Teach one another according to the office I have appointed you (v. 23).

    b.   Every man is to esteem his brother as himself, and practice virtue and holiness before me (vv. 24–25).

    c.   A parable is given to show that they must be one, or they are not Christ's.

➤ 38:28–33   Again He warns of the enemy in secret places who seeks to
             destroy your lives.

   a.   You hear of wars in far countries, and say there will be
        great wars there, but you know not the hearts of men in
        your own land (v. 29).

   b.   Treasure up wisdom lest the wickedness of men shake the
        whole earth, but if you are prepared you shall not fear
        (v. 30).

   c.   You can escape the enemy's power, and gather as a righ-
        teous people (v. 31).

   d.   Gather to the Ohio, and I will give you my law and endow
        you with power from on high (v. 32).

   e.   Christ will go among all nations with a great work and
        save Israel, and no power shall stay his hand (v. 33).

➤ 38:34–39   A commandment to the Church in these parts: Certain men
             shall be appointed by the voice of the church.

   a.   They shall look to the poor and the needy, and administer
        relief to them (v. 35).

   b.   Their work shall be to govern the affairs of the property
        of the church (v. 36).

   c.   Sell their farms, or rent or leave them (v. 37).

   d.   When men are endowed with power from on high, all
        these things will be gathered into the bosom of the church
        (v. 38).

   e.   If you seek for riches, you will be the richest of all people,
        but beware lest you become as the Nephites of old (v. 39).

➤ 38:40–42   Every man, elder, priest, teacher, or member shall labor with
             his might to accomplish what is commanded.

   a.   Let your preaching be a warning voice to your neighbors
        in mildness and meekness (v. 41).

   b.   Go ye out from among the wicked, save yourselves, be
        clean (v. 42).

TEXT AND COMMENTARY

D&C 37:1–4 • Go to the Ohio, But Not Yet

1 Behold, I say unto you that it is not expedient in me that ye should translate any more until ye shall go to the Ohio, and this because of the enemy and for your sakes.

2 And again, I say unto you that ye shall not go until ye have preached my gospel in those parts, and have strengthened up the church whithersoever it is found, and more especially in Colesville; for, behold, they pray unto me in much faith.

3 And again, a commandment I give unto the church, that it is expedient in me that they should assemble together at the Ohio, against the time that my servant Oliver Cowdery shall return unto them.

4 Behold, here is wisdom, and let every man choose for himself until I come. Even so. Amen.

The Lord gave the Church some time to wrap up their work in the Colesville branch at New York (v. 2). Oliver Cowdery was on his mission to the Lamanites, which ended in mid-February, 1831 due to Indian agents and sectarian missionaries (*Autobiography of Parley P. Pratt* [1970], 57). The Prophet and his family left at the end of January and arrived in Kirtland about the first of February, 1831 (*HC*, 1:145). The New York members began their migration to Kirtland in the spring of 1831.

D&C 38:1–6 • All Present Before My Eyes

1 Thus saith the Lord your God, even Jesus Christ, the Great I AM, Alpha and Omega, the beginning and the end, the same which looked upon the wide expanse of eternity, and all the seraphic hosts of heaven, before the world was made;

2 The same which knoweth all things, for all things are present before mine eyes;

3 I am the same which spake, and the world was made, and all things came by me.

4 I am the same which have taken the Zion of Enoch into mine own bosom; and verily, I say, even as many as have believed in my name, for I am Christ, and in mine own name, by the virtue of the blood which I have spilt, have I pleaded before the Father for them.

5 But behold, the residue of the wicked have I kept in chains of darkness until the judgment of the great day, which shall come at the end of the earth;

6 And even so will I cause the wicked to be kept, that will not hear

my voice but harden their hearts, and wo, wo, wo, is their doom.

Jesus Christ knew and understood the past. He knew all the eternities and all the seraphic [the angels and spirits constituting the] hosts of heaven even before the world was created (v. 1). The present was before his eyes (v. 2). He created the world and all things therein (v. 3; see also D&C 93:10), or by His light, He had governed the world (see D&C 88:13). He was the one who had translated the city of Enoch by His power (D&C 38:4), the subject of the revelation received during the recent translation work on the Bible (Moses 7; see *HC*, 1:133–139). He had made the Atonement for all the inhabitants of the earth, past, present, and future, and He continually pleads their cause before the Father (D&C 38:4). He had kept the prior wicked inhabitants of the earth in chains of darkness until the judgment day (v. 5, see 2 Peter 2:4–9; Jude 1:6), and will continue to do so (D&C 38:6). Therefore, as quoted in the Introduction above, "the past, the present, and the future were and are, with him, one eternal 'now'" (*TPJS,* 220; see also "General Authority Quotes," The Prophet Joseph Smith). Since He knew and did all these things, He certainly was qualified to direct the Saints to Ohio and to continue to care for them there.

D&C 38:7–12 • I Am in Your Midst

7 But behold, verily, verily, I say unto you that mine eyes are upon you. I am in your midst and ye cannot see me;

8 But the day soon cometh that ye shall see me, and know that I am; for the veil of darkness shall soon be rent, and he that is not purified shall not abide the day.

9 Wherefore, gird up your loins and be prepared. Behold, the kingdom is yours, and the enemy shall not overcome.

10 Verily I say unto you, ye are clean, but not all; and there is none else with whom I am well pleased;

11 For all flesh is corrupted before me; and the powers of darkness prevail upon the earth, among the children of men, in the presence of all the hosts of heaven—

12 Which causeth silence to reign, and all eternity is pained, and the angels are waiting the great command to reap down the earth, to gather the tares that they may be burned; and, behold, the enemy is combined.

Christ is with His saints in the conference being held, but they cannot see Him (v. 7). At His Second Coming, only those who have purified themselves will be able to see Him (v. 8). Thus, He admonishes them to be prepared (v. 9). The only way to prepare is through the restored Church (v. 10). "All flesh is corrupted" (v. 11) confirms the apostasy was universal except for the Saints that had started to gather. "In the presence of all the hosts of heaven" (v. 11) shows that the happenings on earth are known to those who have not come to earth. The corruption on earth has stopped any revelation that had previously been available. "All eternity being pained" (v. 12) suggests that those in the spirit world were also aware of the conditions on earth.

The Prophet Joseph Smith said: "The spirits of the just are exalted to greater and more glorious work: hence they are blessed in their departure to the world of spirits. Enveloped in flaming fire, they are not far from us, and know and understand our thoughts, feelings, and motions, and are often pained therewith" (*TPJS*, 326). Therefore, the angels are waiting to have the gathering of the tares completed so that they can be burned (Matthew 13:40; D&C 86:7). "That the enemy is combined" (D&C 38:12) seems to be saying that all evil is coming together, or the time has begun that was spoken of by Nephi, when the Lord has caused "a great division among the people, and the wicked will he destroy" (2 Nephi 30:10; see also D&C 1:35–36).

After quoting verses 10 through 12 regarding all flesh being corrupted, and darkness prevailing among all nations President Wilford Woodruff said in 1875 "The angels of God are waiting to fulfill the great commandment given forty-five years ago, to go forth and reap down the earth because of the wickedness of men. How do you feel eternity feels today? Why there is more wickedness, a thousand times over, in the United States now, than when that revelation was given. The whole earth is ripe in iniquity" (*JD*, 18:128). How must "eternity" feel now, over a hundred and thirty years later than Presidents Woodruff's analysis? There is certainly much more corruption and darkness now than there was in 1875.

D&C 38:13–15 • Secret Chambers Seek Your Destruction

13 And now I show unto you a mystery, a thing which is had in secret

chambers, to bring to pass even your destruction in process of time, and ye knew it not;

14 But now I tell it unto you, and ye are blessed, not because of your iniquity, neither your hearts of unbelief; for verily some of you are guilty before me, but I will be merciful unto your weakness.

15 Therefore, be ye strong from henceforth; fear not, for the kingdom is yours.

The world has become more wicked, and Satan still seeks to destroy the kingdom and the individual members of it (v. 14). The Lord is still merciful towards our iniquities and unbelief to some degree (v. 14), but we still must fear not for the kingdom is still ours (v. 15). The kingdom will continue to go forward until He comes. The great division spoken of by Nephi (2 Nephi 30:10) is becoming more pronounced. The big question is; will we be a part of that kingdom or will we be among the wicked?

D&C 38:16–22 • I Will Be Your King and Watch Over You

16 And for your salvation I give unto you a commandment, for I have heard your prayers, and the poor have complained before me, and the rich have I made, and all flesh is mine, and I am no respecter of persons.

17 And I have made the earth rich, and behold it is my footstool, wherefore, again I will stand upon it.

18 And I hold forth and deign to give unto you greater riches, even a land of promise, a land flowing with milk and honey, upon which there shall be no curse when the Lord cometh;

19 And I will give it unto you for the land of your inheritance, if you seek it with all your hearts.

20 And this shall be my covenant with you, ye shall have it for the land of your inheritance, and for the inheritance of your children forever, while the earth shall stand, and ye shall possess it again in eternity, no more to pass away.

21 But, verily I say unto you that in time ye shall have no king nor ruler, for I will be your king and watch over you.

22 Wherefore, hear my voice and follow me, and you shall be a free people, and ye shall have no laws but my laws when I come, for I am your lawgiver, and what can stay my hand?

The Lord hears the prayers of all people, and He answers them on the basis of their needs and worthiness and in accordance to the law of justice and mercy (v. 16). He has also provided the earth to accommodate the earth's inhabitants. He will come to the earth to complete its destiny (v. 17). A land of milk and honey (v. 18) is the description of the land promised to Israel when they were led out of Egypt by Moses; it reflects prosperity (see Exodus 3:8; 1 Nephi 2:20, Ether 2:7). This earth will be the eternal home of those inhabitants of this earth who attain the celestial kingdom (D&C 38:19–20; see also D&C 88:17–19; Matthew 5:5; 3 Nephi 12:5). That there was to be no king or ruler on this land (D&C 38:21–22) was promised earlier. Jacob, brother of Nephi, recorded God's promise that "this land shall be a land of liberty unto the Gentiles, and there shall be no kings upon the land. . . . for I, the Lord, the king of heaven, will be their king" (2 Nephi 10:11–14). Jacob quoted this in conjunction with Isaiah, so perhaps it was originally stated by Isaiah, and was part of the plain and precious parts of the Bible that were lost (see 1 Nephi 13:26–29). The promise of liberty is conditional (D&C 38:22), and was subject to a commandment (v. 16) to hear His voice and follow Him (v. 22) The promise and the commandment extended to the whole of North and South America (see Alma 46:17; *TPJS, 362*).

D&C 38:23–27 • If Ye Are Not One Ye Are Not Mine

> 23 But, verily I say unto you, teach one another according to the office wherewith I have appointed you;
>
> 24 And let every man esteem his brother as himself, and practice virtue and holiness before me.
>
> 25 And again I say unto you, let every man esteem his brother as himself.
>
> 26 For what man among you having twelve sons, and is no respecter of them, and they serve him obediently, and he saith unto the one: Be thou clothed in robes and sit thou here; and to the other: Be thou clothed in rags and sit thou there—and looketh upon his sons and saith I am just?
>
> 27 Behold, this I have given unto you as a parable, and it is even as I am. I say unto you, be one; and if ye are not one ye are not mine.

The conditions of the promised prosperity were to teach one another as called to offices and positions, to esteem one's brother as one's self, and to practice virtue and holiness in one's life (vv. 23–25). The parable exemplifying these conditions (v. 26) was quoted again by the Savior sometime after the Quorum of the Twelve was called. He explained:

> "Ye will answer and say, no man; and ye answer truly; therefore, verily thus saith the Lord your God, I appoint these Twelve that they should be equal in their ministry, and in their portion, and in their evangelical rights; wherefore they have sinned a very grievous sin, inasmuch they have made themselves unequal, and have not hearkened unto my voice; let them repent speedily, and prepare their hearts for the solemn assembly, and for the great day which is to come, verily thus saith the Lord. Amen. [*HC*, 2:301]

To be equal is to be one in accordance with the Savior, who will give them revelation, and the Comforter, who will "teach [them] all things, and bring all things to [their] remembrance, whatsoever I have said unto you" (John 14:26). The same practice of esteem, virtue and holiness should be followed by all Church members (D&C 38:27), "for God hath not revealed anything to Joseph, but what he will make known to the Twelve, and even the least Saint may know all things as fast as he is able to bear them" (*TPJS*, 149).

D&C 38:28–33 • Great Wars In Your Own Lands?

28 And again, I say unto you that the enemy in the secret chambers seeketh your lives.

29 Ye hear of wars in far countries, and you say that there will soon be great wars in far countries, but ye know not the hearts of men in your own land.

30 I tell you these things because of your prayers; wherefore, treasure up wisdom in your bosoms, lest the wickedness of men reveal these things unto you by their wickedness, in a manner which shall speak in your ears with a voice louder than that which shall shake the earth; but if ye are prepared ye shall not fear.

31 And that ye might escape the power of the enemy, and be gathered unto me a righteous people, without spot and blameless—

32 Wherefore, for this cause I gave unto you the commandment that ye should go to the Ohio; and there I will give unto you my law; and there you shall be endowed with power from on high;

33 And from thence, whosoever I will shall go forth among all nations, and it shall be told them what they shall do; for I have a great work laid up in store, for Israel shall be saved, and I will lead them whithersoever I will, and no power shall stay my hand.

Wars and rumors of war continued and were fought in far countries, and in our own land, after this revelation was given (vv. 28–30). They will continue as long as Satan, the father of contention, is loose to stir up wars and conflict (see 3 Nephi 11:29). Our challenge is to gather together physically and spiritually become "without spot and blameless" (D&C 38:31). The Lord then gave two specific reasons for going to the Ohio: to receive His law for the Church, and to be endowed with power from on high (v. 32). Section 42, the "law of the Church," was given about a month later, and the commandment to build a temple, to fulfill the need to be endowed with power from on high was given in December of 1832. The endowment was also needful for those who were to go among all the world to gather and save all nations. No earthly power could stop the Lord's great work, of saving all the tribes of Israel, that was ahead (D&C 38:33).

D&C 38:34–39 • The Law of Consecration

34 And now, I give unto the church in these parts a commandment, that certain men among them shall be appointed, and they shall be appointed by the voice of the church;

35 And they shall look to the poor and the needy, and administer to their relief that they shall not suffer; and send them forth to the place which I have commanded them;

36 And this shall be their work, to govern the affairs of the property of this church.

37 And they that have farms that cannot be sold, let them be left or rented as seemeth them good.

38 See that all things are preserved; and when men are endowed with power from on high and sent forth, all these things shall be gathered unto the bosom of the church.

39 And if ye seek the riches which it is the will of the Father to give unto you, ye shall be the richest of all people, for ye shall have the riches of eternity; and it must needs be that the riches of the earth are mine to give; but beware of pride, lest ye become as the Nephites of old.

Part of the law of the Church was the law of consecration (see chapter 21 of this work; D&C 42:29–39). The above verses are just a preview of this law. The men appointed to this law would be named later, and their duties would be outlined as they were appointed (D&C 38:34–37). The temple endowment was also connected with this law (v. 38), as will be shown later. Members of the Church who do not understand how the law of consecration operates will be unable to see how it will make them the richest people on the earth and it is this author's experience that many Church members do not fully understand it. The riches of eternity and the riches of the earth will also be discussed later, in the context of the law of consecration. However, with or without this law, we must heed the caution to not let the riches of the earth make us prideful as they did the Nephites (v. 39).

D&C 38:40–42 • Be Ye Clean that Bear the Vessels of the Lord

40 And again, I say unto you, I give unto you a commandment, that every man, both elder, priest, teacher, and also member, go to with his might, with the labor of his hands, to prepare and accomplish the things which I have commanded.

41 And let your preaching be the warning voice, every man to his neighbor, in mildness and in meekness.

42 And go ye out from among the wicked. Save yourselves. Be ye clean that bear the vessels of the Lord. Even so. Amen.

Just as the priesthood was intended for all men to receive (see Alma 13:4–5; D&C 1:20), the law of consecration is designed for all men to be blessed (D&C 38:40). The warning voice of mildness and meekness (v. 41) is similar to Alma's instructions to his son Shiblon: "Use boldness, but not overbearance; and also see that ye bridle all your passions, that ye may be filled with love; see that ye refrain from idleness" (Alma 38:12). Going out from among the wicked and being saved (D&C 38:42) is the division of the righteous and the wicked spoken of by Nephi, and quoted above (2 Nephi 30:10). "Be ye clean that bear the [priesthood] vessels of the Lord" another quote from Isaiah 52:11, an oft-repeated reminder in the Book of Mormon and the Doctrine and Covenants (see 3 Nephi 20:41; Mormon 7:31; D&C 76:33; 133:5).

*H*istorical Setting—Sections 39 and 40:

Not long after this conference of the 2ⁿᵈ of January closed, there was a man came to me by the name of James Covill, who had been a Baptist minister for about forty years, and covenanted with the Lord that he would obey any command that the Lord would give to him through me, as his servant, and I received the following: [D&C 39]. [*HC*, 1:143]

As James Covill rejected the word of the Lord, and returned to his former principles and people, the Lord gave unto me and Sidney Rigdon the following revelation. Explaining why he obeyed not the word: [D&C 40]. [*HC*, 1:145]

SECTIONS 39 & 40 • OUTLINE

➤ 39:1–6   Listen to the voice of Christ, who is from all eternity to all eternity.

   a.   He is the light and life of the world that darkness does not comprehend (v. 2).

   b.   He came unto His own and they received Him not (v. 3).

   c.   Those who receive Him are given power to become His sons (v. 4).

   d.   Those who receive His gospel receive him (v. 5).

   e.   His gospel is repentance, and baptism by water, and of the Holy Ghost (v. 6).

➤ 39:7–13   Christ knows James Covill, and his heart is now right before Him, and He has bestowed great blessings upon him.

   a.   James has seen great sorrow because he has rejected Christ because of the cares of the world (v. 9).

   b.   The days of his deliverance are come, if he will be baptized and wash away his sins (v. 10).

   c.   He has prepared him for a greater work, to preach the fulness of my gospel, the covenant to recover my people the house of Israel (v. 11).

   d.   Great power shall rest upon him, and Christ will be with him (v. 12).

      e. James is called to labor in Christ's vineyard, build up the church, and bring forth Zion (v. 13).

➤ 39:14–24   James is called to go to the Ohio, not to the eastern countries.

      a. Christ's people in Ohio shall receive a blessing not known among the children of men, and shall then go to all nations (v. 15).

      b. The people in Ohio call upon Christ to stay His judgment, but He cannot deny His word (v. 16).

      c. Call faithful laborers to prune Christ's vineyard for the last time, and He will stay His hand in judgment (vv. 17–18).

      d. Cry with a loud voice, the kingdom of heaven is at hand (v. 19).

      e. Go forth baptizing with water, preparing for His coming (v. 20).

      f. The time is at hand, the day and the hour knoweth no man (v. 21).

      g. He that receiveth these things receiveth Christ, and will be gathered in time and in eternity (v. 22).

      h. Those whom James baptizes will receive the Holy Ghost, and be looking for the signs of His coming (vv. 23–24).

➤ 40:1–3   James Covill's heart was right, and he covenanted to obey Christ's word.

      a. Satan tempted him, and the fear of persecution and the cares of the world caused him to reject it (v. 2).

      b. He broke the covenant, it remains for the Lord to do as seemeth Him good (v. 3).

TEXT AND COMMENTARY

D&C 39:1–6 • He That Receives the Gospel Receives Christ

1 Hearken and listen to the voice of him who is from all eternity to all eternity, the Great I AM, even Jesus Christ—

2 The light and the life of the world; a light which shineth in darkness and the darkness comprehendeth it not;

3 The same which came in the meridian of time unto mine own, and mine own received me not;

4 But to as many as received me, gave I power to become my sons; and even so will I give unto as many as will receive me, power to become my sons.

5 And verily, verily, I say unto you, he that receiveth my gospel receiveth me; and he that receiveth not my gospel receiveth not me.

6 And this is my gospel—repentance and baptism by water, and then cometh the baptism of fire and the Holy Ghost, even the Comforter, which showeth all things, and teacheth the peaceable things of the kingdom.

The Lord's introduction to this revelation includes several identities and phrases that are used in the Bible, and many of them were used in previous revelations. A possible reason for the multiple titles is that James Covill was a minister and thus acquainted with the Bible. The Lord wanted him to know that the same person was speaking that he had been reading and quoting in his ministerial work. The gospel definition was a repetition, but one to which the minister could relate.

D&C 39:7–13 • Thine Heart is Now Right Before Me

7 And now, behold, I say unto you, my servant James, I have looked upon thy works and I know thee.

8 And verily I say unto thee, thine heart is now right before me at this time; and, behold, I have bestowed great blessings upon thy head;

9 Nevertheless, thou hast seen great sorrow, for thou hast rejected me many times because of pride and the cares of the world.

10 But, behold, the days of thy deliverance are come, if thou wilt hearken to my voice, which saith unto thee: Arise and be baptized, and wash away your sins, calling on my name, and you shall receive my Spirit, and a blessing so great as you never have known.

11 And if thou do this, I have prepared thee for a greater work. Thou shalt preach the fulness of my gospel, which I have sent forth in these last days, the covenant which I have sent forth to recover my people, which are of the house of Israel.

12 And it shall come to pass that power shall rest upon thee; thou shalt have great faith, and I will be with thee and go before thy face.

13 Thou art called to labor in my vineyard, and to build up my

church, and to bring forth Zion, that it may rejoice upon the hills and flourish.

The personal knowledge of James Covill (vv.7–11) came from the Lord, for how would Joseph Smith have known his background of sorrow and rejection? The blessing so great as James had never known was first the Spirit (v.10), but secondly, could refer to the law of consecration and the temple. James Covill was called to go the Ohio where these items were to be revealed (v.14; below). The greater work of Brother Covill, for which he had been prepared, was similar to that of Sidney Rigdon but not as specific. The work to recover the house of Israel (v.11) shows again that those who would gather would be primarily the literal blood of Israel, whose ancestors had been scattered among all nations as Amos had prophesied (Amos 9:8–9; see also Abraham 2:11). The Lord's promise to be with him (D&C 39:12) should have assured him of being successful in his new calling. As a minister, the calling to the Lord's vineyard (see Isaiah 5:1–7; Matthew 21:33–44), His Church (see Matthew 16:13–19), and bringing Zion to flourish (see Isaiah 59:20–60:22) should have been a scriptural and spiritual challenge and incentive to him (D&C 39:13).

D&C 39:14–24 • The Blessings in Store for Ohio

14 Behold, verily, verily, I say unto thee, thou art not called to go into the eastern countries, but thou art called to go to the Ohio.

15 And inasmuch as my people shall assemble themselves at the Ohio, I have kept in store a blessing such as is not known among the children of men, and it shall be poured forth upon their heads. And from thence men shall go forth into all nations.

16 Behold, verily, verily, I say unto you, that the people in Ohio call upon me in much faith, thinking I will stay my hand in judgment upon the nations, but I cannot deny my word.

17 Wherefore lay to with your might and call faithful laborers into my vineyard, that it may be pruned for the last time.

18 And inasmuch as they do repent and receive the fulness of my gospel, and become sanctified, I will stay mine hand in judgment.

19 Wherefore, go forth, crying with a loud voice, saying: The kingdom of heaven is at hand; crying: Hosanna! blessed be the name of the Most High God.

20 Go forth baptizing with water, preparing the way before my face for the time of my coming;

21 For the time is at hand; the day or the hour no man knoweth; but it surely shall come.

22 And he that receiveth these things receiveth me; and they shall be gathered unto me in time and in eternity.

23 And again, it shall come to pass that on as many as ye shall baptize with water, ye shall lay your hands, and they shall receive the gift of the Holy Ghost, and shall be looking forth for the signs of my coming, and shall know me.

24 Behold, I come quickly. Even so. Amen.

As mentioned above, the blessings and ordinances that were not known among the children of men were certainly those of the temple. Once more the Lord indicates the temple endowment was needed for the missionaries before going into all nations (v. 15). The faith of the people in Ohio, and the Lord's declaration that His word would not be denied (v. 16) should have turned James Covill's mind to the scriptures. The last pruning of the vineyard was again mentioned (v. 17; see also D&C 33:3). Should not this have whetted James Covill's appetite? (see Romans 11:13–27). Sanctification is the gospel requirement for salvation in the celestial kingdom (see D&C 20:34; Alma 13:12; Helaman 3:35; 3 Nephi 27:20). For those who were sanctified, the judgment would be stayed (D&C 39:18), but the Lord knew that the nations collectively would not attain that sanctified state.

The mission of the Church was to announce the restoration of the kingdom, and invite the people to be baptized in preparation for His coming (vv. 19–20). "Hosanna" is a word spoken in adoration, a recognition of the plan of salvation that the Father had provided and Jesus had carried out. (v. 19). The time of Christ's coming is not known to man, but those who would be baptized would be given the Holy Ghost, which was the source for becoming sanctified (vv. 21–23, see the references above on sanctification). Those who were prepared would know Him when He came quickly (v. 24).

D&C 40:1–3 • Satan Triumphs

1 Behold, verily I say unto you, that the heart of my servant James

Covill was right before me, for he covenanted with me that he would obey my word.

2 And he received the word with gladness, but straightway Satan tempted him; and the fear of persecution and the cares of the world caused him to reject the word.

3 Wherefore he broke my covenant, and it remaineth with me to do with him as seemeth me good. Amen.

This revelation was given to both Joseph and Sidney, probably because Sidney had also been a Protestant minister and would understand the situation. James Covill is an example of a man who was a combination of stony ground and among thorns in Jesus' parable of the sower:

20 But he that received the seed into stony places, the same is he that heareth the word, and anon with joy receiveth it;

21 Yet hath he not root in himself, but dureth for a while: for when tribulation or persecution ariseth because of the word, by and by he is offended.

22 He also that received seed among the thorns is he that heareth the word; and the care of this world, and the deceitfulness of riches, choke the word, and he becometh unfruitful. [Matthew 13:20–22]

Jesus honored the agency of James Covill, but would undoubtedly still do whatever He could for Him "as seemeth me good" (v. 3). It was probably another time that Jesus wept.

General Authority Quotes

—*The Prophet Joseph Smith* • D&C 38:1–6

The great Jehovah contemplated the whole of the events connected with the earth, pertaining to the plan of salvation, before it rolled into existence, or ever "the morning stars sang together" for joy: the past, the present, and the future were and are, with him, one eternal "now:" He knew of the fall of Adam, the iniquities of the antediluvians, of the depth of iniquity that would be connected with the human family, their weakness and strength, their power and glory, apostasies, their crimes, their righteousness and iniquity; He comprehended the fall of man and his redemption; he knew the plan of salvation and pointed it out; He was acquainted with the situation of all nations and with

their destiny; He ordered all things according to the council of His will; He knows the situation of both the living and the dead, and has made ample provision for their redemption, according to their several circumstances, and the laws of the kingdom of God, whether in this world, or in the world to come. [*TPJS*, 220]

—The Prophet Joseph Smith • D&C 38:7

I saw the Twelve Apostles of the Lamb, who are now upon the earth, who hold the keys of this last ministry, in foreign lands, standing together in a circle, much fatigued, with their clothes tattered and feet swollen, with their eyes cast downward, and Jesus standing in their midst, and they did not behold Him. The Savior looked upon them and wept. [*TPJS*, 107]

—Elder John Taylor • D&C 38:7

We never ought to do a thing that we would be afraid of God seeing us do; and if we are not afraid of God seeing us, we should not be afraid of man seeing us. [*JD*, 5:263]

—President Wilford Woodruff • D&C 38:11–12

God has held the angels of destruction for many years, lest they should reap down the wheat with the tares. But I want to tell you now, that those angels have left the portals of heaven, and they stand over this people and this nation now and are hovering over the earth waiting to pour out the judgments. And from this day they shall be poured out. [*Young Women's Journal*, 5:512]

—Elder Marion G. Romney • D&C 38:11–12

Now the basis for the hope and courage that will keep us from being troubled does not lie in the expectation that enough people will accept and obey the restored gospel to turn aside the oncoming calamities. Nor does it depend on any such contingency. As already indicated, it lies in the assurance that everyone who will accept and obey the restored gospel of Jesus Christ shall reap the promised rewards, and this regardless of what others do. And certain it is those who receive the blessings will have to prevail against great opposition, for the world in general is not improving. It is ripening in iniquity. [CR, October 1966, 53]

—Elder Harold B. Lee • D&C 38:27

The absolute test of the divinity of the calling of any officer in the Church is this: Is he in harmony with the brethren of that body to which he belongs? When we are out of harmony, we should look to ourselves first to find the way to unity. [CR, April 1966, 66]

—President Ezra Taft Benson • D&C 38:39

In the scriptures there is no such thing as righteous pride. It is always considered as a sin. We are not speaking of a wholesome view of self-worth, which is best established by a close relationship with God. But we are speaking of pride as the universal sin, as some have described it.

Mormon writes that "the pride of this nation, or the people of the Nephites, hath proven their destruction" (Mormon 8:27). [quotes D&C 38:39]

Essentially pride is "my will" rather than "thy will" approach to life. The opposite of pride is humbleness, meekness, submissiveness (see Alma 13:28), or teachableness. . . .

Pride does not look up to God and care about what is right. It looks sideways to man and argues who is right. Pride is manifest in the spirit of contention.

Was it not through pride that the devil became the devil? Christ wanted to serve. The devil wanted to rule. Christ wanted to bring men to where he was, The devil wanted to be above men. . . . [CR, April 1986, 5–6]

Chapter Twenty

The Law of God for the Church

D&C 41; 42:1–28, 74–93

*H*istorical Setting: Joseph and Emma lived in the home of Newel K. Whitney for several weeks after arriving in Kirtland about February 1, 1831. At their first meeting Joseph Smith walked into the store and said:

> "Newel K. Whitney! Thou art the man!" he exclaimed, extending his hand cordially, as if to an old and familiar acquaintance, "You have the advantage of me" replied the merchant, as he mechanically took the proffered hand. "I could not call you by name as you have me." "I am Joseph the Prophet," said the stranger smiling. "You've prayed me here, now what do you want of me?" The Prophet, it is said, while in the east, had seen the Whitneys, in vision, praying for his coming to Kirtland. [*HC*, 1:146]

The local branch of the Church, which now numbered nearly one hundred members, received section 41 on February 4, 1831. (*HC*, 1:146–47)

On February 9th, section 42 was given (see section heading). Verses 74–93 were given some days after the first 73 verses. (*HC*, 1:152).

INTRODUCTION

The Psalmist declared that "the law of the Lord is perfect, converting the soul" (Psalm 19:7). The law of the Lord comes by revelation, but it does not come all at once. During the first year after the Church was organized, many commandments, principles, ordinances, and counsels had been given. Now, it was time that the promised law of the Church should be revealed.

SECTIONS 41 & 42 • OUTLINE

➤ 41:1–6   The Lord delights to bless those that hear Him, and curses those who hear Him not that have professed His name.

    a.   The elders are called to assemble to agree upon his word (v. 2).

    b.   By the prayer of faith you shall receive my law and know how to govern my church and have things right before me (v. 3).

    c.   I will be your ruler when I come, and my law will be kept (v. 4).

    d.   He that receiveth my law and doeth it is my disciple, and he that receiveth my law and doeth it not is not my disciple and shall be cast out (v. 5).

    e.   The things of the kingdom are not to be given to the unworthy (v. 6).

➤ 41:7–12   It is meet that Joseph Smith have a house built in which to live and translate.

    a.   Sidney Rigdon should live as seems good if he keep my commandments (v. 8).

    b.   Edward Partridge is called to be ordained a bishop unto the church, and spend all his time laboring in the church to see to all things given (vv. 9–10).

    c.   Edward's heart is pure, like Nathanael of old, in whom there is no guile (v. 11).

    d.   These words are pure and answerable for in the day of judgment (v. 12).

➤ 42:1–3   The elders are to hearken, hear, and obey the law that was asked of the Father.

➤ 42:4–11   The first commandment is the law of preaching the gospel in my name.

    a.   All are to go forth except Joseph and Sidney (v. 4).

b.   Joseph and Sidney shall go forth until the Spirit tells them to return (v. 5).

    c.   Ye shall go forth in the power of my Spirit, two by two as angels (v. 6).

    d.   Ye shall baptize by water, saying repent, the kingdom is at hand (v. 7).

    e.   Ye shall go into the regions westward, and build up my church (v. 8).

    f.   Ye shall go until the time the city of the New Jerusalem is revealed (v. 9).

    g.   Edward Partridge shall stand in the office appointed him (v. 10).

    h.   No one shall go to preach my gospel except he be regularly ordained by some one having authority (v. 11).

    i.   It shall be known to the church that he has authority and has been regularly ordained by the heads of the church (v. 11).

➤ 42:12–17   The elders, priests, and teachers shall teach the principles that are in the Bible and the Book of Mormon, in which is the fullness of the gospel.

    a.   Observe the covenants and church articles as directed by the Spirit (v. 13).

    b.   If ye receive not the Spirit, ye shall not teach (v. 14).

    c.   Do as commanded until the fullness of the scriptures is given (v. 15).

    d.   Speak and prophesy as seems good, and as directed by the Spirit (vv. 16).

    e.   The Comforter knows all things, and bears record of the Father and Son (v. 17).

➤ 42:18–28   The law of moral behavior to the Church.

    a.   Thou shalt not kill, and he that kills shall not have forgiveness in this world nor in the world to come (v. 18).

    b.   He that kills shall die (v. 19).

    c.   Thou shalt not steal, he that steals and does not repent shall be cast out (v. 20).

d. Thou shalt not lie, he that lies and does not repent shall be cast out (v. 21).

e. Thou shalt cleave unto thy wife and none else (v. 22).

f. He that lusts after a woman shall deny the faith and not have the Spirit, and shall be cast out if he does not repent (v. 23).

g. Thou shalt not commit adultery, he that committeth adultery and does not repent shall be cast out (v. 24).

h. He that commits adultery and repents, and forsakes it, shall be forgiven, but if he does it again, he shall not be forgiven, but be cast out (vv. 25–26).

i. Thou shalt not speak evil of thy neighbor nor do him any harm (v. 27).

j. The laws concerning these things are given in the scriptures, he that sins and does not repent shall be cast out (v. 28).

➤ 42:74–77   Persons who have put away their companions because of their own fornication shall be cast out.

a. Persons who left because of adultery, and are the offenders, and the companions are living, shall be cast out (v. 75).

b. None such that are married shall be received (v. 76).

c. If not married, they must repent of all their sins or not be received (v. 77).

➤ 42:78   All who belong to the church must keep all the commandments and covenants.

➤ 42:79   Any persons who kills shall be dealt with according to the laws of the land.

a. He hath no forgiveness (v. 79).

b. It shall be proved according to the law of the land (v. 79).

➤ 42:80–83   If any commit adultery, they are to be tried before two elders, or more.

a. Every word must be established by two or more witnesses of the church (v. 80).

b. If condemned by two witnesses, the church shall lift up

the law of God (v. 81).

    c. If it can be, it is necessary for the bishop to be present (v. 82).

    d. All cases shall be dealt with in the same manner (v. 83).

➤ 42:84–86   If any rob, or steal, or lie they shall be delivered unto the law of the land.

➤ 42:87   If any do any manner of iniquity, they shall be delivered unto the law of God.

➤ 42:88–89   If any offend thee, take him or her before thee alone, and if he or she confess thou shalt be reconciled.

    a. If he or she confess not, deliver he or she to the elders of the church, not the members (v. 89).

    b. It shall be done in a meeting, not before the world (v. 89).

➤ 42:90–93   If any offend many, he or she shall be chastened before many.

    a. If any offend openly, he or she shall be rebuked openly (v. 91).

    b. If they confess not, he or she shall be delivered to the law of the land (v. 92).

    c. If any offend in secret, rebuke them in secret that they may confess in secret to those offended and to God (v. 92).

    d. The church shall not speak reproachfully of him or her (v. 92).

    e. Thus shall ye conduct in all things (v. 93).

TEXT AND COMMENTARY

D&C 41:1–6 • What Is a Disciple?

1 Hearken and hear, O ye my people, saith the Lord and your God, ye whom I delight to bless with the greatest of all blessings, ye that hear me; and ye that hear me not will I curse, that have professed my name, with the heaviest of all cursings.

2 Hearken, O ye elders of my church whom I have called, behold

I give unto you a commandment, that ye shall assemble yourselves together to agree upon my word;

3 And by the prayer of your faith ye shall receive my law, that ye may know how to govern my church and have all things right before me.

4 And I will be your ruler when I come; and behold, I come quickly, and ye shall see that my law is kept.

5 He that receiveth my law and doeth it, the same is my disciple; and he that saith he receiveth it and doeth it not, the same is not my disciple, and shall be cast out from among you;

6 For it is not meet that the things which belong to the children of the kingdom should be given to them that are not worthy, or to dogs, or the pearls to be cast before swine.

The greatest of all blessings (v. 1) was undoubtedly the temple endowment that had been promised to them after they had moved to the Ohio. "To agree upon my word" when they assemble (v. 2), was the law of common consent (see D&C 26:2). It was to be followed on all the commandments, including the ones to be revealed in Ohio. The law of the Church, previously promised (D&C 37:3; 38:32) would show them how to govern the Church (D&C 41:3). Christ would be the ruler when He came the second time. The law to govern the Church would be used then, but should be kept now (v. 4). The true disciples are those whom received His law and keep it. Those who did not keep the law would be cast out from among them (v. 5). The governing law, revealed in section 42, belongs to the children of the kingdom (v. 6). The dogs symbolize those among them who were not worthy. In the New Testament, Christ referred to the scribes, the Pharisees, and the priests as the dogs (see JST, Matthew 7:6–7). The swine symbolize the world, or the Gentiles, who would not understand the mysteries of the kingdom. They would wrest them against the truths of the gospel to bring persecution and ridicule upon the Saints (see JST, Matthew 7:10–11).

D&C 41:7–12 • Edward Partridge Like Nathaniel of Old

7 And again, it is meet that my servant Joseph Smith, Jun., should have a house built, in which to live and translate.

8 And again, it is meet that my servant Sidney Rigdon should live as seemeth him good, inasmuch as he keepeth my commandments.

9 And again, I have called my servant Edward Partridge; and I give a commandment, that he should be appointed by the voice of the church, and ordained a bishop unto the church, to leave his merchandise and to spend all his time in the labors of the church;

10 To see to all things as it shall be appointed unto him in my laws in the day that I shall give them.

11 And this because his heart is pure before me, for he is like unto Nathanael of old, in whom there is no guile.

12 These words are given unto you, and they are pure before me; wherefore, beware how you hold them, for they are to be answered upon your souls in the day of judgment. Even so. Amen.

Joseph was to continue to translate and needed a place to work on the project (v. 7). He used the upstairs of the Newel K. Whitney Store for some time. Sidney was to help Joseph as scribe in the translation (see D&C 35:20), but was given freedom to govern his own living conditions (D&C 41:8). Perhaps that was because the law of consecration had not yet been given (see chapter 21), and because Sidney's financial situation was better than Joseph's. Edward Partridge was the first of many called and appointed by the voice of the church as a part of the law of consecration (see D&C 38:34). He was to be the first bishop in Zion, a full-time position as overseer of the new law yet to be given (D&C 41:9–10). For his comparison to Nathanael of old, see John 1:45–51. The law of consecration made everyone accountable for their stewardships (D&C 38:12; see D&C 70:9).

D&C 42:1–3 • Ask and Ye Shall Receive

1 Hearken, O ye elders of my church, who have assembled yourselves together in my name, even Jesus Christ the Son of the living God, the Savior of the world; inasmuch as ye believe on my name and keep my commandments.

2 Again I say unto you, hearken and hear and obey the law which I shall give unto you.

3 For verily I say, as ye have assembled yourselves together according to the commandment wherewith I commanded you, and are agreed as touching this one thing, and have asked the Father in my name, even so ye shall receive.

The law of the Church, as now revealed, was given in answer to prayer

(v. 3), though there appears to be no additional record of this request. The "law of the Church" is really several laws.

THE LAW OF PREACHING THE GOSPEL

The first law is the law of preaching the gospel (42:1–17). It gave the guidelines for the time referred to earlier, when "men shall go forth into all nations" from Kirtland (D&C 39:15). It divides into two parts; *who* is to teach, and *what* should be taught.

D&C 42:4–11 • The Law of Preaching the Gospel

4 Behold, verily I say unto you, I give unto you this first commandment, that ye shall go forth in my name, every one of you, excepting my servants Joseph Smith, Jun., and Sidney Rigdon.

5 And I give unto them a commandment that they shall go forth for a little season, and it shall be given by the power of the Spirit when they shall return.

6 And ye shall go forth in the power of my Spirit, preaching my gospel, two by two, in my name, lifting up your voices as with the sound of a trump, declaring my word like unto angels of God.

7 And ye shall go forth baptizing with water, saying: Repent ye, repent ye, for the kingdom of heaven is at hand.

8 And from this place ye shall go forth into the regions westward; and inasmuch as ye shall find them that will receive you ye shall build up my church in every region—

9 Until the time shall come when it shall be revealed unto you from on high, when the city of the New Jerusalem shall be prepared, that ye may be gathered in one, that ye may be my people and I will be your God.

10 And again, I say unto you, that my servant Edward Partridge shall stand in the office whereunto I have appointed him. And it shall come to pass, that if he transgress another shall be appointed in his stead. Even so. Amen.

11 Again I say unto you, that it shall not be given to anyone to go forth to preach my gospel, or to build up my church, except he be ordained by someone who has authority, and it is known to the church that he has authority and has been regularly ordained by the heads of the church.

At this time period, all the elders (v. 4), every one of them except Joseph and Sidney, were to go forth. Joseph and Sidney were to go for a little season until the Spirit said to return (vv. 4–5). The missionaries were to go "two by two" (v. 6), the same as in New Testament times (see Luke 10:1). The "regions westward" were only the beginning. "Every region," until the city of the New Jerusalem was prepared (D&C 42:8–9), would include all around the city since it was the center place of Zion (D&C 57:3). The Lord's plan is to eventually teach all people, but he had designated on sequence in teaching the nations of the earth. The Gentiles shall be taught the gospel first, then the house of Israel, and then the heathen [non-Christian] nations (see Matthew 19:30; D&C 90:8–11). When the city of the New Jerusalem is built, the people in that city and in the supporting regions round about will be one They will be the Lord's people, and He will be their God (D&C 42:9). This promise has been given to Israel whenever they are or will be gathered (see Exodus 6:7; Zacharias 8:8). The reason why the calling of Edward Partridge was repeated (D&C 42:10) is not known, but perhaps it was because he would hold such a prominent position in the city of Zion.

No formal calls for preaching the gospel were to be given unless three requirements were met. First, that the one called is ordained by someone having authority; second, that it is known to the Church generally that he has the authority; and third, that he has been regularly ordained by the heads of the Church (v. 11). These requirements refute the claims of any offshoot group of the Church, or any individuals who attempt to "steady the ark" or correct the Church leadership.

D&C 42:4–11 • What to Teach

12 And again, the elders, priests and teachers of this church shall teach the principles of my gospel, which are in the Bible and the Book of Mormon, in the which is the fulness of the gospel.

13 And they shall observe the covenants and church articles to do them, and these shall be their teachings, as they shall be directed by the Spirit.

14 And the Spirit shall be given unto you by the prayer of faith; and if ye receive not the Spirit ye shall not teach.

15 And all this ye shall observe to do as I have commanded concern-

ing your teaching, until the fulness of my scriptures is given.

16 And as ye shall lift up your voices by the Comforter, ye shall speak and prophesy as seemeth me good;

17 For, behold, the Comforter knoweth all things, and beareth record of the Father and of the Son.

What those who are called to preach the gospel are to teach is now designated. The Bible and the Book of Mormon were to be the texts for the missionaries (v. 12). A careful reading again designates only the Book of Mormon as containing the fulness of the gospel. "In *the* which is" (v. 12) is singular, the Book of Mormon containing the fulness, not both books (see also JS—H 1:34; D&C 20:9; 27:5; 35:17). The Bible contains most of these same principles, but due to the loss of plain and precious parts is not as clear as the Book of Mormon is in teaching them. The fullness of the gospel is defined in 3 Nephi 27:13–22. The "covenants and church articles," also mentioned in section 33 verse 14, consisted of sections 20 and 22 of today's Doctrine and Covenants. A copy of these revelations was carried with the elders as they went away teaching.[34] The elder, or teacher, should first know and understand the principles, and then the Spirit will direct which principles he or she should teach. Hyrum Smith was told to "study my word" before declaring it (see D&C 11:21–22). A teacher must pray for the guidance of the Spirit, and then as he or she teaches the Spirit will bring to mind those principles. If the Spirit does not prompt, the principle should not be taught even if the principle is clearly understood (D&C 42:14). The prophet Nephi is a good example to follow: "And now I, Nephi, cannot say more; the Spirit stoppeth mine utterance, and I am left to mourn because of the unbelief, and the wickedness, and the ignorance, and the stiffneckedness of men; for they will not search knowledge, nor understand great knowledge, when it is given unto them in plainness, even as plain as word can be" (2 Nephi 32:7).

"Until the fullness of my scriptures is given" (D&C 42:15), refers to Joseph Smith's completion of the translation of the Bible. Although it was never completed, the Lord later gave approval for using what had been done so far (see D&C 124:89). As the missionaries teach, or are led

---

[34] The Articles and Covenants of the Church of Christ were first printed in *The Evening and the Morning Star,* vol. 1, Independence Mo., June 1832, No.1.

to prophesy, the Comforter will direct them and bear record of the Father and the Son (D&C 42:16–17; see also 3 Nephi 11:32). They will be effective teachers.

THE LAW OF MORAL BEHAVIOR

The second law revealed in section 42 was the law of moral behavior. The basic principles of the law were given in verses 18–28. Verses 74–93 were revealed two weeks later, when seven elders met together to inquire of the Lord.[35] The two revelations are discussed together.

The Ten Commandments have long been the basis of moral conduct among the Christian nations of the earth. In the law of the Church, many of the Ten Commandments pertaining to men's relationship with each other were given again, although in a sometimes modified and more explanatory nature.

D&C 42:18–19, 79 • Thou Shalt Not Kill

> 18 And now, behold, I speak unto the church. Thou shalt not kill; and he that kills shall not have forgiveness in this world, nor in the world to come.
>
> 19 And again, I say, thou shalt not kill; but he that killeth shall die.
>
> 79 And it shall come to pass, that if any persons among you shall kill they shall be delivered up and dealt with according to the laws of the land; for remember that he hath no forgiveness; and it shall be proved according to the laws of the land.

The Lord classes murder as an unforgivable sin, both in time or in eternity (v. 18). It is the "most abominable above all sin" except "denying the Holy Ghost." (Alma 39:5). The punishment pronounced by the Lord is "he that killeth shall die" (D&C 42:19). The controversial capital punishment law is substantiated by the Lord. Capital punishment has been the same from the beginning: "Whoso sheddeth man's blood, by man shall his blood be shed: for in the image of God made he man" (Genesis 9:6). Therefore, the Atonement of Christ will not usually cover it (see Alma 39:6). The guilty are to be dealt with according to the law

---

[35] Lyndon W. Cook, *The Revelations of the Prophet Joseph Smith* [1981], 59, 131.

of the land (D&C 42:79), or their crime is to be tried by the political government.

It is sometimes argued that capital punishment is an Old Testament law and not a New Testament law. While it was an Old Testament law, it was given long before the law of Moses, which was a lesser law. While there are no direct statements in the New Testament on the issue, there are indirect references supporting capital punishment "and almost all things are by the law purged with blood; and without shedding of blood is no remission." (Hebrews 9:22; see also 1 Corinthians 5:5). The Nephites, who lived the higher law (see 2 Nephi 25:24–27), had the law of capital punishment among them: "But if he murdered he was punished unto death" (Alma 30:10). They also gave good reasons for the law:

> Now there is not any man that can sacrifice his own blood which will atone for the sins of another. Now, if a man murdereth, behold will our law, which is just, take the life of his brother? I say unto you, Nay.

> But the law requireth the life of him who hath murdered; therefore there can be nothing which is short of an infinite atonement which will suffice for the sins of the world. [Alma 34:11–12]

> Now, if there was no law given—if a man murdered he should die—would he be afraid he would die if he should murder? [Alma 42:19]

The responsibility of enforcing the law was declared by Alma, the chief judge, in pronouncing the sentence upon Nehor.

> 13 And thou hast shed the blood of a righteous man, yea, a man who has done much good among this people; and were we to spare thee his blood would come upon us for vengeance.

> 14 Therefore thou art condemned to die, according to the law which has been given us by Mosiah, our last king; and it has been acknowledged by this people; therefore this people must abide by the law. [Alma 1:13–14]

Finally, the necessity of capital punishment was emphasized by the Prophet Joseph Smith. Regarding eternal judgment, he explained:

> That the doctrine of eternal judgment was perfectly understood by the Apostles, is evident from several passages of Scripture. Peter preached repentance and baptism for the remission of sins to the Jews who had been led to acts of violence and blood by their leaders; but to the rulers he said, 'I wot that through ignorance ye did it, as did also your rulers.'

'Repent ye therefore, and be converted that your sins may be blotted out, when the times of refreshing (redemption) shall come from the presence of the Lord, and He shall send Jesus Christ, which before was preached unto you,' &c. The time of redemption here had reference to the time when Christ should come; then, and not till then, would their sins be blotted out. Why? Because they were murderers, and no murderer hath eternal life. Even David must wait for those times of refreshing, before he can come forth and his sins be blotted out. For Peter, speaking of him says, 'David hath not yet ascended into heaven, for his sepulcher is with us to this day.' His remains were then in the tomb. Now, we read that many bodies of the Saints arose at Christ's resurrection, probably all the Saints, but it seems that David did not. Why? Because he had been a murderer. If the ministers of religion had a proper understanding of the doctrine of eternal judgment, they would not be found attending the man who had forfeited his life to the injured laws of his country, by shedding innocent blood; for such characters cannot be forgiven, until they have paid the uttermost farthing. The prayers of all the ministers in the world cannot close the gates of hell against a murderer. [*TPJS*, 188–189]

On a later occasion, the Prophet declared:

A murderer, for instance, one that sheds innocent blood, cannot have forgiveness. David sought repentance at the hand of God carefully with tears, for the murder of Uriah; but he could only get it through hell: he got a promise that his soul should not be left in hell.

Although David was a king, he never did obtain the spirit and power of Elijah and the fullness of the Priesthood; and the Priesthood that he received, and the throne and kingdom of David is to be taken from him and given to another by the name of David in the last days, raised up out of his lineage.

Peter referred to the same subject on the day of Pentecost, but the multitude did not get the endowment that Peter had; but several days after, the people asked, 'What shall we do?' Peter says, 'I would ye had done it ignorantly,' speaking of crucifying the Lord &c. He did not say to them, 'Repent and be baptized for the remission of your sins'; but he said, 'Repent ye therefore, and be converted, that your sins may be blotted out, when the times of refreshing shall come from the presence of the Lord.' [Acts 3:19.]

This is the case with murderers. They could not be baptized for the remission of sins, for they had shed innocent blood. [*TPJS*, 339]

There is apparently some exceptions to be considered. Alma said: "whosoever murdereth against the light and knowledge of God, it is not easy for him to obtain forgiveness" (Alma 39:6). This qualification, by Alma, implies that those who have little or no knowledge of God may be given some leniency. This would be left up to the courts of the land to judge on earth, *and to God on the eternal level.*

The law of the Church in these latter days on murder is consistent with the law of the Lord in other dispensations.

D&C 42:20–21, 84–86 • Thou Shalt Not Steal; Thou Shalt Not Bear False Witness

> 20 Thou shalt not steal; and he that stealeth and will not repent shall be cast out.
>
> 21 Thou shalt not lie; he that lieth and will not repent shall be cast out.
>
> 84 And if a man or woman shall rob, he or she shall be delivered up unto the law of the land.
>
> 85 And if he or she shall steal, he or she shall be delivered up unto the law of the land.
>
> 86 And if he or she shall lie, he or she shall be delivered up unto the law of the land.

The Lord divides the eighth commandment into two categories, to *rob* and to *steal* (vv. 20; 84–85). To rob is to take property unlawfully by force; to steal is to take property unlawfully in secret. Such sins, if he or she does not repent, were to result in the perpetrator's being cast out of the Church. Today, such action is called being disfellowshipped, not having full benefits of the Church; or being excommunicated, loss of membership in the Church. In both instances, the Church member was also to be dealt with according to the law of the land (vv. 84–85).

The ninth commandment is worded differently in the Doctrine and Covenants than in the Bible; to lie, instead of to bear false witness. The same punishment as robbing or stealing was to be given in the Church, and was also to be dealt with by the law of the land (vv. 21; 86).

D&C 42:22–28, 80–83 • Thou Shalt Not Commit Adultery

22 Thou shalt love thy wife with all thy heart, and shalt cleave unto her and none else.

23 And he that looketh upon a woman to lust after her shall deny the faith, and shall not have the Spirit; and if he repents not he shall be cast out.

24 Thou shalt not commit adultery; and he that committeth adultery, and repenteth not, shall be cast out.

25 But he that has committed adultery and repents with all his heart, and forsaketh it, and doeth it no more, thou shalt forgive;

26 But if he doeth it again, he shall not be forgiven, but shall be cast out.

27 Thou shalt not speak evil of thy neighbor, nor do him any harm.

28 Thou knowest my laws concerning these things are given in my scriptures; he that sinneth and repenteth not shall be cast out.

80 And if any man or woman shall commit adultery, he or she shall be tried before two elders of the church, or more, and every word shall be established against him or her by two witnesses of the church, and not of the enemy; but if there are more than two witnesses it is better.

81 But he or she shall be condemned by the mouth of two witnesses; and the elders shall lay the case before the church, and the church shall lift up their hands against him or her, that they may be dealt with according to the law of God.

82 And if it can be, it is necessary that the bishop be present also.

83 And thus ye shall do in all cases which shall come before you.

The Lord turns to the positive to introduce the law regarding sexual sin. To love one's wife with all one's heart would eliminate the possibility of sin in this area (v. 22). To cleave is to adhere firmly and closely, or loyally and unwaveringly. The Lord divides the sin into categories as He did in the New Testament (Matthew 5:27–28): spiritual adultery, or the lust of the heart; and physical adultery (42:23–24). Those who are not repentant, in either case, are to be cast out. Both sins, physical or spiritual, lead to a denial of the faith because of the withdrawal of the Spirit (v. 23; see also 63:12–19; 1 Corinthians 6:18–19). John Smith, a member of the Church, unknowingly verified the Lord's statement concerning the denial of the faith as he accused the Prophet Joseph Smith of being a false prophet:

> I have been conversant with early Elders, and I am satisfied that a large number of them fell from their positions in the kingdom of God because they yielded to the spirit of adultery; this was the cause of their destruction. There was an Elder named John Smith who lived in Indiana, who was quite popular in that part of the country as a preacher. He apostatized, but he did not know it. In talking about his faith and how firm it was, he said, I have proven the revelation given to Joseph Smith untrue, which says that if a man shall commit adultery he shall lose the spirit of God, and deny the faith. I have proven that not to be true, for I have violated that commandment and have not denied the faith. He was so blind that he could not see through the darkness that the spirit of adultery had placed upon his head, the great apostasy which seemed to shake the Church, and tried men's souls. [George A. Smith, *JD*, 11:10–11]

Adulterers or adulteresses are to be taken before two or more elders of the Church, and every word shall be established against him or her by two witnesses of the Church, and not of the enemy (D&C 42:80). This is undoubtedly to eliminate the tendency to attack the character of individuals with false accusations, or because of rumors. It does not seem coincidental that the Lord warns against speaking evil of one's neighbor immediately after speaking of the sin of adultery (D&C 42:27).

Forgiveness is held out to those who have committed adultery and repented with all their heart (D&C 42:25). However, a second offense, after repenting and fully forsaking the sin, is not forgivable but requires him or her to be cast out. Furthermore, this revelation was given before the temple endowment was given, and does not apply to those who have received their temple endowments. President John Taylor quoted the revelation and commented:

> This was in the early ages of the Church, in February, 1831. But who is here referred to? Is it a man who has entered into the new and everlasting covenant, and has been sealed by the Holy Spirit of promise, and by that covenant has been united to his wife for time and all eternity, and his wife to him? No, it refers to those who have not entered into this covenant, who have not taken upon themselves obligations of that nature in a Temple or Endowment House; to the latter class who shall be found guilty of this sin, the word of the Lord comes unqualifiedly, they shall

be destroyed. The Lord does expect us to be a pure people, a virtuous people, a people whose bodies and spirits are pure before Him. If wrong doing be practiced in our midst, the Lord expects His Priesthood to ferret it out, or he will hold them responsible. We cannot commit sin with impunity. We cannot violate the laws of God and enjoy His Spirit; nor can we permit the laws of God to be trampled upon and still receive His approbation. [*JD*, 24:170]

President Joseph Fielding Smith further commented on the seriousness of adultery after having received the temple endowment:

Now this revelation was given before the endowment was made known. Since that time when a man is married in the temple, he takes a solemn covenant before God, angels, and witnesses that he will keep the law of chastity. Then, if he violates that covenant it is not easy to receive forgiveness. I call your attention to this statement by the Prophet Joseph Smith: "If a man commit adultery, he cannot receive the celestial kingdom of God. Even if he is saved in any kingdom, it cannot be the celestial kingdom."

Of course, a man may, according to the Doctrine and Covenants, 132:26, receive forgiveness, if he is willing to pay the penalty for such a crime: that is he "shall be destroyed in the flesh, and shall be delivered unto the buffetings of Satan unto the day of redemption," which is the time of the resurrection. We cannot destroy in the flesh, so what will the Lord require in lieu thereof, I do not know. Anciently when the Church was a theocratic power with authority in all things, this law was carried out. "And the man that committeth adultery with another man's wife, the adulterer and the adulteress shall surely be put to death."

We have been taught that adultery is a crime second only to the shedding of innocent blood. We cannot treat it lightly. For a man to destroy another man's home is too serious an offense to be readily forgiven. Such a man should not be permitted to come back in the Church, under any circumstances, at least until years have elapsed. He should be placed on probation for that length of time to see if he can, or will, remain clean. Even then I confess I do not know what disposition the Lord will make of him. To permit him to come back within a short time has a very evil effect upon other members of the Church who begin to think that this enormous crime is not serious after all. [*Doctrines of Salvation*, 2:93–94]

The Lord expects his people to be morally clean, and this includes clean thoughts as well as actions. While the sin is very serious, it becomes even more so after the temple endowments have been received. However, Church discipline is governed by revelation, and it captions to these commandments are occasionally granted. The Lord, fully understanding the circumstances and knowing the hearts of the individuals involved, may direct His servants to be more lenient. He may direct more leniency for one participant than for the other. Church discipline is meted out to save people and not to condemn or punish them. That latter responsibility He has placed on the political government. The Lord reveals what is best for the situation of each individual.

The Lord acknowledges that His instructions concerning these things [adultery] are not complete, but we must go to His scriptures for more information (42:28). An example of further information from the scriptures is Alma 39:5–6, where Alma labels the three most abominable sins: Denial of the Holy Ghost, which is unpardonable; the shedding of innocent blood, for which it is not easy to obtain forgiveness, and for which the law of the Church calls unforgivable; and sexual immorality, which is forgivable under certain conditions as explained above. An unpardonable sin is also unforgivable, but an unforgivable sin is not unpardonable. It may be pardoned by the offender going through the buffetings of Satan (see D&C 78:12; 82:21–22; 132:26).[36]

D&C 42:75–77 • No Divorce Except For Fornication

74 Behold, verily I say unto you, that whatever persons among you, having put away their companions for the cause of fornication, or in other words, if they shall testify before you in all lowliness of heart that this is the case, ye shall not cast them out from among you;

75 But if ye shall find that any persons have left their companions for the sake of adultery, and they themselves are the offenders, and their companions are living, they shall be cast out from among you.

76 And again, I say unto you, that ye shall be watchful and careful, with all inquiry, that ye receive none such among you if they are married;

77 And if they are not married, they shall repent of all their sins or ye shall not receive them.

The Lord gave the Church the same law concerning divorce that He

---

[36] For a more complete explanation see Monte S. Nyman, *The Record of Alma, Book of Mormon Commentary* [2004], 3:499–504.

gave the Saints in New Testament times, the only cause being fornication (v. 74, Matthew 5:31–32;19:9). This instruction has been generally interpreted to mean that the only just grounds for divorce are adultery; in the past, and presently, several states and nations have adopted laws to this effect. The Lord said to accept those who had left their partners because of fornication, but if they had committed adultery themselves and had left their partners, they were not to be accepted (D&C 42:75). Therefore, the Lord makes a distinction between the two sins. An examination of biblical passages will explain the difference:

> 8 And I saw, when for all the causes whereby backsliding Israel committed adultery I had put her away, and given her a bill of divorce; yet her treacherous sister Judah feared not, but went and played the harlot also.
>
> 9 And it came to pass through the lightness of her whoredom, that she defiled the land, and committed adultery with stones and with stocks.
>
> 10 And yet for all this her treacherous sister Judah hath not turned unto me with her whole heart, but feignedly, saith the LORD.
>
> 11 And the LORD said unto me, The backsliding Israel hath justified herself more than treacherous Judah. [Jeremiah 3:8–11]

The children of Israel forsook Jehovah to worship the pagan god Baal. The Lord termed this sin adultery since He (Jehovah) was symbolically married to Israel to produce His children. This He classifies as a physical violation of the marriage covenant. The Lord invites Israel to repent and return unto Him from this sin (see Jeremiah 3:12–14).

In New Testament times, the Lord accuses the kings of the earth of committing fornication with Babylon: "For all nations have drunk of the wine of the wrath of her fornication, and the kings of the earth have committed fornication with her, and the merchants of the earth are waxed rich through the abundance of her delicacies" (Revelation 18:3). This seems to refer to perverted Christianity being adopted as a state religion. Because of this the Lord does not invite their return, but pronounces her destruction after the people are come out of her (see Revelation 18:4–8). Fornication is aptly described by Isaiah when he says: "this people draw near unto me with their mouth, and with their lips do honour me, but have removed their heart far from me, and their fear toward me is taught by the precept of men" (Isaiah 29:13). Thus, fornication may be classified as a spiritual violation of the marriage covenant. The Apostle Paul seems aware of this definition: "Lest there be any fornicator, or profane person, as Esau, who for one morsel of meat sold his birthright" (Hebrews 12:6). The author of Chronicles supports the interpretation also: "Moreover he made high places in the mountains of Judah, and caused the inhabitants of Jerusalem to commit fornication, and compelled Judah thereto" (2 Chronicles 21:11).[37]

The law of the Church concerning divorce is thus one of a spiritual violation of the covenant, and not a physical one Although the physical violation could lead to the spiritual dissolving of a marriage, the divorce should not be given unless the spiritual bond is broken, and even then divorce should be a last resort. Moses allowed divorce, according to the Savior, due to the hardness of people's hearts (Matthew 19:5). The same policy is apparently the law of the Church today. A reconciliation should be sought first (42:88; quoted below), but if this does not work then church disciplinary action should be taken, in private and not before the world (D&C 42:89; also quoted below).

D&C 42:78, 88–93 • Church Discipline

78 And again, every person who belongeth to this church of Christ, shall observe to keep all the commandments and covenants of the church.

88 And if thy brother or sister offend thee, thou shalt take him or her between him or her and thee alone; and if he or she confess thou shalt be reconciled.

89 And if he or she confess not thou shalt deliver him or her up unto the church, not to the members, but to the elders. And it shall be done in a meeting, and that not before the world.

90 And if thy brother or sister offend many, he or she shall be chastened before many.

91 And if any one offend openly, he or she shall be rebuked openly, that he or she may be ashamed. And if he or she confess not, he or she shall be delivered up unto the law of God.

92 If any shall offend in secret, he or she shall be rebuked in secret, that he or she may have opportunity to confess in secret to him or her

---

[37] See also Bruce R. McConkie's definition in *Mormon Doctrine* [1966], 298.

whom he or she has offended, and to God, that the church may not speak reproachfully of him or her.

93 And thus shall ye conduct in all things.

The first responsibility for correct moral behavior rests upon the individual members. They should privately attempt to settle their grievances (v. 88). The next step is to seek the help of the Church. Once more the Lord tells them to do so in privacy, before the elders, or leadership of the Church (v. 89). The counsel given for certain sins being handled by the law of the land must be maintained (see vv. 79; 84–85). There is a separation of church and state "until he reigns whose right it is to reign" (D&C 58:22). The confessions and chastising of the offenders, for any of the sins of moral behavior, is determined by the number of people offended and the knowledge of the offense. Offenses must be confessed to other individuals, Church leaders when the Church is offended, and to God in all things (D&C 42:90–93). Church discipline is intended to save the individuals, not to punish them. There must be a balance of justice and mercy in the Church as well as in eternity (see Alma 42:22–26).

The third law revealed as part of "the Law of the Church," is the law of consecration. Because of the length of the revelation, and the subsequent revelations regarding this law, it will be discussed separately in the next chapter.

General Authority Quotes

—President Joseph Fielding Smith • D&C 42:11–14

> As agents of the Lord we are not called or authorized to teach the philosophies of the world or the speculative theories of our scientific age. Our mission is to preach the doctrines of salvation in *plainness* and simplicity as they are revealed and recorded in the scriptures....
>
> In harmony with the spirit of these revelations, and with a heart full of love for all men, I ask the members of the Church to learn and live the gospel and to use their strength, energy, and means in proclaiming it to the world. We have received a commission of the Lord. He has given a divine mandate. [CR, October 1970, 5–6]

—Elder Spencer W. Kimball • D&C 42:12–14

There are those today who seem to take pride in disagreeing with the orthodox teachings of the Church and who present their own opinions which are at variance with the revealed truth. Some may be partially innocent in the matter; others are feeding their own egotism; and some seem to be deliberate. Men may think as they please, but they have no right to impose upon others their unorthodox views. Such persons should realize that their own souls are in jeopardy. [CR, April 1948, 109]

—President Howard W. Hunter • D&C 42:14

I take this verse to mean not only that we *should not* teach without the Spirit, but also that we *cannot* teach without it. Learning of spiritual things simply cannot take place without the instructional and confirming presence of the Spirit of the Lord. Joseph Smith would seem to agree: "All are to preach the Gospel by the power and influence of the Holy Ghost; and no man can preach the Gospel without the Holy Ghost." [*The Teachings of Howard W. Hunter*, ed. Clyde J. Williams (1997), 209–10]

—President Spencer W. Kimball • D&C 42:22

The words *none else* eliminate everyone and everything. The spouse then becomes preeminent in the life of the husband or wife, and neither social life nor occupational life nor political life nor any other interest nor person nor thing shall ever take precedence over the companion spouse. We sometimes find women who absorb and hover over the children at the expense of the husband, sometimes even estranging them from him. This is in direct violation of the command: *None else.* [*The Teachings of Spencer W. Kimball* (1982), 311]

—Elder Adam S. Bennion • D&C 42:27

To bear false witness is to testify or to pass along *reports, insinuations, speculations, or rumors* as if they were true, to the hurt of a fellow human being. Sometimes the practice stems from a lack of correct information—sometimes from lack of understanding— sometimes from misunderstandings—sometimes from a vicious disposition to distort and misrepresent.

Whereas murder involves the taking of human life, *bearing false witness* centers in the destruction of character or its defamation. It reaches to the ruin of reputation. [*The Ten Commandments Today* (1955), 136]

—*President George F. Richards* • D&C 42:28

It is possible for us by bearing false witness, to destroy the faith of others. It may be a child, a parent, a wife, or some other dear friend. We may later repent, but we cannot repent for them. We should be doubly careful not to do any injury we cannot repair. When we bear false witness, we injure at least four: ourselves, him about whom we speak, him to whom we speak, and the Lord. [CR, April 1947, 25]

Chapter Twenty-One

The Law of Consecration

D&C 42:29–73; 48; 51; 53; 55; 70:5–9

*H*istorical Setting:

> The branch of the Church in this part of the Lord's vineyard, . . . were striving to do the will of the God, so far as they knew it, though some strange notions and false spirits had crept in among them. With a little caution and some wisdom, I soon assisted the brethren and sisters to overcome them. The plan of "common stock" which had existed in what was called "the family," whose members generally had embraced the everlasting Gospel, was readily abandoned for the more perfect law of the Lord; and the false spirits were easily discerned and rejected by the light of revelation. [*HC*, 1:146–47; see also section heading of section 42].

INTRODUCTION

Following the resurrected Christ's ascension into heaven, it is recorded that the New Testament Saints "had all things common" (Acts 2:44). This incomplete account of the law of consecration in the New Testament has led to many attempts at communal-type living since that time. Although a more detailed account is recorded later (Acts 4:32–37) that is closer to "the law of the Lord," it does not reveal enough information to fully practice the law that was revealed in February 1831. "The law of the Lord" is still not generally understood by most members of the Church today, in this writer's opinion. When the law is discussed, we still hear: "When will we *have to* live this law?" The Lord said, in June of 1831, "I grant unto this people a privilege of organizing themselves according to my laws" (D&C 51:15). Hopefully the following treatise will show why it is a privilege to live this law.

SECTION 42 • OUTLINE

➤ 42:29–32   If thou lovest me thou shalt serve me and keep my commandments.

    a.   Consecrate thy properties for the support of the poor with a covenant and a deed which cannot be broken (v. 30).

    b.   Lay thy substance before the bishop and his counselors (v. 31).

    c.   Consecrated properties cannot be taken from the church (v. 32).

➤ 42:32–33   Every man shall be accountable as a steward over his own property received by consecration.

    a.   It shall be sufficient for himself and family (v. 32).

    b.   Properties of the church, or individuals, that is more than necessary after the first consecration, shall be administered to the needy from time to time (v. 33).

➤ 42:34–37   The residue shall be kept in the Lord's storehouse to administer to the poor and the needy as appointed by the high council and the bishop.

    a.   For the purpose of purchasing lands for the public's benefit, building houses of worship, and building up the New Jerusalem (v. 35).

    b.   For the gathering of the Lord's people when he comes to his temple (v. 36).

    c.   Unrepentant sinner shall be cast out, and not retain what he consecrated (v. 37).

➤ 42:38–42   If you do good for the least of these, you do it for Christ, unto the fulfilling of the prophets.

    a.   The rich of the Gentiles, who embrace Christ's Gospel, shall help the poor of Christ's people, who are of the house of Israel (v. 39).

    b.   Do not be proud, let thy garments be plain, the work of thy hands (v. 40).

    c.   Let all things be done in cleanliness before the Lord (v. 41).

    d.   Do not be idle, the idler shall not eat the bread, nor wear the garment of the laborer (v. 42).

➤ 42:43–52   Nourish the sick, who have not faith to be healed, with herbs and mild food.

    a.   Two or more elders shall lay hands on them in Christ's name (v. 43).

    b.   If they die, they die unto Christ, if they live they live unto Christ (v. 44).

    c.   Live together in love, and weep for the loss of those that die (v. 45).

    d.   Those who die in Christ shall not taste death, it shall be sweet (v. 46).

    e.   For those who die not in Christ, death shall be bitter (v. 47).

    f.   Those who have faith, and are not appointed to death, shall be healed (v. 48).

    g.   The blind, the deaf, and the lame shall be healed (vv. 49–51).

    h.   Those who have not faith to be healed can be the sons of Christ (v. 52).

➤ 42:53–55   Stand in the place of thy stewardship.

    a.   Do not take thy brother's garments, but pay for what you receive (v. 54).

    b.   If more is obtained than needed for thy support, give it to the storehouse (v. 55).

➤ 42:56–61   Ask and Christ's scriptures shall be given and preserved in safety.

    a.   Do not teach them until given in full (v. 57).

    b.   Teach them to all nations, kindreds, tongues and people (v. 58).

    c.   That which is given shall be Christ's law to govern the church (v. 59).

    d.   Those who follow the scriptures shall be saved, and those who don't will be damned (v. 60).

e. Ask and you shall know the mysteries and peaceable things that bring joy and eternal life (v. 61).

➤ 42:62–69   The place of the New Jerusalem shall be revealed in due time.

a. Christ's servants shall be sent east, west, north, and south (v. 63).

b. Go now to the east and teach; those converted shall flee to the west (v. 64).

c. Observe these things and you shall know the mysteries of the kingdom (v. 65).

d. Observe the laws you have received, and you shall receive church covenants to establish you here and in the New Jerusalem (vv. 66–67).

e. Ask and you shall receive, the keys of the church have been given (vv. 68–69).

➤ 42:70–73   Priests and teachers shall have their stewardships even as members.

a. Counselors to the bishop shall be supported from consecrations (vv. 71–72).

b. The bishop shall be supported for his service to the church (v. 73).

TEXT AND COMMENTARY

D&C 42:29–32 • The First Step of the Law of Consecration

29 If thou lovest me thou shalt serve me and keep all my commandments.

30 And behold, thou wilt remember the poor, and consecrate of thy properties for their support that which thou hast to impart unto them, with a covenant and a deed which cannot be broken.

31 And inasmuch as ye impart of your substance unto the poor, ye will do it unto me; and they shall be laid before the bishop of my church and his counselors, two of the elders, or high priests, such as he shall appoint or has appointed and set apart for that purpose.

32 And it shall come to pass, that after they are laid before the bishop of my church, and after that he has received these testimonies concerning the consecration of the properties of my church, that they cannot be taken from the church, . . .

To "serve me and keep all my commandments" (v. 29) implies that the law of consecration is a higher law for those who are already keeping most of the laws of God. The Lord then reveals three basic steps of that higher law, and follows with several governing principles for administering the law. The first step is to consecrate thy properties unto the Church. This is done with a covenant and a deed. Its purpose is to remember the poor (v. 30). The covenant is a spiritual commitment, and the deed is a legal commitment that binds one to the law of the land and must be abided by. Consecrated properties "cannot be taken from the Church" (v. 32). The consecration is administered by the bishop [of Zion] and his counselors, as appointed and set apart for that purpose (v. 31).

D&C 42:32–33 • The Second Step—A Steward Over His Own Property

32 . . . agreeable to my commandments, every man shall be made accountable unto me, a steward over his own property, or that which he has received by consecration, as much as is sufficient for himself and family.

33 And again, if there shall be properties in the hands of the church, or any individuals of it, more than is necessary for their support after this first consecration, which is a residue to be consecrated unto the bishop, it shall be kept to administer to those who have not, from time to time, that every man who has need may be amply supplied and receive according to his wants.

The second basic step in the law of consecration is the appointment of every man as "a steward over his own property," or that which he has received by consecration, "as much as is sufficient for himself and family." He is the legal owner of that property on earth, but in conjunction with the Lord to whom he is accountable (v. 32). If, through the exercise of his enterprise, he is able to accumulate more of the worlds goods than is necessary for the support of himself and family from the initial consecration, the residue [surplus] properties are to be consecrated to the bishop that the needs and wants of every man may be satisfied.

In a letter to Bishop Partridge, the Prophet answered the Bishop's questions "concerning the consecration of property." He stated as fact:

. . . a man is bound by law of the church, to consecrate to the Bishop, before he can be considered a legal heir to the kingdom of Zion; and this, too, without constraint; and unless he does this, he cannot be acknowledged before the Lord on the Church Book; therefore, to condescend to particulars, I will tell you that every man must be his own judge how much he should receive, and how much he should suffer to remain in the hands of the Bishop. I speak of those who consecrate more than they need for the support of themselves and their families.

The matter of consecration must be done by the mutual consent of both parties; for to give the Bishop power to say how much every man shall have, and to be obliged to comply with the Bishop's judgment, is giving to the Bishop more power than a king has; and, upon the other hand, to let a man say how much he needs, and the Bishop be obliged to comply with his judgment, is to throw Zion into confusion, and make a slave of the Bishop. The fact is, there must be a balance or equilibrium of power, between the Bishop and the people; and thus harmony and good-will may be preserved among you.

Therefore, those persons consecrating property to the Bishop in Zion, and then receiving an inheritance back, must reasonably show to the Bishop that they need as much as they claim. But in case the two parties cannot come to a mutual agreement, the Bishop is to have nothing to do about receiving such consecrations; and the case must be laid before a council of twelve High Priests, the Bishop not being one of the council, but he is to lay the case before them. [*HC*, 1:364–65]

These instructions are concise and explicit enough to show the relationship between the Bishop and the member of the society.

D&C 42:34–37 • The Third Step—the Bishop's Storehouse

34 Therefore, the residue shall be kept in my storehouse, to administer to the poor and the needy, as shall be appointed by the high council of the church, and the bishop and his council;

35 And for the purpose of purchasing lands for the public benefit of the church, and building houses of worship, and building up of the New Jerusalem which is hereafter to be revealed—

36 That my covenant people may be gathered in one in that day when I shall come to my temple. And this I do for the salvation of my people.

37 And it shall come to pass, that he that sinneth and repenteth not shall be cast out of the church, and shall not receive again that which he has consecrated unto the poor and the needy of my church, or in other words, unto me—

The third basic step in the law of consecration is the establishment of the Bishop's storehouse. The residue or surplus properties from the individual stewardships are kept in the Lord's storehouse, which is administered by the bishop for at least four specific purposes. The Bishop is assisted by his council [counselors] and the high council (v. 34). The first primary purpose of the storehouse is "to administer to the poor and the needy" (v. 34). The second purpose is for "purchasing lands for the public benefit of the church" (v. 35). These lands might be areas for parks or recreational areas. The Church in this context is the covenant society of that regional area. The money to purchase lands, as implied, would come from the sale of surplus goods to them who need them, and can afford to pay for them (see v. 54). They may also be sold to outside people or businesses. The third purpose of the storehouse is for the building of houses of worship; ward and stake chapels, or meeting houses, and temples. The fourth purpose is for the building of the New Jerusalem. This purpose may include land, administrative buildings, and the New Jerusalem temple. The third and fourth purposes would be accomplished similarly to the second purpose. The covenant people would then be gathered, the Lord could then come to His temple, and the salvation of His people would be imminent (v. 36).

Those who enter into the law of consecration and fail to live up their covenant will be cast out if they do not repent. Since they have received a stewardship by legal deed they would retain that property, but they could not receive their original property that they had deeded to the Lord and the Church (v. 37). The Lord is the central figure in the law of consecration.

D&C 42:38–42 • The Idle Shall Not Eat the Bread of the Laborer

38 For inasmuch as ye do it unto the least of these, ye do it unto me.

39 For it shall come to pass, that which I spake by the mouths of my prophets shall be fulfilled; for I will consecrate of the riches of those who embrace my gospel among the Gentiles unto the poor of my people who are of the house of Israel.

40 And again, thou shalt not be proud in thy heart; let all thy

garments be plain, and their beauty the beauty of the work of thine own hands;

41 And let all things be done in cleanliness before me.

42 Thou shalt not be idle; for he that is idle shall not eat the bread nor wear the garments of the laborer.

The Saints in Jerusalem had been taught the same principle, although in a different context, that He now taught the Kirtland Saints: "Forasmuch as ye do it unto the least of these, ye do it unto me" (v. 38; compare Matthew 25:40). The Old Testament prophets had foretold this law that would bring about the New Jerusalem (D&C 42:39; see D&C 58:8 and comments).

Those of Kirtland who embraced the gospel were expected to consecrate their properties as part of their coming into the Church (D&C 42:39). Apparently, those who were already in the Church were not as well off as were the Gentiles living in the Ohio area. The "Gentiles" designation is speaking culturally, since Israel was scattered among them (see D&C 109:60). The first governing principle of the law is to beware of pride (D&C 42:40), which had destroyed the Nephites of old (D&C 38:39). To avoid being prideful, the Lord admonished the Saints to "let their garments be plain, and their beauty the beauty of the work of thine own hands" (D&C 42:40). They were to put forth their best efforts in learning the skills of self-sufficiency, but not in trying to outdo or overshadow others of the society. In other words, they were to take pride in their work, but not in their hearts, supposing that they were better than others of the society (see Jacob 2:13). The plainness of the garment suggests its usefulness, not its stylishness or attractiveness. They were to seek "cleanliness before [the Lord]" (D&C 42:41), knowing that they were seeking first to build His kingdom and not their own aggrandizement (see Jacob 2:18).

The second governing principle was work. Those who were idle "shall not eat the bread nor wear the garments of the laborer" (D&C 42:42). Thus, they were not to receive food or clothing from the storehouse if they could produce their own, but were too lazy and didn't work. However, if they unable to work for a good reason, such as sickness, they would receive the help they needed.

D&C 42:43–52 • The Principle Governing the Sick

43 And whosoever among you are sick, and have not faith to be healed, but believe, shall be nourished with all tenderness, with herbs and mild food, and that not by the hand of an enemy.

44 And the elders of the church, two or more, shall be called, and shall pray for and lay their hands upon them in my name; and if they die they shall die unto me, and if they live they shall live unto me.

45 Thou shalt live together in love, insomuch that thou shalt weep for the loss of them that die, and more especially for those that have not hope of a glorious resurrection.

46 And it shall come to pass that those that die in me shall not taste of death, for it shall be sweet unto them;

47 And they that die not in me, wo unto them, for their death is bitter.

48 And again, it shall come to pass that he that hath faith in me to be healed, and is not appointed unto death, shall be healed.

49 He who hath faith to see shall see.

50 He who hath faith to hear shall hear.

51 The lame who hath faith to leap shall leap.

52 And they who have not faith to do these things, but believe in me, have power to become my sons; and inasmuch as they break not my laws thou shalt bear their infirmities.

The third governing principle was regarding the sick. Those who were "sick, and have not faith to be healed, but believe" were to be nourished and cared for, but not by an enemy (v. 43). The "enemy" was probably the unbelievers who had no faith. Therefore, the believers who were not healed were to call the elders and have them be administered to by the laying on of hands. The outcome was then in the hands of the Lord (v. 44). The same principle was taught in the New Testament. The anointing with oil was included in the New Testament, and also the declaration that those who were healed would be forgiven of their sins. This is the doctrine of justification; evidence that the Lord's requirements for forgiveness had been met, and they were justified in His sight to be forgiven (see James 5:14–15; see also Moses 6:60; D&C 20:30).

In the event of death, the Lord acknowledged the feelings of love and loss, but more so for those not worthy of "a glorious resurrection" (D&C 42:45). Those whose mortal probation was over, and died unto the Lord, would not taste of death. It would be sweet unto them (v. 46). For those who did not die unto the Lord, it would be a bitter experience (v. 47). For those whose mortal probation was not over, they would be healed if they had faith. Therefore, faith is a condition of healing without being blessed by the elders, as well as for those who receive a priesthood blessing (v. 48). There are no limitations on what diseases or infirmities can be healed: even the blind; the deaf; or the lame (vv. 49–51; see also 1 Nephi 11:31; 3 Nephi 17:7; 4 Nephi 1:5). Those who lacked faith, but were believers in Christ, were still acceptable to the Lord, and would become His sons (or daughters) if they kept the commandments. The Church was to help those people in their infirmities (D&C 42:52).

D&C 42:53–55 • Pay For What Is Received From thy Brother

53 Thou shalt stand in the place of thy stewardship.

54 Thou shalt not take thy brother's garment; thou shalt pay for that which thou shalt receive of thy brother.

55 And if thou obtainest more than that which would be for thy support, thou shalt give it into my storehouse, that all things may be done according to that which I have said.

The fourth governing principle of the law of consecration was that the members of the society were to earn their own living from working their stewardship (v. 53). If items were needed for their living comfort, they could be purchased from another person's stewardship, but were not to be taken without purchase (v. 54). If items were produced beyond their needs, the surplus was to be given to the storehouse for the bishop's use (v. 55).

D&C 42:56–61 • The Scriptures Given As Appointed

56 Thou shalt ask, and my scriptures shall be given as I have appointed, and they shall be preserved in safety;

57 And it is expedient that thou shouldst hold thy peace concerning them, and not teach them until ye have received them in full.

58 And I give unto you a commandment that then ye shall teach

them unto all men; for they shall be taught unto all nations, kindreds, tongues and people.

59 Thou shalt take the things which thou hast received, which have been given unto thee in my scriptures for a law, to be my law to govern my church;

60 And he that doeth according to these things shall be saved, and he that doeth them not shall be damned if he so continue.

61 If thou shalt ask, thou shalt receive revelation upon revelation, knowledge upon knowledge, that thou mayest know the mysteries and peaceable things—that which bringeth joy, that which bringeth life eternal.

Other principles for governing one's stewardship were to be revealed through Joseph Smith's translation of the Bible (vv. 56–57). The New Testament accounts would then be more fully revealed. The principles learned therein were not to be taught until they were received in full, and then were to be taught to all nations (v. 58). Those principles were to become a law to govern the Church (v. 59), and the means of salvation or condemnation to the individual members (v. 60). The Lord later gave a commandment to publish what had been translated by Joseph, even though the work had not been completed (see D&C 104:58–59; 124:89).

D&C 42:62–69 • The New Jerusalem to be Revealed

62 Thou shalt ask, and it shall be revealed unto you in mine own due time where the New Jerusalem shall be built.

63 And behold, it shall come to pass that my servants shall be sent forth to the east and to the west, to the north and to the south.

64 And even now, let him that goeth to the east teach them that shall be converted to flee to the west, and this in consequence of that which is coming on the earth, and of secret combinations.

65 Behold, thou shalt observe all these things, and great shall be thy reward; for unto you it is given to know the mysteries of the kingdom, but unto the world it is not given to know them.

66 Ye shall observe the laws which ye have received and be faithful.

67 And ye shall hereafter receive church covenants, such as shall be sufficient to establish you, both here and in the New Jerusalem.

68 Therefore, he that lacketh wisdom, let him ask of me, and I will

give him liberally and upbraid him not.

69 Lift up your hearts and rejoice, for unto you the kingdom, or in other words, the keys of the church have been given. Even so. Amen.

The place of the New Jerusalem was revealed five months later, in July of 1830 (v. 62; see D&C 57:1–3). The servants have been sent in all directions as the Lord directed, although there are even today places yet to go and the gathering of converts continues (D&C 42:63). The principles are being observed by many individually; however, the time to observe it collectively has not come (vv. 64–65). Although there were many hindrances to Joseph's completing the work, the essentials were revealed sufficient to practice it collectively for a season. When the New Jerusalem is established and the law of consecration is practiced again, the Lord will reveal more. As the Lord said, the keys of the Church had been given (vv. 67–69). Many other revelations were received (v. 67) that we will consider below and later.

D&C 42:70–73 • A Just Remuneration For Services

70 The priests and teachers shall have their stewardships, even as the members.

71 And the elders or high priests who are appointed to assist the bishop as counselors in all things, are to have their families supported out of the property which is consecrated to the bishop, for the good of the poor, and for other purposes, as before mentioned;

72 Or they are to receive a just remuneration for all their services, either a stewardship or otherwise, as may be thought best or decided by the counselors and bishop.

73 And the bishop, also, shall receive his support, or a just remuneration for all his services in the church.

The last principle revealed in section 42 was that priesthood holders, whose stewardship was to administer the Zion Society, were to have themselves and family supported "out of the property which is consecrated to the bishop, for the good of the poor, and for other purposes, as before mentioned" (vv. 71–73). Their services, supported with a "just remuneration," suggests either a full or partial support, depending on the individual circumstances. The partial support would be given to supplement a small stewardship to work privately.

*H*istorical Setting—Sections 48; 51; 53; 55; 70:

> Upon inquiry how the brethren should act in regard to purchasing lands to settle upon, and where they [New York Saints] should finally make a permanent location, I received [section 48, March 1831]. [*HC*, 1:166]

> Not long after the foregoing was received (section 50), the Saints from the State of New York began to come on, and it seemed necessary to settle them; therefore at the solicitation of Bishop Partridge, I inquired of the Lord and received [section 51, May 20, 1831]. [*HC*, 1:173]

Shortly after the foregoing was received (section 52), at the request of Algernon Sidney Gilbert I inquired, and received [section 53]. [*HC*, 1:179].

About the middle of June, while we were preparing for our journey to Missouri, William W. Phelps and family arrived among us—"to do the will of the Lord," he said: so I inquired of the Lord and received [section 55]. [*HC*, 1:184–85]

Section 70 was partially discussed in chapter 1. The remainder of the section is discussed at the end of this chapter.

SECTIONS 48; 51; 53 & 55 • OUTLINE

➤ 48:1–6 It is necessary to remain in your places of abode, and impart the lands that ye have to the eastern brethren.

    a. Let the eastern brethren purchase lands as seemeth them good (v. 3).

    b. Save the money you can to obtain in righteousness land for a city of inheritance (v. 4).

    c. After the eastern brethren come, certain men shall have revealed to them the place of the land (v. 5).

    d. They shall purchase the land and begin laying the foundation of the city (v. 6).

    e. Then begin to gather, and every man shall be appointed land according to the law and commandments you have received (v. 6).

➤ 51:1–6   Edward Partridge will receive direction on how to organize the people according to Christ's law.

    a.   He shall appoint equal portions according to family, circumstances, wants, and needs (v. 3).

    b.   He shall give a writing to each to secure his portion (v. 4).

    c.   The portion shall be his inheritance until he transgress and is not worthy (v. 4).

    d.   The unworthy shall not have claim on what he consecrated, but on what he received (v. 5).

    e.   All things are made sure according to the law of the land (v. 6).

➤ 51:7–12   That which belongs to this people is appointed to this people.

    a.   An agent shall be appointed to take the money and provide for their wants (v. 8).

    b.   Every man must deal honestly, and receive alike (v. 9).

    c.   That which belongs to this people shall not be given to another church (v. 10).

    d.   If another church receives money, let them pay as agreed (v. 11).

    e.   All things shall be done through the bishop or the agent (v. 12).

➤ 51:13–20   All things shall be in the storehouse, and kept in the hands of the bishop.

    a.   The bishop shall receive for his own wants and his family's (v. 14).

    b.   The Lord grants to his people according to his laws (v. 15).

    c.   The land [Thompson] is consecrated for a little season (v. 16).

    d.   The hour and the day is not given, but act as if for years (v. 17).

    e.   This land shall be an example in other places, to all churches (v. 18).

    f.   The faithful will enter into the joy of the Lord and receive eternal life (v. 19).

    g.   The Lord will come in an hour you think not (v. 20).

➤ 53:1–7   Algernon Sidney Gilbert is given his calling and election in the church.

     a.   He is to forsake the world (v. 2).

     b.   He is to be ordained an elder and preach (v. 3).

     c.   He is to be an agent unto the church as appointed by the bishop (v. 4).

     d.   He is to journey with Joseph and Sidney (v. 5).

     e.   These are the first ordinances, the residue shall be given later (v. 6).

     f.   Learn that you must endure to the end to be saved (v. 7).

➤ 55:1–6   William Phelps is called and chosen to be baptized and receive the Holy Ghost.

     a.   Be ordained an elder to preach, baptize, and confer the Holy Ghost (vv. 2–3).

     b.   Be ordained to assist Oliver Cowdery in printing, select and write books for children, that they may receive instruction (v. 4).

     c.   He is to journey with Joseph and Sidney, and be planted in the land of his inheritance to do his work (v. 5).

     d.   Joseph Coe is to journey with them, and the residue shall be known later (v. 6).

TEXT AND COMMENTARY

D&C 48:1–6 • Save All the Money That You Can

1 It is necessary that ye should remain for the present time in your places of abode, as it shall be suitable to your circumstances.

2 And inasmuch as ye have lands, ye shall impart to the eastern brethren;

3 And inasmuch as ye have not lands, let them buy for the present time in those regions round about, as seemeth them good, for it must needs be necessary that they have places to live for the present time.

4 It must needs be necessary that ye save all the money that ye can, and that ye obtain all that ye can in righteousness, that in time ye may be enabled to purchase land for an inheritance, even the city.

5 The place is not yet to be revealed; but after your brethren come

from the east there are to be certain men appointed, and to them it shall be given to know the place, or to them it shall be revealed.

6 And they shall be appointed to purchase the lands, and to make a commencement to lay the foundation of the city; and then shall ye begin to be gathered with your families, every man according to his family, according to his circumstances, and as is appointed to him by the presidency and the bishop of the church, according to the laws and commandments which ye have received, and which ye shall hereafter receive. Even so. Amen.

The individual circumstances, such as family size and needs, are again recognized by the Lord among the people of Kirtland as well as those coming from the east (vv. 1–3; 6). The law of consecration was not a communal plan. The long range goal was apparently for the city of the New Jerusalem (4–6). The Lord probably waited to reveal the place of the New Jerusalem (v. 5) until more people were there to carry out the plan.

D&C 51:1–6 • The Individual Circumstances

1 Hearken unto me, saith the Lord your God, and I will speak unto my servant Edward Partridge, and give unto him directions; for it must needs be that he receive directions how to organize this people.

2 For it must needs be that they be organized according to my laws; if otherwise, they will be cut off.

3 Wherefore, let my servant Edward Partridge, and those whom he has chosen, in whom I am well pleased, appoint unto this people their portions, every man equal according to his family, according to his circumstances and his wants and needs.

4 And let my servant Edward Partridge, when he shall appoint a man his portion, give unto him a writing that shall secure unto him his portion, that he shall hold it, even this right and this inheritance in the church, until he transgresses and is not accounted worthy by the voice of the church, according to the laws and covenants of the church, to belong to the church.

5 And if he shall transgress and is not accounted worthy to belong to the church, he shall not have power to claim that portion which he has consecrated unto the bishop for the poor and needy of my church; therefore, he shall not retain the gift, but shall only have claim on that portion that is deeded unto him.

6 And thus all things shall be made sure, according to the laws of the land.

Two months after section 48 had been given in May of 1831, the newly-appointed bishop, Edward Partridge, through revelation to Joseph Smith, was to do as the Lord had instructed in section 48. He was to organize the Colesville saints, who had settled in Thompson, Ohio, "according to my laws," and "to appoint this people their portion, every man equal according to his circumstances, and his wants and needs" (D&C 51:1–3). "Equality" in the eyes of the Lord was not a fixed measurement, but a subjecting consideration of the individual's respective wants and needs. The writing given to secure each man his portion (v. 4) was not the deed, but the certainty of the covenant he had made with the Lord, mentioned in section 42 verse 30. It would become invalid upon his unworthiness in the Church. However, the laws of the land would secure the portion he had been given by deed according to the laws of the land (D&C 42:5–6).

D&C 51:7–12 • An Agent to be Appointed

7 And let that which belongs to this people be appointed unto this people.

8 And the money which is left unto this people—let there be an agent appointed unto this people, to take the money to provide food and raiment, according to the wants of this people.

9 And let every man deal honestly, and be alike among this people, and receive alike, that ye may be one, even as I have commanded you.

10 And let that which belongeth to this people not be taken and given unto that of another church.

11 Wherefore, if another church would receive money of this church, let them pay unto this church again according as they shall agree;

12 And this shall be done through the bishop or the agent, which shall be appointed by the voice of the church.

Each order or community was also to be independent (v. 7). The agent to be appointed (v. 8) was to be somewhat of a business manager to help fulfill the needs of the people. He was to assist the bishop in his duties. The people's honesty must be impeccable to bring about the spiritual oneness or unity required by the Lord, as well as the success of the order (v. 9). To not give to another church (v. 10), obviously means to another order or community of the Church, which was following the same law of the Church. The other church may lend or borrow, but it must be done through mutual agreement (v. 11). The arrangements were to be made by the bishop or the agent, but must be approved by the voice of the people (v. 12), the law of common consent (D&C 26:2).

D&C 51:13–20 • A Privilege to Organize According to My Laws

13 And again, let the bishop appoint a storehouse unto this church; and let all things both in money and in meat, which are more than is needful for the wants of this people, be kept in the hands of the bishop.

14 And let him also reserve unto himself for his own wants, and for the wants of his family, as he shall be employed in doing this business.

15 And thus I grant unto this people a privilege of organizing themselves according to my laws.

16 And I consecrate unto them this land for a little season, until I, the Lord, shall provide for them otherwise, and command them to go hence;

17 And the hour and the day is not given unto them, wherefore let them act upon this land as for years, and this shall turn unto them for their good.

18 Behold, this shall be an example unto my servant Edward Partridge, in other places, in all churches.

19 And whoso is found a faithful, a just, and a wise steward shall enter into the joy of his Lord, and shall inherit eternal life.

20 Verily, I say unto you, I am Jesus Christ, who cometh quickly, in an hour you think not. Even so. Amen.

The storehouse was to establish both surplus money and meat [food] (v. 13). The bishop's needs were to be taken out of the storehouse, since he was employed by the Church (v. 14). The establishment of this society was "a privilege," not an obligation. As will be shown further, it would enable every man to raise his standard of living. It was like the ideal taught to the Nephites: "Think of your brethren like unto yourselves, and be familiar with all and free with your substance, that they may be rich like unto you" (Jacob 2:17). The plan was not permanent (D&C 42:16)

because the Lord had plans for Missouri and the New Jerusalem as will be discussed later. However, they were to enter the order as if it were long term. By so doing, it would be for their good in the future (v. 17). For Edward Partridge, it was a pilot program for all future places and churches (v. 18). It also has eternal rewards if lived in earnest (v. 19). It is the law of the celestial kingdom (see D&C 105:3–5).

D&C 53:1–7 • The Agent—Sidney Gilbert

1 Behold, I say unto you, my servant Sidney Gilbert, that I have heard your prayers; and you have called upon me that it should be made known unto you, of the Lord your God, concerning your calling and election in the church, which I, the Lord, have raised up in these last days.

2 Behold, I, the Lord, who was crucified for the sins of the world, give unto you a commandment that you shall forsake the world.

3 Take upon you mine ordination, even that of an elder, to preach faith and repentance and remission of sins, according to my word, and the reception of the Holy Spirit by the laying on of hands;

4 And also to be an agent unto this church in the place which shall be appointed by the bishop, according to commandments which shall be given hereafter.

5 And again, verily I say unto you, you shall take your journey with my servants Joseph Smith, Jun., and Sidney Rigdon.

6 Behold, these are the first ordinances which you shall receive; and the residue shall be made known in a time to come, according to your labor in my vineyard.

7 And again, I would that ye should learn that he only is saved who endureth unto the end. Even so. Amen.

Sidney Gilbert was called to be the first agent under the law of consecration (v. 4). His duties were partially discussed above. Why he was to journey with Joseph and Sidney (v. 5) is not stated, but was probably to receive instruction and experience. As with all of us, his calling was the first of many he would be given in the Church (v. 6), and of course, we must all endure to the end (v. 7).

D&C 55:1–6 • The Work of Printing

1 Behold, thus saith the Lord unto you, my servant William, yea,

even the Lord of the whole earth, thou art called and chosen; and after thou hast been baptized by water, which if you do with an eye single to my glory, you shall have a remission of your sins and a reception of the Holy Spirit by the laying on of hands;

2 And then thou shalt be ordained by the hand of my servant Joseph Smith, Jun., to be an elder unto this church, to preach repentance and remission of sins by way of baptism in the name of Jesus Christ, the Son of the living God.

3 And on whomsoever you shall lay your hands, if they are contrite before me, you shall have power to give the Holy Spirit.

4 And again, you shall be ordained to assist my servant Oliver Cowdery to do the work of printing, and of selecting and writing books for schools in this church, that little children also may receive instruction before me as is pleasing unto me.

5 And again, verily I say unto you, for this cause you shall take your journey with my servants Joseph Smith, Jun., and Sidney Rigdon, that you may be planted in the land of your inheritance to do this work.

6 And again, let my servant Joseph Coe also take his journey with them. The residue shall be made known hereafter, even as I will. Amen.

William W. Phelps stewardship to assist Oliver Cowdery in printing, and in selection and writing of children's books for their instruction (v. 4), is a good example of the variety of stewardships needed in a complete community. The law of consecration was not just an agricultural program. As it is practiced again in the New Jerusalem, it will undoubtedly include many stewardships that were not even known in Kirtland at the time. The rest of this section is self-explanatory.

D&C 70:5–9 • What the Lord Requires of Every Man

5 Wherefore, I have appointed unto them, and this is their business in the church of God, to manage them and the concerns thereof, yea, the benefits thereof.

6 Wherefore, a commandment I give unto them, that they shall not give these things unto the church, neither unto the world;

7 Nevertheless, inasmuch as they receive more than is needful for their necessities and their wants, it shall be given into my storehouse;

8 And the benefits shall be consecrated unto the inhabitants of Zion,

and unto their generations, inasmuch as they become heirs according to the laws of the kingdom.

9 Behold, this is what the Lord requires of every man in his steward-ship, even as I, the Lord, have appointed or shall hereafter appoint unto any man.

Section 70 is a good example of the law of consecration in a non-agricultural situation. The leadership of the Church: Joseph Smith, Jr., Oliver Cowdery, John Whitmer, Sidney Rigdon, and William W. Phelps (see D&C 70:1), were to manage the publication of the revelations. These men spent their full time governing the Church. The benefits, or profits from the sale of these revelations, were to be used for their wants and needs, or living expenses (v. 5). They were not to give those benefits to the Church or to the world (v. 6). However, if they did receive more benefits than was needful for their living expenses, the surplus was to go to the Lord's storehouse (v. 7). The storehouse was used for the needs of the inhabitants of Zion as they enter into the law of consecration (v. 8). They were following the same laws as every other person who was given a stewardship (v. 9).

D&C 70:10–14 • None Are Exempt From This Law

10 And behold, none are exempt from this law who belong to the church of the living God;

11 Yea, neither the bishop, neither the agent who keepeth the Lord's storehouse, neither he who is appointed in a stewardship over temporal things.

12 He who is appointed to administer spiritual things, the same is worthy of his hire, even as those who are appointed to a stewardship to administer in temporal things;

13 Yea, even more abundantly, which abundance is multiplied unto them through the manifestations of the Spirit.

14 Nevertheless, in your temporal things you shall be equal, and this not grudgingly, otherwise the abundance of the manifestations of the Spirit shall be withheld.

No one in the society of Zion, and eventually of the whole Church, would be exempt from this the law of consecration, whether they had a temporal or a spiritual stewardship (vv. 10–12). The only differences would be the manifestations of the Spirit that some receive more abundantly than others (v. 13). Those who lived this law should not be grudgingly made equal, or the manifestations of the Spirit would be withheld (v. 14).

D&C 70:15–18 • A Blessing and Reward of Diligence and For Security

15 Now, this commandment I give unto my servants for their benefit while they remain, for a manifestation of my blessings upon their heads, and for a reward of their diligence and for their security;

16 For food and for raiment; for an inheritance; for houses and for lands, in whatsoever circumstances I, the Lord, shall place them, and whithersoever I, the Lord, shall send them.

17 For they have been faithful over many things, and have done well inasmuch as they have not sinned.

18 Behold, I, the Lord, am merciful and will bless them, and they shall enter into the joy of these things. Even so. Amen.

The law of consecration was to benefit all while in their mortal probation (vv. 15–16). Those who have been faithful (v. 17) refers to the leaders named in the first verse. They will be blessed further and will find joy in this law, as will all others who will be faithful in accepting and following its principles. Other revelations given later will shed further light on the law of consecration, and will be discussed in their various sections where recorded. The Law of consecration would make everyone equally rich in both physical and spiritual materials.

General Authority Quotes

—President J. Reuben Clark • D&C 42:30–34

The fundamental principle of this system was the private ownership of property. Each man owned his own portion, or inheritance, or stewardship, with an absolute title, which he could alienate, or hypothecate, or otherwise treat as his own. The church did not own the property, and the life under the United Order was not a communal life, as the Prophet Joseph, himself, said. The United Order or the Law of Consecration is an individualistic system, not a communal system.

We have all said that the Welfare Plan is not the United Order and was not intended to be. However, I should like to suggest to you that perhaps, after all, when the Welfare Plan gets thoroughly into operation—it is not so yet—we shall not be very far from carrying out the great fundamentals of the United Order. [*J. Reuben Clark Selected Papers,* (see also 35–43) ed. David H. Yarn Jr. (1984), 38]

—Elder Marion G. Romney • D&C 42:30–37

This procedure [D&C 42:30; 51:3] preserved in every man the right to private ownership and management of his property. At his own option he could alienate it or keep and operate it and pass it on to his heirs.

The intent was, however, for him to so operate his property as to procure a living for himself and his dependents. So long as he remained in the order, he consecrated to the Church the surplus he produced above the needs and wants of his family. This surplus went into a storehouse from which stewardships were given to others and from which the needs of the poor were supplied.

These divine principles are very simple and easily understood. A comparison of them with the underlying principles of socialism reveal similarities and basic differences.

The following are similarities: Both (1) deal with production and distribution of goods; (2) aim to promote the well-being of man by eliminating their economic inequalities; (3) envision the elimination of the selfish motives in our private capitalistic industrial system.

Now the differences:

(1) The cornerstone of the United Order is belief in God and acceptance of Him as Lord of the earth and author of the United Order.

Socialism, wholly materialistic, is founded in the wisdom of men, and not of God.

Although all socialists may not be atheists, none of them in theory or practice seek the Lord to establish His righteousness.

(2) The United Order is implemented by the voluntary free-will actions of men, evidenced by a consecration of all their property to the Church of God.

One time the Prophet Joseph Smith was asked a question by the brethren about the inventories they were taking. His answer was to the effect, "You don't need to be concerned about the inventories. Unless a man is willing to consecrate everything he has, he doesn't come into the United Order." On the other hand, Socialism is implemented by external force, the power of the state.

(3) In harmony with Church belief, as set forth in the Doctrine and Covenants, "that no government can exist in peace, except such laws are framed and held inviolate as will secure to each individual the free exercise of conscience, the right and control of property" (D&C 134:2), the United Order is operated upon the principle of private ownership and individual management.

Thus in both implementation and ownership and management of property, the United Order preserves to men their God-given agency, while socialism deprives them of it.

(4) The United Order is non-political.

Socialism is political, both in theory and practice. It is thus exposed to, and riddled by, the corruption which plagues and finally destroys all political governments which undertake to bridge man's agency.

(5) A righteous people is a prerequisite to the United Order.

Socialism argues that it as a system will eliminate the evils of the profit motive.

The United Order exalts the poor and humbles the rich. In the process both are sanctified. The poor, released from the bondage and humiliating limitations of poverty, are enabled as free men to rise to their full potential, both temporally and spiritually. The rich, by consecration and by imparting of their substance for the benefit of the poor, not by constraint, but willingly as an act of free will, evidence that charity for their fellow men characterized by Mormon as the "pure love of Christ." [CR April, 1966, 96–97]

Chapter Twenty-Two

The Great Day of the Lord

D&C 43:17–35; 44; 45

H istorical Setting: For D&C 43:17–35, see section heading of D&C 43 and chapter 16. For sections 44 and 45, the Prophet Joseph Smith recorded:

> The latter part of February I received [section 44] which caused the Church to appoint a conference in the month of early June. [*HC*, 1:157]

> At this age of the Church [i.e., early in the spring of 1831] many false reports, lies, and foolish stories, were published in the newspapers, and circulated in every direction, to prevent people from investigating the work, or embracing the faith. A great earthquake in China, which destroyed from one to two thousand inhabitants, was burlesqued in some papers, as "Mormonism in China." But to the joy of the Saints who had to struggle against every thing that prejudice and wickedness could invent, I received [section 45]. [*HC*, 1:158]

> This earthquake in China is a matter of some interest in connection with the history of the church since it was the means of bringing Simonds Ryder, a somewhat noted preacher of the Campbellite faith, into the Church. According to *Hayden's History of the Disciples on the Western Reserve* (a Campbellite book), Mr. Ryder was much perplexed over "Mormonism," and for a time was undecided whether to join the Church or not. "In the month of June," (1831), writes Mr. Haydon, "he read in a newspaper an account of the destruction of Pekin[g] in China, and he remembered that six weeks before, a young 'Mormon' girl had predicted the destruction of that city. . . ." It was doubtless this prophecy and the conversion connected with it that led to the papers mentioned in the text to refer to it as Mormonism in China. [fn *HC*, 1:158]

INTRODUCTION

In about the past four months, October 1830 through February 1831, the Lord had stated in five revelations, "I come quickly" (D&C 33:18; 34:12; 35:27; 39:24; and 41:4). In February 1831, He also said, "the great day of the Lord is nigh at hand" (D&C 43:17). Coupled with the vicious false reports, and the foolish stories that were rampant in the area, the Saints were probably anticipating His coming shortly. The Lord apparently gave section 45 to comfort His Saints, and to explain His meaning of "come quickly." It is now over 175 years since those revelations, and He has not yet come. But, certainly many of the things revealed in this revelation and section 43 have happened, or are underway. We are much closer, but still need to be reminded of what we need to do to prepare for that welcome event.

SECTIONS 43 & 45 • OUTLINE

➤ 43:17–18   Hearken, for the great day of the Lord is nigh at hand.

         a.   He shall utter his voice and the heavens and earth shall shake (v. 18).

         b.   The saints shall arise and live, and the sinners shall stay and sleep (v. 18).

➤ 43:19–22   Gird up your loins that ye be not found among the wicked.

         a.   Call on the nations to repent, and prepare for the day of the Lord (v. 20).

         b.   If ye hate me, a man, what will ye say when the thunders utter their voices saying to repent? (v. 21).

         c.   When the lightnings utter their voices to repent, the great day of the Lord is at hand? (v. 22).

➤ 43:23–27   The Lord shall utter his voice and say to the nations, hear the words of the God who made you.

         a.   How oft would I have gathered you, but ye would not? (v. 24).

         b.   How oft have I called you by the mouth of my servants, the ministering of angels, thunderings, lightnings, etc., and ye would not? (v. 25).

c. The day has come when the cup of the wrath of my indignation is full (v. 26).

    d. These words are the Lord's words (v. 27).

➤ 43:28–35 Wherefore, labor in the vineyard and call upon the inhabitants for the last time.

    a. In mine own due time, I will come in judgment (v. 29).

    b. The great millennium, of which I have spoken, shall come (v. 30).

    c. Satan shall be bound for a little season, and then shall the end of the earth come (v. 31).

    d. The righteous shall be changed in the twinkling of an eye (v. 32).

    e. The wicked shall go into unquenchable fire (v. 33).

    f. Treasure these things, and let the solemnities of eternity rest upon you (v. 34).

    g. Be sober, keep all my commandments (v. 35).

➤ 44:1–6 It is expedient for all elders to be called together from all regions.

    a. If they are faithful, I will pour out my Spirit upon their gathering (v. 2).

    b. They shall preach repentance to the people, and many shall be converted and gain power to organize themselves according to the laws of man (v. 3).

    c. Your enemies shall have no power over you that you may keep my laws (v. 4).

    d. You must visit the poor and needy and administer relief (v. 6).

➤ 45:1–5 The people of Christ's church are invited to hearken.

    a. Hearken, lest death overtake you in an hour you think not (v. 2).

    b. Christ is pleading their cause before the Father (vv. 3–5).

➤ 45:6–10 Christ is Alpha and Omega, the beginning and the end, the light and life of the world, who came unto his own and they received him not.

    a. Those who received him were given power to become the

sons of God, and the power to obtain eternal life (v. 8).

b. He sent his everlasting covenant as a light to the world, a standard to his people, the Gentiles to seek unto, and to prepare for the Second Coming (v. 9).

c. Come unto him and hearken to his wisdom (v. 10).

➤ 45:11–15   Christ is the God of Enoch and his brethren, who were separated from the earth and received by him.

a. The city was reserved until a day of righteousness, which was sought by all holy men, but not found (v. 12).

b. The Holy men obtained a promise that they would see it in the flesh (vv. 13–14).

c. I will prophecy as unto men of days of old (v. 15).

➤ 45:16–23   Christ will show Zion as plainly as he did show his disciples about the signs of his coming.

a. As the disciples looked upon the absence of their spirit from the body as a bondage, he said he would show them the restoration of scattered Israel (v. 17).

b. The people in Jerusalem shall be destroyed, and the temple thrown down and not have one stone upon another (vv. 18–20).

c. This generation of Jews shall not pass before their destruction comes (v. 21).

d. The end of the world comes, the heavens and the earth passes away (v. 22–23).

➤ 45:24–27   A remnant of Jerusalem shall be scattered among all nations.

a. They shall be gathered again, but not until the times of the Gentiles be fulfilled (v. 25).

b. In that day, there shall be wars, men's hearts shall fail them, and say; Christ delays his coming, until the end of the earth (v. 26).

c. The love of men shall wax cold (v. 27).

➤ 45:28–33   When the times of the Gentiles is come in, the fullness of the gospel shall break forth among them.

a. They will not receive it, but turn their hearts to the precepts of men (v. 29).

    b.   In that generation shall the times of the Gentiles be fulfilled (v. 30).

    c.   In that generation an overflowing scourge, a desolating sickness, shall cover the land (v. 31).

    d.   Christ's disciples shall stand in holy places, the wicked shall curse God (v. 33).

    e.   There will be earthquakes, desolations, and men will kill one another (v. 33).

➤ 45:34–41   Christ's disciples were troubled, but the promises made shall be fulfilled.

    a.   When the light breaks forth, the parable of the fig tree will show that the hour is nigh at hand (vv. 36–38).

    b.   He who fears Christ will look for signs of the coming of the Son of Man (v. 39).

    c.   They shall see signs and wonders in the heavens and the earth, blood, fire, and smoke (vv. 40–41).

➤ 45:42–47   Before the day of the Lord shall come, the sun shall be darkened, the moon turned to blood, the stars fall from heaven.

    a.   The remnant shall be gathered to Jerusalem (v. 43).

    b.   They shall look for me and see me in the clouds of heaven, clothed with power, with all the holy angels (v. 44).

    c.   An angel sounds his trump, the sleeping saints come forth to meet me (v. 45).

    d.   Those who slept in peace shall come from the four quarters of the earth, and be perfected (v. 46).

    e.   The arm of the Lord shall fall upon all nations (v. 47).

➤ 45:48–55   This mount [Olives] shall cleave in twain, the earth reel, and the heavens shake.

    a.   The ends of the earth shall hear his voice, nations shall mourn, and those in iniquity shall be cast into the fire (v. 49).

    b.   The Jews shall ask; what are these wounds in your hands and feet? (v. 51).

    c.   They shall know who I am, for I will say; These wounds are where I was wounded in the house of my friends (v. 52).

    d.   They shall weep because they persecuted their king (v. 53).

    e.   The heathen nations shall be redeemed and those who knew no law shall have part in the first resurrection (v. 54).

    f.   Satan shall be bound, and have no place in the hearts of men (v. 55).

➤ 45:56–59   When Christ comes in his glory, the parable of the ten virgins shall be fulfilled.

    a.   The wise received the truth, and took the Holy Spirit as their guide (v. 57).

    b.   They will inherit the earth, shall multiply, and their children grow up without sin unto salvation (v. 58).

    c.   The Lord's glory shall be upon them, and be their king and lawgiver (v. 59).

➤ 45:60–64   No more shall be given until the New Testament is translated.

    a.   You may translate that you may be prepared for great things to come (vv. 60–61).

    b.   Not many years hence you will hear of wars in your own lands (vv. 62–63).

    c.   Wherefore, call upon people to repent in the western countries, and build up churches unto me (v. 64).

➤ 45:65–71   With one heart and one mind, gather riches to purchase an inheritance that shall be appointed unto you.

    a.   It shall be called the New Jerusalem, a land of peace, refuge, and safety (v. 66).

    b.   The glory of the Lord and the terror of the Lord shall be there, inasmuch as the wicked will not come unto it, and it shall be called Zion (v. 67).

    c.   Every man who will not take up his sword against his neighbor must flee to Zion for safety (v. 68).

    d.   People out of every nation shall be gathered, and the only people not at war one with another (v. 69).

    e.   The wicked will say: Let us not go up to battle Zion, for the inhabitants are terrible, we cannot stand (v. 70).

    f.   The righteous from all nations shall gather, and come singing songs of everlasting joy (v. 71).

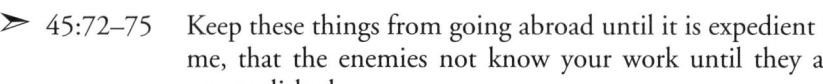

➤ 45:72–75   Keep these things from going abroad until it is expedient in me, that the enemies not know your work until they are accomplished.

     a.   When they know it they may consider these things (v. 73).

     b.   When the Lord appears he shall be terrible, and they shall stand afar off and tremble (v. 74).

     c.   All nations shall be afraid because of his terror and power (v. 75).

TEXT AND COMMENTARY

D&C 43:17–18 • The Great Day of the Lord Is Nigh

17 Hearken ye, for, behold, the great day of the Lord is nigh at hand.

18 For the day cometh that the Lord shall utter his voice out of heaven; the heavens shall shake and the earth shall tremble, and the trump of God shall sound both long and loud, and shall say to the sleeping nations: Ye saints arise and live; ye sinners stay and sleep until I shall call again.

In the New Testament, the Saints were resurrected immediately following Christ's resurrection (see Matthew 27:52–53). The same sequence will follow in the latter days. The Saints will be called out of their graves immediately after his Second Coming appearance (D&C 43:18). Apparently, the trembling of the earth will cause the graves to be opened. The saints, in this context, are those who have qualified for a celestial body in the resurrection. The sinners who will stay and sleep, who are not resurrected, are the telestial spirits. Their sleep will be a thousand years (see D&C 88:101). The terrestrial spirits will also be resurrected as the thousand year millennium begins, but some time after the celestial resurrection (see D&C 88:99).

D&C 43:19–22 • Prepare for the Great Day

19 Wherefore gird up your loins lest ye be found among the wicked.

20 Lift up your voices and spare not. Call upon the nations to repent, both old and young, both bond and free, saying: Prepare yourselves for the great day of the Lord;

21 For if I, who am a man, do lift up my voice and call upon you

to repent, and ye hate me, what will ye say when the day cometh when the thunders shall utter their voices from the ends of the earth, speaking to the ears of all that live, saying—Repent, and prepare for the great day of the Lord?

22 Yea, and again, when the lightnings shall streak forth from the east unto the west, and shall utter forth their voices unto all that live, and make the ears of all tingle that hear, saying these words—Repent ye, for the great day of the Lord is come?

The warnings of the Lord's servants to repent (v. 20) will be attended with thunders and lightnings that also warn the people to repent before He comes (vv. 21–22). Many people do and will pass these warnings off as natural phenomena, caused by mans failure to control the environment. However, Nephi, quoting Isaiah, also equated the thunder and other weather related circumstances "in the last days, or in the days of the Gentiles," as warnings of the Lord: "And when that day [of the Gentiles] shall come, they shall be visited of the Lord of Hosts, with thunder and with earthquake, and with a great noise, and with storm, and with tempest, and with the flame of devouring fire" (2 Nephi 27:1–2; Isaiah 29:6).

D&C 43:23–27 • The Voice of Servants, Angels, and Weather

23 And again, the Lord shall utter his voice out of heaven, saying: Hearken, O ye nations of the earth, and hear the words of that God who made you.

24 O, ye nations of the earth, how often would I have gathered you together as a hen gathereth her chickens under her wings, but ye would not!

25 How oft have I called upon you by the mouth of my servants, and by the ministering of angels, and by mine own voice, and by the voice of thunderings, and by the voice of lightnings, and by the voice of tempests, and by the voice of earthquakes, and great hailstorms, and by the voice of famines and pestilences of every kind, and by the great sound of a trump, and by the voice of judgment, and by the voice of mercy all the day long, and by the voice of glory and honor and the riches of eternal life, and would have saved you with an everlasting salvation, but ye would not!

26 Behold, the day has come, when the cup of the wrath of mine indignation is full.

27 Behold, verily I say unto you, that these are the words of the Lord your God.

Again the voice of the Lord will speak to the nations of the earth, reminding them of His offering to gather them as a hen gathers her chicks under her winds, but they would not gather (vv. 23–24). During His mortal ministry, He told the people of Jerusalem of His many attempts to gather them in Old Testament times, using the same symbolism (see Matthew 23:37). He used the same symbolism to the Nephites, when He spoke to them during the three days of darkness following His crucifixion, adding how oft He would have gathered them, and how oft He would yet attempt to gather them if they would repent (see 3 Nephi 10:4–6). He spoke to the Jews in person, and to the Nephites who were spared, with a voice that was heard by all. The latter-day voice will apparently be like unto the Nephites, but will include the ministering of angels. This voice may verify the visits of the angels who have appeared; Moroni, Moses, Elias, Elijah, and all from "Adam to the present time, all declaring their dispensation, their rights, their keys, their honors, their majesty and glory, and the power of their priesthood" (D&C 128:21).

The voices will include the expanded weather related warnings, and all other means that He had used (D&C 43:25). The Lord enumerated, to the Old Testament prophet Amos, the many "weather warnings" He had given to Israel (see Amos 4:6–13). The voice of judgment, and mercy, glory and honor that "would have saved" modern inhabitants (D&C 43:25) suggests that these voices will be before the wicked inhabitants are destroyed; and will leave them without excuse for their being destroyed. It will undoubtedly bring the same results as it did to the Nephites: "O that we had repented before this great and terrible day" (3 Nephi 8:24), except they may be lamenting for the preservation of their own lives as well as their brethren who had already been destroyed. It could also be terrestrial type people who will not be destroyed, but will recognize their failure to heed the warnings. This was the case with the Nephites: "And it was the more righteous part of the people who were saved, and it was they who received the prophets and stoned them not [celestial type]; and it was they who had not shed the blood of the saints [terrestrial type], who were spared" (3 Nephi 10:12). "The wrath of mine indignation is full" (D&C 43:26) tells us they were about to be destroyed.

The Lord destroys a people when they are ripe in iniquity (see 1 Nephi 17:35–37; Genesis 15:16). The Lord will have spoken (D&C 42:27).

D&C 43:28–35 • Satan Bound For a Little Season

28 Wherefore, labor ye, labor ye in my vineyard for the last time—for the last time call upon the inhabitants of the earth.

29 For in mine own due time will I come upon the earth in judgment, and my people shall be redeemed and shall reign with me on earth.

30 For the great Millennium, of which I have spoken by the mouth of my servants, shall come.

31 For Satan shall be bound, and when he is loosed again he shall only reign for a little season, and then cometh the end of the earth.

32 And he that liveth in righteousness shall be changed in the twinkling of an eye, and the earth shall pass away so as by fire.

33 And the wicked shall go away into unquenchable fire, and their end no man knoweth on earth, nor ever shall know, until they come before me in judgment.

34 Hearken ye to these words. Behold, I am Jesus Christ, the Savior of the world. Treasure these things up in your hearts, and let the solemnities of eternity rest upon your minds.

35 Be sober. Keep all my commandments. Even so. Amen.

Again the Lord verifies the allegory of Zenos concerning the house of Israel. We are in the last dispensation when the Lord will prune His vineyard by calling on the inhabitants of earth to repent (v. 28; Jacob 5). Those who accept the message will be grafted into the natural branches of Israel. Those who do not repent will be cut off because they bring forth bitter fruit (Jacob 5:62–65). The end of the world (JS—M 1:4) is the end of the telestial people's habitation of the earth. The master of the vineyard, Jesus Christ, will redeem His people and reign with them on the earth (D&C 43:29). The house of Israel will produce natural fruit for a long time (Jacob 5:76), the thousand years of the great Millennium (D&C 43:30). During this time, Satan will be bound (v. 31) by the righteousness of the people (see 1 Nephi 22:26). The earth will "receive its paradisiacal glory" (A of F 10), or become a terrestrial earth during the Millennium. Satan will be loosed when the vineyard begins to produce evil fruit, (see Jacob 5:77), but only for a little season (D&C 43:32), and then the vineyard will be burned (see Jacob 5:77). The end of the earth is the time when the earth becomes a celestial earth, and the people who lived on this earth and obtained the celestial resurrection shall inherit it (see D&C 88:17, 25–28).

Righteous mortals who are living on the earth at the end of the Millennium will be changed or transfigured instantly as the earth is cleansed of all unrighteousness (D&C 42:32). The wicked that go into unquenchable fire (v. 33) seem to be the sons of perdition who will receive no glory, and remain filthy still (see D&C 88:35). Only those "who are ordained unto this condemnation" will know of their judgment (D&C 43:33; 76:46–48). The solemnities of eternity (D&C 43:34) are the eternal laws of justice and mercy which cannot be changed or varied (see Alma 42:22–25). As these laws rest upon our minds, we will be sober, knowing that we must keep all of the commandments (D&C 43:35).

D&C 44:1–6 • The Elders Are to Assemble and Then Preach

1 Behold, thus saith the Lord unto you my servants, it is expedient in me that the elders of my church should be called together, from the east and from the west, and from the north and from the south, by letter or some other way.

2 And it shall come to pass, that inasmuch as they are faithful, and exercise faith in me, I will pour out my Spirit upon them in the day that they assemble themselves together.

3 And it shall come to pass that they shall go forth into the regions round about, and preach repentance unto the people.

4 And many shall be converted, insomuch that ye shall obtain power to organize yourselves according to the laws of man;

5 That your enemies may not have power over you; that you may be preserved in all things; that you may be enabled to keep my laws; that every bond may be broken wherewith the enemy seeketh to destroy my people.

6 Behold, I say unto you, that ye must visit the poor and the needy and administer to their relief, that they may be kept until all things may be done according to my law which ye have received. Amen.

This revelation was received a short time after section 43. It seems to be a follow-up to the commandment to call upon the nations of the world to repent and prepare for the great day of the Lord to come (see D&C 43:20). The pruning of the vineyard is to commence, in this part of the vineyard, with the Spirit giving them power to organize themselves according to the laws of man (D&C 44:2–4). This apparently means to organize in such a manner that they are preserved against the laws of man. Their enemies will organize themselves in opposition to the Saints calling upon the nations to repent, but through keeping the law of God, every effort of their enemies will be broken (v. 5). In addition, they must not neglect the poor and the needy, but administer to them according to Christ's law (v. 6). Thus a conference for that purpose was called for in June.

D&C 45:1–5 • Hearken to My Voice Lest Death Overtake You

1 Hearken, O ye people of my church, to whom the kingdom has been given; hearken ye and give ear to him who laid the foundation of the earth, who made the heavens and all the hosts thereof, and by whom all things were made which live, and move, and have a being.

2 And again I say, hearken unto my voice, lest death shall overtake you; in an hour when ye think not the summer shall be past, and the harvest ended, and your souls not saved.

3 Listen to him who is the advocate with the Father, who is pleading your cause before him—

4 Saying: Father, behold the sufferings and death of him who did no sin, in whom thou wast well pleased; behold the blood of thy Son which was shed, the blood of him whom thou gavest that thyself might be glorified;

5 Wherefore, Father, spare these my brethren that believe on my name, that they may come unto me and have everlasting life.

The opposition of the enemies, warned of in section 44, had begun. False reports and foolish stories were circulating. The first thing the people of the Church were to remember was that Christ was on their side. He had made the earth and all things on the earth (v. 1). He would give them revelation, but they must follow it or they would be overtaken before they realized it, and would have lost their salvation (v. 2). He was their advocate with the Father, and was pleading their cause before Him. He was reminding the Father that He (Jesus) had shed His blood, that the Father might be glorified in saving His children (vv. 3–4). Christ also asked for the Father's help in bringing the faithful to obtain everlasting life (v. 5).

D&C 45:6–10 • Mine Everlasting Covenant

> 6 Hearken, O ye people of my church, and ye elders listen together, and hear my voice while it is called today, and harden not your hearts;
>
> 7 For verily I say unto you that I am Alpha and Omega, the beginning and the end, the light and the life of the world—a light that shineth in darkness and the darkness comprehendeth it not.
>
> 8 I came unto mine own, and mine own received me not; but unto as many as received me gave I power to do many miracles, and to become the sons of God; and even unto them that believed on my name gave I power to obtain eternal life.
>
> 9 And even so I have sent mine everlasting covenant into the world, to be a light to the world, and to be a standard for my people, and for the Gentiles to seek to it, and to be a messenger before my face to prepare the way before me.
>
> 10 Wherefore, come ye unto it, and with him that cometh I will reason as with men in days of old, and I will show unto you my strong reasoning.

"Today" (v. 6) is until the coming of the Son of Man (see D&C 64:23). He again introduces himself as Alpha and Omega, and reminds them that though the Jews collectively rejected Him, many became the sons of God (D&C 45:7–8). The beginning of verse 9 shows His Jewish experience to be a parallel to the latter days. As John the Baptist had come among the Jews to prepare the way before Christ's first earthly ministry, in the latter days He had sent the everlasting covenant among the Gentiles for the same purposes as John had done (v. 9). The everlasting covenant is the blood shed by Jesus Christ, both spiritually in the Garden of Gethsemane and physically upon the cross, in making the Atonement (see Hebrews 13:20). The light to the world is the fullness of Christ's gospel (see D&C 45:28 below). The standard for the people is all the commandments that have been restored in these latter days (see D&C 42:29). The Gentiles are given the first opportunity to receive the gospel, and the blessings promised to the house of Israel. They were the last to receive the gospel in the meridian of time, and were to be the first to receive it in the last days (see Matthew 19:30; D&C 90:8–10). Those who come unto Him will see that He had foretold all these things to men in days of old (D&C 45:10).

D&C 45:11–15 • The City of Enoch Returns

11 Wherefore, hearken ye together and let me show unto you even my wisdom—the wisdom of him whom ye say is the God of Enoch, and his brethren,

12 Who were separated from the earth, and were received unto myself—a city reserved until a day of righteousness shall come—a day which was sought for by all holy men, and they found it not because of wickedness and abominations;

13 And confessed they were strangers and pilgrims on the earth;

14 But obtained a promise that they should find it and see it in their flesh.

15 Wherefore, hearken and I will reason with you, and I will speak unto you and prophesy, as unto men in days of old.

Robert J. Matthews has written:

An extensive revelation about Enoch and his people was received by Joseph Smith in December 1830 while he and Sidney Rigdon were translating from the fifth chapter of the King James Version of Genesis. . . .

Consider the situation of the Church in December 1830. What did anyone in the Church know about Enoch or the New Jerusalem or the city of Zion or any of these things at this time? We certainly cannot learn much from the King James Version about Enoch or his city of Zion or the laws that governed the people of Zion. None of the Bibles available today say Enoch had a city or that his people were called "Zion" or that his people were translated. The entire offering in the Bible about Enoch can be read in less than two minutes and consists of only nine verses totaling thirty-eight lines of type, found in Genesis 5:18–24, Hebrews 11:5, and Jude 1:14–15. All of that together would amount to about three-fourths of one column of print in a Bible. The Book of Mormon does not help on this subject, for it does not mention or allude to Enoch. [*Selected Writings of Robert J. Matthews* (1999), 328]

In this revelation, three months after the Enoch revelation, the Lord refers to His being "the God of Enoch, and his brethren" (D&C 45:11). The following verse (12) is a second witness with the Joseph Smith

Translation about Enoch. All the holy men after Enoch had sought for, but not attained, that Zion condition. They were promised they would see it in their flesh (vv. 13–14). This promise, it seems, would not be fulfilled until the Millennium when the city returns. The Lord's purpose in telling the elders seems obvious. He would now reason with His elders of the latter days that they also could build a Zion city before the Second Coming (v. 15).

D&C 45:16–23 • The Long Absence of Your Spirits From Your Bodies

16 And I will show it plainly as I showed it unto my disciples as I stood before them in the flesh, and spake unto them, saying: As ye have asked of me concerning the signs of my coming, in the day when I shall come in my glory in the clouds of heaven, to fulfil the promises that I have made unto your fathers,

17 For as ye have looked upon the long absence of your spirits from your bodies to be a bondage, I will show unto you how the day of redemption shall come, and also the restoration of the scattered Israel.

18 And now ye behold this temple which is in Jerusalem, which ye call the house of God, and your enemies say that this house shall never fall.

19 But, verily I say unto you, that desolation shall come upon this generation as a thief in the night, and this people shall be destroyed and scattered among all nations.

20 And this temple which ye now see shall be thrown down that there shall not be left one stone upon another.

21 And it shall come to pass, that this generation of Jews shall not pass away until every desolation which I have told you concerning them shall come to pass.

22 Ye say that ye know that the end of the world cometh; ye say also that ye know that the heavens and the earth shall pass away;

23 And in this ye say truly, for so it is; but these things which I have told you shall not pass away until all shall be fulfilled.

The above verses are a parallel to Joseph Smith—Matthew 24, now included in the Pearl of Great Price. It adds materials that was apparently neither recorded by Matthew nor added by Joseph's translation; but the Lord saw a need for it being made known. What He would show plainly is His wisdom (see D&C 45:11), and He illustrates it by the signs of His coming given to His New Testament disciples (v. 16). The fathers, to whom He had made promises, were the Old Testament prophets (v. 16). The bondage they perceived of being without their bodies for such a long time, about two thousand years, was explained as His wisdom in restoring scattered Israel (v. 17). The people of that Jewish generation would be destroyed unexpectedly, or scattered among all nations (v. 19). The temple, which was said would never fall, would be completely destroyed (vv. 18, 20). The desolations which He had foretold, i.e. the people falling by the sword, led captive into other nations, and the city trodden down by the Gentiles (Luke 21:24), would all come to pass (D&C 45:21–23). These things were not the Lord's doings, but the people having rejected Him, He would let the wicked destroy the wicked (see Mormon 4:5). He then shows His wisdom.

D&C 45:24–27 • The Jews Scattered Until the Times of the Gentiles

24 And this I have told you concerning Jerusalem; and when that day shall come, shall a remnant be scattered among all nations;

25 But they shall be gathered again; but they shall remain until the times of the Gentiles be fulfilled.

26 And in that day shall be heard of wars and rumors of wars, and the whole earth shall be in commotion, and men's hearts shall fail them, and they shall say that Christ delayeth his coming until the end of the earth.

27 And the love of men shall wax cold, and iniquity shall abound.

A remnant of Judah, the more righteous part (see 1 Nephi 17:38), would be scattered among all nations (D&C 45:24). They would remain scattered until the times of the Gentiles were fulfilled (v. 25). In His wisdom, as had been prophesied, all nations of the Gentiles would be given the opportunity to hear the gospel. In honoring their agency, this could not happen sooner because of wars, commotions, and loss of love among them (vv. 26–27). In man's wisdom, they would say, the Lord was delaying His coming (v. 26), but this was Alpha and Omega speaking, who knows the end from the beginning (D&C 45:7; Isaiah 46:9–10; Abraham 2:8). The day of the Lord is known, but is not revealed to man because of their agency (JS—M 1:40; JST, Mark 13:32).

D&C 45:28–33 • The Times of the Gentiles

> 28 And when the times of the Gentiles is come in, a light shall break forth among them that sit in darkness, and it shall be the fulness of my gospel;
>
> 29 But they receive it not; for they perceive not the light, and they turn their hearts from me because of the precepts of men.
>
> 30 And in that generation shall the times of the Gentiles be fulfilled.
>
> 31 And there shall be men standing in that generation, that shall not pass until they shall see an overflowing scourge; for a desolating sickness shall cover the land.
>
> 32 But my disciples shall stand in holy places, and shall not be moved; but among the wicked, men shall lift up their voices and curse God and die.
>
> 33 And there shall be earthquakes also in divers places, and many desolations; yet men will harden their hearts against me, and they will take up the sword, one against another, and they will kill one another.

The times of the Gentiles began with the publication of the Book of Mormon in March of 1830, which was the light that contained the fullness of the gospel (v. 25, see JS—H 1:34; 3 Nephi 16:6–7). The majority of the Gentiles would reject the light that came among them because of the precepts of men (D&C 45:29). However, this rejection would be some time after the Book of Mormon came forth. It would come:

> At that day when the Gentiles shall sin against my gospel, and shall reject the fulness of my gospel, and shall be lifted up in the pride of their hearts above all nations, and above all the people of the whole earth, and shall be filled with all manner of lyings, and of deceits, and of mischiefs, and all manner of hypocrisy, and murders, and priestcrafts, and whoredoms, and of secret abominations; and if they shall do all those things, and shall reject the fulness of my gospel, behold, saith the Father, I will bring the fulness of my gospel from among them. [3 Nephi 16:10]

This rejection will not happen all at the same time, but nation by nation or area by area. When the missionaries are permanently withdrawn from them, the fullness of the gospel will be brought from among them. In that generation, shall the times of the Gentiles be fulfilled (D&C 45:30). In that same generation, "an overflowing scourge; for a desolating sickness shall cover the land" (v. 31). The *Church News* editorial page made the following observation in 1970:

> Mankind is suffering from two modern plagues. Both have been known in the past, but they are essentially new to us today as far as their present extent is concerned.
>
> They are plagues in reality. They are taking life. They are causing severe mental and physical breakdowns and are affecting men, women, and even little children.
>
> These plagues are drug use and venereal disease. [*Church News*, editorial. December 5, 1970]

Almost forty years later, these two plagues have increased significantly. Are these the fulfillment of the Lord's warning in this revelation? We don't know, but they certainly are part of and good candidates for the desolating scourge fulfillment.

The holy places where the disciples may stand include the stakes of Zion. The Prophet Joseph said:

> . . . the devil will use his greatest efforts to trap the Saints. You must make yourselves acquainted with those men who like Daniel pray three times a day toward the house of the Lord. Look to the Presidency and receive instructions. Every man who is afraid, covetous, will be taken in a snare. The time is soon coming. when no man will have any peace but in Zion and her stakes.
>
> I saw men hunting the lives of their own sons, and brother murdering brother, women killing their own daughters, and daughters seeking the lives of their mothers. I saw armies arrayed against armies. I saw blood, desolation, fires. The Son of Man has said that the mother shall be against the daughter, and the daughter against the mother. These things are at our doors. They will follow the saints of God from city to city. Satan shall rage, and the spirit of the devil is now enraged. I know not how soon these things shall take place; but with a view of them, shall I cry peace? No; I will lift up my voice and testify of them. How long will you have good crops, and the famine be kept off, I do not know; but when the fig tree leaves, know then that summer is now nigh at hand. [*TPJS*, 161]

The earthquakes and many desolations, the sword one against another

(D&C 45:33) are prevalent throughout the world. The great day of the Lord is certainly very nigh at hand.

D&C 45:34–41 • The Promises Made Shall be Fulfilled

34 And now, when I the Lord had spoken these words unto my disciples, they were troubled.

35 And I said unto them: Be not troubled, for, when all these things shall come to pass, ye may know that the promises which have been made unto you shall be fulfilled.

36 And when the light shall begin to break forth, it shall be with them like unto a parable which I will show you—

37 Ye look and behold the fig trees, and ye see them with your eyes, and ye say when they begin to shoot forth, and their leaves are yet tender, that summer is now nigh at hand;

38 Even so it shall be in that day when they shall see all these things, then shall they know that the hour is nigh.

39 And it shall come to pass that he that feareth me shall be looking forth for the great day of the Lord to come, even for the signs of the coming of the Son of Man.

40 And they shall see signs and wonders, for they shall be shown forth in the heavens above, and in the earth beneath.

41 And they shall behold blood, and fire, and vapors of smoke.

The promises to the disciples in Jerusalem were that their people would be gathered again (v. 24), and that Jerusalem and its temple would be rebuilt. These two events would take time. Again we quote the Prophet Joseph Smith:

Judah must return, Jerusalem must be rebuilt, and the temple, and water come out from under the temple, and the Dead Sea healed. It will take some time to rebuild the walls of the city and the temple, etc.; and all this must be done before the Son of Man will make his appearance. There will be wars and rumors of wars, signs in the heavens above and on the earth beneath, the sun turned into darkness, and the moon to blood, earthquakes in divers places, the seas heaving beyond their bounds; then will appear one grand sign of the Son of Man in heaven. But what will the world do? They will say it is a planet, a comet, etc. But the Son of man will come as the sign of the coming of the Son of Man, which will be as the light of the morning coming out of the east. [*HC*, 5:336–337]

The Book of Mormon also foretold the Jews' return: "And I will remember the covenant which I have made with my people; and I have covenanted with them that I would gather them together in mine own due time, that I would give unto them again the land of their fathers for their inheritance, which is the land of Jerusalem, which is the promised land unto them forever, saith the Father." (3 Nephi 20:29; see also vv. 30–37 which imply the temple being built).

The parable of the fig tree was appropriate for the disciples in Jerusalem, but pertaining to our day and location it is the earthquakes, desolations, and the sword mentioned above; "the signs of the coming of the Son of Man" (D&C 45:39). Those looking for the day of the Lord shall see signs in the heavens and the earth (v. 40). These signs are given more specifically below. The blood, fire, and smoke (v. 41) are probably the effects of the sword, earthquakes, and desolations.

D&C 45:42–46 • The Jews Shall Look For Me and I Will Come

42 And before the day of the Lord shall come, the sun shall be darkened, and the moon be turned into blood, and the stars fall from heaven.

43 And the remnant shall be gathered unto this place;

44 And then they shall look for me, and, behold, I will come; and they shall see me in the clouds of heaven, clothed with power and great glory; with all the holy angels; and he that watches not for me shall be cut off.

45 But before the arm of the Lord shall fall, an angel shall sound his trump, and the saints that have slept shall come forth to meet me in the cloud.

46 Wherefore, if ye have slept in peace blessed are you; for as you now behold me and know that I am, even so shall ye come unto me and your souls shall live, and your redemption shall be perfected; and the saints shall come forth from the four quarters of the earth.

The signs in the heavens (vv. 41–42) will be given before the great day of the Lord. While men may speculate about how these will happen, the specifics of these signs fall into the category of Isaiah's prophecies which will be understood, as explained be Nephi: "at the times when they shall come to pass" (2 Nephi 25:7).

The remnant of the Jews being gathered to Jerusalem is well under way (D&C 45:43). However, there are more Jews throughout the world who have not gathered than those who have gathered. There will undoubtedly be many more who will yet gather. Elder Orson Hyde, who was about to embark to dedicate the land of Jerusalem for the return of the Jews, "requested to know if converted Jews are to go to Jerusalem or to come to Zion." The Prophet Joseph replied: "I therefore wish you to inform him that converted Jews are to come here" (*TPJS* 180). At the present time, the Church is not actively proselyting to the Jews in Jerusalem, and may not be until the time of His coming. Their conversion will seemingly come in large numbers at that time, as shown below.

The Jews who have gathered are divided into several groups, but fall generally within two categories: religious Jews, and secular Jews who follow the Jewish culture, but do not look for a Messiah. Again speaking generally, the latter ones are those who will be cut off (D&C 45:44). Those resurrected (v. 45) are apparently the Saints throughout the world, not those in Jerusalem. A Saint, in this context, is someone who is or has been a member of Christ's true Church (see Romans 1:7; 1 Corinthians 1:2). The Lord speaks of His coming in the clouds, and the holy angels with Him (D&C 45:44), which include those who were resurrected from the four quarters of the earth (vv. 45–46).

D&C 45:47–55 • The Arm of the Lord Shall Fall

47 Then shall the arm of the Lord fall upon the nations.

48 And then shall the Lord set his foot upon this mount, and it shall cleave in twain, and the earth shall tremble, and reel to and fro, and the heavens also shall shake.

49 And the Lord shall utter his voice, and all the ends of the earth shall hear it; and the nations of the earth shall mourn, and they that have laughed shall see their folly.

50 And calamity shall cover the mocker, and the scorner shall be consumed; and they that have watched for iniquity shall be hewn down and cast into the fire.

51 And then shall the Jews look upon me and say: What are these

wounds in thine hands and in thy feet?

52 Then shall they know that I am the Lord; for I will say unto them: These wounds are the wounds with which I was wounded in the house of my friends. I am he who was lifted up. I am Jesus that was crucified. I am the Son of God.

53 And then shall they weep because of their iniquities; then shall they lament because they persecuted their king.

54 And then shall the heathen nations be redeemed, and they that knew no law shall have part in the first resurrection; and it shall be tolerable for them.

55 And Satan shall be bound, that he shall have no place in the hearts of the children of men.

When the arm of the Lord falls, the destruction of the wicked will take place (v. 47). The Lord then speaks of Jerusalem again. The Lord will set His foot on the Mount of Olives in Jerusalem (v. 48) as foretold by the prophet Zechariah: "And his feet shall stand in that day upon the Mount of Olives, which [is] before Jerusalem on the east, and the Mount of Olives shall cleave in the midst thereof toward the east and toward the west, [and there shall be] a very great valley; and half of the mountain shall remove toward the north, and half of it toward the south" (Zechariah 14:4). The earth trembling, and reeling to and fro, is described as an earthquake by Zecharias, and he says that "the Lord my God shall come, and all the saints with thee" (Zechariah 14:5). This wording supports the Saints being those resurrected from the four quarters of the earth.

The Lord's standing on the Mount of Olives, and His voice being heard to all the ends of the earth (D&C 45:49), is given a second witness in section 133, verses 20–21, and enlarged upon there. We will discuss it more in that context in a later volume. The destruction of the wicked is then categorized by listing the types of people who will be cast into the fire (D&C 45:49–50).

Returning to the Jews in Jerusalem, the revelation again states what was foretold by Zechariah (vv. 51–52; see Zechariah 13:6; 12:10). While the wording of Zechariah is slightly different, the message is the same. The Doctrine and Covenants text acknowledges that Jesus was the Son of God, and that the Jews will acknowledge Him as their king (D&C 45:53).

The chronology to follow the destruction of the wicked is important. The heathen [non-Christian] nations, and those "that knew no law," will be redeemed during the Millennium, but will still be a part of the first resurrection (v. 54). The first resurrection includes the celestial and the terrestrial beings, and will continue during the millennium as the people qualify for one or the other category of beings (see D&C 88:96–99). Satan being bound during this time (D&C 45:55) is repeated (see 43:31). His having "no place in the hearts" of men is another way of saying he is bound by "the righteousness of [Christ's] people" (1 Nephi 22:26).

D&C 45:56–59 • The Ten Virgins Parable Explained

56 And at that day, when I shall come in my glory, shall the parable be fulfilled which I spake concerning the ten virgins.

57 For they that are wise and have received the truth, and have taken the Holy Spirit for their guide, and have not been deceived—verily I say unto you, they shall not be hewn down and cast into the fire, but shall abide the day.

58 And the earth shall be given unto them for an inheritance; and they shall multiply and wax strong, and their children shall grow up without sin unto salvation.

59 For the Lord shall be in their midst, and his glory shall be upon them, and he will be their king and their lawgiver.

The parable of the ten virgins (Matthew 25:1–13) is well enough known that it will not be included here. The important contribution of this revelation is the identifying of the wise virgins as those who have received the truth—the everlasting gospel—and the oil in the lamps as those who have taken the Holy Spirit as their guide (D&C 45:57). This distinction may be interpreted two ways. First of all, the parable refers to members of the Church, and only half of them will be prepared at the time of the Second Coming (see "General Authority Quotes" at the end of this chapter). The broader interpretation is that it refers to all believing Christians, and only about half of them will be prepared for His coming. In both interpretations, the other half will be cast into the fire (v. 57). Perhaps both interpretations are correct. Since only telestial people will be destroyed, the terrestrial and celestial will "abide the day," and live on the earth during the Millennium (v. 57). However, while the inhabitants of the earth will have their agency to choose between a celestial and terrestrial life style, it is the celestial type people to whom "the earth will be given as an inheritance" (v. 58; D&C 88:17–19). It is they whose children will "grow up without sin unto salvation" (D&C 45:58). The Lord will be among them, but they must choose whether to receive the testimony of Jesus only, or to also receive the gospel of Jesus Christ (see D&C 76:51, 74–76). They may accept Him as their King and Lawgiver, but not the fullness of the Father (see D&C 76:77). The end of the world has come, but not the end of the earth. More about this parable is said in section 64 verse 54, which will be discussed with that section.

D&C 45:60–64 • More Promised In the New Testament Translation

60 And now, behold, I say unto you, it shall not be given unto you to know any further concerning this chapter, until the New Testament be translated, and in it all these things shall be made known;

61 Wherefore I give unto you that ye may now translate it, that ye may be prepared for the things to come.

62 For verily I say unto you, that great things await you;

63 Ye hear of wars in foreign lands; but, behold, I say unto you, they are nigh, even at your doors, and not many years hence ye shall hear of wars in your own lands.

64 Wherefore I, the Lord, have said, gather ye out from the eastern lands, assemble ye yourselves together ye elders of my church; go ye forth into the western countries, call upon the inhabitants to repent, and inasmuch as they do repent, build up churches unto me.

There was only one change made in the Joseph Smith Translation of the parable of the ten virgins, and that does not shed further light on what the Lord said in this revelation. Therefore, we must wait further for more information in the Millennium. A revelation on wars was given on December 25, 1832 that added significantly to verses 63–64 above. The Church did go into the western lands, and did build up churches, as we will learn in our continuing study.

D&C 45:65–71 • A New Jerusalem For The Saints of God

65 And with one heart and with one mind, gather up your riches that

ye may purchase an inheritance which shall hereafter be appointed unto you.

66 And it shall be called the New Jerusalem, a land of peace, a city of refuge, a place of safety for the saints of the Most High God;

67 And the glory of the Lord shall be there, and the terror of the Lord also shall be there, insomuch that the wicked will not come unto it, and it shall be called Zion.

68 And it shall come to pass among the wicked, that every man that will not take his sword against his neighbor must needs flee unto Zion for safety.

69 And there shall be gathered unto it out of every nation under heaven; and it shall be the only people that shall not be at war one with another.

70 And it shall be said among the wicked: Let us not go up to battle against Zion, for the inhabitants of Zion are terrible; wherefore we cannot stand.

71 And it shall come to pass that the righteous shall be gathered out from among all nations, and shall come to Zion, singing with songs of everlasting joy.

The city of Enoch, a Zion society, is described as a people of one heart and one mind, and no poor among them (Moses 7:18). The New Jerusalem will have the same conditions among the people. The Lord is challenging His Saints to become a Zion society (D&C 45:64–66). As quoted above (*TPJS*, 161), the Prophet Joseph expounded on these conditions surrounding Zion (D&C 45:67–68). The only nation not at war (v. 69) is further explained in section 87, referred to above. We will discuss it in the next volume. Zion's being "terrible" will be because the wicked cannot penetrate their ranks, and they will be protected by the cloud of the Lord (v. 70; see D&C 84:5; Isaiah 4:5). The songs of everlasting joy, sung as they come to Zion, is the fulfillment of Isaiah 35:10; "And the ransomed of the LORD shall return, and come to Zion with songs and everlasting joy upon their heads: they shall obtain joy and gladness, and sorrow and sighing shall flee away." The Prophet Joseph Smith equated these songs with their being "delivered from the overflowing scourge that shall pass through the land" (*TPJS*, 17; D&C 45:31).

D&C 45:72–75 • Keep These Things From Going Abroad

72 And now I say unto you, keep these things from going abroad unto the world until it is expedient in me, that ye may accomplish this work in the eyes of the people, and in the eyes of your enemies, that they may not know your works until ye have accomplished the thing which I have commanded you;

73 That when they shall know it, that they may consider these things.

74 For when the Lord shall appear he shall be terrible unto them, that fear may seize upon them, and they shall stand afar off and tremble.

75 And all nations shall be afraid because of the terror of the Lord, and the power of his might. Even so. Amen.

Apparently, the time came for these things to go forth to the world (v. 72) was when the Book of Commandments was published. The revelation constituted 48 in that book. The destruction of the printing press at that time illustrates the danger from the enemies to the work (v. 72; *HC*, 1:390). Now, over 175 years later, many have had opportunity to learn of these things. When the Lord appears, the enemies of the Church will tremble and all nations will fear Him (vv. 73–75). The great day of the Lord will have come.

General Authority Quotes

—*The Prophet Joseph Smith* • D&C 45:29

[The Gentiles] have become high-minded, and have not feared; therefore few of them will be gathered with the chosen family. Have not the pride, high-mindness, and unbelief of the Gentiles, provoked the Holy One of Israel to withdraw His Holy Spirit from them, and sent forth His judgments to scourge them for their wickedness? This is certainly the case. [*TPJS*, 15]

—*The Prophet Joseph Smith* • D&C 45:42

I will prophesy that the signs of the coming of the Son of Man are already commenced. One pestilence will desolate after another. We shall soon have war and bloodshed. The moon shall be turned to blood. I testify of these things and that the coming of the Son of Man is nigh, even at our doors. If our souls and our bodies are not

looking forth for the coming of the Son of Man; and after we are dead, if we are not looking forth, we shall be among those who are calling for the rocks to fall upon them. [*TPJS*, 160]

—*Elder Harold B Lee* • D&C 45:56–59

The bridegroom of the parable was the master, the Savior of mankind. The marriage feast symbolized the second coming of the Savior to receive the church unto himself. The virgins were those who were professed believers in Christ, because they were expectantly waiting for the coming of the bridegroom to the marriage feast, or they were connected with the church and the events which were to transpire with reference to it.

That this parable did refer particularly to the believers in Christ with a warning to them is further indicated by what the Lord has in modern revelation in which He said: "These things are the things that ye must look for, . . . even in the day of the coming of the Son of Man. And until that hour there will be foolish virgins among the wise, and at that hour cometh an entire separation of the righteous and the wicked" (D&C 64:53–54)—undoubtedly meaning a separation of the wicked from the righteous among the professing believers in the Lord Jesus Christ.

The Lord defines the wise virgins of His parable in still another parable in which he said: [quotes D&C 45:57]

Here is clearly indicated a truth we must all recognize, that among the people of God, the believers in Savior of the world, are those wise and keep the commandments, and yet there are those who are foolish, who are disobedient, and who neglect their duties. [*The Teachings of Harold B. Lee* (1996), 146–147]

—*Elder Spencer W. Kimball* • D&C 45:56–59

I believe the ten virgins represent the people of the Church of Jesus Christ and not the rank and file of the world. All the virgins, wise and foolish, had accepted the invitation to the wedding super; they had knowledge of the program and had been warned of the important day to come. They were not the Gentiles, or the heathens or the pagans, nor were they necessarily corrupt and reprobate, but they were knowing people who were foolishly unprepared for the vital happenings that were to affect their eternal lives.

They had the saving, exalting gospel, but it had not been the center of their lives. They knew the way but gave only a small measure of loyalty and devotion. . . . [*Faith Precedes the Miracle* (1972), 253–56]

Chapter Twenty-Three

Seek Ye Earnestly the Best Gifts

D&C 46; 47

H istorical Setting:

> The next day (March 8, 1831) I received [D&C 46], relative to the gifts of the Holy Ghost: [*HC*, 1:163]

> With references to the matters mentioned in verses 1–7, John Whitmer writes: "In the beginning of the Church, while yet in her infancy, the disciples used to exclude unbelievers, which caused some to marvel and converse of this matter because of the things written in the Book of Mormon. Therefore the Lord deigned to speak on this subject, that His people might come to understanding, . . . [*HC*, 1:163–64]

INTRODUCTION

There are three scriptural sources that discuss the gifts of the Spirit: 1 Corinthians 12 and 14; Moroni 10:8–26; and D&C 46. The Prophet Joseph Smith gave three enlightening treatises on this subject that clear up many misunderstandings and questions that are often asked about these gifts. The first was an editorial in the *Times and Seasons* entitled "Try the Spirits," April 1, 1842 (*HC*, 4:571–581). The second treatise was his remarks to the Relief Society, April 28, 1842 (*HC*, 4:602–607). The third treatise was another editorial in the *Times and Seasons* entitled "The Gift of the Holy Ghost," June 15, 1842 (*HC*, 5:26–32). There were also other periodic statements made by the Prophet on the gifts of the Spirit. We will coordinate these sources with the revelation discussed here.

SECTION 46 • OUTLINE

➤ 46:1–7   These things [in the Book of Mormon] were spoken for your profit and learning.

       a.   Elders of my church have and shall always conduct meetings as directed and guided by the Holy Spirit (v. 2).

       b.   You are commanded to never cast any one out from your public meetings which are held before the world (v. 3).

       c.   Never cast out a member of the church from your sacrament meetings, but if they have transgressed, let him not partake of the sacrament (v. 4).

       d.   Do not cast out any who are not members from your sacrament meetings who are earnestly seeking the kingdom (v. 5).

       e.   Do not cast out any who are not members from your confirmation meetings who are earnestly seeking the kingdom (v. 6).

       f.   Ask God, and that which the Spirit testifies should you do in all holiness before me, walking uprightly before me (v. 7).

       g.   Consider the end of your salvation, doing all things with prayer and thanksgiving that ye not be deceived (v. 7).

➤ 46:8–12   Seek ye earnestly the best gifts, remembering for what they are given.

       a.   They are given for them who love me and keep my commandments, and him who seeketh so to do, and do not seek a sign (v. 9).

       b.   Always remember and retain in your minds what the gifts are that are given to the church (v. 10).

       c.   All have not every gift, there are many, but every man is given a gift by the Spirit of God (v. 11).

       d.   Some is given one gift, some another, that all may be edified (v. 12).

➤ 46:13–26   Some of the gifts are enumerated (but will not be listed here), and all come from God to benefit the children of God.

> 46:27–33   The bishop, and such as are appointed of God, is given to discern all the gifts.

    a.   He that asks in the Spirit shall receive in the Spirit (v. 28).

    b.   Some may be given all the gifts that there may be a head (v. 29).

    c.   He that asks in the Spirit does according to the will of God (v. 30).

    d.   All things must be done in the name of Christ (v. 31).

    e.   You must give thanks unto God for whatsoever you are blessed (v. 32),

    f.   You must practice virtue and holiness before me continually (v. 33).

TEXT AND COMMENTARY

D&C 46:1–7 • Never Cast Out Anyone From Your Public Meetings

1 Hearken, O ye people of my church; for verily I say unto you that these things were spoken unto you for your profit and learning.

2 But notwithstanding those things which are written, it always has been given to the elders of my church from the beginning, and ever shall be, to conduct all meetings as they are directed and guided by the Holy Spirit.

3 Nevertheless ye are commanded never to cast any one out from your public meetings, which are held before the world.

4 Ye are also commanded not to cast any one who belongeth to the church out of your sacrament meetings; nevertheless, if any have trespassed, let him not partake until he makes reconciliation.

5 And again I say unto you, ye shall not cast any out of your sacrament meetings who are earnestly seeking the kingdom—I speak this concerning those who are not of the church.

6 And again I say unto you, concerning your confirmation meetings, that if there be any that are not of the church, that are earnestly seeking after the kingdom, ye shall not cast them out.

7 But ye are commanded in all things to ask of God, who giveth liberally; and that which the Spirit testifies unto you even so I would that ye should do in all holiness of heart, walking uprightly before me,

considering the end of your salvation, doing all things with prayer and thanksgiving, that ye may not be seduced by evil spirits, or doctrines of devils, or the commandments of men; for some are of men, and others of devils.

Before analyzing the gifts of the Spirit, the Lord answers the question on excluding some people from their meetings. The things written in the Book of Mormon, to which the Lord refers in verse 1, are: "And their meetings were conducted by the church after the manner of the workings of the Spirit, and by the power of the Holy Ghost; for as the power of the Holy Ghost led them whether to preach, or to exhort, or to pray, or to supplicate, or to sing, even so it was done" (Moroni 6:9). Earlier revelations to the Church had taught the same thing, although not as complete (see D&C 20:45; 43:8, 16). The Apostle Paul taught a similar concept: "Let the word of Christ dwell in you richly in all wisdom; teaching and admonishing one another in psalms and hymns and spiritual songs, singing with grace in your hearts to the Lord" (Colossians 3:16). Some Christian churches use this passage from Paul's writings to justify a spontaneous meeting with no organized procedure. However, as we study the gifts of the Spirit that follow in this revelation, we see that a head is appointed to direct the kingdom (46:29). The kingdom of God is a kingdom of order. Public meetings held before the world are open to any who desire to attend (D&C 46:3). Nevertheless, there are private meetings of the leadership of the Church at ward, stake, and general levels of the organization, and the temple is attended by only those who obtain recommends to enter by living the standards required.

The sacrament meetings of the Church are also open to all, but the partaking of the sacrament is limited to those members who are not guilty of serious transgressions (v. 4). One's worthiness to partaking of the sacrament may be determined by the bishop, or other leaders of the Church, but in general it is a self-evaluation of worthiness. Those who are earnestly seeking the kingdom are certainly welcome (v. 5), but any who may come to disrupt or argue may be ask to leave. The same conditions are given for confirmation meetings, the conferring of the gift of the Holy Ghost (v. 6).

The Spirit is the source of guidance for everything we do, and all we have to do to receive it is to ask God for it, and live the principles of the

gospel. With the goals of eternal salvation in our minds, and thanksgiving in our hearts, the devil and the precepts of man will not have power over us (v. 7). While this seems a simple formula to follow, it is a constant challenge. The following chapter will enlarge upon these influences and this challenge.

D&C 46:8–12 • Seek Earnestly the Best Gifts

8 Wherefore, beware lest ye are deceived; and that ye may not be deceived seek ye earnestly the best gifts, always remembering for what they are given;

9 For verily I say unto you, they are given for the benefit of those who love me and keep all my commandments, and him that seeketh so to do; that all may be benefited that seek or that ask of me, that ask and not for a sign that they may consume it upon their lusts.

10 And again, verily I say unto you, I would that ye should always remember, and always retain in your minds what those gifts are, that are given unto the church.

11 For all have not every gift given unto them; for there are many gifts, and to every man is given a gift by the Spirit of God.

12 To some is given one, and to some is given another, that all may be profited thereby.

The way to prevent being deceived by the devils, or led astray by the commandments of men, is to "seek earnestly the best gifts" of the Spirit (v. 8). After writing about the various gifts of the Spirit, Paul taught the doctrine: ". . . I have shown unto you a more excellent way, therefore covet earnestly the best gifts" (JST, 1 Corinthians 12:31). To covet spiritual gifts, in this context, means to enviously endeavor to obtain them. To know that Jesus is the Christ is the best gift, but the best "gifts" (plural) are the ones that you need at the present time. We must remember that they are given to benefit those who love Christ and keep all His commandments. The Lord recognizes our imperfections and shows His mercy by adding, "and him that seeketh so to do" (D&C 46:9). Furthermore, we should seek those gifts that will benefit all with whom we are among, and not for just our own self-satisfaction or as a lustful sign. To "consume it upon their lusts" (v. 9) suggests they squander it wastefully upon themselves and not to benefit others.

The gifts are given to the Church (v. 10), or are given for the benefit of the Church. Every man who is in the Church is given a gift by the Spirit (v. 11), or is entitled to receive one. The "church," as used here, seems to refer to the local ward or branch; but would be applicable to the whole Church as it uses the gifts. Moroni taught: "And again, I exhort you, my brethren, that ye deny not the gifts of God, for they are many; and they come from the same God. And there are different ways that these gifts are administered; but it is the same God who worketh all in all; and they are given by the manifestations of the Spirit of God unto men, to profit them" (Moroni 10:8). Paul said: "But the manifestation of the Spirit is given to every man to profit withal" (1 Corinthians 12:7). If all the individual gifts in each ward or branch were used effectually, the whole unit would "be profited thereby" (D&C 46:12), and would eventually become perfected. Thus, one of the missions of the Church, to perfect the Saints, would be accomplished (see Ephesians 4:12).

The various gifts listed in this revelation will be treated individually, and compared to other sources mentioned in the introduction above.

D&C 46:13–14 • To Know That Jesus Christ Is the Son of God

13 To some it is given by the Holy Ghost to know that Jesus Christ is the Son of God, and that he was crucified for the sins of the world.

14 To others it is given to believe on their words, that they also might have eternal life if they continue faithful.

Paul told the Corinthians "that no man can say that Jesus is the Lord, but by the Holy Ghost" (1 Corinthians 12:3). The Prophet Joseph said that this passage "should be translated 'no man can *know* that Jesus is the Lord, but by the Holy Ghost'" (*TPJS*, 223; italics added). Those who "believe on [others'] words" (D&C 46:13) must gain their own testimony later. President Heber C. Kimball said: "The time will come when no man nor woman will be able to stand on borrowed light. Each of you will have to be guided by the light within himself." (*LHCK*, 450) President Harold B. Lee quoted this passage and then said: "this is the time of which President Kimball spoke, . . . Each, for himself, must have an unshaken testimony of the divinity of this work if he is to stand in this day!" Several years later, he said:

"Some of you may not have a testimony, and so I have said to other groups like you, if you don't have a testimony today, why don't you cling to mine for a little while? Hold on to our testimonies, the testimonies of your bishops, your stake presidents, until you can develop it. If you can say nothing more today than I believe because my president, or my bishop, believes, I trust him, do this until you can get a testimony for yourselves; but I warn you that won't stay with you until you continue to cultivate it and live the teachings. [*THBL*, 144]

In every organized unit of the Church there are people who have a testimony of Jesus Christ. As they bear their testimony to others, and "when a man speaketh by the power of the Holy Ghost the power of the Holy Ghost carrieth it unto the hearts of the children of men" (2 Nephi 33:1). The primary purpose of our fast and testimony meetings each month is to strengthen the members who need to be uplifted. We can believe on their words until we obtain our own testimony.

D&C 46:15–16 • Differences of Administrations and Operations

15 And again, to some it is given by the Holy Ghost to know the differences of administration, as it will be pleasing unto the same Lord, according as the Lord will, suiting his mercies according to the conditions of the children of men.

16 And again, it is given by the Holy Ghost to some to know the diversities of operations, whether they be of God, that the manifestations of the Spirit may be given to every man to profit withal.

The Apostle Paul briefly spoke of these gifts:

4 Now there are diversities of gifts, but the same Spirit.

5 And there are differences of administrations, but the same Lord.

6 And there are diversities of operations, but it is the same God which worketh all in all. [1 Corinthians 12:4–6]

Administration is management or doing one's duties. The Prophet Joseph explained:

. . . That which is wrong under one circumstance, may be, and often is right in another.

God said, 'Thou shalt not kill;' at another time He said, 'Thou shalt utterly destroy.' This is the principle upon which the government of heaven is conducted—by revelation adapted to the circumstances in which the children of the kingdom are placed. Whatever God requires is right, no matter what it is, although we may not see the reasons thereof till long after the events transpire. [*TPJS*, 256][38]

The diversities of operations probably depend upon the talents which the various servants of the Lord are given (D&C 46:6). "And unto one he gave five talents, to another two, and to another one; to every man according to his several ability; and straightway took his journey" (Matthew 25:15). As the rest of the parable of the talents shows, we must develop other talents or lose the ones we are given (Matthew 25:16–30). "For unto every one who hath obtained other talents, shall be given, and he shall have an abundance. But from him that hath not obtained other talents, shall be taken away even that which he hath received" (JS—Matthew 25:29–30).

D&C 46:17–18 • The Word of Wisdom and the Word of Knowledge

17 And again, verily I say unto you, to some is given, by the Spirit of God, the word of wisdom.

18 To another is given the word of knowledge, that all may be taught to be wise and to have knowledge.

Wisdom is the application of knowledge, and these two gifts are included together in all three of the scriptural accounts. Moroni's account adds teaching to the gift of wisdom:

9 For behold, to one is given by the Spirit of God, *that he may teach* the word of wisdom;

10 And to another, that he may teach the word of knowledge by the same Spirit; [Moroni 10:10; italics added]

Paul's account adds nothing to the other two accounts and so is not given here.

---

[38] An example of what Joseph said is the commandment to Nephi to kill Laban. For a further explanation of this incident, see Monte S. Nyman, *I Nephi Wrote This Record, Book of Mormon Commentary* 1:65–68. 2003.

Knowledge is learning or being educated. Jacob, brother of Nephi, cautioned:

O that cunning plan of the evil one! O the vainness, and the frailties, and the foolishness of men! When they are learned they think they are wise, and they hearken not unto the counsel of God, for they set it aside, supposing they know of themselves, wherefore, their wisdom is foolishness and it profiteth them not. And they shall perish.

But to be learned is good if they hearken unto the counsels of God. [2 Nephi 9:28–29]

The two gifts' compatibility is further illustrated by the Lord's admonition "that all may be taught to be wise and to have knowledge," (46:18). The gift of knowledge is to know what and when to teach, but we cannot know that if we do not seek the gift of knowledge.

D&C 46:19–20 • Faith to be Healed and Faith to Heal

19 And again, to some it is given to have faith to be healed;

20 And to others it is given to have faith to heal.

These two gifts also go together. Moroni and Paul both list faith as a gift preceding these two gifts, but we will not comment on faith as a gift here because the revelation does not include it. Moroni and Paul both combine the two as "the gifts of healing." Since the manner of dealing with the sick was mentioned with the law of consecration, in chapter 22, we will say no more here except that some are given this power as a special gift.

D&C 46:21 • The Working of Miracles

21 And again, to some is given the working of miracles; [D&C 46:21]

Moroni worded the gift as: "he may work *mighty* miracles" (Moroni 10:12; italics added). Paul's wording is the same as the Doctrine and Covenants (see 1 Corinthians 12:10).

Mormon had previously spoken about miracles, and Moroni had included his father's words in his record. After bearing testimony of the miracles among the Nephites, Mormon says:

. . . it is by faith that miracles are wrought; and it is by faith that angels appear and minister unto men; wherefore, if these things have ceased wo be unto the children of men, for it is because of unbelief, and all is vain.

> For no man can be saved, according to the words of Christ, save they shall have faith in his name; wherefore, if these things have ceased, then has faith ceased also; and awful is the state of man, for they are as though there had been no redemption made. [Moroni 7:37–38]

There are miracles occurring among us all the time. Without the gift of the Spirit, these miracles will cease.

D&C 46:22 • The Gift to Prophesy

> 22 And to others it is given to prophesy;

Moroni says: "that he may prophesy concerning all things" (Moroni 10:13). Paul uses it as a noun instead of a verb: ". . . to another prophecy" (1 Corinthians 12:10).

The Prophet Joseph said:

> . . . there are only two gifts that could be made visible—the gift of tongues and the gift of prophecy. . . .
>
> The greatest, the best, and the most useful gifts would be nothing known about by an observer. It is true that a man might prophesy, which is a great gift, and one that Paul told the people—the Church—to seek after and to covet, rather than to speak in tongues; but what does the world know about prophesying? Paul says it serveth only those that believe. [*TPJS*, 246]

D&C 46:23 • The Discerning of Spirits

> 23 And to others the discerning of spirits.

Moroni uses different wording of the same gift: "And again, to another, the beholding of angels and ministering spirits (Moroni 10:14). Paul words it the same (see 1 Corinthians 12:10).

Mormon bore testimony that:

> 29 . . . neither have angels ceased to minister unto the children of men.
>
> 30 For behold, they are subject unto him, to minister according to

the word of his command, showing themselves unto them of strong faith and a firm mind in every form of godliness.

31 And the office of their ministry is to call men unto repentance, and to fulfil and to do the work of the covenants of the Father, which he hath made unto the children of men, to prepare the way among the children of men, by declaring the word of Christ unto the chosen vessels of the Lord, that they may bear testimony of him. [Moroni 7:29–31]

There had been many false spirits among the Saints prior to this revelation being given. The Prophet Joseph said:

It is evident from the [New Testament] Apostles' writings, that many false spirits existed in their day, and had "gone forth into the world," and that it needed intelligence which God alone could impart to detect false spirits, and to prove what spirits were of God. The world in general have been grossly ignorant in regard to this one thing, and why should they be otherwise—for "the things of God knoweth no man, but the Spirit of God"

The Egyptians were not able to discover the difference between the miracles of Moses and those of the magicians until they came to be tested together; and if Moses had not appeared in their midst, they would unquestionably have thought that the miracles of the Egyptians were performed through the mighty power of God, for they were great miracles that were performed by them—a supernatural agency was developed, and great power manifested. [*TPJS*, 202]

One great evil is, that men are ignorant of the nature of spirits; their power, laws government, intelligence, etc., and imagine that whenever there is anything like power, revelation, or vision manifested, that it must be of God. . . .

. . . who can drag into daylight and develop the hidden mysteries of the false spirits that so frequently are made manifest among the Latter-day Saints? We answer that no man can do this without the priesthood, and having the knowledge of the laws by which spirits are governed; for no man knows the things of God but by the spirit of God, . . . [*TPJS*, 203; 204–205]

False spirits are still manifest among the Saints today. The power to recognize and control false spirits is given to some as a gift of the Spirit.

D&C 46:24–25 • Speak With Tongues and Interpretation of Tongues

24 And again, it is given to some to speak with tongues;

25 And to another is given the interpretation of tongues.

Moroni's wording is:

15 And again, to another, all kinds of tongues;

16 And again, to another, the interpretation of languages and of divers kinds of tongues. [Moroni 10:15–16]

Paul says: "to another *divers* kinds of tongues; to another the interpretation of tongues" (1 Corinthians 12:10)

The other visible gift will now be discussed. The Prophet Joseph continued:

. . . these are things that are most talked about, and yet if a person spoke in an unknown tongue, according to Paul's testimony, he would be a barbarian to those present. . . . The gift of tongues is the smallest gift perhaps of the whole, and yet it is the most sought after. [*TPJS*, 246]

Tongues were given for the purpose of preaching among those whose language is not understood; as on the day of Pentecost, etc., and it is not necessary for tongues to be taught to the Church particularly, for any man that has the Holy Ghost, can speak of the things of God in his own tongue as well as speak in another, for faith comes not by signs, but by hearing the word of God. [*TPJS*, 148–49]

. . . the gift of tongues was necessary in the Church; but that if Satan could not speak in tongues, he could not tempt a Dutchman, or any other nation, but the English, for he can tempt an Englishman, for he has tempted me, and I am an Englishman; but the gift of tongues by the power of the Holy Ghost in the Church, is for the benefit of the servants of God to preach to unbelievers, as on the day of Pentecost. When devout men from every nation shall assemble to hear the words of God, let the Elders speak to them in their own mother tongue, whether it be German, French, Spanish, or Irish, or any other, and let those interpret who understand the language spoken, in their own mother tongue, and this is what the Apostle meant in 1 Corinthians 14:27. [*TPJS*, 195]

Be not curious about tongues, do not speak in tongues except there be an interpreter present; the ultimate design of tongues is to speak to foreigners, and if persons are very anxious to display their intelligence, let them speak to such in their own tongues. The gifts of God are all useful in their place, but when they are applied to that which God does not intend, they prove an injury, a snare and a curse instead of a blessing. [*TPJS*, 247–48]

If you have a matter to reveal, let it be in your own tongue; do not indulge too much in the exercise of the gift of tongues, or the devil will take advantage of the innocent and unwary. You may speak in tongues for your own comfort, but I lay this down for a rule, that if anything is taught by the gift of tongues, it is not to be received for doctrine. [*TPJS*, 229]

D&C 46:26 • All Gifts Come From God

26 And all these gifts come from God, for the benefit of the children of God.

Moroni recognizes Christ as the God who gives of the gifts:

17 And all these gifts come by the Spirit of Christ; and they come unto every man severally, according as he will.

18 And I would exhort you, my beloved brethren, that ye remember that every good gift cometh of Christ. [Moroni 10:17–18]

Paul's wording is still different:

11 But all these worketh that one and the selfsame Spirit, dividing to every man severally as he will. [1 Corinthians 12:11]

Some people have been in the habit of calling every supernatural manifestation the effects of the spirit of God, whilst there are others that think there are no manifestations connected with it at all; and that it is nothing but a mere impulse of the mind, or an inward feeling, impression, or secret testimony of evidence, which men possess, and that there is no such a thing as an outward manifestation. . . .

. . . We believe in it [this gift of the Holy Ghost] in all its fullness, and power, and greatness and power, and glory; but whilst we do this, we believe in it rationally, consistently, and scripturally, and not according to the wild vagaries, foolish notions and traditions of men. [*TPJS*, 243]

D&C 46:27–33 • The Bishop and Other Presiding Officers

27 And unto the bishop of the church, and unto such as God shall appoint and ordain to watch over the church and to be elders unto the church, are to have it given unto them to discern all those gifts lest there shall be any among you professing and yet be not of God.

28 And it shall come to pass that he that asketh in Spirit shall receive in Spirit;

29 That unto some it may be given to have all those gifts, that there may be a head, in order that every member may be profited thereby.

30 He that asketh in the Spirit asketh according to the will of God; wherefore it is done even as he asketh.

31 And again, I say unto you, all things must be done in the name of Christ, whatsoever you do in the Spirit;

32 And ye must give thanks unto God in the Spirit for whatsoever blessing ye are blessed with.

33 And ye must practice virtue and holiness before me continually. Even so. Amen.

The bishop, and other people who preside over other members, is given the gift of discernment for those over whom he presides (v. 27). This special gift comes with his calling and ordination. Members of his ward should confer with him if there is any doubt about a manifestation being from God. That spirit of discernment is also given for him to know the spiritual status of his ward members. The ward members may also know for themselves if they will ask of God (v. 28), but they should consult with him if their understanding differs with the accepted policy or practice of the Church.

The President of the Church, the head of the Church, has all of the gifts (v. 29; D&C 107:92). Others who may be considered heads, and have all the gifts needed for that region would include Area Presidents, Mission Presidents (over their missionaries), or others who function as presiding authorities.

Those who ask for the gift, or guidance of the Spirit, are asking to know the will of the Lord for them (D&C 46:30). Nephi, son of Helaman, apparently had this gift. He was promised "even that all things shall be done unto thee, according to thy word, for thou shalt not ask that which is contrary to my will" (Helaman 10:5). What a tremendous promise and gift to receive. Again, the Lord reminds us that all things are to be done in His name (D&C 46:31), and in thanksgiving for the blessings received (v. 32). Of course our living the gospel is required for our receiving any of the gifts or blessings of the Lord (v. 33). As told us in the Book of Mormon; "there was not any man who could do a miracle in the name of Jesus save he were cleansed every whit from his iniquity: (3 Nephi 8:1). The Lord is willing to give us all things that are for our good if we will seek His will.

*H*istorical Setting—Section 47:

> The same day (March 8, 1831) . . . I also received the [D&C 47] setting apart John Whitmer as a historian inasmuch as he is faithful.

> . . . John Whitmer, according to his own representations, said he would rather not keep the Church history, but observed—"The will of the Lord be done, and if he desires it, I wish that he would manifest it through Joseph the seer." [*HC*, 1:166]

D&C 47:1–4 • John Whitmer—Church Historian

> 1 Behold, it is expedient in me that my servant John should write and keep a regular history, and assist you, my servant Joseph, in transcribing all things which shall be given you, until he is called to further duties.

> 2 Again, verily I say unto you that he can also lift up his voice in meetings, whenever it shall be expedient.

> 3 And again, I say unto you that it shall be appointed unto him to keep the church record and history continually; for Oliver Cowdery I have appointed to another office.

> 4 Wherefore, it shall be given him, inasmuch as he is faithful, by the Comforter, to write these things. Even so. Amen.

John Whitmer's call to be Church Historian was the will of the Lord, as manifest to His mortal leaders (v. 1). It did not exclude him from being a participant in the meetings he attended (v. 2). Our callings are from the same source and for the same duration, not for life, but until we are released (v. 3). If we are faithful in our callings, the Comforter will guide us just as was promised to John Whitmer (v. 4). The revelation calling him to this office is included here because of the historical sequence. His calling was mentioned earlier, but the revelation was not included.

General Authority Quotes

—*Elder Bruce R. McConkie* • D&C 46:11–12

Spiritual gifts are endless in number and infinite in variety. Those listed in the revealed word are simply illustrations of the boundless outpouring of divine grace that a gracious God gives those who love and serve him. [*A New Witness for the Articles of Faith* (1985), 371]

—*Elder Marion G. Romney* • D&C 46:13

Everyone who has a testimony of Jesus has received it by revelation from the Holy Ghost. The Holy Ghost is a revelator, and everyone who receives him receives revelation.

Wherever and whenever revelation is operative, manifestations of other gifts of the Holy Ghost are prevalent. [CR, April 1956, 67–69]

—*President Harold B. Lee* • D&C 46:21

Over the last thirty-two years that I have been a General Authority, I have gathered stories of miraculous things that have happened. The greatest miracles that I have seen are not necessarily miracles of healing sick bodies, but the miracles of healing sick souls. That is one of the greatest miracles, to see people, who by human measure would have seemed to be hopeless, come back and become refined with the miracle of forgiveness. [*THBL*, 120]

—*Elder Bruce R. McConkie* • D&C 46:26

It [the restoration] is all of the gifts of the Spirit—the miracles, signs, and wonders of the past. It is revelation and visions and a knowledge of the wonders of the eternity. It is the way and the means and the power whereby the Holy Spirit of God can make of man a new creature—can burn dross and evil out of him as though by fire; can bring him forth in a newness of life, free from carnality and sin; and can sanctify his soul and make him a fit companion for Gods and angels. [*The Millennial Messiah* (1982), 88]

Chapter Twenty-Four

Doctrines of Devils—Commandments of Men

D&C 49; 50; 52; 54

*H*istorical Setting: Joseph Smith records:

> At about this time came Leman Copely, one of the sect called Shaking Quakers and embraced the fulness of the everlasting Gospel, apparently honest-hearted, but still retaining the idea that the Shakers were right in some particulars of their faith. In order to have more perfect understanding on the subject, I inquired of the Lord, and received [section 49]. [*HC*, 1:167]

> This sect of Christians arose in England, and Ann Lee has the credit of being their founder. They derive their name from their manner of worship, which is performed by singing and dancing, and clapping their hands in regular times, to a novel but rather pleasant kind of music. . . . Their dress and manners are similar to those of the society of Friends (Quakers). . . . "They assert, with the Quakers, that all external ordinances, especially baptism and the Lord's supper, ceased in the apostolic age; and that God had sent no one to preach since that time till they were raised up, to call in the elect in a new dispensation. They deny the doctrine of the Trinity and a vicarious atonement, as also the resurrection of the body." [fn, *HC*, 1:167]

INTRODUCTION

The Prophet Joseph Smith taught: "In relation to the kingdom of God, the devil always sets up his kingdom at the very same time in opposition to God" (*TPJS*, 365). The conditions in Kirtland at this time certainly verify the Prophet Joseph's statement. Section 46 verse 7 also warned the Saints against being "seduced by evil spirits, or doctrines of devils, or the commandments of men." The revelations considered in this chapter are an extension of that warning, telling us how to defend against those problems.

SECTION 49 • OUTLINE

➤ 49:1–4   Sidney and Parley are commanded to preach Christ's gospel to the Shakers.

    a.   They desire to know the truth in part but not all, and need to repent (v. 2).

    b.   Leman Copley shall be ordained, and reason with them according to what is taught him by you (v. 4).

➤ 49:5–10   God sent His Only Begotten Son for the redemption of the world, those who receive Him shall be saved, and those who reject Him shall be damned.

    a.   He reigns in heaven until He descends to put all enemies under His feet (v. 6).

    b.   No man or angels know the hour or the day of His coming, nor shall know until He comes (v. 7).

    c.   All men are under sin and shall repent, except those holy men which are reserved unto God (v. 8).

    d.   I have sent you mine everlasting covenant which was from the beginning (v. 9).

    e.   What was promised was fulfilled, and the nations shall bow down to it, either by themselves or laid low by power (v. 10).

➤ 49:11–14   A commandment is given to go among this people and say as did Peter of old:

    a.   Believe on the name of the Lord, who was on the earth and is to come, the beginning and the end (v. 12).

    b.   Repent, be baptized in the name of Jesus Christ for the remission of sins (v. 13).

    c.   These shall receive the gift of the Holy Ghost by the laying on of hands (v. 14).

➤ 49:15–17   Whoso forbids to marry is not of God, for marriage is ordained of God.

    a.   Man should have one wife, and they shall be twain, that the earth might answer the end of its creation (v. 16).

    b.   The earth is to be filled with the measure of man according to what was agreed before the world was made (v. 17).

➤ 49:18–21   Whoso forbids to abstain from meats is not ordained of God.

    a.   The beasts, fowls, and things that come from the earth are ordained for the use of man in abundance (v. 19).

    b.   One man should not possess above another, thus the world lies in sin (v. 20).

    c.   Wo to man that sheds blood or wastes flesh (v. 22).

➤ 49:22–28   The Son of Man comes not in the form of a woman, or man traveling on earth.

    a.   Be not deceived, look for the heavens to shake, the earth to tremble, the valleys exalted, the mountains made low as the angel sounds his trump (v. 23).

    b.   Before the great day of the Lord comes, Jacob shall flourish in the wilderness, and the Lamanites blossom as a rose (v. 24).

    c.   Zion shall flourish on the hills and mountains, and assemble in one place (v. 25).

    d.   Go forth, repent of your sins, ask and receive, knock and it shall open (v. 26).

TEXT AND COMMENTARY

D&C 49:1–4 • Preach My Gospel to the Shakers

1 Hearken unto my word, my servants Sidney, and Parley, and Leman; for behold, verily I say unto you, that I give unto you a commandment that you shall go and preach my gospel which ye have received, even as ye have received it, unto the Shakers.

2 Behold, I say unto you, that they desire to know the truth in part, but not all, for they are not right before me and must needs repent.

3 Wherefore, I send you, my servants Sidney and Parley, to preach the gospel unto them.

4 And my servant Leman shall be ordained unto this work, that he may reason with them, not according to that which he has received of them, but according to that which shall be taught him by you my servants; and by so doing I will bless him, otherwise he shall not prosper.

Leman Copley and the Shakers are a good example of those who want to mix the teachings of the world with the gospel of Jesus Christ. "Even as ye have received it" (v. 1), and "not according to that which he has received of them" (v. 4) makes it clear that the Lord expects us to teach the gospel, not the commandments of men or the philosophies of men. As Isaiah instructed Israel: "To the law [of Moses] and to the testimony [of the Prophet]; if they speak not according to this word, it is because there is no light in them" (Isaiah 8:20; 2 Nephi 18:20). Jesus warned the Nephites:

10 And if it so be that the church is built upon my gospel then will the Father show forth his own works in it.

11 But if it be not built upon my gospel, and is built upon the works of men, or upon the works of the devil, verily I say unto you they have joy in their works for a season, and by and by the end cometh, and they are hewn down and cast into the fire, from whence there is no return. [3 Nephi 27:10–11]

We must measure all teachings of the world against the teachings of the scriptures, especially those that have been given to us in the latter days.

D&C 49:5–10 • Mine Everlasting Covenant

5 Thus saith the Lord; for I am God, and have sent mine Only Begotten Son into the world for the redemption of the world, and have decreed that he that receiveth him shall be saved, and he that receiveth him not shall be damned—

6 And they have done unto the Son of Man even as they listed; and he has taken his power on the right hand of his glory, and now reigneth in the heavens, and will reign till he descends on the earth to put all enemies under his feet, which time is nigh at hand—

7 I, the Lord God, have spoken it; but the hour and the day no man knoweth, neither the angels in heaven, nor shall they know until he comes.

8 Wherefore, I will that all men shall repent, for all are under sin,

except those which I have reserved unto myself, holy men that ye know not of.

9 Wherefore, I say unto you that I have sent unto you mine everlasting covenant, even that which was from the beginning.

10 And that which I have promised I have so fulfilled, and the nations of the earth shall bow to it; and, if not of themselves, they shall come down, for that which is now exalted of itself shall be laid low of power.

Jesus is the giver of this revelation (see v. 28). However, He speaks as the Father and refers to "mine Only Begotten Son" (v. 5). He spoke by "divine investiture of authority," as explained by the First Presidency in June of 1916: ". . . in all His dealings with the human family Jesus the Son has represented and yet represents Elohim His Father in power and authority. This is true of Christ in His pre-existent, antemortal, or unembodied state, in the which He was known as Jehovah; . . ." (*Messages of the First Presidency*, 5:31–32) He now reigns "in the heavens, and will reign till he descends on the earth to put all enemies under his feet" (v. 6). Although no man or even the angels know the hour or the day of His coming (v. 7), He and His Father know. The Gospel of Mark says: "But of that day and [that] hour knoweth no man, no, not the angels which are in heaven, *neither the Son*, but the Father" (Mark 13:32; emphasis added); but Joseph Smith deleted "neither the Son" in the Joseph Smith Translation.

The "holy men that ye know not of" (D&C 49:8) probably refer to the three Nephites and John the Revelator who were transfigured and permitted to remain on earth to bring souls unto Christ until He came in His glory (see 3 Nephi 28:6–8). At the conference held in June, when Doctrine and Covenants 52 was given, "The Spirit of the Lord fell upon Joseph in an unusual manner, and he prophesied that John the Revelator was then among the Ten Tribes of Israel, who had been led away by Shalmaneser, king of Assyria, to prepare them for their return from their long dispersion, to again possess the land of their fathers." (*HC*, 1:176) The everlasting gospel having been sent, and to which all must "bow to it" or "be laid low of power" (D&C 49:9–10), is another expression of the gospels superiority to the commandments and philosophies of men.

D&C 49:11–14 • Like Unto the Apostle Peter

11 Wherefore, I give unto you a commandment that ye go among this people, and say unto them, like unto mine apostle of old, whose name was Peter:

12 Believe on the name of the Lord Jesus, who was on the earth, and is to come, the beginning and the end;

13 Repent and be baptized in the name of Jesus Christ, according to the holy commandment, for the remission of sins;

14 And whoso doeth this shall receive the gift of the Holy Ghost, by the laying on of the hands of the elders of the church.

The commandment to say to this people what the Apostle Peter had said is a paraphrase of Acts 2:38, or perhaps the translation of the original wording. Peter was teaching the gospel pure and simple, and did not mingle it with the philosophies of men.

D&C 49:15–17 • Marriage is Ordained of God

15 And again, verily I say unto you, that whoso forbiddeth to marry is not ordained of God, for marriage is ordained of God unto man.

16 Wherefore, it is lawful that he should have one wife, and they twain shall be one flesh, and all this that the earth might answer the end of its creation;

17 And that it might be filled with the measure of man, according to his creation before the world was made.

The Shakers "neither condemn nor oppose marriage, but they assert the possibility of attaining a higher or angelic order of existence to which virginity is a prime requisite." (Sidney B. Sperry, *Doctrine and Covenants Compendium* [1960], 205.) The Lord not only endorses marriage, but declares that the earth was created for the purpose of marriage and procreation (vv. 15–17). Adam and Eve were commanded: "Be fruitful, and multiply, and replenish the earth" (Genesis 1:28). As noted in the footnote to that verse in the LDS edition of the Bible, the word "replenish" in Hebrew word means "fill," and the same Hebrew word is so translated in Genesis 1:22: "Be fruitful and multiply, and fill the waters." The Book of Mormon bears similar testimony: "the Lord hath created the earth that it should be inhabited; and he hath created his children that they should possess it" (1 Nephi 17:36; see also Jacob 2:21). Furthermore, section 132, the great revelation on eternal marriage, was made known at about this same time although it was not given to the Church until 1843.

D&C 49:18–21 • Meat is Ordained For the Use of Man

18 And whoso forbiddeth to abstain from meats, that man should not eat the same, is not ordained of God;

19 For, behold, the beasts of the field and the fowls of the air, and that which cometh of the earth, is ordained for the use of man for food and for raiment, and that he might have in abundance.

20 But it is not given that one man should possess that which is above another, wherefore the world lieth in sin.

21 And wo be unto man that sheddeth blood or that wasteth flesh and hath no need.

Some, if not all, of the Shakers abstained from eating meat. This revelation is the first of three in the Doctrine and Covenants that teach that meat from animals and fowls were ordained for the use of food and raiment for man (v. 19). Section 59 mentions beasts, fowls, and that which climbs trees or walks on the earth were made for the benefit and use of man (vv. 16–19). Section 89 states that the beasts and fowls are to be used with thanksgiving, but sparingly, and in times of cold and famine (vv. 12–13). This revelation stresses that there is plenty of meat for all to have it in abundance (D&C 49:19). However, the Lord considers one possessing more than another a sin (v. 20). While wild animals and fowls are also for man's use, they should not be killed and not eaten, or wasted in any other way (v. 21).

D&C 49:22–28 • The Son of Man Comes Not In the Form of a Woman

22 And again, verily I say unto you, that the Son of Man cometh not in the form of a woman, neither of a man traveling on the earth.

23 Wherefore, be not deceived, but continue in steadfastness, looking forth for the heavens to be shaken, and the earth to tremble and to reel to and fro as a drunken man, and for the valleys to be exalted, and for

the mountains to be made low, and for the rough places to become smooth—and all this when the angel shall sound his trumpet.

24 But before the great day of the Lord shall come, Jacob shall flourish in the wilderness, and the Lamanites shall blossom as the rose.

25 Zion shall flourish upon the hills and rejoice upon the mountains, and shall be assembled together unto the place which I have appointed.

26 Behold, I say unto you, go forth as I have commanded you; repent of all your sins; ask and ye shall receive; knock and it shall be opened unto you.

27 Behold, I will go before you and be your rearward; and I will be in your midst, and you shall not be confounded.

28 Behold, I am Jesus Christ, and I come quickly. Even so. Amen.

Another belief of the Shakers was: "The Deity is dual in nature. God is both male and female. The male principle of Christ came to earth as Jesus, the son of a Jewish carpenter. The female is represented as 'Mother Ann,' and in her the promise of our Lords' Second Advent was fulfilled." (*DCC*, 205) The Lord corrects this strange doctrine, and adds that He will not be a man traveling on the earth, or another human being (v. 22). He then repeats the signs of Christ's coming as He had given in section 45 verses 45–48, and adds what Isaiah had prophesied about the valleys and mountains (D&C 49:23; see Isaiah 40:4).

Jehovah also added to some of the things that must happen before the great day shall come. "Jacob shall flourish in the wilderness" has reference to the Church that had been brought out of the wilderness (Revelation 12:6; D&C 5:14; 33:5). He later calls His people "a remnant of Jacob" (D&C 52:1). The Lamanites blossoming as a rose (D&C 49:24), identifies at least some of the people of Israel whom Isaiah had prophesied would do this (see Isaiah 35:1). "Zion shall flourish upon the hills and rejoice upon the mountains" (D&C 49:25), again has reference to the Church. The hills are the "utmost bounds of the everlasting hills" that are to "be on the head of Joseph" as he was blessed by his father Jacob, father of the tribes of Israel (Genesis 49:26). The mountains are where the temples were to be built in the last days as prophesied also by Isaiah (Isaiah 2:2). The city of Zion, to where the people of Zion were to assemble as appointed by the Lord (D&C 49:25), is the New Jerusalem in Independence, Missouri. The Lord identified it as the center place of

Zion shortly after this revelation was given (see D&C 57:3). All of these things were to happen as the Church would repent, ask (pray), and knock (live righteously) (D&C 49:26). The Lord again promises to go before them and prepare the way for these glorious events, and to be in their midst as they prepare to do as He commands (v. 27). In the Lord's time, this would come quickly (v. 28).

*H**istorical Setting*—Section 50:

> During the month of April, I continued to translate the Scriptures as time would allow. In May, a number of Elders being present, and not understanding the different spirits abroad in the earth, I inquired and received from the Lord [section 50]. [*HC*, 1:170]

> . . . some very strange spiritual operations were manifested, which were disgusting rather than edifying. Some persons would seem to swoon away and make unseemly gestures, and be drawn or disfigured in their countenances. Others would fall into ecstasies, and be drawn into contortions, cramps, fits, etc. Others would seem to have visions and revelations, which were not edifying and which were not congenial to the doctrine and spirit of the Gospel. In short, a false and lying spirit seemed to be creeping into the Church. . . . [*HC*, 1:170]

SECTION 50 • OUTLINE

➤ 50:1–5 The Lord gives words of wisdom concerning the spirits abroad in the land.

    a. Many false spirits are on the earth, deceiving the world (v. 2).

    b. Satan seeks to deceive and overthrow you (v. 3).

    c. There are abominations in the church that profess my name (v. 4).

    d. The faithful who endure in life or death, inherit eternal life (v. 5).

➤ 50:6–9 Wo unto the deceivers and hypocrites, I will bring them to judgment.

    a. The hypocrites have deceived some, and given the adversary power, but they shall be reclaimed (v. 7).

      b.   The hypocrites shall be cut off in life or death, and overcome by the world (v. 8).

      c.   Every man beware lest he do what is not in truth or righteousness (v. 9).

➤ 50:10–16   The Lord reasons with the Elders, as one man to another face to face, that they may understand.

      a.   Unto what were you ordained? To preach my gospel by the Spirit (vv. 13–14).

      b.   Ye received spirits, which you could not understand, to be of God. Are you justified? (v. 15).

      c.   Answer this question; I will be merciful, if weak ye shall be made strong (v. 16).

➤ 50:17–25   He that is ordained of God and set forth, does he preach by the Spirit or some other way which is not of God?

      a.   Does he receive the word of truth by the Spirit of truth, or some other way? If by some other way it is not of God (vv. 19–20).

      b.   He that receives the word by the Spirit of truth receives it as preached by the Spirit of truth (v. 21).

      c.   He that preaches and he that receive it understand one another, and are edified and rejoice (v. 22).

      d.   That which doth not edify is not of God, and is darkness (v. 23).

      e.   That which is of God is light, and he that receives light, and continues in God, receives more light (v. 24).

      f.   I say this that you may receive the truth, and chase darkness from you (v. 25).

➤ 50:26–30   He that is ordained of God and sent forth is appointed to be the greatest, but is the least and the servant of God.

      a.   He is possessor of all things, and all things are subject to him (v. 27).

      b.   No man possesses all things unless purified and cleansed from all sin (v. 28).

      c.   If ye are purified, ye shall ask in the name of Jesus and it shall be do Nephi (v. 29).

      d.   It shall be given you what to ask, and as you are appointed to the head, the spirits shall be subjected unto you (v. 30).

➤ 50:31–35   If you behold a spirit manifest that you cannot understand, ask in the name of Jesus, and if he give it not, it is not of God.

    a.   You shall be given power over that spirit, and proclaim it is not of God (v. 32).

    b.   Proclaim not with railing accusation or boasting, lest ye be overcome (v. 33).

    c.   He that receives of God, let him account it of God (v. 34).

    d.   By giving heed and doing these things which ye shall receive, the kingdom is given you of the Father, and power to overcome all things (v. 35).

➤ 50:36–40   Blessed are you who are now hearing my words, for your sins are forgiven.

    a.   Joseph Wakefield and Parley P. Pratt are to go among the churches and strengthen them by exhortation (v. 37).

    b.   John Corrill and others who are ordained, are to labor in the vineyard (v. 38).

    c.   Edward Partridge is not justified, repent and be forgiven (v. 39).

    d.   Ye are little children and cannot bear all things, grow in grace and truth (v. 40).

➤ 50:41–46   Fear not little children, you are mine, I have overcome the world, and the Father hath given you unto me.

    a.   None that the Father hath given shall be lost (v. 42).

    b.   The Father and I are one, ye have received me, ye are in me, and I in you (v. 43).

    c.   I am in your midst, the good Shepherd, the stone of Israel, build on this rock and never fail (v. 44).

    d.   The day cometh that ye shall hear my voice, see me, and know that I am (v. 45).

    e.   Watch that ye may be ready (v. 46).

Text and Commentary

D&C 50:1–5 • Many False Spirits Deceive the World

1 Hearken, O ye elders of my church, and give ear to the voice of the living God; and attend to the words of wisdom which shall be given unto you, according as ye have asked and are agreed as touching the church, and the spirits which have gone abroad in the earth.

2 Behold, verily I say unto you, that there are many spirits which are false spirits, which have gone forth in the earth, deceiving the world.

3 And also Satan hath sought to deceive you, that he might overthrow you.

4 Behold, I, the Lord, have looked upon you, and have seen abominations in the church that profess my name.

5 But blessed are they who are faithful and endure, whether in life or in death, for they shall inherit eternal life.

As promised in the previous revelation, "ask and ye shall receive" (49:26), the Lord answers their question concerning "the spirits which have gone abroad in the earth" (D&C 50:1). There are many false spirits who were then and are now deceiving the world (v. 2). They are and were seeking to overthrow the Church (v. 3). The ability to discern false spirits was one of the gifts of the Spirit discussed in section 46 verse 23. More will be given in later revelations (see D&C 129). While they may be and are successful with some, the faithful who endure in life or in death, shall inherit eternal life (D&C 50:4–5).

D&C 50:6–9 • Wo to the Hypocrites and Deceivers

6 But wo unto them that are deceivers and hypocrites, for, thus saith the Lord, I will bring them to judgment.

7 Behold, verily I say unto you, there are hypocrites among you, who have deceived some, which has given the adversary power; but behold such shall be reclaimed;

8 But the hypocrites shall be detected and shall be cut off, either in life or in death, even as I will; and wo unto them who are cut off from my church, for the same are overcome of the world.

9 Wherefore, let every man beware lest he do that which is not in truth and righteousness before me.

A hypocrite is someone who says one thing and does another. In the Church, it is someone who does not live up to the covenants he or she has made. Hypocrisy opens the door for Satan. The Prophet Joseph warned: "The moment we revolt at anything which comes from God, the devil takes power" (*TPJS*, 181). Those who were or are deceived by the hypocrites can "be reclaimed" (D&C 50:7), but the hypocrites who are brought to judgment, whether in life or death, and are cut off from the Church, "are overcome by the world" (v. 8). Therefore, each member must beware of what he or she does (v. 9).

D&C 50:10–16 • Let Us Reason With the Lord

> 10 And now come, saith the Lord, by the Spirit, unto the elders of his church, and let us reason together, that ye may understand;
>
> 11 Let us reason even as a man reasoneth one with another face to face.
>
> 12 Now, when a man reasoneth he is understood of man, because he reasoneth as a man; even so will I, the Lord, reason with you that you may understand.
>
> 13 Wherefore, I the Lord ask you this question—unto what were ye ordained?
>
> 14 To preach my gospel by the Spirit, even the Comforter which was sent forth to teach the truth.
>
> 15 And then received ye spirits which ye could not understand, and received them to be of God; and in this are ye justified?
>
> 16 Behold ye shall answer this question yourselves; nevertheless, I will be merciful unto you; he that is weak among you hereafter shall be made strong.

The Lord invites the elders of the Church, to reason with Him as a man face to face, but they must reason by the Spirit (vv. 10–11). This invitation is another example of "the condescension of God." To condescend is to go from a higher level to a lower one. In the Book of Mormon, the angel who appeared to Nephi asked him whether he knew of this principle (1 Nephi 11:16). He then showed him how God the Father condescended to become the Father of the Lamb of God (see 1 Nephi 11:18–21), and the condescension of Jesus Christ first as He submitted Himself to John the Baptist to be baptized and then as He ministered to the multitudes healing their infirmities (1 Nephi 11:26–32).

The Lord also invited Isaiah to come and reason together with Him (see Isaiah 1:18). In both situations, with the elders and Isaiah, the Lord is offering to come down to man's level and speak, in order that man may better communicate with Him and understand (D&C 50:12). In His reasoning with him, He asks questions that are simple and yet profound. In the revelation, the Lord sometimes answers His own questions because there are really no other logical answers. The first question, "unto what were you ordained?" (v. 13) has no other answer. The elders were not sent to teach their own ideas or opinions, but to teach the restored truths as prompted by the Comforter (v. 14). Had the false spirits taught the truth, the elders would have understood (v. 15). The second question; were "ye justified?" is asking if they had any scriptural or spiritual guidelines that had supported those teachings of the false spirits to be from God? He lets them answer the question individually, because it is an obvious "no." It is self-evident that they were not justified because of His extending mercy to them, and a promise to make them strong (v. 16). They had obviously been weak before because they were without the Spirit.

D&C 50:17–25 • Preach the Truth By the Spirit

17 Verily I say unto you, he that is ordained of me and sent forth to preach the word of truth by the Comforter, in the Spirit of truth, doth he preach it by the Spirit of truth or some other way?

18 And if it be by some other way it is not of God.

19 And again, he that receiveth the word of truth, doth he receive it by the Spirit of truth or some other way?

20 If it be some other way it is not of God.

21 Therefore, why is it that ye cannot understand and know, that he that receiveth the word by the Spirit of truth receiveth it as it is preached by the Spirit of truth?

22 Wherefore, he that preacheth and he that receiveth, understand one another, and both are edified and rejoice together.

23 And that which doth not edify is not of God, and is darkness.

24 That which is of God is light; and he that receiveth light, and continueth in God, receiveth more light; and that light groweth brighter and brighter until the perfect day.

25 And again, verily I say unto you, and I say it that you may know the truth, that you may chase darkness from among you;

The above verses (vv. 17–21) are teaching the same doctrine as taught by Nephi:

> . . . when a man speaketh by the power of the Holy Ghost the power of the Holy Ghost carrieth it unto the hearts of the children of men.
>
> 2 But behold, there are many that harden their hearts against the Holy Spirit, that it hath no place in them; wherefore, they cast many things away which are written and esteem them as things of naught. [2 Nephi 33:1–2]

When the Spirit is with both the speaker and the hearer, both are edified. To be edified is to be improved in spirit and in knowledge. It is a feeling within the heart as well as the mind. It is a personal revelation from God (D&C 50:22). He has told you in your heart and in your mind (see D&C 8:2–3). When darkness and a bad feeling come it is not from God, but from the devil. It may cause anger and confusion (see 2 Nephi 28:10–20; D&C 50:23–24). When truth is received, more will follow until that perfect day of judgment (D&C 50:24). When truth is rejected, they will lose even that truth that they had attained (see 2 Nephi 28:30). The truth chases away darkness. As Jesus said: "And ye shall know the truth, and the truth shall make you free" (John 8:32).

D&C 50:26–30 • The Greatest Is Purified and Cleansed From All Sin

> 26 He that is ordained of God and sent forth, the same is appointed to be the greatest, notwithstanding he is the least and the servant of all.
>
> 27 Wherefore, he is possessor of all things; for all things are subject unto him, both in heaven and on the earth, the life and the light, the Spirit and the power, sent forth by the will of the Father through Jesus Christ, his Son.
>
> 28 But no man is possessor of all things except he be purified and cleansed from all sin.
>
> 29 And if ye are purified and cleansed from all sin, ye shall ask whatsoever you will in the name of Jesus and it shall be done.
>
> 30 But know this, it shall be given you what you shall ask; and as ye are appointed to the head, the spirits shall be subject unto you.

An ordination of God gives one the potential to become the greatest of all missionaries, bishops; or whatever calling it may be. However, to do so one must put himself last in priority of concerns, serving all others ahead of him (v. 26). The Gospel of Mark teaches the same concept in slightly different words. "If any man desire to be first, the same shall be last of all, and servant of all" (Mark 9:35; see also 10:44).

The one ordained has the power of God or the priesthood conferred upon him. The priesthood is the power to call upon the power of God, and it will obey. It can control all of the elements and peoples on the earth, and the holder of the priesthood can call upon the powers of heaven to accomplish this (see Jacob 4:6). However, he can only draw on this power when he knows it is the will of God for which he is asking (D&C 50:27). He must also be purified and cleansed from all sin (vv. 28–29; see 3 Nephi 8:1 quoted in the end of the last chapter). Nephi, son of Helaman, was granted power over all the people, and over the earth, because the Lord knew he "had not sought thine own life but hast sought my will, and to keep my commandments" (Helaman 10:4; see vv. 7–18). As a man is appointed to the head of a ward, a stake, a quorum, or the whole church, the spirits are subject to him (D&C 50:30). This apparently means the spirits over which he presides, as well as the false spirits who are attempting to overthrow the work in his domain. As Paul said: "And the spirits of the prophets are subject to the prophets. For God is not [the author] of confusion, but of peace, as in all churches of the saints" (1 Corinthians 14:32–33). When the false spirits are in control, the prophets, or heads, are not present, or they are not magnifying their priesthood (see *TPJS*, 209, 212; Jacob 1:19).

D&C 50:31–35 • Proclaim Against That Spirit With a Loud Voice

31 Wherefore, it shall come to pass, that if you behold a spirit manifested that you cannot understand, and you receive not that spirit, ye shall ask of the Father in the name of Jesus; and if he give not unto you that spirit, then you may know that it is not of God.

32 And it shall be given unto you, power over that spirit; and you shall proclaim against that spirit with a loud voice that it is not of God—

33 Not with railing accusation, that ye be not overcome, neither with boasting nor rejoicing, lest you be seized therewith.

34 He that receiveth of God, let him account it of God; and let him

rejoice that he is accounted of God worthy to receive.

35 And by giving heed and doing these things which ye have received, and which ye shall hereafter receive—and the kingdom is given you of the Father, and power to overcome all things which are not ordained of him.

Spirits of the devil "possess a power that none but those who have the priesthood can control" (*TPJS*, 208). Jesus' disciples could not cast out a devil that had possessed a body, yet Jesus did cast it out. When asked why they were not able to do so, Jesus answered: "Howbeit this kind goeth not out but by prayer and fasting" (Matthew 17:15–21). If the priesthood holder does not understand whether the spirit is of God or not, he must ask the Father in the name of Jesus (D&C 50:31). His power over that false spirit must also be used cautiously. What Alma taught his son Shiblon regarding teaching the word is also applicable to using the priesthood: "Use boldness, but not overbearance; and also see that ye bridle all your passions: (Alma 38:12). Railing accusations, boasting, and rejoicing are overbearing, and give "the adversary power" (D&C 50:33, 7). Boldness, or confidence, is shown to false spirits when proclaiming against them in a loud voice (v. 32). The right kind of rejoicing is the recognition that the priesthood holders power comes from God (v. 34). Living as the gospel teaches brings the power to overcome that which is not ordained of God (v. 35). The formula for proper use of the priesthood was given to Joseph Smith in the Liberty Jail: "Let thy bowels also be full of charity towards all men, and to the household of faith, and let virtue garnish thy thoughts unceasingly; then shall thy confidence wax strong in the presence of God; and the doctrine of the priesthood shall distil upon thy soul as the dews from heaven" (D&C 121:45).

D&C 50:36–40 • Strengthen the Churches By Exhortation

36 And behold, verily I say unto you, blessed are you who are now hearing these words of mine from the mouth of my servant, for your sins are forgiven you.

37 Let my servant Joseph Wakefield, in whom I am well pleased, and my servant Parley P. Pratt go forth among the churches and strengthen them by the word of exhortation;

38 And also my servant John Corrill, or as many of my servants as are ordained unto this office, and let them labor in the vineyard; and

let no man hinder them doing that which I have appointed unto them—

39 Wherefore, in this thing my servant Edward Partridge is not justified; nevertheless let him repent and he shall be forgiven.

40 Behold, ye are little children and ye cannot bear all things now; ye must grow in grace and in the knowledge of the truth.

Forgiveness of sins (v. 36) comes from the doctrine of justification; doing the things that the Lord has commanded (see 3 Nephi 27:16; Moses 6:60). Those sins will return if we sin again (see D&C 82:7). Therefore, we must be justified repeatedly. If we continue to grow in the church, by laboring in the vineyard (D&C 50:36–37), we are no longer little children, but come to more knowledge of the truth (v. 40).

D&C 50:40–46 • None That the Father Gives Me Shall Be Lost

41 Fear not, little children, for you are mine, and I have overcome the world, and you are of them that my Father hath given me;

42 And none of them that my Father hath given me shall be lost.

43 And the Father and I are one. I am in the Father and the Father in me; and inasmuch as ye have received me, ye are in me and I in you.

44 Wherefore, I am in your midst, and I am the good shepherd, and the stone of Israel. He that buildeth upon this rock shall never fall.

45 And the day cometh that you shall hear my voice and see me, and know that I am.

46 Watch, therefore, that ye may be ready. Even so. Amen.

The faithful in the kingdom are given to Christ as His spiritually adopted sons and daughters (see Mosiah 5:7). None of these are lost (D&C 59:42), and they become one with Him and the Father (v. 43). The stone of Israel is the "mighty God of Israel, the shepherd who strengthened Joseph who was sold into Egypt, and he became second unto the Pharaoh (see Genesis 49:22–26). The stone of Israel is also the rock of Christ, or the foundation upon which the Church is built (see Matthew 16:18–19; 3 Nephi 11:39; D&C 10:69). The promise to see Him and know Him (D&C 50:45) was a conditional promise to the faithful members at this time, and to all future members who remain faithful (see D&C 93:1).

*H*istorical Setting—Section 52:

On the 3rd of June, the Elders from the various parts of the country where they were laboring, came in; and the conference before appointed (see D&C 44), convened in Kirtland; and the Lord displayed His power to the most perfect satisfaction of the Saints. The man of sin was revealed, and the authority of the Melchizedek Priesthood was manifested and conferred for the first time upon several of the Elders. It was clearly evident that the Lord gave us power in proportion to the work to be done, and strength according to the race set before us, and grace and help as our needs required. . . .

The next day, as a kind continuation of this great work of the last days, I received [section 52]. [*HC*, 1:175–177]

SECTION 52 • OUTLINE

➤ 52:1–8   The elders are told what to do until the next conference held in Missouri.

   a.   This land is to be consecrated to my people who are a remnant of Jacob, and heirs according to the covenant (v. 2).

   b.   Joseph and Sidney are to journey to Missouri, and if faithful it shall be made known what they shall do, and the land of their inheritance (vv. 3–5).

   c.   If they are not faithful, they shall be cut off (v. 6).

   d.   Others are called to make their journey (vv. 7–8).

➤ 52:9–13   The elders are to preach the word as they journey, saying only what the prophets and apostles have written, and what the Comforter teaches them.

   a.   Go two by two, preaching in every congregation, baptizing and laying on hands (v. 10).

   b.   I will cut short my work in righteousness (v. 11).

   c.   Lyman Wight is to beware of Satan, who desires to sift him as chaff (v. 12).

   d.   He that is faithful shall be made ruler over many things (v. 13).

➤ 52:14–21   The Lord gives a pattern for all things, for Satan is abroad in the land, deceiving the nations.

    a. He is accepted, if he prays, has a contrite heart, obeys my ordinances (v. 15).

    b. He speaks in meekness and edifies, is of God, and obeys ordinances (v. 16).

    c. He that trembles under my power shall be made strong and bring fruits (v. 17).

    d. He that brings not forth fruit is not mine (v. 18).

    e. By this pattern ye shall know the spirits in all cases under heaven (v. 19).

    f. The days come that according to men's faith shall it be done unto them (v. 20).

    g. This commandment is given to all elders whom he has chosen (v. 21).

➤ 52:22–34   Twenty-two elders are called two by two to take their journey to one place.

    a. One shall not build upon another's foundation, nor journey in his tracks (v. 33).

    b. The faithful shall be blessed with much fruit (v. 34).

➤ 52:35–36   Two more elders are to travel to the eastern lands.

    a. Labor with their families, declaring only what the prophets and apostles have seen and heard, believing that the prophecies shall be fulfilled (v. 36).

    b. In consequence of transgression, let that bestowed be placed on another (v. 37).

➤ 52:37–40   Two are called to be priests, the residue of the elders are to watch over the churches, and declare the word in the regions round about.

    a. Labor with their hands that there be no idolatry or wickedness practiced (v. 39).

    b. My disciples remember the poor, the needy, the sick and afflicted (v. 40).

➤ 52:41–44   Joseph, Sidney, and Edward Partridge are to take a recommend

from the church, and obtain one for Oliver Cowdery to take to Missouri.

   a. Missouri is now the land of your enemies (v. 42).

   b. The Lord will hasten the city in its time, and crown the faithful with joy (v. 43).

   c. Jesus Christ will lift them up at the last day (v. 44).

TEXT AND COMMENTARY

D&C 52:1–8 • The Purpose of Conferences

1 Behold, thus saith the Lord unto the elders whom he hath called and chosen in these last days, by the voice of his Spirit—

2 Saying: I, the Lord, will make known unto you what I will that ye shall do from this time until the next conference, which shall be held in Missouri, upon the land which I will consecrate unto my people, which are a remnant of Jacob, and those who are heirs according to the covenant.

3 Wherefore, verily I say unto you, let my servants Joseph Smith, Jun., and Sidney Rigdon take their journey as soon as preparations can be made to leave their homes, and journey to the land of Missouri.

4 And inasmuch as they are faithful unto me, it shall be made known unto them what they shall do;

5 And it shall also, inasmuch as they are faithful, be made known unto them the land of your inheritance.

6 And inasmuch as they are not faithful, they shall be cut off, even as I will, as seemeth me good.

7 And again, verily I say unto you, let my servant Lyman Wight and my servant John Corrill take their journey speedily;

8 And also my servant John Murdock, and my servant Hyrum Smith, take their journey unto the same place by the way of Detroit.

Conferences of the Church were and are to give instructions to the Saints until the next conference is held (v. 2). The conference held at Kirtland was a great spiritual experience for the young Church (see section heading). In addition to Joseph's prophecy of John the Revelator being among the ten tribes, mentioned previously:

Joseph Smith, Lyman Wight, and Harvey Whitlock received a vision of both God the Father and his Son, Jesus Christ, in the log schoolhouse on the Isaac Morley farm during a conference held from June 3 to 6, 1831. Levi Hancock recorded that the Prophet was speaking to the elders when he "stepped out on the floor and said, "I now see God and Jesus Christ at his right hand, let them kill me, I should not feel death as I am now.

John Whitmer, the official Church historian and recorder; wrote of this same appearance:

> The spirit of the Lord fell upon Joseph in an unusual manner. . . . After he had prophesied he laid his hands upon Lyman Wight [and ordained him] to the high priesthood. . . . And the spirit fell upon Lyman, and he prophesied, concerning the coming of Christ. . . . He saw the heavens opened and the Son of Man sitting on the right hand of the Father. Making intercession for the Saints. He said that God would work a work in these last days that tongue cannot express, and the mind is not capable to conceive. The glory of the Lord shone round about.

> Zebedee Coltrin, who was also present, said that an evil spirit seized Harvey Whitlock. "Joseph rebuked the power that had seized [Harvey], and it left him, and he testified, as Lyman [Wight] had done, that he saw the heavens opened, and Jesus standing on the right hand of the Father. [Karl Ricks Anderson, *Joseph Smith's Kirtland* (1989), 107–108]

The next conference of the Church was to be held in Missouri. The land to be consecrated to the remnant of Jacob (D&C 52:2) again confirms that those Saints who had been gathered, and would continue to be gathered, were the descendants of the ten tribes. It does not seem coincidental that the Prophet Joseph had prophesied of John the Revelator's being among the ten tribes in the Kirtland conference. This remnant had been dispersed after Shalmaneser, king of Assyria, had led them away, as prophesied by the Old Testament prophet Amos:

> 8 Behold, the eyes of the LORD GOD [are] upon the sinful kingdom, and I will destroy it from off the face of the earth; saving that I will not utterly destroy the house of Jacob, saith the LORD.

> 9 For, lo, I will command, and I will sift the house of Israel among all nations, like as [corn] is sifted in a sieve, yet shall not the least grain fall upon the earth. [Amos 9:8–9]

President Spencer W. Kimball quoted the above passage and added

"and be lost" to the last verse (*Ensign,* December 1975, 4). The Lord knows where the remnant of Jacob is, and has sent His servants to gather them from among all nations. "Those who are heirs according to the covenant" (D&C 52:2) are "[Abraham's] seed after [him] (that is to say, the literal seed, or the seed of the body) [thus] shall all the families of the earth be blessed, even with the blessings of the Gospel, which are the blessings of salvation, even of life eternal" (Abraham 2:11). As the gospel is taken among the nations of the earth, those who are not of the seed of Abraham are also invited to "be called after [Abraham's] name, and shall be accounted [adopted as] thy seed" (Abraham 2:10; see also 1 Nephi 22:8–9). The move to Missouri was to begin "as soon as preparations can be made" (D&C 52:3, 7–8), and the faithful will have further revelation given to them there (vv. 4–6).

D&C 52:9–13 • What the Apostles and Prophets Have Written

> 9 And let them journey from thence preaching the word by the way, saying none other things than that which the prophets and apostles have written, and that which is taught them by the Comforter through the prayer of faith.
>
> 10 Let them go two by two, and thus let them preach by the way in every congregation, baptizing by water, and the laying on of the hands by the water's side.
>
> 11 For thus saith the Lord, I will cut my work short in righteousness, for the days come that I will send forth judgment unto victory.
>
> 12 And let my servant Lyman Wight beware, for Satan desireth to sift him as chaff.
>
> 13 And behold, he that is faithful shall be made ruler over many things.

The missionary work was not to be slackened, and the Lord reminds them again of what they are to teach: what "the prophets and apostles have written, and that which is taught them by the Comforter" (vv. 9–10). It must be remembered that the Nephites had Apostles and Prophets whose words were recorded in the Book of Mormon (see *HC*, 4:538), and that Joseph and the Three Witnesses were Apostles (see D&C 18:9, 37; 20:2–3).

The work of the Lord that was to be cut short in righteousness (v. 11) was the scourging and eventual destruction of the wicked at the day of judgment (see D&C 84:96–97). The desire of Satan to sift Lyman Wight as chaff (v. 12) was the same desire he had for the Apostle Peter (see Luke 22:31). Satan must have known what the Lord had in mind for Lyman. The promise to be made ruler over many things (D&C 52:13) was also made to the disciples in Jerusalem in the parable of the talents (see Matthew 25:21–23).

D&C 52:14–21 • Satan Goes Forth Deceiving the Nations

14 And again, I will give unto you a pattern in all things, that ye may not be deceived; for Satan is abroad in the land, and he goeth forth deceiving the nations—

15 Wherefore he that prayeth, whose spirit is contrite, the same is accepted of me if he obey mine ordinances.

16 He that speaketh, whose spirit is contrite, whose language is meek and edifieth, the same is of God if he obey mine ordinances.

17 And again, he that trembleth under my power shall be made strong, and shall bring forth fruits of praise and wisdom, according to the revelations and truths which I have given you.

18 And again, he that is overcome and bringeth not forth fruits, even according to this pattern, is not of me.

19 Wherefore, by this pattern ye shall know the spirits in all cases under the whole heavens.

20 And the days have come; according to men's faith it shall be done unto them.

21 Behold, this commandment is given unto all the elders whom I have chosen.

To be a good person is not enough to avoid being deceived by Satan, we must receive and obey the ordinances given to us by Christ (vv. 14–16). As stated above, "none but those who have the priesthood can control" the power of Satan (*TPJS*, 208). To tremble under my [Christ's] power [the priesthood] (D&C 59:17) is to use it as the Lord intends it to be used: "No power or influence can or ought to be maintained by virtue of the priesthood, only by persuasion, by long-suffering, by gentleness and meekness, and by love unfeigned; By kindness, and pure knowledge, which shall greatly enlarge the soul without hypocrisy, and without guile—" (D&C 121:41–42). Those who misuse it are not of Christ (D&C 50:18). The Lord says of those: "Amen to the priesthood or the authority of that man" (D&C 121:37). By following the pattern given here by the Lord, the spirits in the earth will be known, whether good or evil (D&C 50:19). In this day, things must be done according to faith (v. 20). This commandment is for all elders to know how to use the priesthood (v. 21).

D&C 52:22–38 • Preaching the Word By the Way

NOTE: Verses 22 through 32, and 35 name thirty men who are called, ordained, or directed, to journey "Preaching the word by the way." They will not be included here, but can be found in the Doctrine and Covenants.

> 33 Yea, verily I say, let all these take their journey unto one place, in their several courses, and one man shall not build upon another's foundation, neither journey in another's track.

> 34 He that is faithful, the same shall be kept and blessed with much fruit.

> 36 Let them labor with their families, declaring none other things than the prophets and apostles, that which they have seen and heard and most assuredly believe, that the prophecies may be fulfilled.

The assignment of missionary companions was done by the Lord (vv. 22–32, 35). While this may not be generally recognized, it is still done today. Mission Presidents earnestly seek revelation in assigning companions. Companions are to work together, and not seek self aggrandizement (v. 35). Those who are faithful in their companionship will be "blessed with much fruit" (v. 34).

Verse 36 is basically the same instructions as given in verse 9, except they were called to labor with their families. The revelation seems to refer to the families to whom they would teach the gospel, because they were leaving their own families to go to the eastern lands. The Lord, in His foreknowledge, would know the families whom they would be teaching. What they had "seen and heard" (v. 36) would refer to the restoration of the fullness of the gospel in the latter days. Their purpose was to show how the restoration was fulfilling the prophecies of the Old Testament [prophets] and the New Testament [Apostles] (v. 36).

D&C 52:39–44 • Instructions to the Residue of the Elders

39 Let the residue of the elders watch over the churches, and declare the word in the regions round about them; and let them labor with their own hands that there be no idolatry nor wickedness practiced.

40 And remember in all things the poor and the needy, the sick and the afflicted, for he that doeth not these things, the same is not my disciple.

41 And again, let my servants Joseph Smith, Jun., and Sidney Rigdon and Edward Partridge take with them a recommend from the church. And let there be one obtained for my servant Oliver Cowdery also.

42 And thus, even as I have said, if ye are faithful ye shall assemble yourselves together to rejoice upon the land of Missouri, which is the land of your inheritance, which is now the land of your enemies.

43 But, behold, I, the Lord, will hasten the city in its time, and will crown the faithful with joy and with rejoicing.

44 Behold, I am Jesus Christ, the Son of God, and I will lift them up at the last day. Even so. Amen.

The association of idolatry with not working with your own hands (v. 39) is perhaps not immediately evident. Perhaps it is the worship of the mind, or the reasoning of men, to obtain wealth. The Lord accused Almon Babbitt of setting up a golden calf when he aspired to set up his own counsel instead of the counsel of the Presidency of the Church, which really came from God. (D&C 124:84). The care of the poor and needy, the sick and afflicted, take top priority with the Lord (D&C 52:40; see Alma 34:28; D&C 104:18).

Section 50 verse 41 is the first mention of a Church recommend in the Doctrine and Covenants. It is the same concept as members taking a letter to another branch of the church "certifying that they are regular members in good standing," as directed on the day the Church was organized (D&C 20:84). Similar practices are followed today for performing ordinances in other areas, or temple attendance. The Lord ends by pointing to the great city that is promised to be established in Missouri (D&C 52:42–44).

Historical Setting—Section 54:

The branch of the Church in Thompson, on account of breaking the covenant, and not knowing what to do, they sent in Newel Knight and other Elders, to ask me to inquire of the Lord for them; which I did and received [section 54]. [*HC*, 1:180]

SECTION 54 • OUTLINE

➤ 54:1–6   Newel Knight shall stand in the office I have appointed him.

    a.   If your brethren desire to escape their enemies, let them repent (v. 3).

    b.   The covenant they have broken is void and of no effect (v. 4).

    c.   Wo to whom this offense comes, it were better to be drowned in the sea (v. 5).

    d.   Blessed are they who have kept the covenant (v. 6).

➤ 54:7–10   The Colesville saints are to flee and journey to the land of Missouri, the borders of the Lamanites.

    a.   Seek a living like unto men until I prepare a place for you (v. 9.

    b.   Be patient in tribulation until I come, I come quickly, and they who seek me early shall find rest (v. 10).

TEXT AND COMMENTARY

D&C 54:1–6 • Stand Fast In the Office Appointed

1 Behold, thus saith the Lord, even Alpha and Omega, the beginning and the end, even he who was crucified for the sins of the world—

2 Behold, verily, verily, I say unto you, my servant Newel Knight, you shall stand fast in the office whereunto I have appointed you.

3 And if your brethren desire to escape their enemies, let them repent of all their sins, and become truly humble before me and contrite.

4 And as the covenant which they made unto me has been broken, even so it has become void and of none effect.

5 And wo to him by whom this offense cometh, for it had been better for him that he had been drowned in the depth of the sea.

6 But blessed are they who have kept the covenant and observed the commandment, for they shall obtain mercy.

The philosophies or attributes of men, certainly with help from the devil, had disrupted the Thompson, Ohio branch of the Church. Newel Knight was to stand fast (v. 2) because he was apparently still following the Lord. Others, such as Leman Copley who had broken his law of consecration covenant, were warned of the eternal consequences that would follow. The comparison of death by drowning, being better than their eternal status (v. 5), was used in the New Testament concerning the offending, or abusing, of little children (Matthew 18:6). The symbolism used is that those who are drowned die by violating a physical law, and will continue their life in the spirit world under the mercy of the Lord (D&C 59:6). Those who break covenants violate a spiritual law, and will have to suffer the buffetings of Satan until the day of their redemption (see D&C 78:12; 82:21).

D&C 54:7–10 • Be Patient In Tribulation Until I Come

7 Wherefore, go to now and flee the land, lest your enemies come upon you; and take your journey, and appoint whom you will to be your leader, and to pay moneys for you.

8 And thus you shall take your journey into the regions westward, unto the land of Missouri, unto the borders of the Lamanites.

9 And after you have done journeying, behold, I say unto you, seek ye a living like unto men, until I prepare a place for you.

10 And again, be patient in tribulation until I come; and, behold, I come quickly, and my reward is with me, and they who have sought me early shall find rest to their souls. Even so. Amen.

The work of the Lord in Missouri had been detained but not stopped. But "it is not the work of God that is frustrated, but the work of men" (D&C 3:3). The work in Missouri would proceed. The Thompson branch was to join them, and live normal lives until they receive further instructions (vv. 7–10).

General Authority Quotes

—*President Joseph F. Smith* • D&C 49:2

Among the Latter-day Saints, the preaching of false doctrines disguised as truths of the gospel, may be expected from people of two classes, and practically from these two only; they are:

First—The hopelessly ignorant, whose lack of intelligence is due to their indolence and sloth, who make but feeble effort, if indeed at all, to better understand themselves by reading and study; those who are afflicted with a dread disease that may develop into an incurable malady—laziness.

Second—The proud and self-vaunting ones, who lead by the light of their own conceit; who interpret by the rules of their own contriving, who have become a law unto themselves, and so pose as the sole judges of their own doings. More dangerously ignorant than the first.

Beware of the lazy and the proud, their infection in each case is contagious, better for them and for all when they are compelled to display the yellow flag of warning, that the clean and the uninfected may be protected. [*Gospel Doctrine* (1959), 373]

—President Gordon B. Hinckley • D&C 49:2–3

From the day of Cain to the present, the adversary has been the great mastermind of the terrible conflicts that have brought so much suffering. Treachery and terrorism began with him. And they will continue until the Son of God returns to rule and reign with peace and righteousness among the sons and daughters of God. [*Discourses of President Gordon B. Hinckley* (2005), 2:133]

—President Howard W. Hunter • D&C 49:15–17

With a knowledge of the plan of salvation as a foundation, a man who holds the priesthood looks upon marriage as a sacred privilege and obligation. It is not good for man nor for woman to be alone. Man is not complete without woman. Neither can fill the measure of their creation without the other (see 1 Corinthians 11:11, Moses 3:18). Marriage between a man and a woman is ordained of God (see D&C 49:15–17). Only through the new and everlasting covenant of marriage can they realize the fullness of eternal blessings (see D&C 131:1–4; 132:15–19). [*THWH*, 133]

—The First Presidency and the Council of the Twelve • D&C 49:15–17

The first commandment that God gave to Adam and Eve per-
tained to their potential for parenthood as husband and wife. We
declare that God's commandment for his children to multiply and
replenish the earth remains in force. We further declare that God has
commanded that the sacred powers of procreation are to be employed
only between man and woman, lawfully wedded as husband and wife.
[*The Family: A Proclamation To The World*, September, 1995]

—Elder Ezra Taft Benson • D&C 49:25

Our assemblage today in these mountains beneath the shadow
of the temple, hewn from the stone of these mountains, stand as a
fulfillment of these prophesies. [*The Teachings of Ezra Taft Benson*
(1988), 247]

—President Harold B. Lee • D&C 50:21–24

I speak with a limited vocabulary and sometimes my listeners have
a less efficient vocabulary, and with that limited equipment we try to
get across a few ideas—sometimes with garbled results, I've found to my
sorrow. It's imperative, therefore, that when we speak and as we listen
we heed to the counsel of the Lord, who said: (quotes D&C 50:21–24)

My challenge, then, is to speak by the Spirit. Your challenge is
to listen by the Spirit, hopefully, that we might be edified together.
[*THBL*, 467]

Chapter Twenty-Five

The Center Place of Zion

D&C 56; 57; 58

H istorical Setting:

Elder Thomas B. Marsh came to inquire what he should do, as Elder Ezra Thayre, his yoke fellow in the ministry, could not get ready to start on his mission as soon as he (Marsh) would; and I inquired of the Lord, and received [section 56, June 1831]. [*HC*, 1:186]

INTRODUCTION

Joseph had recently been told by the Lord that He wanted to "reserve unto himself a pure people" (D&C 43:14). The building of Zion had been a theme running throughout the revelations he had previously received. Joseph's work on the translation of the Bible had revealed to him the Zion society of Enoch (Moses 7). A revelation had described: "A land of peace, a city of refuge, a place of safety for the saints of the Most High God, And the glory of the Lord shall be there, . . . and it shall be called Zion" (D&C 45:66–67). For the past few months, Joseph had been dealing with members who were deceived by false spirits, were rebellious, and more recently those who had broken their covenants (section 56). He had apparently been studying Isaiah who had prophesied that the desert would blossom as a rose (Isaiah 35:1). This had been further verified in section 49, verse 24. Isaiah had foreseen the glory of the Lord upon Zion (Isaiah 60:1–2), and had foretold of the temple of the last days unto which all nations would flow (Isaiah 2:2). We are living in the day when Isaiah's and other prophets' prophecies are being fulfilled.

SECTION 56 · OUTLINE

➤ 56:1–13   The Lord's anger is kindled against the rebellious, and they shall know His indignation in the day of wrath against the nations.

       a.   He that will not take up his cross and follow Christ will not be saved (v. 2).

       b.   He that will not obey shall be cut off in the Lord's own due time (v. 3).

       c.   The Lord commands and revokes, all will be answered by the rebellious (v. 4).

       d.   The commandments are revoked and new ones are given (v. 6).

       e.   Other servants are to obey the former commandments (v. 7).

       f.   If Ezra Thayre does not do as commanded, he will be cut off the church (v. 8–10).

       g.   These words will not pass away, but will all be fulfilled (v. 11).

       h.   If Joseph Smith pays the money, he shall be rewarded again (v. 12).

➤ 56:14–20   My people have many things to do and repent of, and are not pardoned.

       a.   Wo unto the rich men who will not give their substance to the poor (v. 16).

       b.   Wo unto the poor men who lay hold of other's goods, and do not labor (v. 17).

       c.   Blessed are the poor whose hearts are broken; the earth shall be theirs (v. 18).

       d.   Every such poor man will be rewarded, and their generation shall inherit the earth from generation to generation (vv. 19–20).

NOTES AND COMMENTARY

D&C 56:1–13 • The Lord Commands and Revokes

1 Hearken, O ye people who profess my name, saith the Lord your God; for behold, mine anger is kindled against the rebellious, and they shall know mine arm and mine indignation, in the day of visitation and of wrath upon the nations.

2 And he that will not take up his cross and follow me, and keep my commandments, the same shall not be saved.

3 Behold, I, the Lord, command; and he that will not obey shall be cut off in mine own due time, after I have commanded and the commandment is broken.

4 Wherefore I, the Lord, command and revoke, as it seemeth me good; and all this to be answered upon the heads of the rebellious, saith the Lord.

5 Wherefore, I revoke the commandment which was given unto my servants Thomas B. Marsh and Ezra Thayre, and give a new commandment unto my servant Thomas, that he shall take up his journey speedily to the land of Missouri, and my servant Selah J. Griffin shall also go with him.

6 For behold, I revoke the commandment which was given unto my servants Selah J. Griffin and Newel Knight, in consequence of the stiffneckedness of my people which are in Thompson, and their rebellions.

7 Wherefore, let my servant Newel Knight remain with them; and as many as will go may go, that are contrite before me, and be led by him to the land which I have appointed.

8 And again, verily I say unto you, that my servant Ezra Thayre must repent of his pride, and of his selfishness, and obey the former commandment which I have given him concerning the place upon which he lives.

9 And if he will do this, as there shall be no divisions made upon the land, he shall be appointed still to go to the land of Missouri;

10 Otherwise he shall receive the money which he has paid, and shall leave the place, and shall be cut off out of my church, saith the Lord God of hosts;

11 And though the heaven and the earth pass away, these words shall not pass away, but shall be fulfilled.

12 And if my servant Joseph Smith, Jun., must needs pay the money, behold, I, the Lord, will pay it unto him again in the land of Missouri, that those of whom he shall receive may be rewarded again according to that which they do;

13 For according to that which they do they shall receive, even in lands for their inheritance.

To rebel is to oppose or disobey one in authority (v. 1). To take up the cross (v. 2) "is to deny himself all ungodliness, and every worldly lusts" (JS—Matthew 16:26). Therefore, those members of the Church, of whom the Lord speaks, were not committing sins of omission, but were opposing the revealed word of the Lord. They were not pure in heart, or a Zion people. The law of consecration, whether lived collectively or individually, is entered into by covenant (see D&C 42:30). Although the Lord revoked the commandments given to some, they were accountable for their breaking of a covenant (D&C 56:3–4).[39] The Church will move on without them, as Thomas B. Marsh and Newel Knight are instructed (vv. 5–7). Others may repent and still obtain the promised blessings (vv. 8–9). If they do not repent, especially after being warned, they will be cut off of the church (v. 10). The binding power of a covenant is stronger than the permanency of the earth in its present heaven (v. 11). Other members may have to take up the slack, or carry an additional load, as Joseph Smith is used as an example in this revelation (v. 12), but the Lord will reward him both temporally and spiritually (v. 12). The final choice is up to each individual (v. 13).

D&C 56:14–20 • Wo Unto the Rich Man, Wo Unto the Poor Man

14 Behold, thus saith the Lord unto my people—you have many things to do and to repent of; for behold, your sins have come up unto me, and are not pardoned, because you seek to counsel in your own ways.

15 And your hearts are not satisfied. And ye obey not the truth, but have pleasure in unrighteousness.

16 Wo unto you rich men, that will not give your substance to the poor, for your riches will canker your souls; and this shall be your lamentation in the day of visitation, and of judgment, and of indignation: The harvest is past, the summer is ended, and my soul is not saved!

17 Wo unto you poor men, whose hearts are not broken, whose

---

[39] Ezra Thayre remained active and prominent in the Church until after the martyrdom of the Prophet and Hyrum, and later affiliated with the Reorganized Church. Hoyt Brewter Jr., *Doctrine and Covenants Encyclopedia* [1988], 588–89.

spirits are not contrite, and whose bellies are not satisfied, and whose hands are not stayed from laying hold upon other men's goods, whose eyes are full of greediness, and who will not labor with your own hands!

18 But blessed are the poor who are pure in heart, whose hearts are broken, and whose spirits are contrite, for they shall see the kingdom of God coming in power and great glory unto their deliverance; for the fatness of the earth shall be theirs.

19 For behold, the Lord shall come, and his recompense shall be with him, and he shall reward every man, and the poor shall rejoice;

20 And their generations shall inherit the earth from generation to generation, forever and ever. And now I make an end of speaking unto you. Even so, Amen.

Some sins are forgiven under the conditions of repentance, and others may be pardoned after they have suffered the consequences (see Matthew 5:26; Alma 39:6; D&C 78:12). Rebelling is knowingly opposing the will of God. Some members were guilty of this sin (D&C 56:1, 14). They were finding pleasure in unrighteousness (v. 15).

The Lord uses three examples: First, the rich men who will not help the poor (v. 16). A canker is a spreading sore. Obtaining money often brings pride to their hearts, and it spread to a desire for more money, expensive clothes, arrogant thinking, and persecution of those who do not have money (see Jacob 1:13). They procrastinate the day of repentance and must suffer for their sins (see Alma 34:32–33). As they suffer these consequences, they will lament as prophesied by the prophet Jeremiah. "The harvest is past," [my deeds are done]; "the summer is ended," [the day of repentance is past]; "my soul is not saved," [I did not take advantage of the atonement and obtain forgiveness] (D&C 56:16; Jeremiah 8:20).

The second example: The poor men, "whose hearts are not broken, whose spirits are not contrite," are not spiritually oriented or concerned. The poor, whose "bellies are not satisfied," think the world owes them a living and expect others to feed, clothe, and shelter them. The poor, "whose hands are not stayed from laying hold upon other men's goods," say it is not dishonest to steal because I'm hungry and they have plenty. Those, "whose eyes are full of greediness," are given food but think the food should be better quality. Those who "will not labor with their own hands," will not take menial type employment, or humble themselves sufficiently to change their environmental, educational, or emotional status (D&C 56:17).

The third example is a positive one. "Blessed are the poor who are pure in heart;" they want to do what is right. The poor, "whose hearts are broken, and whose spirits are contrite;" mourn over their sins and are teachable. The poor, "who see the kingdom of God coming in great power and glory unto their deliverance," have faith in the Lord Jesus Christ, and turn to Him for their comfort and help. "The fatness of the earth will be theirs," for the Lord has promised "that the poor and the meek of the earth shall inherit it" (D&C 56:18; 88:17). These poor people will rejoice when they are rewarded for their deeds (D&C 56:19). Because these people "will train up a child in the way he should go" (Proverbs 22:6), their generations will also inherit the earth with them (D&C 56:20).

*H*istorical Setting—Section 57:

> The meeting of our brethren (in Missouri, July 1831), who had long awaited our arrival, was a glorious one, and moistened with many tears. It seemed good and pleasant for brethren to meet together in unity. But our reflections were many, coming as we had from a highly cultivated state of society in the east, and standing now upon the confines or western limits of the United States, and looking into the vast wilderness of those who sat in darkness; how natural it was to observe the degradation, leanness of intellect, ferocity, and jealousy of a people that were nearly a century behind the times, and to feel for those who roamed about without the benefit of civilization, refinement, or religion; yea, and exclaim in the language of the Prophets: "When will the wilderness blossom as a rose? When will Zion be built up in her glory, and where will Thy temple stand, unto which all nations shall come in the last days?" Our anxiety was soon relieved by receiving [section 57, July 1831]. [*HC*, 1:189]

As Joseph viewed the people in Missouri, he was obviously disappointed with what he saw there. Thus, the three yearning questions were asked: "*When will the wilderness blossom as a rose? When will Zion be built up in her glory, and where will thy Temple stand, unto which all nations shall come in the last days?*" (section heading).

SECTION 57 • OUTLINE

➤ 57:1–3   The land of Missouri is appointed and consecrated for the gathering of the saints.

a.   It is the place for the city of Zion (v. 2).

b.   Independence is the center place, and the temple spot lies westward (v. 3).

➤ 57:4–10   It is wisdom for the saints to purchase lands to the line between Jew and Gentile.

a.   The lands they buy shall be an everlasting inheritance (v. 5).

b.   Sidney Gilbert is to stand in the office of agent and purchase lands (v. 6).

c.   Edward Partridge is to stand in the office of bishop to divide the lands (v. 7).

d.   Sidney Gilbert is to establish a store to sell goods and buy lands (v. 8).

e.   He shall obtain a license and send goods unto the people (v. 9).

f.   He is to provide for the saints that the gospel may be preached (v. 10).

➤ 57:11–14   William W. Phelps shall be established as a printer unto the church.

a.   If the world receives his writing, obtain what he can in righteousness (v. 12).

b.   Oliver Cowdery shall assist him as proved by the spirit (v. 13).

c.   These shall be planted in the land of Zion, with their families speedily (v. 14).

➤ 57:15–16   The bishop is to make preparations for the families commanded to come.

a.   Come as soon as possible (v. 15).

b.   Further directions will be given to elders and members after arrival (v. 16).

TEXT AND COMMENTARY

D&C 57:1–3 • Where Will Thy Temple Stand?

1 Hearken, O ye elders of my church, saith the Lord your God, who have assembled yourselves together, according to my commandments, in this land, which is the land of Missouri, which is the land which I have appointed and consecrated for the gathering of the saints.

2 Wherefore, this is the land of promise, and the place for the city of Zion.

3 And thus saith the Lord your God, if you will receive wisdom here is wisdom. Behold, the place which is now called Independence is the center place; and a spot for the temple is lying westward, upon a lot which is not far from the courthouse.

The Prophet Joseph's questions were answered by the Lord in the next two revelations being treated in this chapter. He reminds the elders of the significance of the whole land of Missouri, the place appointed and consecrated for the gathering of the Saints, the remnant of Jacob (v. 1; see 52:2). This land was the promised place for the city of Zion to be built (v. 2). The place in Missouri called Independence is the center place, and the spot for the temple "is not far from the courthouse" (v. 3).

As for the New Jerusalem gathering, Independence was to be the center place, not the center stake as some are inclined to say. The symbolism of the gathering of Israel had also been used by the Prophet Isaiah: "Enlarge the place of thy tent, and let them stretch forth the curtains of thy habitations; spare not, lengthen thy cords and strengthen thy stakes" (Isaiah 22:2; 3 Nephi 22:2). In the center of the tent was normally a large pole, and cords were fastened to it, and each cord was extended to a perimeter surrounding the tent. A large tent pin or stake was driven into the ground, and the cord extended from the center pole was fastened to the stake and pulled tight to raise the tent. Thus stakes were to be established all around Independence so that the tent of Israel, the New Jerusalem, could be equally supported on all sides. The establishing of stakes around Independence has been underway since this revelation was given. The Lord will determine when there are sufficient stakes in place to raise the center pole.

D&C 57:4–10 • The Line Between Jew and Gentile

4 Wherefore, it is wisdom that the land should be purchased by the saints, and also every tract lying westward, even unto the line running directly between Jew and Gentile;

5 And also every tract bordering by the prairies, inasmuch as my disciples are enabled to buy lands. Behold, this is wisdom, that they may obtain it for an everlasting inheritance.

6 And let my servant Sidney Gilbert stand in the office to which I have appointed him, to receive moneys, to be an agent unto the church, to buy land in all the regions round about, inasmuch as can be done in righteousness, and as wisdom shall direct.

7 And let my servant Edward Partridge stand in the office to which I have appointed him, and divide unto the saints their inheritance, even as I have commanded; and also those whom he has appointed to assist him.

8 And again, verily I say unto you, let my servant Sidney Gilbert plant himself in this place, and establish a store, that he may sell goods without fraud, that he may obtain money to buy lands for the good of the saints, and that he may obtain whatsoever things the disciples may need to plant them in their inheritance.

9 And also let my servant Sidney Gilbert obtain a license—behold here is wisdom, and whoso readeth let him understand—that he may send goods also unto the people, even by whom he will as clerks employed in his service;

10 And thus provide for my saints, that my gospel may be preached unto those who sit in darkness and in the region and shadow of death.

The purchasing of lands was to acquire the necessary ground to be able to raise the tent of Israel when the time came. The size of the city of Zion is indicated by the direction to buy tracts of land "even unto the borders of the line between Jew and Gentile; And every tract bordering by the prairies" (vv. 4–5). In this context, the Jews are the Lamanites who had left Jerusalem to be brought to the Americas. Although they were of the blood line of Manasseh (see Alma 10:3) and Ephraim,[40] they (or

---

[40] The book of Lehi, the lost 116 pages of manuscript, stated that Ishmael, the family traveling with Lehi (1 Nephi 7:5) was of the lineage of Ephraim. See *JD*, 23:184 and chapter 4 of this work.

their ancestors were culturally Jews (see 2 Nephi 33:8; D&C 19:27). The members of the church today are Israelites who were scattered among the Gentiles, or adopted into the house of Israel, but are culturally Gentiles (see D&C 86:8–9; 109:60). The "everlasting inheritance" of these lands (D&C 57:5) shows the possession of these lands was to extend to the time of the building of the New Jerusalem. More will be said on this concept in later revelations.

The appointment of Sidney Gilbert as agent to purchase lands, and Edward Partridge as bishop to divide the lands that were purchased (vv. 6–7), was not only for the time at hand, but will be the responsibility of those offices when the city of Zion will be built. Sidney's directions to establish a store (vv. 8–9) is another illustration of a non-agricultural stewardship at that time. All that was directed to the Saints in Missouri at that time was for the furthering of missionary work until the time for the city of Zion to be built (v. 10). The same emphasis for missionary work is still appropriate.

D&C 57:11–16 • A Printer For the Good of the Saints

11 And again, verily I say unto you, let my servant William W. Phelps be planted in this place, and be established as a printer unto the church.

12 And lo, if the world receive his writings—behold here is wisdom—let him obtain whatsoever he can obtain in righteousness, for the good of the saints.

13 And let my servant Oliver Cowdery assist him, even as I have commanded, in whatsoever place I shall appoint unto him, to copy, and to correct, and select, that all things may be right before me, as it shall be proved by the Spirit through him.

14 And thus let those of whom I have spoken be planted in the land of Zion, as speedily as can be, with their families, to do those things even as I have spoken.

15 And now concerning the gathering—Let the bishop and the agent make preparations for those families which have been commanded to come to this land, as soon as possible, and plant them in their inheritance.

16 And unto the residue of both elders and members further directions shall be given hereafter. Even so. Amen.

The importance to the Lord for the Church members to be learned is shown again in his directions to Brother Phelps, "for the good of the saints" (vv. 11–12). Jacob, brother of Nephi said: "To be learned is good if they hearken to the commandments of God" (2 Nephi 2:29). The Prophet Joseph instructed: "Whatever principle of intelligence we attain unto in this life, it will rise with us in the resurrection. And if a person gains more knowledge and intelligence in this life through his diligence and obedience than another, he will have so much the advantage in the world to come" (D&C 130:18–19). The printing was also apparently intended to be sold for the good of the Saints financially (D&C 57:12). The accuracy of his writing, honed by Oliver Cowdery, and proved by the Spirit (vv. 13–14), also exemplifies the Lord's desire for perfection.

The Lord's commandment "to come to this land as soon as possible" (v. 15) reminds us of President Spencer W. Kimball's motto—" Do it Now." The further direction to "be given hereafter" (v. 16) was given 12 days later (D&C 58), and answers the other two questions posed by the Prophet Joseph.

*H*istorical Setting—Section 58:

> The first Sabbath after our arrival in Jackson County, Brother W. W. Phelps preached to a western audience over the boundary of the United States, wherein were present specimens of all the families of the earth; Shem, Ham, and Japeth; several of the Lamanites or Indians— representative of Shem; quite a respectable number of Negroes— descendants of Ham; and the balance was made up of citizens of the surrounding county, and fully represented themselves as pioneers of the West. At this meeting two were baptized, who had previously believed in the fullness of the gospel.
>
> During this week the Colesville branch, referred to in the latter part of the last revelation, and Sidney Rigdon, Sidney Gilbert and wife, and Elders Morley and Booth, arrived. I received [section 58, August 1831]. [*HC*, 1:190–191]

SECTION 58 • OUTLINE

➤ 58:1–5   The elders are to learn concerning themselves and the land of Missouri.

    a. Blessed are they who keep the commandments, whether in life or death, and are faithful in tribulation (v. 2).

    b. You cannot behold with your natural eye the glory and blessing that shall follow tribulation (vv. 3–4).

    c. Remember what I tell you, and receive what is to follow (v. 5).

➤ 58:6–12   You were sent that you might be obedient and prepared to bear testimony of things to come.

    a. Also, you might be honored in laying the foundation of the city, and bear record of the land of Zion (v. 7).

    b. Also, a feast of fat things prepared for the poor (v. 8).

    c. And a supper for the house of the Lord, and all nations shall be invited (v. 9).

    d. First the rich and the learned, the wise and the noble (v. 10).

    e. Afterwards, the poor, lame, blind, and deaf will come unto the marriage of the Lamb (v. 11).

    f. The Lord has spoken it from the mouth of the city (v. 12).

➤ 58:13–23   For this cause Edward Partridge was appointed his mission in this land.

    a. He must repent of unbelief and blindness lest he fall, and his mission will not be given again (vv. 15–16).

    b. He is to be a judge in Israel, and divide the lands unto God's children (v. 17).

    c. He is to judge by the testimony of the just, assisted by his counselors, according to the laws of the kingdom (v. 18).

    d. God's law shall be kept in the land (v. 19).

    e. Let no man think he is ruler, but let God rule him who judges (v. 20).

    f. Let no man break the laws of the land, if you keep the laws of God, there is no need to break the laws of the land (v. 21).

      g.   Be subject to the powers that be until he reigns whose right it is to reign (v. 22).

      h.   The laws received of God are the law of the church (v. 23).

➤ 58:24–33   This land is the residence of Edward Partridge, his counselors, and the keeper of the storehouse.

      a.   Bring their families as they counsel between themselves and me (v. 25).

      b.   It is not meet to be commanded in all things, the compelled is a slothful and not a wise servant (v. 26).

      c.   Men should be anxiously engaged and do many things of their free will (v. 27).

      d.   The power is in them wherein they are agents unto themselves (v. 28).

      e.   He that does nothing till commanded, is doubtful and slothful, is damned (v. 29).

      f.   The Lord will not hold him guiltless who does not obey (v. 30).

      g.   The Lord promises and fulfills (v. 31).

      h.   I command and men obey not, I revoke and they receive not the blessing (v. 32).

Text and Commentary

D&C 58:1–5 • When Will Zion Be Built Up in Her Glory?

1 Hearken, O ye elders of my church, and give ear to my word, and learn of me what I will concerning you, and also concerning this land unto which I have sent you.

2 For verily I say unto you, blessed is he that keepeth my commandments, whether in life or in death; and he that is faithful in tribulation, the reward of the same is greater in the kingdom of heaven.

3 Ye cannot behold with your natural eyes, for the present time, the design of your God concerning those things which shall come hereafter, and the glory which shall follow after much tribulation.

4 For after much tribulation come the blessings. Wherefore the day cometh that ye shall be crowned with much glory; the hour is not yet, but is nigh at hand.

5 Remember this, which I tell you before, that you may lay it to heart, and receive that which is to follow.

The Lord now answers the second question asked by the Prophet: "When will Zion be built up in her glory"? (v. 1). He prefaces the answer with the declaration that those who are faithful in tribulation, and keep the commandment, will receive the same greater reward whether it is built now or after their death (v. 2). The glory of Zion is beyond their ability to see with their natural eyes (v. 3). The answer to the question is: Zion will not be built up until after much tribulation, and after their lifetime, when they will be crowned with much glory (v. 4). They need to realize this, lay it to heart, and accept the tribulation that will follow in their lifetime (v. 5). It seems that collectively the elders did not understand the Lord's words.

D&C 58:6–12 • Three Purposes For Being in Zion Now

6 Behold, verily I say unto you, for this cause I have sent you-that you might be obedient, and that your hearts might be prepared to bear testimony of the things which are to come;

7 And also that you might be honored in laying the foundation, and in bearing record of the land upon which the Zion of God shall stand;

8 And also that a feast of fat things might be prepared for the poor; yea, a feast of fat things, of wine on the lees well refined, that the earth may know that the mouths of the prophets shall not fail;

9 Yea, a supper of the house of the Lord, well prepared, unto which all nations shall be invited.

10 First, the rich and the learned, the wise and the noble;

11 And after that cometh the day of my power; then shall the poor, the lame, and the blind, and the deaf, come in unto the marriage of the Lamb, and partake of the supper of the Lord, prepared for the great day to come.

12 Behold, I, the Lord, have spoken it.

The Lord's explanation of His three purposes for their being in Zion at this time was a further hint that Zion was not to be built up in this hour (v. 5 above). The first purpose was a test of their obedience, and that their hearts might be prepared to bear testimony of the future building of Zion (v. 6). This may be considered as two purposes, but counted as one here. The second purpose was to give these elders, who had already been tested by their coming to Missouri, the honor of laying the foundation of this city (v. 7). The foundation, in this context, was to mark the area of the city, including the buying, the dedication and consecration of the spot for the temple (see v. 57). Thus, they could bear record of the land upon which Zion would be built (v. 3). It would be much easier to bear record having been there and seen the sites.

The third purpose was probably not understood by many of the Saints then, or by few of them today. It was to prepare "a feast of fat things" for the poor "that the mouths of the prophets shall not fail" (v. 8). While many prophets had obviously foretold of the city of Zion, the one that included this purpose, at least in today's Bible, was Isaiah: "And in this mountain shall the LORD of hosts make unto all people a feast of fat things, a feast of wines on the lees, of fat things full of marrow, of wines on the lees well refined" (Isaiah 25:6). The feast of fat things was the law of consecration (see D&C 42:30–34; 78:3; 82:12). All nations were to be invited to this well prepared supper of the Lord (D&C 58:9), but the first to be invited were the Gentiles, "the rich and the learned" according to the world's standard (v. 10). The riches, of those among the Gentiles [scattered Israelites] who would embrace the gospel, were to be consecrated to the poor of the house of Israel (D&C 42:39). After the Gentile nations had all been invited to the Lord's supper, the invitation would be extended to the house of Israel. The Lamanites, the Jews, and the Ten Tribes are the nations of Israel, or the grafting back of the natural branches into their mother tree (see Jacob 5:60–63). These are represented as the poor, the lame, the blind and the deaf. The symbolism of their being physically impaired is possibly because their [spiritual] handicaps kept them from being first. They will also attend the marriage of the Lamb, as well as His supper (D&C 58:11). The marriage of the Lamb is the bridegroom [Christ] coming in the clouds to receive the bride [the Church] who has prepared herself for the wedding, or the Second Coming (see Revelation 19:7–9). The Lord had spoken (D&C 58:12), the elders were now responsible to understand when Zion would be built up by the Spirit.

D&C 58:13–23 • How to Accomplish the Three Purposes

13 And that the testimony might go forth from Zion, yea, from the mouth of the city of the heritage of God—

14 Yea, for this cause I have sent you hither, and have selected my servant Edward Partridge, and have appointed unto him his mission in this land.

15 But if he repent not of his sins, which are unbelief and blindness of heart, let him take heed lest he fall.

16 Behold his mission is given unto him, and it shall not be given again.

17 And whoso standeth in this mission is appointed to be a judge in Israel, like as it was in ancient days, to divide the lands of the heritage of God unto his children;

18 And to judge his people by the testimony of the just, and by the assistance of his counselors, according to the laws of the kingdom which are given by the prophets of God.

19 For verily I say unto you, my law shall be kept on this land.

20 Let no man think he is ruler; but let God rule him that judgeth, according to the counsel of his own will, or, in other words, him that counseleth or sitteth upon the judgment seat.

21 Let no man break the laws of the land, for he that keepeth the laws of God hath no need to break the laws of the land.

22 Wherefore, be subject to the powers that be, until he reigns whose right it is to reign, and subdues all enemies under his feet.

23 Behold, the laws which ye have received from my hand are the laws of the church, and in this light ye shall hold them forth. Behold, here is wisdom.

The first purpose was; He had brought His people here that the testimony might go forth from the mouth of the city that would become Zion (v. 13). Edward Partridge, or his successor if he did not repent, as the Bishop in Zion was to be the judge in Israel. This was Edward's last chance to correct his unbelief and blindness of heart (vv. 14–16). He perhaps did not understand that they were only to lay the foundation, the second purpose. The Bishop in Zion had two responsibilities, which were "like as it was in ancient times:" He was to divide the lands, or give stewardships, to the members as they entered into the law of consecration, the third purpose (v. 17). Secondly, he was to judge the people's worthiness according to the testimony of the just, or those who had proven their worthiness. He would be assisted by his counselors, who collectively must act according to the laws of the kingdom as given to the prophets (v. 18). The prophets would certainly include both ancient, e.g., Isaiah, and modern, e.g., Joseph Smith. "My law," being singular, must refer to the law of consecration that must be kept in this land of Missouri. When the gathered Saints return, they will be privileged to live this law (see D&C 51:15; 105:29).

The Lord cautioned that the leaders in Zion were not to consider themselves as rulers, but they should be ruled by God (D&C 58:20). However, no man was to break the laws of the land, since the two laws were not in conflict with each other (v. 21). The basis of the Twelfth Article of Faith comes from verse 22: "We believe in being subject to kings, presidents, rulers, and magistrates, in obeying, honoring, and sustaining the law." The laws of the church, given by God, are to be held forth, or advocated to others as we live by the law of common consent, or by the voice of the people (v. 23).

D&C 58:24–33 • The Lord Does Not Command in All Things

24 And now, as I spake concerning my servant Edward Partridge, this land is the land of his residence, and those whom he has appointed for his counselors; and also the land of the residence of him whom I have appointed to keep my storehouse;

25 Wherefore, let them bring their families to this land, as they shall counsel between themselves and me.

26 For behold, it is not meet that I should command in all things; for he that is compelled in all things, the same is a slothful and not a wise servant; wherefore he receiveth no reward.

27 Verily I say, men should be anxiously engaged in a good cause, and do many things of their own free will, and bring to pass much righteousness;

28 For the power is in them, wherein they are agents unto themselves. And inasmuch as men do good they shall in nowise lose their reward.

29 But he that doeth not anything until he is commanded, and

receiveth a commandment with doubtful heart, and keepeth it with slothfulness, the same is damned.

30 Who am I that made man, saith the Lord, that will hold him guiltless that obeys not my commandments?

31 Who am I, saith the Lord, that have promised and have not fulfilled?

32 I command and men obey not; I revoke and they receive not the blessing.

33 Then they say in their hearts: This is not the work of the Lord, for his promises are not fulfilled. But wo unto such, for their reward lurketh beneath, and not from above.

The Lord's program was to be initiated as soon as it was convenient (v. 24). He honors their agency by instructing them to "counsel between themselves and me" (v. 25), or to "study it out in your mind; then ask me if it be right' (D&C 9:8–9). The Lord further explained that He should not command in all things (v. 26). Alma also cautioned against being compelled to be humble (see Alma 32:13–16). The Lord expects us to use our own resources and reasoning power to make decisions (D&C 58:27), but He does expect us to verify those decisions with Him. Throughout the years, this writer has observed that these verses are often taken out of context and greatly misunderstood by some members of the Church. They justify their failure to consult the Lord on major decisions with the excuse that the Lord doesn't want to be bothered in matters that they have the ability to think through themselves, quoting verses 26 and 27 and disregarding verses 25 and 28. The power in them to be agents unto themselves is the power of the Spirit (see v. 38). They also have the light of Christ to enable them to do good or evil (see Moroni 7:12–16). This power is implied in "inasmuch as men do good they shall in nowise lose their reward" (D&C 58:28). The Lord is not pleased with those who do nothing but expect Him to, in robot style, tell them what to do. On the other hand, He wants his children to confirm their well-thought-out decisions with Him so as not to make a mistake. The Lord had earlier told Joseph Smith: "you cannot always tell the wicked from the righteous" (D&C 10:37). If the Prophet was unable to tell, then certainly we need to rely on the Lord for confirmation of our decisions.

The Lord repeats the warning to those who do nothing until com-

manded, but adds that commandments kept with doubtful heart and slothfulness is damned (D&C 58:29; 56:2). Again we note the meaning of the word "damned," to stop their progression. He also repeats man's accountability (D&C 58:30; D&C 56:14), and the command and revoke principle (vv. 31–32; 56:4). Those who fail to acknowledge the Lord's work receive the devils rewards, not God's (v. 33).

D&C 58:34–39 • The Spirit—the Power Within You

> 34 And now I give unto you further directions concerning this land.
>
> 35 It is wisdom in me that my servant Martin Harris should be an example unto the church, in laying his moneys before the bishop of the church.
>
> 36 And also, this is a law unto every man that cometh unto this land to receive an inheritance; and he shall do with his moneys according as the law directs.
>
> 37 And it is wisdom also that there should be lands purchased in Independence, for the place of the storehouse, and also for the house of the printing.
>
> 38 And other directions concerning my servant Martin Harris shall be given him of the Spirit, that he may receive his inheritance as seemeth him good;
>
> 39 And let him repent of his sins, for he seeketh the praise of the world.

In accordance with the law of consecration, Martin Harris was to set the example to every man in the Church by consecrating his money to the bishop. In further accordance with the law of consecration, land was to be purchased for the storehouse and the house of printing (v. 37). This money would come through the donations to the storehouse (see D&C 42:34–35). In spite of all the blessings and experiences that Martin Harris had received, he still could not receive an inheritance or stewardship in the Zion society until he repented (D&C 58:38–39).

D&C 58:40–43 • Repentance of Sins Defined

> 40 And also let my servant William W. Phelps stand in the office to which I have appointed him, and receive his inheritance in the land;
>
> 41 And also he hath need to repent, for I, the Lord, am not well

pleased with him, for he seeketh to excel, and he is not sufficiently meek before me.

42 Behold, he who has repented of his sins, the same is forgiven, and I, the Lord, remember them no more.

43 By this ye may know if a man repenteth of his sins—behold, he will confess them and forsake them.

Since W. W. Phelps also needed to repent, the Lord took the opportunity to enlarge upon the principle of repentance. Once more we have some who do not understand what the Lord revealed here. The Lord says he does not remember those sins for which a person has repented (v. 42). One interpretation taken from this verse is that as long as you can remember a sin, you have not been forgiven. However, there is a difference between "not remembering" and "forgetting." The Lord is not remembering means He does not keep it in the front of His mind, but in the back of His mind. He does not remember what we once did whenever we have some association with Him. But He has not forgotten it because if a person is forgiven, and sins again, the former sins return (D&C 82:7). How can the Lord return the sins, if He has forgotten what the sins were? The Lord leaves the sins in our minds so we will remember our pain and not sin again. Years after Alma had sinned, he recounted his sins to his son. He could remember the pains of the sins no more, but was filled with the joy of forgiveness (see Alma 36:19–20).

The way to know if repentance has taken place is if he has confessed to the proper authority, and has forsaken those sins (D&C 58:43). There are other steps of repentance, but these are the ones revealed here, and the essential ones needed to be recognized.

D&C 58:44–48 • When Will the Wilderness Blossom as a Rose?

44 And now, verily, I say concerning the residue of the elders of my church, the time has not yet come, for many years, for them to receive their inheritance in this land, except they desire it through the prayer of faith, only as it shall be appointed unto them of the Lord.

45 For, behold, they shall push the people together from the ends of the earth.

46 Wherefore, assemble yourselves together; and they who are not appointed to stay in this land, let them preach the gospel in the regions

round about; and after that let them return to their homes.

47 Let them preach by the way, and bear testimony of the truth in all places, and call upon the rich, the high and the low, and the poor to repent.

48 And let them build up churches, inasmuch as the inhabitants of the earth will repent.

The Lord now answers the first question asked by the Prophet Joseph when he beheld the degenerate conditions in Missouri: "When will the wilderness blossom as a rose?" The answer: "The time has not yet come for many years." There was a condition placed on the many years, "except they desire it through the prayer of faith," as appointed unto them by the Lord (D&C 58:44). It seems apparent today that He was speaking of the generations of elders to follow, but to that general present day residue of elders they probably thought it was to their generation. Again, another misunderstood revelation was the meaning of "Jacob shall flourish in the wilderness" (D&C 49:24). As hindsight now makes it obvious, the wilderness referred to was the wilderness of the Rockies where the Saints would be driven and eventually flourish. When the Prophet Joseph understood this concept, is not clear, but he knew it while in Nauvoo if not before.

The next verse also could also have been understood as future generations. The elders of the Church "shall push the people together from the ends of the earth" (v. 45). This movement was a blessing pronounced upon the head of Joseph's descendants by Moses:

15 And for the chief things of the ancient mountains, and for the precious things of the lasting hills,

16 And for the precious things of the earth and fulness thereof, and [for] the good will of him that dwelt in the bush: let [the blessing] come upon the head of Joseph, and upon the top of the head of him [that was] separated from his brethren.

17 His glory [is like] the firstling of his bullock, and his horns [are like] the horns of unicorns: with them he shall push the people together to the ends of the earth: and they [are] the ten thousands of Ephraim, and they [are] the thousands of Manasseh. [Deuteronomy 33:15–17]

The seed of Joseph was given the land of America by the Father, as proclaimed to the Nephites by the Savior when He visited them. "Ye are my disciples; and ye are a light unto this people, who are a remnant of the house of Joseph. And behold, this is the land of your inheritance; and the Father hath given it unto you." (3 Nephi 15:12–13).

Again through hindsight, we see the gathering of "the ten thousands of Ephraim, and the thousands of Manasseh" (Deuteronomy 33:17) was broader than Missouri. The present day elders, who were not to remain in Missouri, were to get at the task of preaching the gospel "in the regions round about" (D&C 58:46–47). They were also to "build up churches inasmuch as the inhabitants of the earth will repent" (v. 48). The "inhabitants of the earth" is another indication of the breadth of the work yet to come. As will be seen later (section 105), the Gentiles were to have the opportunity to be a part of building Zion in that day if they would respond to the gospel.

D&C 58:49–57 • Purchase Lands in Zion

49 And let there be an agent appointed by the voice of the church, unto the church in Ohio, to receive moneys to purchase lands in Zion.

50 And I give unto my servant Sidney Rigdon a commandment, that he shall write a description of the land of Zion, and a statement of the will of God, as it shall be made known by the Spirit unto him;

51 And an epistle and subscription, to be presented unto all the churches to obtain moneys, to be put into the hands of the bishop, of himself or the agent, as seemeth him good or as he shall direct, to purchase lands for an inheritance for the children of God.

52 For, behold, verily I say unto you, the Lord willeth that the disciples and the children of men should open their hearts, even to purchase this whole region of country, as soon as time will permit.

53 Behold, here is wisdom. Let them do this lest they receive none inheritance, save it be by the shedding of blood.

54 And again, inasmuch as there is land obtained, let there be workmen sent forth of all kinds unto this land, to labor for the saints of God.

55 Let all these things be done in order; and let the privileges of the lands be made known from time to time, by the bishop or the agent of the church.

56 And let the work of the gathering be not in haste, nor by flight; but let it be done as it shall be counseled by the elders of the church at

the conferences, according to the knowledge which they receive from time to time.

57 And let my servant Sidney Rigdon consecrate and dedicate this land, and the spot for the temple, unto the Lord.

The purposes of the elders present generation must also be fulfilled. An agent was to be appointed in Ohio "to receive moneys to purchase lands in Missouri" (v. 49; see D&C 57:4). Sidney Rigdon was to write a description of the land (v. 50; see 58:7). He was also to write an epistle and subscription to help churches obtain moneys to send to the bishop in Zion and purchase more lands (v. 51). Why the Lord wanted them to purchase as much land as possible to prevent the shedding of blood (vv. 52–53) will be explained in section 63 verse 29. The present generation was to do as much as possible at this time, as shown by the command to send all kinds of workmen to the area (v. 54). The work was to be done orderly, and the available opportunities be sufficiently advertised to the members (v. 55). Once more quoting scripture, this time the Prophet Isaiah, the Lord admonished them to not gather "in haste nor by flight" (Isaiah 52:12) as did the children of Israel had left Egypt under Moses. The extent and speed of the gathering was to be regulated by the elders of the Church as directed at the conferences of the Church (D&C 58:56). This process of instructions to the general membership has always been followed in these latter days. Sidney Rigdon was also to consecrate and dedicate the land, and the spot for the temple (v. 57). This he did, and the spot is marked and still visible today (see *HC*, 1:196)

D&C 58:58–65 • Preach the Gospel By the Way

58 And let a conference meeting be called; and after that let my servants Sidney Rigdon and Joseph Smith, Jun., return, and also Oliver Cowdery with them, to accomplish the residue of the work which I have appointed unto them in their own land, and the residue as shall be ruled by the conferences.

59 And let no man return from this land except he bear record by the way, of that which he knows and most assuredly believes.

60 Let that which has been bestowed upon Ziba Peterson be taken from him; and let him stand as a member in the church, and labor with his own hands, with the brethren, until he is sufficiently chastened for all his sins; for he confesseth them not, and he thinketh to hide them.

61 Let the residue of the elders of this church, who are coming to this land, some of whom are exceedingly blessed even above measure, also hold a conference upon this land.

62 And let my servant Edward Partridge direct the conference which shall be held by them.

63 And let them also return, preaching the gospel by the way, bearing record of the things which are revealed unto them.

64 For, verily, the sound must go forth from this place into all the world, and unto the uttermost parts of the earth—the gospel must be preached unto every creature, with signs following them that believe.

65 And behold the Son of Man cometh. Amen.

These directions again explain the importance of doing business in conferences by the voice of the people, repentance, and preaching the gospel to every creature as they go about their duties.

General Authority Quotes

—*The Prophet Joseph Smith* • D&C 57:3

I received by a heavenly vision, a commandment in June following [1831], to take a journey to the western boundaries of the state of Missouri, and there designate the very spot which was to be the central place for the commencement of the gathering together of those who embrace the fullness of the everlasting gospel. Accordingly I undertook the journey, with certain of my brethren, and after a long and tedious journey, suffering many privations and hardships, arrived in Jackson County, Missouri, and after viewing the country, seeking diligently at the hand of God, He manifested Himself unto us, and designated, to me and others, the very spot upon which he designed to commence the work of the gathering, and the upbuilding of an "holy city," which should be called Zion—Zion because it is a place of righteousness, and all who build thereon are to worship the true and living God. and all believe in one doctrine, even the doctrine of our Lord and Savior Jesus Christ: Thy watchman shall lift up the voice; with the voice together shall they sing: for they shall see eye to eye, when the Lord shall bring again Zion" (Isaiah 52:8). [*TPJS*, 79–80]

—*President Harold B. Lee* • D&C 58:22

Wherever you are, wherever you live, pray for the leaders of your country, for remember that they too hold in their hands all that you hold dear. Again I repeat the Lord's injunction (quotes D&C 58:22). [*THBL*, 361]

—*Elder Boyd K. Packer* • D&C 58:26–28

We have become very anxious over the amount of counseling that we seem to need in the Church. Our members are becoming dependent.

We must not set up a network of counseling services without at the same time emphasizing the principal of emotional self-reliance and individual independence.

If we lose our emotional and spiritual independence, our self-reliance, we can be weakened quite as much, perhaps even more, than when we become dependent materially.

If we are not careful, we can lose the power of individual revelation. What the Lord said to Oliver Cowdery, has meaning for all of us. (quotes D&C 9:8–9).

Spiritual independence and self-reliance is a sustaining power in the Church. If we rob the members of that how can they get revelation for themselves? How will they know there is a prophet of God? How can they get answers to prayers? How can they know for *sure* for themselves? [*That All May Be Edified*, 90]

—*President Howard W. Hunter* • D&C 58:26–30

The Lord requires obedience not because it is our duty nor because we fear him (quotes D&C 58:26–30).

We recognize that much good comes from individuals and organizations who reach out to remedy the ills of the world. We encourage you to follow the scriptural admonition to be anxiously engaged or actively involved in good causes in the Church and in your neighborhoods, communities, and even throughout the world (see D&C 58:27). Yet we also maintain that without taking Christ into your lives and accepting the gospel, with its saving ordinances and covenants, people will not reach their true potential in this life or in the hereafter. [*THWH*, 269]

—President Ezra Taft Benson • D&C 58:41

Humility responds to God's will—to the fear of his judgments and to the needs of those around us. To the proud, the applause of the world rings in their ears; to the humble, the applause of heaven warms their heart. Someone has said, "Pride gets no pleasure out of having something, only out of having more of it than the next man." Of one brother, the Lord said, [quotes D&C 58:41]. [*TETB*, 436]

—President J. Reuben Clark • D&C 58:43

I would like to point out that to me there is a great difference between confession and admission, after transgression is proved. I doubt much the efficacy of an admission as a confession, [after quoting 58:43]. [CR, April 1950, 166]

—Elder Harold B. Lee • D&C 58:43

And then you immediately say, "To whom does he confess?" Well, it depends on the sin. If it is a sin that affects no one but yourself, and known to no other one but you and God, then your confession should be to Him in secret. If it is something where you injure some other person, then your confession would be to that person whom you have injured. If you have offended the community—you burned the meeting house down, you do something to a whole group—then your confession would be to the group. But if it affects your rights to the privileges in the Church, then that sin should be confessed to the judge in Israel, the bishop of the ward, who has the instruction to hear in secret and forgive the penalty in secret, or do as the Spirit of his higher office shall prompt him to do. [*THBL*, 13–14]

Chapter Twenty-Six

Keep Unspotted from the World

D&C 59

*H*istorical Setting:

On the 7th [August, 1831] I attended the funeral of Polly Knight, wife of Joseph Knight, Sen. This was the first death in the Church in this land, and I can say a worthy member sleeps in Jesus till the resurrection. [*HC*, 1:199]

[Polly Knight] was very ill during her journey from Kirtland to Missouri. "Yet" says her son, she would not consent to stop traveling: her only, or her greatest desire was to set her feet upon the land of Zion, and to have her body interred in the land. [fn *HC*, 1:199]

INTRODUCTION

How do you spell Holy Day in one six letter word? Answer: Sabbath or Sunday. How do many people spell Holy Day in one seven letter word? Answer: Holiday! Americans have become very poor spellers.

SECTION 59 • OUTLINE

➤ 59:1–4   Blessed are those who come to the land of Missouri with an eye single to the glory of God.

    a. Those that live shall inherit the earth, and those who die shall receive a crown in the mansions of my Father (v. 2).

    b. Blessed are those who have obeyed Christ's gospel, they shall receive the good things of the earth (v. 3).

c. They shall be crowned with blessings from above, commandments not a few, and revelations in their time (v. 4).

➤ 59:5–8 They are commanded to love God with all their heart, might, mind, and strength, and in the name of Christ serve him.

a. Thou shalt love thy neighbor as thyself, and not steal, commit adultery, nor kill, nor do anything like unto it (v. 6).

b. Thank the Lord in all things (v. 7).

c. Offer a sacrifice of a broken heart and a contrite spirit (v. 8).

➤ 59:9–14 To more fully keep thyself unspotted from the world, go to the house of prayer and offer up thy sacraments on my holy day.

a. Rest from your labors, and pay your devotions to the Most High (v. 10).

b. Thy vows shall be offered up in righteousness on all days and times (v. 11).

c. On the Lord's day, offer thine oblations, and sacraments, and confess thy sins to thy brethren before the Lord (v. 12).

d. Prepare thy food with singleness of heart, that thy fasting may be perfect (v. 13).

e. This is fasting and prayer, or rejoicing and prayer (v. 14).

➤ 59:15–20 Do these things with thanksgiving and cheerful hearts, not with much laughter.

a. The fullness of earth is yours; beasts, fowls, all that climbs, and walks (v. 16).

b. The herb and good things of the earth, for food, raiment, or other needs (v. 17).

c. All things of the earth are made for the benefit and use of man (v. 18).

d. Food, raiment, taste, and smell, to strength the body and enliven the soul (v. 19).

e. It pleases God to use these things with judgment, not to excess or by extortion.

➤ 59:21–24 It offends God if they confess not his hand in all things, and obey not his commandments.

    a.   This is according the law and the prophets (v. 22).

    b.   He that does these things shall have peace in this life, and eternal life in the world to come (v. 23).

    c.   The Lord has spoken, the Spirit bears record (v. 24).

TEXT AND COMMENTARY

D&C 59:1–4 • Whose Feet Stand Upon the Land of Zion

1 Behold, blessed, saith the Lord, are they who have come up unto this land with an eye single to my glory, according to my commandments.

2 For those that live shall inherit the earth, and those that die shall rest from all their labors, and their works shall follow them; and they shall receive a crown in the mansions of my Father, which I have prepared for them.

3 Yea, blessed are they whose feet stand upon the land of Zion, who have obeyed my gospel; for they shall receive for their reward the good things of the earth, and it shall bring forth in its strength.

4 And they shall also be crowned with blessings from above, yea, and with commandments not a few, and with revelations in their time—they that are faithful and diligent before me.

These verses apparently refer to Polly Knight, the faithful wife to Joseph Knight Sr. and the faithful daughter of her Father in Heaven; her funeral had just been held when this revelation was given. Her eye was certainly single to God's glory (v. 1). She would now rest from her earthly labors, and her sickness that she had so patiently endured in traveling to Zion. She was now to receive a crown in the mansions of her Father that had been prepared for her (v. 2). As a comfort to His beloved apostles, Jesus had promised, shortly before His death, to go and prepare a place for them in the mansions of his Father (see John 14:1–4). The Prophet Joseph gave a plainer meaning to this promise: "It should be—'In my Father's kingdom are many kingdoms,' in order that ye may be heirs of God, and joint heirs with me" (*TPJS*, 366).

Sister Knight's desire to set her foot on the soil of Zion had been achieved. She had obeyed the gospel. Those who remained in Zion would have the physical blessings of the earth; the good things produced through the strength of the earth's elements (D&C 59:3). If faithful and diligent, they would also receive great spiritual blessings of further commandments and revelations as they were needed and appropriate (v. 4). These same blessings are promised to us on the same conditions.

D&C 59:5–8 • Love the Lord God and Your Neighbor

5 Wherefore, I give unto them a commandment, saying thus: Thou shalt love the Lord thy God with all thy heart, with all thy might, mind, and strength; and in the name of Jesus Christ thou shalt serve him.

6 Thou shalt love thy neighbor as thyself. Thou shalt not steal; neither commit adultery, nor kill, nor do anything like unto it.

7 Thou shalt thank the Lord thy God in all things.

8 Thou shalt offer a sacrifice unto the Lord thy God in righteousness, even that of a broken heart and a contrite spirit.

The above commandments were part of the ones promised above (v. 4). Although they were previously given to other dispensations, they were of special significance to the inhabitants of Zion. Those who came to this land, and were to lay the foundation of the city of Zion, must be a pure people, "of one heart and one mind, and [dwell] in righteousness, and there [be] no poor among them" (Moses 7:18).

The first commandment of the Ten Commandments was to love God (D&C 59:5; see Exodus 20:3; Deuteronomy 10:12; Matthew 22:36–38). The word heart is used to represent the innermost character of man. To love God with all thy heart is to submit your spirit to do His will. It is to follow what He tells us to do by revelation in our heart (see D&C 8:2). To love Him with our might is to put all of your physical efforts towards doing His will as directed by the scriptures. "If you love me, keep my commandments" (John 14:15). To love Him with all of your mind is to put all your intellectual efforts towards finding out His will for you. "Study it out in your mind, and then you must ask me if it be right" (D&C 9:8). To love Him with all of your strength is to combine and coordinate all of your spiritual, physical, and intellectual powers towards serving Him. All these efforts must be in the name of Jesus Christ who has been delegated the authority and the power to carry out the plan of salvation. "This is My Beloved Son. Hear Him!" (JS—H 1:17).

The second commandment is like unto the first: "Thou shalt love thy neighbor as thyself" (D&C 59:6, Matthew 22:37). To steal or commit adultery is to take something that does not belong to you. No one likes to have something the prize taken from then. "Therefore all things whatsoever ye would that men should do to you, do ye even so to them: for this is the law and the prophets" (Matthew 7:12). For additional things like unto stealing and adultery, see the quote from Ezra Taft Benson, in the end of the chapter.

All that we have we owe to the Lord our God. Our eternal indebtedness is eternal and never ends. As King Benjamin taught:

> 23 And now, in the first place, he hath created you, and granted unto you your lives, for which ye are indebted unto him.
>
> 24 And secondly, he doth require that ye should do as he hath commanded you; for which if ye do, he doth immediately bless you; and therefore he hath paid you. And ye are still indebted unto him, and are, and will be, forever and ever; therefore, of what have ye to boast? [Mosiah 2:23–24]

We certainly need to thank Him (D&C 59:7). The way we thank Him is to offer a sacrifice in righteousness (v. 8). We willingly pay our tithing, or take the time to home teach. To sacrifice is to willingly give up one thing for something else. We give up our favorite TV program to comfort a grieving Church member or friend. We give up a physical craving or appetite for our bodily or moral cleanness. To offer a broken heart to God is to give up the pride of one's heart, and recognize that one's contributed to the inexplicable suffering of Jesus Christ in the Garden of Gethsemane. One's heart is broken because of what one caused Him to suffer, and for what He did for us. To offer a contrite spirit is to give up the arrogance of self-conceit, and recognize that the source of all intelligence is Jesus Christ (see D&C 88:11–12). One desires to absorb some of that intelligence into one's life.

D&C 59:9–14 • Go to the House of Prayer On My Holy Day

> 9 And that thou mayest more fully keep thyself unspotted from the world, thou shalt go to the house of prayer and offer up thy sacraments upon my holy day;

10 For verily this is a day appointed unto you to rest from your labors, and to pay thy devotions unto the Most High;

11 Nevertheless thy vows shall be offered up in righteousness on all days and at all times;

12 But remember that on this, the Lord's day, thou shalt offer thine oblations and thy sacraments unto the Most High, confessing thy sins unto thy brethren, and before the Lord.

13 And on this day thou shalt do none other thing, only let thy food be prepared with singleness of heart that thy fasting may be perfect, or, in other words, that thy joy may be full.

14 Verily, this is fasting and prayer, or in other words, rejoicing and prayer.

Once a year we commemorate one day to honor each of our mortal parents, our earthly mother and our earthly father. We rightfully honor them with accolades and presents. However, each week has one day set apart to honor our Father in Heaven. The law of Moses set up many things that we could not do on this holy day, and the rabbis added their interpretations of what could not be done. In the Christian world, the list of don'ts is often further multiplied. Among the Church members, we also have lists, or justifications, for what is not appropriate for the Sabbath. In this revelation, the Lord gives us a positive list of what we should do. He does not mention what we should not do. Furthermore, the Lord gives us presents, or blessings for keeping the Sabbath, instead of our giving Him gifts, as the world does to honor their mothers and fathers.

Our first present of the Sabbath is "to more fully keep thyself unspotted from the world" (v. 9). This statement implies that we are, or should be, unspotted from the world. Jesus told His apostles that He had "overcome the world" (John 16:33). The Savior reaffirmed this accomplishment to our dispensation (see D&C 50:41). He also warned us against being overcome by the world (D&C 50:8), and commands us to "forsake the world" (D&C 53:2). How do we forsake the world and overcome it? The New Testament Apostle John answers this question: "For whatsoever is born of God overcometh the world: and this is the victory that overcometh the world, [even] our faith. Who is he that overcometh the world, but he that believeth that Jesus is the Son of God?"

(1 John 5:4–5). The Sabbath day is to help those who have been born again to keep their unspotted condition and proceed towards sanctification (see D&C 84:23). Of course those who have not been born again are helped towards their rebirth by keeping the Sabbath day commandments.

The list of what to do on the Sabbath day begins with "thou shalt go to the house of prayer and offer up our sacraments [covenants]" (D&C 59:9). We are expected to go to our sacrament meeting, and secondly, renew our covenants by partaking the sacrament.

The third item to do on the Lord's day is to rest from our labors (v. 10). However, we are to do the Lord's work instead of sleeping, or doing our own projects and desires. The rest of the Lord "is the fullness of his glory." The Sabbath is to prepare ourselves to come into his presence when that time comes (see D&C 84:23–24). We are also to pay our devotions unto the Most High (D&C 59:10). We pay our devotions, or worship Him, through prayer, meditation, and music (see D&C 25:12). As we are instructed and edified, we meditate on how we are following the Lord's commandments (see D&C 43:8). The Lord takes this opportunity to remind His Saints that religion is not a one-day-a-week ritual, as exemplified by the apostate Zoramites (see Alma 31:12–23), but that we should offer up our vows "in righteousness on all days and at all times" (D&C 59:11).

On the Lord's day "thou shalt offer thine oblations" (v. 12). As defined in the dictionary, an oblation is a religious offering. The sacraments probably represent our offering of time and talents to the service of God, and others of His children (v. 12). Wherefore, we are to pay our tithes and offerings, and do other church callings and service on this day. Confessing our sins unto our brethren, and before the Lord (v. 12) is probably not a reference to our present day fast and testimony meetings. While it may include individual consulting, it is not to replace our meeting with the bishop as a condition of repentance spoken of in the last chapter. The confessions to other members are general statements of humility, or acknowledgments of our imperfections, one to another as we carry out our duties on the Sabbath. It is to assure our brothers and sisters in the gospel, that we are also striving to overcome our weaknesses, and not setting ourselves up as examples to follow as we teach the principles of perfection.

To do "none other thing" (v. 13) is a commandment to devote the whole day to doing what the Lord would want done. We may visit the lonely, our families, friends, or whomever the Spirit may direct us to visit. It is not to just attend our required meetings and then pursue our own pleasures. The Prophet Isaiah summarized it beautifully: "If thou turn away thy foot from the Sabbath, [from] doing thy pleasure on my holy day; and call the Sabbath a delight, the holy of the LORD, honourable; and shalt honour him, not doing thine own ways, nor finding thine own pleasure, nor speaking [thine own] words" (Isaiah 58:13).

Our food should be "prepared with singleness of heart that our fasting may be perfect" (v. 13) is saying that food should be a secondary objective, not the primary one for the Sabbath. While we are doing the Lord's work, we should be fully focused on what we are doing, and not about what or when we will eat. Food may be prepared the day before, or selected on the basis of not requiring a lot of Sabbath time to prepare. As suggested above, the Sabbath is a good time for family to be together if it does not interfere with our Church callings. Our joy of service in the Church will be full when we do it for the right purpose, or with all our heart. We rejoice in what we were able to do for others on the Sabbath, and yet were able to go to the house of prayer for our personal worship and devotion. This is in keeping with loving our God, and loving our neighbors as ourselves (vv. 5–6). This is "rejoicing and prayer" (v. 14).

D&C 59:15–20 • All Things For the Benefit and Use of Man

15 And inasmuch as ye do these things with thanksgiving, with cheerful hearts and countenances, not with much laughter, for this is sin, but with a glad heart and a cheerful countenance—

16 Verily I say, that inasmuch as ye do this, the fulness of the earth is yours, the beasts of the field and the fowls of the air, and that which climbeth upon the trees and walketh upon the earth;

17 Yea, and the herb, and the good things which come of the earth, whether for food or for raiment, or for houses, or for barns, or for orchards, or for gardens, or for vineyards;

18 Yea, all things which come of the earth, in the season thereof, are made for the benefit and the use of man, both to please the eye and to gladden the heart;

19 Yea, for food and for raiment, for taste and for smell, to strengthen the body and to enliven the soul.

20 And it pleaseth God that he hath given all these things unto man; for unto this end were they made to be used, with judgment, not to excess, neither by extortion.

As stated above, the Sabbath was designed by God to bless His children for keeping it holy. It is the spiritual foundation of a Zion society. Many of these blessings are enumerated here. We are to keep the Sabbath willfully and cheerfully, with a glad heart [thanksgiving] and cheerful countenance [rejoicing] (v. 15). We should not feel compelled, nor be slothful (see D&C 58:20). The Lord made the earth for the benefit of His children (see 1 Nephi 17:36). There are conditions upon which the blessings of this earth are given. By keeping the Sabbath, the fulness of the earth is promised to its inhabitants, and especially to his people in Zion. Where "much is given much is required" (D&C 82:3). The fullness of the earth includes all of its living creatures, and all the good things that come from the earth (D&C 59:16–17). They may be used for food and clothing [raiment], and for their personal buildings and grounds (v. 17). The seasons of the earth were designed to produce a variety of foods and clothes to suit those times, that man could use and strengthen his body. They were also intended to gladden the heart, or beautify themselves, their homes, their environment, and thus enliven the soul (vv. 18–19).

Again the Lord admonishes the members to use judgment in their use of the things of the earth, and warns of excessive use and misuse of them (v. 20; see 49:21). Men will be accountable for how they use the things the Lord has provided. An appropriate hymn to acknowledge this blessing is: "For the Beauty of the Earth" (*Hymns of The Church of Jesus Christ of Latter-day Saints*, 92).

D&C 59:21–24 • Confess the Lord's Hand In All Things

21 And in nothing doth man offend God, or against none is his wrath kindled, save those who confess not his hand in all things, and obey not his commandments.

22 Behold, this is according to the law and the prophets; wherefore, trouble me no more concerning this matter.

23 But learn that he who doeth the works of righteousness shall

receive his reward, even peace in this world, and eternal life in the world to come.

24 I, the Lord, have spoken it, and the Spirit beareth record. Amen.

The Lord wants man to recognize His hand in all things (v. 21) so that man knows where to turn to obtain His wants, needs, and desires. It is the same concept of man being less than the earth. The earth obeys God, but man often does not obey Him (see Helaman 12:3–22). Therefore, man is not blessed. "There is a law, irrevocably decreed in heaven before the foundations of this world, upon which all blessings are predicated—And when we obtain any blessing from God, it is by obedience to that law upon which it is predicated" (D&C 130:21). God wants men to obey the Sabbath, and other laws, so that He can bring them to eternal life. This doctrine was originally in the law of Moses, and taught by the Old Testament prophet Amos and others. Thus, it was according to the law and the prophets (D&C 59:22; see Moses 1:39; Amos 4:7–13; Haggai 2:17), and also in the Book of Mormon (Helaman 12:23–24). There are other blessings; peace in this life, and eternal life in the world to come (D&C 59:23). We cannot serve God, and Mammon (Matthew 6:24; 3 Nephi 13:24). The choice of keeping the Sabbath or being overcome by the world is ours.

Before moving on, a word about the correct day to observe the Sabbath seems appropriate. Throughout the Old Testament, the seventh day of the week, or today's Saturday was observed as the holy day. The Christian world has observed Sunday as the Sabbath day since the resurrection of Christ occurred on the first day of the week (see Matthew 28:1), and apparently observed by the Apostles after that time (see Acts 20:7). Thus it commemorated the glorious resurrection as a holy day. Furthermore, the revelation which we have just reviewed (D&C 59) was given on Sunday, August 7, 1831. This is an indirect confirmation of the Christian day observance of the Sabbath on Sunday. There has been no direct revelation in this dispensation to worship on any other day.

General Authority Quotes

—President Ezra Taft Benson • D&C 59:6, 9

[A priesthood holder] will not commit adultery "nor do anything like unto it" (D&C 59:6). This means fornication, homosexual behavior, self abuse, child molestation, or any other sexual perversion. This means that a young man will honor young women and treat them with respect. He would never do anything that would deprive them of that, which in Mormon's words, is "most dear and precious above all things, which is virtue and chastity" (Moroni 9:9).

Virtue is akin to holiness, an attribute of godliness. A priesthood holder should actively seek for that which is virtuous and lovely and not for that which is debasing or sordid [dirty, filthy]. Virtue will "garnish [his] thoughts unceasingly (D&C 121:45). How can any man indulge himself in the evils of pornography, profanity, or vulgarity and consider himself totally virtuous? [CR, October 1986, 60]

The purpose of the Sabbath is for spiritual uplift, for a renewal of our covenants, for worship, for rest, for prayer. It is for the purpose of feeding the spirit, that we may keep ourselves unspotted from the world by obeying God's command (D&C 59:9). [*TETB*, 438]

—*Elder Harold B. Lee* • D&C 59:9

For Latter-day Saints, to offer up "sacraments" in the house of prayer as the Lord commands (see D&C 59:9) means for you to present your devotions before the Lord in the form of songs of praise, prayers and thanksgiving, testimonies, and the partaking of the sacrament and the study of the word of God. In its most widely accepted usage it means for you to stand for any sacred right or ceremony whereby you affirm your allegiance to your Heavenly Father and His Son. [*THBL*, 209–10]

Any dating you do on the Lord's day should be done with a clear understanding of the kind of activities that would be in harmony with what the Lord has commanded. . . .

Therefore, make your dates on the Sabbath, if you desire to associate together on that day, to include faithful attendance at Sunday School and sacrament meeting. Make it a day to become acquainted with each other's family in the home.

Now you might well ask: Why is the proper observance of the Sabbath of importance in dating? The Lord answers in one terse statement: "That thou mayest more fully keep thyself unspotted from the world" (D&C 59:9). Don't trade a soul full of spiritual strength which might be yours to help you resist temptation with which you may be daily confronted for a thimble full of worldly pleasure in which you might otherwise indulge. [*THBL*, 211–212]

—*Elder Howard W. Hunter* • D&C 59:9–11

Are we entitled to the blessings of the Lord as a nation, communities, families, or individuals if we fail to keep his commandments? To know God, one must know his laws. To receive the blessings of God, one must keep his laws. I pray that we may come to observe the Sabbath day and to keep it holy.

There are wide areas of our society from which the spirit of prayer and reverence and worship has vanished. Men and woman in many circles are clever, interesting or brilliant, but they lack one crucial element in a complete life. They do not look up. They do not offer vows in righteousness (see D&C 59:11). . . . Their conversation sparkles, but it is not sacred. Their talk is witty, but it is not wise. Whether it be in the office, the locker room, or the laboratory, they have come too far down the scale of dignity who display their own limited powers and then find it necessary to blaspheme those unlimited powers that come from above.

Unfortunately we sometimes find this lack of reverence even within the Church. Occasionally we visit too loudly, enter and leave meetings too disrespectfully in what should be an hour of prayer and purifying worship. Reverence is the atmosphere of heaven. [*THWH*, 103]

—*President Gordon B. Hinckley* • D&C 59:13

The Lord wrote concerning the sanctity of the Sabbath day when His finger touched the tablets of stone on Sinai: Keep the Sabbath day holy. And that commandment has been reiterated in modern times as set forth in the fifty-ninth section of the Doctrine and Covenants. Let us be a Sabbath-keeping people. Now I do not want to be prudish. I do not want you to lock your children in the house and read the Bible all afternoon to them. Be wise. Be careful. But make that day a day when you can sit down with your families and talk about sacred and good things. "Keep the Sabbath holy," saith

the Lord to all people and particularly to this people. [*TGBH*, 559–60]

—President Spencer W. Kimball • D&C 59:13

I would again urge upon all Saints everywhere a more strict observance of the Sabbath day. The Lord's holy day is fast losing its sacred significance throughout the world, at least our world. More and more, man destroys the Sabbath's sacred purposes in pursuit of wealth, pleasure, recreation, and the worship of false and material gods. We continue to urge all Saints and Godfearing people everywhere to observe the Sabbath day and keep it holy. Businesses will not be open on the Sabbath day if they are not patronized on that holy day. The same is true of resorts, sporting events, and recreation areas of all kinds. Pursuit of the mighty dollar is winning, it seems, over the Lord's commandment, "Keep my Sabbaths, and reverence my sanctuary." [CR, October 1978, 5]

Chapter Twenty-Seven

It Matters Not Unto Me

Sections 60; 61; 62

Historical Setting:

On the 8th (August 1831), as there had been some inquiry among the Elders what they were to do, I received [section 60]. [*HC,* 1:201]

INTRODUCTION

The Prophet Joseph Smith declared: "After all that has been said, the greatest and the most important duty is to preach the Gospel (*TPJS,* 113). The importance of missionary work is exemplified to the elders as they are traveling. The Lord said many times: "It mattereth not to me" what you do, or where you go, or how you go, as long as you preach the gospel as you are doing or going. We will see the Lord's priority upon the work as we review these chapters.

SECTION 60 • OUTLINE

➣ 60:1–4 The Lord is pleased with the elders who are returning to Kirtland.

    a. He is not pleased when they don't open their mouths and hide their talents (v. 2).

    b. If they are not more faithful, their talents shall be taken away (v. 3).

    c. When the Lord makes up his jewels, all men shall know the power of God (v. 4).

➤ 60:5–11   Those returning are to make or buy a craft and go speedily to St. Louis.

     a.   Joseph, Sidney and Oliver are to journey on to Cincinnati (v. 6).

     b.   In Cincinnati declare my word without wrath or doubting (v. 7).

     c.   The residue go two by two and preach to the congregations of the wicked (v. 8)

     d.   The intent for their being sent was to preach the gospel (v. 9)

     e.   Edward Partridge is to impart money to those commanded to return (v. 10).

     f.   Those able are to return the money by way of the agent (v. 11).

     g.   He that is not able is not required to return the money (v. 11).

➤ 60:12–17   The residue of the elders are to preach the gospel to the wicked.

     a.   They shall not idle away their time nor bury their talents (v. 13).

     b.   In Zion, proclaim the word among the wicked, not in haste or strife (v. 14).

     c.   Shake the dust off thy feet in secret against those who do not receive you (v. 15).

     d.   Wash your feet as a testimony against them in the day of judgment (v. 15).

     e.   This is the intent and will of him who sent you (v. 17).

     f.   By Joseph's mouth, it shall be made known about Sidney and Oliver (v. 18).

TEXT AND COMMENTARY

D&C 60:1–4 • They Will Not Open Their Mouths

1 Behold, thus saith the Lord unto the elders of his church, who are to return speedily to the land from whence they came: Behold, it pleaseth me, that you have come up hither;

2 But with some I am not well pleased, for they will not open their

mouths, but they hide the talent which I have given unto them, because of the fear of man. Wo unto such, for mine anger is kindled against them.

3 And it shall come to pass, if they are not more faithful unto me, it shall be taken away, even that which they have.

4 For I, the Lord, rule in the heavens above, and among the armies of the earth; and in the day when I shall make up my jewels, all men shall know what it is that bespeaketh the power of God.

The elders addressed are to return to their homes in the Kirtland area (v. 1). The Lord was pleased that they had come to Missouri, but not pleased with some who had been reluctant to preach the gospel as they traveled. They had not opened their mouths to the people they met, and used their talents to inform them of the restoration. They apparently feared that they might be rejected or ridiculed for their beliefs (v. 2). The Lord's warning that they might have their talents taken away (v. 3) was a principle of the Lord. The Prophet Isaiah warned: "For behold, thus saith the Lord God: I will give unto the children of men line upon line, precept upon precept, here a little and there a little; and blessed are those who hearken unto my precepts, and lend an ear unto my counsel, for they shall learn wisdom; for unto him that receiveth I will give more; and from them that shall say, We have enough, from them shall be taken away even that which they have" (2 Nephi 28:30).[41] The Lord's jewels (D&C 60:4) are those who reflect the light of His gospel by word and by example with His power. The biblical reference for this concept is Malachi 3:17, and is also quoted in 3 Nephi 24:17 (see also D&C 101:3).

D&C 60:5–11 • Let there Be a Craft Made or Bought

5 But, verily, I will speak unto you concerning your journey unto the land from whence you came. Let there be a craft made, or bought, as seemeth you good, it mattereth not unto me, and take your journey speedily for the place which is called St. Louis.

6 And from thence let my servants, Sidney Rigdon, Joseph Smith, Jun., and Oliver Cowdery, take their journey for Cincinnati;

7 And in this place let them lift up their voice and declare my word

---

[41] While the reference used here is 2 Nephi, it is obviously a quote from the plates of brass text of Isaiah 28:13, before plain and precious parts were taken away (see 1 Nephi 13:24–29).

with loud voices, without wrath or doubting, lifting up holy hands upon them. For I am able to make you holy, and your sins are forgiven you.

8 And let the residue take their journey from St. Louis, two by two, and preach the word, not in haste, among the congregations of the wicked, until they return to the churches from whence they came.

9 And all this for the good of the churches; for this intent have I sent them.

10 And let my servant Edward Partridge impart of the money which I have given him, a portion unto mine elders who are commanded to return;

11 And he that is able, let him return it by the way of the agent; and he that is not, of him it is not required.

The Lord now lets the elders apply what He had taught them in section 58 verses 27–28; to make choices as they are directed by the Spirit. They can make a boat (a "craft") to get to St. Louis, or buy one (D&C 60:5). Why Sidney, Joseph, and Oliver are to go to Cincinnati is to preach the gospel (vv. 6–7), the elders' "greatest and most important duty" (*TPJS*, 113). The congregations of the wicked, to whom the St Louis bound elders are to go, is later defined as "the inhabitants of the earth" (D&C 62:5). In a later revelation, the Lord declares that the inhabitants of the whole world "are under the bondage of sin . . . because they come not unto me" (D&C 84:49–50). In other words, they have not been baptized for the remission of sins (see 3 Nephi 21:6; 27:20).

The churches "from whence they came" (D&C 62:8) are the branches of the churches around the Kirtland area. How their missionary work will be for the good of those churches (v. 9) is probably the experiences they will have and report to their fellow members. These reports will bolster and build the members testimonies. When the missionaries, in our day, report their missionary experiences, it has the same effect. Another good outcome could be, it would swell their memberships.

Bishop Partridge imparting money to the elders (v. 10) is an example of the storehouse money being used "for the building up of the New Jerusalem" (D&C 42:34–35). The return of the money by those who are able to do so is an example of "more than is necessary for their support" being consecrated to the bishop (D&C 42:33). Those who are not able are not required to return the money is also an example of the law of consecration; "the same is worthy of his hire" (D&C 70:12).

D&C 60:12–17 • Do Not Idle Away Thy Time

12 And now I speak of the residue who are to come unto this land.

13 Behold, they have been sent to preach my gospel among the congregations of the wicked; wherefore, I give unto them a commandment, thus: Thou shalt not idle away thy time, neither shalt thou bury thy talent that it may not be known.

14 And after thou hast come up unto the land of Zion, and hast proclaimed my word, thou shalt speedily return, proclaiming my word among the congregations of the wicked, not in haste, neither in wrath nor with strife.

15 And shake off the dust of thy feet against those who receive thee not, not in their presence, lest thou provoke them, but in secret; and wash thy feet, as a testimony against them in the day of judgment.

16 Behold, this is sufficient for you, and the will of him who hath sent you.

17 And by the mouth of my servant Joseph Smith, Jun., it shall be made known concerning Sidney Rigdon and Oliver Cowdery. The residue hereafter. Even so. Amen.

The elders who are yet to come to the land of Zion are also to preach the gospel to the congregations of the wicked. Their time and their talents should be devoted to the work (v. 13). They will have the same responsibility on their return to the Kirtland area, and should do it thoroughly, in love, and not be argumentative (v. 14). The New Testament practice of dusting the feet (Matthew 10:14) against those who reject their message was to be followed, but in secret (D&C 60:15). Its secrecy was probably an act of mercy so that those who reject the message might respond when a later opportunity was given. The washing of feet was obviously also done in secret, but the person would be accountable for their rejection "in the day of judgment." The same mercy could also come to them if they later responded to the gospel. The Lord's explanation being "sufficient for you" (v. 16) suggests the practice could be altered later. The conclusion of the revelation shows that Joseph Smith was still their appointed leader, and that the Church was to follow him (v. 17).

H istorical Setting—Section 61:

On the 9th [August 1831], in company with ten Elders, I left Independence landing for Kirtland. We started down the river in canoes, and went the first day as far as Fort Osage, where we had an excellent wild turkey for supper. Nothing very important occurred till the third day, when many of the dangers so common upon the western waters, manifested themselves; and after we had encamped upon the bank of the river, at McIlwaines Bend, Brother Phelps, in open vision by daylight, saw the destroyer in his most horrible power, ride upon the face of the waters; others heard the noise, but saw no vision. The next morning after prayer, I received [section 61]. [*HC*, 1:202–203]

SECTION 61 • OUTLINE

➤ 61:1–6   Alpha and Omega speaks to the elders of the church and forgives their sins.

a.   It is not needful for the whole company to move swiftly on the waters while inhabitants on either side are perishing in unbelief (v. 3).

b.   They are to bear record of the many dangers on the waters (v. 4).

c.   Many destructions are decreed upon the waters, especially these (v. 5).

d.   All flesh is in his hands and the faithful will not perish by water (v. 6).

➤ 61:7–13   It is expedient that Sidney Gilbert and W. W. Phelps be in haste.

a.   They should not depart until they were chastened for all their sins (v. 8).

b.   Depart now with their former company and fill their mission (v. 9).

c.   As they are faithful, they shall be preserved (v. 10).

d.   Let the residue take what is needful for clothing (v. 11).

e.   Let Sidney Gilbert take what is not needful as you shall agree (v. 12).

f.   For your good I command you and will reason with you (v. 13).

➤ 61:14–22   In the beginning, the Lord blessed the waters, in the last days he cursed them.

    a.   The days will come that no flesh shall be safe on the waters (v. 15).

    b.   None shall be safe to go up to the land of Zion upon the waters except the upright in heart (v. 16).

    c.   In the beginning the land was cursed, in the last days it shall be blessed for the use of the Saints (v. 17).

    d.   Forewarn thy brethren that they journey not by water (v. 18).

    e.   The destroyer rides upon the water, and I revoke not the decree (v. 19).

    f.   I was angry with you yesterday, but mine anger is turned away (v. 20).

    g.   The Lord again commanded some to take their journey in haste (v. 21).

    h.   Go by water or by land as it is made known to them (v. 22).

➤ 61:23–29   Sidney Rigdon, Joseph Smith, and Oliver Cowdery shall not come again upon the waters save it be upon the canal to journey to their homes.

    a.   The way to journey for the saints is by canal, and then by land when commanded to go to Zion (v. 24).

    c.   All thy brethren go like the Israelites, pitching their tents by the way (vv. 25–26).

    d.   Unto whom is given power to command the waters, the Spirit will tell him whether to go by land or water (vv. 27–28).

    e.   Unto Joseph Smith is given the course for the camp of the Lord (v. 29).

➤ 61:30–32   Sidney, Joseph, and Oliver shall not preach to the congregations of the wicked until they arrive in Cincinnati.

    a.   There lift up voices unto God against a people who are well nigh ripened to destruction (v. 31).

    b.   From there go to the congregations of their brethren who want them (v. 32).

➤ 61:33–39 The residue of the elders are to journey among the wicked as
it is given.

    a. As they do this they shall rid their garments and be
spotless before me (v. 34).

    b. Go two by two as seems good save Reynolds Cahoon and
Samuel Smith, with whom I am well pleased, be they not
separated.

    c. To all, be of good cheer, I am in your midst and have not
forsaken you (v. 36).

    d. The humble shall have the blessings of the kingdom
(v. 37).

    e. Look for the coming of the Son of Man, who comes when
you think not (v. 38).

    f. Pray always that ye enter not into temptation and abide
my coming (v. 39).

TEXT AND COMMENTARY

D&C 61:1–6 • Many Dangers Upon the Waters

1 Behold, and hearken unto the voice of him who has all power, who
is from everlasting to everlasting, even Alpha and Omega, the beginning
and the end.

2 Behold, verily thus saith the Lord unto you, O ye elders of my
church, who are assembled upon this spot, whose sins are now forgiven
you, for I, the Lord, forgive sins, and am merciful unto those who confess
their sins with humble hearts;

3 But verily I say unto you, that it is not needful for this whole
company of mine elders to be moving swiftly upon the waters, whilst
the inhabitants on either side are perishing in unbelief.

4 Nevertheless, I suffered it that ye might bear record; behold, there
are many dangers upon the waters, and more especially hereafter;

5 For I, the Lord, have decreed in mine anger many destructions upon
the waters; yea, and especially upon these waters.

6 Nevertheless, all flesh is in mine hand, and he that is faithful among
you shall not perish by the waters.

Again the Lord emphasizes the importance of missionary work. There

were eleven people in the company of elders, counting Joseph. Being in canoes, there would be no association with the near river inhabitants at all (v. 3). The vision of the destroyer, given to Brother Phelps, was the power of Satan of which the Lord desired the elders to bear record (v. 4). The Lord's decree of "destruction upon the waters" was a warning for the people to repent (v. 5; see Amos 4:6–13; 3 Nephi 9:1–12). If the people repented, or were faithful, the Lord would keep them from perishing upon those waters (D&C 61:6).

D&C 61:7–13 • Take That Which Is Needful

> 7 Wherefore, it is expedient that my servant Sidney Gilbert and my servant William W. Phelps be in haste upon their errand and mission.
>
> 8 Nevertheless, I would not suffer that ye should part until you were chastened for all your sins, that you might be one, that you might not perish in wickedness;
>
> 9 But now, verily I say, it behooveth me that ye should part. Wherefore let my servants Sidney Gilbert and William W. Phelps take their former company, and let them take their journey in haste that they may fill their mission, and through faith they shall overcome;
>
> 10 And inasmuch as they are faithful they shall be preserved, and I, the Lord, will be with them.
>
> 11 And let the residue take that which is needful for clothing.
>
> 12 Let my servant Sidney Gilbert take that which is not needful with him, as you shall agree.
>
> 13 And now, behold, for your good I gave unto you a commandment concerning these things; and I, the Lord, will reason with you as with men in days of old.

The first five above verses need no comment. The permission for Sidney Gilbert to take more than was needful with him (v. 12) was undoubtedly because of his being the agent for the Church, and his responsibilities connected with that office. "As you shall agree" is apparently referring to Joseph Smith, another recognition by the Lord of his being the President of the Church.

D&C 61:14–22 • John Cursed the Waters

> 14 Behold, I, the Lord, in the beginning blessed the waters; but in

the last days, by the mouth of my servant John, I cursed the waters.

15 Wherefore, the days will come that no flesh shall be safe upon the waters.

16 And it shall be said in days to come that none is able to go up to the land of Zion upon the waters, but he that is upright in heart.

17 And, as I, the Lord, in the beginning cursed the land, even so in the last days have I blessed it, in its time, for the use of my saints, that they may partake the fatness thereof.

18 And now I give unto you a commandment that what I say unto one I say unto all, that you shall forewarn your brethren concerning these waters, that they come not in journeying upon them, lest their faith fail and they are caught in snares;

19 I, the Lord, have decreed, and the destroyer rideth upon the face thereof, and I revoke not the decree.

20 I, the Lord, was angry with you yesterday, but today mine anger is turned away.

21 Wherefore, let those concerning whom I have spoken, that should take their journey in haste—again I say unto you, let them take their journey in haste.

22 And it mattereth not unto me, after a little, if it so be that they fill their mission, whether they go by water or by land; let this be as it is made known unto them according to their judgments hereafter.

The blessing of the waters in the beginning (v. 14) was: "And God said, Let the waters bring forth abundantly the moving creature that hath life, . . . And God created great whales, and every living creature that moveth, which the waters brought forth abundantly, after their kind" (Genesis 1:20–21). The cursing by His servant John (D&C 61:14) was:

8 And the second angel sounded, and as it were a great mountain burning with fire was cast into the sea: and the third part of the sea became blood;

9 And the third part of the creatures which were in the sea, and had life, died; and the third part of the ships were destroyed.

10 And the third angel sounded, and there fell a great star from heaven, burning as it were a lamp, and it fell upon the third part of the rivers, and upon the fountains of waters;

11 And the name of the star is called Wormwood: and the third part

of the waters became wormwood; and many men died of the waters, because they were made bitter. [Revelation 8:8–11; see also 16:2–3]

For this author, the symbolism of John's curse falls into the category of Nephi's words concerning Isaiah: "in the days that the prophecies of Isaiah shall be fulfilled men shall know of a surety, at the times when they shall come to pass" (2 Nephi 25:7). However, the curse will affect the sea life, the ships, and drinking water. While only a third part of the waters will be affected, the curse will definitely be upon the waters leading to the land of Missouri since only the "upright in heart" will be able to go "up to the land of Zion" (D&C 61:16).

The land was cursed for Adam's sake, or for his good: . . . "cursed shall be the ground for thy sake; in sorrow shalt thou eat of it all the days of thy life. Thorns also, and thistles shall it bring forth to thee, and thou shalt eat the herb of the field. By the sweat of thy face shalt thou eat bread, until thou shalt return unto the ground— (Moses 4:23–25). Idleness is a curse, and Adam's working for his bread was to his benefit. In the last days the thorn and thistles, and other detriments to the production of the good things of the earth, will somehow be eliminated from the land of Zion and it will bring forth its fatness for the Saints (D&C 61:17).

The Lord has forewarned us of those waters. Those asked to go to Zion in the future will probably be warned again at that time (v. 18). The decree of the destroyer riding upon those waters is still in effect (v. 19).

Again, the Lord tells those who are now journeying, "it mattereth not to me," but use your judgment and it will be made known "whether to go by water or by land." The important thing is fulfill your mission, and do it in haste (vv. 21–22).

D&C 61:23–29 • Do As the Spirit of God Commands

23 And now, concerning my servants, Sidney Rigdon, Joseph Smith, Jun., and Oliver Cowdery, let them come not again upon the waters, save it be upon the canal, while journeying unto their homes; or in other words they shall not come upon the waters to journey, save upon the canal.

24 Behold, I, the Lord, have appointed a way for the journeying of my saints; and behold, this is the way—that after they leave the canal

they shall journey by land, inasmuch as they are commanded to journey and go up unto the land of Zion;

25 And they shall do like unto the children of Israel, pitching their tents by the way.

26 And, behold, this commandment you shall give unto all your brethren.

27 Nevertheless, unto whom is given power to command the waters, unto him it is given by the Spirit to know all his ways;

28 Wherefore, let him do as the Spirit of the living God commandeth him, whether upon the land or upon the waters, as it remaineth with me to do hereafter.

29 And unto you is given the course for the Saints, or the way for the saints of the camp of the Lord, to journey.

The commandment to Sidney, Joseph, and Oliver to go on the canal, then on land, and pitch their tents like the children of Israel did, was to be the pattern for all the brethren (vv. 23–26). A canal is man-made and generally smaller. It is usually manually controlled. Therefore, Satan will probably focus on the larger bodies of water. Pitching their tents by the way was not a literal commandment, but a way of telling them to stop and stay over where the inhabitants were receptive to the message of the restoration. The children of Israel stopped where they could satisfy their temporal needs. The Saints were to stop where they were able to satisfy the spiritual needs of others.

The canal referred to was the Erie Canal, which was built shortly before the time of Joseph Smith. Was the Lord involved in the decision to build the Erie Canal that assisted the Saints in many ways? He well could have been. The Lord's hand is in all things (see D&C 59:21–22).

"Unto whom is given power to command the waters" (D&C 61:27) implies that only a select few will have that power. While it is a priesthood power, all will not have the faith, or the gift of the Spirit developed to use it. Those few will know when to travel the waters, or when to go by land, because the Lord will tell him what to do through the Spirit (v. 28). Once more the Lord designates Joseph as the one who will give directions to the Church as a whole (v. 29). In the future, when some are sent to establish the city of Zion, the Lord "shall manifest unto my servant [the President of the Church], by the voice of the Spirit, those that are chosen,"

(D&C 105:36). He will certainly also manifest to him the course and manner of travel.

D&C 61:30–32 • Nigh Ripe For Destruction

30 And again, verily I say unto you, my servants, Sidney Rigdon, Joseph Smith, Jun., and Oliver Cowdery, shall not open their mouths in the congregations of the wicked until they arrive at Cincinnati;

31 And in that place they shall lift up their voices unto God against that people, yea, unto him whose anger is kindled against their wickedness, a people who are well-nigh ripened for destruction.

32 And from thence let them journey for the congregations of their brethren, for their labors even now are wanted more abundantly among them than among the congregations of the wicked.

Why Joseph and his companions were not to preach on the way to Cincinnati is not stated (v. 30). Apparently the situation there was urgent. They were ripe for destruction (v. 31), but the city was not destroyed. Perhaps the three men had something to do with its not being destroyed. Apparently, little is known about what they did there. Someday that experience may be made known. Meanwhile, it seems that Joseph was sorely missed in Kirtland, and the Saints there were praying for his return (v. 32).

D&C 61:33–39 • Magnify Your Priesthood

33 And now, concerning the residue, let them journey and declare the word among the congregations of the wicked, inasmuch as it is given;

34 And inasmuch as they do this they shall rid their garments, and they shall be spotless before me.

35 And let them journey together, or two by two, as seemeth them good, only let my servant Reynolds Cahoon, and my servant Samuel H. Smith, with whom I am well pleased, be not separated until they return to their homes, and this for a wise purpose in me.

36 And now, verily I say unto you, and what I say unto one I say unto all, be of good cheer, little children; for I am in your midst, and I have not forsaken you;

37 And inasmuch as you have humbled yourselves before me, the blessings of the kingdom are yours.

38 Gird up your loins and be watchful and be sober, looking forth for the coming of the Son of Man, for he cometh in an hour you think not.

39 Pray always that you enter not into temptation, that you may abide the day of his coming, whether in life or in death. Even so. Amen.

The elders "shall rid their garments" (v. 34) is a conditional promise of magnifying their priesthood. If they are commanded to warn a people and do it they are no longer accountable. Otherwise, the sins of those people are also upon the heads of the priesthood holder (see Jacob 1:19; 2 Nephi 9:44; Ezekiel 33:8–9). The Lord does not always tell us why He does certain things, but we can rest assure it is "for a wise purpose," as He says regarding Reynolds Cahoon and Samuel Smith (D&C 61:35). The last verses (36–39) are assurances He has given them before, so we will not comment on them again.

DOCTRINE AND COVENANTS 62

*H*istorical Setting—Section 62:

On the 13th [August 1831] I met several of the Elders on their way to the land of Zion, and after the joyful salutations with which brethren meet each other, who are actually "contending for the faith once delivered to the Saints received the following": [section 62]. [*HC*, 1:205]

SECTION 62 • OUTLINE

➢ 62:1–5   The Lord knows the weaknesses of man, and how to succor them in temptation.

    a.   His eyes are upon those not yet in Zion, their mission is not yet full (v. 2).

    b.   Their testimony is recorded in heaven for angels to look upon, and their sins are forgiven (v. 3).

    c.   Continue to Zion, hold a meeting, and offer a sacrament to the Most High (v. 4).

    d.   Return and bear record, altogether or two by two, as seemeth good (v. 5).

➤ 62:6–9   The Lord brought them together to fulfill the promise, and
            to rejoice in Zion.

    a. If you desire to ride upon horses, or upon mules, or in
       chariots you shall be blessed, if received with thankful
       heart (v. 7).

    b. It remains for you to do according to judgment and
       direction of the Spirit (v. 8).

    c. The kingdom is yours, and I am with the faithful always
       (v. 9).

TEXT AND COMMENTARY

D&C 62:1–5 • Congregations of the Wicked or Inhabitants of the Earth

1 Behold, and hearken, O ye elders of my church, saith the Lord your God, even Jesus Christ, your advocate, who knoweth the weakness of man and how to succor them who are tempted.

2 And verily mine eyes are upon those who have not as yet gone up unto the land of Zion; wherefore your mission is not yet full.

3 Nevertheless, ye are blessed, for the testimony which ye have borne is recorded in heaven for the angels to look upon; and they rejoice over you, and your sins are forgiven you.

4 And now continue your journey. Assemble yourselves upon the land of Zion; and hold a meeting and rejoice together, and offer a sacrament unto the Most High.

5 And then you may return to bear record, yea, even altogether, or two by two, as seemeth you good, it mattereth not unto me; only be faithful, and declare glad tidings unto the inhabitants of the earth, or among the congregations of the wicked.

The Lord knows how to succor us in our weaknesses (v. 1) because of His experience on the cross, when He took "upon him death; . . . and he will take upon Him their infirmities, that his bowels may be filled with mercy, according to the flesh, that he may know according to the flesh how to succor his people according to their infirmities" (Alma 7:12). He is watching us in our assignments, and is with us to the end (D&C 62:2).

He knows our needs and our desires as well as our strengths and weaknesses. He knows us better than we know ourselves. He also knows those to whom we speak or teach the gospel. Therefore, we should rely on what He tells us to do and say, as directed by the Spirit, rather than follow our own reasoning and knowledge.

The testimonies of the elders were recorded in heaven, and their sins were forgiven (v. 3). Some have concluded from this verse, that whenever we bear our testimony our sins are forgiven. However, the Lord also said those who were assembled on this spot [McIlwaine's Bend] were forgiven. We cannot conclude that any person who went to that spot would have their sins forgiven (D&C 61:2). We could quote many other references where the Lord told someone that their sins were forgiven, and draw the same irrational conclusion. The forgiveness of sins comes by fire and the Holy Ghost upon keeping the commandments of God (2 Nephi 31:17; Moroni 8:25). As stated before, this is the doctrine of justification (Moses 6:60).

The sacrament to be offered in Zion (D&C 62:4) would be a thanksgiving offering of prayer or dedication; not the partaking of the sacrament. This is the third time, once in each section under consideration in this chapter, that the Lord says "it mattereth not to me" (60:5; 61:22; 62:5). The Lord possibly used it here as Three Witnesses to the principle He had taught before. We are to do many things of our own free will as confirmed to us by the Spirit (see D&C 58:26–28). While we should always seek the direction of the Lord, through the Spirit, He expects us to follow the doctrines and principles that we have learned previously, but not to become robots. If there are exceptions to what we have learned, He will inspire us to do differently. As we learned in Doctrine and Covenants 58:26: "it is not meet that I should command in all things; for he that is compelled in all things, the same is a slothful and not a wise servant; wherefore he receiveth no reward."

D&C 62:6–9 • The Lord Promises the Faithful and Cannot Lie

6 Behold, I, the Lord, have brought you together that the promise might be fulfilled, that the faithful among you should be preserved and rejoice together in the land of Missouri. I, the Lord, promise the faithful and cannot lie.

7 I, the Lord, am willing, if any among you desire to ride upon horses, or upon mules, or in chariots, he shall receive this blessing, if he receive

it from the hand of the Lord, with a thankful heart in all things.

8 These things remain with you to do according to judgment and the directions of the Spirit.

9 Behold, the kingdom is yours. And behold, and lo, I am with the faithful always. Even so. Amen.

The promises to Missouri will still be fulfilled. The Lord cannot lie (v. 6). The right choices must still be made (v. 7). With all the instructions given in these three revelations, there seems to be one theme running through to the conclusion: "do according to judgment and the directions of the Spirit" (v. 8). The kingdom is still here, and the Lord is still with the faithful (v. 9). The faithful will follow the theme given here.

General Authority Quotes

—*Elder Boyd K. Packer* • D&C 60:5; 61:22; 62:5, 8

. . . We often find young people who will pray with great exertion over matters that they are free to decide for themselves. Suppose, if you will, that a couple had money available to build a house. Suppose they had prayed endlessly over whether they should build an Early American style, a ranch style, modern style architecture, or perhaps a Mediterranean style. Has it ever occurred to you that perhaps the Lord just plain doesn't care? Let them build what they want to build. It's their choice. In many things we can do just what we want.

Now there are some things he cares very much about. If you're going to build, then be honest and pay for the material that goes in it. When you move in it, live righteously in it. Those are the things that count.

. . . The Lord is very generous with the freedom he gives us. The more we learn to follow the right, the more we are spiritually self-reliant, the more our freedom and our independence are affirmed. . . . [*Ensign*, August 1975, 89]

—*President Joseph F. Smith* • D&C 60:13

I desire to say to this congregation at this time that I have felt very strongly of late a desire, a responsibility, I may say, to admonish the Latter-day Saints everywhere to cease loitering away their precious time, to cease from all idleness. [*Gospel Doctrine*, 235]

—President Joseph Fielding Smith • D&C 61:5

. . . We have every reason to believe that the torrents, floods, and the dangers upon the waters were not as great as they are today, and by no means as great as what the Lord has promised us. The early mariners among the ancient traversed the seas as they knew them in that day in comparative safety. . . .

. . . Today this manner of travel in such boats would be of the most dangerous and risky nature. Moreover, we have seen the dangers upon the waters increase until the hearts of men failed them and only the brave, and those who were compelled to sail the seas, ventured out in them. In regard to the Missouri-Mississippi waters, we have seen year by year great destruction upon them, and coming from them. Millions and millions of dollars almost annually are lost by these great streams overflowing their banks. Many have lost their lives in these floods as they sweep over the land, and even upon this apparently tranquil or sluggish stream there can arise storms that bring destruction. Verily the word of the Lord has been, and is being, fulfilled in relation to these waters. [*Church History and Modern Day Revelation,* 1:124]

—Elder Ezra Taft Benson • D&C 62:39

. . . we are told we should pray always (Luke 21:34–36; 2 Nephi 32:9; D&C 62:39; 88:126; 93:49). This not only shows we should pray frequently but also continually have a prayer in our heart (Alma 34:27). Even when the Lord's time was most in demand, He was not too busy to pray (Luke 5:15–16). [*TETB,* 425]

Chapter Twenty-Eight

Overcome the World

D&C 63; 64

H istorical Setting:

In these infant days of the Church, there was a great anxiety to obtain the word of the Lord upon every subject that in any way concerned our salvation; and as the land of Zion was the most important temporal object in view. I enquired of the Lord for further information upon the gathering of the saints, and the purchase of the land, and other matters, and received [section 63]. [*HC*, 1:207]

INTRODUCTION

Following the last Passover that Jesus observed with His disciples, the Savior gave some great doctrinal teachings (John 14–16). In conclusion He announced: "These things I have spoken unto you, that in me ye might have peace. In the world ye shall have tribulation: but be of good cheer; I have overcome the world" (John 16:33). In these latter days, having set the example in His ministry, He told the inquisitive Latter-day Saints: "I will that ye should overcome the world" (D&C 64:2). The two revelations considered here illustrate the way to accomplish this commandment of the Savior.

SECTION 63 • OUTLINE

➤ 63:1–5   The Lord's word and will concerning his people.

     a.   His anger is kindled against the wicked and rebellious (v. 2).

     b.   He will take whom He will and preserve whom He will (v. 3).

     c.   He builds up at His own will, and destroys and casts down to hell (v. 4).

     d.   He utters His voice, and it shall be obeyed (v. 5).

➤ **63:6–12**   Let the wicked, the rebellious, and the unbelieving take heed, for all flesh shall know that he is God.

     a.   He that seeks signs shall see them, but not unto salvation (v. 7).

     b.   Some of His people seek signs, and have from the beginning (v. 8).

     c.   Faith comes not from signs, but follows those that believe (v. 9).

     d.   Signs come by faith and by the will of God (v. 10).

     e.   Without faith no man pleaseth God, the only sign is His wrath unto their condemnation (v. 11).

     f.   He is not pleased with those who seek signs, and not for the good of men unto the glory of God (v. 12).

➤ **63:13–19**   The Lord has given commandments, and many have not kept them.

     a.   There are adulterers and adulteresses among them, and shall be revealed (v. 14).

     b.   Beware and repent lest judgment come upon them and be manifest (v. 15).

     c.   He that lusts after a woman shall not have the Spirit, and deny the faith (v. 16).

     d.   The liars and whoremongers, and those who love and make a lie, shall suffer a second death (v. 17).

     e.   They will not have part in the first resurrection (v. 18).

     f.   Those people are not justified because these things are among them (v. 19).

➤ **63:20–23**   He that endures in faith, and does the Lord's will, shall receive an inheritance upon the earth when the day of transfiguration comes.

   a. The pattern of transfiguration was shown to the apostles on the mount, but the fullness of that account was not received (v. 21).

   b. He makes His will known, but many do not observe His commandments (v. 22).

   c. Those who keep His commandments will be given the mysteries of the kingdom and eternal life (v. 23).

➤ 63:24–31 The saints should not assemble in Zion in haste lest there be confusion and pestilence.

   a. The Lord holds the land of Zion in his own hands (v. 25).

   b. The Lord renders to Caesar the things that are Caesar's (v. 26).

   c. The Lord wills that you purchase the land and have claim on the world (v. 27).

   d. Satan stirs the world up to anger and the shedding of blood (v. 28).

   e. The land of Zion shall only be purchased or obtained by blood (v. 29).

   f. If by purchase you are blessed (v. 30).

   g. If by blood you shall be scourged, and few will receive an inheritance (v. 31).

➤ 63:32–35 I am angry with the wicked and holding my Spirit from the inhabitants.

   a. I have decreed wars on the earth, the wicked shall slay the wicked (v. 33).

   b. The saints shall hardly escape, and by and by I will come and consume the wicked by fire (v. 34–35).

   c. I will that my saints be assembled upon the land of Zion (v. 36).

   d. Every man should take righteousness in his hands, and lift a warning voice that desolation shall come (v. 37).

➤ 63:38–45 Let my disciples on this farm in Kirtland arrange their temporal affairs (v. 38).

   a. Let Titus Billings dispose of the land and come to Zion in the spring (v. 39).

    b.   Let all of the moneys, little or much, be sent to the land of Zion (v. 40).

    c.   Joseph Smith, Jun. shall determine by the Spirit who shall go to Zion, and who shall tarry (v. 41).

    d.   Let Newel K. Whitney retain his store for a little season (v. 42).

    e.   He shall impart all the money he can to the land of Zion (v. 43).

    f.   Let him do with the things in his hands according to his wisdom (v. 44).

    g.   Let him be ordained an agent to the disciples that tarry (v. 45).

➢ **63:46–48**   The Lord's will is that Oliver Cowdery expound these things to the churches.

    a.   He that is faithful and endures shall overcome the world (v. 47).

    b.   He that sends treasures to Zion shall receive an inheritance in this world, and a reward in the world to come (v. 48).

➢ **63:49–54**   Blessed are the dead that die in the Lord henceforth, when the Lord comes, they will receive an inheritance in the holy city.

    a.   He that lives and kept the commandments is blessed, and shall live to the age of man (v. 50).

    b.   Little children shall grow up, old men shall die, but be changed in the twinkling of an eye (v. 51).

    c.   For this cause preached the Apostles the resurrection of the dead (v. 52).

    d.   Look for the things that are nigh, according to the manner of the Lord (v. 53).

    e.   Until that hour, foolish virgins shall be among the wise (v. 54).

➢ **63:55–60**   I am not pleased with Sidney Rigdon; he exalts himself, receives not counsel, and grieves the Spirit.

    a.   His writing is not acceptable, he must rewrite and it be acceptable, or he shall lose his office to which he is appointed (v. 56).

    b.   Ordain those who desire in their hearts to warn sinners to this power (v. 57).

    c.   This is a day of warning and not a day of many words, and I will not be mocked (v. 58).

    d.   The day comes when all things shall be subject unto me (v. 59).

    e.   I am Alpha and Omega, even Jesus Christ (v. 60).

➤ 63:61–66   Let all men beware how they take my name in their lips.

    a.   Many use my name in vain, having not authority (v. 62).

    b.   Let the church repent of their sins or they shall be cut off (v. 63).

    c.   What comes from above is sacred, and must be spoken with constraint (v. 64).

    d.   Let Joseph and Sidney Rigdon seek a home as taught through the Spirit (v. 65).

    e.   These things remain to be overcome through patience to receive a more eternal weight of glory (v. 66).

TEXT AND COMMENTARY

D&C 63:1–5 • The Lord's Voice Shall Be Obeyed

1 Hearken, O ye people, and open your hearts and give ear from afar; and listen, you that call yourselves the people of the Lord, and hear the word of the Lord and his will concerning you.

2 Yea, verily, I say, hear the word of him whose anger is kindled against the wicked and rebellious;

3 Who willeth to take even them whom he will take, and preserveth in life them whom he will preserve;

4 Who buildeth up at his own will and pleasure; and destroyeth when he pleases, and is able to cast the soul down to hell.

5 Behold, I, the Lord, utter my voice, and it shall be obeyed.

The land of Zion was the most important subject on the minds of the Church members. They called themselves "the people of the Lord," and were to hear the word of the Lord concerning themselves (vv. 1–2). With this subject in mind, the Lord contrasts them with the wicked and rebellious people of the world, and reminds them of His power to separate and control both groups (vv. 3–5).

D&C 63:6–12 • The Sign Seekers

6 Wherefore, verily I say, let the wicked take heed, and let the rebellious fear and tremble; and let the unbelieving hold their lips, for the day of wrath shall come upon them as a whirlwind, and all flesh shall know that I am God.

7 And he that seeketh signs shall see signs, but not unto salvation.

8 Verily, I say unto you, there are those among you who seek signs, and there have been such even from the beginning;

9 But, behold, faith cometh not by signs, but signs follow those that believe.

10 Yea, signs come by faith, not by the will of men, nor as they please, but by the will of God.

11 Yea, signs come by faith, unto mighty works, for without faith no man pleaseth God; and with whom God is angry he is not well pleased; wherefore, unto such he showeth no signs, only in wrath unto their condemnation.

12 Wherefore, I, the Lord, am not pleased with those among you who have sought after signs and wonders for faith, and not for the good of men unto my glory.

The wicked and rebellious were to suffer the wrath of God, and would also come to "know that [the Lord is] God" (v. 6). On the other hand, many of the people of the Lord, who were to overcome the world, had not forsaken the way of the world and were seeking for signs. They would see signs, but not unto salvation (vv. 7–8). As the Savior had taught His disciples, at the close of His ministry, "signs follow those that believe" (v. 9; c.f. Mark 16:17). The signs come by faith, and the Lord's will, not man's (v. 10). Without faith, no man pleaseth God, and the Lord was not pleased with those who sought signs for the wrong reason, not for the good of man and Christ's glory (vv. 11–12).

D&C 63:13–19 • Adulterers and Adulteresses

13 Nevertheless, I give commandments, and many have turned away from my commandments and have not kept them.

14 There were among you adulterers and adulteresses; some of whom have turned away from you, and others remain with you that hereafter shall be revealed.

15 Let such beware and repent speedily, lest judgment shall come upon them as a snare, and their folly shall be made manifest, and their works shall follow them in the eyes of the people.

16 And verily I say unto you, as I have said before, he that looketh on a woman to lust after her, or if any shall commit adultery in their hearts, they shall not have the Spirit, but shall deny the faith and shall fear.

17 Wherefore, I, the Lord, have said that the fearful, and the unbelieving, and all liars, and whosoever loveth and maketh a lie, and the whoremonger, and the sorcerer, shall have their part in that lake which burneth with fire and brimstone, which is the second death.

18 Verily I say, that they shall not have part in the first resurrection.

19 And now behold, I, the Lord, say unto you that ye are not justified, because these things are among you.

In His Jerusalem ministry, Jesus identified the sign seekers as being evil, or wicked and adulterous (Matthew 12:39; 16:4) He implied the same connections with the Saints who called themselves "the people of the Lord." Many had turned away from [Christ's] commandments" (D&C 63:13), including the moral conduct revealed in "the law of the Church" (D&C 42:18–28). There had been, and still were, adulterers and adulteresses among them (D&C 63:14). The teaching that sign seekers were adulterers was verified by the Prophet Joseph Smith:

> When I was preaching in Philadelphia, a Quaker called out for a sign. I told him to be still. After the sermon, he asked again for a sign. I told the congregation the man was an adulterer; that a wicked and adulterous generation seeketh after a sign, and that the Lord had said to me in a revelation, that any man who wanted a sign was an adulterous person, "It is true," cried one, "for I caught him in the very act," which the man afterwards confessed when he was baptized. [*TPJS*, 278]

Elder George A. Smith tells of another occasion when the Prophet Joseph responded to a sign seeker:

> When the Church of Jesus Christ of Latter-day Saints was first founded, you could see persons rise up and ask, "What sign will you show us that we may be made to believe?" I recollect a Campbellite preacher

who came to Joseph Smith, . . . and said that he had come a considerable distance to be convinced of the truth. Why, said he, Mr. Smith, I want to know the truth, and when I am convinced, I will spend all my talents and time in defending and spreading the doctrines of your religion, and I will give you to understand that to convince me is equivalent to convincing all my society, amounting to several hundreds."

Well, Joseph commenced laying before him the coming forth of the work, and the first principles of the Gospel, when Mr. Hayden exclaimed, "O this is not the evidence I want, the evidence that I wish to have is a notable miracle; I want to see some powerful manifestation of the power of God, I want to see a notable miracle performed, and if you perform such a one, then I will believe with all my heart and soul, and will exert all my power and all my extensive influence to convince others, and if you will not perform a miracle of this kind, then I am your worst and bitterest enemy."

"Well. Said Joseph, "what will you have done? Will you be struck blind, or dumb? Will you be paralyzed, or will you have one hand withered? Take your choice, choose which you please, and in the name of Jesus Christ it shall be done."

"That is not the kind of miracle I want," said the preacher.

"Then, sir," replied Joseph, "I can perform none, I am not going to bring any trouble upon any body else, sir, to convince you. I will tell you what you make me think of—the very first person who asked a sign of the Savior, for it is written, in the New Testament, that Satan came to the Savior in the desert, when he was hungry with forty days' fasting, and said, 'If you be the Son of God, command these stones to be bread.' "And now," said Joseph, "the children of the devil and his servants have been asking for signs ever since; and when the people in that day continued asking him for signs to prove the truth of the Gospel which he preached, the Savior replied, "It is a wicked and an adulterous generation that seeketh a sign, &c."

But the poor preacher had so much faith in the power of the Prophet that he daren't risk being struck blind, lame, dumb, or having one hand withered, or anything of the kind.[*JD*, 2:326–27]

Signs follow those that believe (D&C 63:9), but a wicked and adulterous person and generation seeks for a sign.

The Lord's people were admonished to repent speedily of their immorality among them (D&C 63:15). He then adds that looking upon a woman with lust, or spiritual adultery, has need for repentance. "As I have said before" (v. 16) would include his New Testament, and Book of Mormon, admonitions (see Matthew 5:27–28; 3 Nephi 12:27–28). The two accounts are identical, except the New Testament account adds "committed adultery *with her,*" which was undoubtedly done after the original text was given. The modern day revelation gives the negative effects of "they shall not have the Spirit, but shall deny the faith and shall fear" (D&C 63:16). Elder George A. Smith confirmed the Lord's accusation of there being adultery among the people at this time, and also confirms the result of denying of the faith:

> I have been conversant with early Elders, and I am satisfied that a large number of them fell from their positions in the kingdom of God because they yielded to the spirit of adultery; this was the cause of their destruction. There was an elder . . . who lived in Indiana, who was quite popular in that part of the country as a preacher. He apostatized, but he did not know it . . . , he said, I have proven the revelation given to Joseph Smith untrue, which says if a man shall commit adultery he shall lose the spirit of God, and deny the faith. I have proved that not to be true, for I have violated that commandment and have not denied the faith. He was so blind that he could not see the darkness that the spirit of adultery had placed upon his head . . . [*JD*, 11:10–11]

The Lord equates the immoral with "all liars, and whosoever loveth and maketh a lie, and the whoremonger, and the sorcerer" who will suffer the second death, and "not have part in the first resurrection" (D&C 63:17–18). These people are not trustworthy to live among. The Lord again declares that these people have not met the conditions for His atonement paying for their sins, and "are not justified" (v. 19).

D&C 63:20–23 • The Day of Transfiguration

> 20 Nevertheless, he that endureth in faith and doeth my will, the same shall overcome, and shall receive an inheritance upon the earth when the day of transfiguration shall come;

> 21 When the earth shall be transfigured, even according to the pattern which was shown unto mine apostles upon the mount; of which account the fulness ye have not yet received.

> 22 And now, verily I say unto you, that as I said that I would make known my will unto you, behold I will make it known unto you, not by the way of commandment, for there are many who observe not to keep my commandments.

> 23 But unto him that keepeth my commandments I will give the mysteries of my kingdom, and the same shall be in him a well of living water, springing up unto everlasting life.

In contrast to those who would suffer the second death, the Lord promises those who do His will an inheritance upon the earth, when the earth is transfigured (v. 20). The Lord only whetted the appetite of the Saints with His reference to "the day of transfiguration" (v. 20). The pattern for the transfiguration of the earth "was shown unto [Christ's] apostles upon the mount," but we do not have the full account as yet (v. 21). "The mount" has reference to Peter, James, and John, accompanied by Jesus, receiving the keys of the kingdom (Matthew 17:1–3; JST, Mark 9:4–5; Luke 9:28–36)[42] Moses, Elijah, and others appeared to the three Apostles and conferred their keys and authority upon them. Apparently the Apostles were not given the full account either, just the pattern, or preview, for the great millennial condition of the earth. Joseph Smith and others have taught, or given suggestions on some things that may have occurred.

The Prophet Joseph taught: "The Savior, Moses, and Elias [Elijah], gave the keys [of the everlasting Priesthood] to Peter, James, and John, on the mount, when they were transfigured before them. . . . Peter, James, and John had [the keys] given to them and they gave [them] to others" (*TPJS*, 158). This statement implies that the three Apostles were transfigured. As Joseph translated the Bible, he had other truths revealed to him. In JST, Mark 9:4, we read: "And there appeared unto them Elias and Moses, or in other words, John the Baptist and Moses." This is not to imply that John the Baptist instead of Elias was on the mount, but that John the Baptist was also present in the role as an Elias. It is possible that John, who had already been beheaded, was there to behold the transfer of the spirit of Elias, which was to prepare the way of the kingdom, to the spirit of Elijah, which was to build up the kingdom (see *TPJS*, 335–340). That Elijah, the New Testament translates his name Elias, was personally present on the mount seems obvious because of his having been translated rather than tasting of death (2 Kings 2:11). Thus he had a

---

[42] The exact mount in question has been claimed to be both Mount Tabor and Mount Hermon. In this writer's opinion, it happened on Mount Tabor, but the evidence is not vital to our discussion here.

physical body to lay on hands for the conferral of the priesthood, as did Moses (see Alma 45:19). Elijah's personal appearance in the Kirtland Temple is additional evidence and testimony for his personal appearance on the mount to the apostles. The JST also teaches us that these two personages "appeared in glory and spoke of [Jesus'] death, and also of his resurrection" (JST, Luke 9:30–31). This was probably an act of encouragement and strengthening to Jesus for His coming trials, as suggested by Elder James E. Talmage (*Jesus the Christ*, 345).

From the Apostle Peter's writings, we learn that the Apostles were eye witnesses of Jesus' glory, and heard the voice of God the Father declare, "This is my Beloved Son, in whom I am well pleased." Peter also recorded that Jesus "received from God the Father honour and glory" (2 Peter 1:16–18). President Joseph Fielding Smith has proposed that the temple endowments were given on this occasion, not only to Jesus, but to Peter, James, and John. (*Doctrines of Salvation*, 2:165) Some have suggested that Peter, James and John had their calling and election made sure on this occasion, but a careful analysis of Joseph Smith's teachings does not confirm this happening:

> Now, there is some grand secret here, and keys to unlock the subject. Notwithstanding the apostle exhorts them to add to their faith, virtue, knowledge, temperance, etc., yet he exhorts them to make their calling and election sure. And though they had heard an audible voice from heaven bearing testimony that Jesus was the Son of God, yet he says we have a more sure word of prophecy, whereunto ye do well that ye take heed as unto a light shining in a dark place. Now, wherein could they have a more sure word of prophecy than to hear the voice of God saying, This is my Beloved Son,
>
> Now for the secret and grand key. Though they might hear the voice of God and know that Jesus was the son of God, this would be no evidence that their election and calling was made sure, that they had part with Christ, and were joint heirs with Him. They then would want that more sure word of prophecy, that they were sealed in the heavens, and had the promise of eternal life in the kingdom of God. Then having this promise sealed unto them, it was an anchor to the soul, sure and steadfast . . . [*TPJS*, 298].

A week later, the Prophet Joseph again said: "It is one thing to be on the mount and hear the excellent voice, etc., and another to hear the voice declare into you, You have a part and lot in the kingdom" (*TPJS*, 306).

Undoubtedly many other great and marvelous things transpired on that glorious mount. Someday we will know more, as the statement "the fullness ye have not yet received" implies (D&C 63:21). The Lord has made known His will unto us as a Church (v. 22). We are to overcome the world, and become a Zion people by keeping the commandments, that we may receive "the mysteries of [Christ's] kingdom" and make them "a well of living water, springing up with everlasting life" (v. 23; cf. John 4:14). We will then have an inheritance on this celestial earth (see D&C 88:17–20).

D&C 63:24–31 • The Land of Zion

24 And now, behold, this is the will of the Lord your God concerning his saints, that they should assemble themselves together unto the land of Zion, not in haste, lest there should be confusion, which bringeth pestilence.

25 Behold, the land of Zion—I, the Lord, hold it in mine own hands;

26 Nevertheless, I, the Lord, render unto Caesar the things which are Caesar's.

27 Wherefore, I the Lord will that you should purchase the lands, that you may have advantage of the world, that you may have claim on the world, that they may not be stirred up unto anger.

28 For Satan putteth it into their hearts to anger against you, and to the shedding of blood.

29 Wherefore, the land of Zion shall not be obtained but by purchase or by blood, otherwise there is none inheritance for you.

30 And if by purchase, behold you are blessed;

31 And if by blood, as you are forbidden to shed blood, lo, your enemies are upon you, and ye shall be scourged from city to city, and from synagogue to synagogue, and but few shall stand to receive an inheritance.

The Saints did not comply with the Lord's commandment to assemble in Zion, but "not in haste lest there be confusion, which bringeth pestilence" (v. 24). Apparently many came in haste. The same principles that that He revealed at that time must be followed by those who overcome the world and who will eventually establish Zion. The first principle to be followed is to abide by the laws of the land, or in the biblical terms used by the Lord, "render to Caesar the things which are Caesars" (v. 26; see Luke 20:26). "We believe . . . in obeying, honoring, and sustaining the law" (A of F 12).

The Saints were to observe the law by purchasing the lands. The Lord gave the reason, "that you may have *advantage of the world,* that you may have *claim on the world,* that they may *not be stirred up to anger*" (D&C 63:27; italics added). Thus, those of the world would not have an excuse to abuse the Saints. Satan was working hard not only to get the people of the world angry, but to get them to shed the blood of the Saints (v. 28). He will do so again. The other way to obtain the land was by physical force, or by blood (v. 29). Purchasing would bring blessings, by blood was forbidden, and besides, their enemies were much superior in numbers. They were more experienced, and unless the Lord interceded for them, they would be scourged and driven, and few Saints would survive (vv. 30–31). Furthermore, King David was forbidden to build the temple in Jerusalem because he was a man of war (1 Chronicles 28:2–6). The same restrictions were undoubtedly applicable to Latter-day Saints then and now.

D&C 63:32–37 • The Wicked Will Slay the Wicked

32 I, the Lord, am angry with the wicked; I am holding my Spirit from the inhabitants of the earth.

33 I have sworn in my wrath, and decreed wars upon the face of the earth, and the wicked shall slay the wicked, and fear shall come upon every man;

34 And the Saints also shall hardly escape; nevertheless, I, the Lord, am with them, and will come down in heaven from the presence of my Father and consume the wicked with unquenchable fire.

35 And behold, this is not yet, but by and by.

36 Wherefore, seeing that I, the Lord, have decreed all these things upon the face of the earth, I will that my saints should be assembled upon the land of Zion;

37 And that every man should take righteousness in his hands and faithfulness upon his loins, and lift a warning voice unto the inhabitants of the earth; and declare both by word and by flight that desolation shall come upon the wicked.

In connection with the Saints being forbidden to shed blood, the Lord announced that He had decreed war upon the face of the earth. This should not be interpreted as the Lord being the cause of, or His endorsement of war, but it was the results of the Spirit being withheld because of the people's wickedness. Thus the wicked will slay the wicked (vv. 32–33; c.f. Mormon 4:5). These terrible wars will be so intense that the Saints shall hardly escape, but the Lord will save them by coming down and consuming the wicked (D&C 63:34). Nephi, quoting the prophet (either Isaiah or Zenos), from the plates of brass, said He would "preserve the righteous by his power" and destroy "their enemies by fire" (1 Nephi 22:17). However, His coming was not to happen for some time (D&C 63:35)

Those who will be saved from the wars are the righteous who will gather to Zion and her stakes (v. 36). These righteous Saints are to lift up a warning voice to the inhabitants of the earth both by word and by flight (v. 37). In other words, by preaching the gospel to them, and by their seeing them flee to places of safety. The Prophet Joseph was shown in vision and prophesied:

> . . . The time is soon coming, when no man will have any peace but in Zion and her stakes.
>
> I saw men hunting the lives of their own sons, and brother murdering brother, women killing their own daughters, and daughters seeking the lives of their mothers. I saw armies arrayed against armies. I saw blood, desolations, fires. The Son of Man has said that the mother shall be against the daughter, and the daughter against the mother. These things are at our doors. They will follow the Saints of God from city to city. Satan will rage, and the spirit of the devil is now enraged. I know not how soon these things shall take place; but with a view of them, shall I cry peace? No; I will lift up my voice and testify of them. How long will you have good crops, and the famine be kept off, I do not know; when the fig tree leaves, know that summer is nigh at hand. [*TPJS*, 161]

While there have been many wars that the Saints have witnessed, and have been involved in, to some extent, since Joseph was shown the above vision, the time when there will be no peace but in Zion and her stakes has not yet happened, but cannot be far off.

D&C 63:38–45 • The Disciples In Kirtland

38 Wherefore, let my disciples in Kirtland arrange their temporal concerns, who dwell upon this farm.

39 Let my servant Titus Billings, who has the care thereof, dispose of the land, that he may be prepared in the coming spring to take his journey up unto the land of Zion, with those that dwell upon the face thereof, excepting those whom I shall reserve unto myself, that shall not go until I shall command them.

40 And let all the moneys which can be spared, it mattereth not unto me whether it be little or much, be sent up unto the land of Zion, unto them whom I have appointed to receive.

41 Behold, I, the Lord, will give unto my servant Joseph Smith, Jun., power that he shall be enabled to discern by the Spirit those who shall go up unto the land of Zion, and those of my disciples who shall tarry.

42 Let my servant Newel K. Whitney retain his store, or in other words, the store, yet for a little season.

43 Nevertheless, let him impart all the money which he can impart, to be sent up unto the land of Zion.

44 Behold, these things are in his own hands, let him do according to wisdom.

45 Verily I say, let him be ordained as an agent unto the disciples that shall tarry, and let him be ordained unto this power;

The land in Kirtland was to be disposed of, but not in haste. Some members were to remain there until the Lord commanded otherwise (vv. 38–39). However, whatever money could be spared should be sent to Zion for the purchase of lands (v. 40). The establishment of Zion was still top priority. Today the instructions may vary, but they will come from the President of the Church. The same discernment will come to him as was promised to Joseph Smith (v. 41; c.f. D&C 105:35–36). The Whitney store was to function in like manner (vv. 42–45), but was to follow the instructions of agency given in section 58 verses 27–28.

D&C 63:46–54 • The Faithful Overcome the World

46 And now speedily visit the churches, expounding these things unto them, with my servant Oliver Cowdery. Behold, this is my will, obtaining moneys even as I have directed.

47 He that is faithful and endureth shall overcome the world.

48 He that sendeth up treasures unto the land of Zion shall receive an inheritance in this world, and his works shall follow him, and also a reward in the world to come.

49 Yea, and blessed are the dead that die in the Lord, from henceforth, when the Lord shall come, and old things shall pass away, and all things become new, they shall rise from the dead and shall not die after, and shall receive an inheritance before the Lord, in the holy city.

50 And he that liveth when the Lord shall come, and hath kept the faith, blessed is he; nevertheless, it is appointed to him to die at the age of man.

51 Wherefore, children shall grow up until they become old; old men shall die; but they shall not sleep in the dust, but they shall be changed in the twinkling of an eye.

52 Wherefore, for this cause preached the apostles unto the world the resurrection of the dead.

53 These things are the things that ye must look for; and, speaking after the manner of the Lord, they are now nigh at hand, and in a time to come, even in the day of the coming of the Son of Man.

54 And until that hour there will be foolish virgins among the wise; and at that hour cometh an entire separation of the righteous and the wicked; and in that day will I send mine angels to pluck out the wicked and cast them into unquenchable fire.

After being taught by Oliver, the faithful could overcome the world and would be rewarded in this world as well as the world to come (vv. 47–48). Even if they pass from this world, they will rise from the dead and be eternal, and receive an inheritance in the holy city of Zion (v. 49).

Those who are alive at the time of the Lord's coming will remain in their mortal state, and "die at the age of man," or live out their normal mortal life (v. 50). "Children shall grow up until they become old." However, they will not experience death, but will be changed from mortality to immortality "in the twinkling of an eye" (v. 51). Other scriptures give the age of man's transfiguration to immortality at one hundred years (see Isaiah 65:20), or the age of a tree (see D&C 101:30) In this writer's opinion, it will vary for each individual, as it does now, when they have completed their mortal mission. The average age of man will apparently be lengthened. The New Testament and the Book of

Mormon Apostles also taught this comforting doctrine of the resurrection (D&C 63:52; see 1 Corinthians 15:21–23; Mormon 7:6).

Although the Lord's coming was nigh at hand in 1831; that time frame was "speaking after the manner of the Lord" (D&C 63:53). Now, over 175 years later, the Lord's declaration that there would "be foolish virgins among the wise" is saying that there would be many members who will not be prepared for His coming, but that "an entire separation of the righteous and the wicked" would happen among the earth's inhabitants. Also, the destroying angel's work would then begin (v. 54). This separation will probably happen among Church members as well as in the world. As we learned in a previous revelation, the oil in the lamps of the wise virgins, or the Church members who are the bride to be at the marriage supper, is the truth and the Holy Spirit (D&C 45:57).

D&C 63:55–60 • Not a Day of Many Words

55 And now behold, verily I say unto you, I, the Lord, am not pleased with my servant Sidney Rigdon; he exalted himself in his heart, and received not counsel, but grieved the Spirit;

56 Wherefore his writing is not acceptable unto the Lord, and he shall make another; and if the Lord receive it not, behold he standeth no longer in the office to which I have appointed him.

57 And again, verily I say unto you, those who desire in their hearts, in meekness, to warn sinners to repentance, let them be ordained unto this power.

58 For this is a day of warning, and not a day of many words. For I, the Lord, am not to be mocked in the last days.

59 Behold, I am from above, and my power lieth beneath. I am over all, and in all, and through all, and search all things, and the day cometh that all things shall be subject unto me.

60 Behold, I am Alpha and Omega, even Jesus Christ.

The above verses illustrate some of the worldly aspirations that must be overcome as we prepare for the Second Coming (v. 55). They also illustrate the Lord's mercy and yet His ultimate justice. He offers repentance and yet His standards will be met; if not by us, He will call others to do it (vv. 56–57). The people must be warned, but He will not be mocked (v. 58). He has all power, but will not fully exercise it until the day of His coming (v. 59). He started the plan for this world, and He will end it (v. 60).

D&C 63:61–66 • Beware How You Take My Name

61 Wherefore, let all men beware how they take my name in their lips—

62 For behold, verily I say, that many there be who are under this condemnation, who use the name of the Lord, and use it in vain, having not authority.

63 Wherefore, let the church repent of their sins, and I, the Lord, will own them; otherwise they shall be cut off.

64 Remember that that which cometh from above is sacred, and must be spoken with care, and by constraint of the Spirit; and in this there is no condemnation, and ye receive the Spirit through prayer; wherefore, without this there remaineth condemnation.

65 Let my servants, Joseph Smith, Jun., and Sidney Rigdon, seek them a home, as they are taught through prayer by the Spirit.

66 These things remain to overcome through patience, that such may receive a more exceeding and eternal weight of glory, otherwise, a greater condemnation. Amen.

The first reaction to the warning of how one takes the name of the Lord upon his lips is probably one of profanity or swearing. While profanity is not acceptable, the Lord also equates man's condemnation with using the name of the Lord "in vain, having not authority" (v. 62). The Lord will not suffer [allow] His name to be polluted (Isaiah 48:11; 1 Nephi 20:11). Vain mean useless or of no benefit. The way to avoid the use of the name of the Lord's name in vain is to speak by the Spirit. That which is given by the Spirit is sacred and if misused will bring condemnation (v. 64). The Spirit will not only tell us what to speak, but will constrain us when we are not to speak. Nephi taught that the Spirit enables one "to speak with the tongue of angels," but the Spirit also "stoppeth mine utterance, and I am left to mourn because of the unbelief, and the wickedness, and the ignorance, and the stiffneckedness of men" (2 Nephi 32:2, 7).

Having no authority (D&C 63:62) sounds like those who speak without the priesthood. However, those who have the priesthood must be even more careful of how they speak. When they speak without the guidance of the Spirit, they are speaking their own mind or will and may be moved by their emotions or aspirations rather than what the Lord wants them to say. When a man speaks "by the power of the Holy Ghost the Holy Ghost carrieth it unto the hearts of the children of men" (2 Nephi 33:1). This should be the objective of all priesthood holders.

Historical Setting—Section 64:

The early part of September was spent in making preparations to remove to the town of Hiram, and renew our work on the translation of the Bible. The brethren who were commanded to go up to the land of Zion were earnestly engaged in getting ready to start in the coming October. On the 11th of September I received [section 64]. [*HC*, 1:211]

SECTION 64 • OUTLINE

➤ 64:1–4   The Lord wills that his elders overcome the world.

      a.   Many have sinned, but for this once, for my glory and for their salvation, I have forgiven them (v. 3).

      b.   He is merciful for he has given them the kingdom (v. 4).

➤ 64:5–14   The keys of the mysteries of the kingdom shall not be taken from Joseph Smith inasmuch as he obeys mine ordinances.

      a.   There are those who sought occasion against Joseph without cause (v. 5).

      b.   Joseph has sinned, but the Lord forgives those who confess and ask forgiveness, who have not sinned unto death (v. 6).

      c.   My disciples in days of old sought occasion against one another, and were afflicted and sorely chastened (v. 8).

      d.   He that forgives not his brother stands condemned and has the greater sin (v. 9).

      e.   The Lord forgives whom he will, but you are required to forgive all men (v. 10).

      f.   Ye should say in your hearts, let God judge between me and thee and reward thee according to thy deeds (v. 11).

      g.   Those who repent not shall be brought before the church and do with him as the scriptures say (v. 12).

h. Do this for the cause that God may be glorified, and you be justified in the eyes of the law and not offend the lawgiver (vv. 13–14).

➤ 64:15–16   The Lord was angry with Ezra Booth and Isaac Morley for not keeping the commandments, and sought evil in their hearts. I withheld my Spirit, but I forgave Isaac.

➤ 64:17   Edward Partridge sinned and Satan seeks to destroy his soul, but when they repent, they shall be forgiven.

➤ 64:18–19   Sidney Gilbert shall return to his agency in the land of Zion in a few weeks, and make known what he has seen and heard to my disciples that they perish not.

➤ 64:20   That Isaac Morley not be tempted above what he is able to bear, and counsel wrongfully, his farm shall be sold.

➤ 64:21–22   Frederick G, Williams should not sell his farm that a strong hold may be retained for five years.

a. In which time I will overthrow the wicked and save some (v. 21).

b. After that, all that go to Zion with an open heart will be held guiltless (v. 22),

➤ 64:23–25   It is called today until the coming of the Son of Man.

a. It is a day of sacrifice and a day of tithing of my people (v. 23).

b. He that is tithed shall not be burned at my coming (v. 23).

c. Tomorrow, after the manner of the Lord, comes the burning of the proud and the wicked that remain in Babylon (v. 24).

d. If ye believe me, ye will labor while it is called today (v. 25).

➤ 64:26–31   Newel K. Whitney and Sidney Gilbert should not sell their store and possessions until those who remain in the church go to Zion.

a. In my laws it is forbidden to get into debt to thine enemies (v. 27).

b. The Lord may take when he pleases and pay as seemeth him good (v. 28).

c. As agents, ye are on the Lord's errand and are to do the Lord's business (v. 29).

d. You provide for the saints that they may obtain an inheritance in Zion (v. 30).

e. My words are sure and shall nor fail, that they shall obtain it (v. 3).

➤ 64:32–36   All things shall come to pass in their time.

a. Be not weary in well doing, ye are laying the foundation of a great work (v. 33).

b. The Lord requires the heart and a willing mind, who will eat the good of the land of Zion in these last days (v. 34).

c. The rebellious shall be cut off out of the land, and not inherit it (v. 35).

d. The rebellious are not of the blood of Ephraim, and shall be plucked out (v. 36).

➤ 64:37–43   The church is like a judge sitting on a hill to judge the nations.

a. The inhabitants of Zion shall judge all things pertaining to Zion (v. 38).

b. Liars and hypocrites shall be proved by them, and those who are not apostles and prophets shall be made known (v. 39).

c. The bishop, who is a judge, and his counselors, if not faithful, shall be condemned and others planted in their stead (v. 40).

d. Zion shall flourish, and the glory of the Lord be upon her (v. 41).

e. Zion shall be an ensign unto the people, and there shall come unto her out of every nation (v. 42).

f. The day comes when the nations of the earth shall tremble because of her (v. 43).

TEXT AND COMMENTARY

D&C 64:1–4 • Forgiveness of Sins

1 Behold, thus saith the Lord your God unto you, O ye elders of my church, hearken ye and hear, and receive my will concerning you.

2 For verily I say unto you, I will that ye should overcome the world; wherefore I will have compassion upon you.

3 There are those among you who have sinned; but verily I say, for this once, for mine own glory, and for the salvation of souls, I have forgiven you your sins.

4 I will be merciful unto you, for I have given unto you the kingdom.

Since "all have sinned, and come short of the glory of God" (Romans 6:23), all who desire to overcome the world and become a Zion people must have their sins forgiven. The Lord reminds the elders of His church that He wants them to overcome the world (D&C 64:2). The salvation of their souls is the first reason that He has forgiven them (v. 3). The second reason is that He has given them His kingdom, and they represent Him upon the earth (v. 4). King Benjamin reminded his people that they must "walk guiltless before God" to retain a remission of their sins, and enumerated several things to do in remaining guiltless (see Mosiah 4:26–30; see also Alma 4:12–14). The elders, to whom this revelation was given, must retain a remission of their sins.

D&C 64:5–14 • It is Required to Forgive All Men

5 And the keys of the mysteries of the kingdom shall not be taken from my servant Joseph Smith, Jun., through the means I have appointed, while he liveth, inasmuch as he obeyeth mine ordinances.

6 There are those who have sought occasion against him without cause;

7 Nevertheless, he has sinned; but verily I say unto you, I, the Lord, forgive sins unto those who confess their sins before me and ask forgiveness, who have not sinned unto death.

8 My disciples, in days of old, sought occasion against one another and forgave not one another in their hearts; and for this evil they were afflicted and sorely chastened.

9 Wherefore, I say unto you, that ye ought to forgive one another; for he that forgiveth not his brother his trespasses standeth condemned before the Lord; for there remaineth in him the greater sin.

10 I, the Lord, will forgive whom I will forgive, but of you it is required to forgive all men.

11 And ye ought to say in your hearts—let God judge between me and thee, and reward thee according to thy deeds.

12 And him that repenteth not of his sins, and confesseth them not, ye shall bring before the church, and do with him as the scripture saith unto you, either by commandment or by revelation.

13 And this ye shall do that God may be glorified—not because ye forgive not, having not compassion, but that ye may be justified in the eyes of the law, that ye may not offend him who is your lawgiver—

14 Verily I say, for this cause ye shall do these things.

To retain their forgiveness, the members must not be critical of their prophet, Joseph Smith, as some of them had done without cause (vv. 5–6). Being human he had sinned, but the Lord had forgiven him, and they must forgive him also. Satan is an "accuser of our brethren" (Revelation 12:10). Those who criticize the brethren are "placing themselves in the seat of Satan" (*TPJS*, 212). "That man who rises up to condemn others, finding fault with the Church, saying that they are out of the way, while he himself is righteous, then know assuredly, that that man is in the high road to apostasy; and if he does not repent, will apostatize, as God lives" (*TPJS*, 156–57). Those who would confess their sins would be forgiven if they had "not sinned unto death" (D&C 64:7). A sin unto death is one serious enough to lose one's possibility for attaining the celestial glory, such as murder or denying the Holy Ghost (see 1 John 5:16–17; Hebrews 10:26; Galatians 5:19–21).

The second requirement to retain their forgiveness was to forgive one another. The New Testament disciples were sorely chastened for not forgiving one another (D&C 64:8–9). Although the specific incident of their not forgiving one another is not in our present New Testament, the doctrine is taught: "And when ye stand praying, forgive, if ye have ought against any: that your Father also which is in heaven may forgive you your trespasses. But if ye do not forgive, neither will your Father which is in heaven forgive your trespasses" (Mark 11:25–26). The Book of Mormon teaches the same doctrine: "And ye shall also forgive one another your trespasses; for verily I say unto you, he that forgiveth not his neighbor's trespasses when he says that he repents, the same hath brought himself under condemnation" (Mosiah 26:31). "The greater sin" of not forgiving (D&C 64:9) is probably because the Lord, who was sinless, has forgiven all of us, and we therefore are "required to forgive all men" (v. 10). The sins against us are minimal when compared to the suffering He went through for each of us. Forgiveness of others is sometimes a very difficult commandment to keep, but its rewards are great. We must learn to leave the judgment of those who offend or harm us in the Lord's hands (v. 11). He knows the thoughts and intents of him who sinned, and we do not. He will see that appropriate punishment or forgiveness is given.

The Lord further instructs the elders that those in the Church who fail to repent should be brought before the Church for discipline (v. 12). The purpose of church discipline is for the Lord's glory (v. 13), or to protect the character of the Lord and His Church. It is also to bring justification to the sinner; or to assure a proper balance between justice and mercy (see Alma 42:21–25). These were the causes for which the Lord's instructions were given (D&C 64:14). The procedure for such discipline will be treated with that instruction (see D&C 102). The law of forgiveness is also amplified in a later revelation, and will be discussed with that section (D&C 98:39–48).

D&C 64:15–22 • Chastening and Instructions for Kirtland Saints

15 Behold, I, the Lord, was angry with him who was my servant Ezra Booth, and also my servant Isaac Morley, for they kept not the law, neither the commandment;

16 They sought evil in their hearts, and I, the Lord, withheld my Spirit. They condemned for evil that thing in which there was no evil; nevertheless I have forgiven my servant Isaac Morley.

17 And also my servant Edward Partridge, behold, he hath sinned, and Satan seeketh to destroy his soul; but when these things are made known unto them, and they repent of the evil, they shall be forgiven.

18 And now, verily I say that it is expedient in me that my servant Sidney Gilbert, after a few weeks, shall return upon his business, and to his agency in the land of Zion;

19 And that which he hath seen and heard may be made known unto my disciples, that they perish not. And for this cause have I spoken these things.

20 And again, I say unto you, that my servant Isaac Morley may not be tempted above that which he is able to bear, and counsel wrongfully to your hurt, I gave commandment that his farm should be sold.

21 I will not that my servant Frederick G. Williams should sell his farm, for I, the Lord, will to retain a strong hold in the land of Kirtland, for the space of five years, in the which I will not overthrow the wicked, that thereby I may save some.

22 And after that day, I, the Lord, will not hold any guilty that shall go with an open heart up to the land of Zion; for I, the Lord, require the hearts of the children of men.

The Lord told the elders of several individuals who had violated His commandments, and in some cases told of the consequences that had followed. Some had sought evil in their hearts by calling evil what was not evil, and in consequence, the Lord had withheld His Spirit. He that repented was forgiven, and the other apostatized (vv. 15–16). Satan sought to destroy one brother's soul. He was apparently not aware of Satan's efforts, and when he became aware and repented he would be forgiven (v. 17). These were not physical sins of commission, but sins of the heart and mind. The Lord made these sins known that may not be repeated by others.

The Lord's foreknowledge of His people was illustrated through His revealing why or why not certain farms were sold. Isaac Morley's farm was sold so that he would not be tempted above his ability to withstand temptation (D&C 64:20). The Lord does not say what the temptation was, but selling the farm avoided it. This principle of the Lord providing "a way of escape, that ye may be able to bear it" was taught by the Apostle Paul (1 Cor. 10:13). The Lord was providing the escape for Isaac Morley. The Prophet Alma admonished: "watch and pray continually, that ye may not be tempted above that which ye can bear, and thus be led by the Holy Spirit, becoming humble, meek, submissive, patient, full of love and all long-suffering" (Alma 13:28). This is applicable to all, and shows how the temptation will be avoided. Frederick G. William's farm was to be retained as a stronghold in Kirtland area for five years so that some people may be saved before the wicked were overthrown (D&C 64:21). Those who turn their hearts to the Lord, as required, and seek His advice, will not only be guided in their decisions, but will overcome the world and be held guiltless (D&C 64:22).

D&C 64:23-25 • Called Today, Until the Second Coming

23 Behold, now it is called today until the coming of the Son of Man, and verily it is a day of sacrifice, and a day for the tithing of my people; for he that is tithed shall not be burned at his coming.

24 For after today cometh the burning—this is speaking after the manner of the Lord—for verily I say, tomorrow all the proud and they that do wickedly shall be as stubble; and I will burn them up, for I am the Lord of Hosts; and I will not spare any that remain in Babylon.

25 Wherefore, if ye believe me, ye will labor while it is called today.

The context of the "day of sacrifice" suggests that tithing is a sacrifice (v. 23). Since there are many blessings associated with the paying of tithing, some would argue that complying with this principle is not a sacrifice. While this is true, to the new investigator and the new convert, it does represent a sacrifice to them initially. The long-range blessing of tithe paying is the promise to not be burned with the proud and the wicked at the Second Coming. The burning is described in the language of the Old Testament Prophet Malachi (vv. 23–24, see Malachi 4:1). Malachi preceded this description with the challenge to prove the Lord by paying tithes and offerings (Malachi 3:10). It seems apparent that Malachi was also aware of the promise to the tithe payer of not being burned. Of course, we must not overlook the warning given by Mormon regarding the giving of gifts with real intent, or it is counted unto him as if he had retained the gift (Moroni 7:6–8).

The designation of "today" as the time period until the coming of the Son of Man (D&C 64:23) helps us identify other time periods. Jesus is identified as being the same God "yesterday, today, and forever" in the New Testament (Hebrews 13:8), the Book of Mormon (1 Nephi 10:18), and the Doctrine and Covenants (D&C 20:12). Therefore, the "today" period that is until the Second Coming probably began with His ministry, being crucified and resurrected and reigning at the right hand of God (D&C 20:21–24). The "yesterday period would thus describe His reigning in the spirit during Old Testament times, and the "forever" period would be His millennial reign upon the earth and into the eternities. The sameness of Jesus in all three time periods has reference to His eternal attributes. To accept and believe in Him having these attributes will give us an incentive to "labor while it is [still] called today" (D&C 64:25).

D&C 64:26–31 • Not Get Into Debt to Thine Enemies

26 And it is not meet that my servants, Newel K. Whitney and Sidney Gilbert, should sell their store and their possessions here; for this is not wisdom until the residue of the church, which remaineth in this place, shall go up unto the land of Zion.

27 Behold, it is said in my laws, or forbidden, to get in debt to thine enemies;

28 But behold, it is not said at any time that the Lord should not take when he please, and pay as seemeth him good.

29 Wherefore, as ye are agents, ye are on the Lord's errand; and whatever ye do according to the will of the Lord is the Lord's business.

30 And he hath set you to provide for his saints in these last days, that they may obtain an inheritance in the land of Zion.

31 And behold, I, the Lord, declare unto you, and my words are sure and shall not fail, that they shall obtain it.

Having labeled their day as one of sacrifice, the Lord again illustrates His foreknowledge in advising Brothers Whitney and Gilbert not to sell their store and possessions until all the Kirtland residents go up to Zion (v. 26). He also gives some other monetary laws to help them overcome the world. They are to not get in debt to their enemies (v. 27). Where this is said in His laws (the Scriptures) is not identifiable in the Bible today. Apparently it was there before plain and precious parts were removed (see 1 Nephi 13:26–29). While any debt is undesirable, there are times that necessitate it. The admonition implies it is acceptable to be in debt to those who are not enemies. Also, it was acceptable for other churches to borrow from the storehouse (see D&C 51:11). We are all in the Lord's debt (see Mosiah 2:21–24), thus He may take from us, or from the Church, whatever He pleases, or "pay as seemeth him good" (D&C 64:28). Being in debt to an enemy gives him power to prevent one's attaining his goals. This is especially vital when a servant is "on the Lord's errand" (v. 29). Since the servant is doing the Lord's business, He will provide the way for the servant to accomplish his task, and will also give the servant an inheritance in Zion (v. 30). The Lord's words are sure, and there is no question about the servant's attaining Zion if he follow His commandments, both collectively and individually (v. 31).

D&C 64:32–36 • Eat the Good of the Land of Zion

32 But all things must come to pass in their time.

33 Wherefore, be not weary in well-doing, for ye are laying the foundation of a great work. And out of small things proceedeth that which is great.

34 Behold, the Lord requireth the heart and a willing mind; and the willing and obedient shall eat the good of the land of Zion in these last days.

35 And the rebellious shall be cut off out of the land of Zion, and shall be sent away, and shall not inherit the land.

36 For, verily I say that the rebellious are not of the blood of Ephraim, wherefore they shall be plucked out.

Laying the foundation of Zion was one of the basic reasons for the Lord sending some of the Saints to Missouri (see D&C 57:7). This small foundation would become a great and holy city in the due time of the Lord. (D&C 64:32–33). The requirement of "the heart and a willing mind" was vital. The heart is used synonymously with the spirit. The Lord reveals His will "to our spirits precisely as though we had no body at all; and those revelations which will save our spirits will save our bodies" (*TPJS*, 355). To overcome the world, we must tune our spirits to His revelations. He also expects us to use our minds by reasoning with Him through prayer (see Isaiah 1:18; D&C 50:10), or to study it out and ask for confirmation of his Spirit (see D&C 9:8). Thus we come to know His will and meet the requirement for the blessing sought.

The promise to eat the good of the land of Zion in these last days (v. 34) is a fulfillment of a prophecy of Isaiah: "If ye be willing and obedient, ye shall eat the good of the land" (Isaiah 1:19). While it may be a dual prophecy, relating to both Isaiah's day of warning northern Israel and to the latter days, Isaiah was shown and he prophesied of our day. Oliver Cowdery, in speaking of the Angel Moroni's visit to Joseph Smith in September 1823, declared that: "Isaiah, who was on the earth at the time the ten tribes were led away captive from the land of Canaan, was shown not only their calamity and affliction, but the time they were to be delivered" (*MA*, April 1835, 109–110). Therefore, it is no coincident that Isaiah is quoted. One of the purposes of the Restoration in the latter days was to fulfill that "which was written by the prophets" (D&C 1:18). The above prophecy of Isaiah is yet to be fulfilled.

The rebellious who would be cut off, and are not of the "blood of Ephraim," and would be plucked out (D&C 64:34–35), are referring to members of the Church. Ephraim was the first born, or the birthright holder, who was to be the first tribe of ancient Israel gathered (see Jeremiah 31:8–9; Jacob 5:52–54, 63). While there is a prevalent theory among Church members that the large majority of them are adopted into Israel, the Doctrine and Covenants and Church leaders teach otherwise.[43] As President Joseph F. Smith testified: "A striking peculiarity of the Saints gathered from all parts of the earth is that they are almost universally of the blood of Ephraim" (*Gospel Doctrine*, 115). As stated previously, Amos prophesied that Israel would be scattered among all the nations of the earth or among the Gentiles (see Amos 9:8–9). The work of the Restoration was and is to gather those Israelites who were scattered among the nations. As the gospel is preached to the nations," my sheep hear my voice" (John 10:27) and are gathered or grafted back into their mother branch of Israel (see Jacob 5:54–56; Jeremiah 31:6–9).

The rebellious not being of Israel is similar to the Apostle Paul's teaching to the Romans: "For they are not all Israel, which are of Israel" (Romans 9:6). Even though many of the gathered are literal descendants of Ephraim, they will not be given the blessings of Israel if they are rebellious. If they rebel against their birthright responsibilities, they have become of the world and will lose their birthright as happened often in ancient times (i.e. 1 Chronicles 5:1). The Savior also taught this principle to the Jews during his earthly ministry (see Matthew 8:10–12).

D&C 64:37–43 • The Church to Judge the Nations

37 Behold, I, the Lord, have made my church in these last days like unto a judge sitting on a hill, or in a high place, to judge the nations.

38 For it shall come to pass that the inhabitants of Zion shall judge all things pertaining to Zion.

---

[43] See Wayne Shute; Monte S. Nyman, and Randy L. Bott, *Ephraim: Chosen Servant of the Lord* [1999], 111–119.

39 And liars and hypocrites shall be proved by them, and they who are not apostles and prophets shall be known.

40 And even the bishop, who is a judge, and his counselors, if they are not faithful in their stewardships shall be condemned, and others shall be planted in their stead.

41 For, behold, I say unto you that Zion shall flourish, and the glory of the Lord shall be upon her;

42 And she shall be an ensign unto the people, and there shall come unto her out of every nation under heaven.

43 And the day shall come when the nations of the earth shall tremble because of her, and shall fear because of her terrible ones. The Lord hath spoken it. Amen.

The Church judging all nations (v. 37) will not be until the New Jerusalem, or the city of Zion, is fully established. To be a judge, the Church and its members must be a Zion people who have overcome the world (v. 38). They shall be the Lord's standard of measurement against other nations and their inhabitants. Those who do not measure up to these standards, such as liars and hypocrites shall be detected. Those who have pretended to be Apostles and Prophets, or have usurped authority and led the Church members astray shall be made known (v. 39). Even a bishop, who is a judge in Israel, and his counselors may be removed (v. 40).

Zion flourishing, the glory of the Lord being upon her, and Zion being an ensign to the people is a summation of the Prophet Isaiah's description of her in the latter days. "Arise, shine; for thy light is come, and the glory of the LORD is risen upon thee" (D&C 64:41; Isaiah 60:1). "And the Gentiles shall come to thy light" (D&C 64:42; Isaiah 60:3). "For the nation and kingdom that will not serve thee shall perish; yea, [those] nations shall be utterly wasted" (D&C 64:43; Isaiah 60:12, see the whole chapter). Those who affiliate with The Church of Jesus Christ of Latter-day Saints, and overcome the tribulations of the world, shall become a Zion people and a part of the ensign to the world.

General Authority Quotes

—*Elder Spencer W. Kimball* • D&C 63:7, 10

Certainly we should not be interested in signs. Signs are available and anyone, I believe, can have signs who wants them. I believe if one wants revelations enough to crave them beyond the rightness of it, that eventually he will get his revelations—but they may not come from God. I am sure that there can be many spectacular things performed, because the devil is very responsive. He is listening and he is eager to do it. And so he gives strange experiences. I think some actually do get unusual experiences and revelations.

However, the Lord does make specific promises: Signs will follow them that believe. He makes no promise that signs will create belief nor save nor exalt. Signs are the product of faith. They are born in the soil of unwavering sureness. They will be prevalent in the Church in about the same degree to which the people have true faith. [*TSWK*, 458, 500]

—President Joseph Fielding Smith • D&C 63:20–21

When our Savior comes, the earth will be changed to a terrestrial condition and will then be made the fit abode for terrestrial brings, and this condition will last until the close of the millennium when the earth will die and be raised again in a resurrection to receive its glory as a celestial body, which is its final state. [*Doctrines of Salvation*, 1:84]

—The Prophet Joseph Smith • D&C 63:34

. . . it is a false idea that the Saints will escape all the judgments, whilst the wicked suffer; for all flesh is subject to suffer, and "the righteous shall hardly escape;" still many of the Saints will escape, for the just shall live by faith; yet many of the righteous shall fall prey to disease, to pestilence, etc., by reason of the weakness of the flesh, and yet be saved in the kingdom of God. So that it is an unhallowed principle to say that such and such have transgressed because they have been preyed upon by disease or death, for all flesh is subject to death; and the Savior said, "Judge not, lest ye be judged." [*TPJS*, 162–63]

—President Spencer W. Kimball • D&C 64:9–10

For if ye forgive men their trespasses, your heavenly Father will also forgive you: But if ye forgive not men their trespasses, neither will your Father forgive your trespasses (Matthew 6:14–15).

Hard to do? Of course. The Lord never promised an easy road, nor a simple gospel, nor low standards, nor a low norm. The price is high, but the goods attained are worth all they cost. The Lord himself turned the other cheek; he suffered himself to be buffeted and beaten without remonstrance; he suffered every dignity and yet spoke no word of condemnation. And the question to all of us is: "Therefore, what manner of men ought ye to be?" And his answer to us is: "Even as I am" (3 Nephi 27:27). [*TSWK*, 102]

Chapter Twenty-Nine

What Is Scripture?

D&C 65; 67:10–14; 68

*H*istorical Setting:

> In the fore part of October, I received the following prayer [section 65] through revelation. [*HC*, 1:218]

> After this revelation [section 66] was received, some conversation was had concerning revelations and language. I received [section 67]. [*HC*, 1:224]

Note: The first 9 verses of this revelation were discussed in chapter 1 of this work, concerning the coming forth of the Doctrine and Covenants. sections 66; 69; and part of section 70 were also discussed there. Since verses 10–14 are more fitting to our subject of a Zion people, they were held over to be discussed here.

INTRODUCTION

What is scripture? Many define it according to the words of Peter: "Holy men of God spake as they were moved upon by the Holy Ghost" (2 Peter 1:21). This definition is enlarged upon in this revelation as an example to the priesthood holders.

SECTIONS 65 & 67 • OUTLINE

➤ 65:1–6   A voice as one sent down from on high to all men.

    a.   Prepare ye the way of the Lord, make His paths straight (v. 1).

    b.   The keys of the kingdom are committed that the gospel may roll forth as a stone cut out of the mountain without hands until it fills the whole earth (v. 2).

    c.   A voice crying, prepare a supper of the Lamb; make ready the bridegroom (v. 3).

    d.   Call on His holy name to make known his works among the people (v. 4).

    e.   Call on the Lord that his kingdom may roll forth to prepare for the Son of Man to come down and meet the kingdom of God on the earth (v. 5).

    f.   May the kingdom of God go forth, that the kingdom of heaven may come and subdue thine enemies (v. 6).

➤ 67:10–14   A privilege and a promise to those ordained to the priesthood.

    a.   Strip yourselves from jealousies and fear, and humble yourselves, and you shall see me with spiritual eyes, and know that I am (v. 10).

    b.   No man has seen God in the flesh except quickened by the Spirit of God (v. 11).

    c.   Natural man cannot abide the presence of God, neither the carnal mind (v. 12).

    d.   Ye are not able to abide the presence of God, nor the ministering of angels, wherefore continue in patience until ye are perfected (v. 13).

    e.   When ye are worthy, in mine own due time, you will know what was conferred upon you by my servant Joseph Smith (v. 14).

TEXT AND COMMENTARY

D&C 65:1–6 • May the Kingdom of God Go Forth

1 Hearken, and lo, a voice as of one sent down from on high, who is mighty and powerful, whose going forth is unto the ends of the earth, yea, whose voice is unto men—Prepare ye the way of the Lord, make his paths straight.

2 The keys of the kingdom of God are committed unto man on the

earth, and from thence shall the gospel roll forth unto the ends of the earth, as the stone which is cut out of the mountain without hands shall roll forth, until it has filled the whole earth.

3 Yea, a voice crying—Prepare ye the way of the Lord, prepare ye the supper of the Lamb, make ready for the Bridegroom.

4 Pray unto the Lord, call upon his holy name, make known his wonderful works among the people.

5 Call upon the Lord, that his kingdom may go forth upon the earth, that the inhabitants thereof may receive it, and be prepared for the days to come, in the which the Son of Man shall come down in heaven, clothed in the brightness of his glory, to meet the kingdom of God which is set up on the earth.

6 Wherefore, may the kingdom of God go forth, that the kingdom of heaven may come, that thou, O God, mayest be glorified in heaven so on earth, that thine enemies may be subdued; for thine is the honor, power and glory, forever and ever. Amen.

The Lord's voice to "Prepare ye the way of the Lord, make his paths straight" (v. 1) is the same commandment given to John the Baptist before the Savior began His earthly ministry (see Matthew 3:3; Mark 1:3; Luke 3:40). The Prophet Isaiah had prophesied of John's mission, and had extended his mission to the Second Coming (see Isaiah 40:3–5; see also JST, Luke 3:4–10). Sidney Rigdon had been a part of that preparation and was discussed earlier (see D&C 35:4–6).

The keys of the kingdom committed to man on the earth, and the gospel rolling to the ends of the earth (D&C 65:2), verifies the interpretation of the dream given to Nebachadnezzar, king of Babylon, by the young Old Testament prophet Daniel. He told the king that the God of heaven would "set up a kingdom which should never be destroyed," and would consume all earthly kingdoms and "stand forever" (Daniel 2:44). Joseph Smith was the man to whom those keys were given. "As the stone cut out of the mountain without hands," and "roll forth, until it has filled the whole earth" (D&C 65:2) further verifies Daniel's interpretation. Daniel's interpretation of the stone "that it brake in pieces the iron [Roman kingdom], the brass [Macedonian kingdom], the clay [kingdoms to come out of the Roman Empire], the silver [Medes and Persian kingdom], and the gold [Babylonian kingdom] . . . what shall come to pass hereafter"

(Daniel 2:45) has happened as Daniel said it would, and the Lord here confirms it.[44]

The preparation for the wedding supper of the Lamb is the mission now given to the Saints (D&C 65:3). The bride is the Church, who was to be prepared for her symbolic marriage to the Lord (see JST, Revelation 19:7; Revelation 19:6–9). The Church had been driven into the wilderness at the time of the apostasy (see Revelation 12:6), and had been brought out at the time of the Restoration (see D&C 5:14; 33:5). Her being prepared and adorned in purity for her wedding was the "wonderful works" to be made known "among the people" (D&C 65:4). To be prepared, she must overcome the world. The time of the wedding is His Second Coming, when He will come down from the heaven "clothed in the brightness of his glory" (v. 5). The kingdom of God on earth must go forth and be prepared so that Christ will come down and subdue the Church's enemies (v. 6). The kingdom has gone forth, but her members must continue to overcome the world.

D&C 67:10–14 • Quickened By the Spirit of God

10 And again, verily I say unto you that it is your privilege, and a promise I give unto you that have been ordained unto this ministry, that inasmuch as you strip yourselves from jealousies and fears, and humble yourselves before me, for ye are not sufficiently humble, the veil shall be rent and you shall see me and know that I am—not with the carnal neither natural mind, but with the spiritual.

11 For no man has seen God at any time in the flesh, except quickened by the Spirit of God.

12 Neither can any natural man abide the presence of God, neither after the carnal mind.

13 Ye are not able to abide the presence of God now, neither the ministering of angels; wherefore, continue in patience until ye are perfected.

14 Let not your minds turn back; and when ye are worthy, in mine own due time, ye shall see and know that which was conferred upon you by the hands of my servant Joseph Smith, Jun. Amen.

---

[44] For the bracketed interpretations of the kingdoms represented see Rudger Clawson, President of the Quorum of the Twelve in 1930, CR April 1930, 33.

The Lord declared, in a conference held shortly after, what must be done by those ordained to the ministry to have the privilege and the promise to see God (v. 10). While the revelation speaks of them individually, it applies to the Church collectively as a requirement to be present at the supper of the Lamb. Moses was able to endure the presence of God because the glory of God was upon him (see Moses 1:2). He later said: "But now mine own eyes have beheld God; but not my natural, but my spiritual eyes, for my natural eyes could not have beheld; for I should have withered and died in his presence; but his glory was upon me; and I beheld his face, for I was transfigured before him" (Moses 1:11). The brother of Jared was able to endure the presence of the pre-mortal Jesus Christ because he was redeemed from the fall (see Ether 3:14–15). He was no longer a natural man. From the Joseph Smith Translation we learn: "No man hath seen God at any time, except them who believe" (JST, 1 John 4:12). "And no man hath seen God at any time, except he hath borne record of the Son; for except it is through him no man can be saved" (JST, John 1:19). The Apostle Paul, speaking of himself said: "I knew a man in Christ above fourteen years ago, (whether in the body, I cannot tell; or whether out of the body, I cannot tell: God knoweth;) such an one caught up to the third heaven" (2 Corinthians 12:2). All of these accounts are consistent with section 67 verses 11–12.

The Aaronic Priesthood holds the keys of the ministering of angel (see D&C 13). However there are requirements to have angels appear. Mormon testified:

> 29 . . . neither have angels ceased to minister unto the children of men.
>
> 30 For behold, they are subject unto him, to minister according to the word of his command, showing themselves unto them of strong faith and a firm mind in every form of godliness.
>
> 31 And the office of their ministry is to call men unto repentance, and to fulfil and to do the work of the covenants of the Father, which he hath made unto the children of men, to prepare the way among the children of men, by declaring the word of Christ unto the chosen vessels of the Lord, that they may bear testimony of him.
>
> 32 And by so doing, the Lord God prepareth the way that the residue of men may have faith in Christ, that the Holy Ghost may have place in their hearts, according to the power thereof; and after this manner

bringeth to pass the Father, the covenants which he hath made unto the children of men. [Moroni 7:29–32]

The Melchizedek Priesthood holds the keys of the knowledge of God.

22 For without this no man can see the face of God, even the Father, and live.

23 Now this Moses plainly taught to the children of Israel in the wilderness, and sought diligently to sanctify his people that they might behold the face of God;

24 But they hardened their hearts and could not endure his presence; therefore, the Lord in his wrath, for his anger was kindled against them, swore that they should not enter into his rest while in the wilderness, which rest is the fulness of his glory. [D&C 84:19, 22–24]

The Lord chastised the members of the Church, at the above mentioned conference, by saying that they were not prepared to have angels minister to them let alone be in the presence of God (D&C 65:13). He wanted them to look forward, and not back, that they may appreciate the Melchizedek Priesthood that had been conferred upon them, and be worthy to use it (v. 14).

*H*istorical Setting—Section 68:

The first Sunday in October, Orson Hyde, a clerk in Brother Sidney Gilbert and Newel K, Whitney's store, in Kirtland was baptized, and became a member of the Church. He was soon after designated as one of the chosen men of the Lord, to bear his word to the nations. [*HC*, 1:217]

As the following Elders—Orson Hyde, Luke Johnson, Lyman E. Johnson, and William E. McLellin—were desirous to know the mind of the Lord concerning themselves, I inquired, and received [section 68, November 1831]. [*HC*, 1: 227]

SECTION 68 • OUTLINE

➤ 68:1–6   Orson Hyde was called to proclaim the everlasting gospel, by the Spirit, from land to land, reasoning and expounding all scripture unto them.

    a.   This is an ensample unto all who are ordained to the priesthood (v. 2).

    b.   They shall speak as they are moved upon by the Holy Ghost (v. 3).

    c.   What they speak shall be scripture, from the Lord, and bring salvation (v. 4).

    d.   Be of good cheer and do not fear, the Lord will be with you as you bear record of him and his coming (vv. 5–6).

➤ 68:7–12   The word of the Lord to Orson Hyde, Luke Johnson, Lyman Johnson, and William E McLellin, and all the faithful elders of the church.

    a.   Go into the world and preach the gospel to every creature, in authority, baptizing in the name of the Father, Son, and Holy Ghost (v. 8).

    b.   He that believes and is baptized shall be saved, and he that believes not shall be damned (v. 9).

    c.   He that believes shall be blessed with signs as it is written (v. 10).

    d.   The signs of the times shall be given, and the coming of the Son of Man (v. 11).

    e.   As many as the Father shall bear record, to you shall be given power to seal up unto eternal life (v. 12).

➤ 68:13–24   Items in addition to the covenants and commandments.

    a.   In due time other bishops will be set apart to minister like the first (v. 14).

    b.   They shall be high priests who are worthy, appointed by the First Presidency, except he be a literal descendant of Aaron and the first born (vv. 15–16).

    c.   The first born has the legal right of presidency over this priesthood, and the keys or authority (vv. 17–18).

    d.   A high priest of the Melchizedek Priesthood has authority to minister in the lesser offices and may officiate as bishop when no legal descendant of Aaron is found, if called and set apart by the first Presidency (v. 19).

    e.   A legal descendant of Aaron must be designated by the First Presidency, found worthy, and ordained under the hands of this Presidency (v. 20).

f. Aaron's lineage from father to son may claim this anoint-
    ing if they prove their lineage, or ascertain it by revelation
    from the Lord to this Presidency (v. 21).

g. No bishop or high priest who is set apart for this ministry
    shall be tried or convicted of any crime save by the First
    Presidency (v. 22).

h. If found guilty, he shall be condemned, if he repents he
    shall be forgiven according to the covenants and com-
    mandments of the church (vv. 23–24).

➤ 68:25–30   Parents who do not teach their children the first principles of
             the gospel when eight years old, the sin be upon the parents.

a. This shall be the law unto Zion or any of her stakes
    (v. 26).

b. Children shall be baptized when eight years old, and
    receive the laying on of hands (v. 27).

c. Children are to be taught to pray, and walk uprightly
    before the Lord (v. 28).

d. The inhabitants of Zion shall keep the Sabbath day holy
    (v. 29).

e. They are to labor as appointed in faithfulness, and not be
    idle (v. 30).

➤ 68:31–35   The Lord is not pleased with the inhabitants of Zion because
             of idleness, not teaching their children, and they're not seeking
             the riches of eternity.

a. These things ought not to be; Oliver shall carry these
    sayings to Zion (v. 32).

b. The Lord commands that those who observe not their
    prayers be reported to the judge of his people (v. 33).

c. These sayings are true and faithful, transgress them not
    (v. 34).

d. I am Alpha and Omega, I come quickly (v. 35).

TEXT AND COMMENTARY

D&C 68:1–6 • What Is Scripture?

1 My servant, Orson Hyde, was called by his ordination to proclaim

the everlasting gospel, by the Spirit of the living God, from people to people, and from land to land, in the congregations of the wicked, in their synagogues, reasoning with and expounding all scriptures unto them.

2 And, behold, and lo, this is an ensample unto all those who were ordained unto this priesthood, whose mission is appointed unto them to go forth—

3 And this is the ensample unto them, that they shall speak as they are moved upon by the Holy Ghost.

4 And whatsoever they shall speak when moved upon by the Holy Ghost shall be scripture, shall be the will of the Lord, shall be the mind of the Lord, shall be the word of the Lord, shall be the voice of the Lord, and the power of God unto salvation.

5 Behold, this is the promise of the Lord unto you, O ye my servants.

6 Wherefore, be of good cheer, and do not fear, for I the Lord am with you, and will stand by you; and ye shall bear record of me, even Jesus Christ, that I am the Son of the living God, that I was, that I am, and that I am to come.

Orson Hyde was sent by the Prophet Joseph Smith, shortly after the Kirtland Temple was dedicated, to dedicate the land of Jerusalem for the return of the Jews. After suffering great physical hardships, he dedicated the land on the Mount of Olives on October 24, 1841. This was a major part of the fulfillment of his priesthood ordination; "from people to people, and from land to land" (v. 1). All priesthood holders are to follow his example (v. 2).

There are two kinds of scripture, according to the world's definition. Scripture that is voted on and accepted as binding upon that group of people, or faith, is called "canonized scripture." But scripture, in the broader sense, is what is spoken by man when moved upon by the Holy Ghost (v. 3). It is also binding upon the people to whom it is spoken, or to whom it is made available. As defined in this revelation (v. 4), scripture is the will of the Lord, or what He desires or commands to be given to His people. Scripture is the mind of the Lord, above and beyond the mind of man, or that which He reveals to man that he could not otherwise know. The word of the Lord is scripture or revelation, that you are told "in your mind and in your heart, by the Holy Ghost" (D&C 8:2–3). Scripture is the voice of the Lord, spoken to His prophets either audibly (see 3 Nephi 11:3–7; Helaman 5:30), or into the mind (see Enos 1:10; 1 Kings 19:12–13; D&C 85:6). Lastly, scripture is the power of God unto salvation, or what it will do for a person. It is to persuade men to come unto God, and be saved (see 1 Nephi 6:4; 2 Nephi 25:23; 31:20–21). The Apostle Paul also gave this last definition of the gospel, or scripture: "I am not ashamed of the gospel of Christ, for it is the power of God unto salvation to every one that believeth" (Romans 1:16). The promise of the Lord (D&C 68:5) is that revelation will be given to His ordained priesthood through all of these sources. He promises further to be with them as they bear record of Him as their past, the present, and their God who will come again (v. 6).

D&C 68:7–12 • Unto All the Faithful Elders

7 This is the word of the Lord unto you, my servant Orson Hyde, and also unto my servant Luke Johnson, and unto my servant Lyman Johnson, and unto my servant William E. McLellin, and unto all the faithful elders of my church—

8 Go ye into all the world, preach the gospel to every creature, acting in the authority which I have given you, baptizing in the name of the Father, and of the Son, and of the Holy Ghost.

9 And he that believeth and is baptized shall be saved, and he that believeth not shall be damned.

10 And he that believeth shall be blest with signs following, even as it is written.

11 And unto you it shall be given to know the signs of the times, and the signs of the coming of the Son of Man;

12 And of as many as the Father shall bear record, to you shall be given power to seal them up unto eternal life. Amen.

The Lord now gives scripture, the word of the Lord, to the collective group that sought the mind of Him, and to all the faithful elders of His Church (v. 7, see the section heading). They are to do as Christ commanded His Apostles after His resurrection; to go to all the world, and with authority, preach the gospel and baptize (v. 8, see Matthew 28:19; Mark 16:15). The promise to the New Testament believers was extended to present dispensation believers; those who believed and were baptized would be saved, and the unbelievers would be damned, and the believers would be blessed with signs. He acknowledged that these promises had been written before (D&C 68:9–10; Mark 16:16–17). This is significant in light of many Bible scholars' rejection of the ending of Mark as being the words of the biblical text.[45]

The Lord extended a further promise to the priesthood holders of this generation; to know the signs of the times, and the signs of the coming of the Son of Man (v. 11). Note that He does not tell them the day or the hour, which no man knows (see D&C 39:21; 49:7 and comments).

The power to seal up unto eternal life (v. 12) had been promised at this same time in the Preface to the Doctrine and Covenants (see D&C 1:8). This revelation is part of the evidence that Joseph Smith knew of the revelation on eternal marriage (D&C 132) as early as 1831, although it was not recorded until 1843 (see section heading of D&C 132). We will not discuss this power here, but leave it until later revelations are discussed.

D&C 68:13–15 • Literal Descendants of Aaron

13 And now, concerning the items in addition to the covenants and commandments, they are these—

14 There remain hereafter, in the due time of the Lord, other bishops to be set apart unto the church, to minister even according to the first;

15 Wherefore they shall be high priests who are worthy, and they shall be appointed by the First Presidency of the Melchizedek Priesthood, except they be literal descendants of Aaron.

Edward Partridge was the first bishop in the Church, called in February 1831 (see D&C 41:9–11). He had served for nine months, often assisted by the agent of the Church, when this revelation was received. There were other bishops to be "set apart" like unto the first (D&C 68:14). The words "set apart" are significant. A bishop is appointed and ordained to the office (see D&C 72:8), but is set apart to preside over a ward. They are to be high priests in the Melchizedek Priesthood, or be ordained to that office, and be worthy to serve. They are all appointed

---

[45] See Frederick C. Grant, The Gospel According to Mark, Exegesis, *The Interpreters Bible,* Vol.7, 915–16 Abington Press.

by the First Presidency except he be a literal descendant of Aaron, the brother of Moses (D&C 68:14). The office of bishop in the Church is an extremely important office in the eyes of the Lord. One month later, Newel K. Whitney was called as the first of those other bishops (D&C 72:8). The Lord gave further directions concerning the literal descendants of Aaron.

D&C 68:16–18 • The Firstborn Son

16 And if they be literal descendants of Aaron they have a legal right to the bishopric, if they are the firstborn among the sons of Aaron;

17 For the firstborn holds the right of the presidency over this priesthood, and the keys or authority of the same.

18 No man has a legal right to this office, to hold the keys of this priesthood, except he be a literal descendant and the firstborn of Aaron.

The first requirement for Aaron's descendant to be a bishop was that he be the first born son among the sons of Aaron (v. 16). This practice apparently began in the days of Aaron. When Aaron died, his third son Eleazar succeeded him, since his first two sons were dead (see Numbers 20:26–28). The office continued through the firstborn of Eleazar. The Lord made a covenant of an everlasting priesthood with Phineas, Eleazar's firstborn, and his seed after him (see Numbers 25:10–13). Thus, they hold the right of presidency and the keys of authority of the Aaronic Priesthood (D&C 68:17–18).

D&C 68:19–21 • A High Priest May Officiate

19 But, as a high priest of the Melchizedek Priesthood has authority to officiate in all the lesser offices he may officiate in the office of bishop when no literal descendant of Aaron can be found, provided he is called and set apart and ordained unto this power, under the hands of the First Presidency of the Melchizedek Priesthood.

20 And a literal descendant of Aaron, also, must be designated by this Presidency, and found worthy, and anointed, and ordained under the hands of this Presidency, otherwise they are not legally authorized to officiate in their priesthood.

21 But, by virtue of the decree concerning their right of the priesthood descending from father to son, they may claim their anointing if at any time they can prove their lineage, or do ascertain it by revelation

from the Lord under the hands of the above named Presidency.

A high priest has been appointed and ordained as the Presiding Bishop of the Church, and the President of the Aaronic Priesthood, since the days of Joseph Smith (v. 19). Even if a first born descendant of Aaron was found in the Church, they must prove their lineage—a very difficult thing to do at this much later date. Therefore, the more possible way for him to take his legal position would be by revelation from the Lord (v. 21). This of course would come to the President of the Church. He would still have to be found worthy, and anointed, and ordained under the hands of the First Presidency (v. 20).

D&C 68:22–24 • Tried Only By the First Presidency

22 And again, no bishop or high priest who shall be set apart for this ministry shall be tried or condemned for any crime, save it be before the First Presidency of the church;

23 And inasmuch as he is found guilty before this Presidency, by testimony that cannot be impeached, he shall be condemned;

24 And if he repent he shall be forgiven, according to the covenants and commandments of the church.

According to President Joseph Fielding Smith, these verses apply only to the Presiding Bishop of the Church.

In case of the transgression of the Presiding Bishop of the Church, he could not be tried by a high council in the stake in which he lives, but he would have to be tried by the First Presidency of the Church. The reason for this is that he holds the keys of presidency of the Aaronic Priesthood and is not under the jurisdiction of any ward or stake in this capacity. This order given for the trial of the presiding bishop does not apply to a local bishop in a ward, who is under the jurisdiction of the presidency of the stake. [*Church History and Modern Day Revelation*, 2:30–31]

The importance of the office of Presiding Bishop is emphasized by the Lord in His judiciary system for the Church. Only the first Presidency may hold a disciplinary council for him, whether he be a high priest called to serve in this hereditary office, or the firstborn descendant of Aaron (v. 22). Certainly he is not exempt from being tried, nor is the President of the Church (see D&C 107:76), but it must be based on unquestionable evidence (D&C 68:23). Of course, forgiveness is always held out to any member of the Church when the requirements are met (v. 24). More information on the hereditary office of the firstborn descendant of Aaron is given later in D&C 107.

D&C 68:25–30 • The Age of Accountability

25 And again, inasmuch as parents have children in Zion, or in any of her stakes which are organized, that teach them not to understand the doctrine of repentance, faith in Christ the Son of the living God, and of baptism and the gift of the Holy Ghost by the laying on of the hands, when eight years old, the sin be upon the heads of the parents.

26 For this shall be a law unto the inhabitants of Zion, or in any of her stakes which are organized.

27 And their children shall be baptized for the remission of their sins when eight years old, and receive the laying on of the hands.

28 And they shall also teach their children to pray, and to walk uprightly before the Lord.

29 And the inhabitants of Zion shall also observe the Sabbath day to keep it holy.

30 And the inhabitants of Zion also shall remember their labors, inasmuch as they are appointed to labor, in all faithfulness; for the idler shall be had in remembrance before the Lord.

The age of accountability being eight years of age (v. 25–27) can be traced back to at least the time of Abraham: "And I will establish a covenant of circumcision with thee, and it shall be my covenant between me and thee, and thy seed after thee, in their generations; that thou mayest know for ever that children are not accountable before me until they are eight years old" (JST, Genesis 17:11). To "know for ever" strongly implies that it was known before that time, and has been the age for children to be baptized since the time of Adam. The circumcision of the male children at the age of eight days old was a token of the covenant, or a symbolic reminder of the accountability age (Genesis 17:10–12; JST, Genesis 17:15–17). The teaching of their children to pray and to walk uprightly before the Lord (D&C 68:28), the keeping of the Sabbath, and the reminder that they are to labor in their stewardships, are other characteristics of good parenting of children (vv. 29–30).

D&C 68:31–35 • The Lord Not Well Pleased

31 Now, I, the Lord, am not well pleased with the inhabitants of Zion, for there are idlers among them; and their children are also growing up in wickedness; they also seek not earnestly the riches of eternity, but their eyes are full of greediness.

32 These things ought not to be, and must be done away from among them; wherefore, let my servant Oliver Cowdery carry these sayings unto the land of Zion.

33 And a commandment I give unto them—that he that observeth not his prayers before the Lord in the season thereof, let him be had in remembrance before the judge of my people.

34 These sayings are true and faithful; wherefore, transgress them not, neither take therefrom.

35 Behold, I am Alpha and Omega, and I come quickly. Amen.

The displeasure of the Lord with the inhabitants of Zion for not keeping these principles (v. 31) is another declaration that they have not overcome the world, or become a people that are pure in heart. To overcome the world they must learn the Lord's will, mind, word, and voice, which is scripture. Oliver is to carry this message and commandment to Zion (v. 32). These commandments are true and faithful, and must be followed with exactness, or they will not achieve their Zion status. The bishop of Zion, Edward Partridge, is to be informed, that he may work to eliminate these transgressions from among them (vv. 33–34). Again the Lord reminds them of His being the beginning and the end, and the end is coming quickly, according to His time (v. 35).

General Authority Quotes
—The Prophet Joseph • D&C 65:2–4

Where did the kingdom of God begin? Where there is no kingdom of God there is no salvation. What constitutes the kingdom of God? Where there is a prophet, a priest, or a righteous man unto whom God gives His oracles, there is the kingdom of God; and where the oracles of God are not, there the kingdom of God is not. [*TPJS*, 272]

We consider that God has created man with a mind capable of

instruction, and a faculty which may be enlarged in proportion to the heed and diligence given to the light communicated from heaven to the intellect; and that the nearer man approaches perfection, the clearer are his views, and the greater his enjoyments, till he has overcome the evils of his life and lost every desire for sin; and like the ancients, arrives at that point of faith where he is wrapped in the power and glory of His Maker and is caught up to dwell with Him. But we consider that this is a station to which no man arrived in a moment: he must have been instructed in the government and laws of that kingdom by proper degrees, until his mind is capable in some measure of comprehending the propriety, justice, equality, and consistency of the same . . . it is necessary for men to receive an understanding concerning the laws of the heavenly kingdom, before they are permitted to enter it; we mean the celestial glory. [*TPJS*, 51]

—Elder James E. Talmage • D&C 65:4–6

The expression "kingdom of God" is used synonymously with the term "Church of Christ;" but the Lord has made plain that He sometimes used the term "kingdom of heaven" in a distinctive sense. . . . [quotes D&C 65:1–6].

Such was the prayer, such is the prayer, prescribed for this people to pray, not to utter in words only, not to say only, but to pray—that the kingdom of God may roll forth in the earth to prepare the earth for the coming of the kingdom of heaven. That provision in the Lord's prayer, "Thy kingdom come, thy will be done on earth as it is in heaven" has not been abrogated. We are praying for the kingdom of heaven to come, and are endeavoring to prepare the earth for its coming. The kingdom of God, already set up upon the earth, does not aspire to temporal domination among the nations. It seeks not to overthrow any existing forms of government; it does not profess to exercise control in matters that pertain to the governments of the earth, except by teaching correct principles and trying to get men to live according to the principles of true government, before the kingdom of heaven shall come and be established upon the earth with a king at the head. But when He comes, He shall rule and reign, for it is His right. [CR, April 1916, 128–29]

—President Harold B. Lee • D&C 67:11–13

[After quoting D&C 67:11–13, and Moses 1:11], Now, if you will read carefully the testimony of the Prophet Joseph Smith, you will find him relating the experience of how the Father and the Son came to him and delivered that great message as to what he should do, what church he should join and not join; he says this: "When I came to myself again, I found myself lying on my back, looking up into heaven." In other words, he had exactly the same kind of experience that Moses had. One must be transfigured, then, to see with his spiritual eyes and not his natural eyes. If you will read the first chapter of the book of Revelation, where this great revelation came to John the Revelator, you will find that same thing being said by John. He fell at His feet, he was overcome, he was witnessing by the Spirit things that he could not have beheld with his natural eyes.

So if we understand, then, that no man can see the Lord, or be in His presence, except quickened by the Spirit, except by that we could not endure His presence. [*THBL,* 5]

—The Prophet Joseph Smith • D&C 68:1–4

. . . a brother and sister from Michigan, who thought that "a prophet is always a prophet;" but I told them that a prophet was a prophet only when he was acting as such— [*TPJS,* 278]

—President Joseph Fielding Smith • D&C 68:1–6

What is Scripture? When one of the brethren stands before a congregation of the people today, and the inspiration of the Lord is upon him, he speaks that which the Lord would have him speak. It is just as much scripture as anything you will find written in any of these records, and yet we call these the standard works of the Church. We depend, of course, upon the guidance of the brethren who are entitled to inspiration.

There is only one man in the Church at a time who has the right to give revelation for the Church, and that is the President of the Church. But that does not bar any other member in this Church from speaking the word of the Lord, as indicated here in this revelation, section 68, but a revelation that is to be given as these revelations are given in this book, to the Church, will come through the presiding officer of the church; yet, the word of the Lord, as spoken by other servants at the general conferences and stake conferences, or wherever they may be when they speak that which the Lord has put into their mouths, is just as much of the Lord as the writings and the words of other prophets in other dispensations. [*Doctrines of Salvation*, 1:186]

—President Harold B. Lee • D&C 68:2–4

This is so when a General Authority is speaking by the power of the Holy Ghost. . .

It is not to be thought that every word spoken by the General Authorities is inspired, or that they are moved upon by the Holy Ghost in everything they write. I don't care what his position is, if he writes something or speaks something that goes beyond anything that you can find in the standard Church works, unless that one be the prophet, seer, and revelator—please note that one exception— you may immediately say, "Well that is his own idea." . . . we can know or have the assurance that they are speaking under inspiration if we so live that we can have a witness that what they are speaking is the word of the Lord. . . . [*THBL*, 540–1]

If you want to know what the Lord would have the Saints know and to have His guidance and direction for the next six months, get a copy of the proceedings of this conference, and you will have the latest word of the Lord as far as the Saints are concerned, and [also] all others who are not of us, but who believe what has been said has been "the mind of the Lord, . . . the word of the Lord, . . . the voice of the Lord, and the power of God unto salvation" (D&C 68:4). [*THBL*, 471]

—President J. Reuben Clark • D&C 68:2–4

The question is, how shall we know when the things they have spoken were said as they were "moved upon by the Holy Ghost?"

I have given some thought to this question, and the answer thereto so far as I can determine, is: We can tell when the speakers are "moved upon by the Holy Ghost" only when we, ourselves, are "moved upon by the Holy Ghost."

In a way, this completely shifts the responsibility from them to us to determine when they so speak. [*J. Reuben Clark, Selected Papers*, ed. David H. Yarn (1984), 95–96]

—*President George Albert Smith* • D&C 68:14

There is no position in the Church that will bring a greater blessing to any man than the office of Bishop if he will honor that office and be a real father over the flock over whom he is called to preside. [*Latter-day Prophets and the Doctrine and Covenants*, 2:403]

—*President Joseph Fielding Smith* • D&C 68:16–17; 22–24

. . . This [legal right to the Presiding Bishop] has reference only to one who presides over the Aaronic Priesthood. It has no reference whatever to bishops of wards. Further, such a one must be designated by the First Presidency of the Church and receive the anointing and ordination under their hands. The revelation comes from the Presidency not from the patriarch, to establish a claim to the right to preside in this office. . . . [*Doctrines of Salvation*, 3:92]

. . . The reason for [the Presiding Bishop being tried by the First Presidency] is that he . . . is not under the jurisdiction of any ward or stake in this capacity. This order for the trial of the presiding bishop does not apply to a local bishop in a ward, who is under the jurisdiction of the presidency of the stake. [*CHMR*, 1:259–260]

—*Elder Gordon B. Hinckley* • D&C 68:25–30

Fathers and mothers are needed who will rise and stand upon their feet to make of their homes a sanctuaries in which children will grow in a spirit of obedience, industry, and fidelity to tested standards of conduct. If our society is coming apart at the seams, it is because the tailor and the seamstress in the home are not producing the kind of stitching that will hold under stress. . . . [*TGBH*, 200]

—*Elder Harold B. Lee* • D&C 25–32

By revelation, the Lord gave us what we might style as a five-point program by which parents could teach faith. First, He said, their children were to be baptized when they had reached the age of accountability at eight years; second; they were to be taught to pray; third, they were to be taught to walk uprightly before the Lord;

fourth, they were to keep the Sabbath day holy; and fifth, they were to be schooled not to be idle, either in the Church, or in their private lives (see D&C 68:25–32).

All parents who have followed that formula and have so taught their children have reaped the reward of an increased faith in their family, which has stood and will yet stand the rest of the difficulties into which their children will still go. [*THBL*, 270]

—*President N. Eldon Tanner* • D&C 68:25, 28

Don't let us be fooled or misled by the claim extant in the world today that restraints and conventions are damaging to the psyche of a child. In promoting a permissive and unrestricted society, they would have a child undisciplined for misbehavior. This is a false premise, and we are better advised to heed the counsel of the Lord when he said: [quotes D&C 68:25, 28]

Children do not learn by themselves how to distinguish right from wrong. Parents have to determine the child's readiness to assume responsibility and his capacity to make sound decisions, to evaluate alternatives, and the results of doing so. While we are teaching them, we have the responsibility to discipline them, and to see that they do what is right. If a child is besmudged with dirt, we do not let him wait until he grows up to decide whether or not he will bathe. We do not let him wait to decide whether or not he will take his medicine when sick, or go to school or to church. By example, persuasion, and love we see that he does what we know what is best for him. We cannot overemphasize the importance of example. The late J. Edgar Hoover said that if fathers and mothers would take their children to Sunday School and church regularly, they could strike a felling blow against the forces that contribute to juvenile delinquency. [CR, April 1973, 58]

—*President Spencer W. Kimball* • D&C 68:25–30

A higher and higher percentage of children grow up with only one parent. This is certainly not the way of the Lord. He expected for a father and a mother to raise their children. Certainly any who deprive their children of a parent will have some very stiff questions to answer. The Lord used both parents in the plural and said if children were not properly trained "the sin be upon the heads of the parents" (D&C

68:25). That makes it a bit hard to justify broken homes. Numerous of the divorces are the result of selfishness. The day of judgment is approaching, and parents who abandon their families will find that excuses and rationalizations will hardly satisfy the Great Judge. [CR, October 1974, 9]

—Elder Boyd K. Packer • D&C 68:25–30

The measure of our success as parents, however, will not rest solely on how our children turn out. That judgment would be just only if we could raise our families in a perfectly moral environment, and that now is not possible.

It is not uncommon for responsible parents to lose one of their children, for a time, to influences over which they have no control. They agonize over rebellious sons or daughters. They are puzzled over why they are so helpless when they have tried so hard to do what they should.

It is my conviction that those wicked influences one day will be overruled.

—Elder Orsen F. Whitney • D&C 68:25–30

"The Prophet Joseph Smith declared—and he never taught a more comforting doctrine—that the eternal sealing of faithful parents and the divine promises made to them for valiant service in the Cause of Truth, would save not only themselves, but likewise their posterity. Though some of the sheep may wander, the eye of the Shepherd is upon them, and sooner or later they will feel the tentacles of Divine Providence reaching out after them and drawing them back to the fold. Either in this life or the life to come, they will return. They will have to pay their debt to justice; they will suffer for their sins; and may tread a thorny path; but if it leads them at last, like the penitent Prodigal, to a loving and forgiving father's heart and home, the painful experience will not have been in vain. Pray for your careless and disobedient children; hold on to them with your faith. Hold on, trust on, till you see the salvation of God.

We cannot overemphasize the value of temple marriage, the binding ties of the sealing ordinance, and the standards of worthiness required of them. When parents keep the covenants they have made at the altars of the temple, their children will be forever bound to them. President Brigham Young said:

. . . I care not where those children go, they are bound up to their parents by an ever-lasting tie. And no power of earth or hell can separate them from their parents in eternity; they will return again to the fountain from whence they sprang. [CR, April 1992, 94–95]

Abbreviations used in this Book

CHC	–	*A Comprehensive History of the Church*
CHMR	–	*Church History and Modern Day Revelation*
CR	–	Conference Report
DBY	–	*Discourses of Brigham Young*
GD	–	*Gospel Doctrine*
HC	–	*History of the Church*
HJSM	–	*History of Joseph Smith by His Mother*
JD	–	*Journal of Discourses*
LDPDC	–	*The Latter-day Prophets and the Doctrine and Covenants*
LHCK	–	*Life of Heber C. Kimball*
MFP	–	*Messages of the First Presidency*
TABE	–	*That all May be Edified*
TETB	–	*The Teachings of Ezra Taft Benson*
TBGH	–	*Teachings of Gordon B. Hinckley*
THBL	–	*The Teachings of Harold B. Lee*
THWH	–	*The Teachings of Howard W. Hunter*
TPJS	–	*Teachings of the Prophet Joseph Smith*
TSWK	–	*The Teachings of Spencer W. Kimball*

&c. = and etc.

Scripture Index

OLD TESTAMENT

JOSEPH SMITH TRANSLATION

THE BOOK OF MORMON

DOCTRINE AND COVENANTS

THE PEARL OF GREAT PRICE

Topical Index

written for the intent that ye may
believe, 32
written in a language unknown, 32
Booth, Ezra, 540, 544
Bott, Randy L.
Ephraim, chosen of the Lord, 71
Ephraim: chosen servant of the Lord,
549
breastplate, 105, 106, 240, 247, 248, 250
Brewter, Hoyt Jr.
Doctrine and Covenants Encyclopedia
(book), 466
Bridegroom
Christ, 477
make ready the, 554, 555
oil in the lamps, 305
parable was the master, 414
to the marriage feast, 415
brimstone, 166, 283, 527
broken heart and a contrite spirit, 194,
196, 490, 492
brother of Jared, 105, 106, 557
brotherly kindness, 87
buffetings of Satan, 167, 357, 358, 460
bullock, 483
Burroughs, Philip, 256, 262

—C—

Cahoon, Reynolds, 510, 515, 516
Callis, Charles A., 292
camp of Washington, 243
Campbellites, 312
capital punishment, 351, 352
carnal, 556
carnality and sin, 432
commandments, 133, 135
desires, 54
law of carnal commandments, 135
mind, 554, 556
nor sensual, 274, 285
ordinances, 135
sensual, and devilish lyrics, 233
carpenter, 440
Celestial, 281, 284, 397, 411
body, 395, 551
earth, 399, 532
glory, 161, 543, 568

kingdom, 36, 45, 241, 281, 284, 286,
289, 294, 329, 337, 357, 383
receive their crowns, and robes of
righteousness, 281
resurrection, 284, 395, 399
saints, 281
world, 293
chaff
sift him as, 451, 455
charity
pure love of Christ, 87, 148, 388
Christ created all things spiritual, 274
Christ's disciples, 31, 393
Church at Ephesus
Apostle Paul taught, 141
Church Historian, 15, 113, 431, 454
*Church History and Modern Day
Revelation* (book), 94, 155,
565
Church News, 406
church organization, 8
church patriarch, 216
circumcised, 291
circumcision
law of, 200
baptism instituted in the place of,
291
covenant of, 291, 566
eight days of age, 291
is not baptism, 200, 291
symbolic reminder, 566
token of the covenant, 566
city of Enoch, 326, 402, 413
Clark, J. Reuben, 236, 386, 387, 487, 570
Clark, James R. (comp.)
*Messages of the First Presidency of
The Church of Jesus* (book),
270
Cobb, Mrs, 56
Coe, Joseph, 379, 384
Colesville, 203-205, 218, 220, 322, 325
branch, 473
branch at New York, 325
Broome county, 141
saints, 381, 459
Coltrin, Zebedee, 454
Columbus, 26, 45, 243

same yesterday, today and forever,
182
Savior, 1, 9, 16, 29, 34, 41, 42, 53,
56-58, 71, 72, 81, 99, 104,
117, 129, 144, 153, 155,
156, 158, 160, 170,
172-174, 180-182, 188,
196, 201, 202, 242, 260,
267, 294, 307, 318, 330,
339, 347, 360, 398, 414,
415, 483, 486, 494, 521,
526, 528, 530, 549, 551, 555
Savior in Gethsemane, 196
Savior of the world, 181, 398
Second Coming of, 28, 269
Son of God, 13, 61, 72, 89, 92, 93, 117,
158, 184, 185, 311, 318,
347, 384, 410, 422, 458,
494, 531
Son of the Eternal Father, 181
testimony of, 432
the beginning and end, 322
the Great I AM, 276, 322, 325, 334
the Light and Light of men, 306
the Son, the Only Begotten of the
Father, 185
voice of, 241
Jew, 149, 169, 293, 469, 471
convincing of the, 163
declare Christ's gospel to, 149
declare my gospel to, 143
from the mouth of, 71
Jewish
culture, 409
experience, 401
generation, 404
people, 10
Job
biblical, 66
John the Baptist, 49, 69, 104, 131, 132,
135, 137, 139, 153, 244,
245, 303, 312, 401, 445,
530, 555
John the Revelator, 24, 27, 33, 48, 180,
181, 243, 288, 302, 307,
437, 453, 454, 569
Johnson, Lyman E., 558, 559, 562

Jones, Gracia N.
Emma and Lucy (book), 227
Joseph, 240
of Egypt, 123, 216, 450
son of Jacob, 71
Joseph, Jacob, Isaac, Abraham, 240
Josephites, 53, 57
Joshua, 290
Journal of Discourses, 35, 45, 129, 140, 155,
212, 293, 308, 320, 327,
339, 356, 471, 528, 529
Judah, 276, 359, 360
descendants of, 169
house of, 30
king of, 169
mountains of, 359
must return, 407
remnant of, 404
judge in Israel, 474, 478, 488, 550
judged, 182, 183, 551
according to his works, 27
according to the words, 183
according to your works, 280
by our thoughts, 249
by the other twelve, 280
by the twelve, 280
of their works, 161
of your works, 280
work shall be, 176
judgment
endless torment, 158
condemn us, 281
endless punishment, 158
eternal damnation, 158
exonerate us, 281
gnashing of teeth, 158
wailing, 158
weeping, 158
judgment-seat, 280
judgment-seat of Christ, 280
apostles with Christ at the judgment
bar, 280
prophets will also be there, 280
special witnesses of the name of
Christ, 280
justice, 164, 204, 319, 537, 568, 573
and mercy, 230

—T—